The Best of Beta Sigma Phi Cookbook

The Best of
Beta Sigma Phi
Cookbook

EDITORIAL STAFF

Managing Editor	Mary Jane Blount
Project Manager	Debbie Seigenthaler
Editors	Georgia Brazil Ashlee Brown Mary Cummings Jane Hinshaw Linda Jones Mary Wilson
Associate Editors	Christie Carlucci Judy Jackson Rachel Lawson Charlene Sproles
Typography	Pam Newsome Sara Anglin
Panel of Judges	Bill Ross Mary Jane Blount Pat Coker

Cover Photograph: Courtesy of Pet Incorporated; Page 1: Courtesy of The Dow Chemical Company, makers of SARAN WRAP™; Page 2: Courtesy of the California Beef Council

© Favorite Recipes® Press, A Division of Heritage House, Inc. MCMLXLI
   P.O. Box 305141, Nashville, Tennessee 37230

ISBN: 0-87197-306-5
Library of Congress Number: 91-16600

Manufactured in the United States of America
First Printing 1991

Recipes for photographs are on page 19.

Contents

*A Time For Us
60 Years of
Beta Sigma Phi*

July 1, 1991

Dear Beta Sigma Phis,

As Professor Henry Higgins of "My Fair Lady" would say: "By George, we've got it!"

After 23 years of compiling cookbooks with your recipes and the able help of the staff at Favorite Recipes® Press, we think we've finally put together the collection that beats them all. That's why we're calling this year's cookbook *THE BEST OF BETA SIGMA PHI COOKBOOK*. Simply put, there is none better.

Inside this book, you will find the perfect recipe for a scrumptious hors d'oeuvre, an entrée to impress your mother-in-law, or a dessert that'll have sisters singing your praises! We've also included some of the best recipes from our past Beta Sigma Phi cookbooks, and some quick and easy craft projects as well. (As usual, we have awarded prizes in various food categories; these 'best-of-the-best' recipes are specially marked by a rose in the book.)

We hope you'll enjoy *THE BEST OF BETA SIGMA PHI COOKBOOK* as much as Favorite Recipes® Press has enjoyed putting it together for you. Won't these cookbooks make wonderful holiday gifts? There's no better present you can give a loved one than a "gift from the heart" of the best cooks on earth!

Yours in Beta Sigma Phi,
Beta Sigma Phi International Executive Committee
Brenda Evans
Linda Rostenberg
Laura Ross-Wingfield

1800 West 91st Place   *P.O. Box 8500* ▲ *Kansas City, MO 64114-0500* ▲ *(816) 444-6800*

Memorable Moments

It's not enough that you've sent us great recipes
for more than two decades: this year we
asked for, and received, your very best. You know
the recipes we mean. The one on the ancient
index card stuck between the pages of Mom's old
cookbook. The one you've never even written
down because you know it so well. The one you
picked up on that summer vacation. The one
you invented in a last-minute panic that
has become a family favorite. We've divided
these one-of-a-kind recipes into nine categories,
each with three special prize winners, including
unusual ideas for appetizers and
snacks, entrées, salads and side dishes, drinks,
breads, desserts and wonderful ethnic dishes.
These tried-and-true favorites have stood the test
of time and taste buds. We think they'll
become classics in your kitchen too.

Heritage Recipes

1968 – Meats

Including Seafood and Poultry

CITY CHICKEN

2 eggs, lightly beaten
3 tablespoons milk
¾ cup cracker crumbs
1 cup cornflake crumbs
Salt and pepper to taste
Garlic salt to taste
Poultry seasoning

2½-pound boneless
veal shoulder, cut in 1-
to 2-inch cubes
2 tablespoons fat
1 bouillon cube
¾ cup hot water

Mix eggs and milk; mix together cracker and cornflake crumbs and seasonings. Dip veal cubes in egg batter, then in crumb mixture. Brown in fat. Melt bouillon cube in hot water; add to meat. Simmer about 1 hour or until meat is done. Use liquid from meat for gravy. May cover and bake in 325- to 350-degree oven about 1 hour or until tender.
Yield: 8 servings.

Pat White, Alpha Delta
Aberdeen, Maryland

STEAK DIANE

2 boneless sirloin
steaks, ¾ inch thick
6 tablespoons butter or
margarine
2 teaspoons dry mustard
½ teaspoon salt
2 tablespoons sliced
green onions

2 tablespoons olive oil
1 teaspoon freshly
ground pepper
1 tablespoon
Worcestershire sauce
2 tablespoons lemon
juice

Pound steaks well with mallet or side of saucer. Melt 4 tablespoons butter in a large skillet. Stir in mus-tard, salt and green onions; sauté 1 minute. Press 1 tablespoon olive oil into steaks; sprinkle with half the pepper. Cook with oil-pepper side down for about 2 minutes, spooning pan juices over meat. Rub remaining oil and pepper into uncooked side of steaks; turn and cook 2 minutes or to desired degree of doneness. Remove from pan. Add remaining butter, Worcestershire sauce and lemon juice to pan juices; blend and heat. Pour over steaks just before serving. Garnish with chopped parsley.
Yield: 4 servings.

Mrs. Mary C. Pittman, Pres., Xi Beta Delta
DeFuniak Springs, Florida

1969
Dorothy Ross' Cookbook

"A Labor of Love"

SPICED PECANS

3 cups confectioners'
sugar
¼ cup cornstarch
1 teaspoon salt
2 teaspoons cinnamon
½ teaspoon cloves
½ teaspoon allspice

½ teaspoon chili
powder
2 egg whites
4 tablespoons cold
water
4 cups pecans

Sift dry ingredients together. Dip pecans in egg white; drain on absorbent paper. Roll in sugar mixture. Spread on cookie sheet so they do not touch. Put in very slow oven (250 degrees) until dry, about 30 to 35 minutes. Makes 4 cups.

1969 – Casseroles

Including Breads

KING RANCH CHICKEN

1 5-pound hen or 2 fryers	12 tortillas, cut in fourths
1 can Ro-Tel tomatoes and chilies	2 cups cheese, grated
1 can cream of mushroom soup	1 large onion, chopped
1 can cream of chicken soup	1 green pepper, chopped (optional)
1 cup chicken broth	Crushed potato chips (optional)

Boil hen; cube. Combine tomatoes, soups and broth for sauce. Layer chicken, tortillas, cheese, onion, green pepper and sauce in casserole. Repeat. Top with crumbs. Bake in 350-degree oven for 1 hour. Cover pan with foil in order to keep tortillas moist. Yield: 10 servings.

Neloise Blasingame, Pres., Kappa Gamma No. 3292
Corpus Christi, Texas
Judy Clack, 2nd VP, Alpha Alpha Alpha No. 6535
Alice, Texas

HONEY TWIST

1 cup milk, scalded	5 to 6 cups sifted flour
1/4 cup butter	Honey Topping
1/2 cup sugar	Chopped nuts (optional)
1 teaspoon salt	Chopped candied
2 cakes yeast	cherries and pineapple
1/4 cup lukewarm water	(optional)
2 eggs, well beaten	

Pour milk over butter, sugar and salt; crumble yeast into lukewarm water to soften. Cool milk to lukewarm; add yeast and eggs. Beat in flour to make a soft dough; turn out on floured board. Knead until smooth. Form into ball; place in greased bowl. Cover; let rise until doubled in bulk. Shape into long roll about 1-inch in diameter. Coil roll into greased cake pan, beginning at outside edge and covering bottom. Brush with Honey Topping. Let rise until doubled in bulk. Sprinkle with nuts, cherries and pineapple. Bake in 375-degree oven for 25 to 30 minutes.

HONEY TOPPING

1/4 cup butter	1 egg white
2/3 cup confectioners' sugar	2 tablespoons honey, warmed

Cream all ingredients together.

Mrs. Annetta Godochik, Rec. Sec., Gamma Upsilon No. 6437
Weirton, West Virginia
Marie LaCroix, Pres., Delta Upsilon No. 6145
Hanmer, Ontario, Canada

1970 – Salads

Including Appetizers

ARTICHOKE-OLIVE SALAD WITH HERB DRESSING

2 packages frozen artichoke hearts	1/2 teaspoon tarragon leaves
3 teaspoons salt	1/2 teaspoon basil leaves
1 teaspoon lemon juice	1 teaspoon sugar
1/2 cup tarragon vinegar	4 tomatoes, cut into eighths
1 cup olive or salad oil	1 cup pitted black olives
1/4 cup parsley	1 to 2 heads Bibb
2 tablespoons finely chopped onion	lettuce, washed and crisped
1/8 teaspoon pepper	

Cook artichokes with 2 teaspoons salt and lemon juice according to package directions; drain. Combine vinegar, oil, parsley, onion, pepper, tarragon leaves, basil leaves, sugar and remaining salt in jar; cover. Shake well. Spoon 2/3 of the dressing over warm artichokes; cover. Refrigerate for at least 4 hours, turning artichokes occasionally. Cover remaining dressing; refrigerate. Place tomatoes in medium bowl; add olives and chilled dressing. Toss to mix. Arrange artichokes around edge of lettuce on serving dish; pile tomato mixture in center of lettuce. Yield: 6-8 servings.

Martha True, VP, Mu Tau No. 6316
Carol Stream, Illinois

PECTIN FRENCH DRESSING

1/2 teaspoon salt	Few grains of pepper
1/2 teaspoon sugar	1/2 cup Pectin Solution
1/4 teaspoon celery salt	2 tablespoons vinegar or lemon juice
1/2 teaspoon dry mustard	1 garlic clove, crushed
1/8 teaspoon paprika	

Combine first 6 ingredients; stir in Pectin Solution well. Add vinegar and garlic; combine thoroughly, stirring and shaking. One-half cup contains only 10 calories.

PECTIN SOLUTION

1 1/2 ounces pectin powder	1/2 cup boiling water

Add pectin to boiling water. Bring to a boil; boil for 30 seconds. Pectin is used in preserving.

Mrs. Barbara Ross, Pres., Kappa Sigma No. 3543
Amarillo, Texas

1971
Holiday Cookbook

Plus a Collection of Festive Menus

SPECTER'S SUNDAE

3 tablespoons butter	4 large bananas, sliced
1 cup brown sugar	Ice cream
1/2 teaspoon cinnamon	Toasted coconut
1/2 cup light cream	

Melt butter in saucepan; add brown sugar and cinnamon. Heat gently until sugar melts. Remove from heat; stir in cream. Return to low heat; continue stirring. Drop in bananas gently. Serve hot over ice cream; sprinkle with toasted coconut.

Verna Kidd, Xi Alpha Beta X 557
Nelson, British Columbia, Canada

HOLIDAY PIE

1 1/2 cups Brazil nuts	1 1/2 cups milk
Sugar	1/2 cup thinly sliced
1 envelope unflavored	glacé cherries
gelatin	2 tablespoons light rum
3 eggs, separated	3/4 cup heavy cream
1/8 teaspoon salt	

Grind 1 1/4 cups nuts fine. Pour 1 cup boiling water over remaining nuts and let stand for 30 minutes. Drain nuts and shave thin. Combine ground nuts and 3 tablespoons sugar; mix well. Press mixture against bottom and side of 9-inch pie plate building up rim. Bake at 400 degrees for 8 minutes or until lightly browned. Cool. Soften gelatin in 1/4 cup cold water. Beat egg yolks with salt and 1/4 cup sugar. Scald milk in top of double boiler; add small amount of hot milk to egg yolk mixture. Mix well and return to remaining milk. Cook, stirring, until smooth and thickened. Stir in gelatin until dissolved. Chill until partially congealed; whip until smooth and fold in cherries and rum. Beat egg whites until stiff, adding 1/4 cup sugar gradually; fold into custard mixture. Mound into baked crust and refrigerate overnight. Whip cream and sweeten to taste. Spoon whipped cream around edge of pie; sprinkle with shaved nuts. Keep pie refrigerated until ready to serve. Yield: 6-8 servings.

Mrs. R. E. Sink
San Diego, California

Make Coconut Milk for Shrimp Curry by simmering 2 1/2 cups milk and 1 package coconut in double boiler for 1 hour. Chill overnight and strain through cheesecloth.

1972
Fondue & Buffet Cookbook

One of the Most Unusual Cookbooks

INDONESIAN SHRIMP CURRY

2 large onions, chopped	2 tablespoons (about)
2 pieces of gingerroot,	curry powder
peeled	1 tablespoon sugar
2 cloves of garlic, minced	1 cup chicken stock
4 apples, finely diced	2 cups Coconut Milk
2 bay leaves	Salt to taste
1/4 teaspoon cinnamon	2 pounds cooked
Butter	shrimp, chicken or
3 tablespoons flour	lamb

Sauté onions, gingerroot, garlic, apples, bay leaves, and cinnamon in small amount of butter in top of double boiler until lightly browned. Combine flour, curry powder, and sugar; stir into apple mixture. Simmer, stirring, for 5 minutes. Blend in stock; simmer for 10 minutes longer. Place top of double boiler over hot water. Stir Coconut Milk into mixture; simmer for 45 minutes. Remove gingerroot. Stir in salt and shrimp just before serving; heat through. Transfer to chafing dish; keep warm over hot water. Serve with rice and following condiments: mango chutney, chopped peanuts, chopped candied ginger, Bombay duck, and chopped green onions.

Dr. Hope S. Ross, International Honorary Member, BSP
Enid, Oklahoma

CHAMPAGNE SWISS FONDUE

1 pound Swiss cheese,	1/8 teaspoon ground
shredded	nutmeg
3 tablespoons flour	1/8 teaspoon pepper
1 clove of garlic, cut	1/8 teaspoon paprika
1 cup champagne	2 loaves Italian or
1 cup dry white wine	French bread, cubed
1 tablespoon lemon juice	
3 tablespoons kirsch or	
brandy	

Dredge cheese lightly in flour. Rub inside of fondue pot completely with garlic; pour in champagne and wine. Bring champagne mixture just to a boil; add lemon juice. Stir in cheese gradually. Cook, stirring constantly with a wooden spoon, until cheese is melted and fondue is smooth. Bring to a rolling boil; add kirsch and spices. Reduce heat; cook, stirring constantly, until blended. Spear bread cubes through soft side into crust with fondue forks; swirl in fondue. Yield: 10-12 servings.

Linda Singer, Beta Phi No. 3154
Clearwater, Florida

1973 – Party Book

Hundreds of Proven Party Ideas

MILLIONAIRE'S PARTY

Time and Place: 8 PM in a home.
Invitations: Written on blank checks.
Special Dress: Costume to go with the millionaire theme—girls came in silks, satins and jewels. Two members dressed as waitresses and two as butlers to take wraps and serve and announce guests' names on arrival.

We decorated with ticker tape and little money trees covered with play money and old checks. A red carpet was placed in the entrance and we used red velvet coasters. All the food was served on crystal and silver. The menu included wine and pink champagne. Dessert was flaming cherries jubilee served on crystal and silver trays. We also had a variety of finger sandwiches and coffee espresso. We played games involving money—blackjack, roulette and bingo. Prizes were awarded for the best costume and for games winners. Prizes were small bags of chocolate coin money covered in gold paper in gold mesh bags.

Trudi Landreth, Pres. Xi Kappa Omega X2691
LaMesa, California

ALICE IN WONDERLAND'S MAD HATTER TEA PARTY

Time: 7:00 PM.
Invitations: Individual invitations were sent in shape of a teapot.

Our chapter members wore hats of our choice or creations for a tea party. Decorations were of huge paper flowers to resemble a flower garden. There was a cardboard doorway and boxes to walk through to resemble going down a rabbit's hole and through a tunnel to garden. Name tags were in the form of cups and saucers. Huge tissue butterflies were also used for decorations. A menu of punch and miniature cookies, cakes and sandwiches were served in children's tea set on low tables and chairs; nut cups with mints were in teapots. Guests were given paper bonnets and paper pinafores of hearts. The guests were divided into teams and each team had to make up a nursery rhyme. The winners got candy rolls. There were pictures of national brand ads on the wall; guests had to guess them. We played miniature croquet on tables in teams. Prizes were large, inexpensive serving trays and products from the ads.

Nancy H. Burns, W and M Chairman, Xi Alpha Theta X2813
Scottsdale, Arizona

1973 – Gourmet

Elegant Gourmet Recipes

ARTICHOKES MILANESE

1/2 cup butter	1 tablespoon fine dry
2 cups sliced fresh	bread crumbs
mushrooms	2 tablespoons fresh
1 teaspoon salt	lemon juice
1 teaspoon crushed	2 8-ounce packages
sweet basil	frozen artichoke
1/2 teaspoon crushed	hearts, thawed
oregano	1/2 cup Parmesan cheese
1/4 teaspoon garlic	
powder	

Melt butter in large, heavy skillet; sauté mushrooms in butter until golden. Sprinkle with salt, sweet basil, oregano and garlic powder during cooking. Stir in bread crumbs and lemon juice; mix well. Arrange artichoke hearts in greased shallow baking dish. Spoon mushroom mixture over artichokes. Sprinkle cheese over all. Bake at 350 degrees for 25 minutes or until bubbly and cheese is browned. Yield: 8 servings.

Shirley Ayers, Pres., Xi Gamma Rho X3864
Federal Way, Washington

OYSTERS BIENVILLE

1 dozen shrimp	1/4 teaspoon celery seed
1 2-ounce can	1 tablespoon sherry
mushroom stems	1 1/2 pints oysters
and pieces	Grated Parmesan
1/4 cup butter	cheese
3 tablespoons flour	Paprika
1 clove of garlic, minced	Salt to taste
1 tablespoon onion juice	
1 tablespoon	
Worcestershire sauce	

Cook shrimp in boiling water for 5 minutes. Drain shrimp; reserve liquid. Chop shrimp. Drain mushrooms; add enough reserved shrimp liquid to mushroom liquid to make 3/4 cup liquid. Melt butter; stir in flour, garlic, onion juice, Worcestershire sauce and celery seed. Add mushroom liquid mixture; cook, stirring, until thickened. Add mushrooms, shrimp and sherry; mix well. Drain oysters; place in shallow pan. Broil until edges just curl; pour off liquid. Sprinkle oysters liberally with Parmesan cheese; cover with mushroom sauce. Sprinkle with paprika; broil for 5 to 8 minutes longer or until bubbly. Season with salt. Yield: 4-6 servings.

Sherry Bullock, Pres., Theta Gamma No. 8845
Ames, Iowa

1974
Money-Saving Casseroles

Ideas for Stretching the Food Dollar

BEEF-MACARONI STROGANOFF

1 7-ounce package Creamettes macaroni	1 can cream of mushroom soup
1 pound ground beef	1 cup sour cream
1 cup chopped onions	1 tablespoon cooking sherry (optional)
1/4 teaspoon pepper	1 17-ounce can green peas, drained
1 teaspoon salt	

Prepare macaroni according to package directions. Cook beef, onions and seasonings in large skillet until beef is brown. Stir in soup and simmer for 10 minutes. Remove from heat and stir in sour cream, sherry, macaroni and peas. Pour into 2 1/2-quart casserole. Bake in preheated 350-degree oven for 35 minutes.

Brenda Tipton, Pres., Eta Mu No. 5752
Tampa, Florida

1975 – Save and Win

Personalized Craft Projects

PARTY FAVOR IDEA

Materials: Spray paint (optional), empty thread spools, tiny strawflowers.

Paint spools or leave unfinished. Insert several strawflowers in the hole of each spool; place 1 at each place setting. If full spools of thread are used, the colors can be coordinated with colors of candles and napkins for a custom-decorated effect.

Rue Haddock, Pres., Preceptor Alpha Rho
Arvada, Colorado

PERMANENT BREAD CENTERPIECE

Equipment: Paintbrush, glue.
Materials: Loaf of unsliced bread, Mod-Podge, ribbon, small berries or flowers.

Bake bread at lowest oven temperature, about 200 degrees, for 12 hours; let cool. Brush on Mod-Podge with paintbrush. This produces glossy finish and seals loaf so that it will not crumble. Let dry. Tie with ribbon. Decorate with berries or flowers as desired. Loaf may be glued to breadboard or any desired base.

Neda Bean, Alpha Epsilon No. 6905
Rock Springs, Wyoming

1976
Bicentennial Heritage Recipes

Special Limited Edition

OLD VIRGINIA COUNTRY HAM

1 15-pound Virginia country ham	2 tablespoons whole cloves
6 medium onions	1 teaspoon mustard
3 1/2 cups (packed) brown sugar	1 teaspoon ground cloves
2 cups blackberry wine	1 teaspoon allspice
3 bay leaves	Pepper to taste

Soak ham overnight in enough water to cover; scrub to remove mold. Place ham, skin side down, in large roaster; cover with cold water. Add onions, 3 cups brown sugar, wine, bay leaves and whole cloves; cover. Bring to a boil; reduce heat. Simmer for 25 minutes per pound; cool in water. Remove skin; cut off excess fat. Place ham in water in which cooked; let stand overnight. Drain; place, fat side up, in roaster. Score fat. Mix remaining sugar with remaining ingredients and small amount of additional wine; rub on ham. Bake in preheated 400-degree oven for 25 minutes or until brown.

Mrs. Jackie Farley, VP, Epsilon Rho No. 8379
Verona, Virginia

BEAN POT BAKED BEANS

1 quart pea beans	2 teaspoons salt
10 ounces salt pork	1/8 teaspoon ginger
3/4 teaspoon dry mustard	2 tablespoons sugar
	1/4 cup molasses

Soak beans overnight in water to cover; drain. Pour boiling water over salt pork; scrape until white. Place beans and salt pork in bean pot. Combine mustard, salt, ginger, sugar, molasses and 1 1/2 cups boiling water; mix well. Pour over beans and salt pork. Cover. Bake in preheated 250 to 300-degree oven for about 9 hours. Add 1/2 cup hot water every 30 minutes or as needed. Water should never cover beans completely.

Bettye W. King, Pres., Alpha Kappa Delta No. 8897
Lindale, Texas

BAKED BEANS—*Baked Beans were the perfect food for the Sabbath-respecting Puritans. The homemaker baked her beans all day Saturday and when the Sabbath began at sundown, the meals for the next 24 hours were ready. The Saturday evening and Sunday morning Baked Bean meal still feeds thousands of New England families to this very day.*

1977
Dieting to Stay Healthy

Better Nutrition and Healthier Meal Planning

HEALTH BREAD

7¹/2 to 8¹/2 cups unbleached flour	1¹/2 cups cottage cheese
1 cup whole wheat flour	¹/2 cup molasses
1 tablespoon salt	2 tablespoons margarine
2 envelopes yeast	2¹/2 cups boiling water
1 cup rolled oats	³/4 cup chopped walnuts
1 cup whole bran cereal	³/4 cup chopped dates
	³/4 cup raisins

Combine 1 cup flour, whole wheat flour, salt and yeast in bowl. Combine oats, bran, cottage cheese, molasses and margarine in separate large bowl. Stir in water; let cool to 120 degrees. Add to flour mixture gradually. Beat for 2 minutes. Stir in enough remaining flour with wooden spoon to make soft dough. Knead for 10 minutes. Place in greased bowl; cover. Let rise 45 minutes or until doubled in bulk. Punch down. Turn out onto lightly floured surface. Knead in walnuts, dates and raisins. Divide in thirds; place in greased 9x5x3-inch loaf pans. Cover with cloth. Let rise 45 minutes or until doubled in bulk. Bake at 375 degrees for 35 minutes. This bread freezes well.

Peggy Swanke, Alpha Zeta No. 6717
Valley City, North Dakota

SLIM LEMON CHEESECAKE

2 envelopes gelatin	3 cups low-fat creamed
³/4 cup sugar	cottage cheese
2 eggs, separated	¹/3 cup graham cracker
1¹/2 cups skim milk	crumbs
1¹/2 tablespoons lemon	¹/4 teaspoon ground
juice	cinnamon
1¹/2 teaspoons grated	¹/8 teaspoon ground
lemon peel	nutmeg

Mix unflavored gelatin and ¹/2 cup sugar in medium saucepan. Beat egg yolks with 1 cup milk; add to saucepan. Stir over low heat until gelatin dissolves, about 5 minutes. Add remaining ¹/2 cup milk, lemon juice and peel. Beat cottage cheese until smooth in large bowl. Beat in gelatin mixture gradually. Chill, stirring occasionally, until mixture mounds slightly when dropped from spoon. Beat egg whites until soft peaks form in large bowl. Add remaining ¹/4 cup sugar gradually. Beat until stiff. Fold in cheese mixture. Turn into 8 or 9-inch springform pan. Sprinkle top with graham cracker crumbs mixed with cinnamon and nutmeg. Chill until firm, about 3 hours. Yield: 12 servings/150 calories per serving.

Karen A. Zillner, Treas., Xi Tau X2485
Milwaukee, Wisconsin

1978
World of Beta Sigma Phi

Elegance Is Back

FRENCH ALMOND CRÊPES

¹/3 cup flour	Melted butter
1 tablespoon sugar	Almond Cream Filling
Dash of salt	Grated unsweetened
1 egg	chocolate
1 egg yolk	Confectioners' sugar
³/4 cup milk	

Place first 6 ingredients and 1 tablespoon melted butter in mixing bowl. Beat until smooth. Refrigerate several hours or until thick. Heat heavy 6-inch skillet; grease lightly. Pour in 2 tablespoons batter. Lift skillet from heat; tilt from side to side until batter covers bottom evenly. Return to heat. Cook until underside of crêpe is lightly browned, about 1¹/2 minutes. Invert skillet over paper towels to remove. Repeat. Spread about 2 tablespoons Almond Cream Filling on unbrowned side of each crêpe. Roll up. Place folded side down in buttered 13x9x2-inch baking dish. Brush crêpes with additional melted butter. Bake at 350 degrees for 20 to 25 minutes. Sprinkle with grated unsweetened chocolate. Sift confectioners' sugar over all. Serve warm with whipped cream.

ALMOND CREAM FILLING

1 cup sugar	2 teaspoons vanilla
¹/4 cup flour	extract
1 cup milk	¹/2 teaspoon almond
2 eggs	extract
2 egg yolks	¹/2 cup ground toasted
3 tablespoons butter	blanched almonds

Mix sugar and flour together in saucepan. Add milk. Cook, stirring until thick. Cook, stirring for 1 or 2 minutes longer. Beat eggs and egg yolks slightly; stir a small amount of hot mixture into eggs; return to hot mixture. Bring just to a boil, stirring constantly; remove from heat. Stir in butter and flavorings. Add ground almonds; mix until well blended. Cool to room temperature.

Sandra Bell, Pres., Zeta Gamma No. 2720
Shelby, Ohio

CRÊPE: *Thin, delicate pancakes spread with jam or jelly, or stuffed with savory meat or vegetable, then rolled up, and served as hors d'oeuvres or main dish (or dessert).*

1979
The Dining Room

Breakfast, Brunch, Lunch and Dinner

BAKED EGGS MORNAY

15 eggs, hard-boiled	1¼ teaspoons salt
Mayonnaise to taste	Pepper to taste
3 teaspoons horseradish	½ cup heavy cream
Sweet pickle juice to taste	4 tablespoons Parmesan cheese
Butter	4 tablespoons Swiss cheese
5 tablespoons flour	Buttered bread crumbs
2½ cups milk	

Slice eggs in half lengthwise; scoop out yolks. Mash yolks. Add mayonnaise, horseradish and sweet pickle juice. Return yolk mixture to egg halves. Place deviled eggs in buttered 13x9-inch casserole. Melt 5 tablespoons butter in saucepan over low heat. Blend in flour; stir in milk slowly. Cook until thickened. Add salt, pepper, cream, Parmesan cheese, Swiss cheese and 2½ tablespoons butter. Stir until cheese melts. Pour over deviled eggs. Sprinkle with buttered bread crumbs. Bake at 350 degrees for 20 to 30 minutes. Yield: 6-8 servings.

Rita Burke, Epsilon Eta No. 3703
Hawarden, Iowa

1980–81
Golden Anniversary Cookbook

A Special Love of Cooking

CORNED BEEF MOLD

1 enveloped unflavored gelatin	1 small onion, grated
1 cup mayonnaise	2 cups chopped celery
2 tablespoons lemon juice	1 can corned beef, chopped
1 4-ounce jar sliced mushrooms, drained	4 hard-cooked eggs, chopped

Soften gelatin in small amount of cold water. Dissolve gelatin in 1½ cups hot water; cool. Add remaining ingredients; mix well. Pour into mold. Chill overnight. Garnish with parsley.

Donna M. Stoddard, International Honorary Member
Xi Theta Pi
Lakeland, Florida

NOODLE-SPINACH RING

1 8-ounce package wide noodles	1 onion, chopped
2 10-ounce packages frozen chopped spinach, thawed and drained	½ cup butter
	3 eggs, slightly beaten
	1 cup sour cream

Prepare noodles according to package directions; drain. Combine noodles and spinach; mix well. Sauté onion in butter until browned. Add to noodle mixture; mix well. Fold in eggs. Add sour cream; blend well. Pour into greased 6-cup ring mold; place in pan of hot water. Bake at 350 degrees for 45 minutes. Serve on heated platter with steamed mushrooms in center. Yield: 8 servings.

Tina Duncan, Librarian, Epsilon Rho
North Wilkesboro, North Carolina

1982
Desserts & Party Foods Cookbook

Entertaining with a Flair!

CROWN JEWEL DESSERT

1½ cups fine graham cracker crumbs	1 package lemon gelatin
Sugar	1 9-ounce can crushed pineapple, drained
½ cup melted butter	3 tablespoons lemon juice
1 package strawberry gelatin	1½ cups Cool Whip
1 package black cherry gelatin	

Combine crumbs, ⅓ cup sugar and butter in bowl. Press over bottom and sides of 9x13-inch pan. Chill in refrigerator. Dissolve strawberry gelatin in 1 cup hot water. Stir in ½ cup cold water. Pour into 8-inch square pan. Chill until firm. Cut into ½-inch cubes. Repeat process with black cherry gelatin. Dissolve lemon gelatin and ¼ cup sugar in 1 cup hot water. Add pineapple, lemon juice and ½ cup cold water. Chill until partially set. Whip until fluffy. Fold in gelatin cubes and Cool Whip. Pour into prepared crust. Chill until firm.

Margaret Smith, Pi Alpha
McHenry, Illinois

1983
All-Occasion Casserole Cookbook

Magic for Your Menus

PHYLLIS' REUBEN CASSEROLE

1 16-ounce can sauerkraut, drained	1/4 cup Thousand Island dressing
1 12-ounce can corned beef, crumbled	2 medium tomatoes, sliced
2 cups shredded Swiss cheese	1/4 cup bread crumbs
1/2 cup mayonnaise	2 tablespoons butter, melted

Layer first 3 ingredients in order given in casserole. Mix mayonnaise and salad dressing in bowl. Spread over cheese. Top with tomatoes. Mix bread crumbs with butter. Sprinkle over tomatoes. Bake at 325 degrees until heated through.

Phyllis Emmel, Phi Alpha Zeta
Jefferson City, Missouri

GULLIVER'S CREAMED CORN

4 cups frozen corn	Butter
1 cup whipping cream	2 teaspoons flour
1 teaspoon salt	Parmesan cheese
1/2 teaspoon each sugar, MSG	

Cook corn in cream in saucepan until heated through. Stir in salt, sugar and MSG. Melt 2 teaspoons butter in small saucepan. Add flour, mixing well. Stir into corn mixture. Cook until slightly thick, stirring frequently. Spoon into casserole. Sprinkle Parmesan cheese over top. Dot with butter. Bake at 350 degrees for 25 minutes. Yield: 8-10 servings.

Verda Alfson, Preceptor Laureate Alpha
Williston, North Dakota

1984
The New Holiday Cookbook

Twelve Months of Festive Recipes

BUTTER CREAM EASTER EGGS

Butter	1 8-ounce package semisweet chocolate
1 8-ounce package cream cheese, softened	1 2-inch square paraffin
3 boxes confectioners' sugar	1/4 teaspoon vanilla extract

Cream 1/2 pound butter and cream cheese. Mix in sugar gradually. Shape into eggs. Melt remaining ingredients and 1 tablespoon butter in double boiler. Dip eggs in chocolate mixture; cool. Yield: 8 dozen.

Nancy S. Sykes, Zeta Psi
Grayson, Georgia

QUICHE NOËL

1 recipe 1-crust pie pastry	6 eggs, beaten
3/4 cup chopped cooked chicken	1 cup half and half
1 cup shredded Cheddar cheese	1 tablespoon minced onion
2 tablespoons chopped pimento	1/2 teaspoon seasoned salt
1/4 cup chopped green pepper	1/4 teaspoon white pepper

Line 9-inch quiche dish with pastry; trim. Prick bottom and side. Bake at 400 degrees for 3 minutes; remove from oven. Prick. Bake for 5 minutes longer; cool. Sprinkle chicken, cheese, pimento and green pepper in pie shell. Mix remaining ingredients; pour over layers. Bake at 425 degrees for 30 minutes or until set. Let stand for 10 minutes before serving. Yield: 6-8 servings.

Eileen Ueckermann, Xi Alpha Iota
Pleasantville, New Jersey

1985
Cook Quick Cookbook

1,000 Time-Saving Recipes

ALMOND CREME STRAWBERRIES

2 pints large strawberries	1 cup whipping cream, whipped
1 small package vanilla instant pudding mix	1 teaspoon almond extract
1 cup milk	

Stem strawberries. Cut deep X in stem end of each berry; spread apart to make petals. Prepare pudding mix according to package directions using 1 cup milk. Fold in whipped cream and flavoring gently. Pipe pudding mixture into strawberries using large writing tip. Arrange in serving dishes. Yield: 8-10 servings.

Debbi Smith, Xi Gamma Sigma
Elma, Washington

CHICKEN BREASTS WITH TARRAGON SAUCE

³/4 cup chicken stock	1 cup whipping cream
³/4 cup dry white wine	1 tablespoon tarragon
1¹/2 pounds chicken	2 teaspoons salt
breast filets, skinned	¹/4 teaspoon white
3 egg yolks, beaten	pepper
2 tablespoons	¹/4 teaspoon celery salt
cornstarch	1 cup green peas

Combine chicken stock and wine in 2-quart glass baking dish. Microwave on High for 4 minutes or until mixture boils. Add chicken. Microwave for 2 minutes or until tender; remove chicken. Mix egg yolks, cornstarch and whipping cream in bowl. Stir ¹/4 cup hot stock into egg mixture; stir egg yolk mixture into hot stock. Add seasonings. Microwave on High for 5 minutes, stirring 4 times. Fold in peas and chicken. Serve with buttered noodles.
Yield: 4-6 servings.

Jane Gabel, Xi Mu Eta
Houston, Texas

1986
Cook Light Cookbook

Nearly 1,000 Recipes for Cooking Light

ASPARAGUS-SHRIMP SALAD

1¹/2 cups torn spinach	¹/4 cup unsalted butter
¹/2 cup sliced	1 red pepper, cut into
mushrooms	strips
16 fresh asparagus	1 tablespoon olive oil
spears	2 teaspoons lemon juice
12 peeled raw shrimp	

Arrange spinach on 4 salad plates. Sprinkle mushrooms over spinach. Cut asparagus into ¹/2-inch pieces. Combine with ³/4 cup water in saucepan. Cook until tender-crisp. Drain, reserving ¹/2 cup liquid. Cut shrimp into thirds. Stir-fry in butter in skillet just until cooked through. Add red pepper. Stir-fry until tender-crisp. Add asparagus. Cook just until heated through. Remove to salad plates with slotted spoon. Stir reserved asparagus liquid into pan juices. Add olive oil. Cook until reduced to ¹/3 cup liquid. Remove from heat. Whisk in lemon juice and salt and freshly ground pepper to taste. Spoon over salads. Yield: 4 servings.

Approx per serving: Cal 182, Prot 7.6 gr, Fat 15.4 gr, Chol 61.5 mg, Carbo 5.7 gr, Sod 187 mg, Potas 384 mg.

Nancy F. Otte, Preceptor Alpha Kappa
Freeport, Illinois

FLANK STEAK FLORENTINE

2 1-pound flank steaks	³/4 cup soft bread crumbs
1 egg, beaten	2 tablespoons oil
1 10-ounce package	1 8-ounce can tomato
frozen chopped spinach,	sauce
cooked, drained	¹/2 cup dry red wine
¹/2 cup shredded sharp	¹/2 cup chopped onion
American cheese	1 clove of garlic, minced
¹/2 teaspoon sage	2 tablespoons flour
Salt and pepper to taste	

Pound steaks to ¹/4-inch thickness with meat mallet. Combine egg, spinach, cheese and sage with salt and pepper to taste in bowl. Stir in bread crumbs. Spread on steaks. Roll from narrow side to enclose filling; secure with string. Brown steak rolls in oil in skillet. Place in shallow baking dish. Combine tomato sauce, wine, onion and garlic in bowl. Pour over steak. Bake at 350 degrees for 1¹/2 hours. Remove rolls to serving plate. Stir in mixture of flour and ¹/4 cup water. Cook over low heat until thickened, stirring constantly. Serve with steak rolls. Yield: 8 servings.

Approx per serving: Cal 263, Prot 27.8 gr, Fat 11.7 gr, Chol 108.3 mg, Carbo 9.9 gr, Sod 374.1 mg, Potas 484.0 mg.

Ann Clapper, Kappa Omicron
Shawnee on Delaware, Pennsylvania

1987
All-New Holiday Cookbook

Festive Recipes, Ideas and Menus

WHITE WINE SANGRIA

3¹/4 cups dry white	1 small orange, thinly
wine, chilled	sliced
¹/2 cup orange juice	1 small red Delicious
¹/4 cup lime juice	apple, thinly sliced
¹/4 cup Brandy	1 7-ounce bottle of
¹/3 cup sugar	club soda, chilled
1 cup strawberry halves	
1 small lime, thinly	
sliced	

Combine wine, orange and lime juices and Brandy in large pitcher. Add sugar, stir until dissolved. Stir in strawberries and fruit slices. Chill until serving time. Mix in club soda and ice just before serving time. Yield: 8 to 9 servings.

Lois Maine, Laureate Zeta
Duluth, Minnesota

FROSTED CRANBERRY SALAD

1 6-ounce package raspberry gelatin	1 8-ounce can crushed pineapple
2 cups boiling water	1/4 cup sugar
1 11-ounce can mandarin oranges	1 tablespoon all-purpose flour
1 16-ounce can whole cranberry sauce	1 egg, beaten
1/4 cup chopped nuts	1/2 cup whipping cream, whipped

Dissolve gelatin in boiling water in bowl. Drain oranges, reserving 1/3 cup juice. Chop oranges coarsely. Add juice and cranberry sauce to gelatin mixture. Chill until partially set. Drain pineapple, reserving 1/3 cup juice. Add oranges, 1/4 cup nuts and pineapple to gelatin mixture; mix gently. Pour into 8-inch glass dish. Chill until firm. Combine pineapple juice, sugar, flour and egg in saucepan. Cook until thickened, stirring constantly. Cool. Fold in whipped cream. Spread over congealed layer. Garnish with additional nuts. Serve on lettuce-lined plates. Yield: 8 to 10 servings.

Linda Robinson, Beta Alpha
Mt. Vernon, Ohio

1988 – Party Cookbook

Prize-Winning Menus and Recipes

THANKSGIVING CELEBRATION

Red Pepper Pasta with
Salmon Champagne Cream Sauce
Frozen Waldorf Salad
Barbecued Turkey
Carrots in Champagne
Whipped Potatoes
Swedish Braid Loaf
Pecan Black Bottom Pie

Diane Runo, Xi Beta
Peoria, Arizona

SALMON CHAMPAGNE CREAM SAUCE

2 cups Champagne	2 1/2 cups whipping cream
2 cups water	Salt and pepper to taste
1 teaspoon whole allspice	Red Pepper Pasta
1 bay leaf	1/2 cup minced green onions
1 pound salmon fillets	

Bring Champagne to a boil in skillet with water, allspice and bay leaf. Add salmon. Simmer, covered, for 7 to 10 minutes or until salmon is opaque in the thickest part. Lift out salmon; flake. Strain liquid; return to skillet. Add cream. Boil rapidly until reduced to 2 1/2 cups, stirring occasionally. Add salmon to reduced mixture; season with salt and pepper to taste. Serve over hot Red Pepper Pasta. Garnish with green onions.

RED PEPPER PASTA

2 teaspoons dried hot pepper flakes	1/2 teaspoon salt
2 tablespoons boiling water	1 tablespoon corn oil
1 cup semolina flour	1 tablespoon tomato paste
1 cup all-purpose flour	2 eggs, slightly beaten
	1 tablespoon olive oil

Combine red pepper flakes and boiling water in small bowl. Let steep for 15 minutes. Combine flours and salt in food processor container. Add pepper flakes, corn oil, tomato paste and eggs, processing constantly until mixture forms ball. Let rest, wrapped in plastic wrap, for 20 minutes. Roll out; cut into strips by hand or with pasta machine. Place in boiling water in saucepan with 1 tablespoon olive oil added. Cook for 2 minutes; drain. Yield: 4 servings.

1989
Comfort Foods

Recipes to Comfort You Today

DEATH BY CHOCOLATE

1 2-layer package chocolate cake mix	32 ounces whipped topping
1/2 cup Kahlua	1 1.4-ounce milk chocolate candy bar
4 packages chocolate mousse mix	
8 Skor candy bars, crushed	

Prepare cake mix using package directions. Pour into 3 greased and floured 8-inch round cake pans. Bake at 350 degrees for 30 minutes. Cool slightly. Pierce cake layers with fork. Drizzle Kahlua over layers. Prepare all packages chocolate mousse in large bowl using package directions. Break cake layers into pieces. Layer cake pieces, mousse, crushed candy and whipped topping 1/3 at a time in large bowl. Shave milk chocolate candy over top. Yield: 12 servings.

Anne Stone, Alpha Kappa
Montgomery, New York

1990
Celebrations Cookbook

Recipes • Crafts • Decorations

AMARETTO CHEESE MOLD

This is nice served at Christmas, Valentine's Day and Secret Sister Revealing parties.

2 egg yolks	2 tablespoons water
8 ounces cream cheese, softened	1/4 cup sugar
	2 tablespoons Amaretto
1 1/2 teaspoons unflavored gelatin	Fruit slices
	Water wafers

Cream egg yolks and cream cheese in bowl until light and fluffy. Soften gelatin in water in saucepan. Heat over low heat until dissolved. Add to egg yolk mixture; mix well. Add sugar and Amaretto. Beat until smooth and creamy. Pour into 1-cup mold. Chill for several hours. Unmold onto platter. Serve with fruit slices or water wafers. Yield: 8 servings.

Barbara Firor, Laureate Delta Nu
Santa Ana, California

1991
The Best of Beta Sigma Phi

Special Friends

STEAMED DUMPLINGS

1 pound ground turkey	1/2 teaspoon sugar
1/2 cup chopped water chestnuts	1 tablespoon soy sauce
1/4 cup chopped green onions	1 package wonton wrappers
1/2 cup chopped bamboo shoots	Lettuce leaves
	1/2 cup soy sauce
1 tablespoon cornstarch	2 tablespoons rice vinegar
1/2 teaspoon garlic powder	2 teaspoons sesame oil
1 teaspoon salt	1/2 teaspoon Tabasco sauce
1/4 teaspoon pepper	

Combine turkey and vegetables in bowl; mix well. Add cornstarch, seasonings and 1 tablespoon soy sauce; mix well. Spoon a small amount onto each wonton wrapper; moisten edges with water. Pleat or crimp with pot sticker maker to seal. Place in single layer in lettuce-lined steamer. Steam over boiling water for 6 minutes or until cooked through. Repeat with remaining dumplings. Serve with mixture of remaining 1/2 cup soy sauce, vinegar, oil and Tabasco sauce for dipping. Yield: 8 servings.

Laura Ross-Wingfield
daughter of Jack Ross

SUGAR AND SPICE MUFFINS

These are great made as mini-muffins! They've been served at many a sorority brunch; makes great lunch box treats; snacks; breakfast!

1 3/4 cups all-purpose flour	3/4 cup sugar
1 1/2 teaspoons baking powder	1 egg
	3/4 cup milk
1/2 teaspoon salt	2/3 cup melted butter or margarine
1/2 teaspoon nutmeg	3/4 cup sugar
1/3 cup vegetable oil	1 teaspoon cinnamon

Preheat oven to 350 degrees. Sift flour, baking powder, salt and nutmeg together into bowl. Add mixture of oil, 3/4 cup sugar, egg and milk; stir until blended. Fill greased unlined muffin cups 1/3 full. Bake for 15 minutes for medium muffins or 12 minutes for miniature muffins. Remove from pan. Dip hot muffins into melted butter. Coat with mixture of 3/4 cup sugar and cinnamon. Yield: 12 servings.

Marilyn Ross
wife of Bill Ross

SMALL DEVIL'S FOOD CAKE

1 cup all-purpose flour	1/2 cup butter, softened
1 cup sugar	3 1/2 cups sifted confectioners' sugar
1 egg	
1/2 cup milk	Pinch of salt
1 tablespoon vinegar	4 to 5 tablespoons hot coffee
1/2 cup boiling water	
1 teaspoon soda	1 1/2 teaspoons vanilla extract
1 teaspoon vanilla extract	
2 ounces unsweetened baking chocolate, melted	

Preheat oven to 350 degrees. Combine flour, sugar, egg and mixture of milk and vinegar in bowl; mix well. Add water, soda and 1 teaspoon vanilla; mix well. Stir in chocolate. Batter will be thin. Pour into greased and floured 8-inch square cake pan. Bake for 35 minutes or until cake tests done. Cream butter in mixer bowl until light and fluffy. Add confectioners' sugar gradually, beating constantly. Add salt and enough coffee to make of spreading consistency; beat until fluffy. Blend in remaining 1 1/2 teaspoons vanilla. Spread over cooled cake. Yield: 9 servings.

Jean Ross
wife of Jack Ross

1991
The Best of Beta Sigma Phi

Photograph Recipes

PEAR-BERRY PIE

2 PET-RITZ deep-dish pie crust shells	3 tablespoons cornstarch
4 cups canned sliced pears	1/4 teaspoon salt
1/2 cup packed light brown sugar	3/4 teaspoon cinnamon
	1/4 teaspoon nutmeg
	1 16-ounce can whole cranberry sauce

Preheat oven and baking sheet to 400 degrees. Remove pie shells from freezer. Invert 1 pie shell onto waxed paper. Let thaw until flat. Combine pears, brown sugar, cornstarch, salt and spice in medium bowl. Stir in cranberry sauce gently. Spoon into pie shell. Place flattened pastry on top. Recrimp edges, sealing completely; cut slits. Bake on preheated baking sheet for 35 to 40 minutes or until brown and bubbly. Yield: 8 servings.

Photograph for this recipe is on the Cover.
Recipe developed by Pet Incorporated

FUDGE PECAN PIE

1/2 cup butter	1/8 teaspoon salt
3 tablespoons unsweetened baking cocoa	1 teaspoon vanilla extract
3/4 cup hot water	1 cup pecan halves
2 cups sugar	1 PET-RITZ deep dish pie crust shell
1/2 cup all-purpose flour	La Creme Whipped Topping, thawed
1 5-fluid ounce can PET Evaporated Milk	

Preheat oven and baking sheet to 350 degrees. Melt butter in saucepan; remove from heat. Add cocoa and hot water. Stir until dissolved. Blend in sugar, flour, evaporated milk, salt and vanilla with wire whisk. Stir until batter is smooth. Add pecans. Pour into pie shell. Bake on preheated baking sheet for 50 minutes or until knife inserted 1 inch from edge comes out clean. Serve cooled pie with La Creme. May bake in miniature tart shells for 20 minutes or until set. Yield: 8 servings.

Photograph for this recipe is on the Cover.
Recipe developed by Pet Incorporated

HOT BROCCOLI VINAIGRETTE

1 bunch broccoli	2 teaspoons dry mustard
1/3 cup water	2 teaspoons sugar
2 tablespoons cider vinegar	3/4 teaspoon salt
3 tablespoons olive oil	2 tablespoons cider vinegar

Cut broccoli into 1/2-inch thick spears. Arrange in 8-by-12-inch glass baking dish with flowerets toward center. Add water and 2 tablespoons vinegar. Microwave, covered with SARAN WRAP™, turning back edge to vent, on High for 8 to 10 minutes or until tender-crisp, turning dish once. Combine remaining ingredients in 2-cup glass measure. Microwave on High for 1 minute. Pour over drained broccoli on serving plate. Yield: 4 to 6 servings.

Photograph for this recipe is on page 1.
Recipe developed by the Dow Chemical Co.

TOMATO ASPIC

2 envelopes unflavored gelatin	1 stalk celery, finely chopped
2 cups tomato juice	3 tablespoons lemon juice
1 6-ounce can tomato paste	2 tablespoons cider vinegar
1/2 small green pepper, finely chopped	3/4 teaspoon salt
1 small onion, minced	1/2 teaspoon oregano

Soften gelatin in tomato juice in 2-quart glass bowl for 3 minutes. Stir in remaining ingredients. Microwave, covered with SARAN WRAP™, turning back edge to vent, on High for 7 minutes, stirring once. Pour into 4- to 5-cup mold. Chill, tightly covered with SARAN WRAP™, for 4 hours or until firm. Unmold onto lettuce-lined serving plate. Garnish with lemon wedges. Yield: 8 servings.

Photograph for this recipe is on page 1.
Recipe developed by the Dow Chemical Co.

BEEF STEAK WITH ARTICHOKES

2 pounds beef top sirloin steak	1/2 cup beef broth
1 teaspoon vegetable oil	2 9-ounce packages frozen artichokes, thawed
1 pound fresh mushrooms, sliced	2 teaspoons oregano
2/3 cup dry white wine	2 teaspoons thyme
2 teaspoons grated lemon rind	1/2 teaspoon salt

Preheat oven to 200 degrees. Trim steak. Brush nonstick 12-inch skillet with oil. Place steak in skillet. Cook over medium heat until done to taste, turning occasionally to brown steak evenly on both sides. Remove steak; keep warm in oven. Add mushrooms to skillet. Cook over medium heat until mushrooms are coated with pan drippings, stirring frequently. Stir in wine. Increase heat to high. Cook until wine is reduced by 2/3. Stir in remaining ingredients. Simmer, covered, for 3 minutes or until artichokes are tender-crisp. Cut steak into slices. Serve artichoke topping with steak. Yield: 8 servings.

Photograph for this recipe is on page 1.
Recipe developed by California Beef Council

Menus Through the Year

New Year's Day
Black-Eyed Pea Party

Black-Eyed Pea Spread
Black-Eyed Pea Pâté — Black-Eyed Pea Dip
Black-Eyed Pea Pinwheels
Pineapple Baked Ham — Potato Casserole
Black-Eyed Pea Spaghetti
Best-Ever Plain Ole Peas — Cajun Peas
Sweet and Sour Peas — Chinese Peas
Plentiful P's Salad
Lucky Almond Tassies
Brandy Slush

See Index for similar recipes.

For several years, my husband and I have hosted a Black-Eyed Pea Party on New Year's Day. I have assembled a menu of dishes made with black-eyed peas. With so many selections, even people who don't especially like black-eyed peas can find something they like. We serve Brandy Slush and other assorted drinks with the appetizers. The person who finds the lucky almond in the dessert receives a surprise gift. This year the invitations were decorated with big black P's with eyes drawn in the round part of the letters.

 Lavada Harrison, Xi Delta Xi
Poplar Bluff, Missouri

BLACK-EYED PEA SPREAD

1 16-ounce can black-eyed peas, drained	8 ounces sour cream
1 10-ounce package frozen chopped spinach, thawed, well drained	1/2 cup mayonnaise
	1/3 cup vegetable soup mix
1 8-ounce can sliced water chestnuts, drained, chopped	1/8 teaspoon garlic powder
	40 party pumpernickel bread slices

Combine peas, spinach, water chestnuts, sour cream, mayonnaise, soup mix and garlic powder in bowl; mix well. Spread on bread slices. Yield: 40 servings.

BLACK-EYED PEA PÂTÉ

6 ounces cream cheese, softened	3 tablespoons Worcestershire sauce
2 16-ounce cans black-eyed peas, drained	2 envelopes unflavored gelatin
1 medium onion, cut into quarters	2 tablespoons cold water
1 or 2 cloves of garlic	Chopped parsley
1/2 cup medium picante sauce	Red, yellow and green bell peppers, cut into pieces
1 teaspoon hot sauce	

Combine cream cheese, peas, onion, garlic, picante sauce, hot sauce and Worcestershire sauce in food processor container fitted with steel blade; process for 1 minute or until smooth. Soften gelatin in cold water in small saucepan. Let stand for 1 minute. Cook over low heat until gelatin dissolves, stirring constantly. Add to pea mixture in food processor; process for 30 seconds. Spoon into oiled 9-inch round pan. Chill, covered, until set. Unmold onto serving plate; sprinkle with parsley. Serve with bell pepper pieces. Yield: 16 servings.

BLACK-EYED PEA DIP

1³/4 cups dried black-
  eyed peas
5 cups water
5 jalapeño peppers,
  seeded, chopped
¹/3 cup chopped onion
1 clove of garlic
1 cup butter or
  margarine

2 cups shredded sharp
  American cheese
1 4-ounce can chopped
  green chilies
1 tablespoon jalapeño
  pepper liquid
Corn chips

Combine peas with water to cover in heavy sauce-pan. Bring to a boil. Cook for 2 minutes; remove from heat. Let stand, covered, for 1 hour; drain. Combine peas with 5 cups water in saucepan. Simmer, covered, for 1 hour and 15 minutes or until tender; drain. Combine peas, jalapeño peppers, onion and garlic in blender container; process until smooth. Melt butter and cheese in double boiler over boiling water, stirring to mix well. Add green chilies, pepper liquid and pea mixture; mix well. Serve with corn chips. Yield: 24 servings.

BLACK-EYED PEA PINWHEELS

1 15-ounce can black-
  eyed peas, drained
¹/4 cup butter or
  margarine
2 dashes of hot sauce
Garlic powder to taste
¹/4 teaspoon seasoned
  salt

6 ounces cream cheese,
  softened
1 10-ounce package
  4-by-6-inch ham
  slices
10 green onions,
  trimmed to 6 inches

Combine peas, butter, hot sauce, garlic powder and seasoned salt in saucepan. Bring to a boil; reduce heat. Simmer for 15 minutes, stirring occasionally. Cool to room temperature. Combine pea mixture with cream cheese in food processor container fitted with steel blade. Process for 3 to 5 seconds or until smooth, scraping side of container. Spread mixture on ham slices. Place 1 green onion on each slice. Roll ham to enclose filling and green onion. Chill until firm. Cut into slices. Yield: 20 servings.

BLACK-EYED PEA SPAGHETTI

1 cup chopped onion
3 cloves of garlic, minced
2 tablespoons bacon
  drippings
1 pound ground beef
2 16-ounce cans
  stewed tomatoes,
  chopped
1 teaspoon seasoned salt
1¹/2 teaspoons chili
  powder

2 teaspoons garlic salt
¹/2 teaspoon oregano
¹/2 teaspoon basil
1¹/2 teaspoons sugar
1 to 2 tablespoons
  Worcestershire sauce
1 teaspoon salt
¹/4 teaspoon pepper
1 cup elbow spaghetti
5 cups frozen black-
  eyed peas

Sauté onion and garlic in bacon drippings in large skillet until onion is tender. Add ground beef. Cook until brown, stirring frequently; drain. Add un-drained tomatoes and seasonings; mix well. Simmer for 25 minutes, stirring occasionally. Cook spaghetti using package directions; drain. Cook peas using package directions; drain. Add spaghetti and peas to ground beef mixture. Simmer for 5 minutes. Yield: 8 to 10 servings.

BEST-EVER PLAIN OLE PEAS

1 16-ounce package
  dried black-eyed peas
6 cups water
4 slices hickory-smoked
  bacon
1 tablespoon sugar

1 tablespoon white
  wine vinegar
¹/4 teaspoon garlic salt
1 tablespoon salt
¹/4 teaspoon pepper

Combine peas with water to cover by 2 inches in heavy saucepan. Soak for 8 hours; drain. Add 6 cups water, bacon, sugar, vinegar, garlic salt, salt and pep-per; mix well. Simmer, covered, for 1¹/2 hours or until peas are tender. Yield: 6 cups.

Cajun Peas: Preheat oven to 350 degrees. Layer 3 cups cooked rice, mixture of 1 cup sour cream and 1 tea-spoon poultry seasoning and mixture of 16 ounces red beans, drained, and 2 cups Best-Ever Peas in baking dish. Bake for 30 minutes. Sprinkle ¹/2 cup chopped cooked hickory-smoked sausage and ¹/2 cup shredded Monterey Jack cheese over layers. Bake for 5 minutes. Yield: 9 cups.

Chinese Peas: Sauté 2 bunches sliced green onions in 2 teaspoons butter or margarine in skillet. Mix 8 ounces each sliced drained water chestnuts and drained bamboo shoots, ¹/2 teaspoon instant chicken bouillon, 1 teaspoon each teriyaki and soy sauce to half the green onions. Add 4 cups Best-Ever Peas. Heat to serving temperature. Garnish with remain-ing green onions. Yield: 6¹/2 cups.

PLENTIFUL P'S SALAD

4 cups cooked black-
  eyed peas
2 cups cooked rotini
1 medium red bell
  pepper, chopped
1 medium green bell
  pepper, chopped
1 medium purple onion,
  chopped
6 ounces provolone
  cheese, cut into strips
1 2-ounce jar chopped
  pimento, drained

3 ounces sliced
  pepperoni, cut into
  strips
1 4-ounce jar sliced
  mushrooms, drained
2 tablespoons minced
  fresh parsley
1 envelope Italian
  salad dressing mix
¹/2 cup vinegar
¹/4 cup sugar
¹/4 cup vegetable oil
¹/4 teaspoon pepper

Combine first 10 ingredients in large bowl. Add mix-ture of salad dressing mix, vinegar, sugar, oil and pepper. Chill for 2 hours. Yield: 8 servings.

Valentine Tea

Finger Sandwiches — Watercress Pinwheels
Shortbread — Almond Fingers
Dainty Chocolate Chip Cookies
Whole Wheat Digestives
Pecan Tarts — Orange Tea Loaf
Applesauce Cake with Sour Cream
Chocolate Cake — Varieties of Tea

See Index for similar recipes.

Every member of our chapter made one of these recipes for our Valentine Tea in February. We crowned our Valentine Queen, had our annual "teacup exchange," and sampled a variety of teas in our new teacups while enjoying a program on tea history and the English tea ceremony.

Kristie Gray, Epsilon Tau
Stafford, Virginia

FINGER SANDWICHES

1 4-ounce can shrimp	1/4 cup drained crushed
3 tablespoons	pineapple
mayonnaise	3 tablespoons minced
2 tablespoons finely	green bell pepper
chopped celery	1 tablespoon minced
1/4 teaspoon onion	onion
flakes	1/4 cup raisins
1 tablespoon chili sauce	1/2 cup chopped apple
2 4-ounce cans deviled	1/4 cup chopped celery
ham	1/4 cup chopped pecans
12 ounces cream cheese,	1/4 cup mayonnaise
softened	Party bread

Combine shrimp, 3 tablespoons mayonnaise, 2 tablespoons celery, onion flakes and chili sauce in bowl; mix well. Blend ham and cream cheese in bowl. Add pineapple, green pepper and onion; mix well. Mix remaining ingredients in bowl. Spread fillings on bread. Arrange on serving plate. Yield: 5 dozen.

Elaine Lavelett, Preceptor Alpha Beta, Colorado Springs, Colorado, served "Champagne and Valentines" for a Chapter Sweetheart Cocktail Party. The menu included hearty appetizers, heart-shaped cookies and Pink Champagne Punch. Soak 1 quart strawberries sprinkled with 1/2 cup sugar in 3 ounces Brandy and 1 bottle of Sauterne for 1 hour. Add 2 bottles of pink Champagne and 1 bottle of sparkling water.

ALMOND FINGERS

1 cup butter, softened	1 teaspoon almond
1/2 cup confectioners'	extract
sugar	2 cups chopped toasted
1 1/2 cups all-purpose	almonds
flour	Sifted confectioners'
Salt to taste	sugar

Cream butter and 1/2 cup confectioners' sugar in mixer bowl until light and fluffy. Sift in flour and salt; mix well. Beat in almond extract. Stir in almonds. Chill for 1 hour. Preheat oven to 325 degrees. Shape dough by tablespoonfuls into 1/2-by-2-inch fingers. Place on lightly greased baking sheet. Bake for 20 minutes or until very light brown. Remove to tray sprinkled with sifted confectioners' sugar; sift additional confectioners' sugar over tops. Cool to room temperature. Store in layers separated with waxed paper in airtight container. Yield: 6 dozen.

WHOLE WHEAT DIGESTIVES

1 cup all-purpose	1/4 cup vegetable
flour	shortening, chilled,
1/2 teaspoon salt	cut into chunks
2 cups whole wheat	1/2 cup packed light
flour	brown sugar
6 tablespoons cold	1 egg
margarine, chopped	1/4 cup water

Preheat oven to 350 degrees. Sift all-purpose flour and salt into large bowl; stir in whole wheat flour. Rub in margarine and shortening with fingers until crumbly. Add brown sugar; mix well. Add mixture of egg and water; mix to form soft dough. Roll 1/8 inch thick on lightly floured surface. Cut into 2-inch circles. Place on greased baking sheet; prick tops with fork. Bake for 15 minutes or until light brown. Remove to wire rack to cool. Yield: 50 servings.

ORANGE TEA LOAF

2 cups self-rising flour	3/4 cup sugar
2 1/2 teaspoons baking	1 egg
powder	Grated rind of 1/2 orange
Salt to taste	2 tablespoons orange
1/4 cup butter or	juice
margarine, softened	2 tablespoons milk

Preheat oven to 375 degrees. Sift flour, baking powder and salt into medium bowl. Cream butter and sugar in mixer bowl until light and fluffy. Beat in egg, orange rind, orange juice and milk. Fold in sifted dry ingredients. Spoon into greased 4-by-8-inch loaf pan. Bake for 40 to 50 minutes or until wooden pick inserted in center comes out clean. Cool in pan for 5 minutes. Remove to wire rack to cool completely. Store, tightly wrapped, for 1 to 2 days before serving. Slice and serve with butter.
Yield: 8 to 10 servings.

Mardi Gras Magic

Sensational Salad
Chicken and Sausage Gumbo
French Bread
King's Cake

See Index for similar recipes.

I served this menu at our February dinner and did a program on the history of Mardi Gras and the tradition of the King's Cake. Invitations instructed members to wear costumes relating to New Orleans jazz, and the member with the best costume won a decorated Champagne bottle. The member who found the baby in her piece of cake also won a prize.

Deana Bowles, Xi Alpha Phi
Columbia, South Carolina

SENSATIONAL SALAD

1/2 cup vegetable oil	1 bunch parsley,
1/2 cup olive oil	chopped
2 1/2 tablespoons lemon	1 cup grated Romano
juice	cheese
1 1/2 tablespoons vinegar	1/4 cup crumbled bleu
2 cloves of garlic,	cheese
crushed	Freshly ground pepper
3/4 teaspoon salt	to taste
2 large heads lettuce,	
torn	

Combine vegetable oil, olive oil, lemon juice, vinegar, garlic and salt in bowl; mix well. Combine lettuce and parsley in salad bowl. Add dressing; toss to coat well. Sprinkle with cheeses; toss again. Sprinkle with pepper. Yield: 10 servings.

CHICKEN AND SAUSAGE GUMBO

1 chicken	1 large onion, chopped
Salt, pepper and	3 bay leaves
cayenne pepper to taste	1 teaspoon basil
1/2 to 1 pound sausage,	2 teaspoons thyme
chopped	2 fresh or canned
2 cups sliced okra	tomatoes, chopped
(optional)	3 tablespoons bacon
1 green bell pepper,	drippings or
chopped	shortening
3 cloves of garlic,	3 tablespoons
chopped	all-purpose flour

Rinse chicken inside and out. Combine with salt, pepper, cayenne pepper and water to cover in large saucepan. Cook until tender. Drain, reserving stock. Remove chicken from bones in slivers, discarding bones and skin. Brown sausage in large saucepan, stirring frequently. Remove with slotted spoon. Add okra, green pepper, garlic, onion, bay leaves, basil and thyme to drippings in skillet. Sauté until tender. Stir in tomatoes. Simmer for 15 minutes, stirring frequently. Add sausage, chicken and all but 1 cup reserved stock. Simmer while preparing roux. Heat bacon drippings in cast-iron saucepan or skillet until nearly smoking. Stir in flour. Cook for 3 to 5 minutes or until dark brown, stirring constantly to prevent burning. Cool for 5 minutes. Add remaining 1 cup reserved stock, stirring constantly. Add to gumbo. Adjust salt and cayenne pepper. Simmer for 2 to 3 hours. Remove bay leaves. Serve over rice. Yield: 12 servings.

KING'S CAKE

2 envelopes dry yeast	1/2 cup butter, sliced
2 teaspoons sugar	1 cup all-purpose flour
1/2 cup lukewarm water	1 1-inch plastic baby,
3 1/2 cups all-purpose	dried bean or pecan
flour	half
1/2 cup sugar	1 egg
1 teaspoon nutmeg	1 tablespoon milk
2 teaspoons salt	3/4 cup sugar
1/2 cup lukewarm milk	1 drop each of green,
1 teaspoon grated	yellow, red and blue
lemon rind	food coloring
5 egg yolks	Melted butter

Sprinkle yeast and 2 teaspoons sugar over lukewarm water. Let stand until yeast is softened; stir to mix well. Let stand for 10 minutes or until bubbly. Mix 3 1/2 cups flour, 1/2 cup sugar, nutmeg and salt in bowl. Add yeast mixture, 1/2 cup lukewarm milk and lemon rind; mix well. Beat in egg yolks. Add 1/2 cup butter, beating until smooth. Knead with dough hook or on floured surface until smooth and elastic, kneading in 1 cup flour. Place in greased bowl, turning to coat surface. Let rise, covered, in warm place for 1 1/2 to 2 hours or until doubled in bulk. Shape into 14- or 15-inch roll on floured surface. Shape into ring on buttered baking sheet, pressing ends to seal. Press baby into cake from bottom. Let rise for 45 minutes or until doubled in bulk. Brush with mixture of egg and 1 tablespoon milk. Preheat oven to 375 degrees. Bake cake for 25 minutes or until brown. Remove to wire rack to cool. Tint 1/4 cup sugar with green food coloring. Repeat with yellow coloring and mixture of red and blue colorings to form purple. Brush top of cake with melted butter. Sprinkle 1/3 of cake with each color of the tinted sugars which are the traditional colors of Mardi Gras. May knead candied citron or raisins into dough or frost with confectioners' sugar frosting before adding sugars. Yield: 12 to 15 servings.

St. Patrick's Day Luncheon

Spinach and Bacon Dip
Broccoli and Cheese Quiche
Caesar Salad — Pistachio Salad
Vegetable and Fruit Platter
Ambrosia Lime Cake — Lime Bars
Limeade Punch

See Index for similar recipes.

We combined our spring luncheon social with a rush party and a party to honor our daughter legacies. The decorations and menu were selected to carry out the theme of a "Very Green Day" in spring. Invitations asked guests to wear something green and plates, napkins, tablecloths and candles carried out the color scheme. Name tags had shamrocks and the table had a "Pot of Gold." Guests took home potted shamrock plants.

Brenda Gervais, Delta Gamma
Lively, Ontario, Canada

SPINACH AND BACON DIP

16 ounces cream cheese, softened	1 cup chopped onion
1 cup mayonnaise	1/2 package fresh spinach, chopped
1 teaspoon garlic powder	1 cup shredded Cheddar cheese
2 teaspoons dillweed	1 loaf French, Italian
8 ounces bacon, chopped	or pumpernickel bread

Preheat oven to 250 degrees. Combine cream cheese, mayonnaise, garlic powder and dillweed in bowl; mix until smooth. Fry bacon in skillet until crisp; remove with slotted spoon to drain. Add onion to drippings in skillet. Sauté until tender. Add bacon, onion, spinach and Cheddar cheese to cream cheese mixture; mix well. Cut off top of bread and scoop out center. Spoon dip into bread cavity; replace top. Wrap in double layer of foil; place on baking sheet. Bake for 1 1/2 hours. Yield: 10 to 15 servings.

BROCCOLI AND CHEESE QUICHE

3 eggs	1 cup shredded Monterey Jack cheese
1 cup half and half	
1/4 teaspoon salt	2 cups chopped broccoli
1/8 teaspoon pepper	1 unbaked 9-inch deep-dish pie shell
1/4 cup chopped green onions	

Preheat oven to 350 degrees. Beat eggs in mixer bowl. Beat in half and half, salt and pepper. Add green onions, cheese and broccoli; mix well. Spoon into pie shell. Bake for 40 minutes or until knife inserted in center comes out clean. Let stand for several minutes. Cut into wedges. Yield: 6 to 8 servings.

AMBROSIA LIME CAKE

1 2-layer package white cake mix	1 teaspoon grated lime rind
1 14-ounce can sweetened condensed milk	1 cup whipped cream
	1/3 cup coconut (optional)
2 tablespoons lime juice	Lime slices

Preheat oven to 350 degrees. Prepare and bake cake mix using package directions for 9-by-13-inch cake pan. Cool on wire rack. Pierce holes halfway through cake at 1-inch intervals with knife handle. Combine condensed milk, lime juice and lime rind in bowl; mix well. Drizzle into holes and over top of cake. Chill for 1 hour or longer. Spread with whipped cream; sprinkle with coconut. Garnish with lime slices. Store in refrigerator. Cut into squares. Yield: 12 to 16 servings.

LIME BARS

2 cups all-purpose flour	1 teaspoon baking powder
1/4 cup sugar	
1 cup butter or margarine, softened	3 eggs
	2/3 cup lime juice
1/4 cup all-purpose flour	Grated rind of 2 limes
2 cups sugar	

Preheat oven to 350 degrees. Combine 2 cups flour and 1/4 cup sugar in bowl; mix well. Cut in butter until crumbly. Pat into 9-by-13-inch baking pan. Bake for 15 minutes or until brown. Combine remaining 1/4 cup flour, remaining 2 cups sugar, baking powder, eggs, lime juice and lime rind in mixer bowl; mix well. Pour over baked layer. Bake for 20 minutes longer or until set. Cool on wire rack. Cut into squares. Yield: 24 servings.

LIMEADE PUNCH

1 48-ounce can apple juice, chilled	2 bottles of club soda, chilled
1 12-ounce can frozen lime juice, thawed	1 lime, sliced
	1 pint lime sherbet (optional)
1 6-ounce can frozen limeade concentrate, thawed	

Combine apple juice, lime juice and limeade concentrate in punch bowl; mix well. Add club soda; mix gently. Top with lime slices. Top with spoonfuls of lime sherbet. Yield: 15 servings.

Woman of the Year Dinner

Roast Beef
Green Beans — Parslied Potatoes
Tossed Green Salad — Coleslaw
Green Fruit Salad — Green Condiment Tray
Hot Rolls
Green Wine — Lime Punch

See Index for similar recipes.

We honored our Woman of the Year on St. Patrick's Day, so we planned the menu and decorations to carry out the green theme. Invitations were in a green shamrock. The centerpiece was geranium foliage in a white container with gold ribbons on a white tablecloth with green napkins. Each of the dishes brought to the potluck dinner to go with the roast beef were either green or accented with green. The fruit salad was made of kiwifruit, honeydew melon, Granny Smith apples, green grapes and bananas.

Dorothy Malo, Preceptor Beta Omega
San Diego, California

Easter Brunch

Make-Ahead Breakfast Brunch
Fruit Platter — Fruit Dip
Tiny Hot Cross Buns — Oat Bran Muffins
Mimosas

See Index for similar recipes.

I used this menu on a festive, but slightly sad occasion, for it was served at the brunch we gave to say goodbye to friends who were moving away. After brunch we exchanged gifts and had an Easter egg hunt for the children. Adults celebrated with Mimosas made of equal parts of orange juice and Champagne, garnished with strawberries.

Diane Klikus, Iota Epsilon
Fayetteville, Georgia

MAKE-AHEAD BREAKFAST BRUNCH

12 eggs, beaten	8 ounces sour cream
1/2 cup milk	12 slices bacon, crisp-
1/2 teaspoon salt	fried, crumbled
1/4 teaspoon pepper	1 cup shredded sharp
1 tablespoon butter or	Cheddar cheese
margarine	

Scramble mixture of eggs, milk, salt and pepper in butter in skillet. Stir in sour cream. Spoon into buttered shallow 2-quart baking dish. Top with bacon and cheese. Chill, covered, overnight. Preheat oven to 300 degrees. Bake, uncovered, for 15 to 20 minutes or until bubbly. Yield: 12 servings.

FRUIT DIP

8 ounces Neufchâtel	1/2 cup drained canned
cheese, softened	crushed pineapple or
1 small banana, mashed	chopped fresh
1/4 teaspoon nutmeg	pineapple

Combine all ingredients in bowl; mix well. Chill, covered, for 1 hour or longer. Yield: 1 3/4 cups.

TINY HOT CROSS BUNS

1 1-pound loaf frozen	1/4 teaspoon nutmeg
bread dough, thawed	1 egg, slightly beaten
2 tablespoons sugar	1 cup confectioners'
1/3 cup raisins	sugar
3/4 teaspoon cinnamon	1 tablespoon milk

Knead bread dough with sugar, raisins, cinnamon and nutmeg on unfloured surface for 10 minutes. Shape into ball; cover with damp cloth. Let rise for 30 minutes. Shape into 12 rolls. Place on greased baking sheet. Cover with damp towel. Let rise for 30 minutes. Preheat oven to 375 degrees. Brush buns with egg. Bake for 15 minutes or until golden brown. Pipe mixture of confectioners' sugar and milk in X on top of each bun. Let stand for 30 minutes or until icing is set. Yield: 12 servings.

OAT BRAN MUFFINS

1 cup boiling water	1/2 cup shortening
1 cup natural bran	1 3/4 cups sugar
2 1/2 cups all-purpose	2 eggs
flour	2 cups buttermilk
2 1/2 teaspoons soda	2 cups oats
1/2 teaspoon salt	1 cup raisins

Preheat oven to 375 degrees. Pour water over bran in bowl; mix well. Let stand for several minutes. Mix flour, soda and salt in large bowl. Cream shortening and sugar in mixer bowl until light and fluffy. Beat in eggs and buttermilk. Add to dry ingredients; mix well. Stir in oats, raisins and bran. Fill greased muffin cups 3/4 full. Bake for 15 to 20 minutes or until muffins test done. Yield: 2 1/2 dozen.

Derby Day Fling

Mint Juleps
Ham Balls — Rumaki
Shrimp Dip — Assorted Crackers
Honey-Glazed Baked Ham
Kentucky Burgoo
Sweet Potato Soufflé
Seven-Layer Salad
Homemade Biscuits
Chocolate Chip Pecan Pie
Coffee

See Index for similar recipes.

This is the menu for our chapter's annual Derby Day Party. We decorate with green and white pennants, silk magnolia blossoms or red-rose horseshoe, loving cups and blue ribbons. The Mint Juleps and appetizers are served until race time, when we gather around the television set to see who wins the pool for the race. After dinner, we stage our own version of the Derby with play money, wooden horses, and a 6-lane paper race track of 8 furlongs. Players progress with the throw of a die. Winners of the preliminary heats meet for the final run and a nice prize. Coffee and conversation round out the evening.

Sue Chase, Laureate Lambda
Port St. Lucie, Florida

MINT JULEPS

1 12-ounce can frozen limeade concentrate	1 quart water Fresh mint leaves
1 12-ounce can frozen lemonade concentrate	1 cup bourbon 1 1-liter bottle of 7-Up

Combine first 3 ingredients in large container; mix well. Add mint leaves, bourbon and 7-Up. Pour over shaved ice in large punch bowl. Serve with garnish of fresh mint. Yield: 12 servings.

HAM BALLS

2 pounds ground ham	1 cup cracker crumbs
1 pound ground pork	1 cup vinegar
1 egg	2 cups packed light
1 5-ounce can evaporated milk	brown sugar 1 teaspoon dry mustard

Combine ground ham, ground pork, egg, evaporated milk and cracker crumbs in bowl; mix well. Shape into 1-inch balls. Arrange around outer edge of 2-quart glass dish. Microwave on High for 4 to 5 minutes; drain. Combine vinegar, brown sugar and dry mustard in bowl; mix well. Pour over ham balls. Microwave, covered, on High for 11 to 13 minutes or until done to taste, stirring once. Yield: 4 dozen.

HONEY-GLAZED BAKED HAM

1 cooked boneless ham	1 cup honey
Whole cloves	3 tablespoons
1 cup packed light brown sugar	pineapple juice

Preheat oven to 325 degrees. Slice ham; tie with string to retain shape. Place in roasting pan; stud with cloves. Combine remaining ingredients in bowl; mix well. Pour over ham. Bake for 1½ to 2 hours, basting every 30 minutes. Yield: 8 servings.

KENTUCKY BURGOO

4 whole boneless chicken breasts	6 carrots, sliced 4 cups whole kernel corn
2 pounds beef cubes	2 16-ounce cans lima
2 pounds pork cubes	beans
1 tablespoon salt	2 28-ounce cans stewed
Pepper to taste	tomatoes
3 quarts water	1 large green bell
4 large onions, chopped	pepper, chopped
5 large potatoes, chopped	2 cups sliced okra ½ cup chopped parsley

Rinse chicken and pat dry. Combine with beef, pork, salt, pepper and water in large stockpot. Bring to a boil; skim surface. Simmer, loosely covered, for 1 hour or until chicken is tender. Remove chicken. Cook remaining mixture for 1½ hours longer or until tender. Remove beef and pork with slotted spoon. Add next 8 ingredients to stockpot; mix well. Simmer, covered, for 1 hour, adding additional water if needed. Cut beef, pork and chicken into small pieces. Add to burgoo. Add parsley and adjust seasonings. Yield: 16 servings.

CHOCOLATE CHIP-PECAN PIE

1 cup chocolate chips	½ cup sugar
½ cup chopped pecans	½ cup light corn syrup
1 unbaked deep-dish pie shell	¼ cup melted butter Ice cream or whipped
2 eggs, beaten	topping

Preheat oven to 375 degrees. Sprinkle chocolate chips and pecans in pie shell. Add mixture of eggs, sugar, corn syrup and butter. Bake for 10 minutes. Reduce oven temperature to 350 degrees. Bake for 35 minutes longer. Serve warm with ice cream or whipped topping. Yield: 8 servings.

Mother's Day Luncheon

Raspberry Fizz
Lemon Chicken
Broccoli and Rice Casserole
Apple Coffee Cake

This menu was a delightful treat for a Mother's Day Luncheon.

Marguerite Siedlicke, Preceptor Beta
Liverpool, New York

RASPBERRY FIZZ

1 scoop raspberry sherbet	Carbonated water, chilled
1/2 cup Dubonnet, chilled	

Scoop sherbet into wine glass. Add wine and enough carbonated water to fill glass. Serve with small straw. Yield: 1 serving.

LEMON CHICKEN

8 pieces of chicken	Grated rind of 1 lemon
Juice of 1 lemon	2 tablespoons light brown sugar
1/3 cup all-purpose flour	1 lemon, sliced
1/2 teaspoon paprika	1 cup chicken broth
1 teaspoon salt	Mint sprig
1/4 cup corn oil	

Preheat oven to 375 degrees. Rinse chicken and pat dry. Sprinkle with lemon juice. Combine flour, paprika and salt in small bag. Add chicken a few pieces at a time, shaking to coat well. Brown in oil in wide skillet over medium heat; remove to shallow 9-by-13-inch or 3-quart baking dish. Sprinkle with lemon rind and brown sugar. Arrange lemon slices over chicken; pour broth over top. Bake, covered, for 40 to 45 minutes or until done to taste. Garnish with mint. Yield: 4 to 6 servings.

BROCCOLI AND RICE CASSEROLE

1 10-ounce can cream of mushroom soup	3 tablespoons minced onion
1 tablespoon melted butter	2 10-ounce packages frozen chopped broccoli, thawed
1 8-ounce jar Cheez Whiz	1 cup instant rice

Preheat oven to 350 degrees. Combine soup, butter, Cheez Whiz and onion in bowl; mix well. Stir in broccoli and rice. Spoon into baking dish. Bake for 45 minutes. Yield: 10 servings.

APPLE COFFEE CAKE

1 2-layer package yellow cake mix	1 cup sour cream
	1/2 cup vegetable oil
1 4-ounce package vanilla instant pudding mix	1/2 cup sugar
	2 teaspoons cinnamon
	2 apples, chopped
4 eggs	

Preheat oven to 350 degrees. Combine cake mix, pudding mix, eggs, sour cream and oil in mixer bowl. Beat for 5 minutes. Mix sugar and cinnamon in small bowl. Layer cake batter, apples and cinnamon-sugar 1/2 at a time in greased 10-inch tube pan. Bake for 1 hour. Cool in pan for 30 minutes. Remove to serving plate with cinnamon-sugar side up. Yield: 16 servings.

June Wedding Brunch

Fruit Plate — Praline Dip
Assorted Pastries
Overnight Omelet or Potato Medley
Side Dishes — Mimosas

See Index for similar recipes.

The members of our chapter form a support group that extends to our personal lives as well as our relationships as sorority sisters. We always try to entertain for out-of-town guests and the wedding party when our children marry, allowing the mother of the bride or groom to really enjoy this special occasion. We have found this brunch to be one of the most popular entertainments. The pastries can be purchased from the bakery; side dishes can be salads from the local deli. The potato medley can be your own combination of chopped cooked potatoes, scrambled eggs, chopped cooked ham, green and red bell peppers and mushrooms. The sorority symbol of yellow roses can be used as the centerpiece and then presented to the sister who is being honored.

Nancy I. Nicholson, Preceptor Epsilon Xi
Woodridge, Illinois

For Praline Dip, combine 8 ounces softened cream cheese, 1/4 cup packed light brown sugar, 1/4 cup sugar and 1 tablespoon vanilla extract in mixer bowl; beat until smooth. Stir in 1 can praline ice cream topping. Chill until serving time. Serve with fresh fruit.

Icelandic Celebrations Day

Ruelupylsa — Brown Bread
Lobster Chowder — Roast Leg of Lamb
Vegetables — Vinarterta
See Index for similar recipes.

The first day of June is the day Canada celebrates Icelandic Day. All Icelandic descendants celebrate with music, telling of sagas, picnics and children's games held outdoors. In the evening adults celebrate at a dinner party with a menu such as this. All the recipes are typical Icelandic fare.

Loa Monteith, Kappa Psi
Orangeville, Ontario, Canada

RUELUPYLSA

1 2-pound lamb flank	2 tablespoons salt
2 shoulder lamb chops	3/4 teaspoon pepper
2 tablespoons saltpetre	1 medium onion,
3/4 teaspoon cloves	chopped
1 teaspoon allspice	Salt to taste

Bone and trim lamb flank and chops. Sprinkle with mixture of saltpetre, cloves, allspice, 2 tablespoons salt and pepper. Sprinkle with onion. Arrange lamb chops crosswise over flank. Roll flank to enclose chops; sew ends and edges closed with string, winding string around roll. Sprinkle with additional salt. Chill, wrapped in waxed paper, for 3 days. Bring to a boil in water to cover in stockpot; reduce heat. Simmer for 1½ hours. Cool to room temperature. Chill overnight. Remove string; slice into rounds. Serve with Brown Bread. Yield: 16 servings.

BROWN BREAD

2 envelopes dry yeast	2 cups boiling water
2 teaspoons sugar	2 cups water
2/3 cup warm water	1 cup dry milk powder
1 cup packed dark	1 cup wheat germ
brown sugar	9 cups whole wheat
1 cup molasses	flour
1/3 cup shortening	4 cups (about)
2 teaspoons salt	all-purpose flour

Dissolve yeast and sugar in 2/3 cup warm water in small bowl. Combine brown sugar, molasses, shortening and salt in bowl. Add 2 cups boiling water, stirring to melt shortening. Add 2 cups water. Add dry milk powder, wheat germ and half the whole wheat flour; beat until smooth. Beat in yeast mixture. Add remaining whole wheat flour gradually, mixing well. Add all-purpose flour, mixing and kneading on floured surface until smooth and elastic. Place in greased bowl, turning to coat surface. Let rise in warm place for 45 minutes or until doubled in bulk. Shape into 4 loaves; place in greased loaf pans. Let rise for 30 minutes. Preheat oven to 400 degrees. Reduce oven temperature to 325 degrees. Bake loaves for 1 hour. Cool on wire rack. Yield: 4 loaves.

LOBSTER CHOWDER

4 medium potatoes,	1 tablespoon sugar
chopped	2 cups milk or
1 medium onion, chopped	evaporated milk
Salt to taste	1/2 cup (or less)
1 12-ounce can lobster	margarine

Cook potatoes with onion and salt in water to cover in saucepan until tender. Add lobster, sugar, milk and margarine. Heat to serving temperature. Yield: 8 servings.

ROAST LEG OF LAMB

1 5-pound leg of lamb	1 teaspoon ginger
1 clove of garlic, cut	Salt and pepper to taste
into 4 slivers	

Preheat oven to 300 degrees. Cut 4 slits in lamb; push garlic into slits. Rub with ginger, salt and pepper. Place fat side up in roasting pan. Roast for 30 to 35 minutes per pound or until done to taste. Remove garlic. Yield: 10 servings.

VINARTERTA

32 ounces prunes	1 teaspoon baking
2 cups sugar	powder
1 teaspoon cardamom	1 teaspoon soda
1/2 cup butter or	1 teaspoon cardamom
margarine, softened	1 teaspoon salt
1/2 cup shortening	1/2 cup sour cream
2 cups sugar	1 teaspoon vanilla
4 eggs	extract
6 cups all-purpose flour	

Soak prunes in water to cover in saucepan overnight. Cook until tender; mash. Stir in 2 cups sugar. Bring to a boil. Add 1 teaspoon cardamom; remove from heat. Cream butter, shortening and 2 cups sugar in mixer bowl until light and fluffy. Beat in eggs. Mix flour, baking powder, soda, 1 teaspoon cardamom and salt together. Add to batter alternately with sour cream and vanilla, mixing well after each addition. Divide into 15 portions. Chill, individually wrapped in plastic wrap, overnight. Preheat oven to 350 degrees. Roll dough into 8-inch circles on floured surface. Place each on bottom of 8-inch round pan, shaping by hand to fit. Bake for 8 minutes. Remove to wire rack to cool. Spread prune filling between layers. Frost top as desired. Yield: 16 servings.

A Summer Evening of Divine Elegance

Limeade — Lemon Sorbet
Prawns — Cracked Crab
Oysters on the Half Shell
Lemon Wedges — Nut Crackers
Lemon Dill Dip — Marinara Dip
Avocado Dip
Red and Green Cabbage Bowls
Baked Camembert
Baked Brie in Puff Pastry
Red and Green Apple Slices
Chutney Cheese Balls
Miniature Chicken and Beef Floutas
Sour Cream Basil Sauce
Pesto Pasta Salad — Crusty Breadsticks
Chocolate Fondue — Strawberries
Frosted Grapes
Butter Cookies — Hazelnut Coffee

See Index for similar recipes.

This elegant but easy menu was served at an afternoon buffet on the lawn of a home on the river. Guests, dressed in white, arrived in limousines and vintage cars. The earlier part of the afternoon was spent playing croquet on the lawn as we watched boats sail by and refreshed ourselves with limeade and lemon sorbet. A group from the local college played jazz. Faux palm trees, which can be inexpensively rented, decorated the grounds and patio area. Tall clear vases filled with water, black marbles, one bird-of-paradise flower and 1 goldfish were placed on tables and grounds; the goldfish were great conversation pieces. Other black and white containers had floating gardenias and votive candles. The tables were simply black-sprayed shelving placed across the flat rungs of borrowed and rented ladders. Pots of ivy were placed at the bases of the ladders to twine up the legs. Rather than one large buffet table, various smaller tables, each with a variety of dishes, were spaced about the grounds. Small paper plates and convenient waste containers encouraged guests to graze and mingle. Most of the food was finger food, much of which could be prepared in advance. It was served in as many odd dishes as could be assembled. A couple of waiters, dressed in white aprons and black ties, helped to serve and police the grounds. The dessert was not served until about one hour before the party was over in order to bring guests back together at the close of a wonderful evening.

Colleen Kelly-Ginter, Xi Beta Omega
Portland, Oregon

LEMON DILL DIP

½ cup clarified butter	*4 teaspoons tarragon*
Juice of 1 lemon	*4 teaspoons chopped*
2 teaspoons dill	*parsley*
2 teaspoons chopped	*Mayonnaise*
chives	

Combine butter, lemon juice, dill, chives, tarragon and parsley in saucepan. Heat until bubbly; remove from heat. Add enough mayonnaise to make of desired consistency. Chill until serving time. Yield: 1 cup.

MARINARA DIP

½ cup olive oil	*¼ cup wine vinegar*
1 pound Roma	*Dash of Tabasco sauce*
tomatoes, peeled,	*1 teaspoon oregano*
seeded, chopped	*Salt and pepper to taste*
1 large green bell	*12 stuffed olives, sliced*
pepper, chopped	*2 avocados, chopped*
½ cup chopped parsley	

Heat olive oil in skillet. Add tomatoes, green pepper and parsley. Sauté for several minutes. Stir in vinegar, Tabasco sauce, oregano, salt and pepper. Chill until serving time. Stir in olives and avocados. Yield: 12 servings.

BAKED BRIE IN PUFF PASTRY

8 sheets phyllo dough	*1 round of Brie*
Melted butter	

Preheat oven to 350 degrees. Layer sheets of phyllo dough on baking sheet, brushing each sheet with butter. Place cheese in center. Bring up sides of dough to enclose cheese, folding ends down. Brush with butter. Bake for 20 to 30 minutes or until light brown. Yield: 8 to 12 servings.

For Crusty Breadsticks, buy long plain breadsticks from bakery before they are baked. Dip in melted butter and sprinkle with favorite seasonings. Bake just before serving.

Fall Luau

Watermelon Fruit Boat
Barbecued Pork and Chicken
Almond Sweet Potato Puffs
Spinach Salad — Baked Apples
Banana Bread — Lemon Bread
Luau Banana Dessert

See Index for similar recipes.

This is typical of the menu served at our annual Fall Luau. Last year it was held at a home on a lake. Members and guests dressed Hawaiian style in floral shirts and leis. We enjoyed boating and water skiing after dinner. The men were in charge of the barbecue, which is done on a homemade smoker and takes all day.

Judy Kiriluk, Xi Gamma Tau
Kingston, Tennessee

ALMOND SWEET POTATO PUFFS

3 cups mashed cooked sweet potatoes	5 tablespoons orange marmalade
3 tablespoons melted butter or margarine	1/2 teaspoon salt
1 egg	2/3 cup chopped almonds

Combine sweet potatoes, butter, egg, marmalade and salt in mixer bowl. Beat until smooth. Chill in refrigerator. Preheat oven to 350 degrees. Spread almonds on waxed paper. Drop sweet potato mixture by heaping tablespoonfuls into almonds, rolling to coat well and shape into balls. Arrange in greased shallow 9-by-13-inch baking dish. Bake for 15 minutes or until heated through. Yield: 12 servings.

SPINACH SALAD

3 pounds fresh spinach	1 1/2 teaspoons sugar
3 tablespoons sesame seed	3 tablespoons vinegar
3 tablespoons soy sauce	1 small clove of garlic, minced
3 tablespoons sesame oil	1/2 teaspoon MSG

Trim spinach and tear into 1 1/2-inch pieces. Chill until serving time. Preheat oven to 275 degrees. Toast sesame seed in shallow pan for 20 to 25 minutes. Combine soy sauce, sesame oil, sugar, vinegar, garlic and MSG in salad bowl; mix well. Add spinach; toss to coat well. Sprinkle with toasted sesame seed. Yield: 8 to 10 servings.

BAKED APPLES

12 apples	1 1/2 cups raisins
2 cups packed light brown sugar	1 cup coconut
	2 teaspoons cinnamon

Preheat oven to 350 degrees. Core apples; arrange in 9-by-13-inch baking dish. Combine brown sugar, raisins, coconut and cinnamon in bowl. Spoon into centers of apples. Bake for 20 to 30 minutes or until tender. Serve warm. Yield: 12 servings.

LEMON BREAD

1/4 cup butter or margarine, softened	2 cups all-purpose flour
3/4 cup sugar	1 teaspoon salt
2 eggs, slightly beaten	3/4 cup milk
1 tablespoon grated lemon rind	1/2 cup chopped walnuts
2 1/2 teaspoons baking powder	1 tablespoon fresh lemon juice
	2 tablespoons sugar

Preheat oven to 350 degrees. Cream butter and 3/4 cup sugar in mixer bowl until light and fluffy. Beat in eggs and lemon rind. Sift baking powder, flour and salt together. Add to creamed mixture alternately with milk, beginning and ending with dry ingredients. Stir in walnuts. Spoon into greased 5-by-9-inch loaf pan. Bake for 55 to 60 minutes or until bread tests done. Combine lemon juice and 2 tablespoons sugar in small bowl; mix well. Spoon over hot bread. Remove to wire rack to cool. Yield: 12 servings.

LUAU BANANA DESSERT

12 firm ripe bananas	1/2 cup brandy
1/4 cup confectioners' sugar	1/4 cup melted butter or margarine
1 cup Kirsch	

Split skins of bananas lengthwise. Remove fruit carefully, keeping fruit and skins intact. Mix confectioners' sugar, Kirsch and brandy in shallow dish. Cut slits 1 inch apart in bananas; place in Kirsch mixture. Let stand for 30 minutes, turning occasionally. Preheat oven to 350 degrees. Replace fruit in skins; arrange in 9-by-13-inch baking dish. Pour melted butter and part of the remaining brandy mixture over bananas. Bake for 20 to 30 minutes or until done to taste; skins will be black. Serve in skins with remaining brandy mixture. May substitute 1/2 cup Madeira for Kirsch if preferred. Yield: 12 servings.

For Watermelon Fruit Boat, (on menu above), slice 1/4 from top of watermelon. Scallop edges with knife. Remove watermelon and fill boat with assorted melon balls, fresh pineapple chunks, white seedless grapes and coconut if desired.

Halloween Hobo Dinner

Appetizers — Hamburger Chowder
Corn Bread
Dump Cake — Bar Cookies — Beverages

See Index for similar recipes.

Invitations to this dinner were written on the back of soup can labels. Guests came dressed as hobos and bag ladies. Dinner was served in tin cans, paper plates and fruit jars. The setting was the garage with wooden boxes for seats, cardboard boxes for tables and candles in cans. Games were played after dinner, and prizes were sample sizes of toiletries wrapped in kerchiefs and tied on sticks.

Leslie Peacock, Xi Upsilon Rho
Oxnard, California

HAMBURGER CHOWDER

1 pound ground beef	1 16-ounce package
1 28-ounce can	frozen mixed
tomatoes	vegetables
1 medium onion,	2 teaspoons salt
chopped	1/2 teaspoon pepper
2 medium potatoes,	1 1/2 to 2 cups water
chopped	

Brown ground beef in skillet, stirring until crumbly; drain. Combine with undrained tomatoes, onion, potatoes, mixed vegetables, salt and pepper in pressure cooker. Add enough water to fill halfway. Cook using manufacturer's directions for 15 minutes. Yield: 6 to 8 servings.

Christmas Eve Supper

Bleu Cheese Caesar Salad
New England Clam Chowder
Dilly Casserole Bread
Christmas Cookies

See Index for similar recipes.

My mother had to work on Christmas Eve one year when I was a child and my father was left with the responsibility of preparing supper. He made clam chowder, and it was such a hit that it became a tradition. Eventually, we added the salad, bread and cookies. Over the years, we have made this supper wherever we were and the smell of clam chowder simmering on the stove and the aroma of fresh-baked bread tell me that Christmas has finally arrived.

Betsy Fisher, Preceptor Alpha Epsilon
Nashville, Tennessee

BLEU CHEESE CAESAR SALAD

2 cloves of garlic, cut	1/2 teaspoon salt
into quarters	1/4 teaspoon pepper
1/4 cup vegetable oil	3 1/2 tablespoons lemon
4 slices bread	juice
1 head lettuce	1 tablespoon
1/2 cup grated Parmesan	Worcestershire sauce
cheese	1 egg, beaten (optional)
1/4 cup crumbled bleu	
cheese	

Combine garlic with oil in small bowl. Let stand at room temperature for several hours to overnight. Preheat oven to 300 degrees. Cut bread into cubes; spread on baking sheet. Bake for 25 minutes or until golden brown. Tear lettuce into salad bowl. Sprinkle with cheeses, salt and pepper. Drizzle with oil, discarding garlic. Add lemon juice, Worcestershire sauce and egg; toss lightly. Top with croutons. Yield: 6 to 8 servings.

NEW ENGLAND CLAM CHOWDER

6 6-ounce cans minced	Pepper to taste
clams	4 cups milk, scalded
2 ounces salt pork	2 cups half and half,
1 1/2 cups sliced onions	scalded
6 cups chopped potatoes	3 tablespoons melted
3 cups water	butter or margarine
2 small bay leaves,	2 tablespoons
crumbled	all-purpose flour
1 tablespoon salt	

Drain clams, reserving liquid. Sauté salt pork in saucepan for several minutes. Add onions, potatoes, 3 cups water, bay leaves, salt and pepper. Bring to a boil; reduce heat. Simmer for 15 minutes. Add enough additional water to reserved liquid to measure 3 cups. Add to chowder with clams, milk and half and half; mix well. Blend butter and flour in small bowl. Stir into chowder. Simmer for 20 minutes, stirring occasionally. Yield: 12 servings.

Making Memories

Country Heart Ornament

If you're in need of a pretty and easy ornament idea then you need look no further. A pipe cleaner and bits of ribbon and lace are all you'll need to make this very attractive tree trimming.

MATERIALS

1 green pipe cleaner
1/2 yard (11/2-inch wide) bead lace
Hot glue gun
24 inches (1/2-inch wide) red satin loop-edged ribbon

DIRECTIONS

☐ Insert pipe cleaner through holes in lace.

☐ Bend pipe cleaner into heart shape and twist ends together to secure. Glue lace ends together.

☐ Make bow from ribbon; glue to center of heart.

☐ Glue small ribbon loop to back of ornament.

Kite Sweat Shirt

Kite flying brings out the kid in each of us. Experience that same frolicky feeling every time you wear this fun-loving kite sweat shirt. It's so easy you'll want to make one for each member of your family.

MATERIALS

Sweat shirt
1   (10-by-10-inch) fusible webbing piece
1   (10-by-10-inch) fabric piece
Waxed paper
Tulip® Paints:
     Yellow Slick, White Slick
30 inches (¼-inch wide) green satin ribbon
Cloud-shaped sponge

DIRECTIONS

☐ Wash, dry, and press sweat shirt.

☐ Following manufacturers' instructions, fuse webbing to fabric.

☐ Cut out kite shape from fabric.

☐ Fuse fabric to sweat shirt.

☐ Line sweat shirt with waxed paper.

☐ Apply yellow Slick Paint around edges of fabric to prevent fraying.

☐ Paint wavy line with yellow paint for kite tail.

☐ Cut satin ribbon into 3 equal pieces.

☐ Make 3 bows from ribbon. Attach to shirt by pressing into wet Slick Paint or by sewing.

☐ Dip cloud-shaped sponge into white Slick Paint and press randomly onto shirt.

☐ Let sweat shirt dry for 24 hours.

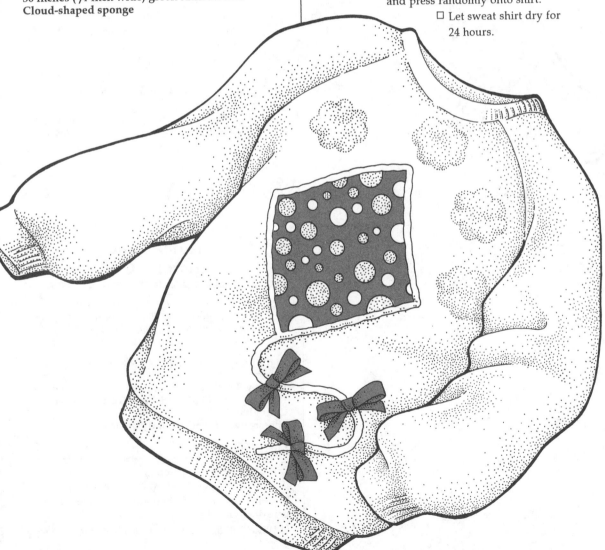

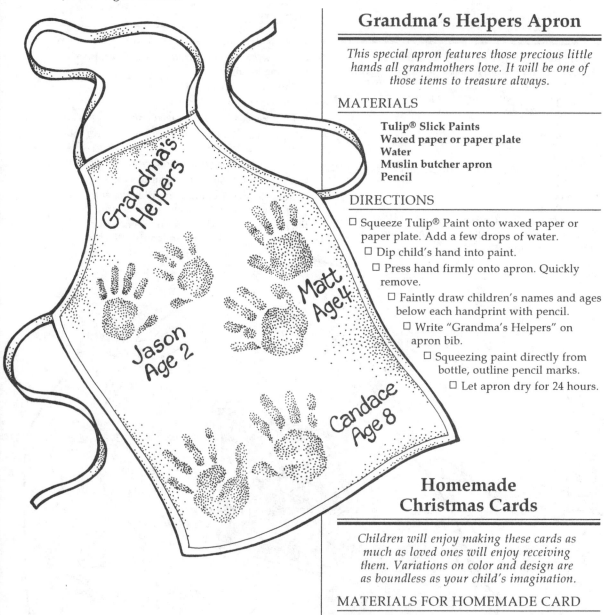

Grandma's Helpers Apron

This special apron features those precious little hands all grandmothers love. It will be one of those items to treasure always.

MATERIALS

Tulip® Slick Paints
Waxed paper or paper plate
Water
Muslin butcher apron
Pencil

DIRECTIONS

☐ Squeeze Tulip® Paint onto waxed paper or paper plate. Add a few drops of water.

☐ Dip child's hand into paint.

☐ Press hand firmly onto apron. Quickly remove.

☐ Faintly draw children's names and ages below each handprint with pencil.

☐ Write "Grandma's Helpers" on apron bib.

☐ Squeezing paint directly from bottle, outline pencil marks.

☐ Let apron dry for 24 hours.

Homemade Christmas Cards

Children will enjoy making these cards as much as loved ones will enjoy receiving them. Variations on color and design are as boundless as your child's imagination.

MATERIALS FOR HOMEMADE CARD

1 (12-by-9-inch) piece green construction paper
1 (5½-by-7-inch) piece red construction paper
Craft glue
Photocopy of favorite family photograph

DIRECTIONS

☐ Fold green construction paper in half to form card. Glue red construction paper to front of card.

☐ Glue photocopy of photograph to center of red construction paper.

☐ Write holiday message on inside of card and sign.

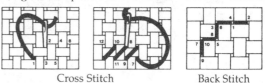

Key – Holiday Finger Tip Towel

▨ DMC #699 Green
⊠ DMC #666 Red

Backstitch Tree Outline in DMC #666 Red
(use 1 strand of floss)
Backstitch Garland and Stars in DMC #666 Red
(use 2 strands of floss)

Stitch Chart
Bring needle up at odd numbers, down at even numbers.

Cross Stitch   Back Stitch

Holiday Fingertip Towel

This fingertip towel will add the holiday spirit to anyone's bath! It's the perfect gift for that person who has everything.

MATERIALS

1 (19-by-10½-inch) fingertip towel with 14-count Aida cloth insert
1 (#24) embroidery needle
DMC® Embroidery Floss = 8m skeins (1 skein each): #666 Red, #699 Green

DIRECTIONS

☐ Mark center of cross-stitch fabric both ways with long running stitch using needle and thread.

☐ Work cross-stitch according to chart and color key, beginning at intersection of arrows on chart to ensure proper placement on fabric.

☐ Each square on chart represents 1 fabric thread. Use 2 strands of floss for cross-stitch and 1 strand of floss for backstitch.

☐ Press finished work.

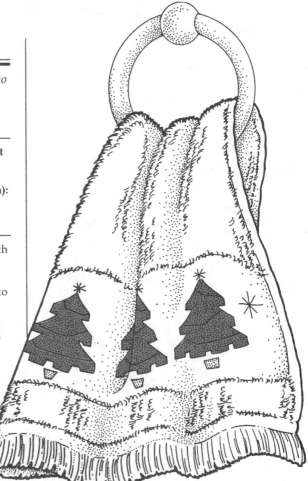

Red mouth

Cut 1
from gray fabric

Cut 1
Tartan plaid bow

Cut 1
from gray fabric

Red

Christmas Eve Pillowcase

Santa never arrives soon enough! This Christmas Eve pillowcase will bring visions of sugarplums to little boys and girls and might even speed Santa's arrival.

MATERIALS

Pillowcase
Fine-point permanent marker
Scrap of gray corduroy fabric
Scrap of tartan plaid fabric
Red thread

DIRECTIONS

☐ Write "Not a creature was stirring not even a" on pillowcase using marker.

☐ Cut mouse from gray fabric using pattern.

☐ Cut bow from plaid fabric using pattern.

☐ Position appliqué at end of words in lower right corner of pillowcase.

☐ Set sewing machine for appliqué. Using satin stitch and red thread, appliqué pieces in the following order: mouse, bow.

☐ Machine-embroider mouth and tail with red thread as indicated on pattern.

Stenciled Flowerpots

Stencil Christmas designs on clay flowerpots.
Line with napkins and fill with holiday treats.

MATERIALS

Stencil-Ease® Japan Paint
Small bowl
Stencil design
Masking tape
Stencil-Ease® Pure Bristle Brushes
Clean clay flowerpots

DIRECTIONS

☐ Place 1 or 2 teaspoons of paint in bowl.

☐ Place stencil in correct position and tape in place with masking tape.

☐ Start at outside of design and work in a clock-wise motion. Reverse direction and move brush in a counter-clockwise motion to build up paint to desired color.

☐ Allow stenciled project to cure for 1 week.

☐ Line pot with a napkin and fill with snacks, cookies or candies.

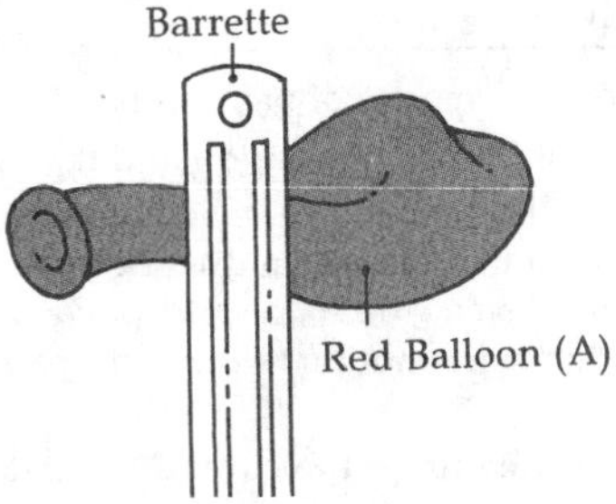

Barrette

Red Balloon (A)

Figure 1

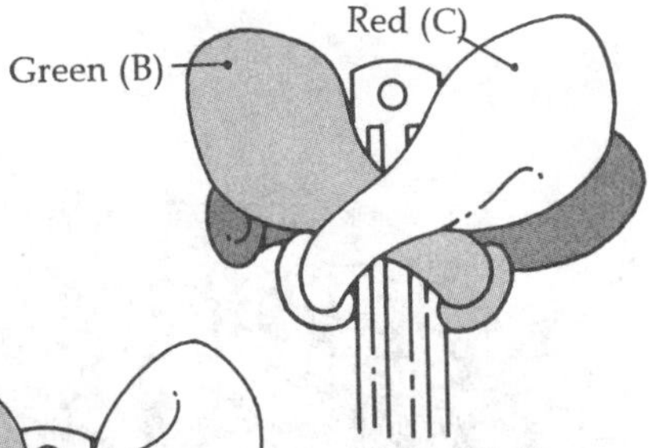

Green (B) Red (C)

Figure 2

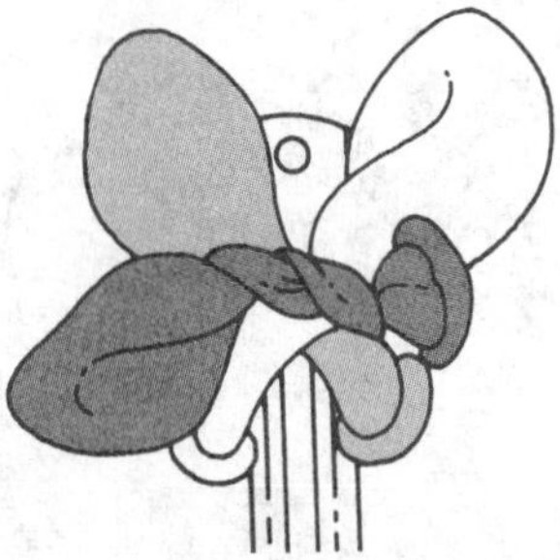

Figure 3

Balloon Barrette

You will want to make a lot of these to give as gifts or to sell as a service project. Vary the colors for different seasons.

MATERIALS

17 (6-inch) red balloons
1   (3-inch) spring-clasp hair barrette
9   (6-inch) green balloons

DIRECTIONS

☐ Place one red balloon (A) under base of barrette, running perpendicular to barrette. Push balloon to end of barrette (Figure 1).

☐ Center 1 green balloon (B) and one red balloon (C) on top of barrette with bulb end of green balloon (B) to the left and bulb end of red balloon (C) to the right (Figure 2).

☐ Wrap both ends of balloon (A) around top of barrette catching balloons (B) and (C) in loop (Figure 3).

☐ Repeat procedure until barrette is completely covered, alternating placement of bulb ends so that colors will be red, green, red, green, etc. Example: 2nd row—bulb end of green balloon to the right and bulb end of red balloon to the left.

Decorative Jelly Jars

Dress up your homemade jams and jellies with one of these charming yet easy designs. You will not want to keep them hidden away in the cupboard anymore.

MATERIALS

Hot glue gun
Artificial berries and greenery
Purchased bird's nests
Homemade jams or sauces
Crocheted doilies
Satin ribbon

DIRECTIONS

☐ Glue artificial berries and greenery around top edge of bird's nest.

☐ Nestle homemade jams or sauces in center of bird's nest.

   ☐ Arrange crocheted doily over lid of canning jar.

      ☐ Tie with satin ribbon.

Bread Centerpiece

This charming centerpiece does double duty. Guests will enjoy the way it tastes as well as the way it looks.

MATERIALS

Favorite monkey bread recipe
Bundt pan
Large votive candle

DIRECTIONS

☐ Bake monkey bread in bundt pan.

☐ Let bread cool.

☐ Place votive candle in center of bread. Place in center of table.

Decorated Gingerbread Cookies

*These make wonderful decorations if they last
that long. Half the fun is making
these delicious cookies.*

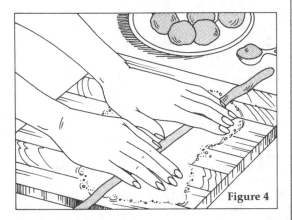

Figure 4

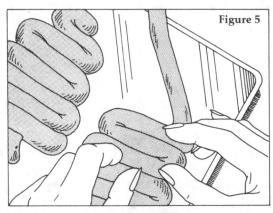

Figure 5

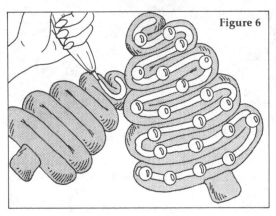

Figure 6

MATERIALS

**1 package Betty Crocker gingerbread cake and
cookie mix**
1/3 cup lukewarm water
Canned frosting
Decorator's Frosting
Red cinnamon candies
Red sugar sprinkles

DIRECTIONS

☐ Preheat oven to 375 degrees.

☐ Combine gingerbread mix and water in bowl;
mix well. Chill for 1 to 2 hours.

☐ Shape or cut into Christmas trees or gift tags.
Place on ungreased cookie sheet.

☐ Bake for 8 to 10 minutes or until edges are firm
and no imprint remains when lightly touched.

☐ Cool on cookie sheet for 1 minute. Remove to
wire rack to cool completely.

☐ Decorate cookies with Decorator's Frosting,
cinnamon candies and sugar sprinkles as directed
below. May use purchased tubes of frosting for
Decorator's Frosting.

☐ **Christmas Trees:** Shape 2 tablespoons dough at a
time into 24-inch long rope (Figure 4). Coil rope
back and forth into shape of tree on
ungreased cookie sheet (Figure 5). Attach small
piece of dough for trunk. Bake and cool as
directed. Spread with frosting. Outline with
Decorator's Frosting (Figure 6). Decorate with cinnamon candies. Sprinkle with sugar sprinkles.

☐ **Gift Tags:** Cut dough into rectangles with pizza
cutter and ruler. Make hole near 1 corner with
plastic straw. Bake and cool as directed. Spread
with frosting. Outline and inscribe name with
Decorator's Frosting.

MATERIALS FOR DECORATOR'S FROSTING

1 1/2 cups confectioners' sugar
1 large egg white
1/8 teaspoon cream of tartar

DIRECTIONS

☐ Combine confectioners' sugar, egg white and
cream of tartar in mixer bowl.

☐ Beat for 5 minutes or until smooth and thickened.
Spoon into decorating tube. Store in covered
container in refrigerator.

☐ Yield: 3/4 cup.

Christmas Card Gift Tags

Those beautiful Christmas cards from years past can be cut and used for tags on this year's Christmas presents. Children will love making these gift tags and being involved in the gift-wrapping process. They also look charming as ornaments on the Christmas tree.

MATERIALS

Christmas cards
Hole Punch
8 inches red craft ribbon per card

DIRECTIONS

☐ Cut pictures from fronts of Christmas cards.

☐ Punch hole at top of each picture.

☐ Thread ribbon through holes and tie in knot at top.

☐ Tape to packages or hang on Christmas tree.

Two Gifts in One

Who could resist delicious homemade goodies wrapped in reuseable baking pans? See Index for suitable recipes.

MATERIALS

Foil cupcake liners
Homemade baked muffins, sweet rolls, tarts and bundt cake
New muffin pans, tart pans and bundt pan identical to pans in which muffins, rolls, tarts and cake were baked
Holiday Ribbon
Plastic Wrap

DIRECTIONS

☐ Line new muffin pans with foil liners.

☐ Place muffins, rolls, tarts and cake in new pans.

☐ Tie with ribbon. Wrap in plastic wrap.

Dowel Feather Tree

Antique and new feather trees are once again gaining in popularity. Follow these simple instructions to make your own version and then reuse it each year by trimming with Dried Apple Ornaments and purchased cookies.

MATERIALS FOR DOWEL TREE

1 (1/2-by-30-inch) dowel
Drill with 1/4-inch and 1/2-inch bits
1 (1/4-by-24-inch) dowel
1 (1/4-by-20-inch) dowel
1 (1/4-by-16-inch) dowel
1 (1/4-by-12-inch) dowel
1 (1/4-by-8-inch) dowel
Hot glue gun
1 (7-by-9-inch) board
1 (9-by-11-inch) board
Artificial greenery roping
Wheat
1 large red apple

DIRECTIONS

☐ Mark 30-inch dowel to drill five 1/4-inch holes as follows: 6 inches from bottom, and at 5-inch intervals. Last mark will be 4 inches from top.

☐ Drill holes. Insert 1/4-inch dowels with longest dowel 6 inches from bottom graduating to smallest dowel 4 inches from top.

☐ Glue smaller board to larger board. Drill 1/2-inch hole 3/4 inch deep in center. Insert large dowel.

☐ Wrap 1/4-inch dowels with greenery. Tie wheat to top. Insert apple on top. Hang Dried Apple Ornaments and purchased cookies on branches.

MATERIALS FOR DRIED APPLE ORNAMENTS

Apples
2 cups lemon juice
3 tablespoons citric acid
3 tablespoons salt
Clear gloss acrylic spray
Nylon line

DIRECTONS

☐ Preheat oven to 150 degrees.

☐ Cut apples into 1/4-inch lengthwise slices which contain portions of core. Soak in mixture of lemon juice, citric acid and salt in bowl for 5 minutes.

☐ Place apples on racks on baking sheets. Dry in oven with door ajar for 6 to 8 hours.

☐ Spray with acrylic spray. Thread nylon line through tops of apple slices for hanger.

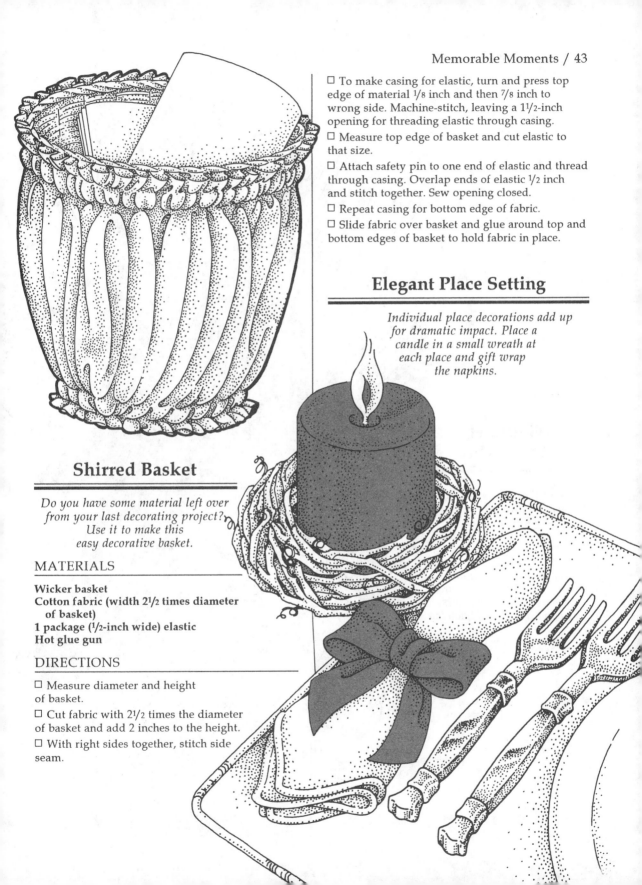

□ To make casing for elastic, turn and press top edge of material 1/8 inch and then 7/8 inch to wrong side. Machine-stitch, leaving a 1 1/2-inch opening for threading elastic through casing.

□ Measure top edge of basket and cut elastic to that size.

□ Attach safety pin to one end of elastic and thread through casing. Overlap ends of elastic 1/2 inch and stitch together. Sew opening closed.

□ Repeat casing for bottom edge of fabric.

□ Slide fabric over basket and glue around top and bottom edges of basket to hold fabric in place.

Elegant Place Setting

Individual place decorations add up for dramatic impact. Place a candle in a small wreath at each place and gift wrap the napkins.

Shirred Basket

Do you have some material left over from your last decorating project? Use it to make this easy decorative basket.

MATERIALS

Wicker basket
Cotton fabric (width 2 1/2 times diameter of basket)
1 package (1/2-inch wide) elastic
Hot glue gun

DIRECTIONS

□ Measure diameter and height of basket.

□ Cut fabric with 2 1/2 times the diameter of basket and add 2 inches to the height.

□ With right sides together, stitch side seam.

Gourmet Oven Mitt

Fill a holiday oven mitt with speciality utensils like these for draining and serving pasta. Vary the utensils to suit the cooking skills and interests of the lucky recipient and use the mitts as place card favors on backs of chairs or beside plates. Add holiday greens, ribbon and bells for a festive touch.

Our Best Recipes

One of the joys of pouring over favorite old
cookbooks is remembering the recipes you enjoyed
and the occasions on which you served them.
More than just lists of ingredients and
measurements, the best cookbooks are full of
memories too. In *Reunion Recipes*, we've
highlighted outstanding recipes, menus and
craft ideas that have made Beta Sigma Phi's
annual cookbooks such favorites with members
around the country. *Menus through the Year*
offers four seasons of delicious food ideas,
from a New Year's Day bash with a new twist
for traditional black-eyed peas, to a cozy
Christmas Eve supper before the fire.
In between, you'll find tips for any special
occasion you can think of—and then some.
To help savor those special times, we've included
a section on *Making Memories*, sure-fire ideas
and directions for crafts, gifts and decorations
you and your family will cherish.

Fresh Beginnings

THREE-CHEESE BALL

4 ounces Cheddar cheese, shredded	1 tablespoon minced onion
8 ounces cream cheese, softened	1 tablespoon Worcestershire sauce
4 ounces bleu cheese, crumbled	1 cup chopped walnuts Assorted crackers

Cream Cheddar cheese, cream cheese and bleu cheese in mixer bowl until light and fluffy. Add onion and Worcestershire sauce; mix well. Shape into ball. Roll in walnuts. Chill, wrapped in plastic wrap, for 24 hours. Serve with assorted crackers.
Yield: 50 servings.

Cathy C. Neese, Preceptor Alpha Zeta
Marietta, Georgia

CHEESE BALL

8 ounces cream cheese, softened	1 5-ounce jar garlic cheese
2 5-ounce jars Old English cheese	2 cups butter or margarine, softened
1 5-ounce jar processed bacon-cheese spread	1 cup finely chopped walnuts

Combine cheeses and butter in bowl; mix well. Shape into ball. Roll in walnuts. Chill until serving time. Serve with crackers. Yield: 100 servings.

Shloe Maurer, Xi Gamma Gamma
Sioux City, Iowa

Toni Olff, Preceptor Beta Iota, Marietta, Ohio, makes an easy freezable cheese ball by combining 16 ounces softened cream cheese, 2½ cups shredded sharp Cheddar cheese, ¼ cup onion flakes and ¼ cup mayonnaise. Coat formed ball with pecans.

HAM AND CHEESE BALL

Whenever I'm in charge of refreshments, my sorority sisters ask me to bring this. I thought the rest of you might like it.

3 ounces thinly sliced ham, frozen	1 tablespoon lemon juice
5 green onions	Dash of MSG
5 jalapeño peppers	Garlic salt to taste
16 ounces cream cheese, softened	¾ cup chopped pecans Crackers

Combine ham, green onions and peppers in food processor container. Process with chopper blade. Add cream cheese, lemon juice, MSG and garlic salt. Process with mixer blade. Shape into 1 large ball or 2 grapefruit-sized balls. Roll in pecans. Serve with crackers. Yield: 50 servings.

Donna Wheeler, Alpha Epsilon Epsilon
Seminole, Texas

PINEAPPLE CHEESE BALL

16 ounces cream cheese, softened	2 tablespoons chopped onion
1 8-ounce can crushed pineapple, drained	1 tablespoon seasoned salt
1 cup chopped pecans	1 cup chopped pecans
¼ cup chopped green bell pepper	

Beat cream cheese with fork in bowl. Add pineapple, 1 cup pecans, green pepper, onion and seasoned salt gradually, mixing well. Shape into 1 to 4 balls. Roll in remaining 1 cup pecans. Chill, wrapped in plastic wrap, until serving time. May be made ahead and frozen. Yield: 60 servings.

Paula K. Myers, Xi Omicron
Cumberland, Maryland

SALMON BALL

1 15-ounce can red
  sockeye salmon
8 ounces cream cheese,
  softened
1 tablespoon lemon juice
1 tablespoon grated
  onion

1 teaspoon prepared
  horseradish
1/4 teaspoon salt
1/4 teaspoon liquid
  smoke
Chopped parsley
Crackers

Combine salmon, cream cheese, lemon juice, onion, horseradish, salt and liquid smoke in bowl; mix well. Chill for several hours. Shape into ball. Sprinkle with parsley. Serve with crackers. Yield: 50 servings.

Lynette Dorsey, Delta Delta
Woodbridge, Virginia

TUNA CHEESE BALL

This is always the recipe I use when at 10:00 P.M. I remember that tomorrow is my day for refreshments.

1 6-ounce can tuna,
  drained
16 ounces cream cheese,
  softened

1 onion, chopped
1 envelope ranch salad
  dressing mix

Combine tuna, cream cheese, onion and dressing mix in bowl; mix well. Shape into ball. Chill for 2 to 4 hours. Yield: 50 servings.

Imogene Graves, Xi Beta Alpha
Bowling Green, Kentucky

ARTICHOKE DREAM DIP

8 ounces cream cheese,
  softened
1 cup sour cream
1 cup mayonnaise
1 cup Parmesan cheese
1/4 teaspoon dillweed

1 16-ounce can
  artichoke hearts,
  finely chopped
Parmesan cheese
Paprika
Wheat crackers

Spray 3-by-7-inch glass dish with nonstick cooking spray. Combine cream cheese, sour cream, mayonnaise, 1 cup Parmesan cheese and dillweed in bowl; mix well. Stir in artichoke hearts. Spoon into prepared dish. Sprinkle with remaining Parmesan cheese and paprika. Serve with wheat crackers. Yield: 80 servings.

Karen McGee, Xi Kappa
Canyon Country, California

ARTICHOKE DIP

Whenever I have a meeting, my sisters request that I make this. It's also requested at family gatherings.

1 cup shredded Cheddar
  cheese
1 cup shredded
  mozzarella cheese

1 cup mayonnaise
1 8-ounce can
  artichoke hearts
Wheat crackers

Preheat oven to 350 degrees. Combine cheeses, mayonnaise and artichoke hearts in bowl; mix well. Spoon into glass dish. Bake for 15 to 20 minutes or until cheeses are melted. Serve with wheat crackers. Yield: 65 servings.

Marion E. Corbett, Preceptor Alpha Eta
Kenmore, New York

DRIED BEEF HOT DIP

1 large round loaf bread
1 cup sour cream
8 ounces cream cheese,
  softened
1 cup shredded sharp
  Cheddar cheese

3 ounces shredded
  dried beef
2 tablespoons dried
  chives
1/2 teaspoon garlic salt

Preheat oven to 325 degrees. Cut top from bread; hollow out loaf in shape of bowl. Combine sour cream, cream cheese, Cheddar cheese, beef, chives and garlic salt in bowl; mix well. Spoon into bread shell; wrap in foil. Bake for 30 minutes. Break extra bread into small pieces. Add to top of mixture in bread shell. Bake for 30 minutes longer. Yield: 50 servings.

Nancy M. Cramer, Eta Omicron
Rogers, Arkansas

CHEESE-OLIVE DIP

8 ounces Cheddar
  cheese, shredded
8 ounces mozzarella
  cheese, shredded
1/2 cup mayonnaise
1/2 cup sour cream

1/2 cup sliced green
  olives
1 cup sliced black olives
6 green onions, chopped
Tortilla chips

Preheat oven to 350 degrees. Combine cheeses, mayonnaise, sour cream, olives and green onions in bowl; mix well. Spoon into ungreased pie plate. Bake for 15 to 20 minutes or until bubbling; do not overbake. Serve with tortilla chips. Yield: 12 servings.

Dianne V. Berthe, Xi Alpha Sigma
Apple Valley, Minnesota

GREAT CHEESE DIP

This recipe was used at a family Christmas party. I would like to thank Julie for bringing and sharing it.

1 10-ounce package
  frozen broccoli,
  thawed
1 10-ounce can cream
  of mushroom soup

1 10-ounce can nacho
  cheese soup
1 10-ounce can
  Cheddar cheese soup
Garlic powder to taste

Combine broccoli, soups and garlic powder in bowl; mix well. Spoon into small slow cooker. Cook until heated through. Serve with nacho or corn chips. Yield: 50 servings.

Sharon Vallett, Omicron Eta
Steeleville, Illinois

TANGY CHEESE DIP

2 cups shredded Colby
  cheese
2 cups shredded
  Monterey Jack cheese
1/2 cup finely chopped
  black olives
3 green onions, chopped
1 7-ounce can green
  chilies, chopped
1 tomato, chopped
1 8-ounce bottle of
  Italian salad dressing

Combine all ingredients in bowl; mix well. Chill, covered, for 2 hours. Yield: 80 servings.

Melany Bradley, Beta Phi
Cortez, Colorado

CHEESE FONDUE

This is part of our family's traditional Christmas Eve dinner. It is our favorite meal with close friends; it's casual and cheery.

4 1/2 teaspoons chopped
  onion
1 small clove of garlic,
  crushed
1 1/2 teaspoons butter or
  margarine
1/2 cup dry white wine
7 1/2 teaspoons butter or
  margarine
3 tablespoons
  all-purpose flour
1 1/2 cups boiling milk
1/2 teaspoon salt
1/8 teaspoon pepper
Pinch of nutmeg
Pinch of cayenne pepper
1 egg yolk
1 cup shredded Swiss
  cheese
2 tablespoons butter or
  margarine

Sauté onion and garlic lightly in 1 1/2 teaspoons butter in skillet. Add wine. Cook until reduced to 1/4 cup. Combine 7 1/2 teaspoons butter and flour in saucepan. Cook for 2 minutes, stirring frequently. Remove from heat. Beat in boiling milk. Add seasonings. Boil for 1 minute or until very thick, stirring constantly. Place egg yolk in center of mixture. Beat with wire whisk. Cool slightly. Beat in cheese and remaining 2 tablespoons butter. Add wine mixture; mix well. Yield: 35 servings.

Marsha Elizabeth Williams, Xi Gamma Chi
Tucson, Arizona

CHILI CON QUESO

1/2 teaspoon margarine
1 onion, chopped
1/2 teaspoon garlic
Dash of Worcestershire
  sauce
2 tomatoes, chopped
1 to 2 tablespoons
  all-purpose flour
10 ounces Monterey
  Jack cheese with
  jalapeño peppers,
  cubed
10 ounces sharp
  Cheddar cheese, cubed
Corn chips

Melt margarine in skillet. Add onion. Sauté until transparent. Add garlic, Worcestershire sauce and tomatoes; mix well. Cook, covered, over low heat for 5 minutes or until tomatoes are tender. Stir in enough flour to absorb liquid. Add cheeses. Cook until

melted, stirring occasionally. Serve with corn chips. Yield: 6 servings.

Barbara Waldron, Delta Theta
Harvard, Massachusetts

EASY CHILI CON QUESO

1 1-pound package
  Velveeta cheese
1 1/4 cups half and half
1 4-ounce can chopped
  green chilies
4 teaspoons chopped
  pimento
1/4 cup finely chopped
  cooked green bell
  pepper

Cut cheese into chunks. Combine with remaining ingredients in double boiler. Cook over low heat until cheese is melted, stirring frequently. Serve warm with tortilla chips. Yield: 6 servings.

Dallas Magrum, Alpha Zeta
Calgary, Alberta, Canada

CLAM DIP

1 6-ounce can chopped
  clams
8 ounces cream cheese
1/2 teaspoon MSG
1 1/2 teaspoons lemon
  juice
1 1/2 teaspoons
  Worcestershire sauce
Chopped green onions
  to taste
Red pepper to taste
Dash of black pepper

Drain clams, reserving a small amount of juice. Soften cream cheese with reserved juice. Combine with MSG, lemon juice, Worcestershire sauce, green onions and peppers in bowl; mix well. Stir in clams. Chill for 2 hours. Serve with corn chips. Yield: 15 servings.

Dottie Hunter, Xi Eta Iota
Jacksonville, Florida

HOT CLAM DIP

Everyone enjoys this recipe. I have been asked for this recipe or to make it for numerous occasions by friends.

2 6-ounce cans minced
  clams
1 teaspoon lemon juice
1/2 cup butter or
  margarine
1 onion, minced
1 clove of garlic, minced
1/2 green bell pepper,
  minced
1 teaspoon parsley
1 teaspoon oregano
Dash of Tabasco sauce
Dash of cayenne pepper
1/2 cup Italian bread
  crumbs
Crumbled Velveeta
  cheese
Grated Parmesan cheese
Paprika to taste
Thin wheat crackers

Preheat oven to 350 degrees. Combine clams and lemon juice in saucepan. Simmer for 15 minutes. Melt butter in skillet. Add next 8 ingredients. Simmer until softened, stirring frequently. Stir into clam mixture. Pour into 9-inch pie plate. Top with cheeses. Sprinkle with paprika. Bake for 20 minutes. Serve with thin wheat crackers. Yield: 12 servings.

Mary Louise Ridgway, Preceptor Lambda
Vineland, New Jersey

CRAB MEAT DIP

My mother-in-law gave this recipe to me; whenever I take it anywhere, it's a great hit. Special thanks to Marge Hersh.

8 ounces cream cheese, softened	1 cup sliced water chestnuts
1/2 cup sour cream	2 6-ounce cans crab meat
2 tablespoons chopped green onions	Crackers
1/2 cup chili sauce	

Combine cream cheese and sour cream in bowl; blend until smooth. Add green onions, chili sauce and water chestnuts; mix well. Stir in crab meat. Chill for 2 hours. Serve with crackers. Yield: 50 servings.

Linda Hersh, Eta Delta
Topeka, Kansas

PACIFIC NORTHWEST CRAB DIP

We had this on visits to my grandmother's house in Washington State. She used fresh crab, right out of the steamer, that had been caught earlier in the day.

3 ounces cream cheese, softened	1 tablespoon lemon juice
1/2 cup mayonnaise	1/8 teaspoon hot pepper sauce
1 6-ounce can crab meat, drained	Small slices French bread or crackers
1/4 cup minced onion	

Preheat oven to 350 degrees. Beat cream cheese in mixer bowl until light and fluffy. Add mayonnaise, crab meat, onion, lemon juice and pepper sauce; mix well. Spoon into small baking dish. Bake for 30 minutes or until bubbly. Serve with small slices French bread or with crackers. Yield: 15 servings.

Susan Nilson, Xi Pi Gamma
Rohnert Park, California

SHEEPHERDERS' CRAB DIP

1 loaf sheepherders' bread	1/3 cup white wine
16 ounces cream cheese, softened	1/4 cup grated green onions
1 cup sour cream	1 pound chopped crab meat
1 teaspoon Worcestershire sauce	Lightly salted or unsalted crackers

Preheat oven to 250 degrees. Cut top from bread; hollow out loaf to make shell. Beat cream cheese, sour cream, Worcestershire sauce, wine and green onions in mixer bowl. Stir in crab meat. Spoon into bread shell. Replace top of bread. Place on baking sheet. Bake for 2 1/2 to 3 hours. Serve with lightly salted or unsalted crackers. Yield: 50 servings.

Janice Prince, Preceptor Beta
Rapid City, South Dakota

DENVER DIP

2 tablespoons mayonnaise-type salad dressing	2 carrots, finely chopped
8 ounces cream cheese, softened	1 bunch green onions, finely chopped
1 tablespoon sugar	1 green bell pepper, finely chopped (optional)
8 radishes, finely chopped	Crackers

Cream mayonnaise, cream cheese and sugar in mixer bowl until light and fluffy. Add radishes, carrots, green onions and green pepper; mix well. Serve with crackers. Yield: 12 servings.

Vicki McMurray, Xi Theta Sigma
Godfrey, Illinois

ALL-PURPOSE DIP

1 cup mayonnaise	1/2 teaspoon curry powder
1/2 cup sour cream	1 teaspoon dried onion
1/2 teaspoon lemon juice	1 teaspoon dried chives
1/4 teaspoon salt	1/2 teaspoon Worcestershire sauce
1/4 teaspoon pepper	1 clove of garlic, minced
1 teaspoon Italian seasoning	

Combine mayonnaise, sour cream, lemon juice, salt, pepper, Italian seasoning, curry powder, onion, chives, Worcestershire sauce and garlic in bowl; mix well by hand. Chill until serving time. Store in refrigerator. Yield: 35 servings.

Cindy Weber, Delta Chi
Mukwonago, Wisconsin

DILL DIP

1 cup mayonnaise	1 teaspoon seasoned salt
1 cup sour cream	1 teaspoon dillweed
1 tablespoon minced dried onion	1 teaspoon Worcestershire sauce
1 tablespoon parsley flakes	1/2 teaspoon MSG
	Sliced fresh vegetables

Combine mayonnaise, sour cream, onion, parsley, seasoned salt, dillweed, Worcestershire sauce and MSG in bowl; mix well. Serve with sliced fresh vegetables such as carrots, celery, green onions, broccoli or cauliflower. Yield: 35 servings.

Becky Brown, Xi Delta Eta
Delta, Colorado

Alison Fitzpatrick, Xi Lambda Gamma, Jefferson City, Missouri, makes Artichoke Chili Dip by combining 14 ounces canned artichoke hearts, chopped, 4 ounces canned chopped green chilies, 1 cup Parmesan cheese and 1 cup mayonnaise in 8-inch baking dish. Bake in preheated 350-degree oven for 20 minutes.

APPLE DIP

This tastes like a candied apple, but it doesn't stick to your teeth!

6 Granny Smith apples, sliced
12 ounces cream cheese, softened
1/2 cup sugar
1 cup packed light brown sugar
1 teaspoon vanilla extract

Arrange apple slices around outer edges of round serving plate. Combine cream cheese, sugar, brown sugar and vanilla in bowl; mix well. Set bowl in center of apple slices. Yield: 25 servings.

Carolyn Goldbach, Tau Eta
Hemet, California

FLUFFY FRUIT DIP

3 ounces cream cheese, softened
1 7-ounce jar marshmallow creme
1 teaspoon vanilla extract
Strawberries, bananas, apples, oranges or kiwifruit

Combine cream cheese, marshmallow creme and vanilla in bowl; mix well. Serve with strawberries, bananas, apples, oranges or kiwifruit. Yield: 15 servings.

Katherine Herrick, Gamma Theta
Cedar Rapids, Iowa

FRUIT "DIP IN"

8 ounces cream cheese, softened
1 7-ounce jar marshmallow creme
1 teaspoon grated orange rind
1 tablespoon frozen orange juice concentrate
Dash of grated ginger

Combine cream cheese and marshmallow creme in bowl; blend well. Add rind, concentrate and ginger; mix well. Chill, covered, overnight. May use as a dip for fresh fruit or spoon over shortcake. Yield: 30 servings.

Kathy Welt, Xi Epsilon Alpha
Paonia, Colorado

KAHLUA DIP

1 7-ounce jar marshmallow creme
8 ounces cream cheese, softened
1/3 cup Kahlua
Sliced fresh fruit

Combine marshmallow creme and cream cheese in bowl; blend well. Stir in Kahlua. Chill, covered, overnight. Serve with sliced fresh fruit. May substitute flavored schnapps for Kahlua. Yield: 30 servings.

Ruby Scharping, Lambda Alpha
Wichita, Kansas

STRAWBERRY-MARSHMALLOW CREME FRUIT DIP

I have memories of fixing this dip in summer and winter; it always went over with a bang.

8 ounces strawberry cream cheese, softened
13 ounces marshmallow creme
2 tablespoons pineapple juice
Bananas, apples, pears strawberries or peaches

Combine cream cheese and marshmallow creme in bowl; blend well. Stir in pineapple juice. Chill until serving time. Serve with fresh bananas, apples, pears, strawberries or peaches. Yield: 30 servings.

Hilda McWilliams, Alpha Sigma
Elkins, West Virginia

MOCK GUACAMOLE

1 10-ounce package frozen English peas
1/4 cup nonfat yogurt
1 tablespoon chopped green chilies
1 teaspoon lemon or lime juice
1/2 teaspoon cumin
1/4 teaspoon salt
Tabasco sauce to taste
3 tablespoons finely chopped purple onion
1 cup peeled, seeded, chopped tomato
Cilantro to taste

Cook peas using package directions; drain well. Purée peas in food processor. Add yogurt, chilies, lemon juice, cumin, salt and Tabasco sauce. Process until well blended. Chill until serving time. Add onion, tomato and cilantro; mix well. Spoon into serving bowl. Yield: 2 cups.

Nancy Maranto, Laureate Delta Gamma
Houston, Texas

HOT HAMBURGER DIP

2 pounds ground beef
2 pounds Velveeta cheese, cubed
1 16-ounce jar picante sauce
1 10-ounce can cream of mushroom soup
Tortilla chips

Brown ground beef in skillet, stirring until crumbly; drain. Combine ground beef, Velveeta cheese, picante sauce and mushroom soup in slow cooker. Cook on High to serving temperature. Serve with tortilla chips. Yield: 20 servings.

Brenda Clarke, Xi Eta
Newcastle, Wyoming

Carolyn Cline, Xi Sigma, Jamestown, New York, serves an Easy Fruit Dip by combining 2 cups sour cream, 1/2 cup packed light brown sugar, 1/2 cup coconut and 1/2 teaspoon vanilla extract. Served with assorted fresh fruit, this dip is good for a luau.

HOT MEXICAN DIP

1 15-ounce can chili without beans	10 drops of Tabasco sauce
1 pound Velveeta cheese, cubed	1/2 2-ounce can sliced black olives
1 bunch green onions, chopped	Nacho or corn chips
1 tablespoon Worcestershire sauce	

Combine chili, Velveeta cheese, green onions, Worcestershire sauce, Tabasco sauce and black olives in slow cooker. Cook until cheese is melted, stirring frequently. Cook on High for 1 hour, stirring occasionally. Serve with nacho or corn chips.
Yield: 12 servings.

Cindy Magnifico, Nu Psi
Lexington, Missouri

MEXICAN DIP FOR CORN CHIPS

2 8-ounce cans jalapeño-flavored bean dip	1 bunch green onions, chopped
3 (or more) avocados	1 2-ounce can sliced black olives
1 tablespoon lemon juice	2 or 3 tomatoes, peeled, chopped
1 cup sour cream	1½ cups shredded Cheddar cheese
½ envelope taco seasoning mix	

Spread bean dip in 8-by-12-inch serving dish. Mash avocados in shallow bowl with lemon juice. Mix sour cream with taco seasoning mix in bowl. Layer avocado, sour cream, green onions, black olives, tomatoes and cheese over bean dip. Serve with plain corn chips. May be refrigerated overnight.
Yield: 20 servings.

Phyllis E. Lindberg, Preceptor Psi
Sedona, Arizona

MEXICAN LAYERED DIP

1 16-ounce can refried beans	8 ounces Monterey Jack cheese, shredded
1 8-ounce can bean dip	1 tomato, finely chopped
8 ounces cream cheese, softened	¼ cup finely chopped green onions
3 tablespoons picante sauce	¼ cup finely chopped black olives
2 cups guacamole	
8 ounces Cheddar cheese, shredded	

Layer refried beans and bean dip in 12-by-12-inch serving dish. Mix cream cheese with picante sauce in bowl. Layer cream cheese mixture, guacamole, Cheddar cheese, Monterey Jack cheese, tomato, green onions and black olives over bean dip. Chill, covered, for 2 hours to 3 days. Yield: 20 servings.

Josephine Martin, Preceptor Delta
Montgomery, Alabama

OLÉ TACO DIP

1 pound ground beef	8 ounces Cheddar cheese, shredded
1 pound sausage	2 cups sour cream
1 medium onion, chopped	Black olives
1 envelope taco seasoning mix	Sliced jalapeño peppers
1 8-ounce can refried beans	Mexican salsa
1 8-ounce can chili beans	Corn chips

Preheat oven to 350 degrees. Brown ground beef with sausage and onion in skillet, stirring frequently; drain. Add taco seasoning mix; mix well. Stir in refried beans and chili beans. Spoon into 9-by-13-inch baking dish. Sprinkle with cheese. Bake for 25 to 30 minutes or until bubbly. Let stand at room temperature for 20 minutes to cool. Spread sour cream over top. Garnish with black olives, jalapeño peppers and salsa. Serve with corn chips.
Yield: 10 servings.

Shirley McInturff, Epsilon
Winchester, Virginia

ROUNDUP NACHO SUPREME

1 pound ground beef	1 10-ounce package frozen avocados
1 envelope taco seasoning mix	2 fresh avocados, mashed
8 drops of Tabasco sauce	2 tablespoons lime juice
1 30-ounce can refried beans	6 green onions, sliced
5 tablespoons sliced jalapeño peppers	1 teaspoon seasoned salt
1½ cups shredded Cheddar cheese	1 cup sour cream
1½ cups shredded Monterey Jack cheese	1 cup sliced jalapeño peppers
1 8-ounce jar picante sauce	1 2-ounce can sliced black olives
	Thinly sliced tomatoes
	Tortilla chips

Preheat oven to 400 degrees. Brown ground beef in skillet, stirring until crumbly; drain. Add taco seasoning mix and water according to package directions. Add Tabasco sauce; mix well. Simmer for 10 minutes. Spread refried beans in 9-by-13-inch baking dish. Add 5 tablespoons jalapeño peppers to ground beef mixture; mix well. Layer ground beef, Cheddar cheese, Monterey Jack cheese and picante sauce over refried beans. Bake for 25 minutes. Mix frozen avocados, mashed avocados and lime juice in bowl. Layer avocado mixture, green onions, seasoned salt and sour cream over baked mixture. Garnish with jalapeño peppers, black olives and sliced tomatoes. Serve with tortilla chips. Yield: 50 servings.

Bettie Hill, Preceptor Kappa Omicron
Dallas, Texas

TACO DIP

1 cup sour cream	1 head lettuce, finely
8 ounces cream cheese,	shredded
softened	2 large tomatoes,
2 avocados, mashed	chopped
1 teaspoon onion	2 large green bell
powder	peppers, chopped
1 teaspoon garlic	1 1/2 pounds Cheddar
powder	cheese, shredded
2 teaspoons seasoned	1 16-ounce package
salt	Tostitos chips

Combine sour cream, cream cheese and avocados in bowl; mix well. Add onion powder, garlic powder and seasoned salt; mix well. Spread on serving dish. Layer shredded lettuce, tomatoes, green peppers and cheese over mixture. Chill for 1 hour before serving. Serve with Tostitos chips. Yield: 8 servings.

Debra Klima, Xi Gamma Pi
Colorado Springs, Colorado

COTTAGE CHEESE TACO DIP

8 ounces cream cheese,	1 small head lettuce,
softened	shredded
16 ounces cottage cheese	2 tomatoes, chopped
1 envelope taco	8 ounces Cheddar
seasoning mix	cheese, shredded
1 8-ounce jar salsa	Taco chips
1 Spanish onion,	
chopped	

Combine cream cheese, cottage cheese and taco seasoning mix in bowl; mix well. Spread on large serving dish. Chill for several hours. Layer salsa, onion, lettuce, tomatoes and cheese over mixture. Serve with taco chips. Yield: 12 servings.

Judy Wright, Laureate Alpha Theta
Peterborough, Ontario, Canada

MIX-MATCH DIPPER

24 ounces cream cheese,	1/2 cup finely chopped
softened	green onions
1 10-ounce can tomato	1/2 cup finely chopped
soup	green bell pepper
1 3-ounce package	Julienne vegetables
lemon gelatin	

Combine cream cheese, soup and gelatin in bowl; mix well. Stir in green onions and green pepper. Spoon into serving bowl. Chill for 2 hours or longer. Serve with vegetables. Yield: 16 servings.

Vicki Massey, Preceptor Mu Xi
Wake Village, Texas

NACHO DIP

1 pound Velveeta	1 15-ounce can chili
cheese, cubed	without beans
1 pound ground beef	Nacho chips

Melt cheese in slow cooker. Brown ground beef in skillet, stirring until crumbly; drain. Add ground beef and chili to melted cheese. Cook to serving temperature. Serve with nacho chips.
Yield: 90 servings.

Tricia Beck, Mu Mu
Colfax, Illinois

PIZZA DIP

8 ounces cream cheese,	1/4 cup sliced green
softened	onions
1/2 cup sour cream	1/2 cup chopped
1/8 teaspoon garlic	pepperoni
powder	1/2 cup shredded
1/2 teaspoon oregano	mozzarella cheese
1/2 cup pizza sauce	Crackers, vegetables or
1/4 cup chopped green	potato chips
bell pepper	

Preheat oven to 350 degrees. Combine cream cheese, sour cream, garlic powder and oregano in bowl; mix well. Spread in glass pie plate. Layer pizza sauce, green pepper, green onions and pepperoni over cream cheese mixture. Bake for 10 to 15 minutes or until green pepper is tender-crisp. Top with mozzarella cheese. Bake for 5 minutes longer. Serve with crackers, vegetables or potato chips.
Yield: 28 servings.

Judith Betters, Xi Zeta Lambda
Cambridge Springs, Pennsylvania

MUSHROOM PIZZA DIP

This is one of those recipes that is embarrassing to give out because it is so simple.

8 ounces cream cheese,	1 2-ounce can sliced
softened	black olives, drained
1/2 15-ounce jar Ragu	16 ounces mozzarella
pizza sauce	cheese, shredded
1 4-ounce jar sliced	Tortilla chips
mushrooms, drained	

Spread cream cheese in pie plate. Layer pizza sauce, mushrooms, olives and mozzarella cheese over cream cheese. Chill until 30 minutes before serving time. Let stand at room temperature for 30 minutes to soften. Serve with tortilla chips. Yield: 50 servings.

Nora Sullivan, Alpha Zeta
Moberly, Missouri

FRESH SALSA DIABOLIQUE

6 tomatoes, peeled,
  chopped
1/4 cup chopped red
  onion
1/4 cup chopped yellow
  onion
1/2 cup beef consommé
3 tablespoons vodka
1 teaspoon cumin

1 teaspoon chopped
  fresh cilantro
1 teaspoon salt
1 tablespoon lime juice
1/2 to 1   2-ounce can
  chopped mild green
  chilies
Corn chips

Combine tomatoes, red onion, yellow onion, consommé, vodka, cumin, cilantro, salt, lime juice and green chilies in bowl; mix well. Let stand for 1 hour to enhance flavor. Serve with corn chips. May substitute canned tomatoes for fresh tomatoes. May substitute 1/2 teaspoon dried coriander for cilantro. Yield: 50 servings.

Pamela Thompson, Omicron Alpha
Osage City, Kansas

SALSA CON CHILI VERDE

3 medium tomatoes,
  finely chopped
1 small onion, finely
  chopped
1 cup chopped cilantro
2 serano chilies, chopped

1/2 teaspoon garlic
  powder
1/2 teaspoon salt
1/2 to 1 lime, chopped
Tortilla chips

Combine tomatoes, onion, cilantro and chilies in bowl; mix well. Add garlic powder and salt; mix well. Add lime to taste. Chill for 45 minutes before serving. Serve with tortilla chips. Yield: 24 servings.

Barbara Cluck, Zeta Xi
Flagstaff, Arizona

SALSA CRUDA

2 to 3 hot peppers,
  minced
1 teaspoon salt
1/2 teaspoon garlic
  powder
1/2 teaspoon oregano
1/2 teaspoon comino seed
4 tomatoes

2 green onions
1 tablespoon (or more)
  lemon juice
1 tablespoon chopped
  cilantro
1 tablespoon cider
  vinegar
Chips

Grind hot peppers with salt, garlic powder, oregano and comino seed. Grind tomatoes and green onions. Do not use blender. Combine peppers, ground seasoning mixture, tomatoes, green onions, lemon juice, cilantro and vinegar in bowl; mix well. May stir in lemon juice a small amount at a time if salsa is too hot. Serve with chips or as a sauce with Mexican dishes. Yield: 2 cups.

Cindy Weber, Delta Chi
Mukwonago, Wisconsin

SPECIAL SEAFOOD DIP

8 ounces cream cheese,
  softened
1/3 cup mayonnaise
1/2 teaspoon prepared
  horseradish
1/2 teaspoon prepared
  mustard
1 1/2 tablespoons dried
  minced onion
1/2 teaspoon salt

1 tablespoon chopped
  parsley
Dash of garlic powder
2 tablespoons white
  wine
1/2 cup sour cream
1 6-ounce can crab
1 6-ounce can shrimp
Vegetables, chips or
  crackers

Combine cream cheese, mayonnaise, horseradish, mustard, onion, salt, parsley, garlic powder, white wine and sour cream in bowl; mix well. Stir in crab and shrimp. Serve with vegetables, chips or crackers. May serve hot or cold. Yield: 15 servings.

Maribeth Stauness, Xi Delta Psi
Surrey, British Columbia, Canada

SHRIMP CHIP DIP

1 cup whipping cream,
  whipped
4 ounces cream cheese,
  softened
1 6-ounce can shrimp,
  drained, rinsed

1 cup chopped green
  onions
Crackers or potato chips

Blend first 2 ingredients in bowl. Stir in shrimp and green onions. Spoon into serving dish; surround with crackers or potato chips. Yield: 40 servings.

Bev Wanamaker, Psi
Regina, Saskatchewan, Canada

SHRIMP DIP

This is a favorite for our chapter get togethers, even for people who usually don't like shrimp.

1 6-ounce can shrimp,
  drained, rinsed
4 ounces sharp Cheddar
  cheese, shredded
1 bunch green onions,
  thinly sliced

1 cup mayonnaise
1 teaspoon Louisiana
  hot sauce
Triscuit crackers

Drain rinsed shrimp on paper towels; pat dry. Combine cheese, green onions, mayonnaise and hot sauce in bowl; mix well. Stir in shrimp. Chill for several hours. Serve with Triscuit crackers. Yield: 6 servings.

Joan Metz, Psi Chi
Sunnyvale, California

Linda Jones, Gamma Theta, Forrest City, Arizona, makes a Shrimp Dip by combining 8 ounces rinsed canned shrimp, 8 ounces softened cream cheese, 1 cup each mayonnaise, chopped celery and chopped onion and 3 tablespoons lemon juice. Chill for several hours.

SPINACH APPETIZER DIP

1 10-ounce package frozen spinach, thawed, drained	1 cup sour cream
	1 envelope Knorr vegetable soup mix
1 8-ounce can water chestnuts	1 clove of garlic, minced
1/2 small onion	1 large round loaf sourdough bread
1 cup mayonnaise	

Combine spinach, water chestnuts and onion in food processor container. Process until finely chopped. Combine mayonnaise, sour cream, soup mix and garlic in bowl; mix well. Add spinach mixture; mix well. Cut top from bread; remove center carefully, leaving shell. Spoon dip into shell. Cut bread from center into cubes. Serve with dip. Yield: 60 servings.

Cynthia Nash, Delta Phi
Salmon Arm, British Columbia, Canada

ELLIE'S VEGETABLE DIP

I served this at the first rush party I attended after I joined Beta Sigma Phi and now I am always asked to bring this great dip.

1 cup plain yogurt	1 tablespoon parsley flakes
1 cup mayonnaise	
1 teaspoon Worcestershire sauce	1 teaspoon dillweed
	1 teaspoon seasoned salt
1 tablespoon dried minced onion	1 teaspoon MSG
	Assorted vegetables

Combine yogurt, mayonnaise and Worcestershire sauce in bowl; mix well. Mix dried onion, parsley flakes, dillweed, seasoned salt and MSG together. Add to yogurt mixture; mix well. Chill, covered, for 2 hours to overnight. Serve with vegetables. Yield: 30 servings.

Eleanor Miller, Preceptor Omicron
Bradenton, Florida

BACON SPREAD

1 3-ounce jar bacon bits	2 cups shredded cheese
	1 16-ounce jar mayonnaise-type salad dressing
1/4 cup chopped green bell pepper	
1/4 cup chopped onion	Ritz crackers

Combine bacon bits, green pepper, onion, cheese and salad dressing in bowl; mix well. Serve with Ritz crackers. Yield: 30 servings.

Tara S. Norris, Beta Rho
Lexington, South Carolina

Phyllis Putnam, Tau Beta, Harris, Missouri, makes Shrimp Spread by layering 8 ounces softened cream cheese, 1 jar shrimp sauce and 1 can tiny shrimp on serving plate. Serve with assorted crackers.

CHAR'S CHUTNEY AND CHEESE SPREAD

8 ounces cream cheese, softened	1 tablespoon dry sherry
	3 to 4 tablespoons chutney
1/2 teaspoon curry powder	
2 ounces Cheddar cheese, shredded	3 to 4 tablespoons chopped green onions
Dash of salt and pepper	Assorted crackers

Combine cream cheese, curry powder, cheese, salt, pepper and sherry in bowl; mix well. Shape into mound on serving plate. Chill until firm. Spread chutney over cheese ball; sprinkle with green onions. Serve with crackers. Yield: 4 to 8 servings.

Charlyne Wirkees, Preceptor Psi
Sedona, Arizona

CRAB SPREAD

1 pound imitation crab meat	Dash of Worcestershire sauce
11 ounces cream cheese, softened	1 tablespoon lemon juice
	2 tablespoons mayonnaise
2 teaspoons minced onion	
1 teaspoon dillweed	Crackers or vegetables

Chop imitation crab meat very fine. Combine with cream cheese, onion, dillweed, Worcestershire sauce, lemon juice and mayonnaise in bowl; mix well. Chill until serving time. Serve with crackers or vegetables. Yield: 15 servings.

June S. Jolley, Alpha Theta
Canton, North Carolina

SURPRISE SPREAD

8 ounces cream cheese, softened	1/2 tomato, finely chopped
1/2 cup sour cream	1 4-ounce can small shrimp, rinsed, drained
1/4 cup mayonnaise	
1/2 cup seafood cocktail sauce	
1/2 green bell pepper, finely chopped	1 cup shredded mozzarella cheese
3 green onions, finely chopped	Assorted party crackers

Combine cream cheese, sour cream and mayonnaise in bowl; mix well. Spread on large rimmed serving plate. Layer cocktail sauce, green pepper, green onions, tomato, shrimp and mozzarella cheese over cream cheese mixture. Chill for 2 hours or longer. Serve with crackers. Yield: 50 servings.

Gail E. Audras, Epsilon Upsilon
Winfield, British Columbia, Canada

SEAFOOD AND AVOCADO MOLD

1 envelope unflavored gelatin	Dash of red pepper sauce
1/4 cup water	8 ounces imitation crab meat, chopped
1 medium avocado, finely chopped	1/2 cup sour cream
1 medium avocado, puréed	1/4 cup chopped parsley
1 tablespoon minced onion	1 large green onion, finely chopped
2 tablespoons lemon juice	Dash of red pepper sauce
	1 tablespoon lemon juice
2 tablespoons mayonnaise	1/2 cup sour cream
1/4 teaspoon salt	2 tablespoons minced onion
	Avocado and parsley
	Tortilla chips

Sprinkle gelatin on water in saucepan. Let stand for 1 minute to soften. Cook over low heat until gelatin dissolves, stirring constantly. Combine chopped avocado, puréed avocado, 1 tablespoon minced onion, 2 tablespoons lemon juice, mayonnaise, salt and pepper sauce in bowl; mix well. Stir in 2 tablespoons gelatin. Spoon into 3-by-7-inch springform pan. Chill, covered, for 30 minutes. Combine next 6 ingredients and 1 tablespoon gelatin in bowl; mix well. Spread over avocado layer. Chill, covered, for 30 minutes. Combine sour cream, 2 tablespoons minced onion and remaining gelatin in bowl; mix well. Spread over seafood layer. Chill, covered, for 8 hours or until set. Remove sides of springform pan. Garnish with avocado and parsley. Serve with tortilla chips. Yield: 60 servings.

Bev Jones, Xi Kappa Omega
Brunswick, Missouri

SHRIMP OR LOBSTER MOLD

1 10-ounce can tomato soup	12 ounces (or more) shrimp or lobster
8 ounces cream cheese, softened	1 teaspoon salt
2 envelopes unflavored gelatin	1/2 teaspoon paprika
	2 dashes of Tabasco sauce
1/4 cup cold water	1 tablespoon Worcestershire sauce
1 cup mayonnaise	
3/4 cup finely chopped celery	2 teaspoons (or more) horseradish
Grated onion	Assorted crackers

Combine tomato soup and cream cheese in saucepan. Cook over low heat until well blended, stirring frequently. Soften gelatin in cold water. Add to soup mixture. Cook until gelatin dissolves, stirring constantly. Add mayonnaise, celery, a small amount of onion and next 6 ingredients; mix well. Pour into lightly greased 1 1/2-quart mold. Chill overnight or until set. Serve with crackers. Yield: 80 servings.

Helen F. Nielsen, Laureate Lambda
Salmon, Idaho

CHEESE AND SHRIMP APPETIZER

12 ounces cream cheese, softened	1 teaspoon lemon juice
2 tablespoons mayonnaise	1 1/2 to 2 cups fresh or frozen cooked shrimp
1 small onion, grated	1/2 12-ounce bottle of chili sauce
2 teaspoons Worcestershire sauce	Assorted crackers

Process first 5 ingredients in blender until well blended. Spoon onto serving plate. Chill, covered, overnight. Combine shrimp and chili sauce in bowl; toss to mix. Chill, covered, overnight. Drain shrimp. Spread over cream cheese. Serve with crackers. Yield: 10 to 12 servings.

Shirley E. Duncan, President, Rho
Victoria, British Columbia, Canada

BACON ROLL-UPS

1 loaf sliced bread	1 pound center-cut bacon
8 ounces cream cheese, softened	

Preheat oven to 450 degrees. Trim crust from bread slices; flatten bread with hand. Spread with cream cheese. Roll as for jelly roll. Secure with wooden pick. Wrap bacon slice around roll; secure with pick. Place in ungreased baking pan. Bake for 20 minutes. May cut into halves. Yield: 20 servings.

Pat Duffield, Preceptor Nu
Orlando, Florida

SWEETENED BACON ROLL-UPS

1 loaf sliced bread	2 tablespoons Worcestershire sauce
1 14-ounce can sweetened condensed milk	1 pound bacon
	3 cups shredded cheese
1/2 cup mustard	

Remove crust from bread slices; flatten bread with rolling pin. Combine condensed milk, mustard and Worcestershire sauce in bowl; mix well. Layer 1 slice bread over 3 slices bacon. Spread with condensed milk mixture; sprinkle with cheese. Roll as for jelly roll. Cut into halves. Place in baking pan. Repeat with remaining ingredients. Chill in refrigerator for 3 hours. Preheat oven to 375 degrees. Bake for 30 minutes. Yield: 20 servings.

Gladys Kelly, Alpha Rho Theta
Friendswood, Texas

Jamie Lambert, Alpha Upsilon Psi, The Colony, Texas, spreads mixture of 16 ounces softened cream cheese, 4 ounces chopped green chilies, 1 can chopped black olives and 1 chopped onion on flour tortillas and rolls them up for Tortilla Pinwheels.

GROUND BEEF TIDBITS

We have used these at our sorority Sweetheart Cocktail Party and had many compliments.

2 pounds ground beef	8 ounces cream cheese,
1/4 cup dried minced	softened
onion	8 10-count cans
1 teaspoon garlic salt	crescent rolls
1 8-ounce package	
mushrooms, chopped	

Preheat oven to 350 degrees. Brown ground beef with minced onion and garlic salt in skillet, stirring frequently; drain. Add chopped mushrooms and cream cheese; mix well. Separate crescent rolls into rectangles. Spoon mixture down middle of rectangle. Roll to enclose filling; pinch ends to seal. Place on ungreased baking sheet. Bake for 12 to 14 minutes or until golden brown. Slice each roll into 4 to 6 slices. Serve warm. Yield: 160 servings.

Lucille Schuer, Laureate Lambda
Sioux Falls, South Dakota

BREAD SALAD SQUARES

2 10-count cans	1 3-ounce can bacon
crescent rolls	bits
6 ounces cream cheese,	8 ounces Cheddar
softened	cheese, shredded
6 to 8 green onions,	
chopped	

Preheat oven to 350 degrees. Separate crescent rolls; line 9-by-13-inch baking sheet with dough. Bake for 10 to 12 minutes or until brown. Cool to room temperature. Spread cream cheese over baked layer; sprinkle with green onions, bacon bits and cheese. Cut into small squares. Yield: 80 servings.

Linda Tiller, Preceptor Beta Mu
Virginia Beach, Virginia

CALIFORNIA DIP CANAPÉS

1 envelope onion soup	Shaved ham and/or
mix	shaved smoked turkey
2 cups sour cream	American cheese slices
2 loaves sliced bread	and/or Swiss cheese
2 16-ounce jars dill	slices
pickle spears	

Combine onion soup mix and sour cream in bowl; mix well. Chill for 2 hours or longer. Remove crust from bread; flatten bread with rolling pin. Cut pickle spears into halves. Spread sour cream mixture on each bread slice. Add ham or turkey, American Cheese or Swiss cheese and pickle. Roll to enclose filling. Slice each roll into 3 pieces. Pack tightly in covered container. Chill until serving time. Yield: 50 servings.

Elaine McCulloch, Lambda Eta
Lamar, Missouri

MISSISSIPPI CAVIAR

2 15-ounce cans	1/4 cup wine vinegar
black-eyed peas	1/2 teaspoon salt
2 small onions, thinly	1 clove of garlic, minced
sliced	1 cup vegetable oil
Cracked pepper to taste	

Rinse black-eyed peas; drain. Layer black-eyed peas and onion slices in serving bowl, sprinkling each layer generously with cracked pepper. Process vinegar, salt, garlic and vegetable oil in blender at high speed for 3 minutes or until well blended. Pour over black-eyed peas and onions. Chill for 2 hours to 2 weeks. Flavor improves after several days. Yield: 50 servings.

Sandra Gorski, Xi Gamma Gamma
Sioux City, Iowa

CHEESE BOAT

4 cups shredded sharp	1/2 teaspoon Tabasco
cheese	sauce
16 ounces cream cheese,	1/2 teaspoon chili
softened	powder
8 ounces corned beef,	1 loaf sourdough or
chopped	French bread
1 tomato, chopped	Tortilla chips
1 bunch green onions,	Sesame crackers
chopped	
1 hot chili pepper, finely	
chopped	

Preheat oven to 350 degrees. Combine sharp cheese, cream cheese and corned beef in mixer bowl; mix well. Add tomato, green onions, chili pepper, Tabasco sauce and chili powder; mix well. Cut top from bread; remove center carefully, leaving shell. Spoon cheese mixture into bread shell. Wrap in foil. Bake for 45 minutes. Place on serving tray with tortilla chips and sesame crackers. Yield: 100 servings.

 Maureen Echols, Preceptor Zeta
Warner Robins, Georgia

QUICK CHEESE FONDUE

1 10-ounce can	2 dashes of cayenne
Cheddar cheese soup	pepper
8 ounces French onion	French bread, cut into
dip	1-inch cubes
1 cup shredded Cheddar	Apples, cut into
cheese	bite-sized pieces
1/2 teaspoon dry mustard	Green seedless grapes

Combine cheese soup, onion dip, cheese, mustard and cayenne pepper in saucepan. Cook over low heat until cheese is melted, stirring constantly. Pour into chafing dish. Serve with bread cubes, apples and grapes. Yield: 2 1/2 cups.

Debbie Minnich, Eta Delta
Winterville, North Carolina

CHEESE PIE

1 egg, beaten	3/4 cup all-purpose flour
1 cup milk	1 cup Muenster cheese
1/2 teaspoon salt	cubes
1/2 teaspoon oregano	1/2 cup cubed pepperoni

Preheat oven to 450 degrees. Combine egg, milk, salt and oregano in mixer bowl; mix well. Blend in flour. Stir in cheese and pepperoni. Pour into 8-inch square baking dish. Bake for 30 minutes. Yield: 16 servings.

Jane C. Newman, Epsilon Psi
Martinsville, Virginia

CHEESE PUFFS

8 ounces cream cheese, softened	1/4 cup grated Parmesan cheese
1 1/2 teaspoons grated onion	1/4 teaspoon cayenne pepper
1/2 cup mayonnaise	1/2 loaf sliced white bread, trimmed
2 tablespoons chopped chives	

Preheat oven to 350 degrees. Combine cream cheese, onion, mayonnaise, chives, Parmesan cheese and cayenne pepper in food processor container. Process until smooth. Cut each bread slice into 4 squares or 4 circles. Spread cheese mixture on bread; place on baking sheet. Bake for 10 to 15 minutes or until golden brown. Yield: 40 servings.

Deborah A. Herod, Eta Xi
Winter Park, Florida

TASTY CHEESE PUFFS

1/2 cup butter or margarine	2 egg whites, stiffly beaten
3 ounces cream cheese, softened	1 large loaf unsliced French bread
5 to 6 ounces Monterey Jack cheese, shredded	

Combine butter, cream cheese and Monterey Jack cheese in top of double boiler. Cook until melted, stirring frequently. Fold in egg whites. Cut bread into cubes. Dip bread into cheese mixture to coat; place on tray. Freeze, covered with waxed paper, until firm. Store in plastic bag in freezer. Preheat oven to 400 degrees. Place cheese puffs on baking sheet. Bake for 8 to 10 minutes or until brown. Yield: 3 dozen.

Marsha Parrish, Laureate Delta Nu
Orange, California

Laura J. Leroy, Xi Beta Tau, Columbus, Kansas, combines 1 cup vegetable oil, 1 package ranch salad dressing mix, 1 teaspoon dillweed, 1/2 teaspoon garlic powder and 24 ounces oyster crackers in airtight container. Makes a Zippy Snack.

CHEESE SNACKS

8 ounces Tilamook cheese	1/2 green bell pepper, chopped
8 ounces Velveeta cheese	1 10-ounce can tomato soup
1 4 1/2-ounce bottle of stuffed green olives	1 12-count package hot dog buns
1 small onion	

Grind Tilamook cheese, Velveeta cheese, olives, onion and green pepper. Combine with tomato soup in bowl; mix well. Chill, covered, overnight. Preheat oven to 400 degrees. Cut hot dog buns into quarters. Spread with cheese mixture. Place on baking sheet. Bake for 2 minutes or until cheese melts. Serve hot. May be heated under broiler. Yield: 40 servings.

Mary Ann Tretteen, Preceptor Delta Omega
Apple Valley, California

CHEESE SNACKS WITH DILL

I served these at a Thanksgiving Brunch at church and everyone requested the recipe. Every time I serve these, they disappear as fast as they come out of the oven.

3 5-ounce jars Old English cheese spread	3/4 teaspoon Tabasco sauce
1 cup margarine	Dash of cayenne pepper
1 teaspoon onion powder	2 loaves extra thin sliced sandwich bread
1 1/4 teaspoons dillweed	
1 tablespoon Worcestershire sauce	

Preheat oven to 350 degrees. Combine cheese spread, margarine, onion powder, dillweed, Worcestershire sauce, Tabasco sauce and cayenne pepper in bowl; mix well. Stack bread 3 slices at a time. Trim crusts; cut each stack into quarters. Spread cheese mixture between layers and over top and sides. Do not spread on bottom. Place on nonstick baking sheet. Bake for 10 to 12 minutes or until edges are brown. Serve warm. Yield: 36 servings.

Tara Smith, Alpha Rho Theta
Friendswood, Texas

CHEESE TRUFFLES

3 tablespoons butter or margarine, softened	1 teaspoon sugar
1 teaspoon sour cream	2 cups fine pumpernickel bread crumbs
3 ounces cream cheese, softened	

Cream butter and sour cream in bowl. Mix cream cheese and sugar in bowl. Add to butter mixture; mix well. Chill until firm. Shape into balls. Roll in bread crumbs. Chill until serving time. Yield: 6 to 8 servings.

Karen Bowe, Xi Gamma Theta
Kitchener, Ontario, Canada

GOUDA BAKE

1 Gouda cheese	Crackers
1 8-count can crescent rolls	

Preheat oven to 350 degrees. Peel red wax covering from cheese. Unroll crescent rolls. Press together to form square; seal perforations. Wrap roll dough around cheese. Place on baking sheet. Bake for 20 minutes or until light brown. May be reheated in microwave. Serve with crackers. Yield: 6 to 8 servings.

Viv Biermann, Lambda
Roswell, Georgia

HOT CHEESE SPREAD

1/2 cup mayonnaise	1 teaspoon
1 cup grated Parmesan cheese	Worcestershire sauce
1 cup shredded Cheddar cheese	1 small loaf sliced French bread
1 tablespoon chopped green onions	

Preheat oven to 450 degrees. Combine mayonnaise, Parmesan cheese, Cheddar cheese, green onions and Worcestershire sauce in bowl; mix well. Spread cheese mixture on bread slices; place on baking sheet. Bake for 5 to 10 minutes or until cheese is melted. Serve hot. Yield: 6 servings.

Connie Noah, Xi Omicron
Roseburg, Oregon

SNAPPY CHEESE APPETIZERS

8 ounces Imperial cheese, softened	1/2 teaspoon salt
1/2 cup butter or margarine, softened	Dash of Tabasco sauce
	Dash of Worcestershire sauce
1 cup all-purpose flour	1 cup crisp rice cereal

Preheat oven to 350 degrees. Combine cheese and butter in bowl; mix well. Blend in flour, salt, Tabasco sauce and Worcestershire sauce. Stir in rice cereal. Shape into balls; place on baking sheet. Flatten with fork. Bake for 15 minutes or until brown. Serve warm. May be reheated at 300 degrees for 5 minutes. Yield: 50 servings.

Wendy Turnbull, Xi Zeta Xi
Angus, Ontario, Canada

Patricia K. Lahey, Xi Alpha Iota, Rochester, Minnesota, marinates 6 pounds chicken wings overnight in mixture of 2 cups each soy sauce, sugar, water and pineapple syrup, 2 teaspoons each garlic and ginger, and 1/2 cup vegetable oil. Bake in marinade in preheated 350-degree oven for 1 hour. Drain and bake at 300 degrees for 1 hour longer.

SPICY CHICKEN NUGGETS

1/2 cup melted butter or margarine	1/2 cup spicy brown mustard
1/2 cup spicy brown mustard	1/2 cup melted butter or margarine
8 chicken breast filets, cubed	1/4 cup sherry
2 cups cracker crumbs	2 tablespoons soy sauce
1/2 cup melted butter or margarine	1/4 teaspoon garlic powder

Preheat oven to 375 degrees. Combine 1/2 cup melted butter and 1/2 cup brown mustard in bowl; mix well. Dip chicken in mixture; roll in cracker crumbs. Place in two 9-by-13-inch baking dishes; drizzle with 1/2 cup melted butter. Bake for 20 to 25 minutes or until golden brown. Drain on paper towels. Combine 1/2 cup brown mustard, remaining 1/2 cup melted butter, sherry, soy sauce and garlic powder in bowl; mix well. Serve with chicken. Yield: 16 to 18 servings.

Kim Adams, Xi Alpha Rho
Danville, Kentucky

BAKED CHICKEN WING APPETIZERS

18 chicken wings (about 3 pounds)	3/4 teaspoon paprika
11/2 cups dried bread crumbs	1/8 teaspoon red pepper
	1 cup plain yogurt
1/4 cup sesame seed	2 tablespoons honey
11/4 teaspoons salt	6 tablespoons melted margarine
3/4 teaspoon ginger	

Preheat oven to 425 degrees. Disjoint chicken wings; discard tips. Mix bread crumbs with next 5 ingredients on waxed paper. Mix yogurt and honey in bowl. Dip chicken in yogurt mixture; roll in crumb mixture to coat. Place on rack in large roasting pan. Drizzle 3 tablespoons margarine over chicken. Bake for 15 minutes. Turn chicken; drizzle with remaining margarine. Bake for 15 minutes longer or until brown and tender. Yield: 36 servings.

Becky Elms, Mu Epsilon
San Angelo, Texas

CHICKEN WINGS

1/2 cup melted butter or margarine	1/2 cup water
1 cup soy sauce	1 teaspoon dry mustard
1 cup packed light brown sugar	3 or 4 pounds chicken drumettes

Combine first 5 ingredients in bowl; mix well. Layer chicken in 9-by-13-inch baking dish; drizzle with butter mixture. Chill, covered, for 2 hours or longer. Preheat oven to 350 degrees. Bake, uncovered, for 1 hour or until brown. Yield: 12 servings.

Janice Yates, Xi Gamma Gamma
Sioux City, Iowa

CHICKEN WINGS SUPREME

2 pounds chicken wings
Salt and pepper to taste
Garlic powder to taste
1 cup orange marmalade
1 cup Italian salad
  dressing
Honey

Disjoint chicken wings; discard tips. Sprinkle with salt, pepper and garlic powder. Mix orange marmalade and Italian salad dressing together in bowl. Add chicken, stirring to coat. Marinate, covered, in refrigerator for several hours to overnight. Preheat oven to 350 degrees. Place chicken in shallow baking pan. Bake for 45 minutes to 1 hour. Drizzle chicken with honey. Bake for 15 minutes longer or until brown. Yield: 4 servings.

Anna New, Alpha Psi
Coronach, Saskatchewan, Canada

HONEY GARLIC WINGS

1/2 cup honey
1/4 cup lemon juice
1/2 cup water
3 tablespoons catsup
2 cloves of garlic,
  minced
1 teaspoon salt
1 teaspoon ginger
3 pounds chicken wings
1/4 cup butter or
  margarine

Combine honey, lemon juice, water, catsup, garlic, salt and ginger in saucepan. Heat just to the boiling point. Pour into 9-by-13-inch baking dish. Disjoint chicken wings; discard tips. Add chicken to baking dish, turning to coat. Marinate in refrigerator for several hours, turning frequently. Preheat oven to 400 degrees. Remove chicken to plate. Drain marinade into saucepan. Place butter in baking dish. Bake until melted. Add chicken, turning to coat with butter. Bake for 25 minutes. Turn chicken. Bake for 20 minutes longer or until tender. Heat marinade to serving temperature. Serve with chicken. Chicken may also be cooked in marinade. It is also good on spareribs. Yield: 6 servings.

Terry Hewitson, Zeta Delta
Prescott, Ontario, Canada

SOUTHWEST WINGS

3/4 cup picante sauce
1/4 cup honey
3/4 teaspoon grated
  fresh ginger
1 tablespoon soy sauce
1 1/2 to 2 pounds chicken
  drumettes

Preheat oven to 350 degrees. Combine picante sauce, honey, ginger and soy sauce in saucepan. Simmer for 10 minutes, stirring occasionally. Place chicken in greased baking pan. Brush with sauce. Bake for 15 minutes. Turn chicken; baste with sauce. Bake for 15 minutes longer or until tender. Yield: 8 to 10 servings.

Ina M. Schreiber, Laureate Beta Beta
Irving, Texas

CHILIES RELLENOS SQUARES

2 4-ounce cans green
  chilies
1 pound Monterey Jack
  or mozzarella cheese,
  shredded
3 eggs
1 cup sour cream
Chopped red bell pepper
1/4 teaspoon salt
1/4 teaspoon pepper

Preheat oven to 350 degrees. Combine green chilies, cheese, eggs, sour cream, bell pepper, salt and pepper in bowl; mix well. Spoon into greased 9-by-13-inch baking dish. Bake for 40 to 45 minutes or until set. Cut into small squares. Yield: 9 servings.

Cheryl Ingeberg, Xi Omicron
Regina, Saskatchewan, Canada

FRUITED HAM BALLS

1 pound ground cooked
  ham
4 ounces ground pork
1 1/2 cups fine bread
  crumbs
1 egg, slightly beaten
1/4 cup milk
Butter or margarine
1/4 cup cornstarch
2/3 cup packed light
  brown sugar
1 20-ounce can
  pineapple chunks
1 cup orange juice
1/2 cup vinegar
1/2 cup each drained red
  and green maraschino
  cherries

Mix ham, pork, bread crumbs, egg and milk in bowl. Shape into small balls. Brown in butter in saucepan over medium heat; keep warm. Mix cornstarch and brown sugar in saucepan. Drain pineapple, reserving juice. Add enough water to reserved juice to measure 1 cup. Stir into brown sugar mixture. Add orange juice and vinegar. Cook over low heat until thickened, stirring frequently. Combine ham balls, cherries and pineapple in chafing dish. Drizzle with sauce. Serve with wooden picks. Yield: 20 servings.

Elizabeth Hogan, Laureate Beta Lambda
Bethany, Missouri

HAM AND ALMOND PINWHEELS

8 ounces cream cheese,
  softened
3 tablespoons finely
  chopped almonds
2 tablespoons
  mayonnaise
1 teaspoon
  Worcestershire sauce
1/4 teaspoon paprika
1/2 teaspoon prepared
  mustard
1/8 teaspoon salt
1/8 teaspoon pepper
4 thin 3-by-6-inch slices
  boiled ham
40 round crackers or
  Melba toast rounds

Beat cream cheese in small bowl until light. Add next 7 ingredients; mix well. Spread evenly over ham slices. Roll ham from long side to enclose filling. Chill, wrapped in foil, for 4 hours or longer. Cut into 1/2-inch slices. Place on crackers. Yield: 40 servings.

Ardis Monarchi, Preceptor Nu
Lakewood, Colorado

LIVER PÂTÉ

This fifth-generation Danish liver pâté recipe is called Liva-Paa-Steig.

1 pound frozen chicken livers	1/4 cup all-purpose flour
1/2 medium onion, chopped	1 cup half and half or whipping cream
1 pound butter or margarine, melted	2 eggs
	1 teaspoon salt
	1/4 teaspoon pepper

Preheat oven to 350 degrees. Grind frozen livers and onion together. Blend butter and flour in bowl. Add liver mixture and half and half; mix well. Mix in eggs, salt and pepper. Spoon into 2 or 3 baking pans. Place in shallow pan of water. Bake, covered, for 1 hour. Bake, uncovered, for 30 minutes longer. Invert onto serving plate. Yield: 20 servings.

Eleanor Taylor, Sigma Lambda
Oaklawn, Illinois

SWEDISH MEATBALLS

2 pounds ground beef	3/4 cup vinegar
2 cups bread crumbs	1 1/2 cups packed light brown sugar
2 eggs, slightly beaten	1 tablespoon dry mustard
1 cup milk	
1 teaspoon salt	
3/4 cup water	

Preheat oven to 325 degrees. Combine ground beef, bread crumbs, eggs, milk and salt in bowl; mix well. Shape into 1-inch balls; place in shallow baking dish. Combine water, vinegar, brown sugar and dry mustard in bowl; mix well. Pour over meatballs. Bake for 40 minutes. Yield: 20 servings.

Teresa Gitto, Xi Alpha
Beaconsfield, Quebec, Canada

COCKTAIL MEATBALLS

1 pound ground beef	1 teaspoon salt
1/2 cup bread crumbs	1/8 teaspoon pepper
1/3 cup chopped onion	1/4 cup shortening
1/4 cup milk	1 16-ounce bottle of chili sauce
1 egg	
1 tablespoon chopped parsley	1 10-ounce jar grape jelly
1/2 teaspoon Worcestershire sauce	

Combine ground beef, bread crumbs, onion, milk, egg, parsley, Worcestershire sauce, salt and pepper in bowl; mix well. Shape into small balls. Brown in shortening in skillet; drain. Heat chili sauce and jelly in saucepan until well mixed. Add meatballs; stir to coat well. Simmer for 30 minutes. Yield: 4 to 6 servings.

Tracy D. Gagnon, Omicron
Hudson, New Hampshire

MEATBALLS IN GINGERSNAP SAUCE

1 pound ground beef	1/3 cup packed light brown sugar
1 egg	
3/4 cup soft bread crumbs	1/4 cup dark raisins
1/4 cup water	2 1/2 tablespoons lemon juice
1/4 cup chopped onion	
1/2 teaspoon salt	1/2 cup coarsely crumbled gingersnaps
1 1/2 cups water	
2 beef bouillon cubes	

Combine ground beef with egg, bread crumbs, 1/4 cup water, onion and salt in bowl; mix well. Shape into 1-inch balls. Bring 1 1/2 cups water to a boil in saucepan. Stir in bouillon cubes, brown sugar, raisins, lemon juice and gingersnap crumbs. Add meatballs. Simmer for 10 minutes. Turn over meatballs and baste with sauce. Simmer for 10 minutes longer. Yield: 6 servings.

Jeannette Daehler, Alpha Zeta
Nevada, Iowa

MARINATED MUSHROOMS

2/3 cup sugar	1 teaspoon paprika
1/3 cup vinegar	1 teaspoon celery seed
1 tablespoon lemon juice	1/4 teaspoon salt
1/3 cup honey	1 cup vegetable oil
1 teaspoon grated onion	3 6-ounce cans whole mushrooms
1 teaspoon mustard	

Combine sugar, vinegar, lemon juice, honey, onion, mustard, paprika, celery seed and salt in bowl; mix well. Whisk in oil. Add mushrooms. Marinate in refrigerator overnight. Yield: 12 servings.

Pat MacArthur, Laureate Beta Mu
Lindsay, Ontario, Canada

SAUSAGE AND CHEESE MUSHROOMS

I served this at a rush party; when our chapter went to a restaurant for the last meeting of the year we were served the same appetizer.

1 1/2 pounds fresh mushrooms	3/4 cup shredded mozzarella cheese
8 ounces pork sausage	Parsley
1/4 cup seasoned bread crumbs	

Preheat oven to 450 degrees. Remove and chop mushroom stems, reserving caps. Cook sausage in 10-inch skillet, stirring until crumbly. Drain, reserving 2 tablespoons drippings. Sauté mushroom stems in reserved drippings in skillet; remove from heat. Stir in sausage, bread crumbs and 1/2 cup cheese. Spoon into mushroom caps. Place on baking sheet; sprinkle with remaining 1/4 cup cheese. Bake for 15 minutes. Garnish with parsley. Yield: 8 to 10 servings.

Mary E. Kolle, Delta Zeta
Traverse City, Michigan

STUFFED MUSHROOMS

1 pound hot sausage
1 pound large fresh
  mushrooms
1 8-ounce jar Cheez
  Whiz

Preheat broiler. Brown sausage in skillet, stirring until crumbly. Drain, reserving 2 to 3 tablespoons drippings. Remove and chop mushroom stems, reserving caps. Sauté stems in reserved drippings in skillet until golden brown. Add sausage and Cheez Whiz; mix well. Spoon into mushroom caps; arrange on baking sheet. Broil 6 inches from heat source for 5 to 7 minutes or until bubbly and brown. Yield: 16 to 24 servings.

Esther Adkins, Xi Delta Beta
Hartford City, Indiana

APPETIZER TORTILLA PINWHEELS

1 cup sour cream
8 ounces cream cheese,
  softened
1 4-ounce can chopped
  green chilies, drained
1 4-ounce can chopped
  black olives, drained
1/2 cup chopped green
  onions
1 cup shredded Cheddar
  cheese
Garlic powder and
  seasoned salt to taste
5 10-inch flour tortillas
Salsa
Parsley

Combine sour cream, cream cheese, chilies, olives, green onions, cheese, garlic powder and seasoned salt in bowl; mix well. Spread evenly on tortillas. Roll tortillas to enclose filling. Wrap individually in plastic wrap, twisting ends. Chill for several hours. Cut each tortilla into 10 slices, discarding ends. Arrange on serving dish with bowl of salsa in center. Garnish with parsley. Yield: 50 servings.

Carolyn Taylor, Preceptor
Baxter Springs, Kansas

MEXICAN PINWHEELS

1 cup sour cream
8 ounces cream cheese,
  softened
1 4-ounce can chopped
  black olives
1/2 cup chopped green
  onions
1 to 2 cups shredded
  Cheddar cheese
1/2 to 1 envelope taco
  seasoning mix
1 10-count package
  flour tortillas
Salsa

Combine sour cream, cream cheese, olives, green onions, cheese and taco seasoning mix in bowl; mix well. Spread evenly on tortillas. Roll tortillas to enclose filling; wrap with plastic wrap. Chill for several hours. Cut into 1/2-inch slices; arrange on serving plate. Top with salsa. Yield: 50 servings.

Tammy Goebel, Zeta Phi
Bryan, Ohio

PARTY PINWHEELS

16 ounces cream cheese,
  softened
2 green onions, minced
1 envelope ranch salad
  dressing mix
4 12-inch flour tortillas
1/2 cup chopped red bell
  pepper
1/2 cup chopped celery
1 4-ounce can sliced
  black olives, drained

Combine cream cheese, green onions and dressing mix in bowl; mix well. Spread on tortillas; sprinkle with red pepper, celery and olives. Roll tortillas to enclose filling; wrap in plastic wrap. Chill for 2 hours. Cut into 1-inch slices, discarding ends. Arrange on serving plate. Yield: 8 to 10 servings.

Amy S. Horby, Preceptor Kappa Omicron
Dallas, Texas

PEPPERONI APPETIZERS

A sorority sister brought this to a cookout and the men devoured it before the women got a taste. Now it is a "must" at every pig-out get-together.

8 ounces mild Cheddar
  cheese, shredded
8 ounces mozzarella
  cheese, shredded
1 4-ounce can sliced
  mushrooms, drained
1 green bell pepper,
  chopped
1 4-ounce can sliced
  black olives, drained
1 6-ounce jar stuffed
  green olives, sliced
1 cup mayonnaise-type
  salad dressing
1 8-ounce package
  sliced pepperoni
Tortilla chips

Mix first 7 ingredients in bowl. Spread in 9-by-13-inch dish. Top with pepperoni slices. Serve with tortilla chips. Yield: 15 servings.

Janet Strouse, Preceptor Beta Beta
Storm Lake, Iowa

CORA'S APPETIZER PIZZA

8 ounces cream cheese,
  softened
1 12-ounce bottle of
  cocktail sauce
2 or 3 drops of Tabasco
  sauce
1 7-ounce can shrimp,
  rinsed, drained
1 4-ounce can chopped
  black olives
Chopped green onions
  to taste
1 green bell pepper,
  chopped
2 cups shredded
  mozzarella cheese
Crackers or tortilla
  chips

Spread cream cheese on 12-inch platter. Combine cocktail sauce and Tabasco sauce in bowl; mix well. Spread over cream cheese. Layer shrimp, olives, green onions, green pepper and cheese over cocktail sauce. Serve with crackers or tortilla chips. Yield: 12 servings.

Sheryl Gage, Theta Zeta
Austin, Texas

GARDEN PIZZA

2 8-count cans crescent
  rolls
8 ounces cream cheese,
  softened
1/2 cup mayonnaise
1 envelope ranch salad
  dressing mix
1 cup chopped green bell
  pepper
1/2 cup chopped broccoli

1/3 cup chopped green
  onions
1 cup drained chopped
  tomatoes
1/2 cup chopped black or
  green olives
1/2 cup chopped
  cauliflower
Shredded Cheddar
  cheese

Preheat oven to 375 degrees. Unroll roll dough and spread on lightly greased 10-by-15-inch baking pan; press edges and perforations to seal. Bake for 9 minutes. Cool to room temperature. Combine cream cheese, mayonnaise and dressing mix in bowl; mix well. Spread over crust. Layer green pepper, broccoli, green onions, tomatoes, olives, cauliflower and Cheddar cheese over cream cheese layer. Cut into squares to serve. Do not make more than 2 hours before serving as crust will not remain crisp. May vary toppings to suit individual tastes. Yield: 20 servings.

Marilyn Beyer, Xi Upsilon
Lincoln, Nebraska

HORS D'OEUVRES PIZZA

I made this dish for our Valentine Party and used a heart-shaped dish.

16 ounces cream cheese,
  softened
1 to 2 tablespoons milk
1 12-ounce bottle of
  chili sauce
1/2 to 3/4 cup sliced red
  onion
1/2 to 3/4 cup thinly
  sliced green bell pepper

1/2 to 3/4 cup sliced
  mushrooms
1/2 cup sliced black
  olives
2 cups shredded
  mozzarella cheese
Corn chips or taco chips

Beat cream cheese with milk in bowl until of spreading consistency. Spread in round 12-inch dish or pan. Spread chili sauce to within 1/2 inch of edge. Sprinkle onion, green pepper, mushrooms and olives on chili sauce. Top with mozzarella cheese. Serve with corn chips or taco chips. Yield: 8 servings.

Barbara M. Allen, Preceptor Pi
Brewer, Maine

PIZZA PUFFS

1 pound ground beef
1 pound sausage
1 pound Velveeta
  cheese, chopped
1 teaspoon oregano

1 1/2 teaspoons parsley
1 teaspoon basil
1/4 teaspoon garlic
  powder
2 loaves party rye bread

Preheat broiler. Brown ground beef and sausage in skillet, stirring until crumbly; drain. Stir in cheese

until melted. Add oregano, parsley, basil and garlic powder; mix well. Spread on bread; place on baking sheet. Broil for 4 to 5 minutes or until bubbly. May freeze on baking sheet and store in freezer in plastic bag until needed. Yield: 20 servings.

Mary H. Kennedy, Xi Alpha Beta
South Windsor, Connecticut

VEGETABLE PIZZA

1 Boboli (prepared
  Italian bread shell)
8 ounces herb and
  garlic-flavored cream
  cheese, softened
1 cucumber, peeled,
  thinly sliced

8 to 10 cherry tomatoes,
  cut into halves
8 mushrooms, thinly
  sliced
Broccoli flowerets

Preheat oven to 450 degrees. Place Boboli on baking sheet. Bake for 8 to 10 minutes. Spread Boboli with cream cheese. Layer cucumber, cherry tomatoes, mushrooms and broccoli in concentric circles on cream cheese. Cut into wedges. May chill for up to 3 hours. May substitute mixture of cream cheese and envelope of ranch salad dressing mix for prepared cream cheese and use vegetables of preference. Yield: 4 to 6 servings.

Jani Bielenberg, Kappa
Denver, Colorado

YANKEE PIZZA

1 pound bacon, chopped
10 to 12 green onions,
  minced
1 pound American
  cheese, coarsely
  shredded
2 teaspoons MSG
  (optional)

1 cup mayonnaise
Dash of cayenne pepper
1/2 teaspoon salt
Pepper to taste
2 12-count packages
  dinner rolls with
  vertical sections

Preheat oven to 450 degrees. Cook bacon in skillet over medium heat until edges curl. Add green onions. Cook until green onions are tender. Drain, reserving half the drippings. Stir in cheese, MSG, mayonnaise, cayenne pepper, salt and pepper; mix well. Separate rolls vertically into 4 or 5 slices. Roll with rolling pin to flatten. Spread with bacon mixture; place on greased baking sheet. Bake for 5 minutes or until heated through. Yield: 96 to 120 servings.

Betty E. Stisser, Xi Beta Upsilon
Angel Fire, New Mexico

Leslie J. Went, Epsilon Epsilon, Spring Hill, Florida, makes Deep-Fried Mushrooms by coating 1 pound mushrooms with batter of 3/4 cup each flour and club soda and 1/2 teaspoon garlic salt. Fry in 400-degree deep vegetable oil until golden brown.

SALAMI-CHEESE APPETIZER SQUARES

This appetizer was a hit with my sorority sisters and their spouses at our annual Christmas-New Year party this year.

1 8-count can crescent rolls	1 clove of garlic, finely chopped
1 4-ounce can pimentos	3 tablespoons finely chopped Bermuda onion
12 ounces Genoa salami, sliced, cut into quarters	2 tablespoons finely chopped black olives
1 pound extra-sharp Cheddar cheese, shredded	5 eggs, at room temperature, beaten
1 medium green bell pepper, finely chopped	2 tablespoons poppy seed
3 tablespoons finely chopped parsley	5 tablespoons grated Parmesan cheese

Preheat oven to 350 degrees. Unroll roll dough. Press over bottom of nonstick 9-by-13-inch baking pan; press edges and perforations to seal. Push up 1/4 inch around edge of pan to form rim. Seed and drain pimentos. Process pimentos and salami in food processor with metal blade until finely chopped. Combine pimentos, salami, Cheddar cheese, green pepper, parsley, garlic, onion, olives, eggs, poppy seed and 3 tablespoons Parmesan cheese in large bowl; mix well. Spoon over roll dough; sprinkle with remaining 2 tablespoons Parmesan cheese. Bake for 30 to 40 minutes or until top is golden and knife inserted in center comes out clean. Cool on wire rack for 15 minutes. Cut into 1-inch squares. Serve on electric hot tray set at Medium-Low. Yield: 30 servings.

 Hope Rose Poveromo, Xi Zeta Eta Bethlehem, Pennsylvania

RIBBON SANDWICHES

2 loaves unsliced white bread	2 pounds chicken salad
2 loaves unsliced whole wheat bread	32 ounces cream cheese, softened
2 pounds pimento cheese spread	Garlic salt and onion salt to taste
2 pounds ham salad	Milk

Trim crusts from bread and cut each loaf into 4 horizontal slices. Spread pimento cheese on bottom slice of each loaf. Top with slice of alternating color of bread. Spread with ham salad; top with slice of alternating color of bread. Spread with chicken salad. Top with remaining bread slices. Combine cream cheese with garlic salt, onion salt and enough milk to make of spreading consistency in bowl; mix until smooth. Spread over loaves. Chill, wrapped, overnight. Cut into vertical slices. Yield: 50 servings.

Donna Tappe, Preceptor Gamma Sigma Quincy, Illinois

PARTY SANDWICHES

People always want to know what kind of meat is in these sandwiches when I serve them to a new group.

8 ounces cream cheese, softened	3 tablespoons chili sauce
3 tablespoons finely chopped onion	3 hard-cooked eggs, finely chopped
3 tablespoons finely chopped green bell pepper	1 large loaf sandwich bread, crusts trimmed
2/3 cup finely chopped pecans	Butter or margarine, softened

Combine cream cheese, onion, green pepper, pecans, chili sauce and eggs in bowl; mix well. Spread bread lightly with butter, covering surface completely. Spread with cream cheese mixture. Cut each slice into triangles or 3 finger sandwiches. Store in refrigerator. Yield: 48 servings.

Dorothy Hambright, Preceptor Epsilon Nu San Angelo, Texas

SAUSAGE BALLS

1 pound Cheddar cheese	3 cups baking mix
1 pound hot sausage	

Preheat oven to 350 degrees. Melt cheese in double boiler. Combine with sausage in bowl; mix well. Add baking mix; mix well. Shape into balls; place on baking sheet. Bake for 20 to 25 minutes or until brown. Yield: 36 servings.

Elaine Cumpton, Preceptor Omega Monroe, Louisiana

TEXAS ARMADILLO EGGS

2 cups shredded Monterey Jack cheese	Cheese
8 ounces hot sausage	1 package Shake 'N Bake for pork
1 1/2 cups baking mix	Eggs, beaten
15 jalapeño peppers, seeded	

Preheat oven to 325 degrees. Combine 2 cups cheese and sausage in bowl; mix well with fingers. Add baking mix 1/3 at a time, mixing well after each addition; mixture will be stiff. Stuff peppers with cheese. Pat sausage mixture into circles 2 inches in diameter and 1/4 inch thick. Place 1 pepper on each circle. Wrap to enclose pepper completely, pressing edges to seal and shaping to resemble egg. Roll in Shake 'N Bake. Dip in beaten eggs, then roll in Shake 'N Bake again. Place on baking sheet. Bake for 20 to 25 minutes or until brown. Yield: 15 servings.

Marie Tennison, Laureate Delta Alpha Silsbee, Texas

ZUCCHINI APPETIZER

3 cups grated zucchini
1 cup baking mix
1/2 cup grated Parmesan
  cheese
2 tablespoons chopped
  parsley
Dash of red pepper

1/2 teaspoon oregano or
  marjoram
1 clove of garlic,
  chopped
1/2 cup olive oil
4 eggs, beaten

Preheat oven to 350 degrees. Combine zucchini, baking mix, cheese, parsley, red pepper, oregano, garlic, olive oil and eggs in bowl; mix well. Pour into greased 9-by-13-inch baking dish. Bake for 25 minutes. Cut into squares. Yield: 20 servings.

Carole Pipetti, Xi Xi
Altoona, Pennsylvania

NEW ENGLAND CLAM CHOWDER QUICHE

I serve this at the staff member luncheon at the end of the year.

8 ounces bacon,
  crisp-fried, crumbled
1 15-ounce can Snow's
  New England clam
  chowder
4 eggs, slightly beaten
1/2 cup chopped onion

1/2 cup sour cream
2 teaspoons parsley
  flakes
1/4 teaspoon pepper
1 unbaked 9- or 10-inch
  pastry shell
4 slices Velveeta cheese

Preheat oven to 400 degrees. Combine bacon, chowder, eggs, onion, sour cream, parsley flakes and pepper in bowl; mix well. Pour 2/3 of the mixture into pie shell. Arrange cheese slices on top. Top with remaining egg mixture. Reduce oven temperature to 325 degrees. Bake quiche for 50 to 55 minutes or until set. Let stand for 20 minutes. Yield: 6 servings.

Norma Thompson
Vero Beach, Florida

CRAB MEAT BITES

1/2 cup margarine
6 to 7 ounces Cheez
  Whiz
1 1/2 teaspoons
  mayonnaise

1 7-ounce can crab
  meat
1/2 teaspoon salt
1/2 teaspoon garlic salt
6 English muffins, split

Preheat broiler. Melt margarine and Cheez Whiz in saucepan, stirring to mix well. Add mayonnaise, crab meat, salt and garlic salt; mix well. Cool to room temperature. Spread on English muffins. Cut into quarters; place on baking sheet. Broil until bubbly. May freeze until needed and broil at serving time. Yield: 48 servings.

Kelly Dennis, Xi Alpha Omicron
Lewiston, Maine

HOT CRAB MEAT CANAPÉS

1 7-ounce can crab
  meat
1/2 cup mayonnaise
1/2 teaspoon prepared
  mustard
1/2 teaspoon
  Worcestershire sauce

1/2 teaspoon prepared
  horseradish
24 crackers or 6 slices
  bread
1/2 cup grated Parmesan
  cheese

Preheat broiler. Combine crab meat, mayonnaise, mustard, Worcestershire sauce and horseradish in bowl; mix well. Spread on crackers; sprinkle with cheese. Place on baking sheet. Broil for 1 to 1 1/2 minutes or until bubbly. Yield: 24 servings.

Amy Autewrieth, Xi Alpha Tau
St. Petersburg, Florida

CRAB DABS

12 ounces crab meat or
  lobster
1/3 cup fine soft bread
  crumbs
2 tablespoons dry sherry
1 teaspoon chopped
  chives

1 teaspoon lemon juice
1 teaspoon dry mustard
Dillweed to taste
1/4 teaspoon salt
10 slices bacon, cut into
  thirds

Preheat broiler. Chop crab meat. Combine with bread crumbs, wine, chives, lemon juice, dry mustard, dillweed and salt in bowl; mix well. Chill for 30 minutes. Shape by tablespoonfuls into 30 rolls. Wrap with bacon; secure with toothpicks. Place in broiler pan. Broil for 12 minutes or until bacon is crisp. Yield: 30 servings.

Debra Curti, Xi Kappa Phi
West Palm Beach, Florida

CRAB NACHOS DELITE

1 10-ounce package
  tortilla chips
8 ounces imitation crab
  meat
1 4-ounce can sliced
  mushrooms
8 ounces Monterey Jack
  cheese, shredded

8 ounces Velveeta
  Mexican cheese,
  shredded
1 4-ounce can chopped
  green chilies
4 ounces real bacon bits

Preheat oven to 400 degrees. Place tortilla chips on baking sheet lined with foil. Layer crab meat, mushrooms, cheeses and green chilies over chips. Top with bacon bits. Bake for 12 to 15 minutes or until heated through. Yield: 12 servings.

Lisa Beck
Pratt, Kansas

SEAFOOD PARTY CRISPS

1 cup mayonnaise	1/2 cup chopped green
3 cups shredded	onions
Monterey Jack cheese	2 tablespoons lemon
1 5-ounce can crab	juice
meat, drained	1/2 teaspoon Tabasco
1 5-ounce can small	sauce
shrimp, drained	18 slices white bread

Preheat oven to 350 degrees. Brush miniature tart cups lightly with 1 to 2 tablespoons mayonnaise. Combine remaining mayonnaise with next 6 ingredients in bowl; mix well. Trim crusts from bread; cut each slice into 4 squares. Press bread squares into prepared tart pans. Spoon seafood mixture into bread shells. Bake for 15 to 20 minutes or until light brown. Yield: 72 servings.

Bev Sammut, Eta Upsilon
Bolton, Ontario, Canada

COQUILLES ST. JACQUES

3 cups water	1/2 cup dry white wine
1 bay leaf	2 tablespoons
1/4 teaspoon thyme	all-purpose flour
Salt and pepper to taste	2 tablespoons melted
2 cups fresh scallops	butter or margarine
8 ounces mushrooms,	1 egg yolk
sliced	2 tablespoons whipping
1 small onion, chopped	cream
1 tablespoon chopped	Buttered bread crumbs
parsley or chives	
2 tablespoons butter or	
margarine	

Preheat oven to 350 degrees. Bring water and seasonings to a boil in saucepan. Add scallops; reduce heat. Simmer for 10 minutes or until tender. Drain, reserving 1 cup cooking liquid. Sauté mushrooms, onion and parsley in 2 tablespoons butter in saucepan. Add wine. Simmer for 10 minutes. Blend flour with melted butter in saucepan. Add reserved cooking liquid gradually. Cook until thickened, stirring constantly. Stir a small amount of hot sauce into mixture of egg yolk and cream; stir egg yolk into hot sauce. Add scallops and mushroom mixture. Spoon into baking shells; sprinkle with buttered crumbs. Bake until crumbs are brown. Yield: 6 servings.

Judy McFadden, Preceptor Zeta
Minnedosa, Manitoba, Canada

Esther Stipp, Xi Gamma Chi, Claremore, Oklahoma, fills chicken breast filets with mixture of 1 1/2 cups chopped cooked shrimp, 3/4 cup softened butter or margarine, 1/4 cup chopped green onions and rolls up. After chilling for several hours, coat with mixture of 1 cup all-purpose flour, 1 1/4 teaspoons baking powder, 1 teaspoon salt and 3/4 cup water. Deep-fry in 370-degree vegetable oil for 10 to 15 minutes.

CHEESE-STUFFED SHRIMP

2 pounds large fresh	4 1/2 ounces cream
shrimp	cheese, softened
Leaves of 1 bunch celery	1 teaspoon finely
2 large sprigs of parsley	chopped onion
1 small onion, sliced	1 teaspoon prepared
4 ounces bleu cheese	mustard
2 12-ounce bottles of	1 teaspoon prepared
beer	horseradish
1/2 teaspoon thyme	1/4 teaspoon savory
Pinch of tarragon	1 cup finely chopped
6 peppercorns	parsley

Bring shrimp and next 8 ingredients to a boil in large saucepan; reduce heat. Simmer for 5 minutes or until shrimp are pink. Drain and cool shrimp. Peel and devein shrimp. Slit backs of shrimp for stuffing. Chill in refrigerator. Combine cream cheese, onion, mustard, horseradish and savory in bowl; mix well. Stuff into shrimp. Dip backs of shrimp into 1 cup parsley. Arrange on serving plate. Yield: 48 to 60 servings.

Beth Sarazin, Preceptor Beta Psi
London, Ontario, Canada

UNSTUFFED SHRIMP

1 pound peeled shrimp	2 tablespoons grated
2 tablespoons lemon	Parmesan cheese
juice	Cayenne pepper to taste
1/2 cup dry bread crumbs	1 large clove of garlic,
1 tablespoon chopped	minced
parsley	3 tablespoons butter or
1 teaspoon oregano	margarine

Preheat oven to 350 degrees. Arrange shrimp in individual baking dishes; sprinkle with lemon juice. Combine bread crumbs, parsley, oregano, cheese and cayenne pepper in bowl; mix well. Brown garlic lightly in butter in skillet. Add bread crumb mixture; mix well. Sprinkle over shrimp. Bake for 15 minutes. Yield: 2 to 3 servings.

Ann Rascoe, Xi Delta Lambda
Niskayuna, New York

MEXICAN SHRIMP COCKTAIL

3 large tomatoes, chopped	1 long green chili pepper,
2 avocados, chopped	seeded, chopped
1 bunch green onions,	1 1/2 tablespoons
chopped	chopped garlic
1 1/2 cups chopped celery	Salt to taste
1 46-ounce can tomato	2 pounds cooked
juice	medium shrimp
3/4 cup chopped cilantro	Celery leaves

Combine first 9 ingredients in bowl; mix well. Add shrimp. Marinate in refrigerator for 2 to 8 hours. Garnish with celery leaves. Yield: 12 servings.

Pat Salgado, Tau Eta
Hemet, California

SHRIMP TARTS

Melted butter or
  margarine
1 loaf white or brown
  bread
3 tablespoons melted
  butter or margarine
3 tablespoons
  all-purpose flour
2 cups milk
1 teaspoon lemon juice
1 tablespoon chopped
  onion
2 cups cooked shrimp
Salt and pepper to taste

Preheat oven to 450 degrees. Brush butter on both
sides of bread. Cut circle from each bread slice. Press
into muffin cups. Bake for 12 to 15 minutes or until
brown. Blend 3 tablespoons butter and flour in
saucepan. Add milk. Cook until thickened, stirring
constantly. Add lemon juice, onion, shrimp, salt and
pepper; mix well. Spoon into prepared bread shells.
Yield: 24 servings.

Kathy Hanbury, Beta Mu
Abbotsford, British Columbia, Canada

VEGETABLE TORTE

14 ounces cheese
  crackers, crushed
10 tablespoons melted
  butter or margarine
4 cups sour cream or
  yogurt
2 tablespoons lemon
  juice
Tabasco sauce to taste
1 teaspoon
  Worcestershire sauce
1/2 teaspoon paprika
1 cup chopped celery
1 cup chopped green
  onions
1 cup chopped green bell
  pepper
1 cup sliced black olives

Combine cracker crumbs and butter in bowl; mix well.
Press half the mixture into bottom of springform
pan. Combine next 5 ingredients in bowl; mix well.
Stir in remaining cracker crumb mixture, celery,
green onions, green pepper and olives. Spoon into
prepared pan. Chill overnight. Place on doily-lined
plate; remove side of pan. Yield: 10 to 12 servings.

Carol Sharp, Gamma Iota
Milwaukie, Oregon

TEXAS TORTE

2 eggs
2 tablespoons
  all-purpose flour
1/3 cup milk
1/2 teaspoon salt
1 4-ounce can chopped
  green chilies
2 cups shredded sharp
  Cheddar cheese
2 cups shredded
  Monterey Jack cheese

Preheat oven to 350 degrees. Beat eggs in bowl. Add
flour, milk and salt; beat until smooth. Add green
chilies and cheeses; mix well. Spoon into greased
8-by-12-inch baking dish. Bake for 35 minutes or
until set. Cut into small squares. Yield: 96 servings.

Beth Sullivan, Epsilon Nu
Birmingham, Alabama

BACON-WATER CHESTNUT APPETIZER

1 pound bacon
1 7-ounce can whole
  water chestnuts,
  drained
1/4 cup soy sauce
3 tablespoons light
  brown sugar

Cut bacon slices into halves. Wrap water chestnuts
with bacon; secure with toothpicks. Place in baking
dish. Combine soy sauce and brown sugar in bowl;
mix well. Pour over water chestnuts. Marinate overnight. Preheat oven to 400 degrees. Bake for 20
minutes. Serve hot. Yield: 12 servings.

Connie Smith, Preceptor Gamma Gamma
Mechanicsburg, Pennsylvania

WATER CHESTNUTS WRAPPED IN BACON

1 pound bacon
2 7-ounce cans whole
  water chestnuts,
  drained
1 14-ounce bottle of
  catsup
1 teaspoon
  Worcestershire sauce
Soy sauce and hot sauce
  to taste
1/2 to 1 cup sugar

Preheat oven to 350 degrees. Cut bacon slices into
halves. Wrap water chestnuts with bacon; secure
with toothpicks. Place in shallow 9-by-13-inch
baking dish. Bake for 30 minutes; drain. Combine
catsup, Worcestershire sauce, soy sauce, hot sauce
and sugar in bowl; mix well. Pour over water
chestnuts. Bake for 30 minutes longer.
Yield: 20 servings.

Jan Gaston, Zeta Phi
Bryan, Ohio

SCRAMBLE

*My college children and their friends loved cans of this
to nibble on during exams.*

1 16-ounce package
  wheat Chex
1 12-ounce package
  rice Chex
1 10-ounce package
  Cheerios
1 12-ounce package
  thin pretzels
1 pound mixed nuts
1 pound peanuts
2 cups vegetable oil
2 tablespoons
  Worcestershire sauce
1 teaspoon garlic salt
1 teaspoon seasoned salt

Preheat oven to 225 degrees. Mix cereals, pretzels
and nuts in large roasting pan. Combine oil, Worcestershire sauce, garlic salt and seasoned salt in
bowl; mix well. Pour over cereal, mixing gently. Bake
for 2 hours, stirring every 30 minutes. Cool to room
temperature. Store in airtight container or plastic bag
for up to 2 months. Yield: 25 servings.

Donna Conley, Laureate Beta
Westbrook, Maine

RUM POPCORN

9 cups popped popcorn
2 cups mixed nuts
1/2 cup butter or
  margarine
1 cup packed light
  brown sugar
1/2 cup light corn syrup
1 1/2 teaspoons rum
  extract
1 teaspoon soda

Preheat oven to 250 degrees. Combine popped popcorn and nuts in lightly greased shallow roasting pan. Bring butter, brown sugar and corn syrup to a boil in saucepan over medium heat. Cook for 5 minutes; remove from heat. Stir in rum extract and soda. Pour over popcorn and nuts; mix well. Bake for 1 hour, stirring every 15 minutes. Spread on waxed paper, stirring to break apart. Cool to room temperature. Store in airtight container. Yield: 10 servings.

Marilyn R. Buchele, Xi Epsilon Nu
Emporia, Kansas

REFRIED BEAN SOUP

8 slices bacon, chopped
1 1/2 cups finely chopped
  onion
1 1/2 cups finely chopped
  celery
2 green bell peppers,
  finely chopped
2 cloves of garlic,
  minced
2 16-ounce cans refried
  beans
2 tablespoons chili
  powder
1/2 teaspoon pepper
Broth
Crushed tortilla chips
Shredded Monterey Jack
  cheese

Cook bacon in skillet until crisp; drain. Add onion, celery, green peppers and garlic. Cook until tender, stirring frequently. Add beans, chili powder, pepper and enough broth to make of desired consistency; mix well. Bring to a boil; remove from heat. Garnish with crushed tortilla chips and cheese. May substitute mashed leftover pinto beans for refried beans. Yield: 6 servings.

Gayla J. Smith, Preceptor Iota Omicron
San Angelo, Texas

BEEF ORZO SOUP

My sisters look forward to keeping warm with this soup at our chapter garage sales in the spring or fall.

1 1/4 pounds ground beef
1 large onion, finely
  chopped
3 16-ounce cans
  tomatoes, crushed
16 cups beef broth
1 16-ounce package
  orzo
1/2 teaspoon MSG
  (optional)
Salt to taste
1/2 teaspoon pepper

Sauté ground beef with onion in 8-quart saucepan, stirring frequently; drain. Add tomatoes, beef broth and pasta. Cook until pasta is tender. Stir in MSG, salt and pepper. Yield: 20 servings.

Justine Mitala, Laureate Delta Zeta
Easton, Pennsylvania

BROCCOLI CHEESE SOUP

1/2 cup chopped onion
1/4 cup margarine
1/4 cup all-purpose flour
3 cups water
2 10-ounce packages
  frozen chopped
  broccoli, thawed,
  drained
8 ounces fresh
  mushrooms, sliced
4 teaspoons instant
  chicken bouillon
1 teaspoon
  Worcestershire sauce
3 cups shredded
  Cheddar cheese
1 cup whipping cream
1 cup milk

Sauté onion in margarine in large saucepan. Stir in flour. Add water gradually, stirring to mix well. Add broccoli, mushrooms, bouillon and Worcestershire sauce; mix well. Cook over medium heat until broccoli is tender. Stir in cheese, cream and milk. Cook just until cheese melts and soup is heated through; do not boil. Yield: 8 servings.

Marsha McCool, Psi
Jerome, Idaho

CREAM OF BROCCOLI SOUP

2 pounds fresh broccoli
2 13-ounce cans
  chicken broth
1 1/2 cups milk
1 10-ounce can cream
  of mushroom soup
1/4 cup butter or
  margarine
1/4 cup white wine
2 cups shredded Swiss
  cheese
1/2 teaspoon seasoned
  salt
1 teaspoon salt
1/8 teaspoon each
  seasoned pepper and
  black pepper

Steam broccoli in saucepan until tender-crisp. Cool to room temperature; chop coarsely. Combine remaining ingredients in large saucepan. Stir in broccoli. Cook until soup is heated through and cheese melts. Yield: 8 servings.

Kathy McReynolds, Xi Nu
Springfield, Missouri

CURRIED CREAM OF BROCCOLI SOUP

2 10-ounce packages
  frozen chopped broccoli
1 cup finely chopped
  celery
1/2 cup finely chopped
  onion
1 clove of garlic, finely
  chopped
2 cups water
1 10-ounce can cream
  of chicken soup
1 cup half and half
Dash of curry powder
1/2 teaspoon salt
1/4 teaspoon pepper

Combine broccoli, celery, onion and garlic in medium saucepan. Add water. Simmer over medium heat for 10 minutes. Stir in soup, half and half, curry powder, salt and pepper. Simmer for 30 minutes or longer. Yield: 6 servings.

Pauline Determan, Laureate Eta
Columbus, Nebraska

CREAMY CAULIFLOWER SOUP

Flowerets of 1 head cauliflower	2 cups half and half
Salt to taste	1/2 teaspoon Worcestershire sauce
2/3 cup chopped onion	3/4 teaspoon salt
1/4 cup butter or margarine	1 cup shredded Cheddar cheese
2 tablespoons all-purpose flour	Chopped chives or parsley
2 cups chicken broth	

Cook cauliflower in salted water in saucepan until tender. Drain, reserving 1 cup cooking liquid. Sauté onion in butter in saucepan until tender. Stir in flour. Add chicken broth. Bring to a boil, stirring constantly. Stir in reserved cooking liquid, half and half, Worcestershire sauce and 3/4 teaspoon salt. Add cauliflower. Cook until heated through. Stir in cheese and chives or parsley. Yield: 8 servings.

Estelline Mikeworth, Laureate Gamma Upsilon
Bellevue, Texas

BEER CHEESE SOUP

1 cup all-purpose flour	1 tablespoon Worcestershire sauce
1/2 cup melted margarine	
4 cups chicken broth	1 1/2 cups half and half
1 16-ounce jar Cheez Whiz	12 ounces dried beef, chopped
1 bottle of beer	

Blend flour and margarine in saucepan. Cook for several minutes, stirring constantly. Stir in chicken broth, Cheez Whiz, beer, Worcestershire sauce, and half and half. Cook until thickened, stirring constantly. Stir in beef. Yield: 8 servings.

Margaret Slinkard, Xi Beta Theta
Nebraska

CHEESE SOUP

1/2 cup finely chopped carrot	1/4 cup all-purpose flour
	1 cup chicken broth
1/2 cup finely chopped onion	1 10-ounce can cream of celery soup
1/2 cup finely chopped celery	1 cup milk
	1 cup half and half
2 tablespoons butter or margarine	1 pound Velveeta cheese, chopped

Sauté carrot, onion and celery in butter in saucepan over low heat until tender. Stir in flour. Add broth. Cook until thickened, stirring constantly. Stir in soup, milk, and half and half. Add cheese gradually, stirring to mix well. Cook until cheese melts and soup is heated through. Serve with French bread and salad or baked potato. Yield: 4 to 6 servings.

Jill McGuire, Theta Iota
Marietta, Georgia

CLAM CHOWDER

2 6-ounce cans minced clams	3/4 cup all-purpose flour
	1 quart half and half
1 cup minced onion	2 tablespoons red wine vinegar
1 cup minced celery	
2 cups chopped potatoes	1 1/2 teaspoons salt
3/4 cup melted butter	Pepper to taste

Drain clams, reserving liquid. Combine reserved liquid with vegetables in 10-inch skillet. Add enough water to cover vegetables. Simmer until tender-crisp. Blend butter and flour in large saucepan. Whisk in half and half gradually. Cook until thickened, whisking constantly. Add vegetables, clams, vinegar and seasonings. Cook until heated through. Yield: 8 to 12 servings.

Eva Lamp, Xi Alpha Tau
Kemmerer, Wyoming

CANADIAN CORN CHOWDER

1 cup chopped Canadian bacon	2 cups milk
	1 1/2 cups chopped potatoes
2 cups chopped onions	
1/2 cup chopped celery	1/4 teaspoon marjoram
1/2 cup shredded carrot	1 to 2 teaspoons salt
8 teaspoons margarine	1/4 teaspoon pepper
2 tablespoons all-purpose flour	2 cups whole kernel corn

Sauté first 4 ingredients in margarine in 8-quart stockpot until onions are tender. Sprinkle with flour; mix well. Stir in milk gradually. Bring to a boil, stirring constantly; reduce heat. Add potatoes, marjoram, salt and pepper. Simmer, covered, for 15 minutes or until potatoes are tender. Stir in corn. Simmer until heated through. Yield: 6 to 8 servings.

Ruth Hochadel, Laureate Beta Eta
Lakeland, Florida

HARVEST CORN CHOWDER

4 slices bacon, chopped	2 cups chicken stock
2 cups chopped peeled potatoes	2 cups whole kernel corn
	1 14-ounce can cream-style corn
1 cup chopped celery	
1 cup chopped carrot	2 cups milk
1/2 cup chopped red or green bell pepper	1/2 teaspoon basil
	Salt and pepper to taste
1 cup chopped onion	

Cook bacon in skillet until crisp. Drain, reserving 1 tablespoon drippings. Sauté next 5 ingredients in reserved drippings in saucepan for 5 minutes. Stir in chicken stock. Simmer for 10 minutes or until vegetables are tender. Add remaining ingredients. Heat, covered, just until heated through; do not boil. Top servings with bacon. Yield: 6 to 8 servings.

Denise Amy, Preceptor Zeta
Minnedosa, Manitoba, Canada

GARLIC SOUP

1 onion, chopped	6 slices white bread,
12 cloves of garlic,	crusts trimmed
chopped	1/8 teaspoon cayenne
1/4 cup olive oil	pepper
2 14-ounce cans	1/2 teaspoon thyme
chicken broth	1/2 cup whipping cream

Sauté onion and garlic in hot olive oil in large sauce-pan for 3 to 4 minutes. Add chicken broth. Bring to a simmer. Add bread slices 1 at a time, pressing into liquid. Pour into food processor container; process until smooth. Combine with cayenne pepper and thyme in saucepan over low heat. Stir in cream gradually. Simmer until heated through. Serve with salad, breadsticks, wine and lowered lights. Yield: 3 to 4 servings.

Synda Prisbrey, Beta Psi
Fredericktown, Missouri

GAZPACHO

1 large red onion,	1 7-ounce jar stuffed
chopped	green olives, chopped
1 green bell pepper,	1 4-ounce can chopped
chopped	green chilies
2 medium carrots,	6 6-ounce cans tomato
chopped	juice
4 medium stalks celery,	6 6-ounce cans
chopped	vegetable juice cocktail
6 medium tomatoes,	2 tablespoons garlic
chopped	juice or 2 crushed
2 2-ounce cans	cloves of garlic
chopped black olives	Salt and pepper to taste

Combine first 8 ingredients in large bowl. Add equal amounts of tomato juice and vegetable juice cocktail until soup is of desired consistency. Season with garlic juice, salt and pepper. Chill until serving time. May store in refrigerator for several days. Yield: 15 servings.

Tonya Blackburn, Xi Xi Tau
Lubbock, Texas

MAMAW'S GUMBO

My grandmother made this for us with vegetables that my grandfather brought in fresh from the garden.

6 to 10 fresh tomatoes,	1 tablespoon sugar
chopped	1 medium onion,
4 to 8 jalapeño peppers,	chopped
seeded, sliced	1 pound okra, sliced
1/2 cup butter or	Salt and pepper to taste
margarine	

Combine tomatoes, peppers, butter, sugar and onion in 6-quart saucepan. Cook until onion is tender. Add okra. Simmer until okra is tender; do not add water. Season with salt and pepper. Yield: 6 to 8 servings.

Trecie Bergt, Xi Rho Gamma
Vernon, Texas

HEARTY HAMBURGER CHOWDER

1 1/2 pounds ground beef	3 cups water
3/4 cup chopped onion	3 10-ounce cans
1 1/2 cups chopped celery	minestrone
1 clove of garlic, minced	1 tablespoon
1 31-ounce can pork	Worcestershire sauce
and beans	1/2 teaspoon oregano

Brown ground beef with onion, celery and garlic in 3-quart saucepan, stirring frequently; drain. Add remaining ingredients. Simmer, covered, for 15 minutes. Yield: 4 servings.

Rebecca M. Gummerson, Beta Rho
Burley, Idaho

LENTIL SOUP

12 ounces dried lentils	1 teaspoon oregano
3 quarts water	Salt to taste
3 medium carrots,	1/4 teaspoon pepper
chopped	4 ounces bacon
4 stalks celery, chopped	4 medium potatoes,
3 medium onions,	chopped
chopped	8 turkey frankfurters,
2 teaspoons minced	sliced (optional)
parsley	

Bring lentils to a boil in water to cover in saucepan. Drain, discarding water. Add 3 quarts water, carrots, celery, onions and seasonings. Simmer, covered, for 1 hour. Cook bacon partially in skillet; drain. Add bacon, potatoes and frankfurters to soup. Simmer until potatoes are tender. Yield: 4 to 6 servings.

Dorothy L. Robinson, Laureate Beta Upsilon
Jacksonville, Florida

FRENCH ONION SOUP

6 large onions, thinly	2 tablespoons
sliced	margarine, softened
1/4 cup margarine	Mrs. Dash seasoning to
1 tablespoon	taste
all-purpose flour	6 slices mozzarella
7 cups beef broth	cheese
6 slices French bread	

Preheat oven to 400 degrees. Simmer onions, covered, in 1/4 cup margarine in large heavy saucepan for 40 minutes, stirring frequently to deglaze pan. Stir in flour. Cook for 3 minutes, stirring constantly. Stir in beef broth. Bring to a boil; reduce heat. Simmer for 20 minutes longer. Spread French bread slices with softened margarine; sprinkle with Mrs. Dash. Toast for 10 minutes or until brown. Cut into cubes. Sprinkle into oven-proof bowls. Ladle soup into bowls; top with cheese. Broil for 3 minutes or until cheese is bubbly and brown. Serve immediately. Yield: 6 servings.

Rita Beaver, Xi Alpha Sigma
Ashland, Ohio

CREAM OF PEANUT SOUP

1 medium onion, chopped	2 quarts chicken stock or chicken broth
2 stalks celery, chopped	2 cups creamy peanut butter
1/4 cup butter or margarine	1 3/4 cups half and half
3 tablespoons all-purpose flour	Chopped peanuts

Sauté onion and celery in butter in saucepan until tender but not brown. Stir in flour. Add chicken stock. Bring to a boil, stirring constantly. Press through a sieve. Combine with peanut butter and half and half in saucepan, mixing well. Heat to serving temperature; do not boil. Garnish with peanuts. Yield: 10 servings.

Betty Farnsworth, Alpha Zeta
Kane, Pennsylvania

PORTUGUESE SOUP

This is a good soup to cook in the slow cooker and serve to friends during a football game.

5 to 6 carrots, sliced 1/4 inch thick	1 16-ounce can Mexican stewed tomatoes
1 16-ounce can peas	
1 16-ounce can corn	1/4 to 1/2 teaspoon each garlic powder, basil, cumin, sage, chili powder, salt and pepper
1 16-ounce can kidney beans	
1 1/2 pounds kielbasa, sliced 1/2 inch thick	
1 16-ounce can tomato sauce	French bread

Combine carrots, peas, corn, kidney beans, sausage, tomato sauce, tomatoes, garlic powder, basil, cumin, sage, chili powder, salt and pepper in slow cooker. Cook on Low for 2 to 3 hours. Serve with French bread. Yield: 10 to 12 servings.

Becky Mahon, Theta Pi
Thornton, Colorado

CREAM OF POTATO SOUP

I prepare this for the soup luncheon for the staff in the school where I teach; I use potatoes my husband grows.

6 cups chicken broth	1/2 cup margarine
2 cups chopped onions	1/2 cup all-purpose flour
4 cups thinly sliced potatoes	1 teaspoon salt
4 cups thinly sliced carrots	Pepper to taste
	4 cups milk
1/4 cup chopped parsley	2 cups cubed Velveeta cheese
2 teaspoons basil	
2 teaspoons dillweed	2 cups finely chopped ham

Combine chicken broth, onions, potatoes, carrots, parsley, basil and dillweed in large soup pot. Bring to a boil; reduce heat. Simmer for 10 to 12 minutes or until vegetables are tender. Melt margarine in saucepan. Blend in flour, salt and pepper. Add milk all at once. Cook until thickened, stirring constantly. Stir in cheese until melted. Add to vegetables; mix well. Add ham. Cook until heated through. Yield: 12 servings.

Sharon Popp, Xi Theta Zeta
Gilbert, Iowa

HEARTY SLOW-COOKER POTATO SOUP

10 to 12 potatoes, peeled, chopped	1 pound bacon
8 ounces French onion dip	1 medium onion, chopped
1/2 cup margarine	Salt and pepper to taste
2 10-ounce cans cream of chicken soup	Milk
	8 ounces Swiss cheese, shredded
2 cups milk	

Parboil potatoes; drain. Combine onion dip, margarine, soup and 2 cups milk in slow cooker. Set temperature on Low. Fry bacon in skillet; drain, reserving a small amount of drippings. Crumble bacon. Sauté onion in reserved drippings in skillet. Add onion, potatoes, half the bacon, salt and pepper to soup mixture. Add enough milk to nearly fill cooker. Cook on Low for 8 hours. Stir in cheese and remaining bacon. Flavor improves if reheated the second day. Yield: 10 servings.

Patricia Price, Lambda Omega
Mt. Vernon, Missouri

POTATO AND LEEK SOUP

1/2 cup chopped onion	Salt and pepper to taste
2 cups chopped leeks	1 egg yolk, beaten
2 tablespoons butter or margarine	2 cups half and half
	2 tablespoons chopped chives or parsley
2 cups sliced potatoes	
4 cups chicken stock	

Sauté onion and leeks in butter in saucepan for 15 minutes or until tender but not brown. Add potatoes, chicken stock, salt and pepper. Cook until potatoes are tender. Process in blender. Stir a small amount of hot mixture into egg yolk; stir egg yolk into hot mixture in saucepan. Stir in half and half. Heat just to serving temperature; do not boil. Garnish with chives or parsley. Yield: 6 servings.

Kelly Dory, Beta Epsilon
Austin, Nevada

Deborah McLeod, Alpha Theta, St. Albert, Alberta, Canada, makes an easy Tomato-Basil Soup by combining 2 large cans tomato soup, 8 ounces cream cheese, sautéed mixture of 1/4 cup onion and 2 cloves of garlic, 1 teaspoon fresh basil and 2 soup cans milk in saucepan. Heat until cream cheese is melted and season to taste.

PUMPKIN SOUP

½ cup chopped onion	1 cup mashed cooked
½ cup chopped celery	pumpkin
1 tablespoon butter or	⅔ cup half and half or
margarine	milk
3 cups chicken broth	Salt and pepper to taste
1 medium potato,	Minced parsley
peeled, chopped	

Sauté onion and celery in butter in saucepan until tender but not brown. Add chicken broth, potato and pumpkin. Bring to a boil; reduce heat. Simmer, covered, for 20 minutes or until potatoes are tender. Process ½ at a time in blender until smooth. Combine with half and half, salt and pepper in saucepan. Heat just to serving temperature; do not boil. Garnish with parsley. May substitute carrots, zucchini, peas, spinach or tomatoes for pumpkin if preferred. Yield: 4 servings.

Marian Bard, Mu Iota
Rio Vista, California

SPINACH AND CARROT CREAM SOUP

I served this at the soup social supper at my home. The presentation is very colorful and eye-catching.

Spinach Cream Soup	Sour cream
Carrot Cream Soup	Chopped fresh herbs

Ladle Spinach Cream Soup and Carrot Cream Soup at the same time into opposite sides of soup bowls. Top with sour cream and chopped fresh herbs. Yield: 8 servings.

SPINACH CREAM SOUP

2 pounds fresh spinach,	1½ cups chicken stock
trimmed	1 cup whipping cream
1 cup chopped onion	¼ teaspoon mace
2 tablespoons unsalted	Salt and pepper to taste
butter or margarine	

Rinse spinach and place undrained in 6-quart saucepan. Cook over high heat until steaming; reduce heat. Simmer, covered, for 6 minutes; drain. Sauté onion in butter in large saucepan. Combine with spinach in blender container; process until smooth. Combine with chicken stock, cream, mace, salt and pepper in saucepan. Heat to serving temperature, stirring frequently. May use two 10-ounce packages spinach if preferred. Yield: 4 servings.

CARROT CREAM SOUP

3 cups sliced carrots	1 cup whipping cream
¾ cup chopped onion	½ teaspoon curry
2 tablespoons unsalted	powder
butter or margarine	Salt and pepper to taste
½ cup chicken stock	

Cook carrots in water to cover in saucepan for 9 to 11 minutes or until tender; drain, reserving 1 cup cooking liquid. Sauté onion in butter in saucepan over medium heat until tender. Combine with carrots and ½ cup reserved cooking liquid in blender container; process until smooth. Combine with chicken stock, remaining ½ cup reserved cooking liquid, cream, curry powder, salt and pepper in saucepan. Heat to serving temperature over medium heat, stirring frequently. Yield: 4 servings.

Caroline Straeck, Preceptor Beta Alpha
Kenmore, New York

TURKEY AND ZUCCHINI SOUP

1 pound ground turkey	2 28-ounce cans
2 cups chopped celery	sodium-free tomatoes
2 pounds zucchini,	1 teaspoon sugar
sliced ½ inch thick	¼ teaspoon minced
1 cup chopped onion	garlic
2 green bell peppers,	1 teaspoon oregano
chopped	1 teaspoon basil

Brown turkey in skillet sprayed with nonstick cooking spray, stirring until crumbly; drain. Add celery. Cook for 10 minutes, stirring frequently. Combine with zucchini, onion, green peppers, tomatoes, sugar, garlic, oregano and basil in saucepan; mix well. Simmer for 2 hours. Yield: 6 servings.

Anne M. Rishe, Laureate Alpha Epsilon
Bloomsburg, Pennsylvania

TURKEY MEATBALL MINESTRONE

1 pound ground turkey	1 stalk celery, sliced
¼ teaspoon garlic	1 medium onion, sliced
powder	1 tablespoon chopped
½ teaspoon each	parsley
oregano, basil,	1 pound cabbage,
thyme, onion salt	shredded
and salt	1 ounce thin spaghetti,
⅛ teaspoon pepper	broken into 1-inch
1 28-ounce can stewed	pieces
tomatoes	Croutons
3 cups water	Cheese
3 bouillon cubes	

Combine ground turkey, garlic powder, oregano, basil, thyme, onion salt, salt and pepper in bowl; mix well. Shape into small balls. Bring tomatoes, water, bouillon cubes, celery, onion and parsley to a boil in heavy saucepan. Add meatballs. Simmer for 5 minutes or until meatballs are cooked through. Add cabbage and spaghetti. Simmer until cabbage and spaghetti are tender. Garnish with croutons and cheese. Serve with salad and carrot sticks. Yield: 6 servings.

Janice Goetzman, Xi Kappa Mu
Keystone Heights, Florida

Thirst Quenchers

BANANA COW

This is an excellent way to use up ripe bananas when you don't have time to make banana bread.

½ cup pineapple juice	1 teaspoon honey
1 medium banana	¼ cup milk
⅛ teaspoon vanilla extract	1 cup ice

Combine pineapple juice, banana, vanilla, honey, milk and ice in blender container. Process at high speed until smooth. May substitute coconut milk for banana. Yield: 1 large or 2 small servings.

Elizabeth Jordan, Xi Alpha Omega
Hanahan, South Carolina

ALCOHOL-FREE BLOODY MARY MIX

1 gallon tomato juice	1 tablespoon lemon juice
2 teaspoons pepper	6 tablespoons
2 teaspoons salt	Worcestershire sauce
¼ teaspoon Tabasco sauce	1 medium lime
2 teaspoons celery salt	Celery stalk

Combine tomato juice, pepper, salt, Tabasco sauce, celery salt, lemon juice and Worcestershire sauce in a 1-gallon container; mix well. Chill in refrigerator. Serve with a squeeze of lime and a stalk of celery. Yield: 16 servings.

Valerie Johnson, Xi Alpha Nu
Baker, Montana

Carol A. Johannigmeier, Laureate Mu, Ft. Collins, Colorado makes Grape Juice Lemonade by combining the juice of 3 lemons, ⅓ cup sugar, 2 cups grape juice and enough ice water to measure 1 quart.

GOLDEN FRUIT DRINK

6 cups water	3 cups water
5 cups sugar	1 46-ounce can
1 12-ounce can frozen orange juice concentrate, thawed	pineapple juice, chilled
	5 medium ripe bananas
1 12-ounce can frozen lemonade concentrate, thawed	8 cups ginger ale or sugar-free lemon-lime soda, chilled

Heat 6 cups water and sugar in saucepan, stirring until sugar is dissolved. Set aside to cool. Combine orange juice concentrate, lemonade concentrate, 3 cups water and pineapple juice in large bowl. Add sugar-water mixture; mix well. Chill in refrigerator until serving time. Purée bananas in blender container. Add bananas and ginger ale to mixture just before serving. May be frozen into ice rings or partially frozen for slush. Yield: 50 servings.

Marilyn Wood
Sullivan, Illinois

PATTI'S HAWAIIAN LEMONADE

1 6-ounce can frozen lemonade concentrate, thawed	1 12-ounce can apricot nectar
	¾ cup water
1 12-ounce can unsweetened pineapple juice	2 7-ounce bottles of ginger ale
	Ice cubes

Mix lemonade concentrate, pineapple juice, apricot nectar and ¾ cup water in large pitcher. Chill in refrigerator. Add ginger ale and ice cubes just before serving. Yield: 8 servings.

Patricia M. Burns, Xi Epsilon
Ashland, Kentucky

SPARKLING LIMEADE

A real winner on a hot summer's day.

1 large lime
1/2 cup sugar
1 1/3 cups water
2 cups club soda
Pinch of salt

Place lime, sugar and water in blender container. Process at high speed for 30 seconds. Strain liquid into pitcher. Add club soda and salt. Serve immediately. Yield: 3 servings.

Sudha Katti, Laureate Alpha Mu
Erie, Pennsylvania

ORANGE JULIUS

1/2 6-ounce can frozen
orange juice
concentrate, thawed
1/2 cup milk
1/2 teaspoon vanilla
extract
1/2 cup water
1/4 cup sugar or 6
packets artificial
sweetener
5 or 6 ice cubes

Process all ingredients in blender until smooth. Serve immediately. Yield: 3 servings.

Faye Williams, Xi Delta Pi
Kennett, Missouri

APPLE PUNCH

1 46-ounce can
pineapple juice
1 46-ounce can apple
juice
3 2-liter bottles of
ginger ale

Mix juices in large container. Freeze for 2 days. Place in large punch bowl. Add ginger ale just before serving. Yield: 30 servings.

Marynelle Bassford, Laureate Phi
Arlington, Virginia

BUBBLY BANANA PUNCH

Great if you have a "bunch." I've used this recipe for lots of showers. Everyone seems to go "bananas" over it.

6 cups water
4 cups sugar
1 12-ounce can frozen
orange juice
concentrate, thawed
1 46-ounce can
pineapple juice
1 12-ounce can frozen
lemonade concentrate,
thawed
5 medium ripe bananas,
mashed
8 cups ginger ale or
Sprite

Bring water to a boil in large saucepan; stir in sugar. Cool. Add orange juice concentrate, pineapple juice, lemonade concentrate and bananas; mix well. Pour into freezer container. Freeze until slushy. Place in chilled punch bowl. Add ginger ale just before serving. Yield: 40 servings.

Kim Swinford, Beta Omicron
Cambria, Illinois

IMITATION CHAMPAGNE PUNCH

1 2-liter bottle of
sugar-free lemon-lime
soda, chilled
1 12-ounce can frozen
apple juice concentrate
Ice ring
Strawberries or slices of
orange, lemon or lime

Mix soda with thawed apple juice concentrate in large punch bowl. Float ice ring in punch. Garnish with strawberries. Yield: 18 to 20 servings.

Virginia Ann Thomas, Preceptor Gamma Eta
Merritt Island, Florida

CRANBERRY-CHERRY PUNCH

This punch has been served at many sorority socials from baby showers to Christmas parties.

1 3-ounce package
cherry gelatin
4 cups boiling water
1 6-ounce can frozen
lemonade concentrate,
thawed
1 32-ounce bottle of
cranberry juice cocktail
1 6-ounce can frozen
orange-pineapple juice
concentrate, thawed
4 cups ginger ale or
lemon-lime soda

Dissolve gelatin in boiling water in large pitcher. Add next 3 ingredients. Chill in refrigerator. Add ginger ale just before serving. Yield: 25 servings.

Ann E. Perdue, Preceptor Epsilon Omega
Chillicothe, Ohio

DIPLOMAT PUNCH

I created this punch to serve at a gathering to welcome the Ambassador from Uganda.

2 64-ounce cans
unsweetened pineapple
juice
1 64-ounce can
unsweetened
grapefruit juice
1 12-ounce can frozen
orange juice
concentrate,
thawed
1 64-ounce can fruit
punch
1 12-ounce can frozen
apple juice concentrate,
thawed
1 8-ounce can
mandarin oranges
8 cups sparkling soda
2 fruit juice ice rings
Ice cubes
Fresh fruit pieces

Combine pineapple juice, grapefruit juice, orange juice concentrate, fruit punch, apple juice concentrate and undrained oranges in large bowl; mix well. Add soda; stir gently. Pour over frozen fruit juice ring in punch bowl. Add ice cubes. Garnish with fruit pieces. Add remaining ice ring and ice as needed. Yield: 70 servings.

Christine Greenleaf, Xi Alpha Theta
Limestone, Maine

FRUIT PUNCH FOR KIDS

1/2 6-ounce can frozen lemonade concentrate, thawed	2 envelopes cherry-flavored drink mix
1 6-ounce can frozen orange juice concentrate, thawed	2 cups sugar
	2 1/2 quarts water
	1 1/2 quarts ginger ale
	Ice cubes

Combine concentrates, drink mix and sugar in large bowl. Stir in water gradually. Add ginger ale and ice just before serving, stirring gently. Yield: 50 servings.

Linda Neary, Preceptor Delta Kappa
Acton, Ontario, Canada

SUMMER FRUIT PUNCH

7 oranges, peeled and sectioned	1 46-ounce can unsweetened pineapple juice
1 16-ounce can frozen orange juice concentrate, thawed	7 medium bananas, mashed
6 cups unsweetened apple juice	Ginger ale or lemon-lime soda

Process oranges in food processor fitted with slicing blade. Add half the concentrate and juices. Process with plastic mixing blade for 2 to 3 seconds. Pour into large bowl. Add bananas, remaining concentrate and juices; mix well. Freeze in small plastic bowls until slushy. Remove from freezer 30 minutes before serving. Stir gently to evenly distribute fruits; add ginger ale. Yield: 25 to 35 servings.

Mary H. Goldberg, Psi Beta
Plattsburg, Missouri

CLEAR LEMON PUNCH

Given to me by a friend, this punch is enjoyed at wedding and baby showers and at our sorority meetings.

1 cup lemon juice	1 tablespoon vanilla extract
3 cups sugar	Water
1 tablespoon almond extract	

Mix lemon juice and sugar in 1-gallon pitcher until sugar is dissolved. Add flavorings; mix well. Add enough water or ice to fill pitcher. Chill for several hours before serving. Yield: 30 to 40 servings.

Kaylyn Geistweidt, Xi Omicron Beta
Fredericksburg, Texas

Colleen Wood, Laureate Alpha, Missoula, Montana, freezes mixture of 46 ounces each apricot nectar and pineapple-grapefruit juice and 16 ounces orange juice concentrate. Thaw for 1 hour and combine with 1 quart 7-Up and 1 quart pineapple sherbet for Yellow Daffodil Punch.

PARTY PUNCH

2 quarts water	1 46-ounce can pineapple juice
1 1/2 cups sugar	1 6-ounce can frozen lemonade concentrate, thawed
2 envelopes any flavor unsweetened drink mix	4 cups ginger ale
1 6-ounce can frozen orange juice concentrate, thawed	

Mix water, sugar, drink mix, orange juice concentrate, pineapple juice and lemonade concentrate together in punch bowl. Add ginger ale just before serving, stirring gently. Choose varied flavors of drink mix to harmonize with your color scheme. Yield: 40 servings.

Mary Lou Powell, Kappa Rho
Springfield, Illinois

PERKY PUNCH

1 46-ounce can pineapple juice, chilled	1 12-ounce bottle of apricot nectar, chilled
1 6-ounce can frozen lemonade concentrate, thawed	4 12-ounce cans lemon-lime soda, chilled
	Mint leaves

Combine pineapple juice, lemonade concentrate and apricot nectar in large punch bowl; mix well. Add lemon-lime soda just before serving. Garnish with mint leaves. Yield: 22 servings.

Arlean Jensen, Laureate Alpha Pi
Los Altos, California

PINK PUNCH

My mom served this to company at Christmas. I use it for Beta gatherings—something special for friends.

2 46-ounce cans unsweetened pineapple juice	2 16-ounce bottles of cranberry juice cocktail
2 cups lemon juice	2 cups sugar
	7 1/2 cups ginger ale

Combine pineapple juice, lemon juice, cranberry juice and sugar in large bowl; stir until sugar is dissolved. Pour into punch bowl. Add ginger ale and ice just before serving. Yield: 24 servings.

Sandra Hague, Lambda
Saskatchewan, Canada

PINEAPPLE-CITRUS PUNCH

1 16-ounce can pineapple juice	Ice cubes
1 16-ounce can orange-grapefruit juice	1 1-liter bottle of lemon-lime soda
	1 cup lime sherbet

Mix juices in punch bowl. Add ice. Add lemon-lime soda and scoops of sherbet just before serving. Yield: 16 to 19 servings.

Gail Ward, Xi Theta
Truro, Nova Scotia, Canada

PINEAPPLE SLUSH PUNCH

2 46-ounce cans unsweetened pineapple juice	1½ tablespoons vanilla extract
1 cup lemon juice	1 tablespoon almond extract
4 cups sugar	Water

Combine pineapple juice, lemon juice, sugar and flavorings in large container; mix well. Add enough water to make 2 gallons of punch; stir. Freeze overnight. Thaw for 3 hours before serving. Yield: 35 servings.

Sandra Nolte, Preceptor Lambda
Houston, Texas

RACY RED PUNCH

1 46-ounce can pineapple-grapefruit juice	¼ cup cinnamon candies
⅓ cup sugar	4 cups ginger ale

Combine juice, sugar and cinnamon candies in large container; mix well. Chill in refrigerator for 30 minutes, stirring occasionally to dissolve candies. Add ginger ale just before serving. Yield: 20 servings.

Becky Strong, Alpha Eta
Green River, Wyoming

SLUSH PUNCH

2 cups boiling water	6 cups cold water
2 3-ounce packages any flavor sugar-free gelatin	Artificial sweetener to equal 2 cups sugar
2 46-ounce cans unsweetened pineapple juice	2 2-liter bottles of sugar-free ginger ale

Pour boiling water over gelatin in large freezer container. Stir in pineapple juice, cold water and artificial sweetener. Freeze for several hours. Thaw for 2 hours before serving; place in punch bowl. Add ginger ale just before serving. Yield: 50 servings.

Bobbie Austin, Preceptor Iota Omicron
San Angelo, Texas

CRANBERRY SPARKLE PUNCH

1 6-ounce can frozen grape juice concentrate, thawed	1 32-ounce bottle of cranberry juice cocktail
1 6-ounce can frozen lemonade concentrate, thawed	1 6-ounce can frozen orange juice concentrate, thawed
1 6-ounce can frozen pink lemonade concentrate, thawed	1 3-liter bottle of lemon-lime soda

Combine grape juice concentrate, lemonade concentrate, pink lemonade concentrate, cranberry juice cocktail and orange juice concentrate in large freezer container; mix well. Freeze until slushy. Spoon into punch bowl. Add lemon-lime soda just before serving; mix well. Yield: 40 servings.

 Renee Fife, Alpha Iota Theta
Georgetown, Texas

SPARKLING LIME PUNCH

1 envelope lime-flavored drink mix	4 to 8 cups lemon-lime soda
1 cup sugar	1 quart vanilla ice cream
2 quarts milk	

Combine drink mix, sugar, milk and soda in large punch bowl; mix well. Add scoops of ice cream just before serving. May also add brandy. Yield: 34 to 42 servings.

Michelle Fox, Zeta Kappa
Harrow, Ontario, Canada

STRAWBERRY PUNCH

Serve at showers, wedding receptions or Christmas open-house parties.

1 46-ounce can pineapple juice	2 16-ounce packages frozen strawberries, thawed
2 envelopes strawberry-flavored drink mix	2 1-liter bottles of ginger ale
1 envelope lemonade-flavored drink mix	Crushed ice

Combine pineapple juice, drink mixes and strawberries in blender container. Process until smooth. Add ginger ale just before serving. Serve over crushed ice. Yield: 25 servings.

Anne Hall, Preceptor Laureate Gamma Alpha
Dallas, Texas

VALENTINE PUNCH

Served at the Xi Beta Zeta Valentine lunch in 1991.

1 32-ounce can cran-apple juice	½ cup lemon juice
1 46-ounce can pineapple juice	½ cup sugar
1 envelope strawberry-flavored drink mix	1 1-liter bottle of ginger ale
1 envelope orange-flavored drink mix	½ gallon orange or strawberry sherbet
	1 quart fresh strawberries, trimmed, frozen

Combine first 6 ingredients in 1-gallon container; mix well. Chill in refrigerator. Pour into punch bowl. Add ginger ale and sherbet just before serving. Place frozen strawberries in punch bowl or use as decoration in each glass. Yield: 30 servings.

Brenda Coartney, Xi Beta Zeta
Milwaukee, Wisconsin

SMOOTHIE

1/2 cup vanilla yogurt	1/2 slice fresh pineapple
1/2 cup ice	1/2 banana
1/2 cup unsweetened pineapple juice	2 large strawberries or 1 large kiwifruit

Combine all ingredients in blender container. Process at high speed for 2 minutes. Yield: 4 to 6 servings.

Cindy H. Salley, Upsilon
Winston-Salem, North Carolina

STRAWBERRY DELIGHT

1 cup strawberries	1 teaspoon instant
2 cups strawberry- flavored drink mix	powdered milk
1 cup ice	1 teaspoon vanilla extract

Combine all ingredients in blender container. Process until smooth. Yield: 4 servings.

Joya Hill, Xi Nu
Weiser, Idaho

STRAWBERRY-CITRUS SLUSH

1 16-ounce package frozen strawberries	3 cups water
1 12-ounce can frozen lemonade concentrate	2 cups pineapple juice Lemon-lime soda or ginger ale
1 6-ounce can frozen limeade concentrate	

Let strawberries and concentrates stand until partially thawed. Spoon into blender container. Process until smooth. Combine with water and pineapple juice in freezer container; mix well. Freeze until slushy, stirring occasionally. Serve with lemon-lime soda. Yield: 20 to 25 servings.

Elaine Warwick, Alpha Theta
St. Albert, Alberta, Canada

RHUBARB DRINK

1 12-ounce can frozen pink lemonade concentrate, thawed	Water 1 1/2 cups sugar 1 cup water
3 pounds red rhubarb, cooked	2 cups ginger ale

Prepare pink lemonade using package directions. Purée rhubarb in food processor. Combine with enough water in 3-quart measure to measure 3 quarts. Heat sugar with 1 cup water in large saucepan for 10 to 15 minutes. Add rhubarb mixture. Cook for 5 minutes. Remove from heat. Add pink lemonade. Pour into large container. Chill in refrigerator. Add ginger ale just before serving. Yield: 24 servings.

Connie Anderson, Xi Alpha Rho
Grand Island, Nebraska

TOMATO JUICE JULEPS

Mint leaves	4 lemon wedges
Finely crushed ice	Sprigs of mint
1 46-ounce can tomato juice	

Crush mint leaves in bottom of each glass. Fill glass with finely crushed ice. Pour tomato juice over ice. Serve with lemon wedge and sprig of mint. Yield: 4 servings.

Marie Crosby, Preceptor Chi
Fanwood, New Jersey

COCOA FOR FIFTY

My mother supervised a "soup kitchen" during the depression era. This was one of her favorite recipes.

2 1/2 cups baking cocoa	2 teaspoons salt
2 cups sugar	2 quarts water
1 tablespoon cornstarch	2 gallons milk

Combine cocoa, sugar, cornstarch, salt and water in large saucepan; mix well. Stir in milk. Heat until steaming hot. Yield: 50 servings.

Mary Alice McClure, Laureate Phi
Council Bluffs, Iowa

HOT COCOA MIX

Give Christmas tins of cocoa mix as gifts.

2 cups instant powdered milk	1 cup confectioners' sugar
1/4 cup cocoa	Dash of salt

Combine powdered milk, cocoa, confectioners' sugar and salt in container; mix well. Dissolve 1/4 cup mix in boiling water or milk in cup to serve. Yield: 13 servings.

Linda Wonder, Xi Gamma Pi
Carroll, Iowa

HOT CHERRY-APPLE CIDER PUNCH

3 cups water	1 3-ounce package
4 cups apple cider	cherry gelatin

Bring water to a boil in saucepan. Add apple cider; reduce heat. Simmer, stirring frequently. Remove from heat. Stir in gelatin until dissolved. Serve hot. Yield: 8 to 10 servings.

Dolores Johnson, Laureate Zeta
Duluth, Minnesota

Betty Jo Savoie, Delta Zeta, Troy, Alabama, makes Key Lime Tea by steeping 6 tea bags in 1 quart very hot water, then adding 1 1/2 cups sugar, the juice of 2 limes and 3 quarts purified water.

HOT APRICOT PUNCH

3 cups water	1 cup strong tea
1 cup sugar	1/2 cup lemon juice
2 cinnamon sticks	2 12-ounce cans
6 whole cloves	apricot nectar

Combine water, sugar, cinnamon sticks and cloves in saucepan. Bring to a boil. Stir in tea, lemon juice and apricot nectar. Serve hot. Yield: 30 servings.

Peggy Davis, Laureate Gamma Alpha
Dallas, Texas

HOT CRAN-APPLE PUNCH

1 64-ounce bottle of	1 teaspoon cinnamon
cran-apple juice	1 teaspoon ground
1/4 cup sugar	cloves
1 cup water	1 teaspoon allspice

Combine cran-apple juice, sugar, water, cinnamon, cloves and allspice in saucepan. Bring to a boil. Simmer for 15 minutes. Serve hot in mugs or cups. Yield: 10 to 12 servings.

Jennifer Mason, Xi Lambda Lambda
North Canton, Ohio

CRANBERRY SPICED TEA

This is a favorite Christmas or Valentine's Day drink for my family.

2 cups water	1 32-ounce bottle of
4 cinnamon sticks	cranberry juice cocktail
1/4 teaspoon salt	2 cups orange juice
1 1/2 cups sugar	1/4 cup lemon juice
1 quart water	

Combine 2 cups water, cinnamon sticks, salt and sugar in large saucepan. Bring to a boil. Boil for 5 minutes. Add remaining 1 quart water, cranberry juice cocktail, orange juice and lemon juice; mix well. Serve hot. May store in refrigerator and heat as needed. Yield: 20 to 25 cups.

Kay Cooper, Xi Epsilon Beta
Prairie Village, Kansas

SPICED TEA MIX

1 cup orange breakfast	1/4 cup sugar
drink mix	1 tablespoon ground
1 envelope lemonade	cloves
mix	1 tablespoon cinnamon
1 cup instant tea powder	

Combine orange drink mix, lemonade mix, tea powder, sugar, cloves and cinnamon in airtight container; mix well. Dissolve 1 to 2 tablespoons mix in 1 cup hot water to serve. Yield: 22 servings.

Barbara Platz, Eta Xi
Sterling Heights, Michigan

TEA QUENCHER

2 quarts water	1 tablespoon grated
1/4 cup tea leaves or 5	lemon rind
tea bags	2 teaspoons grated
1 cup sugar	orange rind
1 cup water	1/2 cup orange juice
2 2-inch cinnamon	1/4 cup lemon juice
sticks	1/2 cup pineapple juice

Bring 2 quarts water to a boil in saucepan; pour over tea leaves in bowl. Steep for 3 to 5 minutes; strain into pitcher, discarding leaves. Combine sugar, 1 cup water, cinnamon sticks, lemon rind and orange rind in saucepan. Simmer for 15 minutes, stirring frequently. Add with remaining juices to tea; mix well. Chill in refrigerator. Serve in punch bowl or in tall ice-filled glasses. Yield: 10 servings.

Liz Cyr, Lambda
Kingston, Ontario, Canada

HOLIDAY PUNCH

1 3-ounce package	3 12-ounce cans frozen
raspberry gelatin	lemonade concentrate,
3 cups cranberry juice	thawed
cocktail	2 32-ounce bottles of
3 tablespoons lemon	cranberry juice cocktail
juice	3 1-liter bottles of
1 1-liter bottle of	lemon-lime soda
lemon-lime soda,	1 1-quart bottle of
chilled	whiskey sour mix
4 cups water	

Mix gelatin with 1 cup cranberry juice cocktail, stirring until dissolved. Stir in 2 cups cranberry juice cocktail, lemon juice and 1 bottle of lemon-lime soda. Pour into round mold. Freeze until solid. Combine remaining ingredients in large punch bowl; mix well. Float frozen ice ring in bowl. Yield: 30 servings.

Anne Schroeder, Preceptor Alpha Zeta
Appleton, Wisconsin

WHITE WINE SANGRIA

1/2 pint strawberries	1/2 cup orange juice
1 small lime	1/3 cup sugar
1 small red Delicious	1/4 cup lime juice
apple	1/4 cup brandy
1 small orange	1 7-ounce bottle of
3 1/4 cups dry white	club soda
wine	

Cut strawberries into halves. Cut lime, apple and orange into thin slices. Combine next 5 ingredients in large pitcher, stirring until sugar is dissolved. Stir in fruit. Chill until serving time. Add club soda just before serving. Yield: 9 servings.

Cindy Bower, Lambda Mu
Hughesville, Pennsylvania

FROZEN ALEXANDERS

The husband of one of our members invented this recipe for us. We always ordered them after dinner and now we serve them at our home parties.

6 ounces 80-proof vodka	1/2 gallon ice cream
3 ounce Crème de Cacao	Whipped cream
3 ounces chocolate syrup	(optional)
1 ounce evaporated milk	Nutmeg (optional)

Combine vodka, Crème de Cacao, chocolate syrup and evaporated milk in blender container. Add enough ice cream to fill blender container. Process at high speed until smooth. Freeze until thickened. Spoon into cocktail glass. Top with whipped cream; sprinkle with nutmeg. May be frozen until firm to serve as dessert. Yield: 10 servings.

Elizabeth Burke, Preceptor Alpha Epsilon
Indianapolis, Indiana

CLAM BLOODY MARYS

1 6-ounce can minced clams	2 tablespoons lemon juice
4 large green onions, minced	1 1/2 teaspoons Worcestershire sauce
1 16-ounce can tomatoes, seeded	6 drops of hot pepper sauce
1 46-ounce can tomato juice	Salt and pepper to taste
2 8-ounce bottles of clam juice	1 1/2 cups vodka
	Additional tomato juice, if needed

Purée undrained clams in blender. Pour into 3-quart pitcher; stir in green onions. Purée undrained tomatoes, tomato juice, clam juice, lemon juice, Worcestershire sauce, hot pepper sauce, salt and pepper in blender. Add to pitcher; mix well. Adjust seasonings to taste. Chill for at least 2 hours. Add vodka just before serving. Add additional tomato juice, if needed. Yield: 12 servings.

Marjorie Lapp, Preceptor Beta Alpha
Portland, Oregon

FROZEN DAIQUIRI QUENCHERS

These were a hit at our 1991 St. Patrick's Day party.

1 12-ounce can frozen pineapple juice concentrate	1/4 cup honey
	1 fifth of light rum
	6 cups water
2 12-ounce cans frozen limeade concentrate	2 drops of green food coloring (optional)

Combine pineapple juice concentrate, limeade concentrate, honey, rum and water in blender container. Process until blended. Tint with food coloring. Freeze in airtight container for 6 hours or until slushy. Yield: 24 servings.

Carol Bulis-Stanion, Beta Omega
Stansbury, Utah

SPARKLING BERRY PUNCH

For children's parties omit the alcohol and serve in tall glasses with a scoop of raspberry sherbet.

2 8-ounce cans frozen raspberry concentrate	1/4 cup lemon juice
	1 cup frozen raspberries
1 12-ounce can frozen cranberry juice concentrate	3 cups ginger ale
	3 cups club soda
	2 cups vodka or gin
1 12-ounce can frozen lemonade concentrate	(optional)

Combine raspberry concentrate, cranberry juice concentrate, lemonade concentrate, and lemon juice in large pitcher. Let stand until thawed; mix well. Add frozen raspberries; do not stir. Chill until serving time. Add ginger ale, club soda and vodka; mix well. Serve over ice. Yield: 16 servings.

Siobhan Irwin, Rho
Blackfalds, Alberta, Canada

BAILEYS

Tastes just like Bailey's Irish Cream. It's great!

4 eggs	2 tablespoons sugar
1 cup whiskey	1 14-ounce can sweetened condensed milk
2 tablespoons instant coffee	
2 tablespoons chocolate syrup	1 cup whipping cream
2 tablespoons vanilla extract	

Beat eggs in mixer bowl. Add whiskey, coffee powder, chocolate syrup, vanilla, sugar and condensed milk; mix well. Add whipping cream; mix well. Pour into pitcher. Keep refrigerated. Yield: 8 servings.

Debbie Tremayne, Beta Epsilon
Austin, Nevada

IRISH CREAM LIQUOR

This is Brenda Sparks' recipe that was a great hit at a New Year's party.

1 3/4 cups brandy	2 tablespoons chocolate syrup
1 cup whipping cream	
1 14-ounce can sweetened condensed milk	1 teaspoon vanilla extract
	1/2 teaspoon almond extract
1 teaspoon instant coffee	4 eggs

Combine brandy, whipping cream, condensed milk, coffee powder, chocolate syrup and vanilla in blender container. Process until blended. Pour into pitcher. Chill until serving time. May store in refrigerator for 5 to 6 weeks. Yield: 9 servings.

Heidi Vose, Beta Beta Chi
Cedar Hill, Texas

A BARREL OF FUN

This is a sorority favorite. It doesn't take much!

1 pint light rum	1 pint vodka
1 pint gin	1 16-ounce bottle of
1 pint Triple Sec	cola
1 pint Tequila	1 cup pineapple-orange
2 32-ounce bottles of	juice
sweet and sour mix	Crushed ice

Combine rum, gin, Triple Sec, Tequila, sweet and sour mix, vodka, cola and pineapple-orange juice in large container; mix well. Serve over ice. Yield: 34 servings.

Sue Fulcher, Xi Alpha Mu
Fayetteville, North Carolina

BOONE COUNTY MINT JULEP

We serve this frequently at the Lake-of-the-Ozarks on our dock.

1½ cups (about) sprigs	Crushed ice
of mint	Lemon-lime soda
1 cup bourbon	

Twist sprigs of mint; place in bottom of 1-gallon bucket. Add bourbon; fill with crushed ice. Fill with lemon-lime soda; stir with neck of upside-down soda bottle. Twist bucket back and forth using bail or handle and wrist action until bucket is frosted. Pass bucket around circle of friends, twisting to maintain frostiness after each "take." I use a rusty bucket. Yield: 30 servings.

Evelyn Fenton, Preceptor Pi
Columbia, Missouri

BRANDY SLUSH

2 cups sugar	1 12-ounce can frozen
4 cups boiling water	orange juice
4 family-size tea bags	concentrate
1 12-ounce can frozen	1 pint apricot brandy
lemonade concentrate	1 2-liter bottle of 7-Up

Dissolve sugar in 2 cups boiling water. Steep tea bags in remaining 2 cups boiling water; remove tea bags. Combine sugar water, tea, lemonade concentrate, orange juice concentrate and brandy in large plastic container. Freeze until slushy. Place a scoop of slush in glass; fill with 7-Up. Yield: 20 to 30 servings.

Carol Lintner, Xi Gamma Mu
Carmel, Indiana

HOT BUTTERED RUM

1 1-pound package	1 teaspoon (rounded)
dark brown sugar	cinnamon
1 1-pound package	1 quart vanilla ice
confectioners' sugar	cream, softened
2 cups butter or	Rum
margarine, softened	Boiling water

Cream brown sugar, confectioners' sugar, butter and cinnamon in large mixer bowl until light and fluffy. Add ice cream; mix well. Freeze in covered container. Spoon a generous tablespoonful of mixture into a mug. Add ½ to ¾ jigger of rum; fill with boiling water. Yield: 128 servings.

C. K. Vugteveen, Kappa
Sioux City, Iowa

CHAMPAGNE PUNCH

This punch is always a big hit at our parties.

2 cups ginger ale	1 8-ounce package
2 cups raspberry or	frozen blueberries or
strawberry soda	strawberries
1 gallon strawberry or	1 750-milliliter bottle
raspberry sherbet	of Champagne

Combine ginger ale and raspberry soda in punch bowl. Unmold sherbet into punch bowl. Add frozen blueberries, stirring 2 times. Top with Champagne. May use non-alcoholic Champagne. Yield: 32 servings.

 Donna C. Zieler, Omicron
Middletown, Connecticut

CRANBERRY COOLER

Be careful! This tasty cooler is deceiving. Many people have claimed there couldn't be any wine in something so refreshing. They have been proven wrong once they attempted to walk across the room.

1 750-milliliter bottle	1 cup orange juice
of Lambrusco wine,	1 lime, cut into eighths
chilled	1 orange, sliced
1 32-ounce bottle of	1 12-ounce can 7-Up
cranberry juice cocktail	

Combine wine, cranberry juice cocktail and orange juice in punch bowl; mix well. Squeeze lime sections into mixture; add sections of lime. Float orange slices in punch. Chill until serving time. Add 7-Up just before serving. Yield: 18 servings.

Mary E. Biehl, Xi Alpha
Raytown, Missouri

CRANBERRY CORDIAL

This cordial recipe can also be used to make wine jelly. Pour into wine glasses; seal top with paraffin.

2 12-ounce packages	3 large bottles of dry
cranberries, coarsely	white wine
chopped	3 cups sugar

Combine cranberries, wine and sugar in large bowl; cover. Let stand for 22 days, stirring every 3 days. Strain through cheesecloth 3 times. Pour into decorative bottles. Yield: 18 servings.

Bonnie L. Scrivener, Xi Gamma Xi
Bremerton, Washington

EGGNOG SWIRL

Great on Christmas Eve around the fire.

3 quarts vanilla ice cream	2/3 cup dark rum
1 quart eggnog	1 cup whipping cream, whipped
2 tablespoons instant coffee	Pinch of cinnamon or nutmeg

Soften ice cream in punch bowl. Stir in eggnog, coffee powder and rum. Swirl whipped cream over top; sprinkle with cinnamon. Yield: 20 servings.

Donna Lofstrom, Iota
Nelson, British Columbia, Canada

IRISH COFFEE EGGNOG PUNCH

2 quarts eggnog	1/2 teaspoon cinnamon
1/3 cup packed light brown sugar	1/2 teaspoon nutmeg
3 tablespoons instant coffee	1 cup Irish whiskey
	1 quart coffee ice cream

Combine first 5 ingredients in large mixer bowl. Beat at low speed until smooth. Stir in whiskey. Chill for 2 hours. Pour into puch bowl. Garnish with scoops of ice cream. Yield: 9 servings.

Patricia K. Lahey, Xi Alpha Iota
Rochester, Minnesota

HOMEMADE KAHLUA

This makes great gifts at Christmas time.

1 2-ounce jar Maxwell House instant coffee	1 750-milliliter bottle of 190-proof alcohol
2 cups boiling water	2 tablespoons vanilla extract
6 cups sugar	
5 1/2 cups water	

Dissolve 3/4 jar (1 1/2 ounces) coffee powder in boiling water, reserving remaining coffee powder for another use. Let stand, covered, until cool. Boil sugar and remaining 5 1/2 cups water for 7 minutes. Let stand until cool. Combine coffee, sugar water, alcohol and vanilla in large container. Let stand, covered, for 7 days. Yield: 24 servings.

Patricia Ann Clopton Honc, Alpha Phi Kappa
Palestine, Texas

HOT DAMN COFFEE

1 cup freshly brewed coffee	1/2 ounce Kahlua
1/2 ounce Hot Damn cinnamon schnapps	1 tablespoon whipped cream

Combine coffee, schnapps and Kahlua in large coffee mug. Top with whipped cream. Yield: 1 serving.

Marka A. Coker, Epsilon Epsilon
Brooksville, Florida

MAI TAIS

Use 1-cup measures for groups.

1 jigger dark rum	1/2 jigger lime juice
1 jigger light rum	1/2 jigger grenadine
1 jigger Triple Sec or Curaçao	2 jiggers pineapple juice
	2 jiggers orange juice

Combine dark rum, light rum, Triple Sec, lime juice, grenadine, pineapple juice and orange juice in pitcher; mix well. Pour over crushed ice in a tall glass. Yield: 2 servings.

Betty Cordrey, Xi Epsilon Mu
Sylvania, Ohio

MARGARITAS

1 tray crushed ice	3 jiggers Tequila
1 6-ounce can frozen limeade concentrate	1 drop of green food coloring (optional)
2 jiggers Triple Sec	

Combine ice, limeade concentrate, Triple Sec, Tequila and food coloring in blender container. Process until blended. Yield: 4 to 6 servings.

Betty Spies, Preceptor Alpha Xi
Chickasha, Oklahoma

PITCHER MARGARITAS

2 cups crushed ice	1/4 cup confectioners' sugar
3/4 cup Tequila	
1/3 cup lime juice	1 tablespoon Triple Sec
1 tablespoon egg white	Lime slices

Combine ice, Tequila, lime juice, egg white, confectioners' sugar and Triple Sec in blender container. Process at high speed until very frothy. Pour into pitcher; garnish with lime slices. Serve in salt-lined cocktail glasses. Yield: 6 servings.

Terri Keefe, Mu Epsilon
Jefferson City, Missouri

BOURBON PUNCH

1 6-ounce can frozen lemon juice	2 1/2 cups bourbon
1 6-ounce can frozen orange juice concentrate	2 1-liter bottles of 7-Up
	Orange slices (optional)
2 6-ounce cans frozen lemonade concentrate	Lemon slices (optional)

Combine lemon juice, orange juice concentrate, lemonade concentrate and bourbon in container; mix well. Chill or freeze until serving time. Pour into punch bowl. Add 7-Up; garnish with orange or lemon slices. Yield: 26 servings.

Willie Cook, Laureate Alpha Rho
Augusta, Kansas

GINNIE'S PARTY PUNCH

1 46-ounce can pineapple-orange fruit drink	1 2- or 3-liter bottle of 7-Up
1 46-ounce can red Hawaiian Punch	1 4-ounce jar maraschino cherries
1 fifth of vodka	Lemon slices
	Orange slices

Combine all ingredients in punch bowl; mix well. Add ice; serve in punch cups. Yield: 40 servings.

Ginnie Schry, Xi Omicron
Cumberland, Maryland

PARTY PUNCH

1 cup sugar	1/2 cup lemon juice
4 cups water	3 2-liter bottles of 7-Up
1 46-ounce can grapefruit juice	1 26-ounce bottle of vodka or gin
1 46-ounce can orange juice	Ice cubes

Boil sugar and water in saucepan for 5 minutes. Let stand until cool. Add grapefruit juice, orange juice and lemon juice; mix well. Chill until serving time. Add 7-Up, vodka and ice just before serving. Ladle into punch cups. Yield: 20 servings.

Irma Ford, Preceptor Lambda
Drumheller, Alberta, Canada

ROSÉ PUNCH

1/2 gallon rosé wine, chilled	1 2-liter bottle of ginger ale, chilled
1/2 cup grenadine, chilled	1/2 fifth of vodka, chilled
1/2 cup lemon juice, chilled	

Combine wine, grenadine, lemon juice, ginger ale and vodka in punch bowl; mix well. Serve in punch cups. Yield: 32 servings.

Wendy McDonald, Theta Chi
Kentwood, Michigan

RUM PUNCH

2 46-ounce cans tropical fruit punch	1 6-ounce can frozen orange juice concentrate
1 6-ounce can frozen lemonade concentrate	2 cups light rum

Combine fruit punch, lemonade concentrate, orange juice concentrate and rum in large container; mix well. Chill for 2 hours. Pour over ice in punch bowl. Serve in punch cups. Yield: 30 servings.

Carolyn Ransom, Alpha Alpha
Alliance, Nebraska

STRAWBERRY SLUSH

1 16-ounce package frozen strawberries, thawed	1 12-ounce can frozen pink lemonade concentrate
1 46-ounce can pineapple juice	1 26-ounce bottle of vodka, gin or rum
1 12-ounce can frozen orange juice concentrate	1 2-liter bottle of ginger ale, Sprite or 7-Up

Purée strawberries in blender. Combine with pineapple juice, orange juice concentrate, lemonade concentrate and vodka in covered container. Freeze for 24 hours, stirring 4 times. Fill serving glass with slush to 3/4 full; add ginger ale to fill. Yield: 40 servings.

Laura Williams, Alpha Xi
Spruce Grove, Alberta, Canada

"SLUSH"

Wonderful for summer sorority parties.

1 12-ounce can frozen limeade concentrate	3¾ cups Wink or Squirt
1 12-ounce can frozen lemonade concentrate	1 8-ounce jar maraschino cherries
4 cups ginger ale	1 fifth (or less) gin

Combine all ingredients in metal container; mix well. Freeze until slushy. Yield: 22 servings.

Brenda Smith, Xi Delta
Montgomery, Alabama

TAHITIANS

8 ounces Tequila	8 ounces pineapple juice
3 ounces frozen lime juice concentrate	2 ounces grenadine

Combine all ingredients in blender container. Fill with ice cubes or crushed ice. Blend until slushy. Yield: 6 to 8 servings.

Dottie Friedley, Beta Alpha Tau
Desert Shores, California

VODKA SLUSH

1 16-ounce can coconut cream	2 12-ounce cans frozen lemonade concentrate
2 46-ounce cans pineapple juice	4 cups vodka
	7-Up

Pour coconut cream into blender container. Add pineapple juice to fill. Process until blended. Combine with remaining pineapple juice, lemonade concentrate and vodka in large container. Freeze until slushy, stirring occasionally. Fill cocktail glass with slush to 2/3 to 3/4 full; add 7-Up to fill. Stir to blend. Yield: 30 servings.

Carol Hecox, Xi Gamma Xi
Logansport, Indiana

Salads and Such

APPLE SALAD

1 20-ounce can pineapple chunks	1 cup pecans
3 cups diced red apples	½ teaspoon salt
1 cup colored miniature marshmallows	½ cup sugar
8 ounces Velveeta cheese, cubed	2 tablespoons cornstarch
	1 teaspoon vinegar
	2 eggs, beaten

Drain pineapple, reserving juice. Mix pineapple, apples, marshmallows, cheese and pecans together in bowl. Combine salt, sugar, cornstarch, vinegar, eggs and reserved pineapple juice in saucepan; mix well. Cook until thickened, stirring constantly. Let stand until cool. Pour over fruits, mixing well. Yield: 12 servings.

Jean Baker, Alpha Beta
Bedford, Indiana

APPLE-SNICKER SALAD

6 medium Granny Smith or red Delicious apples, peeled, cubed	Red or green seedless grapes
6 Snickers bars, cubed	3 medium bananas, sliced
12 ounces whipped topping	

Combine apples and Snickers with whipped topping in bowl. Add grapes and bananas; mix well. Yield: 8 servings.

Janice M. Christensen, Iota Phi
West Bend, Iowa

APRICOT SALAD

1 30-ounce can apricots, drained	¾ cup sugar
1 cup apricot juice	8 ounces whipped topping
8 ounces cream cheese, softened	

Purée apricots with 1 cup apricot juice in blender. Add cream cheese and sugar; process until smooth. Fold in whipped topping. Pour into 2-quart bowl. Freeze until firm. Remove from freezer 30 minutes prior to serving. Yield: 12 to 14 servings.

Susie Henderson, Laureate Eta
Salina, Kansas

BANANA SALAD

1 cup packed light brown sugar	2 to 3 tablespoons mayonnaise-type salad dressing
2 eggs, beaten	Lettuce leaves
1 tablespoon all-purpose flour	3 or 4 bananas, sliced
1 tablespoon vinegar	Crushed walnuts
Pinch of salt	

Combine brown sugar, eggs, flour, vinegar and salt in heavy saucepan. Bring to a boil. Simmer until caramelized, stirring constantly. Let stand until cool. Add salad dressing; mix well. Line 8-by-8-inch serving dish with lettuce leaves. Arrange sliced bananas over lettuce. Pour dressing over bananas; garnish with walnuts. Yield: 6 servings.

Phyllis Williams, Preceptor Beta Iota
Marietta, Ohio

BLUE DEVIL SALAD

A favorite at our family gatherings and sorority potlucks.

1 6-ounce package raspberry gelatin	1 8-ounce can crushed pineapple
1 cup boiling water	1 cup sour cream
1 21-ounce can blueberry pie filling	1 cup whipped topping
	1/2 cup sugar
	1/4 cup slivered almonds

Dissolve gelatin in boiling water in 2-quart bowl. Stir in pie filling and undrained pineapple. Pour into 9-by-13-inch dish. Chill until firm. Mix sour cream, whipped topping and sugar together in small bowl. Spread over gelatin mixture. Garnish with slivered almonds. Yield: 12 to 14 servings.

Lisa Seckora, Xi Zeta
The Dalles, Oregon

BUTTERMILK SALAD

1 cup sugar	1 cup pecans
1 cup buttermilk	8 ounces whipped topping
4 medium bananas, mashed	Lettuce leaves
1 15-ounce can crushed pineapple, drained	Whipped cream

Mix sugar and buttermilk together in bowl. Add mashed bananas, pineapple and pecans; mix well. Fold in whipped topping. Freeze, covered, for 6 hours to overnight. Serve on lettuce leaves with whipped cream on top. Yield: 10 to 12 servings.

Mary Frances Gladen, Preceptor Epsilon Upsilon
Sherman, Texas

BUTTER MINT SALAD

2 15-ounce cans crushed pineapple	1 6-ounce package lime gelatin
1 10-ounce package miniature marshmallows	1 7-ounce package butter mints, crushed
	4 cups whipped topping

Combine undrained pineapple, marshmallows and gelatin in bowl; mix well. Chill in refrigerator overnight. Fold in crushed butter mints and whipped topping. Spoon into 9-by-13-inch dish. Freeze until firm. Remove from freezer 20 minutes before serving time. Serve with crackers. Yield: 12 servings.

Doris E. Galbraith, Xi Beta Mu
Crete, Nebraska

Linda Adkins, Epsilon Nu, Bessemer, Alabama, makes Congealed Buttermilk Salad by bringing 6 ounces strawberry gelatin and 15 ounces undrained crushed pineapple to a boil in saucepan. Add 2 cups buttermilk. Chill until thickened. Fold in 8 ounces whipped topping. Chill until set.

CHERRY COLA SALAD

3/4 cup sugar	1 8-ounce can juice-pack crushed pineapple
3/4 cup water	
1 21-ounce can cherry pie filling	8 ounces whipped topping
2 3-ounce packages cherry gelatin	1/2 cup shredded Cheddar cheese
1 cup cola	
1/2 cup chopped pecans	

Add sugar to boiling water in saucepan. Stir in pie filling. Bring to a boil, stirring constantly. Remove from heat. Stir in gelatin until dissolved. Add cola, pecans and undrained pineapple; mix well. Pour into serving dish. Chill until firm. Top with whipped topping and cheese. Yield: 8 servings.

Susan O'Brien
Manhattan, Kansas

JIM'S COOKIE SALAD

1 cup buttermilk	1 11-ounce can mandarin oranges, drained
1 4-ounce package vanilla instant pudding mix	
8 ounces whipped topping	17 shortbread striped cookies, crumbled
1 8-ounce can crushed pineapple	

Mix buttermilk and pudding mix in large bowl until well blended. Fold in whipped topping. Add undrained pineapple and mandarin oranges; stir gently. Add 3/4 of the cookie crumbs; mix well. Pour into serving dish. Top with remaining cookie crumbs. Yield: 10 to 15 servings.

Merla Webster, Beta Tau
Albany, Oregon

MACAROON SALAD

1 cup sugar	1/2 cup margarine, softened
2 tablespoons all-purpose flour	1 teaspoon vanilla extract
1/4 teaspoon baking powder	12 ounces whipped topping
1/4 teaspoon salt	4 bananas, sliced
1/2 cup flaked coconut	1/2 cup chopped pecans
1/2 cup oats	
1 egg, beaten	

Preheat oven to 350 degrees. Mix first 6 ingredients in bowl. Add egg, margarine and vanilla; mix well. Press onto bottom of greased and floured 9-by-13-inch baking pan. Bake for 30 minutes or until light brown. Crumble with fork; cool. Layer whipped topping, bananas, crumb mixture and pecans in glass serving dish. Chill for 4 hours. Yield: 8 to 10 servings.

Pat McAtee, Xi Alpha Pi
Carrollton, Missouri

CRANBERRY GELATIN SALAD

1 3-ounce package
   black raspberry
   gelatin
1 3-ounce package
   wild strawberry
   gelatin
2 cups boiling water

1 16-ounce can whole
   cranberry sauce
1 20-ounce can crushed
   pineapple, drained
1 cup chopped walnuts
Whipped topping

Mix both packages of gelatin with boiling water in bowl until dissolved. Chill until partially set. Stir in cranberry sauce, pineapple and walnuts. Pour into gelatin mold. Chill until firm. Serve with whipped topping. Yield: 8 to 10 servings.

Caroline Akins, Omicron
Nashua, New Hampshire

CRANBERRY SALAD

2 cups fresh cranberries,
   ground
3/4 cup sugar
3 cups miniature
   marshmallows
2 cups cubed apples

1 cup seedless green
   grape halves
1/2 cup chopped walnuts
1/4 teaspoon salt
1 cup whipped topping

Combine ground cranberries, sugar and marshmallows in bowl, stirring gently. Chill in refrigerator overnight. Stir in apples, grapes, walnuts and salt. Fold in whipped topping. Chill until serving time. Yield: 10 to 12 servings.

Cathy Boeckenheuer, Xi Delta Omega
Calmar, Iowa

FROZEN CRANBERRY SALAD

1 cup sugar
8 ounces cream cheese,
   softened
1 10-ounce package
   frozen cranberry-orange
   sauce, thawed

1 20-ounce can crushed
   pineapple, drained
1 tablespoon lemon juice
1/2 cup chopped pecans
12 ounces whipped
   topping

Cream sugar and cream cheese in mixer bowl until light and fluffy. Add cranberry-orange sauce, pineapple, lemon juice and pecans; mix well. Fold in whipped topping gently. Spoon into salad mold. Freeze until firm. Yield: 10 servings.

Margaret Z. Jack, Rho
Alexandria, Indiana

ORANGE SURPRISE

A nice nippy salad to chase the 'blahs' away.

1 6-ounce package
   orange gelatin
1 3/4 cups boiling water
1 14-ounce jar
   cranberry-orange
   relish

1 15-ounce can crushed
   pineapple
1/2 cup chopped walnuts
3/4 cup chopped celery
Mayonnaise-type salad
   dressing

Dissolve gelatin in boiling water in bowl. Add relish; mix well. Stir in undrained pineapple, walnuts and celery. Pour into 6-cup mold. Chill until firm. Unmold onto lettuce-lined serving plate. Top with mayonnaise-type salad dressing. Yield: 8 servings.

Marilyn J. Murphy, Preceptor Upsilon
Sheridan, Wyoming

DELICIOUS SALAD

1 cup whipping cream
1 16-ounce can fruit
   cocktail
1 21-ounce can lemon
   pie filling

1 10-ounce package
   miniature
   marshmallows

Beat whipping cream in large bowl until soft peaks form. Fold in fruit cocktail, pie filling and marshmallows. Chill until firm. Yield: 8 servings.

Vicki Kenison, Alpha Omega
Sioux Falls, South Dakota

FRESH FRUIT SALAD WITH HONEY-LIME DRESSING

1 apple, sliced
1 small pineapple, cubed
1/2 cantaloupe, cubed
1/2 honeydew melon,
   cubed
12 strawberries
3 cups watermelon
   balls or cubes

2 peaches, peeled, sliced
1/2 cup frozen limeade
   concentrate, thawed
2/3 cup honey
2/3 cup vegetable oil
1 teaspoon poppy seed

Combine apple, pineapple, cantaloupe, honeydew, strawberries, watermelon and peaches in large bowl. Chill in refrigerator. Beat limeade concentrate, honey, oil and poppy seed in small bowl. Pour over fruits; toss to coat. Serve immediately. Yield: 8 servings.

Robin Wind, Delta
San Jose, California

FRUIT SALAD

2 11-ounce cans
   mandarin oranges,
   drained
1 21-ounce can cherry
   pie filling
1 2-ounce package
   chopped pecans
1/2 10-ounce package
   miniature
   marshmallows

1 15-ounce can
   pineapple tidbits,
   drained
1 14-ounce can
   sweetened condensed
   milk
8 ounces whipped
   topping

Mix oranges, pie filling, pecans, marshmallows and pineapple in large bowl. Stir in condensed milk. Fold in whipped topping gently. Pour into serving dish. Chill until serving time. Yield: 8 servings.

Shari Sidler, Kappa Delta
Strong City, Kansas

TWENTY-FOUR-HOUR FRUIT SALAD

1 20-ounce can pineapple chunks	1 cup miniature marshmallows
1/2 cup sugar	1 cup orange sections
2 tablespoons lemon juice	1 cup seedless grape halves
1 tablespoon cornstarch	1/2 cup slivered almonds
1 egg yolk, beaten	
8 ounces whipped topping	

Drain pineapple, reserving juice. Mix pineapple juice with sugar, lemon juice, cornstarch and egg yolk in saucepan. Cook over low heat until thickened, stirring constantly. Cool. Fold into whipped topping in large bowl. Add pineapple chunks and remaining ingredients. Chill for 24 hours. Yield: 8 to 10 servings.

Pearl Clarke, Preceptor Beta Lambda
Grand Rapids, Michigan

FROZEN FRUIT CUPS

1 cup sugar	3 bananas, chopped
2 1/2 cups water	1 6-ounce can frozen orange juice concentrate, thawed
1 10-ounce package frozen strawberries, thawed	1 6-ounce can frozen lemonade concentrate, thawed
1 20-ounce can crushed pineapple	1/2 teaspoon strawberry extract
1 4-ounce jar maraschino cherries, drained	

Bring sugar and water to a boil in saucepan. Cook until sugar is dissolved, stirring constantly. Cool. Pour into large bowl. Add strawberries, undrained pineapple, cherries, bananas, orange juice concentrate, lemonade concentrate and strawberry extract; mix well. Spoon into paper cups. Freeze, covered, until firm. Yield: 25 servings.

Lois Kuehl, Xi Zeta Kappa
Rock Rapids, Iowa

GLAZED GRAPES

2 2 1/2-ounce packages slivered almonds	1 cup sour cream
3/4 cup packed light brown sugar	3 cups seedless red grapes
4 ounces whipped topping	3 cups seedless green grapes

Preheat oven to 350 degrees. Arrange almonds on baking sheet. Toast for 10 minutes, turning frequently. Beat brown sugar, whipped topping and sour cream in mixer bowl. Stir in red grapes, green grapes and toasted almonds. Spoon into serving dish. Chill in refrigerator. Yield: 10 servings.

Jenelle Busse, Preceptor Theta
Pierre, South Dakota

GREEN GRAPE SALAD

No one believes that garlic and grapes go together until they taste this salad.

2 cloves of garlic, crushed	4 cups green grape halves
3 ounces cream cheese, softened	Crackers

Rub serving bowl with garlic. Beat cream cheese in mixer bowl until light and fluffy. Stir in grapes. Serve with crackers. Yield: 4 servings.

Mae M. Bruce, Preceptor Kappa Rho
Hilltop Lakes, Texas

GRAPEFRUIT SALAD

2 1/2 cups grapefruit juice	8 ounces cream cheese, softened
1 cup sugar	Milk
2 1/2 envelopes unflavored gelatin	1/2 cup finely chopped pecans
1/2 cup cold water	1 teaspoon garlic salt
4 cups grapefruit sections	

Combine grapefruit juice and sugar in saucepan. Cook until sugar is dissolved, stirring constantly. Soften gelatin in cold water. Stir into grapefruit juice mixture. Add grapefruit sections; mix well. Pour half the mixture into 9-by-13-inch dish. Freeze until firm. Beat cream cheese with enough milk to obtain spreading consistency. Stir in pecans and garlic salt. Spread over frozen mixture. Pour remaining half of grapefruit mixture over cream cheese. Chill until set. Yield: 10 servings.

Sheila Chatlos, Rho Phi
Frostproof, Florida

HORSERADISH SALAD

2 3-ounce packages lemon gelatin	1/2 cup mayonnaise
1 1/2 cups boiling water	1/4 cup horseradish, drained
1/2 cup whipping cream	2 cups boiling water

Dissolve 1 package gelatin in 1 1/2 cups boiling water in bowl. Cool until partially set. Whip cream until stiff peaks form. Fold into gelatin mixture gently. Add mayonnaise and horseradish; mix well. Spoon into mold. Chill until firm. Dissolve remaining package gelatin in 2 cups boiling water in bowl. Chill until partially set. Spoon over congealed layer. Yield: 10 to 12 servings.

Irene Henderson, Laureate Beta Chi
Cambridge, Ontario, Canada

Terri Bergthold, Kappa Gamma, Davenport, Iowa, lightens congealed salads by using sugar-free gelatin, low-fat milk and low-fat cream cheese.

LEMON SALAD

2 3-ounce packages
   lemon gelatin
2 cups boiling water
1 6-ounce can frozen
   lemonade concentrate,
   thawed

8 ounces whipped
   topping
Lettuce leaves
1 lemon, sliced

Dissolve gelatin in boiling water in bowl. Add lemonade concentrate; mix well. Chill until partially set. Add whipped topping; beat well. Spoon into 2-quart mold. Chill until firm. Unmold onto lettuce-lined serving dish. Top with lemon slices. Yield: 8 to 12 servings.

Judi James
Springfield, Illinois

ORANGE DELIGHT SALAD

My great-grandmother was one of the first women to travel the Oregon Trail. This is an adaptation of one of her recipes, served at all our family gatherings.

1 16-ounce package
   butter-flavored crackers
1/4 cup sugar
1/2 cup margarine,
   melted
1 6-ounce can
   unsweetened frozen
   orange juice
   concentrate, thawed

1 14-ounce can
   sweetened condensed
   milk
8 ounces whipped
   topping
2 11-ounce cans
   mandarin oranges,
   drained

Crush crackers. Mix with sugar and melted margarine in bowl. Reserve 1/2 cup crumb mixture. Press remaining crumb mixture in 9-by-13-inch dish. Blend orange juice concentrate and condensed milk in bowl. Fold in whipped topping gently. Reserve several mandarin orange segments. Stir remaining mandarin oranges into orange juice mixture. Spoon over crumb mixture. Top with reserved crumb mixture and mandarin orange segments. Chill or freeze until serving time. Yield: 10 to 12 servings.

Cathy Brandon, Beta Upsilon
Bradenton, Florida

ORANGE GELATIN SALAD

12 ounces whipped
   topping
1 6-ounce package
   orange gelatin

16 ounces cottage cheese
2 11-ounce cans
   mandarin oranges,
   drained

Combine whipped topping, gelatin and cottage cheese in bowl; stir gently to mix. Stir in mandarin oranges. Chill until serving time. Yield: 8 servings.

Shirley Mackert, Preceptor Delta
Milford, Delaware

ORANGE SHERBET SALAD

2 4-ounce packages
   vanilla tapioca
   pudding mix
1 3-ounce package
   orange gelatin
3 cups water
8 ounces whipped
   topping

1 11-ounce can
   mandarin oranges,
   drained
1 8-ounce can
   pineapple chunks,
   drained

Combine pudding mix, gelatin and water in saucepan. Cook over medium heat until thickened, stirring constantly. Cool. Fold in whipped topping, mandarin oranges and pineapple. Pour into serving dish. Chill until set. Yield: 8 to 10 servings.

Alice Cone, Xi Delta Lambda
Cañon City, Colorado

OUT-OF-THIS-WORLD ORANGE CREAM FRUIT SALAD

1 20-ounce can
   pineapple chunks,
   drained
1 16-ounce can sliced
   peaches, drained
1 11-ounce can
   mandarin oranges,
   drained
2 apples, peeled,
   chopped
3 bananas, sliced

1 4-ounce package
   vanilla instant
   pudding mix
1 1/2 cups milk
1/3 cup thawed frozen
   orange juice
   concentrate
3/4 cup sour cream
Lettuce cups
Mandarin oranges

Combine pineapple, peaches, mandarin oranges, apples and bananas in large bowl. Combine pudding mix, milk and orange juice concentrate in mixer bowl. Beat at high speed for 1 to 2 minutes. Add sour cream; beat well. Pour over fruit mixture. Chill, covered, in refrigerator. Serve in lettuce cups. Garnish with additional orange segments. Yield: 10 servings.

 Mrs. Loy Bressler, Preceptor Sigma
Roswell, New Mexico

HEAVENLY DELIGHT

1 22-ounce can pears
1 3-ounce package
   lime gelatin

8 ounces cream cheese,
   softened
1 cup whipping cream

Drain pears, reserving 1 cup juice; chop pears. Mix reserved pear juice and gelatin in saucepan. Heat until gelatin dissolves, stirring frequently. Combine chopped pears and cream cheese in mixer bowl. Beat at medium speed for 1 to 2 minutes. Stir in gelatin mixture. Beat whipping cream in small bowl until soft peaks form. Fold into gelatin-cream cheese mixture. Spoon into glass serving bowl. Chill until serving time. Yield: 15 servings.

Carolyn Riley, Preceptor Alpha Chi
Phoenix, Arizona

SNOWFLAKE SALAD

1   8-ounce can crushed
   pineapple
1   3-ounce package
   lemon gelatin
1 cup boiling water
1 cup cottage cheese
½ cup sugar
¼ cup chopped
   unsalted English
   walnuts
1 cup whipped cream

Drain pineapple, reserving juice. Add enough water to reserved juice to measure 1 cup. Dissolve gelatin in boiling water in bowl. Stir in reserved juice. Chill until syrupy. Beat until fluffy. Add cottage cheese, pineapple, sugar and walnuts; mix well. Fold in whipped cream. Chill overnight. May use green or red gelatin for seasonal salads. Yield: 8 to 10 servings.

Polly McDonald, Xi Zeta
Rock Rapids, Iowa

WATERGATE SALAD

1   3-ounce package
   pistachio instant
   pudding mix
1   8-ounce can crushed
   pineapple
8 ounces whipped
   topping
½ cup chopped pecans
1 cup miniature
   marshmallows

Combine pudding mix and undrained pineapple in large bowl; mix well. Fold in whipped topping. Stir in pecans and marshmallows gently. Chill in refrigerator until serving time. Yield: 6 to 8 servings.

Kathleen Heronema, Xi Tau Nu
Wink, Texas

WHEAT SALAD

1 cup wheat
2 cups boiling water
1   20-ounce can crushed
   pineapple, drained
12 ounces whipped
   topping
1   6-ounce package
   vanilla instant
   pudding mix
Maraschino cherries

Combine wheat with boiling water in thermos. Let stand overnight. Rinse, drain and cool. Combine with pineapple in bowl. Add whipped topping and pudding mix; mix well. Pour into serving dish. Chill in refrigerator. Garnish with cherries. Yield: 8 servings.

Kim Davis, Theta Delta
Burlington, Colorado

ROAST BEEF SALAD IN PITAS

8 ounces cooked roast
   beef, cut into thin strips
8 stalks celery, chopped
6 green onions, chopped
1 teaspoon capers,
   chopped
1 egg, coddled
2 tablespoons red wine
   vinegar
2 tablespoons olive oil
1 tablespoon Dijon
   mustard
Pinch of sugar
Salt and pepper to taste
Mayonnaise
Pita bread
Alfalfa sprouts

Combine roast beef, celery, green onions and capers in salad bowl; toss to mix. Chill, covered, in refrigerator. Combine coddled egg, vinegar, olive oil, mustard, sugar, salt and pepper in blender container. Process until well blended. Add dressing to salad; toss to mix. Spread mayonnaise on pita bread. Spoon in salad; sprinkle with alfalfa sprouts.
Yield: 3 to 4 servings.

Sue Terveer-Mullins, Upsilon Phi
Aurora, Illinois

LAYERED REUBEN SALAD

1 cup sour cream
¼ cup chili sauce
1 tablespoon sugar
½ teaspoon salt
½ teaspoon dillweed
½ teaspoon Beau
   Monde seasoning
6 cups torn lettuce
1   16-ounce can
   sauerkraut, drained
3 ounces cooked corned
   beef, cut into strips
⅓ cup chopped dill
   pickle
¼ cup sliced green
   onions
6 ounces Swiss cheese,
   cut into strips
2 slices buttered toasted
   rye bread, cubed

Combine sour cream, chili sauce, sugar, salt, dillweed and Beau Monde seasoning in bowl; mix well. Chill, covered, for 2 hours. Layer half the lettuce, sauerkraut, corned beef, pickle, green onions, Swiss cheese, bread cubes and remaining lettuce in 3-quart salad bowl. Chill, covered, for 2 hours. Add dressing to salad just before serving. Yield: 6 to 8 servings.

Verdell Monson, Xi Zeta Kappa
Rock Rapids, Iowa

TACO SALAD

1 pound lean ground beef
1 envelope taco
   seasoning mix
2 green onions, chopped
1 medium green bell
   pepper, chopped
2 large tomatoes,
   chopped
1   2-ounce can sliced
   black olives
1   16-ounce can
   Mexican beans in chili
12 ounces Cheddar
   cheese, shredded
1 large head romaine
   lettuce, torn
2   16-ounce packages
   natural corn chips
½   8-ounce jar taco
   sauce
1   8-ounce bottle of
   Catalina salad
   dressing

Spread ground beef in broiler pan. Cook under hot broiler until light brown, stirring frequently; drain. Combine ground beef, taco seasoning mix, green onions, green pepper, tomatoes, olives, Mexican beans and cheese in salad bowl; mix well. Add lettuce, corn chips, taco sauce and salad dressing just before serving. Yield: 15 servings.

Helena Adolph, Beta Omicron
Prince Rupert, British Columbia, Canada

VEGETABLE TACO SALAD

1/2 pound ground beef (optional)	Flowerets of 1/2 head cauliflower (optional)
1 16-ounce can kidney beans, drained	1/2 head red cabbage, chopped
1 large head lettuce, chopped	8 to 10 scallions, chopped
2 large tomatoes, chopped	1 16-ounce package nacho cheese chips
Chopped carrots and celery to taste	1 12-ounce bottle of Catalina salad dressing
1 small green bell pepper, chopped	

Brown ground beef in skillet, stirring until crumbly; drain. Combine ground beef, kidney beans, lettuce, tomatoes, carrots, celery, green pepper, cauliflower, red cabbage and scallions in salad bowl; toss to mix. Chill, covered, for 1 hour. Add chips and dressing just before serving; toss to mix. Yield: 20 servings.

Ruth Anne Holmes, Xi Omega
Albion, Idaho

NOODLE-GARLIC HAM SALAD

2 packages chicken sesame-flavored ramen noodles	2 green onions, sliced
	1 cup chopped ham
4 cups boiling water	1 4-ounce can chopped olives
1 6-ounce jar marinated artichoke hearts	1 tablespoon sesame seed
2 (or more) cloves of garlic, minced	1 tablespoon olive oil
	Salt and pepper to taste
1 8-ounce can sliced water chestnuts	2 tablespoons chopped cilantro (optional)

Cook noodles with flavor packets in boiling water for 2 minutes. Rinse; drain. Drain artichoke hearts, reserving marinade in bowl. Add sesame oil from noodle package and garlic to artichoke marinade; mix well. Add water chestnuts, green onions, ham, olives and noodles; mix well. Sauté sesame seed in olive oil in skillet until golden brown. Add sesame seed, salt, pepper and cilantro to noodle mixture; toss to mix. Yield: 4 to 5 servings.

Sharon Herndon, Preceptor Lambda Iota
San Jose, California

PEPPERONI SALAD

17 ounces vermicelli	2 medium tomatoes, seeded, chopped
4 ounces sliced pepperoni, cut into quarters	1 cup Cheddar cheese cubes
1 2-ounce can sliced olives	1 cup mayonnaise
	1/2 cup Durkee's dressing

Break vermicelli into 4-inch pieces. Cook in salted water using package directions; drain. Combine ver-

micelli, pepperoni, olives, tomatoes and cheese in bowl. Mix mayonnaise and Durkee's dressing in bowl. Add to salad; toss lightly to mix. Chill, covered, until serving time. May add milk to moisten. Yield: 10 to 12 servings.

Jane Bebermeyer, Theta Delta
Reserve, Kansas

SALAD À LA PRINCIPE

4 ounces salami, finely chopped	1 cup celery chunks
1 small red onion, chopped	1 cup cherry tomato halves
1 cup whole black olives	6 ounces provolone cheese, cubed
8 ounces fresh mushrooms, sliced	Freshly shredded Romano cheese to taste
1/2 cup Italian salad dressing	12 slices salami
8 ounces cooked spiral pasta	

Combine chopped salami, onion, olives and mushrooms in bowl. Add salad dressing; toss to mix. Marinate in refrigerator for 3 hours. Combine pasta, celery, tomatoes, provolone cheese and marinated mixture in salad bowl; toss to mix. Chill for 30 minutes. Garnish with Romano cheese and salami slices. Yield: 8 to 10 servings.

Cynthia Albert, Beta Phi
Clatonia, Nebraska

LAYERED CHICKEN SALAD

3 cups chopped cooked chicken	1 small green bell pepper, chopped
2 cups torn lettuce	1 cup mayonnaise
1 cup cooked long grain rice	1/2 cup sour cream
	1/2 cup raisins
1 10-ounce package frozen green peas, thawed	1/2 cup chopped onion
	1/4 cup sweet pickle relish
1/4 cup chopped parsley	2 tablespoons milk
2 large tomatoes, seeded, chopped	1/2 teaspoon celery seed
	1/2 teaspoon dillseed
1 cup thinly sliced cucumber	1/2 teaspoon dry mustard
1 small red bell pepper, chopped	1/2 teaspoon garlic salt
	2 red pepper rings

Layer 1 1/2 cups chicken, lettuce, rice, peas, parsley, tomatoes, cucumber, chopped red pepper, green pepper and remaining 1 1/2 cups chicken in 3-quart salad bowl. Combine mayonnaise, sour cream, raisins, onion, pickle relish, milk, celery seed, dillseed, dry mustard and garlic salt in bowl; mix well. Spoon dressing over top of salad, sealing edge. Garnish with red pepper rings. Chill, covered, for 8 hours to overnight. Yield: 8 servings.

Colette Gibbs, Xi Iota Psi
College Station, Texas

CHICKEN SALAD PIE

3 5-ounce cans chicken
1 13½-ounce can
   crushed pineapple,
   drained
1½ cups shredded mild
   Cheddar cheese
1 cup finely chopped
   celery
1 teaspoon instant
   chicken bouillon
¾ cup sliced almonds
½ teaspoon dried
   minced onion
½ teaspoon pepper
1 baked 9-inch pie
   shell
1 cup sour cream
2 tablespoons
   mayonnaise
Shredded carrots

Combine chicken, pineapple, cheese, celery, instant
bouillon, almonds, onion and pepper in bowl; mix
well. Spoon into pie shell. Mix sour cream and
mayonnaise in bowl. Spread over chicken salad.
Sprinkle carrots over top. Chill until serving time.
May substitute 1½ cups chopped cooked chicken for
canned chicken. Yield: 8 servings.

Judy Behnke, Xi Gamma Alpha
Norfolk, Nebraska

CHICKEN MELON SALAD

3 cups chopped cooked
   chicken
2½ cups seedless grapes
2 cups finely chopped
   celery
1½ cups mayonnaise
6 tablespoons milk
1½ tablespoons chutney
1½ teaspoons curry
   powder
½ teaspoon salt
1 cantaloupe, cut into
   wedges
Lettuce

Combine chicken, grapes and celery in bowl; mix
well. Process mayonnaise, milk, chutney, curry powder and salt in blender until smooth. Add to chicken
salad; toss to mix. Chill, covered, for 2 hours or until
serving time. Arrange cantaloupe on lettuce-lined
plate. Spoon chicken salad over cantaloupe.
Yield: 6 servings.

Janice Cook, Zeta Delta
White Rock, British Columbia, Canada

CHINESE CHICKEN SALAD

½ teaspoon dry
   mustard
2 tablespoons sugar
2 teaspoons soy sauce
1 teaspoon sesame oil
¼ cup vegetable oil
3 tablespoons rice
   vinegar
¼ teaspoon cayenne
   pepper
1 package Maifun rice
   sticks
Vegetable oil
2 tablespoons sesame
   seed
2 green onions, chopped
2 to 3 cups shredded,
   cooked chicken
2 tablespoons chopped
   fresh cilantro
1 11-ounce can
   mandarin oranges,
   drained
2 quarts shredded lettuce
½ cup peanuts or
   cashews

Process first 7 ingredients in blender until smooth.
Prepare Maifun rice sticks in very hot oil using package directions; drain. Sauté sesame seed in skillet

until medium brown. Combine green onions, chicken,
cilantro, oranges, lettuce, sesame seed and Maifun
rice sticks in large bowl; toss to mix. Add dressing
and peanuts; toss until well mixed.
Yield: 2 to 4 servings.

Barbara Haire, Xi Tau Tau
Valencia, California

SESAME CHICKEN SALAD

This recipe was part of a Chinese dinner I gave as a
program for a meeting.

10 cooked chicken
   breast filets
1 head lettuce, chopped
1 bunch green onions,
   chopped
1 cup chopped celery
½ cup unsalted peanuts
2 packages ramen
   noodles
3 tablespoons soy sauce
6 to 8 tablespoons
   peanut oil
Pinch of ginger
Pinch of sugar
Pinch of garlic powder
¼ cup rice vinegar
¼ cup sesame seed,
   toasted
2 tablespoons sesame oil

Chop cooked chicken. Combine chicken, lettuce,
green onions, celery and peanuts in bowl; mix well.
Mash ramen noodles; add to chicken mixture. Do not
use ramen noodle seasoning pack. Combine soy
sauce, peanut oil, ginger, sugar, garlic powder, rice
vinegar, sesame seed and sesame oil in bowl; mix
well. Pour dressing over salad; toss to mix. Chill,
covered, overnight. Yield: 10 servings.

Juanita McGann, Preceptor Alpha Beta
Colorado Springs, Colorado

MARINATED CHINESE CHICKEN SALAD

⅓ cup corn oil
¼ cup light or dark
   corn syrup
¼ cup soy sauce
2 tablespoons cider or
   white vinegar
½ cup thinly sliced
   green onions
¼ teaspoon minced
   gingerroot
1 clove of garlic, minced
2 cups cooked thin
   chicken strips
Boiling water
8 ounces fresh bean
   sprouts
Cold water
5 cups thinly shredded
   lettuce
½ cup thinly sliced
   radishes

Combine first 7 ingredients in bowl; mix well. Add
chicken; toss to coat. Marinate, covered, in refrigerator for 2 hours. Add boiling water to cover to bean
sprouts in bowl. Let stand for several seconds; drain.
Rinse in cold water; drain. Combine shredded lettuce, radishes, bean sprouts and chicken mixture in
salad bowl at serving time; toss to mix. May substitute 12 ounces cooked shrimp or 2 cups cooked
thin pork strips for chicken. Yield: 4 to 6 servings.

Karen L. Sawyer, Xi Lambda Mu
Bartlett, Illinois

GRANDMA'S TURKEY SALAD

2 cups chopped cooked turkey	3/4 cup chopped celery
2 tablespoons sliced black olives	3/4 cup mayonnaise
2 tablespoons sliced green olives	2 hard-cooked eggs, chopped
2 tablespoons pickle relish	1/4 cup toasted slivered almonds
	Crackers or rolls

Combine turkey, black olives, green olives, pickle relish, celery, mayonnaise and eggs in bowl; mix well. Chill for 2 hours. Add almonds just before serving; toss to mix. Serve with crackers or rolls. Yield: 6 to 12 servings.

Barbara Cluck, Zeta Xi
Flagstaff, Arizona

TURKEY SALAD

I use this for our Christmas Open House.

5 pounds roasted turkey, chopped	1/4 cup pickle juice
1 cup finely chopped celery	1 teaspoon white pepper
1 small onion, chopped	1 1/2 teaspoons dry mustard
2 to 2 1/2 cups Spin Blend salad dressing	1 teaspoon horseradish
	1 teaspoon celery seed
	Party rolls

Combine turkey, celery and onion in bowl; mix well. Combine salad dressing, pickle juice, white pepper, dry mustard, horseradish and celery seed in bowl. Add to salad; toss to mix. Chill for 2 hours to overnight. Serve on party rolls. Yield: 50 servings.

Linda Moen Muth, Xi Zeta Chi
Rolfe, Iowa

LAYERED SALAD WITH CRAB MEAT

I prepare this salad for my sorority sisters and for special occasions.

1 head lettuce, shredded	1/2 carrot, sliced
1 cucumber, sliced	2 hard-cooked eggs, cut into wedges
1 small package radishes, sliced	1 medium onion, sliced into rings
2 or 3 medium tomatoes, cut into wedges	2 6-ounce cans crab meat
1 cup cauliflowerets or broccoli flowerets	Thousand Island salad dressing

Layer lettuce, cucumber, radishes, tomatoes, cauliflowerets, carrot, eggs, onion and crab meat in salad bowl. Serve with Thousand Island salad dressing or your favorite dressing. Yield: 12 to 14 servings.

Aleksandra Stolley, Xi Delta Sigma
Corpus Christi, Texas

DEVILED CRAWFISH EGGS

12 hard-cooked eggs	Salt to taste
10 ounces crawfish tails	Pepper to taste
Mayonnaise to taste	Cayenne pepper or Tabasco sauce to taste
2 teaspoons dry mustard	Paprika to taste
1 teaspoon lemon juice	Parsley
Worcestershire sauce to taste	Olive halves

Cut eggs into halves lengthwise; remove yolks. Combine egg yolks and crawfish in food processor container. Add mayonnaise, dry mustard, lemon juice, Worcestershire sauce, salt, pepper and cayenne pepper. Process until well blended. Spoon into egg white halves. Garnish with paprika, parsley and olive halves. Yield: 12 servings.

Tina G. Kaack, Eta Rho
Folsom, Louisiana

SALMON AND RICE SALAD

3 cups cooked rice	1/4 cup chopped fresh parsley
1 15-ounce can salmon, drained	1/2 cup Italian salad dressing
1 10-ounce package frozen green peas, thawed	Green bell pepper rings
2 carrots, finely chopped	1 tomato, cut into quarters
2 green onions, chopped	

Combine rice, salmon, peas, carrots, onions, parsley and salad dressing in bowl; mix well. Chill, covered, overnight. Garnish with green pepper and tomato. Yield: 6 servings.

Dorothy Sirney, Xi Sigma Eta
Temple, Texas

CARIBBEAN SHRIMP AND PAPAYA SALAD

1/4 cup chili sauce	6 to 8 ounces cooked shrimp
2 green onions, sliced	1 large ripe papaya
1/4 teaspoon cinnamon	Lettuce leaves
2 or 3 drops of hot pepper sauce	

Combine chili sauce, green onions, cinnamon and hot pepper sauce in bowl; mix well. Add shrimp; toss to mix. Let stand, covered, for several minutes. Cut papaya lengthwise; scoop out seeds. Place papaya halves on lettuce-lined salad plates. Spoon shrimp mixture onto papaya. Yield: 2 servings.

Jenny Simmons, Zeta Delta
White Rock, British Columbia, Canada

Kathy Soldwedel, Xi Eta Chi, Morton, Illinois combines chilled Rice-A-Roni, 2 cans chicken, 1/2 cup chutney, 2 cups chopped celery and 1/2 cup French salad dressing to make Easy Chicken Salad. Serve in lettuce cups garnished with slivered almonds.

JAMBALAYA SALAD

I have served this at city council salad suppers.

1/4 cup mayonnaise- type salad dressing	1 clove of garlic, minced
1/2 cup sliced celery	2 cups cooked rice
1/2 cup chopped green bell pepper	1/2 cup cubed cooked ham
1/4 cup chopped onion	6 ounces frozen tiny
1 teaspoon thyme	shrimp, thawed
1/4 teaspoon red pepper	1 cup chopped tomato
1/4 teaspoon salt	6 slices crisp-fried bacon, crumbled

Combine salad dressing, celery, green pepper, onion, thyme, red pepper, salt and garlic in bowl; mix well. Add rice, ham, shrimp and tomato; mix well. Chill until serving time. Add bacon; toss to mix. Yield: 6 to 8 servings.

Pauline Dennis, Laureate Pi
Dallas, Texas

EGG AND SHRIMP SALAD

I was served this at my baby shower 2 weeks before my daughter was born.

1 loaf sliced white bread	2 5-ounce cans shrimp,
1 medium onion, finely chopped	drained
7 hard-cooked eggs, chopped	3 cups mayonnaise-type salad dressing
1 cup chopped celery	Lettuce leaves
	Crackers

Remove crust from bread; cut bread into cubes. Combine bread, onion and eggs in bowl; mix well. Chill overnight. Add celery, shrimp and salad dressing; toss to mix. Chill for 6 hours or longer before serving. Serve on lettuce-lined salad plate with crackers. Yield: 6 to 10 servings.

Angela Jeschke, Alpha Gamma Omega
Lowake, Texas

CRUNCHY TUNA SALAD

2 7-ounce cans tuna	1/4 cup Italian salad
1 8-ounce can sliced water chestnuts, drained	dressing
1/4 cup finely chopped celery	1/2 teaspoon salt
2 tablespoons sliced green onions	1 tablespoon lemon juice
1/2 cup sour cream	Dash of pepper
	1/2 cup chopped pecans
	Salad greens

Combine tuna, water chestnuts, celery and green onions in bowl; mix well. Mix sour cream, salad dressing, salt, lemon juice and pepper in bowl. Add to salad; toss to mix. Chill until serving time. Add pecans; mix well. Serve over salad greens. Yield: 6 servings.

Dianna Haley, Alpha Zeta
Nevada, Iowa

ORIENTAL TUNA SALAD

1 6-ounce package frozen Chinese pea pods	Salt and pepper to taste
1 6-ounce can tuna	1/2 cup mayonnaise- type salad dressing
1 cup chopped celery	1/2 teaspoon soy sauce
1/2 8-ounce can sliced water chestnuts	1 tablespoon lemon juice
1 teaspoon dillweed	1 5-ounce can chow mein noodles
Dash of garlic powder	

Cook Chinese pea pods using package directions. Chill in refrigerator overnight. Combine tuna, celery, water chestnuts, dillweed, garlic powder, salt, pepper and pea pods; mix well. Mix salad dressing, soy sauce and lemon juice in bowl. Add to salad; toss to mix. Add chow mein noodles just before serving; toss lightly. Yield: 8 servings.

Grace E. Black, Preceptor Psi
Aurora, Colorado

TUNA AND RICE SALAD WITH AVOCADO DRESSING

2 avocados, mashed	2 7-ounce cans tuna, drained
1 cup mayonnaise	1 8-ounce can green peas, drained
1 cup sour cream	
3 or 4 drops of hot pepper sauce	1/2 cup chopped onion
1/2 teaspoon Worcestershire sauce	1 cup thinly sliced celery
1/2 teaspoon onion juice	1 teaspoon salt
1/4 teaspoon garlic powder	1/2 teaspoon pepper Dash of hot pepper
1/2 teaspoon salt	sauce
2 cups cooked rice	1/2 cup mayonnaise
	8 tomatoes

Process avocados, mayonnaise, sour cream, 3 or 4 drops of hot pepper sauce, Worcestershire sauce, onion juice, garlic powder and 1/2 teaspoon salt in blender until well blended. Chill in refrigerator. Combine rice, tuna, green peas, onion, celery, 1 teaspoon salt, pepper, dash of hot pepper sauce and mayonnaise in bowl; mix well. Cut blossom end from tomatoes. Remove centers carefully, leaving shells. Fill with tuna and rice salad. Top with avocado dressing. May substitute 1 teaspoon grated onion for onion juice. Yield: 8 servings.

Stacey Keeling, Kappa Tau
Edmond, Oklahoma

Paula Watts, Epsilon Nu, Birmingham, Alabama, makes Layered Macaroni Shrimp Salad. Layer 4 cups mixed greens, 7 ounces cooked macaroni, 1 cup shredded Cheddar cheese, 2 chopped tomatoes, two 4-ounce cans shrimp, 1 package frozen peas and 4 cups shredded cabbage in salad bowl. Top with mixture of 1 1/2 cups mayonnaise and 1/2 cup Italian salad dressing. Sprinkle with 1 cup shredded Cheddar cheese. Chill and toss before serving.

PASTA-BEAN SALAD

This recipe is special. It can be made ahead and is delicious. We tripled it for our sorority and they loved it.

1/2 cup vegetable oil	1/4 cup grated Parmesan
3 tablespoons red wine	cheese
vinegar	8 ounces ziti, cooked
3/4 teaspoon Italian	1 jar artichoke hearts,
seasoning	drained, cut into
1/2 teaspoon salt	quarters
1/4 teaspoon pepper	1 10-ounce can
1/4 teaspoon dry	chick-peas, drained
mustard	1 16-ounce can kidney
1 teaspoon sugar	beans, drained
1/8 teaspoon cayenne	3 stalks celery, sliced
pepper	2 medium tomatoes, cut
1 clove of garlic, crushed	into wedges

Combine oil, vinegar, Italian seasoning, salt, pepper, dry mustard, sugar, cayenne pepper, garlic and Parmesan cheese in small bowl; mix well. Combine pasta, artichoke hearts, chick-peas, kidney beans, celery and tomatoes in large bowl. Pour salad dressing over pasta mixture. Toss lightly. Chill for 2 hours to overnight. Yield: 8 servings.

Alice M. Krol, Laureate Alpha Theta
Washington, Pennsylvania

BROCCOLI TORTELINI

1 7-ounce package	2 1/2 teaspoons fresh
tortelini	basil
1 cup broccoli flowerets	1/2 teaspoon garlic
1/2 cup finely chopped	powder
fresh parsley	1/2 cup Italian salad
1 tablespoon chopped	dressing
pimento	Sliced black olives
1 6-ounce jar artichoke	5 or 6 cherry tomatoes,
hearts	cut into halves
2 green onions, chopped	Grated Parmesan cheese

Cook tortelini using package directions; drain. Combine with broccoli, parsley, pimento, undrained artichoke hearts, green onions, basil, garlic powder, salad dressing and black olives in salad bowl; mix well. Chill, covered, for 4 hours to overnight. Add tomatoes and Parmesan cheese just before serving. Yield: 6 servings.

Betty Ross, Xi Zeta
Rock Rapids, Iowa

MACARONI SALAD CARBONARA

1 3-ounce can sliced	1/2 cup chopped green
mushrooms	bell pepper
1 cup frozen green peas	2 tomatoes, chopped
1 cup ham strips	1 1/4 cups ranch salad
6 ounces macaroni	dressing
twists, cooked	Spinach leaves

Bring undrained mushrooms to a boil in 10-inch skillet; add peas. Cook, covered, for 3 minutes. Remove cover; add ham. Cook until liquid is absorbed and peas are tender-crisp, stirring constantly. Toss macaroni, green pepper and tomatoes with salad dressing in large bowl. Stir in mushroom mixture. Chill in refrigerator. Spoon onto spinach-lined platter. Yield: 6 to 8 servings.

Judy S. Phillips, Preceptor Eta
Whitefish, Montana

MARCO POLO SALAD

1 pound vermicelli,	2 teaspoons pepper
cooked	1/2 cup half and half
3/4 cup olive oil	1 green bell pepper, cut
2 cloves of garlic,	julienne-style
crushed	2/3 pound Monterey Jack
1 1/2 teaspoons basil	cheese, cut into strips
1 tablespoon oregano	1/2 cup chopped pecans
1/2 cup parsley, chopped	3/4 cup Parmesan cheese
2 teaspoons salt	

Toss pasta with 2 tablespoons olive oil in large bowl. Combine remaining olive oil, garlic, basil, oregano, parsley, salt and pepper in medium bowl. Add half and half gradually, whisking constantly. Pour over pasta, tossing to mix. Add green pepper, Monterey Jack cheese and pecans. Sprinkle with Parmesan cheese. Serve at room temperature. Yield: 6 to 10 servings.

Beana Mueller, Delta Iota
St. Cloud, Minnesota

VEGETABLE-PASTA TOSS

Everyone loves this salad, including men!

8 ounces vermicelli,	1/2 teaspoon salt
broken into thirds	1/2 teaspoon basil leaves
4 cups bite-sized	2 cups mayonnaise
broccoli flowerets	1 pound bacon, crisp-
4 cups bite-sized	fried, crumbled
cauliflowerets	2 cups seasoned
1 large red onion, thinly	croutons
sliced into rings	1 8-ounce can sliced
1/3 cup grated Parmesan	water chestnuts,
cheese	drained
1/4 cup sugar	

Cook vermicelli using package directions; drain. Combine broccoli, cauliflower and onion in large bowl. Mix Parmesan cheese, sugar, salt, basil and mayonnaise in small bowl. Add to vegetables; toss lightly. Chill for several hours to overnight. Add bacon, vermicelli, croutons and water chestnuts just before serving; toss lightly. Yield: 20 to 24 servings.

Susan C. Moulton, Laureate Epsilon Kappa
Ridgecrest, California

VERMICELLI WALNUT SALAD

6 to 8 ounces vermicelli, cooked
1/2 cup large walnut pieces, toasted
1 cup green beans, cut into bite-sized pieces
2 6-ounce jars marinated artichoke hearts, drained, chopped
1 cup sliced fresh mushrooms
1/2 cup black olives
1 cup cherry tomatoes
1 red bell pepper, cut julienne-style
3 tablespoons chopped parsley
1/4 cup vegetable oil
1 clove of garlic, minced
1/2 teaspoon basil
1/4 teaspoon salt
Pepper to taste

Combine vermicelli, walnuts, green beans, artichoke hearts, mushrooms, black olives, tomatoes, red pepper and parsley in large bowl. Combine oil, garlic, basil, salt and pepper in small bowl; mix well. Pour over vermicelli and vegetables; toss to mix. Chill until serving time. Yield: 4 to 6 servings.

Jeanne Twenge, Laureate Alpha Iota
Monmouth, Oregon

ARTICHOKE RICE SALAD

1 5-ounce package chicken-flavored rice mix
2 9-ounce jars marinated artichoke hearts
1/2 teaspoon curry powder
1/3 cup mayonnaise
3 green onions, thinly sliced
1/2 green bell pepper, chopped
15 stuffed green olives, sliced

Cook rice using package directions, omitting butter. Let stand until cool. Drain artichoke hearts, reserving marinade from 1 jar. Combine reserved marinade with curry powder and mayonnaise in large bowl; mix well. Add rice, artichoke hearts, green onions, green pepper and green olives; toss to mix. Chill for several hours before serving. May add diced cooked chicken or shrimp for a main dish salad. Yield: 10 servings.

Catherine M. Chitty, Upsilon
Winston-Salem, North Carolina

CURRIED RICE SALAD

I fixed this recipe 10 years ago for my bridge group's Christmas potluck and now they insist that I bring it each year.

1 cup long grain rice, cooked
1 10-ounce package frozen peas, cooked
1 1/2 cups frozen salad shrimp
1/4 cup chopped green onions
1 teaspoon salt
1/2 teaspoon celery salt
1/2 cup sugar
1/2 cup salad oil
3 tablespoons vinegar
2 tablespoons soy sauce
2 teaspoons curry powder
1/2 cup cashews

Combine rice, peas, shrimp, green onions, salt, celery salt, sugar, oil, vinegar, soy sauce and curry powder in large bowl; mix well. Chill for at least 8 hours. Add cashews just before serving. Yield: 8 servings.

Beverly S. Douglass
Cheney, Washington

RICE SALAD

1 6-ounce package long grain and wild rice mix, cooked
1 8-ounce can water chestnuts
1 bunch green onions, chopped
1 10-ounce can water-pack artichoke hearts, drained, chopped
12 stuffed green olives, chopped
1/2 cup mayonnaise
1 teaspoon curry powder

Chill rice in refrigerator. Combine rice, water chestnuts, green onions, artichoke hearts, green olives, mayonnaise and curry powder in bowl; mix well. Chill for several hours to overnight. Yield: 6 servings.

Norma L. Shelp, Laureate Beta Delta
St. Louis, Missouri

AVOCADO MOLDED SALAD

This salad is one of the first ways I tasted avocados.

1 3-ounce package lemon or lime gelatin
1 cup boiling water
1 avocado, chopped
1 green bell pepper, chopped
1 tablespoon onion juice
Juice of 1/2 lemon
3/4 cup chopped celery
1 cup mayonnaise
1 cup whipped cream

Dissolve gelatin in boiling water in bowl; cool slightly. Add avocado, green pepper, onion juice, lemon juice and celery; mix well. Stir in mayonnaise and whipped cream. Pour into mold. Chill until set. Unmold onto serving plate. Yield: 8 servings.

Alta Mae Seiler, Laureate Beta Upsilon
Chico, California

BEAN SALAD

1 16-ounce can green beans, drained
1 16-ounce can yellow wax beans, drained
1 16-ounce can kidney beans, drained
1 16-ounce can chick-peas, drained
1/2 cup water
1 1/2 cups sugar
2/3 cup vegetable oil
2 stalks celery, chopped
2 medium onions, sliced
1 green bell pepper, chopped
1 1/2 cups white vinegar
1 tablespoon salt
1 teaspoon pepper

Combine green beans, wax beans, kidney beans, chick-peas, water, sugar, oil, celery, onions, green pepper, vinegar, salt and pepper in large bowl; mix well. Chill overnight. Yield: 20 servings.

Teresa Gitto, Xi Alpha
Beaconsfield, Quebec, Canada

CANNELLINI BEAN SALAD

1   16-ounce can
    cannellini beans,
    drained
2 green onions, chopped
1 tomato, chopped
½ purple onion,
    chopped
½ cucumber, chopped

¼ cup crumbled feta
    cheese
¼ cup olive oil
2 tablespoons vinegar
1 teaspoon oregano
1 teaspoon dill
1 teaspoon garlic salt
½ teaspoon pepper

Combine beans, green onions, tomato, purple onion, cucumber, feta cheese, olive oil, vinegar, oregano, dill, garlic salt and pepper in bowl; mix well. Chill overnight. Yield: 4 to 6 servings.

Helen L. Newlin, Preceptor Gamma Tau
Oak Grove, Missouri

DILLED GREEN BEANS IN SOUR CREAM

I took this on a sister chapter visitation and we all shared our recipes.

1 pound green beans
1 tablespoon dried
    minced onion
2 tablespoons parsley
2 tablespoons butter or
    margarine
1 tablespoon
    all-purpose flour

1 teaspoon dillweed
1 teaspoon sugar
1 teaspoon vinegar
1 teaspoon salt
½ teaspoon pepper
1 cup sour cream

Cook green beans in water to cover in saucepan until tender. Drain, reserving ½ cup liquid. Sauté onion and parsley in butter in medium saucepan until onion is soft. Stir in flour. Add reserved green bean liquid gradually, stirring constantly until sauce is thickened. Remove from heat. Add green beans, dillweed, sugar, vinegar, salt, pepper and sour cream; mix well. Yield: 10 servings.

Nancy L. Weeks, Xi Beta Phi
Evergreen, Colorado

GREEN BEAN SALAD

1   16-ounce can French-
    style green beans
1   3-ounce package
    lime gelatin
1 small bunch green
    onions, chopped

¼ cup chopped pecans
2 tablespoons vinegar
1 cup sour cream or
    yogurt
Prepared horseradish to
    taste

Drain green beans, reserving liquid. Add enough water to reserved liquid to equal 1 cup. Bring liquid to a boil in saucepan. Stir in gelatin until dissolved. Let stand until cool. Add green beans, green onions, pecans and vinegar. Spoon into 8-inch square dish. Chill until firm. Spread mixture of sour cream and horseradish over congealed salad. Cut into squares to serve. Yield: 6 to 8 servings.

Molly Goodwin, Laureate Gamma Pi
Sequin, Texas

TWO BEANS AND CORN SALAD

3   28-ounce cans green
    beans
2   16-ounce cans kidney
    beans
2   16-ounce cans corn
2 cups sugar

1 cup olive oil
1 cup red vinegar
1 cup water
Oregano and basil to
    taste
Salt and pepper to taste

Combine green beans, kidney beans, corn, sugar, oil, vinegar, water, oregano, basil, salt and pepper in large bowl; mix well. Chill for several hours to overnight before serving. Yield: 16 to 20 servings.

Kathleen J. Shafer, Beta Zeta
Bloomsburg, Pennsylvania

BROCCOLI SALAD

This is a great favorite at sorority or office parties as it is crisp, different and delicious.

2 pounds broccoli, cut
    into flowerets
2 bunches green onions,
    finely chopped
½ 15-ounce package
    white raisins
½ cup sunflower seed

8 slices crisp-fried
    bacon, crumbled
1 cup mayonnaise
1 tablespoon vinegar or
    lemon juice
¼ cup sugar

Combine broccoli, green onions, raisins, sunflower seed and bacon in large bowl; mix well. Combine mayonnaise, vinegar and sugar in small bowl; mix well. Pour over broccoli mixture; toss to mix. Chill for 2 hours to overnight before serving.
Yield: 15 to 20 servings.

Rose Ann Young, Alpha Mu
Martinez, Georgia

ALMOND BOK CHOY

Easy as A. B. C.–Almond Bok Choy. Everyone loves this delicious salad.

3 tablespoons sesame
    seed
6 tablespoons slivered
    almonds
2   3-ounce packages
    ramen noodles, broken
    into pieces
½ teaspoon pepper
1 teaspoon garlic
    powder

¼ cup vegetable oil
¼ cup vinegar
½ cup sugar
2 tablespoons soy sauce
1 large bunch Napa bok
    choy, shredded, chilled
1 large bunch green
    onions, chopped,
    chilled

Brown sesame seed, almonds, ramen noodles, pepper and garlic powder in oil in skillet; cool. Bring vinegar, sugar and soy sauce to a boil in saucepan. Let stand until cool. Mix sesame seed mixture with bok choy and green onions in large bowl. Top with cooled vinegar mixture; toss well. Yield: 6 servings.

Wanda Malin, Preceptor Zeta
Great Falls, Montana

CONFETTI SLAW

1 medium head cabbage,
  shredded
1 cup chopped tomato
2 cups chopped green
  bell pepper
1 cup coarsely chopped
  cucumber
1/2 cup sliced green
  onions

1 cup mayonnaise-type
  salad dressing
1 cup sour cream
1 teaspoon sugar
1 teaspoon salt
1/2 teaspoon garlic salt

Combine cabbage, tomato, green pepper, cucumber and green onions in large bowl. Mix salad dressing, sour cream, sugar, salt and garlic salt in small container. Pour over salad, tossing to coat. Chill for 8 hours to overnight. Yield: 8 to 10 servings.

Margaret Jacobs, Laureate Rho
Hutchinson, Kansas

FRUITY COLESLAW

1 8-ounce can
  pineapple chunks
2 tablespoons cider
  vinegar
2 tablespoons vegetable
  oil
1 tablespoon grated
  onion
2 tablespoons sugar

1/8 teaspoon salt
Pinch of pepper
1 11-ounce can
  mandarin oranges,
  drained
4 cups chopped
  cabbage
2 carrots, chopped

Drain pineapple, reserving 2 tablespoons juice for salad dressing. Combine reserved pineapple juice with vinegar, oil, onion, sugar, salt and pepper in small bowl; mix well. Combine pineapple, mandarin oranges, cabbage and carrots in large bowl. Top with salad dressing; toss to mix. Yield: 6 to 8 servings.

Linda Gafford, Xi Delta
Montgomery, Alabama

ORIENTAL COLESLAW

A delightful change from the ordinary.

3/4 cup mayonnaise
2 tablespoons soy sauce
2 tablespoons sugar
1/2 teaspoon salt
1 medium head cabbage,
  shredded
1/4 cup chopped green
  onions

2 tablespoons chopped
  pimentos
1 8-ounce can water
  chestnuts, thinly sliced
1 8-ounce can bamboo
  shoots, chopped

Whip mayonnaise, soy sauce, sugar and salt in large bowl. Add remaining ingredients, tossing until well coated. Chill for 1 hour before serving. Yield: 6 servings.

Vickie Thomas, Xi Nu
Weiser, Idaho

CORN BREAD SALAD

1 8 1/2-ounce package
  corn bread mix
1 or 2 16-ounce cans
  chili beans, drained
2 tomatoes, chopped

1 onion, chopped
1 1/4 cups mayonnaise-
  type salad dressing
1/2 cup dill pickle juice
1 cup shredded cheese

Prepare corn bread using package directions; cool. Crumble corn bread; place in salad bowl. Spread beans over corn bread; top with tomatoes and onion. Beat salad dressing and dill pickle juice in mixer bowl until smooth. Spread over salad, lifting with fork in several places to mix gently. Sprinkle with cheese. Chill for 2 to 2 1/2 hours before serving. Yield: 4 to 6 servings.

Kim Falkenstien, Kappa Omega
Fredonia, Kansas

SALTINE CRACKER SALAD

1 cup chopped onion
1/2 cup chopped green
  bell pepper
1 cup chopped sweet
  pickles
1 cup mayonnaise

1 7-ounce package
  pimento cheese spread
4 ounces saltine
  crackers, crushed
5 hard-cooked eggs,
  chopped

Combine onion, green pepper, pickles, mayonnaise, cheese spread, cracker crumbs and eggs in bowl; mix well. Serve immediately or chill overnight. Yield: 6 servings.

Janie McKissick, Delta Tau
Woodbury, Georgia

CAESAR SALAD

1 head green leaf
  lettuce, torn
1 bunch green onions,
  chopped
1/2 can 100% real bacon
  bits
Parmesan cheese

1 tablespoon grated
  Romano cheese
Caesar salad croutons
2 tablespoons lemon
  juice
1/2 cup olive oil
Pepper to taste

Combine lettuce, green onions, bacon bits, Parmesan cheese, Romano cheese and croutons in salad bowl. Whip lemon juice, olive oil and pepper in small bowl. Pour over salad just before serving; toss well. May add tomato, olives or hard-cooked eggs. Yield: 4 servings.

Karin Fowler, Rho
Coeur d'Alene, Idaho

Artherene Mahanay, Alpha Rho, Calera, Oklahoma, mixes 2 cups each cubed Cheddar cheese and chopped walnuts, 8 ounces chopped pimentos and enough mayonnaise to moisten. Season with 1/2 teaspoon Mrs. Dash, 1/4 teaspoon celery salt and 1/8 teaspoon each pepper and garlic powder. Chill Cheese and Walnut Salad in refrigerator overnight.

QUICK CAESAR SALAD

1 head romaine lettuce, torn	1 small clove of garlic, crushed
2 tablespoons grated Parmesan cheese	1/2 cup Caesar salad dressing
2 tablespoons crumbled bleu cheese	1 cup croutons
1 egg	1 tablespoon bacon bits

Place lettuce in plastic bag; chill in refrigerator. Combine Parmesan cheese and bleu cheese in small bowl. Add to lettuce 15 minutes before serving; shake well. Cook egg in boiling water in saucepan for 1 minute; cool slightly. Break into lettuce, including any bits of cooked egg white. Stir garlic into Caesar salad dressing. Add dressing, croutons and bacon bits to lettuce; shake well. Yield: 4 to 6 servings.

Harlene Annett, Preceptor Beta Pi
Peterborough, Ontario, Canada

CAULIFLOWER SALAD

Flowerets of 1 head cauliflower	1 large tomato, chopped
3 tablespoons chopped onion	1/2 cup sour cream
1/4 green bell pepper, chopped	4 teaspoons white vinegar
	Dash of salt
	Olives

Combine all ingredients in salad bowl; mix well. Chill for several hours to overnight before serving. Yield: 4 servings.

Marsha Neel, Xi Tau Nu
Wink, Texas

SHOE PEG SALAD

1 16-ounce can Shoe Peg corn, drained	1 2-ounce jar pimento, drained, chopped
1 16-ounce can small peas, drained	1 small onion, chopped
2 16-ounce cans French-style green beans, drained	1/2 cup vegetable oil
	1/3 cup vinegar
	3/4 cup sugar
1/2 cup chopped celery	1 teaspoon salt
	1/2 teaspoon pepper

Combine first 6 ingredients in salad bowl. Bring oil, vinegar, sugar, salt and pepper to a boil in saucepan; reduce heat. Simmer for 15 minutes; cool. Pour over vegetables; toss to mix. Chill for 24 hours before serving. Yield: 10 to 12 servings.

Sarah Bates, Xi Beta Xi
Paris, Missouri

CUCUMBER SALAD

1 or 2 cucumbers, sliced	Pepper to taste
1 red onion, sliced into rings	1 tablespoon vinegar
Salt to taste	2 tablespoons (about) sour cream

Combine cucumbers, onion rings and salt in bowl. Chill, covered, for 45 minutes to 1 hour; drain. Add pepper, vinegar and sour cream, stirring to coat. Chill for several hours or longer to enhance flavor. Yield: 4 to 6 servings.

Helen Grace Young, Preceptor Laureate
McComb, Mississippi

REFRIGERATOR CUCUMBER SALAD

7 cups thinly sliced cucumbers	1 tablespoon salt
	1 tablespoon celery seed
1 cup thinly sliced onion	2 cups sugar
1 medium green bell pepper, finely chopped	1 cup white vinegar

Place cucumbers, onion and green pepper in large bowl. Add mixture of salt, celery seed, sugar and vinegar; mix well. Chill, covered, for 3 hours or longer, stirring several times. Yield: 10 servings.

Billie P. George, Preceptor Alpha Omega
Oklahoma City, Oklahoma

LAYERED SALAD

2 heads lettuce, shredded	2 cups shredded Cheddar cheese
Flowerets of 1 head cauliflower	1 pound crisp-fried bacon, crumbled
Flowerets of 1 bunch broccoli	1 cup mayonnaise
1 to 2 cups fresh mushrooms, sliced	1 cup sour cream
3 or 4 hard-cooked eggs, chopped	Garlic salt to taste
	Salt and pepper to taste

Layer first 7 ingredients in large bowl. Mix mayonnaise, sour cream and seasonings in small bowl. Pour over layered salad. Yield: 20 to 25 servings.

Sandra McCartney, Xi Beta Theta
Jasper, Alabama

COMMITTEE SALAD

1/2 cup sunflower seed	1/2 cup vegetable oil
1/2 cup almonds	3 tablespoons red wine vinegar
2 tablespoons butter	
1 head leaf lettuce, torn	1 tablespoon lemon juice
1 avocado, chopped	1/2 teaspoon salt
1 11-ounce can mandarin oranges, drained	1/2 teaspoon dry mustard
	1 clove of garlic, crushed
1 bunch green onions, chopped	2 teaspoons sugar

Brown sunflower seed and almonds in butter in skillet; drain. Mix with lettuce, avocado, oranges and green onions in bowl. Combine remaining ingredients in covered jar; shake well. Add to salad just before serving; toss well. Yield: 6 servings.

Kim Habetler, Xi Alpha Chi
Maple Ridge, British Columbia, Canada

CHRISTMAS EVE SALAD

1 head romaine lettuce, torn	1/4 cup toasted sesame seed
1 9-ounce can artichokes, drained	1/4 cup toasted slivered almonds
1 11-ounce can mandarin oranges, drained	Coarsely ground pepper to taste
1 avocado, sliced	Italian salad dressing

Combine lettuce, artichokes, mandarin oranges, avocado, sesame seed and almonds in large bowl; mix well. Add pepper. Serve with Italian dressing. Yield: 6 servings.

Starr Byrne, Theta Upsilon
Peachtree City, Georgia

LETTUCE-APPLE SALAD

4 heads leaf lettuce or spinach, torn	1 1/2 cups salad oil
1 cup sliced red onion	3 tablespoons sugar
1 cup chopped walnuts	2 cloves of garlic, minced
1 red Delicious apple, sliced	1 teaspoon salt

Mix lettuce, onion, walnuts and apple in large bowl. Combine oil, sugar, garlic and salt in covered jar; shake well. Let stand for 1 hour before serving. Shake again. Pour over salad just before serving; toss well. Yield: 10 to 12 servings.

Roxanne Nelson, Xi Beta Theta
Hastings, Nebraska

MANDARIN ALMOND SALAD

This is always a favorite for gourmet get-togethers.

Romaine lettuce, torn	1/2 teaspoon salt
Leaf lettuce, torn	Dash of pepper
Spinach, torn	2 tablespoons sugar
1 11-ounce can mandarin oranges, drained	1/4 cup red wine vinegar
1/2 cup sliced almonds	1/2 cup olive oil
Water	7 or 8 dashes of Tabasco sauce
2 tablespoons sugar	Pinch of tarragon, parsley and thyme

Mix salad greens together in large bowl. Arrange mandarin oranges on top. Spread almonds on baking sheet; sprinkle with water and 2 tablespoons sugar. Broil until golden brown. Sprinkle over salad. Combine salt, pepper, remaining 2 tablespoons sugar, vinegar, olive oil, Tabasco sauce and herbs in covered jar; shake well. Pour over salad; toss to coat. Yield: 6 to 8 servings.

Karen Loughborough, Xi Gamma Theta
Kitchener, Ontario, Canada

FRESH MUSHROOM SALAD

This was served at our first Harvest Sampler, a fund raising event for our service projects.

1 pound fresh mushrooms	1/2 teaspoon salt
3 green onions, chopped	1 tablespoon Worcestershire sauce
1/4 cup fresh lemon juice	Shredded lettuce
2/3 cup vegetable oil	10 slices bacon, crisp-fried, crumbled
1/2 teaspoon dry mustard	

Wash mushrooms; remove and discard stems. Slice caps 1/8-inch thick. Combine green onions, lemon juice, oil, dry mustard, salt and Worcestershire sauce in bowl; mix well. Add sliced mushrooms; toss to coat. Marinate in refrigerator for at least 4 hours. Serve on bed of lettuce; sprinkle with crumbled bacon. Yield: 10 servings.

Valerie Beenken
Mount Pleasant, Iowa

PICKLED MUSHROOMS

1/3 cup salad oil	2 teaspoons salt
1/3 cup red wine vinegar	1 bay leaf
1 small onion, thinly sliced	2 teaspoons dried parsley
1 teaspoon prepared mustard	1 teaspoon oregano
1 tablespoon light brown sugar	1 teaspoon dried dillweed
1 clove of garlic, minced	1 pound fresh small mushrooms

Combine oil, vinegar, onion, mustard, brown sugar, garlic, salt, bay leaf and herbs in 3-quart saucepan. Bring to a boil, stirring constantly. Add mushrooms. Cook over medium-low heat for 8 to 10 minutes. Chill overnight; drain before serving. Yield: 10 to 12 servings.

Ruth Osterburg, Laureate Alpha Iota
Womelsdorf, Pennsylvania

UNA'S ONIONS

An onion lover's "must."

1/2 cup water	1/2 cup mayonnaise
1/2 cup sugar	1 teaspoon celery seed
1/2 cup vinegar	Salt and pepper to taste
2 teaspoons salt	
1 1/2 large red onions, thinly sliced into rings	

Mix water, sugar, vinegar and salt in bowl. Add onions. Marinate, covered, in refrigerator for 3 hours to overnight; drain. Mix marinated onions with mayonnaise, celery seed, salt and pepper. Yield: 6 servings.

Lorraine McKenzie, Xi Delta Phi
Langley, British Columbia, Canada

PEANUT PARADISE SALAD

6 cups romaine lettuce,
  torn
3 bananas, sliced
2 apples, chopped
1/2 cup honey-roasted
  peanuts
1/2 cup white raisins
1/2 cup mayonnaise
1/4 cup crunchy peanut
  butter
1/4 cup honey

Mix lettuce, bananas, apples, peanuts and raisins together in large bowl. Combine remaining ingredients in small bowl; mix well. Pour over salad. I use honey-crunch peanut butter. Yield: 6 servings.

Margaret McNary, Xi Xi Chi
Los Altos, California

GREEN PEA SALAD

2/3 cup chopped celery
2/3 cup chopped red
  onion
2/3 cup chopped green
  bell pepper
1 1/2 tablespoons sugar
2 cups mayonnaise
1/4 cup sour cream
2 8-ounce cans early
  green peas
1 cup shredded Cheddar
  cheese
1/2 pound bacon, crisp-
  fried, crumbled

Combine celery, onion and green pepper in bowl. Stir in sugar, mayonnaise and sour cream. Add peas; mix well. Top with cheese and bacon. Chill for 24 hours. Yield: 4 to 6 servings.

Toy Holland, Epsilon Nu
Birmingham, Alabama

SNOW PEA SALAD WITH FRUIT

4 cups fresh snow peas,
  ends trimmed
1 cup whole red seedless
  grapes
2 large oranges, cut into
  sections
2 large grapefruit, cut
  into sections
1 green bell pepper, cut
  julienne-style
1 small red onion, sliced
1/2 cup sunflower seed
2 cups sugar
1 1/4 cups white vinegar
3 1/3 cups vegetable oil
8 teaspoons poppy seed
1/4 cup dried onion
  flakes
2 teaspoons dry mustard

Combine first 7 ingredients in large bowl; mix well. Combine sugar and vinegar in small deep bowl; whisk until blended. Whisk in oil. Add poppy seed, onion flakes and dry mustard; mix well. Pour desired amount over fruits and vegetables; toss well. Dressing will keep in refrigerator for up to 3 weeks. Yield: 8 to 10 servings.

Cindy Layton, Xi Epsilon Nu
Cape Girardeau, Missouri

Alice R. Nicholson, Xi Delta Beta, Olney, Illinois, makes Pea and Peanut Salad by mixing 10 ounces cooked chilled peas, 1/2 cup mayonnaise, 1/3 cup sour cream, 1 cup Spanish peanuts and 1/2 teaspoon Worcestershire sauce. Chill.

DIET POTATO AND GREEN BEAN SALAD

1 1/2 pounds small red
  potatoes, cut into
  halves
1 pound green beans,
  trimmed, cooked
1 sweet white onion,
  chopped
1 bunch scallions,
  chopped
1 pint cherry tomatoes,
  cut into halves
1/4 cup chopped fresh
  parsley
2 teaspoons dried chives
1 teaspoon dried
  dillweed
1 tablespoon onion
  powder
Salt and pepper to taste
1 cup low-calorie
  Italian salad dressing
1/3 cup red wine vinegar

Boil potatoes in salted water until fork-tender; drain. Combine with cooked green beans, onion, scallions, tomatoes, parsley, chives, dillweed, onion powder, salt and pepper in large bowl; mix well. Mix salad dressing with vinegar. Pour over vegetables; toss well to coat. Yield: 8 to 10 servings.

Phyllis B. Painter, Preceptor Omega
Staunton, Virginia

GERMAN POTATO SALAD

Grandma Homer served this on cold winter evenings when I was a child. I serve it at barbecues and picnics.

7 medium potatoes,
  peeled
1/2 cup chopped onion or
  1 tablespoon onion
  flakes
6 slices bacon
6 tablespoons sugar
2 tablespoons
  all-purpose flour
1 1/2 teaspoons salt
Dash of pepper
3/4 cup water
3/4 cup vinegar
Parsley

Cook potatoes until tender; drain. Cool and slice. Combine with onion in large bowl. Fry bacon in skillet until crisp; drain, reserving 1/3 cup bacon drippings. Crumble bacon over potatoes. Add sugar, flour, salt and pepper to reserved bacon drippings in saucepan, stirring well. Add water and vinegar gradually, stirring constantly. Bring to a boil. Cook for 1 minute, stirring constantly. Pour over potatoes; mix well. Serve while warm. Garnish with parsley. Yield: 6 servings.

Lucinda Heape, Xi Alpha Tau
Phoenix, Arizona

ITALIAN POTATO SALAD

6 cups cubed cooked
  potatoes
1/2 cup sliced celery
1/4 cup chopped black
  olives
1 envelope Italian salad
  dressing mix
1 cup mayonnaise

Combine potatoes, celery and olives in bowl; toss gently. Mix salad dressing mix and mayonnaise in small bowl. Spoon over potatoes; mix well to coat. Chill before serving. Yield: 8 servings.

Julie Jones, Mu Omicron
Broken Arrow, Oklahoma

SAUERKRAUT SALAD

4 cups sauerkraut, drained	1 cup chopped celery
1 medium onion, chopped	2/3 cup white vinegar
1 green bell pepper, chopped	1 1/2 cups sugar
	1/3 cup water
	1/2 cup vegetable oil
	1 teaspoon celery seed

Combine sauerkraut, onion, green pepper and celery in large bowl. Mix vinegar, sugar, water, oil and celery seed in saucepan. Bring to a boil. Cook for 1 minute, stirring frequently. Pour over sauerkraut mixture; toss to coat. Chill for 24 hours before serving. May keep in refrigerator for up to 2 weeks. Yield: 8 to 10 servings.

Eleanor Duncanson, Preceptor Rho
St. Catharines, Ontario, Canada

MARION'S SPINACH SALAD

1 1/2 pounds fresh spinach, torn	2 tablespoons sesame seed
8 mushrooms, sliced	1/4 cup vegetable oil
1/2 cup chopped water chestnuts	1/4 cup wine vinegar
1/2 medium onion, cut into rings	1/2 teaspoon salt
6 slices bacon, crisp-fried, crumbled	1/4 cup catsup
	1/4 cup sugar
	1 tablespoon Worcestershire sauce

Combine spinach, mushrooms, water chestnuts, onion, bacon and sesame seed in large bowl; stir well. Mix remaining ingredients in bowl until well blended. Pour over salad; toss well to coat. Yield: 4 to 6 servings.

Lisa Appleby, Xi Alpha Xi
Lenoir, North Carolina

BONNIE'S SPINACH SALAD

This salad was served at a luncheon given by dear friends in Pennsylvania. I serve it on holidays and for guests. It is beautiful in appearance and very tasty.

3/4 to 1 cup sugar	2 cups vegetable oil
3/4 cup vinegar	1 pound fresh spinach, torn
2 tablespoons prepared mustard	1 pint fresh strawberries, sliced
2 teaspoons salt	1 cup fresh blueberries
2 tablespoons poppy seed	3/4 to 1 cup chopped walnuts
1/3 cup grated onion	

Mix first 7 ingredients in bowl, stirring well to blend. Chill in refrigerator overnight. Arrange spinach on individual salad plates. Sprinkle with strawberries, blueberries and walnuts. Pour dressing over salad just before serving. Garnish with additional strawberry slices. Yield: 6 servings.

Betty McCalley, Alpha Omega
Kansas City, Missouri

MANGO CHUTNEY SPINACH SALAD

1 bunch fresh spinach, torn	1/4 cup lemon juice
1 tart green apple, chopped	1/4 cup mango chutney
1/4 cup chopped green onions	1 teaspoon curry powder
1 cup roasted whole peanuts	1/8 teaspoon cayenne pepper
2 tablespoons red wine vinegar	1/4 teaspoon turmeric
	1/2 teaspoon sugar
	1/2 teaspoon salt
	3/4 cup vegetable oil

Toss spinach, apple, green onions and peanuts together in large bowl. Combine vinegar and next 7 ingredients in blender container. Blend for 2 minutes. Add oil in fine stream, processing constantly at high speed until blended. Pour over spinach salad; toss well to coat. Yield: 4 to 6 servings.

Margaret Warbrick, Preceptor Beta
Vancouver, British Columbia, Canada

ORANGE-CASHEW SPINACH SALAD

2 bunches fresh spinach, torn	1 small onion, chopped
1 11-ounce can mandarin oranges, drained, chopped	1/4 to 1/2 cup sugar
	1/2 cup vinegar
	1 tablespoon celery seed
4 ounces cashews, chopped	1 tablespoon dry mustard
	1 cup vegetable oil

Toss spinach, mandarin oranges and cashews in large bowl. Combine onion, sugar, vinegar, celery seed and dry mustard in blender container. Process at high speed until smooth. Add oil in fine stream, processing constantly until completely blended. Pour over spinach salad. Yield: 6 to 8 servings.

Sherry Blyth, Psi Eta
Richmond, Missouri

HONEY-CARAWAY SPINACH SALAD

1/3 bunch fresh spinach, torn	2 large oranges, peeled, chopped
1 head lettuce, torn	1 small cucumber, peeled, sliced
2 tablespoons chopped onion	3/4 cup mayonnaise
2 tablespoons chopped green bell pepper	2 tablespoons honey
2 tablespoons chopped pimento	1 tablespoon lemon juice
	1 tablespoon caraway seed

Toss spinach, lettuce, onion, green pepper, pimento, oranges and cucumber in large bowl. Combine mayonnaise, honey, lemon juice and caraway seed in small bowl; mix well. Spoon desired amount over salad. Yield: 6 to 8 servings.

Kathleen L. Radcliffe, Preceptor Laureate Beta
Lancaster, Pennsylvania

SESAME-BERRY-SPINACH SALAD

2 tablespoons sesame seed	1/4 teaspoon Worcestershire sauce
1/3 cup vegetable oil	1 1/2 pounds fresh spinach, torn
1/3 cup red wine vinegar	
1 tablespoon sugar	2 cups fresh strawberries, cut into halves
2 teaspoons minced green onions	
1/2 teaspoon paprika	

Sauté sesame seed in skillet over medium heat until golden brown. Combine oil, vinegar, sugar, green onions, paprika and Worcestershire sauce in small bowl, stirring vigorously until blended. Mix spinach and strawberries in large glass bowl. Pour dressing over salad; toss well. Sprinkle with sautéed sesame seed. Yield: 6 servings.

Karen K. Timperley, Preceptor Kappa
Huron, South Dakota

STRAWBERRY AND SPINACH SALAD

I have fond memories of a bridal shower for a young co-worker and the lovely women present whenever this salad is served.

1/3 cup (generous) raspberry wine vinegar	1 1/2 teaspoons poppy seed
1/3 cup (scant) balsamic wine vinegar	1 pint strawberries, sliced
1 cup vegetable oil	1 tablespoon grated red onion
3/4 cup sugar	
1 teaspoon salt	1 large bunch fresh spinach, torn
1 teaspoon dry mustard	

Combine raspberry vinegar, balsamic vinegar, oil, sugar, salt and mustard in blender container. Process at high speed until blended. Stir in poppy seed. Sprinkle strawberries and onion over spinach in salad bowl. Pour dressing over salad. Yield: 6 servings.

Linda Seeley, Preceptor Laureate Theta
Boise, Idaho

ITALIAN ANTIPASTO

1 cup diagonally sliced carrots	2 small onions, sliced
1 cup diagonally sliced celery	1/2 cup wine vinegar
	1/2 cup vegetable oil
1 cup cauliflowerets	2 tablespoons sherry
1 4-ounce can mushrooms, drained	1/2 teaspoon salt
1/2 cup green olives	1/4 teaspoon garlic powder
1/2 cup black olives	1/4 teaspoon oregano
1 green bell pepper, cut julienne-style	1/4 teaspoon pepper
	1/4 teaspoon MSG

Cook carrots, celery and cauliflowerets in boiling water in saucepan for 2 minutes; drain. Rinse in cold water. Mix with next 5 ingredients in large bowl.

Combine vinegar, oil, sherry, salt, garlic powder, oregano, pepper and MSG in small bowl, stirring vigorously to blend. Pour over vegetables. Marinate in refrigerator for several hours. Yield: 8 servings.

Jan Bierschbach, Beta Omega
Mobridge, South Dakota

CONFETTI SALAD

Flowerets of 1 head cauliflower	1 7-ounce can black olives, sliced
1 16-ounce can green beans, drained	1 7-ounce can stuffed green olives
1 16-ounce can wax beans, drained	2 tablespoons dried chives
1 stalk celery, sliced	1 8-ounce bottle of Italian salad dressing
1 pint cherry tomatoes	
1 4-ounce jar pickled yellow corn	1 8-ounce bottle of buttermilk or ranch salad dressing
1 small bunch carrots, sliced	

Combine cauliflowerets, beans, celery, tomatoes, corn, carrots and olives in large bowl; mix well. Mix chives with salad dressings in small bowl. Pour over vegetables; toss to coat well. May store in refrigerator for up to 2 weeks. May substitute any creamy salad dressing for buttermilk or ranch dressing. Yield: 10 servings.

Sue Awtry, Nu Alpha
Rock Valley, Iowa

MARINATED VEGETABLE SALAD

This has been a favorite dish at family gatherings, and also a way to get my young daughter to eat vegetables.

1 16-ounce can green beans, drained	1 medium onion, thinly sliced
1 16-ounce can red kidney beans, drained	1/4 cup tarragon vinegar
	3/4 teaspoon MSG
1 7-ounce can black olives, drained	Sugar to taste
1 15-ounce can artichoke hearts, drained	1 tablespoon mixed salad herbs
	1/2 cup salad oil
1 12-ounce jar button mushrooms, drained	1/4 teaspoon hot pepper sauce
1 4-ounce jar chopped pimentos, drained	1/4 cup chopped fresh parsley
1 1/2 cups diagonally sliced celery	

Combine first 8 ingredients in large bowl. Combine vinegar, MSG and sugar in bowl, stirring until sugar is dissolved. Add herbs, oil and pepper sauce; beat well. Pour over vegetables; toss well. Marinate in refrigerator overnight. Spoon into serving bowl. Garnish with chopped parsley. Yield: 8 to 10 servings.

Ginger Wise, Chi Delta
Blue Springs, Missouri

SUSE'S SIX-VEGGIE SALAD

I think of my friend Susan, who first served me this salad, whenever I make it.

1 medium bunch celery, sliced diagonally	4 tomatoes, cut into quarters
1 green bell pepper, chopped	2 tablespoons French salad dressing
1 small onion, chopped	1 cup sugar
2 tablespoons salt	1/2 cup vinegar
1 16-ounce can green beans, drained	1/2 cup vegetable oil
1 16-ounce can peas, drained	1/4 cup water

Combine celery, green pepper, onion and salt with water to cover in bowl for 4 hours; drain. Mix with beans, peas and tomatoes in large bowl. Combine French salad dressing, sugar, vinegar, oil and water in small bowl; mix well until blended. Pour over vegetables; toss well to coat. Chill before serving. Yield: 12 to 16 servings.

Beth Hazen, Xi Epsilon Xi
Dodge City, Kansas

CAESAR SALAD DRESSING

1/3 cup salad oil	1 egg
1/4 cup grated Parmesan cheese	1 large clove of garlic, minced
2 tablespoons lemon juice	1/2 teaspoon salt
	1/8 teaspoon pepper

Process all ingredients in blender until smooth and well blended. Chill in refrigerator for several hours before using. Yield: 3/4 cup.

Margaret Mary Stewart, Preceptor Eta
North Bay, Ontario, Canada

FRENCH SWEET AND SPICY DRESSING

1/2 cup sugar	1/2 cup finely chopped onion
1 tablespoon all-purpose flour	1 clove of garlic, minced
1/2 cup cider vinegar	1 cup salad oil
1 teaspoon salt	1/3 cup catsup
1 teaspoon Worcestershire sauce	1 teaspoon celery seed

Combine sugar, flour and vinegar in saucepan; mix well. Cook over medium heat until thick and bubbly, stirring constantly. Pour into blender container. Add salt, Worcestershire sauce, onion and garlic. Process at low speed until very smooth. Add oil in slow steady stream, increasing blender speed as mixture thickens. Add catsup and celery seed; mix gently. Chill, covered, for several hours to 4 weeks. May serve over spinach salad. Yield: 2 cups.

Lois Pfiefle, Xi Lambda Upsilon
Sterling, Illinois

CARAMEL SAUCE FOR FRUIT SALAD

8 ounces cream cheese, softened	Milk
2/3 cup packed light brown sugar	

Mix first 2 ingredients in bowl. Add enough milk to make of desired consistency. Yield: 1 cup.

Pam Allen, Theta Iota
Aurelia, Iowa

HONEY-MUSTARD DRESSING

1 cup mayonnaise	1/4 cup creamy Italian salad dressing
1/2 cup prepared mustard	
1/2 cup honey	

Combine mayonnaise, mustard, honey and salad dressing in bowl; mix well. Yield: 2 cups.

Lisa Bounds, Theta Zeta
Austin, Texas

LOW-CALORIE RANCH SALAD DRESSING

1 cup buttermilk	2 cups low-fat cottage cheese
1 envelope original recipe ranch salad dressing mix	1 teaspoon Mrs. Dash

Process buttermilk and salad dressing mix in blender container until well mixed. Add cottage cheese and Mrs. Dash. Blend at high speed for 2 minutes or until smooth. Add additional buttermilk if a thinner consistency is desired. Yield: 3 cups.

Mabyl Miller, Laureate Beta Zeta
Fort Worth, Texas

POPPY SEED DRESSING

1/3 cup honey	1 teaspoon dry mustard
6 tablespoons tarragon vinegar	1 teaspoon paprika
3 tablespoons lemon juice	1/4 teaspoon salt
	2 teaspoons poppy seed
1 teaspoon grated onion	1/4 cup sugar
	1 cup salad oil

Whisk together first 8 ingredients in bowl. Whisk in sugar gradually, tasting for desired sweetness. Add oil slowly, beating with whisk until of desired consistency. Store in tightly covered jar in refrigerator. Shake before using. Yield: 2 cups.

Jane Biedermann, Xi Zeta Kappa
Rock Rapids, Iowa

Kim Livingston, Xi Delta Psi, McKean, Pennsylvania, makes Chutney Fruit Dip by mixing together 1/3 cup chutney, 1 teaspoon finely grated orange rind, 1/2 teaspoon grated fresh ginger and 1 cup sour cream. Serve chilled dip with fresh fruit.

The Meat Market

SECRET CROCKERY BARBECUED BEEF

1½ pounds boneless
    chuck roast
2 medium onions,
    chopped
¾ cup cola
¼ cup Worcestershire
    sauce
1 tablespoon vinegar
2 cloves of garlic,
    minced

1 teaspoon instant beef
    bouillon
½ teaspoon dry
    mustard
½ teaspoon chili powder
¼ teaspoon red pepper
½ cup catsup
2 tablespoons margarine
Shredded greens
Flour tortillas

Place roast and onions in crockery slow cooker. Combine cola, Worcestershire sauce, vinegar, garlic, instant bouillon, dry mustard, chili powder and red pepper in bowl; mix well. Reserve ½ cup mixture. Pour remaining cola mixture over roast. Cook on Low for 10 to 12 hours or on High for 5 to 6 hours. Combine reserved cola mixture with catsup and margarine in small saucepan; mix well. Cook until heated through. Place beef on cutting board, discarding cooking liquid; shred beef. Serve on shredded greens in flour tortillas. Serve with hot catsup sauce. Do not use diet cola. Yield: 6 servings.

Sharon Sotvik
Story, Wyoming

SHERRIED BEEF

3 pounds stew beef
1 cup cooking sherry
2 10-ounce cans cream
    of mushroom soup

1 envelope onion soup
    mix
1 4-ounce can
    mushrooms

Preheat oven to 325 degrees. Combine all ingredients in casserole. Bake, covered, for 3 hours. Serve over rice or noodles. Yield: 4 to 6 servings.

Melanie Carroll, Xi Delta Mu
Madras, Oregon

SPICY BEEF AND ASPARAGUS

1 pound top round steak
1 tablespoon cornstarch
1 tablespoon water
1 teaspoon dry sherry
Hot pepper sauce to
    taste
½ teaspoon salt
¼ teaspoon pepper
¼ cup beef broth
1 tablespoon soy sauce
1 tablespoon catsup
1 teaspoon red wine
    vinegar

½ teaspoon sugar
2 tablespoons vegetable
    oil
1 clove of garlic, minced
12 ounces asparagus,
    cut into 1-inch pieces
1 cup cauliflowerets
1 small red or green bell
    pepper, cut into narrow
    strips
1 small onion, cut into
    thin wedges

Trim beef; freeze until partially firm. Slice cross grain into thin strips. Combine cornstarch, water, sherry, pepper sauce, salt and pepper in bowl. Add beef; mix well. Combine beef broth, soy sauce, catsup, vinegar and sugar in small bowl; set aside. Preheat wok or large skillet over high heat. Add 1 tablespoon oil. Stir-fry garlic in oil for 30 seconds. Stir-fry beef mixture ½ at a time until brown, removing to bowl. Add remaining 1 tablespoon oil if needed. Stir-fry asparagus and cauliflowerets for 4 minutes. Add red pepper and onion. Stir-fry for 2 minutes or until vegetables are tender-crisp. Add beef and beef broth mixture. Cook until bubbly, stirring constantly. Cook, covered, for 1 minute longer. May substitute one 10-ounce package frozen asparagus for fresh if preferred. Yield: 6 servings.

Diane Polansky Ward, Xi Gamma Psi
Ankeny, Iowa

MAINE JAILHOUSE CHILI

2 pounds cubed beef	2 tablespoons hot taco
All-purpose flour	sauce
2 tablespoons vegetable	1 4-ounce can chopped
oil	green chilies
2 16-ounce cans	2 medium onions,
stewed tomatoes	chopped
2 29-ounce cans kidney	1¹/2 to 2 teaspoons each
beans	cayenne pepper,
1 16-ounce can kidney	paprika, cumin and
beans	oregano
2 green bell peppers,	3 to 3¹/2 tablespoons
chopped	chili powder
1 6-ounce can tomato	1 teaspoon salt
paste	

Coat beef with flour. Brown in oil in skillet. Drain 1 can tomatoes. Combine beef, tomatoes, beans, green peppers, tomato paste, taco sauce, green chilies and onions in slow cooker. Add cayenne pepper, paprika, cumin, oregano, chili powder and salt; mix well. Cook on Low for 8 to 10 hours or on High for 5 hours. Yield: 10 servings.

Debra Jo Brown, Alpha Omega
Hampden, Maine

TOUGH MAN'S CHILI

1 pound cubed beef	2 16-ounce cans
1 onion, chopped	Mexican chili beans
Vegetable oil	3 tablespoons garlic
1 28-ounce can whole	powder
tomatoes	2 tablespoons chili
2 8-ounce cans tomato	powder
sauce	1 tablespoon cumin
2 (or more) 4-ounce cans	¹/4 teaspoon red pepper
chopped green chilies	

Brown beef with onion in a small amount of oil in large saucepan, stirring frequently; drain. Add tomatoes, tomato sauce, green chilies, beans, garlic powder, chili powder, cumin and red pepper; mix well. Simmer for 1¹/2 hours. May cook in slow cooker on Low for 8 hours if preferred. Yield: 10 servings.

Barbara Lefholz, Laureate Beta Omicron
Oak Grove, Missouri

EASY BRISKET

¹/2 cup soy sauce	1 teaspoon whole
¹/4 cup Worcestershire	allspice
sauce	¹/4 teaspoon pepper
¹/3 cup water	1 6- to 8-pound beef
1 tablespoon lemon juice	brisket, trimmed
1 tablespoon light	1 tablespoon
brown sugar	all-purpose flour
¹/4 teaspoon ginger	

Combine first 8 ingredients in saucepan; mix well. Simmer, covered, for 5 minutes. Cool for 5 minutes. Pour over brisket in shallow dish. Marinate for 2 to 4 hours. Drain, reserving marinade. Preheat gas grill to Low. Grill brisket for 20 minutes, turning once and basting with reserved marinade. Preheat oven to 250 degrees. Coat cooking bag with flour. Add brisket to bag; seal bag. Cut 2 or 3 slits in bag; place in 9-by-13-inch baking pan. Bake for 2¹/2 hours. Slice to serve. Yield: 10 to 12 servings.

Bunny Lane, Xi Nu
Nixa, Missouri

LASAGNA FIESTA

2¹/2 pounds sirloin steak	2 10-ounce cans cream
Vegetable oil	of mushroom soup
¹/4 cup lime juice	1 8-ounce package
1 cup picante sauce	precooked lasagna
2 teaspoons garlic	noodles
powder	6 corn tortillas, torn
6 sprigs of cilantro,	into bite-sized pieces
chopped	1 medium onion, finely
1 teaspoon cumin	chopped
2 teaspoons pepper	2 cups shredded
2 10-ounce cans Ro-Tel	Cheddar cheese
tomatoes with green	Sour cream
chilies	Chopped avocados

Preheat oven to 350 degrees. Cut steak into ¹/2-inch cubes. Sauté in a small amount of oil in saucepan until brown; drain. Add next 6 ingredients; mix well. Cook for 5 minutes. Heat tomatoes and soup in saucepan until bubbly. Spoon a small amount of soup mixture into 9-by-13-inch baking dish. Layer noodles, tortillas, beef mixture, onion, soup mixture and cheese in prepared dish until all ingredients are used, ending with soup and cheese. Bake for 30 minutes. Garnish with sour cream and avocados. Precooked lasagna noodles are a new product and do not have to be cooked before using in casserole. Yield: 6 to 8 servings.

Merline McCoy, Laureate Beta Psi
Port Neches, Texas

MICROWAVE ROAST

1 3-pound rib-eye roast	¹/4 teaspoon pepper
1 teaspoon dry mustard	1 tablespoon catsup
¹/4 teaspoon garlic	1 teaspoon
powder	Worcestershire sauce
1 teaspoon salt	¹/2 cup dry red wine

Place roast fat side down in glass dish; sprinkle with dry mustard, garlic powder, salt and pepper. Microwave on Medium-High for 10 minutes. Combine catsup, Worcestershire sauce and wine in bowl; mix well. Turn roast over; add wine sauce. Place probe in roast. Microwave on Medium to 135 degrees. Let stand for 10 to 15 minutes. Roast will be medium. Yield: 6 to 8 servings.

Loretta F. Hill, Preceptor Beta
Westminster, Maryland

MUSHROOM POT ROAST

1 3½- to 4-pound pot roast	¼ teaspoon each dry mustard, marjoram, rosemary and thyme
All-purpose flour	
2 tablespoons shortening	1 medium bay leaf
	1 6-ounce can mushrooms, drained
Salt and pepper to taste	
2 cups sliced onions	¼ cup cold water
½ cup water	2 tablespoons all-purpose flour
½ cup catsup	
1 clove of garlic, minced	

Coat roast with flour. Brown on both sides in shortening in heavy saucepan. Season with salt and pepper. Add onions, ½ cup water, catsup, garlic, dry mustard, marjoram, rosemary, thyme and bay leaf. Simmer for 2 hours or until tender. Remove roast to serving platter. Skim grease from cooking liquid; discard bay leaf. Stir mushrooms and mixture of ¼ cup water and 2 tablespoons flour into liquid in saucepan. Cook until thickened, stirring constantly. Serve with roast. Yield: 6 to 8 servings.

Lucille Humbert
Greensburg, Indiana

ROAST BEEF CALIFORNIAN

1 cup orange juice	½ teaspoon chili powder
1 cup tomato juice	
¼ cup vegetable oil	2 teaspoons salt
1 clove of garlic, crushed	1 3-pound rolled rump roast
½ teaspoon allspice	

Combine orange juice, tomato juice, oil, garlic, allspice, chili powder and salt in bowl; mix well. Add roast, coating well. Marinate, covered, in refrigerator overnight. Preheat oven to 325 degrees. Drain roast, reserving marinade. Place roast in roasting pan. Roast for 1 hour and 15 minutes or for 25 minutes per pound, basting with marinade. Cool slightly; cut into thin slices. Yield: 6 servings.

Shirley Ann Trice, Preceptor Tau
Davidsonville, Maryland

BEEF RED WINE ROULADEN

2 cups mushrooms	3 tablespoons vegetable oil
2 cups chopped white onions	
	½ cup red wine
1 teaspoon chopped parsley	1 bay leaf
	5 peppercorns
½ teaspoon salt	1 to 2 tablespoons cornstarch
½ teaspoon pepper	
4 to 6 pieces top round steak, ⅛ inch thick	1½ tablespoons water

Remove and chop mushroom stems. Combine stems with onions, parsley, salt and pepper in bowl; mix well. Spoon 1 to 2 tablespoons onion mixture onto each portion of beef. Roll to enclose filling; secure with wooden picks. Brown on all sides in hot oil in large skillet over medium heat. Add wine, bay leaf and peppercorns. Simmer for 1 hour. Add remaining onion mixture and mushroom caps. Simmer for 10 minutes; discard bay leaf. Stir in mixture of cornstarch and water. Cook until thickened, stirring constantly. Yield: 4 to 6 servings.

Beverly E. Oldaker, Laureate Alpha Delta
Pueblo, Colorado

MUSHROOM-STUFFED BEEF

2 1½-to 3-pound round steaks, ½ inch thick	1 teaspoon salt
	⅛ teaspoon pepper
	3 tablespoons shortening
8 ounces fresh mushrooms	
½ cup chopped parsley	1 10-ounce can beef consommé
½ cup chopped onion	¼ teaspoon dry mustard
1 cup shredded sharp Cheddar cheese	
	Cooked noodles
¼ cup all-purpose flour	

Cut steak into 6 serving pieces. Pound to ¼-inch thickness with meat mallet. Remove and chop mushroom stems. Combine stems, parsley, onion and cheese in bowl; mix well. Spoon 3 tablespoons onion mixture onto each piece of steak; reserve unused onion mixture. Roll steak to enclose filling. Secure with skewers or wooden picks; tie with string. Coat with mixture of flour, salt and pepper. Brown in shortening in saucepan; drain. Combine consommé and dry mustard in bowl; mix well. Pour over rolls. Add mushroom caps. Simmer, tightly covered, for 45 minutes. Add reserved onion mixture. Simmer for 45 minutes longer or until tender. Serve with noodles. May thicken pan juices with flour if desired. Yield: 6 servings.

Sue Ford, Beta Tau
Pierre, South Dakota

SIMPLY ELEGANT STEAK

1½ pounds boneless round steak, tenderized	1 10-ounce can cream of mushroom soup
1½ tablespoons vegetable oil	½ cup dry sherry
	1½ teaspoons garlic salt
2 large onions, sliced into ½-inch rings	
	3 cups cooked rice
1 4-ounce can sliced mushrooms	

Cut steak into thin strips. Brown in oil in large skillet over high heat. Add onions. Sauté until tender-crisp. Drain mushrooms, reserving liquid. Combine reserved liquid with soup, wine and garlic salt in bowl. Add to skillet with mushrooms. Simmer, covered, for 1 hour. Serve over rice. Yield: 6 servings.

Nicky Huddleston, Kappa Rho
Springfield, Illinois

ROUND STEAK BIRDS

1 round steak, 1/2 inch thick	1/2 teaspoon poultry seasoning
3 tablespoons all-purpose flour	3 tablespoons drippings
1 teaspoon salt	1 cup hot water
1/8 teaspoon pepper	1 beef bouillon cube
1/2 cup chopped onion	1 1/2 tablespoons all-purpose flour
1/2 cup chopped celery	1 1/2 tablespoons water
1 4-ounce can chopped mushrooms	

Remove bone from steak. Pound mixture of 3 tablespoons flour, salt and pepper into steak with meat mallet. Cut into 5 serving pieces. Combine onion, celery, mushrooms and poultry seasoning in bowl; mix well. Spoon about 1/4 cup mixture onto each piece of steak. Roll to enclose filling; secure with wooden picks. Brown in drippings in 9- or 10-inch skillet; drain. Add 1 cup hot water and bouillon cube. Simmer, covered, for 1 1/2 to 2 hours or until tender. Stir in mixture of 1 1/2 tablespoons flour and 1 1/2 tablespoons water. Cook until thickened, stirring constantly. Yield: 5 servings.

Rita M. Ensminger, Preceptor Eta Nu
Garland, Texas

SKILLET BEEF AND GREEN BEANS

1 pound top round steak	1/2 cup water
1 teaspoon vegetable oil	2 teaspoons chopped fresh basil or 1/2 teaspoon dried basil
3 cups sliced red new potatoes	
2 tablespoons chopped onion	1/4 teaspoon salt
1 10-ounce package frozen cut green beans	1/8 teaspoon pepper
	2 tablespoons vinegar
1/2 teaspoon dry mustard	2 teaspoons cornstarch
	2 tablespoons water

Trim steak and cut into thin strips. Heat oil in skillet over medium heat. Add steak. Stir-fry for 2 to 3 minutes or until brown. Remove with slotted spoon. Add potatoes, onion, green beans, dry mustard, 1/2 cup water, basil, salt and pepper to skillet. Simmer, covered, over medium heat for 10 to 12 minutes or until vegetables are tender. Add steak, vinegar and mixture of cornstarch and 2 tablespoons water. Cook until thickened, stirring constantly. Yield: 4 servings.

Joyce Boor, Laureate Kappa
Great Bend, Kansas

STEAK PIE

3 pounds stew beef	2 tablespoons Bisto or gravy mix
8 ounces ground beef	
8 ounces pork sausage	1/4 teaspoon garlic salt
1 small onion, chopped	2 tablespoons all-purpose flour
1 stalk celery, chopped	
3 bay leaves, crushed	1 package puff pastry

Preheat oven to 350 degrees. Combine stew beef and ground beef with water to cover in saucepan. Cook until stew beef is tender. Brown sausage in skillet, stirring frequently. Remove to saucepan. Add onion and celery to drippings in skillet. Sauté until tender. Add to saucepan. Stir in bay leaves, Bisto, garlic salt and mixture of flour and enough water to blend; mix well. Spoon into 9-inch pie plate. Top with puff pastry. Bake for 20 minutes or until brown. Yield: 6 servings.

Linda Walsh, Alpha Omicron
Canmore, Alberta, Canada

STEAK WITH TARRAGON AND MUSHROOM SAUCE

1 tablespoon butter or margarine	5 teaspoons all-purpose flour
1 1/2 cups fresh mushrooms, sliced	1/2 teaspoon tarragon
	2 cups beef stock
2 tablespoons chopped green onions	2 rib-eye steaks

Preheat coals in grill. Melt butter in saucepan. Add mushrooms and green onions. Sauté until tender. Sprinkle with flour and tarragon. Cook for 2 minutes, stirring constantly. Bring beef stock to a boil in small saucepan. Stir into mushroom mixture. Cook for 10 to 20 minutes or until thickened to desired consistency, stirring frequently. Grill steaks over hot coals for 7 minutes on each side. Serve with mushroom sauce. Yield: 2 servings.

Patricia Allaby, Alpha Zeta
Douglastown, New Brunswick, Canada

BARBADOS BEEF STEW

3 pounds 1 1/2-inch beef cubes	1/4 teaspoon pepper
	1/3 cup cider vinegar
1/2 cup all-purpose flour	1/3 cup molasses
2 tablespoons shortening	1 cup water
	6 carrots, chopped
1 28-ounce can tomatoes	1/2 cup raisins
	1/2 teaspoon ginger
2 medium onions, sliced	Cooked rice or mashed potatoes
1 teaspoon celery salt	
1 teaspoon salt	

Shake beef cubes in several batches in flour in bag, coating well. Brown in shortening in heavy saucepan. Add tomatoes, onions, celery salt, salt and pepper. Combine vinegar, molasses and water in bowl; mix well. Stir into saucepan. Add carrots, raisins and ginger. Simmer for 3 hours. Serve over rice or mashed potatoes. Yield: 8 to 10 servings.

Audrey E. McFadyen, Laureate Alpha Alpha
Kingston, Ontario, Canada

OVEN STEW

This is an easy dish to prepare for a New Year's day spent watching football.

1½ to 2 pounds stew beef	1 cup diagonally sliced celery
4 to 6 potatoes, chopped	3 tablespoons tapioca
4 carrots, thickly sliced	1 cup hot water
1 onion, sliced	1 beef bouillon cube
1 head cabbage, cut into large pieces	1 cup tomato juice
1 tablespoon sugar	1½ teaspoons salt
	1 slice bread

Preheat oven to 325 degrees. Combine beef, potatoes, carrots, onion, cabbage, sugar, celery, tapioca, hot water, bouillon cube, tomato juice and salt in bowl; mix well. Spoon into greased baking pan. Crumble bread over top. Bake, covered, for 2½ hours. Serve with French bread. Yield: 6 to 8 servings.

Jan Olson, Xi Gamma Gamma
Sioux City, Iowa

STEPHENSON COUNTY STIR-FRY

10 ounces tofu	2 cups sliced fresh mushrooms
1 cup water	
1 teaspoon instant chicken bouillon	2 tablespoons vegetable oil
1 tablespoon soy sauce	1 teaspoon instant chicken bouillon
6 ounces beef	
6 ounces pork	1 tablespoon soy sauce
2 tablespoons vegetable oil	½ teaspoon Worcestershire sauce
4 cups chopped fresh broccoli	¼ cup red wine vinegar
	⅓ cup sugar
2 cups sliced carrots	2 tablespoons cornstarch
1 cup chopped onion	
1 cup chopped green bell pepper	⅛ teaspoon garlic powder
1 cup chopped celery	Cooked rice

Cut tofu into ½- to 1-inch cubes. Combine with water, 1 teaspoon bouillon and 1 tablespoon soy sauce in bowl; mix gently. Marinate for 6 to 8 hours. Drain, reserving liquid. Cut beef and pork into ½- to 1-inch cubes. Stir-fry beef, pork and tofu in 2 tablespoons oil in wok or skillet. Add broccoli, carrots, onion, green pepper, celery, mushrooms and remaining 2 tablespoons oil if needed. Stir-fry until vegetables are tender-crisp. Combine reserved tofu liquid with 1 teaspoon bouillon, 1 tablespoon soy sauce, Worcestershire sauce, vinegar, sugar, cornstarch and garlic powder in bowl; mix well. Pour into wok. Cook until thickened, stirring constantly. Serve over rice. Yield: 6 servings.

Linda Werkheiser, Xi Lambda Upsilon
Rock Falls, Illinois

BEEF STROGANOFF

1 pound sirloin steak, ¼ inch thick	1 clove of garlic, chopped
3 tablespoons all-purpose flour	1 10-ounce can consommé or bouillon
1 teaspoon paprika	1 cup water
1 teaspoon salt	1 pound fresh mushrooms, sliced
¼ teaspoon pepper	
¼ cup butter or margarine	½ cup sour cream
	2 tablespoons chopped green onions or chives
½ cup finely chopped onion	

Cut steak into 1-by-1½-inch strips. Toss with mixture of flour, paprika, salt and pepper, coating well. Brown steak in butter in heavy skillet. Add onion and garlic. Cook until onion is tender, stirring constantly. Add consommé, water and mushrooms. Simmer, covered, for 1½ hours or until steak is very tender, stirring occasionally. Simmer, uncovered, until thickened to desired consistency. Stir in sour cream and green onions. Serve with noodles, potatoes or rice. May thicken gravy with mixture of water and remaining flour used for coating steak if necessary for desired consistency. Yield: 4 to 5 servings.

Cheryl Byblow, Lambda
Yorkton, Saskatchewan, Canada

HANCH TIPS

¼ cup vegetable oil	¼ teaspoon basil
1 green bell pepper, cut into strips	1 pound 1-inch beef tip cubes
1 medium onion, cut into strips	1 10-ounce can tomato soup
1 clove of garlic, chopped	1 cup water
¼ teaspoon oregano	1 16-ounce can whole tomatoes

Heat oil in 10-inch skillet over medium heat for 5 minutes. Add green pepper, onion and garlic. Sauté until vegetables are tender. Add oregano and basil. Sauté for several minutes. Add beef cubes. Cook until brown on all sides, stirring frequently. Add soup and water. Cut tomatoes into halves. Add tomatoes and juice to skillet. Simmer for 10 minutes. Serve over rice or noodles. Yield: 6 servings.

Chris Hanchey, Nu Epsilon
Mt. Vernon, Ohio

Carol Kay, Xi Eta Delta, Holland Landing, Ontario, Canada, sprinkles a 5-pound brisket with ¼ cup liquid smoke, wraps in foil and bakes in preheated 225-degree oven for 8 hours. After draining, add mixture of 8 ounces barbecue sauce and apricot jam and 1 teaspoon liquid smoke. Rewrap and bake at 325 degrees for 1 hour.

INDIVIDUAL BEEF WELLINGTONS

This was served with a broccoli casserole and consommé rice for our Christmas Progressive Dinner.

2 cups chopped fresh
  mushrooms
1/4 cup margarine
1 tablespoon sherry
4 1-inch filet mignon
  steaks
1/4 cup margarine
1 8-count can crescent
  rolls

Preheat oven to 425 degrees. Cook mushrooms in 1/4 cup margarine and sherry in skillet until liquid is nearly absorbed. Brown steaks lightly on both sides in 1/4 cup margarine in large skillet. Separate roll dough into 4 squares, pressing diagonal perforations to seal. Place spoonful of mushrooms on each square; top with steak. Bring up corners of dough to enclose steak, pressing edges to seal. Place mushroom side up on baking sheet. Bake for 8 to 10 minutes or until golden brown. May broil for several minutes if necessary to complete browning. Yield: 4 servings.

Amy Tayloe, Epsilon Kappa
Elkin, North Carolina

CONEY ISLAND CORNED BEEF

1 1/2 cups shredded
  corned beef
1 1/2 cups shredded
  Cheddar cheese
1 cup chopped stuffed
  olives
6 tablespoons finely
  chopped green onions
1 tablespoon finely
  chopped green bell
  pepper
2/3 cup catsup
4 teaspoons
  Worcestershire sauce
12 hot dog buns

Preheat oven to 300 degrees. Combine corned beef, cheese, olives, green onions, green pepper, catsup and Worcestershire sauce in bowl; mix well. Spoon into buns; wrap individually in foil. Bake for 20 minutes or until sandwiches are heated through and cheese is melted. Yield: 12 servings.

Frances Parks, Laureate Beta Sigma
St. Charles, Missouri

BARBECUED BEEF PATTIES

1 pound ground chuck
1/2 cup oats
2/3 cup evaporated milk
1/4 cup chopped onion
1/4 teaspoon salt
1/8 teaspoon pepper
2/3 cup catsup
1/3 cup water
2 tablespoons vinegar
4 teaspoons sugar
4 teaspoons
  Worcestershire sauce
1/4 cup chopped onion

Preheat oven to 350 degrees. Combine ground chuck, oats, evaporated milk, 1/4 cup onion, salt and pepper in bowl; mix well. Let stand until milk is absorbed. Shape into 6 patties. Brown on both sides in skillet; drain. Remove to baking dish. Combine catsup, water, vinegar, sugar, Worcestershire sauce and 1/4 cup onion in bowl; mix well. Pour over patties. Bake for 1 hour. May simmer for 1 hour if preferred. Yield: 6 servings.

Marilyn Beeman, Xi Kappa
Independence, Kansas

BEEF IN PASTRY

1 package frozen phyllo
  dough
1 1/2 pounds lean ground
  beef
3 potatoes, peeled,
  shredded
2 cups sliced fresh
  mushrooms
2 tomatoes, chopped
1 onion, chopped
1 cup chopped parsley
1 cup Burgundy
1 1/2 teaspoons allspice
1/2 teaspoon garlic
  powder
1 teaspoon salt
1/2 teaspoon pepper
3/4 cup melted margarine
Grated Parmesan cheese

Let phyllo dough stand in refrigerator for 12 hours. Let stand, unopened, for 2 to 4 hours at room temperature. Preheat oven to 350 degrees. Brown ground beef in skillet, stirring until crumbly; drain. Add next 10 ingredients; mix well. Simmer, covered, for 20 to 30 minutes or until liquid is nearly absorbed, stirring frequently. Cut phyllo dough into twelve 8-by-12-inch sheets; cover with towel to prevent drying out. Brush 8-by-12-inch baking dish with margarine. Layer 6 sheets of dough in dish, brushing each sheet with margarine. Spoon beef mixture into prepared dish. Top with remaining 6 sheets dough, brushing each sheet with margarine. Bake for 30 minutes or until golden brown. Sprinkle with cheese. Yield: 8 servings.

Sandra S. Kelley, Pi Zeta
Monticello, Illinois

CABBAGE PATCH STEW

1 pound ground beef
2 medium onions,
  thinly sliced
1 1/2 cups coarsely
  chopped cabbage
1/2 cup chopped celery
1 16-ounce can stewed
  tomatoes
1 cup water
1 16-ounce can kidney
  beans
1 to 2 teaspoons chili
  powder
1 teaspoon salt
1/4 teaspoon pepper
2 cups baking mix
2/3 cup milk

Brown ground beef in heavy saucepan, stirring until crumbly; drain. Add onions, cabbage and celery. Cook until vegetables are lightly browned, stirring constantly. Stir in tomatoes, water, undrained beans, chili powder, salt and pepper. Bring to a boil; reduce heat. Combine baking mix and milk in bowl; mix well. Drop by spoonfuls into simmering mixture. Cook, uncovered, over low heat for 10 minutes. Cook, covered, for 10 minutes longer. Yield: 5 to 6 servings.

Phyllis J. Wagner, Alpha Psi
Pasadena, Maryland

CHEESY BEEF AND PASTA

2 pounds lean ground beef	1 3-ounce can sliced mushrooms
2 tablespoons vegetable oil	1 8-ounce package shell macaroni
2 medium onions, chopped	3 cups sour cream
1 clove of garlic, chopped	8 ounces provolone cheese, sliced
1 14-ounce jar spaghetti sauce	8 ounces mozzarella cheese, thinly sliced
1 16-ounce can stewed tomatoes	

Preheat oven to 350 degrees. Brown ground beef in oil in large deep skillet, stirring until crumbly; drain. Add onions, garlic, spaghetti sauce, tomatoes and undrained mushrooms; mix well. Simmer for 20 minutes or until onions are tender. Cook pasta using package directions; drain and rinse with cold water. Layer half the pasta, half the meat sauce and half the sour cream in deep baking dish. Top with provolone cheese. Repeat layers of pasta, meat sauce and sour cream. Top with mozzarella cheese. Bake, covered, for 35 to 40 minutes. Bake, uncovered, until cheese melts and is golden brown. Yield: 8 servings.

Madeline Bamsey, Laureate Lambda
Sioux Falls, South Dakota

LAZY DAY LASAGNA

1 pound ground beef	2 cups cottage cheese
1 14-ounce can tomatoes	1/4 cup grated Parmesan cheese
1 6-ounce can tomato paste	1 egg
1 cup water	1 tablespoon parsley flakes
1/8 teaspoon garlic powder	8 uncooked lasagna noodles
1 1/2 teaspoons basil	2 cups shredded mozzarella cheese
1/2 teaspoon oregano	
1 1/2 teaspoons salt	

Preheat oven to 350 degrees. Brown ground beef in skillet, stirring until crumbly; drain. Add next 7 ingredients; mix well. Simmer for 15 minutes. Combine cottage cheese, Parmesan cheese, egg and parsley flakes in bowl; mix well. Spread 1 1/2 cups meat sauce in 9-by-11-inch baking dish. Layer 4 uncooked noodles in prepared dish. Add layers of half the cottage cheese mixture, half the mozzarella cheese, 1 cup meat sauce, remaining noodles, remaining cottage cheese mixture, remaining mozzarella cheese and remaining meat sauce. Cover with foil, shiny side down. Bake for 1 hour to 1 hour and 10 minutes or until bubbly. Let stand for 10 to 15 minutes before serving. Yield: 8 servings.

Karen McCune, Xi Gamma Gamma
Sioux City, Iowa

COMPANY'S COMING MEAT LOAF

1 egg	6 slices mozzarella cheese
1 1/2 cups milk	3/4 cup all-purpose flour
12 ounces bread crumbs	1 cup sour cream
1 medium onion, chopped	3 egg yolks
Salt and pepper to taste	Salt and pepper to taste
1 1/2 pounds extra-lean ground beef	3 egg whites, stiffly beaten
2 tomatoes, sliced	

Preheat oven to 350 degrees. Combine 1 egg and milk in bowl. Stir in bread crumbs, onion, salt and pepper; mix well. Add ground beef; mix well. Press into 8-by-8-inch baking dish. Bake for 25 minutes; drain well. Arrange tomato and cheese slices over top. Combine flour, sour cream, egg yolks, salt and pepper in bowl; mix well. Fold in stiffly beaten egg whites. Spoon over meat loaf. Bake for 30 minutes longer. Serve with salad or green vegetable. Yield: 8 servings.

Ruth F. Jacques, Laureate Beta Iota
Burlington, Ontario, Canada

ORIENTAL MEATBALLS

1 1/2 pounds ground beef	1/2 cup chicken stock or bouillon
1 clove of garlic, crushed	Chopped green bell pepper
1 teaspoon salt	3 tablespoons cornstarch
1/4 teaspoon pepper	
2 eggs	
1/4 cup all-purpose flour	1/2 cup sugar
1 teaspoon salt	1/2 cup vinegar
1/4 teaspoon pepper	3 tablespoons soy sauce
1/2 cup vegetable oil	Cooked rice
1 14-ounce can pineapple chunks	

Combine ground beef, garlic, 1 teaspoon salt and 1/4 teaspoon pepper in bowl; mix well. Shape into balls. Combine eggs, flour, 1 teaspoon salt and 1/4 teaspoon pepper in bowl. Beat until smooth, adding enough water to make thin batter. Heat oil in skillet over low heat. Dip meatballs in batter with tongs, shaking off excess. Brown on all sides in oil in skillet, removing to bowl. Drain skillet, reserving 1 tablespoon oil. Drain pineapple, reserving 1/2 cup juice. Stir chicken stock, green pepper and pineapple into skillet. Simmer, covered, for 5 minutes. Add meatballs. Simmer for 3 minutes. Combine cornstarch, sugar, reserved pineapple juice, vinegar and soy sauce in bowl; mix well. Stir into skillet. Cook until thickened, stirring constantly. Serve over rice. May add chopped tomato just before serving. Yield: 6 to 8 servings.

Glenda Spenrath, Alpha Pi
Lloydminster, Alberta, Canada

MEAT LOAF PLUS

1½ pounds lean ground
  beef
1 pound mild or hot
  Italian sausage
1 pound mushrooms,
  thinly sliced
1 medium onion,
  chopped
3 cloves of garlic,
  minced

2 tablespoons butter or
  margarine
¾ cup dry bread crumbs
1 8-ounce can tomato
  sauce
2 eggs
½ teaspoon each basil,
  oregano, salt and
  pepper

Preheat oven to 350 degrees. Combine ground beef and sausage in large bowl; mix well. Sauté mushrooms, onion and garlic in butter in skillet over medium-high heat for 10 to 15 minutes or until onion is tender. Cool slightly. Add to meat mixture. Add bread crumbs, tomato sauce, eggs, basil, oregano, salt and pepper; mix well with hands. Press into 9-by-13-inch baking pan. Bake for 1 hour and 5 minutes to 1 hour and 10 minutes or until done to taste. Yield: 8 to 10 servings.

Carol Zentmire, Xi Alpha Lambda
Lewistown, Montana

BARBECUED MEATBALLS

½ cup molasses
½ cup catsup
½ cup vinegar
10 drops of Tabasco
  sauce
⅛ teaspoon turmeric
1 pound ground beef
1 cup chopped onion

½ cup bread crumbs
¼ cup milk
1 teaspoon MSG
Salt and pepper to taste
All-purpose flour
Vegetable oil for
  browning

Combine molasses, catsup, vinegar, Tabasco sauce and turmeric in large skillet; mix well. Simmer for 10 minutes. Combine ground beef, onion, bread crumbs, milk, MSG, salt and pepper in bowl; mix well. Shape into balls. Coat with flour. Brown in oil in skillet; drain. Add to sauce in skillet. Simmer for 25 minutes. Yield: 5 to 6 servings.

Joan Batsford, Preceptor Zeta
Laval, Quebec, Canada

CRANBERRY MEATBALLS

1 16-ounce bottle of
  chili sauce
2 cups water
1 16-ounce can whole
  cranberry sauce
1 16-ounce can
  sauerkraut

½ cup packed light
  brown sugar
2 pounds ground beef
1 envelope onion soup
  mix
1 cup dry bread crumbs
3 eggs

Preheat oven to 350 degrees. Combine chili sauce, water, cranberry sauce, sauerkraut and brown sugar in saucepan; mix well. Simmer for several minutes. Combine ground beef, soup mix, bread crumbs and

eggs in bowl; mix well. Shape into 20 meatballs. Place in small baking pan. Pour sauce over meatballs. Bake for 2 hours. Yield: 6 servings.

Kristi Warner, Theta
Gillette, Wyoming

MEATBALL CASSEROLE WITH CHILI CHEESE BISCUITS

1 pound ground beef
4 ounces pork sausage
½ cup dry bread crumbs
1 tablespoon chopped
  onion
⅓ cup evaporated milk
1 teaspoon chili powder
⅛ teaspoon pepper

1 10-ounce can cream
  of mushroom soup
1 10-ounce can cream
  of celery soup
1 cup evaporated milk
½ cup water
Chili Cheese Biscuits

Preheat oven to 400 degrees. Combine ground beef, sausage, bread crumbs, onion, ⅓ cup evaporated milk, chili powder and pepper in bowl; mix well. Shape into balls. Brown on all sides in skillet. Cook, covered, for 10 minutes. Place in 2½-quart baking dish. Combine soups, 1 cup evaporated milk and water in saucepan. Heat until steaming, stirring to mix well. Pour over meatballs. Top with Chili Cheese Biscuits. Bake for 20 to 25 minutes or until biscuits are golden brown. Yield: 6 to 8 servings.

CHILI CHEESE BISCUITS

1⅓ cups all-purpose
  flour
1 teaspoon baking
  powder
½ teaspoon chili powder
¼ teaspoon salt
⅓ cup margarine

1 egg
⅓ cup evaporated milk
1½ cups shredded
  American cheese
1 tablespoon parsley
  flakes

Mix flour, baking powder, chili powder and salt in bowl. Cut in shortening until crumbly. Add mixture of egg and evaporated milk; mix to form dough. Knead on lightly floured surface. Roll to 12-by-12-inch square. Sprinkle with cheese and parsley flakes. Roll up to enclose filling. Cut into 1¼-inch slices. Yield: 10 biscuits.

 Marsha Adamson, Preceptor Lambda
Ely, Nevada

Michele L. Thomason, Upsilon Sigma, Brownstown, Illinois, makes Slow-Cooker Barbecued Meatballs by combining 2 pounds ground beef, 2 eggs, one 5-ounce can evaporated milk, 1½ cups bread crumbs, and salt, pepper and garlic salt to taste. Shape into meatballs. Brown in skillet. Combine 1 sautéed chopped onion, 1 large bottle of catsup, juice of 1 lemon, 2 tablespoons each light brown sugar and Worcestershire sauce in slow cooker. Heat on High. Add meatballs. Cook on Low for 3 hours.

PLANTATION STUFFED PEPPERS

8 medium green bell
  peppers
1 pound ground chuck
1 cup chopped onion
1 clove of garlic,
  chopped
2 10-ounce cans
  tomato soup

2 teaspoons chili
  powder
1 teaspoon salt
2 cups shredded sharp
  Cheddar cheese
1½ cups cooked rice

Preheat oven to 350 degrees. Cut tops off peppers; discard seeds and membranes. Parboil peppers; drain well. Brown ground chuck with onion and garlic in skillet, stirring frequently; drain. Stir in soup, chili powder and salt. Simmer, covered, for 10 minutes. Stir in cheese until melted. Add rice; mix well. Cool to room temperature. Spoon into peppers; place in baking dish. Bake for 20 minutes. Yield: 8 servings.

Juanita W. Gray, Xi Omicron
Bluefield, West Virginia

SPICY SHEPHERD'S PIE

½ cup minced onion
½ cup finely chopped
  celery
2 tablespoons vegetable
  oil
1½ pounds lean ground
  beef
½ cup beef broth
1 cup grated carrot
1 clove of garlic, crushed
2 tablespoons
  Worcestershire sauce

½ teaspoon rosemary
¼ teaspoon salt
½ teaspoon freshly
  ground pepper
6 servings prepared
  instant mashed
  potatoes or 4 large
  potatoes, cooked and
  mashed
Melted butter or
  margarine
Paprika to taste

Preheat oven to 375 degrees. Sauté onion and celery in oil in skillet. Add ground beef. Cook until brown and crumbly; drain. Add beef broth, carrot, garlic, Worcestershire sauce, rosemary, salt and pepper; mix well. Simmer for 30 minutes. Spoon into 8-by-8-inch baking dish or deep pie plate. Top with mashed potatoes. Brush with melted butter; sprinkle with paprika. Bake for 35 to 45 minutes or until heated through. Yield: 6 servings.

Rita McLean, Preceptor Beta Xi
Nanaimo, British Columbia, Canada

UPSIDE-DOWN BEEF PIE

¼ cup chopped onion
2 tablespoons
  shortening
1½ pounds ground beef
2 10-ounce cans
  tomato soup
½ teaspoon salt
1½ cups all-purpose
  flour

1 tablespoon baking
  powder
1 teaspoon paprika
1 teaspoon celery salt
½ teaspoon salt
¼ teaspoon white
  pepper
3 tablespoons shortening
¾ cup milk

Preheat oven to 475 degrees. Sauté onion in 2 tablespoons shortening in 9-inch ovenproof skillet until tender. Add ground beef. Cook until light brown and crumbly; drain. Stir in tomato soup and ½ teaspoon salt. Sift flour, baking powder, paprika, celery salt, ½ teaspoon salt and pepper into bowl. Add 3 tablespoons shortening; work in with fork. Stir in milk. Spread over beef mixture. Bake for 20 minutes or until brown. Invert onto large platter. Yield: 4 to 6 servings.

Eleanor Kartlick, Preceptor Alpha Eta
Shippensburg, Pennsylvania

POOR MAN'S FILET

2 pounds ground chuck
Lemon pepper to taste
Grated Parmesan
  cheese to taste
1 green bell pepper,
  chopped

1 4-ounce can chopped
  mushrooms
6 to 10 slices bacon

Preheat grill. Pat ground chuck into large rectangle on foil. Sprinkle with lemon pepper and cheese. Spread green pepper and mushrooms over ground beef; press in gently. Roll to enclose vegetables. Cut into slices the width of bacon. Wrap slices with bacon; secure with wooden picks. Grill until done to taste. Yield: 6 to 10 servings.

Elizabeth Hiller, Gamma Zeta
McCune, Kansas

SPAGHETTI SAUCE

1 pound ground beef
1 pound ground pork
1 pound ground veal
1 cup chopped onion
1 cup chopped celery
1 cup chopped carrots
2 green bell peppers,
  chopped
1 16-ounce bottle of
  chili sauce
2 10-ounce cans
  tomato soup
1 28-ounce can
  tomatoes
1 13-ounce can tomato
  paste

2 to 6 tablespoons steak
  sauce
2 tablespoons
  Worcestershire sauce
Tabasco sauce to taste
4 to 5 cloves of garlic,
  minced
1 tablespoon sugar
4 bay leaves
1 teaspoon thyme
1 teaspoon sage
½ teaspoon marjoram
¼ teaspoon allspice
Salt and pepper to taste

Brown ground beef, ground pork and ground veal in heavy saucepan, stirring until crumbly; drain. Add onion, celery, carrots, green peppers and remaining ingredients; mix well. Simmer for 1 hour or longer. Remove bay leaves. May use 2 to 4 tablespoons H.P. Sauce for part of the steak sauce. Yield: 12 to 15 servings.

Lois McGibbon, Xi Nu
Petitcodiac, New Brunswick, Canada

SPINACH FANDANGO

1¼ pounds lean ground round	½ teaspoon pepper
1 medium onion, chopped	¼ cup vegetable oil
1 11-ounce can sliced mushrooms	1½ 10-ounce packages frozen chopped spinach
2 cloves of garlic, chopped	1 10-ounce can cream of celery soup
1 teaspoon oregano	1¼ cups sour cream
⅛ to ¼ teaspoon salt	Sliced mozzarella or Monterey Jack cheese
	Paprika

Preheat oven to 350 degrees. Brown ground beef with onion, mushrooms, garlic, oregano, salt and pepper in oil in large skillet, stirring frequently; drain. Place frozen spinach on top of ground beef mixture. Steam, covered, until spinach can be stirred into ground beef. Stir in soup and sour cream. Spoon into medium baking dish. Bake for 20 to 25 minutes or until bubbly. Top with cheese slices; sprinkle with paprika. Broil until cheese is bubbly.
Yield: 6 to 8 servings.

Sue Clapp, Lambda Kappa
Charleston, Arkansas

GROUND BEEF STROGANOFF

1 pound ground beef	¼ teaspoon pepper
1 medium onion, chopped	1 tablespoon all-purpose flour
¼ cup margarine	1 10-ounce can beef broth
3 tablespoons all-purpose flour	2 tablespoons catsup
1 clove of garlic, minced	1 10-ounce can cream of chicken soup
1 8-ounce can mushrooms	1 cup sour cream
1 teaspoon salt	4 cups cooked noodles

Brown ground beef with onion in margarine in skillet, stirring frequently; drain. Stir in 3 tablespoons flour, garlic, mushrooms, salt and pepper. Cook for 5 minutes. Blend 1 tablespoon flour with ⅓ cup of the beef broth. Add remaining beef broth and catsup to skillet. Stir in broth and flour mixture. Cook until bubbly, stirring constantly. Cook for 1 minute longer. Stir in soup and sour cream. Cook just until heated through. Serve over noodles. Yield: 4 servings.

Diana L. Kindred, Xi Eta Chi
Morton, Illinois

HAMBURGER WELLINGTON

1 egg	¼ cup hamburger relish
2 pounds lean ground beef	1 teaspoon Worcestershire sauce
1 cup sour cream	1½ teaspoons salt
½ cup dry whole wheat bread crumbs	⅛ teaspoon pepper
¼ cup finely chopped onion	2 cups baking mix
	1 cup whipping cream

Preheat oven to 425 degrees. Beat egg slightly in bowl. Add next 8 ingredients; mix well. Shape into 12-inch roll. Combine baking mix with whipping cream in bowl; mix well. Knead 10 times on lightly floured surface. Roll into 12-by-12-inch square. Place ground beef roll on dough. Wrap dough to enclose ground beef; moisten edges and press to seal. Place seam side down in 9-by-13-inch baking dish. Cut several vents in top. Bake for 10 minutes. Reduce oven temperature to 325 degrees. Bake for 1 hour longer. Yield: 6 to 8 servings.

Susan Harvey, Gamma Mu
Kennewick, Washington

TAGLIARINI

1 pound lean ground beef	¼ cup olive juice
1 medium onion, chopped	1 teaspoon garlic powder
1 28-ounce can peeled tomatoes	¼ teaspoon salt
1 15-ounce can cream-style corn	¼ teaspoon black pepper
½ teaspoon dried hot peppers	12 ounces uncooked small noodles
½ cup green olives	1 pound longhorn or Colby cheese, shredded
	Grated Parmesan cheese
	Hot pepper sauce

Brown ground beef with onion in large saucepan, stirring frequently; drain. Add next 8 ingredients; mix well. Simmer for 35 to 45 minutes or to desired consistency, stirring frequently. Cook noodles using package directions; drain. Add to ground beef mixture. Simmer for 15 minutes. Stir in longhorn cheese until melted. Top servings with Parmesan cheese and pepper sauce. Yield: 6 to 10 servings.

Debbie Larimore, Xi Delta Tau
Dove Creek, Colorado

STUFFED ZUCCHINI

4 8-inch zucchini	1 medium clove of garlic, minced
8 ounces ground beef	¾ cup bread crumbs
8 ounces Italian sausage	¼ cup chopped onion
½ cup ricotta cheese	1 egg
½ cup shredded mozzarella cheese	1 tablespoon basil
¼ cup grated Parmesan cheese	1 medium jar spaghetti sauce

Preheat oven to 375 degrees. Cut zucchini into halves lengthwise. Scoop out pulp, leaving shells; reserve 1 cup pulp. Combine reserved pulp with ground beef and next 9 ingredients in bowl; mix well. Spoon into zucchini shells; place in large baking dish. Bake for 30 minutes. Heat spaghetti sauce in saucepan until bubbly. Spoon over zucchini. Serve immediately.
Yield: 8 servings.

Linda Davis, Xi Omega Psi
Waco, Texas

ALL-IN-ONE CASSEROLE

3 cups hot mashed
  potatoes
1/2 cup shredded
  Cheddar cheese
1 3-ounce can French-
  fried onions
1 1/2 cups chopped
  cooked ham
1 10-ounce package
  frozen broccoli,
  thawed, drained

1 10-ounce can cream
  of mushroom soup
1/4 cup milk
1/2 teaspoon dry
  mustard
1/4 teaspoon garlic
  powder
1/4 teaspoon pepper
1/2 cup shredded
  Cheddar cheese

Preheat oven to 375 degrees. Combine potatoes, 1/2 cup cheese and half the onions in bowl; mix well. Press over bottom and side of greased 1 1/2-quart baking dish. Combine ham, broccoli, soup, milk, dry mustard, garlic powder and pepper in bowl; mix well. Spoon into prepared dish. Bake for 30 minutes. Top with remaining onions and 1/2 cup cheese. Bake for 3 minutes longer. Let stand for 5 minutes before serving. Yield: 4 to 6 servings.

Dorothy J. Christiansen, Upsilon Kappa
Inverness, Florida

CHRISTMAS MORNING BREAKFAST

16 slices white or whole
  wheat bread
Thin slices of ham or
  back bacon
Thin slices of sharp
  Cheddar cheese
6 eggs
1/2 teaspoon salt
1/4 teaspoon pepper
1/2 teaspoon dry
  mustard

1/4 cup chopped onion
1/4 cup chopped green
  bell pepper
3 cups milk
Tabasco sauce to taste
1 1/2 teaspoons
  Worcestershire sauce
1/2 cup melted butter or
  margarine
Cornflake crumbs

Trim crusts from bread. Arrange 8 slices in 9-by-13-inch baking dish. Layer ham and cheese over bread. Top with remaining bread. Beat eggs with salt and pepper in bowl. Add next 6 ingredients; mix well. Pour over layers. Chill, covered, overnight. Preheat oven to 350 degrees. Drizzle butter over casserole; sprinkle with cornflake crumbs. Bake for 1 hour. Let stand for several minutes before serving. Yield: 8 servings.

Carol R. Munro, Xi Nu
Petitcodiac, New Brunswick, Canada

HAM AND CHEESE CASSEROLE

1 8-ounce package
  medium noodles
1/2 cup chopped onion
1/2 cup chopped green
  bell pepper
2 tablespoons butter or
  margarine

1 10-ounce can cream
  of mushroom soup
1 cup sour cream
2 cups shredded cheese
2 cups chopped cooked
  ham

Preheat oven to 350 degrees. Cook noodles using package directions; drain. Sauté onion and green pepper in butter in 1-quart saucepan; remove from heat. Stir in soup and sour cream. Layer 1/3 of the noodles, 1/3 of the cheese and 1/3 of the ham in buttered 3-quart baking dish. Spread half the soup mixture over layers. Repeat layers and soup mixture. Top with remaining noodles, ham and cheese. Bake for 30 to 45 minutes or until heated through. Yield: 6 to 8 servings.

Beverly Clouse, Alpha
West Fargo, North Dakota

HAM AND BROCCOLI ROYALE

1 cup uncooked rice
2 10-ounce packages
  frozen chopped broccoli
2 cups finely chopped
  onions
1/4 cup butter or
  margarine
3 tablespoons
  all-purpose flour
1 teaspoon salt

1/4 teaspoon pepper
3 cups milk
4 cups chopped cooked
  ham
8 ounces American
  cheese, sliced
2 cups fresh bread
  crumbs
2 tablespoons melted
  butter or margarine

Cook rice using package directions. Spread in greased 9-by-13-inch baking dish. Cook broccoli using package directions; drain well. Arrange in single layer over rice. Sauté onions in 1/4 cup butter in skillet. Stir in flour, salt and pepper. Cook until bubbly, stirring constantly. Stir in milk. Cook until thickened, stirring constantly. Cook for 1 minute longer. Stir in ham. Cook until bubbly. Spoon over broccoli. Arrange cheese slices over ham mixture. Top with mixture of bread crumbs and 2 tablespoons butter. Chill in refrigerator. Preheat oven to 350 degrees. Bake for 45 minutes or until topping is golden brown. Yield: 6 to 8 servings.

Nancy Conroy, Preceptor Kappa
Des Moines, Iowa

HAM LOAVES

3 1/2 pounds ground ham
2 pounds ground beef
1 pound ground sausage
3 cups graham cracker
  crumbs
3 eggs
2 cups milk

1 10-ounce can tomato
  soup
1 tablespoon prepared
  mustard
1 1/2 cups packed light
  brown sugar
1/2 cup vinegar

Preheat oven to 250 degrees. Combine ground ham, ground beef, sausage, cracker crumbs, eggs and milk in bowl; mix well. Shape into 2 loaves. Place close together in 9-by-13-inch baking dish. Combine soup, mustard, brown sugar and vinegar in bowl; mix well. Pour over loaves. Bake for 2 hours. Yield: 20 to 30 servings.

Joan Sothan, Laureate Delta
Lincoln, Nebraska

HAM CROQUETTES

1/4 cup butter or
  margarine
6 tablespoons
  all-purpose flour
2 cups milk
2 cups chopped cooked
  ham
1 teaspoon chopped
  parsley
1/2 teaspoon chopped
  onion

1/2 teaspoon chopped
  green bell pepper
1/4 teaspoon paprika
1/4 teaspoon salt
1 1/2 cups crumbs
1 egg or 2 egg yolks
3 tablespoons cold
  water
Vegetable oil for deep
  frying

Melt butter in saucepan. Blend in flour. Stir in milk. Cook until thickened, stirring constantly. Add ham, parsley, onion, green pepper, paprika and salt; mix well. Cool to room temperature. Shape mixture into croquettes. Roll in crumbs. Dip in mixture of egg and water; coat with crumbs again. Chill in refrigerator. Deep-fry in hot oil until brown. Yield: 4 servings.

Ronda Jo McLean, Beta Kappa
Meeteetse, Wyoming

MICROWAVE HAM MEAL-IN-ONE

3 ounces sliced ham
1 medium potato, sliced
  1/8 inch thick
1/2 medium zucchini,
  sliced 1/4 inch thick
1/2 medium yellow
  squash, sliced 1/4 inch
  thick

1/2 medium red bell
  pepper, cut into 1-inch
  squares
1 tablespoon lemon juice
1/2 teaspoon basil
1/4 teaspoon red pepper
  flakes
Salt and pepper to taste

Cut 15-by-15-inch piece of nonstick microwave cooking paper. Layer ham, potato, zucchini, squash and bell pepper on paper. Sprinkle with lemon juice, basil, red pepper, salt and pepper. Fold paper over layers, tucking in ends. Microwave on High for 5 minutes. Let stand for 3 minutes. Yield: 1 serving.

Helen Ables, Beta Alpha
Mt. Vernon, Ohio

GOLDEN HAM PIE WITH CHEESE BISCUITS

3 tablespoons chopped
  onion
1/4 cup chopped green
  bell pepper
1 tablespoon shortening
6 tablespoons
  all-purpose flour

2 cups milk
1 10-ounce can cream
  of chicken soup
2 cups chopped cooked
  ham
1 tablespoon lemon juice
Cheese Biscuits

Preheat oven to 250 degrees. Sauté onion and green pepper in shortening in saucepan. Stir in flour; add milk and soup. Cook until thickened, stirring constantly; remove from heat. Stir in ham and lemon juice. Spoon into 9-by-13-inch baking dish. Bake until heated through. Top with biscuits. Bake for 10 minutes longer or until biscuits are golden brown. Yield: 6 servings.

CHEESE BISCUITS

1 cup all-purpose flour
1 1/2 teaspoons baking
  powder
1/2 teaspoon salt
2 1/2 tablespoons
  shortening

3/4 cup shredded
  Cheddar cheese
1/2 cup milk

Sift flour, baking powder and salt into bowl. Cut in shortening and cheese. Add milk; mix well. Roll on floured surface; cut into circles. Yield: 6 biscuits.

Linda K. Thompson, Xi Alpha Kappa
Clarksville, Arkansas

HAM AND SPAGHETTI QUICHE

1 8-ounce package
  spaghetti
1 cup chopped cooked
  ham
1 cup chopped green bell
  pepper
1 cup chopped zucchini

4 eggs
2 cups milk
1/2 cup grated Parmesan
  cheese
1 teaspoon salt
1/8 teaspoon pepper

Cook spaghetti in boiling salted water for 5 minutes; drain well. Add ham, green pepper and zucchini; toss to mix well. Spoon into greased 12-inch quiche dish. Chill, covered, for up to 2 days. Preheat oven to 325 degrees. Beat eggs with milk, cheese, salt and pepper in bowl. Pour over spaghetti mixture. Bake for 50 minutes or until light brown and edges are set. Let stand for 10 minutes. Cut into wedges. Yield: 8 servings.

Alice Ackley, Xi Eta Rho
Cerritos, California

FRANKFURTERS PAPRIKA

1 cup minced onion
2 tablespoons butter or
  margarine
1 teaspoon vegetable oil
1 cup hot water
1 beef bouillon cube
1 large green pepper,
  chopped
4 teaspoons paprika
8 frankfurters

Dillseed to taste
Caraway seed to taste
  (optional)
1/4 teaspoon salt
1/8 teaspoon pepper
2 medium tomatoes,
  chopped
Rice, buttered noodles
  or mashed potatoes
Green pepper rings

Sauté onion in butter and oil in large skillet. Add hot water, bouillon cube, chopped green pepper and paprika. Simmer for 3 to 4 minutes. Add frankfurters, dillseed, caraway seed, salt and pepper. Simmer for 8 to 10 minutes. Stir in tomatoes. Cook for 2 minutes longer. Serve with rice, buttered noodles or mashed potatoes. Garnish with green pepper rings. Yield: 4 servings.

Helen F. Nielsen, Laureate Lambda
Salmon, Idaho

RED HOT APPLE WIENERS

4 wieners, chopped	1 cup chopped apple
1/2 cup shredded cheese	Butter or margarine
2 teaspoons chopped onion	Mustard
1/4 cup catsup	8 hot dog buns

Preheat oven to 350 degrees. Combine wieners, cheese, onion, catsup and apple in bowl; mix well. Spread butter and mustard on hot dog buns. Spoon wiener mixture into buns; wrap individually in foil. Bake for 20 minutes. Yield: 8 servings.

Judy Pratt
Estevan, Saskatchewan, Canada

LEG OF LAMB WITH PINEAPPLE AND PEACHES

This makes a special Easter dinner.

1 leg of lamb	1/2 teaspoon whole cloves
Onion salt and pepper to taste	3/4 cup currant jelly
1 20-ounce can sliced pineapple	1 1/2 teaspoons aromatic bitters
1 16-ounce can sliced peaches	Parsley

Preheat oven to 325 degrees. Sprinkle lamb with onion salt and pepper. Place on rack in shallow roasting pan. Roast for 25 to 30 minutes per pound or to 140 degrees on meat thermometer for medium rare. Drain pineapple and peaches, reserving pineapple juice and 1/2 cup peach juice. Combine reserved juices with cloves in saucepan. Boil for 2 minutes. Add jelly and bitters. Simmer for 10 minutes. Place 8 pineapple slices in baking pan. Place 2 peach slices on each pineapple slice. Bake for 5 minutes. Chop remaining fruit. Stir into hot sauce. Place lamb on serving platter. Arrange pineapple slices around lamb. Garnish with parsley. Serve with sauce. Yield: 8 servings.

Mildred Burns, Alpha Master
Alamosa, Colorado

MARINATED BROILED LAMB CHOPS

3 tablespoons lemon juice	2 tablespoons olive oil
2 tablespoons honey	1 teaspoon minced garlic
2 tablespoons red wine vinegar	2 teaspoons oregano
10 tablespoons vegetable oil	1 teaspoon rosemary
	1 teaspoon salt
	6 1-inch lamb chops
	Jalapeño pepper jelly

Combine lemon juice, honey, vinegar, vegetable oil, olive oil, garlic, oregano, rosemary and salt in shallow dish. Add lamb chops, turning to coat well. Marinate in refrigerator overnight, turning occasionally. Preheat broiler. Drain lamb chops, reserving marinade. Place chops on rack in broiler pan. Broil for 5 to 7 minutes on each side or until done to taste. Baste with reserved marinade. Serve with jelly. Yield: 6 servings.

Patricia A. Dubois, Xi Alpha Tau
Sanford, Maine

MAKE-AHEAD EGGS BENEDICT

4 English muffins, split, toasted	1/2 teaspoon nutmeg
16 thin slices Canadian bacon	1/8 teaspoon pepper
	2 cups milk
8 eggs, poached	2 cups shredded Swiss cheese
1/4 cup butter or margarine	1/2 cup dry white wine
1/4 cup all-purpose flour	1/2 cup cornflake crumbs
1 teaspoon paprika	1 tablespoon melted butter or margarine

Arrange muffins cut side up in 9-by-13-inch baking dish. Place 2 slices Canadian bacon on each muffin; top with eggs. Melt 1/4 cup butter in saucepan. Stir in flour, paprika, nutmeg and pepper. Add milk all at once. Cook until thickened, stirring constantly. Stir in cheese until melted. Add wine. Spoon carefully over muffins. Sprinkle with mixture of cornflakes and 1 tablespoon butter. Chill, covered, overnight. Preheat oven to 375 degrees. Bake casserole for 20 to 25 minutes or until heated through. Yield: 8 servings.

Ginger Burrell, Xi Beta Gamma
Monmouth, Illinois

BARBECUED PORK

1 pork roast	1/2 teaspoon salt
1 3/4 cups vinegar	1 1/2 teaspoons cayenne pepper
1/4 teaspoon Worcestershire sauce	1/2 teaspoon red chili pepper
3/4 cup dill pickle juice	2 teaspoons pepper
1/8 teaspoon dry mustard	3 tablespoons vegetable oil
1/4 teaspoon nutmeg	1 cup catsup
1/8 teaspoon cinnamon	8 hamburger buns
1/2 teaspoon celery salt	

Preheat oven to 350 degrees. Roast pork in roasting pan until tender and done to taste. Shred or chop pork; place in shallow baking dish. Reduce oven temperature to 275 degrees. Combine vinegar, Worcestershire sauce, pickle juice, dry mustard, nutmeg, cinnamon, celery salt, salt, cayenne pepper, chili pepper and pepper in saucepan. Simmer for several minutes. Stir in oil and catsup. Spoon over pork. Bake for 2 hours. Serve on hamburger buns with coleslaw and baked beans. Yield: 10 servings.

Diane Sanderfer, Laureate Tau
Silverton, Idaho

BARBECUED PORK CHOPS

8 1-inch loin or shoulder pork chops	1 medium onion, sliced
1 8-ounce can tomato sauce	1 clove of garlic, crushed
½ cup catsup	½ teaspoon Tabasco sauce
¼ cup vinegar	½ cup water
1 tablespoon prepared mustard	⅛ teaspoon cloves
	1 teaspoon celery seed
	1 teaspoon salt

Preheat oven to 350 degrees. Trim fat from pork chops. Render fat in skillet. Add pork chops. Cook for 10 minutes or until brown; drain. Arrange pork chops in single layer in 9-by-13-inch baking dish. Combine remaining ingredients in skillet; mix well. Cook until heated through, stirring to deglaze skillet. Pour over pork chops. Bake for 1 hour and 15 minutes. Yield: 8 servings.

Betty J. Buckles, Laureate Phi
Phoenix, Arizona

FALL PORK CHOPS

6 ½-inch pork chops	1 teaspoon salt
1½ cups apple cider or apple juice	6 pitted prunes
1 tablespoon sugar	12 dried apricot halves
¼ teaspoon curry powder	2 tablespoons cornstarch
	2 tablespoons water

Preheat electric skillet to 325 degrees. Brown pork chops on both sides. Combine next 4 ingredients in bowl; mix well. Pour over pork chops. Spread prunes and apricots over chops. Simmer, covered, for 1 hour or until done to taste. Remove chops and fruit to serving platter. Stir mixture of cornstarch and water into pan juices. Cook until thickened, stirring constantly. Pour over chops. Yield: 6 servings.

Margaret Palmtag, Laureate Alpha Lambda
West Grove, Pennsylvania

PORK CHOP LOAF

6 large pork chops	3 tablespoons chopped parsley
3 tablespoons butter or margarine	¾ teaspoon salt
¾ cup chopped celery	½ teaspoon pepper
¾ cup chopped onion	Candied apple rings
3 cups day-old bread cubes	

Preheat oven to 325 degrees. Cook pork chops in butter in skillet until tender but not brown. Combine celery, onion, bread cubes, parsley, salt and pepper in bowl; mix well. Arrange pork chops on end in loaf pan, spooning stuffing mixture between chops; begin and end with pork chop. Bake for 1 hour. Garnish with candied apple rings. Yield: 6 servings.

Rebecca Currence, Zeta Gamma
Parkersburg, West Virginia

PORK CHOPS WITH ORANGE STUFFING

I served this at our chapter Christmas party last year. It is easy to prepare in advance and bake while you attend to the other details of a dinner party.

1 cup chopped onion	6 double pork chops with pockets
¼ cup margarine	¼ cup packed light brown sugar
1¼ cups water	1 teaspoon Worcestershire sauce
1 6-ounce can frozen orange juice concentrate	½ teaspoon dry mustard
1 8-ounce package stuffing mix	
¼ teaspoon sage	

Preheat oven to 325 degrees. Sauté onion in margarine in small skillet for 2 to 3 minutes. Stir in water and ¼ cup orange juice concentrate. Bring to a boil. Pour over stuffing mix and sage in bowl; mix well. Spoon into pockets in pork chops. Arrange in large baking dish. Pack remaining stuffing between chops. Bake, loosely covered with foil, for 1½ hours. Combine remaining orange juice concentrate with brown sugar, Worcestershire sauce and dry mustard in saucepan. Heat until brown sugar dissolves. Spoon over pork chops. Bake, uncovered, for 30 minutes longer. Yield: 6 servings.

Mary Skinner, Xi Rho Sigma
Morro Bay, California

TOMATO PORK CHOPS

6 pork chops	1 19-ounce can tomatoes
1 teaspoon vegetable oil	1 tablespoon light brown sugar
½ teaspoon oregano	6 green bell pepper rings
½ teaspoon salt	¼ cup grated Parmesan cheese
Freshly ground pepper to taste	
6 large onion slices	

Preheat oven to 350 degrees. Brown pork chops on both sides in lightly oiled skillet. Place in shallow baking dish. Sprinkle with oregano, salt and pepper. Top with onion. Pour tomatoes over top; sprinkle with brown sugar. Bake, covered, for 1 hour. Top with pepper rings and cheese. Bake, uncovered, for 15 minutes longer. Yield: 6 servings.

Lynda Parsons, Xi Alpha Epsilon
Whitecourt, Alberta, Canada

Helene Cable, Laureate Gamma, Charlotte, North Carolina, marinates pork chops in mixture of 3 tablespoons each lemon juice, olive oil and soy sauce, crushed garlic, ¼ teaspoon pepper, ½ teaspoon salt and herbs to taste. Chill in refrigerator for 6 hours or longer before grilling or broiling.

FRUIT-STUFFED PORK LOIN ROAST

3/4 cup chopped prunes	2 teaspoons cider
3/4 cup chopped dried	vinegar
apricots	1/4 cup packed light
1 tablespoon grated	brown sugar
gingerroot	2 teaspoons all-purpose
1 teaspoon grated	flour
orange rind	1 teaspoon dry mustard
1/2 teaspoon cinnamon	1 teaspoon cumin
1/2 teaspoon cumin	1/2 cup water
Salt and pepper to taste	1 teaspoon cornstarch
1 4-pound pork loin	Cold water
roast	

Preheat oven to 325 degrees. Combine prunes, apricots, gingerroot, orange rind, cinnamon, 1/2 teaspoon cumin, salt and pepper in bowl; mix well. Split roast lengthwise, leaving 1 side intact. Spoon fruit mixture into roast; secure halves with string. Place in roasting pan. Combine vinegar, brown sugar, flour, dry mustard and 1 teaspoon cumin in small bowl; mix well. Spread over roast. Bake for 1 1/2 hours or until done to taste, basting occasionally with pan juices. Remove roast to warm platter. Skim grease from pan juices. Add 1/2 cup water to roasting pan, stirring to deglaze. Stir in mixture of cornstarch and a small amount of cold water. Cook on stove top for 1 minute or until thickened to desired consistency, stirring occasionally. May strain if desired. Serve with roast. Yield: 8 servings.

Alice Malachowski, Laureate Omicron
Port Alberni, British Columbia, Canada

PORK POT ROAST

1 3- to 5-pound pork	1 large onion, cut into 4
roast	to 6 wedges
2 cups water	1 tablespoon sugar
1/4 cup sherry	Cooked rice
1 cup soy sauce	
3 or 4 1-inch pieces	
gingerroot	

Combine pork roast and water in heavy saucepan. Bring water to a boil. Add wine, soy sauce, gingerroot and onion; reduce heat. Simmer, covered, for 2 hours, turning roast after 1 hour. Turn roast; sprinkle with sugar. Simmer for 30 minutes longer or until tender enough to fall apart. Serve over rice. Yield: 6 servings.

Mildred L. Siders, Preceptor Beta Delta
Jacksonville, Florida

MARINATED PORK TENDERLOINS

1/4 cup Burgundy	1/2 teaspoon minced
1/2 cup corn oil	garlic
1/4 cup soy sauce	2 or 3 pork tenderloins
2 tablespoons catsup	

Combine wine, oil, soy sauce, catsup and garlic in glass dish. Slice tenderloins as desired. Add to marinade. Marinate in refrigerator overnight; drain. Preheat grill. Grill pork for 2 to 3 minutes on each side or until done to taste. Yield: 4 to 6 servings.

Carlette Rhea Machan, Xi Gamma Gamma
Sioux City, Iowa

PORK SCHNITZEL

6 pork tenderloin cutlets	1 teaspoon paprika
1/4 cup all-purpose flour	1 tablespoon shortening
1 teaspoon seasoned salt	3/4 cup chicken broth
1/4 teaspoon pepper	1 teaspoon all-purpose
1 egg, beaten	flour
2 teaspoons milk	1/2 cup sour cream
3/4 cup dry bread crumbs	1/4 teaspoon dillweed

Pound pork 1/8 to 1/4 inch thick with meat mallet. Cut small slits in edges. Coat with mixture of 1/4 cup flour, seasoned salt and pepper. Dip in mixture of egg and milk. Coat with mixture of bread crumbs and paprika. Cook 3 at a time in shortening in large skillet for 2 to 3 minutes on each side. Remove to warm platter. Add broth to skillet, stirring to deglaze. Stir in 1 teaspoon flour, sour cream and dillweed. Cook until thickened, stirring constantly; do not boil. Serve with cutlets. Yield: 6 servings.

Erin Silva, Alpha Omega
Springerville, Arizona

TOURTIÈRE (Pork Pie)

This is served at a traditional French Canadian Christmas Eve dinner.

1 onion, chopped	1/4 teaspoon pepper
1/2 clove of garlic,	Mace, savory and/or
crushed	sage to taste
2 tablespoons bacon	2 tablespoons chopped
drippings	parsley
1 1/2 pounds ground pork	1 recipe 2-crust pie
3/4 cup broth or bouillon	pastry
1 teaspoon salt	2 tablespoons cream

Preheat oven to 425 degrees. Sauté onion and garlic in bacon drippings in saucepan until light brown. Add ground pork. Cook until light brown, stirring until crumbly; drain. Stir in broth, salt and pepper. Cook for 10 minutes or until liquid is nearly absorbed. Add mace, savory, sage and parsley. Cool to room temperature. Spoon into pastry-lined 9-inch deep-dish pie plate. Top with remaining pastry; seal edges and cut vents. Brush with cream. Bake for 20 minutes. Reduce oven temperature to 350 degrees. Bake for 20 to 30 minutes longer or until golden brown. Serve warm or cold. Yield: 6 servings.

Sue Robbins, Preceptor Delta Kappa
Rockwood, Ontario, Canada

SWEET AND SOUR SPARERIBS

2 pounds spareribs
1 cup packed light
  brown sugar
1 tablespoon chili
  powder
1 tablespoon salt
1 tablespoon celery seed
1 teaspoon paprika
1 12-ounce can tomato
  juice
1/2 cup vinegar

Preheat oven to 350 degrees. Cut ribs into serving pieces. Cook in water to cover for 30 minutes; drain. Place in baking dish. Combine brown sugar, chili powder, salt, celery seed, paprika, tomato juice and vinegar in bowl; mix well. Pour over ribs. Bake for 1 1/2 to 2 hours or until done to taste. Yield: 4 servings.

Elizabeth McDonald, Xi Phi
Melville, Saskatchewan, Canada

BARBECUED SPARERIBS

24 pounds spareribs
3 tablespoons dry
  mustard
3 tablespoons water
4 cups tomato purée
2 cups vinegar
1 cup corn oil
1 cup packed light
  brown sugar
1 cup minced onion
1 tablespoon minced
  garlic
6 tablespoons salt

Preheat oven to 375 degrees. Place spareribs in 3 large baking pans. Bake for 1 1/2 hours; drain. Combine dry mustard with water in saucepan. Let stand for 10 minutes. Add tomato purée, vinegar, oil, brown sugar, onion, garlic and salt. Simmer for 10 minutes. Spoon over spareribs. Bake for 30 minutes longer. Yield: 48 servings.

Sabina I. Beckett, Laureate Alpha Kappa
Milwaukie, Oregon

BAKED SAUSAGE CASSEROLE

1 1/2 pounds sweet
  Italian sausage
1 red bell pepper, sliced
1 green bell pepper,
  sliced
1 small onion, chopped
2 medium potatoes, cut
  into chunks
1 28-ounce can
  tomatoes, chopped
1 tablespoon sweet basil
Salt and pepper to taste

Preheat oven to 350 degrees. Cut sausage into 2-inch pieces. Combine with bell peppers, onion, potatoes, undrained tomatoes, basil, salt and pepper in bowl; mix well. Spoon into 3-quart baking dish. Bake for 1 hour and 15 minutes. Yield: 6 servings.

Michaelene Campana, Preceptor Gamma Epsilon
Monessen, Pennsylvania

Susan Konen, Lambda, Walla Walla, Washington, simmers mixture of 1 cup packed light brown sugar, 1 cup catsup and 1 can beer in saucepan. Simmer for 30 minutes. Add 2 packages hot dogs cut into pieces. Simmer for 30 minutes.

BREAKFAST CASSEROLE

2 12-ounce packages
  sausage
1 loaf French bread,
  cubed
2 cups shredded sharp
  Cheddar cheese
12 eggs, beaten
1 tablespoon dry
  mustard
2 1/2 cups milk
1 onion, chopped
1 or 2 4-ounce cans
  mushrooms, drained
3 tablespoons butter or
  margarine
3 tablespoons
  all-purpose flour
Salt and pepper to taste
1 to 2 cups milk

Brown sausage in skillet, stirring until crumbly; drain. Layer bread cubes, cheese and sausage in 9-by-13-inch baking dish. Combine eggs, dry mustard and 2 1/2 cups milk in bowl; mix well. Pour over layers. Chill, covered, overnight. Preheat oven to 325 degrees. Bake casserole for 1 hour and 15 minutes. Sauté onion and mushrooms in butter in saucepan. Stir in flour, salt and pepper. Cook until light brown, stirring constantly. Add 1 to 2 cups milk. Cook until thickened, stirring constantly. Pour over casserole. Cut into squares. Yield: 12 servings.

Hazel Haynes, Preceptor Upsilon
Boise, Idaho

EASTER CALZONE

This recipe came from Bari, Italy, with my grandparents in the early 1900s. It was Grandma's special treat and was served only at Easter.

7 cups all-purpose flour
3 1/2 teaspoons baking
  powder
3/4 cup sugar
1/2 teaspoon salt
4 eggs
1 cup melted lard
3 1/2 pounds Italian
  sausage
24 hard-cooked eggs
3 pounds ricotta cheese
4 eggs
1/2 cup chopped parsley
Sugar, salt and pepper
  to taste
Egg yolks, beaten
Sugar

Preheat oven to 350 degrees. Mix flour, baking powder, 3/4 cup sugar and 1/2 teaspoon salt in bowl; make well in center. Place 4 eggs and lard in well; mix to form dough. Separate into 2 portions. Roll 1 portion 1/4-inch thick on floured surface. Fit into 10-by-15-inch baking pan, covering bottom and sides. Brown sausage in skillet, stirring until crumbly; drain. Layer hard-cooked eggs and sausage in prepared pan. Combine ricotta cheese, 4 eggs, chopped parsley, sugar, salt and pepper to taste in bowl; mix well. Pour over layers. Top with remaining pastry. Seal edges; cut vents in top. Brush with egg yolks; sprinkle with sugar. Bake for 1 1/2 hours. Yield: 16 servings.

Jan Capodagli, Alpha Upsilon Psi
The Colony, Texas

CREOLE JAMBALAYA

1 pound smoked pork sausage	2 tablespoons chopped fresh parsley
1 cup chopped green bell pepper	2 cups uncooked rice
1 cup chopped onion	2 tablespoons Worcestershire sauce
1 clove of garlic, crushed	1/2 teaspoon thyme
1 tablespoon all-purpose flour	2 teaspoons salt
1 28-ounce can tomatoes	1/4 teaspoon red pepper
2 1/2 cups water	1 pound seafood or chicken (optional)

Cut sausage into 1/2-inch pieces. Brown in large skillet for 5 minutes. Drain, reserving 2 tablespoons drippings. Sauté green pepper, onion and garlic in reserved drippings in skillet. Stir in flour. Cook over low heat until brown, stirring frequently. Stir in tomatoes, water and parsley. Bring to a boil. Add sausage and next 5 ingredients. Simmer, covered, for 20 minutes. Add seafood. Simmer for 10 minutes longer; fluff with fork. Yield: 12 servings.

Stacy E. Stewart, Eta
Winter Springs, Florida

EGG PIZZA

1 pound Italian sausage or bacon	1 6-ounce can sliced olives
12 eggs	6 green onions, chopped
6 tablespoons milk	1 pound mozzarella cheese, shredded
1 4-ounce can mushrooms, drained	

Preheat oven to 350 degrees. Brown sausage in skillet, stirring until crumbly; drain. Beat eggs with milk in bowl. Add mushrooms, sausage, olives and green onions; mix well. Pour into greased 10-by-15-inch baking pan. Sprinkle with cheese. Bake for 15 to 20 minutes or until set. Yield: 6 servings.

Sugar Carpenter, Preceptor Beta
Gresham, Oregon

SAUSAGE LASAGNA WRAPS

6 lasagna noodles	1 16-ounce jar spaghetti sauce
1 pound smoked sausage	Grated Parmesan cheese
3 slices mozzarella cheese, cut into halves	

Preheat oven to 350 degrees. Cook lasagna noodles using package directions; drain well. Cut sausage into 6 portions. Split sausage pieces lengthwise. Place 1 piece mozzarella cheese in each sausage; replace halves. Wrap sausage in noodles. Place in 2-quart baking dish. Top with spaghetti sauce. Bake for 30 minutes. Serve with grated Parmesan cheese. Yield: 4 to 6 servings.

Kayleen Karlin, Mu Theta
Salina, Kansas

SAUCY SAUSAGE SKILLET

8 ounces uncooked ziti	2 tablespoons all-purpose flour
3 quarts water	1 teaspoon salt
1 to 1 1/2 pounds kielbasa, sliced into wedges	1 cup milk
1 cup broccoli flowerets	1/4 cup shredded Monterey Jack cheese
1 cup cauliflowerets	1/4 cup grated Parmesan cheese
2 tablespoons butter or margarine	1 2-ounce jar sliced pimento, drained
1 teaspoon dry mustard	

Cook pasta in water in large saucepan for 5 minutes. Add kielbasa, broccoli and cauliflower. Cook for 5 minutes longer; drain. Melt butter in saucepan. Blend in dry mustard, flour and salt. Add milk. Cook until thickened, stirring constantly. Stir in cheeses until melted. Add pimento, pasta and vegetable mixture; mix well. Serve immediately. Yield: 6 to 8 servings.

Sheryl A. Porter, Beta Theta
Gadsden, Alabama

SPINACH AND SAUSAGE PIE IN CORNMEAL PASTRY

12 ounces sausage	1/2 cup chopped onion
1/2 cup chopped mushrooms	2 tablespoons all-purpose flour
2 10-ounce packages frozen chopped spinach, thawed	1 1/2 cups shredded mozzarella cheese
2 eggs	1/3 cup grated Parmesan cheese
24 ounces cottage cheese, drained	Cornmeal Pastry
	1 egg, slightly beaten

Preheat oven to 425 degrees. Brown sausage with mushrooms in skillet, stirring frequently; drain. Squeeze spinach to remove moisture. Beat 2 eggs and cottage cheese in mixer bowl until smooth. Add sausage mixture, spinach, onion, flour and cheeses; mix well. Spoon into 9-inch pie plate lined with Cornmeal Pastry. Top with remaining pastry. Brush with 1 egg. Place on lower oven rack. Bake for 15 minutes. Reduce oven temperature to 350 degrees. Bake for 35 to 40 minutes longer or until brown. Let stand for 10 minutes. Yield: 6 servings.

CORNMEAL PASTRY

2 cups all-purpose flour	3/4 cup butter or margarine
1/2 cup white cornmeal	6 to 8 tablespoons cold water
1/4 cup grated Parmesan cheese	
1/2 teaspoon salt	

Mix flour, cornmeal, cheese and salt in bowl. Cut in butter until mixture forms coarse crumbs. Stir in enough water to form dough. Chill in refrigerator. Roll into 2 circles on floured surface. Yield: 2 pie shells.

Jill Luna, Rho Xi
Stanton, Texas

SAUSAGE AND GRITS CASSEROLE

1 pound sausage	3 tablespoons butter or
3 cups hot cooked grits	margarine
2½ cups shredded	3 eggs, beaten
Cheddar cheese	1½ cups milk

Preheat oven to 350 degrees. Brown sausage in heavy skillet, stirring until crumbly; drain. Spoon into lightly greased 9-by-13-inch baking dish. Combine grits with cheese and butter in bowl; stir until cheese and butter melt. Stir in mixture of eggs and milk. Spoon over sausage. Bake for 1 hour. Yield: 8 to 10 servings.

Flora E. Bates, Delta Sigma
Flora, Mississippi

CHINESE VEAL

1½ pounds cubed veal	¼ cup soy sauce
2 tablespoons	1 cup water
shortening	1 cup finely chopped
1 cup finely chopped	celery
onion	1 10-ounce package
½ cup uncooked rice	frozen peas
1 10-ounce can chicken	¼ cup toasted almonds
and rice soup	

Preheat oven to 425 degrees. Brown veal in shortening in skillet. Add onion. Cook until golden brown; drain. Stir in rice, soup, soy sauce and water; mix well. Spoon into 2-quart baking dish. Bake, covered, for 40 minutes. Add celery and peas; mix well. Bake, covered, for 20 minutes longer. Sprinkle with almonds. Serve with gelatin salad, scalloped potatoes and French bread. Yield: 8 to 10 servings.

Ann McClintic, Epsilon Iota
Memphis, Missouri

MEXICAN VEAL LOAF

1 cup chopped onion	1 pound ground veal
1 cup chopped mixed red	¾ cup dry bread crumbs
and green bell pepper	½ cup tomato sauce
2 cloves of garlic,	¼ cup plain yogurt
minced	2 tablespoons chopped
1 packet beef broth	parsley
seasoning mix	2 teaspoons
4 teaspoons vegetable	Worcestershire sauce
oil	1 teaspoon chili powder
1 cup shredded Cheddar	Pepper to taste
cheese	

Preheat oven to 375 degrees. Sauté onion, bell pepper and garlic with broth mix in oil in skillet over medium heat. Combine with cheese, ground veal, bread crumbs, tomato sauce, yogurt, parsley, Worcestershire sauce, chili powder and pepper in bowl; mix well. Shape into loaf; place in 8-by-8-inch baking pan. Bake for 45 minutes or until brown. Yield: 4 servings.

Virginia H. Jenkins, Beta Kappa
Middletown, Ohio

VEAL SCALLOPINI

4 veal scallops	1 cup Champagne
¼ cup all-purpose flour	1 cup sliced mushrooms
½ teaspoon salt	1 cup whipping cream
⅛ teaspoon pepper	2 tablespoons Cognac
3 tablespoons butter	Salt and white pepper
or margarine	to taste

Coat veal with mixture of flour, ½ teaspoon salt and ⅛ teaspoon pepper. Brown in butter in skillet for 1 to 1½ minutes on each side. Remove to warm plate. Stir in Champagne. Add mushrooms and cream. Cook for 10 minutes or until thickened, stirring constantly. Stir in Cognac. Season with salt and white pepper. Spoon over veal. Yield: 4 servings.

Judi Davis, Xi Beta Theta
Broken Arrow, Oklahoma

VENISON AND BROCCOLI STIR-FRY

1 10-ounce can chicken	2 teaspoons cornstarch
and rice soup	½ teaspoon sugar
1 pound venison roast	2 tablespoons soy sauce
or steak	4 servings hot cooked
3 tablespoons olive oil	rice
Flowerets of 1 pound	
fresh broccoli	

Strain soup, reserving broth and chicken and rice. Slice venison diagonally cross grain into ¼-by-2-inch strips. Stir-fry in 1 tablespoon olive oil in wok for 2 minutes. Remove to bowl. Add remaining 2 tablespoons olive oil and broccoli to wok. Stir-fry for 2 to 3 minutes. Remove to bowl. Add mixture of cornstarch, sugar, soy sauce and reserved broth. Cook over medium heat until thickened, stirring constantly. Add venison and broccoli. Cook for 2 minutes. Stir reserved chicken and rice from soup into hot cooked rice. Spoon venison mixture over rice. Yield: 4 servings.

Patricia C. Payne, Xi Nu
Summerville, South Carolina

EASY VENISON STROGANOFF

1 pound venison steak	1 3-ounce can sliced
1 tablespoon shortening	mushrooms
1 onion, chopped	2 teaspoons
1 clove of garlic, minced	Worcestershire sauce
1 10-ounce can cream	1½ cups sour cream
of mushroom soup	Cooked wide egg
2 tablespoons catsup	noodles

Cut venison into ¼-inch strips. Brown in hot shortening in large skillet. Add onion and garlic. Cook until onion is tender. Stir in mixture of next 4 ingredients. Stir into skillet. Cook until heated through; do not boil. Stir in sour cream. Cook just until heated through. Serve over noodles. Yield: 4 servings.

Mary K. Hawkins, Psi Beta
Plattsburg, Missouri

CHICKEN AND ANGEL HAIR PASTA

3 chicken breasts
2 tablespoons olive oil
2 tablespoons butter or
  margarine
2 tablespoons
  all-purpose flour
1/2 16-ounce can
  Italian stewed tomatoes
1 cup chicken broth
1/4 cup white wine

1 zucchini, cut
  julienne-style
3 green onions, sliced
3 tablespoons chopped
  parsley
1/4 teaspoon each
  oregano, basil, garlic
  powder, salt and pepper
Cooked angel hair
  pasta or spaghetti

Rinse chicken and pat dry; cut into bite-sized pieces. Brown in olive oil and butter in skillet. Remove chicken. Stir flour into pan drippings. Drain tomatoes, reserving juice. Stir reserved juice, broth and wine into skillet. Simmer until thickened, stirring constantly. Add vegetables, seasonings and chicken. Simmer for 5 to 10 minutes or until heated through. Serve over pasta. Yield: 2 to 3 servings.

Ruth Mullen, Preceptor Mu Upsilon
Thousand Oaks, California

CREAMY CHICKEN CRÊPES

1 1/3 cups all-purpose
  flour
1 teaspoon salt
4 eggs, beaten
2 tablespoons vegetable
  oil
1 1/3 cups milk
1/2 cup sour cream

1 10-ounce can cream
  of mushroom soup
2 1/2 cups chopped
  cooked chicken
Mushroom Sauce
1 cup shredded Cheddar
  cheese
Paprika to taste

Combine flour, salt and eggs in bowl; mix well. Blend in 2 tablespoons oil and milk; beat until smooth. Refrigerate for 2 hours or longer. Brush bottom of 10-inch crêpe pan with oil. Preheat over medium heat. Pour 3 tablespoons batter in pan; tilt pan in all directions so that batter covers pan in thin film. Cook for 1 minute. Turn crêpe. Cook for 30 seconds. Remove crêpe from pan. Repeat procedure with remaining batter. Set aside 10 crêpes. Freeze remaining crêpes for another purpose. Preheat oven to 350 degrees. Combine sour cream and soup in bowl; mix well. Add chicken; mix well. Spoon 1/3 cup into center of each crêpe; roll up. Place seam side down in greased 9-by-13-inch baking dish. Spoon Mushroom Sauce over crêpes. Bake for 15 minutes. Sprinkle cheese over crêpes. Bake for 10 minutes. Sprinkle with paprika. Yield: 10 crêpes.

MUSHROOM SAUCE

1 small onion, finely
  chopped
2 tablespoons butter or
  margarine
1 chicken bouillon cube
2 tablespoons water

1 2 1/2-ounce jar sliced
  mushrooms, drained
1/4 cup Vermouth
1 10-ounce can cream
  of mushroom soup
1/2 cup sour cream

Sauté onion in butter in skillet until tender. Add bouillon cube, water and mushrooms. Cook until bouillon cube dissolves, stirring frequently. Add Vermouth. Cook until reduced by 1/3. Stir in soup and sour cream. Yield: 2 1/2 cups.

Robin Haines, Epsilon Zeta
Corbin, Kentucky

THE WOODLANDS COUNTRY CHICKEN

8 chicken breasts,
  skinned
1/2 cup all-purpose flour
2 teaspoons salt
1 teaspoon pepper
1/4 cup butter or
  margarine
1/4 cup sunflower oil
1 cup chopped green bell
  pepper
1/2 cup chopped red bell
  pepper

1 1/2 cups chopped onions
1 clove of garlic,
  chopped
1 1/2 to 2 tablespoons
  curry powder
2 20-ounce cans
  chunky stewed
  tomatoes
1 cup dark seedlesss
  raisins
6 cups hot cooked rice
1 cup slivered almonds

Rinse chicken and pat dry. Combine flour, salt and pepper in large plastic bag. Shake chicken 1 piece at a time in flour mixture, coating well. Brown on all sides in mixture of hot butter and oil in heavy 6-quart saucepan. Remove to platter. Add bell peppers, onions, garlic and curry powder to drippings in skillet. Cook for 5 minutes, stirring constantly. Add tomatoes, raisins and chicken. Simmer, covered, for 1 hour or until chicken is tender. Spoon onto platter. Spoon rice around chicken. Sprinkle with almonds. May use two 2 1/2-pounds chickens, cut up, if preferred. Yield: 8 servings.

Jeannette Bell Weber, Preceptor Laureate Delta Gamma
Conroe, Texas

GALLIANO CHICKEN

4 to 6 chicken breast
  filets
Mrs. Dash, garlic salt
  and lemon pepper to
  taste
3/4 cup orange juice

2 tablespoons
  all-purpose flour
1/2 cup Galliano liqueur
1 bunch green onions,
  chopped
Chopped parsley

Rinse chicken and pat dry. Sprinkle with Mrs. Dash, garlic salt and lemon pepper. Brown on both sides in 10-inch skillet sprayed with nonstick cooking spray; remove to bowl. Blend orange juice, flour and liqueur in skillet. Cook until thickened, stirring constantly. Add a small amount of water if needed for desired consistency. Add chicken. Simmer for 15 minutes. Add green onions. Simmer for 15 minutes or until tender. Arrange chicken on platter; sprinkle with parsley. Serve with sauce. Serve with cold fruit salad and French bread. Yield: 4 servings.

Yvonne Hendrix, Xi Alpha Delta
Corvallis, Montana

CHICKEN ÉTOUFÉE

9 tablespoons vegetable
  oil
³/4 cup all-purpose flour
4¹/2 cups chicken broth
¹/3 cup butter or
  margarine
¹/3 cup chopped green
  bell pepper
¹/3 cup chopped celery
¹/3 cup chopped onion
²/3 cup butter or
  margarine

³/4 cup finely minced
  green onions with tops
1 3¹/2-pound chicken,
  cooked, boned
¹/4 teaspoon garlic
  powder
1¹/2 teaspoons salt
¹/2 teaspoon cayenne
  pepper
Cooked rice

Heat oil in heavy 9-inch skillet until smoking; remove from heat. Add flour all at once, whisking until smooth. Cook over medium heat until roux is medium brown, stirring constantly; remove from heat. Bring broth to a boil in 4-quart saucepan. Stir in roux. Simmer for 25 minutes; remove from heat. Wipe out skillet used to brown flour. Melt ¹/3 cup butter in skillet. Add green pepper, celery and onion. Cook over low heat for 12 to 18 minutes or until tender. Add to stock mixture. Melt remaining ²/3 cup butter in skillet. Add green onions. Cook over medium heat for 2 minutes. Add to stock mixture. Stir in chicken, garlic powder, salt and cayenne pepper. Heat to serving temperature. Serve over hot rice. Yield: 6 servings.

Rosalyn Thomas, Laureate Mu
Albany, Georgia

GLAZED CHICKEN WITH GRAPES

1 pound chicken breast
  filets
¹/3 cup apple jelly
2 tablespoons dry sherry
2 teaspoons lemon juice

¹/4 teaspoon salt
³/4 cup seedless red
  grape halves
3 sprigs of parsley,
  chopped

Rinse chicken and pat dry. Heat skillet sprayed with nonstick cooking spray over medium-high heat. Add chicken. Cook for 8 to 10 minutes or until cooked through, turning once. Remove to serving platter. Stir jelly, wine, lemon juice and salt into skillet. Cook until jelly melts, stirring constantly. Stir in grapes and parsley. Cook until heated through. Spoon over chicken. Yield: 4 servings.

Donna Bryant, Xi Alpha Omega
Tillson, New York

POACHED CHICKEN WITH FETA CHEESE

2 chicken breast filets
3 green onions, chopped
¹/2 cup chopped parsley
1 tablespoon olive oil
1 cup undrained canned
  whole tomatoes

¹/2 teaspoon oregano
Freshly ground pepper
  to taste
3 tablespoons sherry
1 cup chicken stock
1 ounce feta cheese

Rinse chicken and pat dry. Pound with meat mallet to flatten. Sauté green onions and parsley in olive oil in skillet for 3 minutes or until tender. Add tomatoes, oregano and pepper. Bring to a simmer, mashing tomatoes gently with spoon. Simmer for 20 minutes, stirring occasionally. Add wine. Cook for 1 minute. Bring stock to a simmer in shallow saucepan. Add chicken. Cook for 10 minutes or until chicken tests done; drain well. Arrange on serving plate. Spoon sauce over chicken. Crumble cheese over top. Yield: 2 servings.

Evelyn M. Oberlander, Laureate Nu
Allison Park, Pennsylvania

BREAST OF CHICKEN WITH SHRIMP

2 large chicken breasts
1 clove of garlic, minced
Nutmeg, salt and
  pepper to taste
¹/2 cup all-purpose flour
2 tablespoons butter or
  margarine
¹/2 cup chopped celery
1¹/2 cups sliced fresh
  mushrooms

¹/2 cup chopped onion
³/4 cup dry white wine
1¹/2 cups shrimp
2 tablespoons butter or
  margarine
2 tablespoons chopped
  parsley
¹/2 cup sour cream
Pecan Brown Rice
  (page 150)

Rinse chicken and pat dry. Cut into bite-sized pieces. Sprinkle with seasonings. Let stand in refrigerator for 30 minutes. Coat well with flour. Brown in 2 tablespoons butter in skillet. Add celery, mushrooms, onion and wine. Simmer, covered, for 30 minutes. Sauté shrimp in 2 tablespoons butter in skillet for 5 minutes. Add to chicken mixture. Add parsley and sour cream. Cook until heated through. Serve over Pecan Brown Rice. Yield: 4 servings.

Leona Lanthier, Laureate Nu
Comox, British Columbia, Canada

CHICKEN IN WINE SAUCE

4 chicken breast filets
Salt and nutmeg to taste
¹/4 cup butter or
  margarine
1 red bell pepper, cut
  into strips
¹/4 cup chopped green
  onions

8 ounces fresh
  mushrooms, sliced
1¹/3 cups dry white wine
4 teaspoons cornstarch
2 tablespoons dry white
  wine
Cooked rice

Rinse chicken and pat dry; sprinkle with salt and nutmeg. Brown on both sides in butter in heavy skillet. Add vegetables and 1¹/3 cups wine. Bring to a boil; reduce heat. Simmer, covered, for 15 minutes. Remove chicken to platter. Blend cornstarch and 2 tablespoons wine in small bowl. Stir into skillet. Cook until thickened, stirring constantly. Arrange chicken over rice. Spoon sauce over top. Yield: 4 servings.

Sandra Gilbert, Zeta Alpha
Marion, Kentucky

BOOZED CHICKEN

8 chicken breast filets	1/2 cup margarine, sliced
2 10-ounce cans cream	1 1/2 cups herb-seasoned
of chicken soup	stuffing mix
2 cups shredded	1/2 cup bourbon
Cheddar cheese	

Preheat oven to 350 degrees. Rinse chicken and pat dry. Arrange in 9-by-13-inch baking dish. Layer soup, cheese, margarine and stuffing mix over chicken. Pour bourbon over layers. Bake for 1 hour and 15 minutes. Yield: 8 servings.

Lucille Bennett, Laureate Gamma Phi
Orcutt, California

CHICKEN BREASTS BORDELAISE

4 whole chicken breasts	8 ounces fresh
Juice of 1 lemon	mushrooms, sliced
1/8 teaspoon thyme	1/4 cup all-purpose flour
1/2 teaspoon salt	2 cups chicken stock
1/4 teaspoon pepper	1/2 cup dry white wine
3 tablespoons peanut oil	1/8 teaspoon tarragon or
3 tablespoons butter or	1 bay leaf
margarine	

Split chicken breasts into halves; rinse and pat dry. Rub with lemon juice. Mix thyme, salt and pepper on plate. Roll chicken in mixture. Chill, covered, for 3 hours to overnight. Preheat oven to 300 degrees. Brown chicken in oil in skillet over medium heat. Place in deep baking dish. Heat butter in skillet. Add mushrooms. Cook for 1 minute over high heat. Stir in flour. Add stock and wine. Cook over medium heat until thickened, stirring constantly. Add tarragon. Pour over chicken. Bake, covered, for 1 hour. Serve with parsley rice and green beans. Yield: 6 to 8 servings.

Nicole Milne, Xi Chi
Port Alberni, British Columbia, Canada

CHICKEN CORDON BLEU

Two sorority sisters and I prepared this for 26 guests at our 1990 Christmas party.

8 chicken breast filets	1 cup Italian bread
8 slices Danish ham	crumbs
8 slices Swiss cheese	1/4 cup margarine
3 tablespoons chopped	1 10-ounce can cream
parsley	of mushroom soup
1/4 teaspoon pepper	1 cup sour cream
2 eggs, beaten	

Preheat oven to 350 degrees. Rinse chicken and pat dry. Pound 1/4 inch thick with meat mallet. Top each filet with slice of ham and cheese; sprinkle with mixture of parsley and pepper. Roll to enclose filling; secure with wooden picks. Dip in eggs; roll in bread crumbs. Brown in margarine in large heavy skillet. Place in 9-by-13-inch baking dish. Stir mixture of soup and sour cream into drippings in skillet. Pour over chicken. Bake for 45 minutes. Serve with green vegetable and wild rice. Yield: 8 servings.

Bettie Paoletta, Preceptor Alpha Kappa
San Antonio, Texas

CRANBERRY CHICKEN

12 chicken breast filets	1 12-ounce can
1 16-ounce bottle of	cranberry sauce
Russian salad dressing	
1 envelope onion soup	
mix	

Preheat oven to 375 degrees. Rinse chicken and pat dry. Arrange in 8-by-12-inch baking dish. Combine salad dressing, soup mix and cranberry sauce in bowl; mix well. Spoon over chicken. Bake for 45 to 60 minutes or until tender. Yield: 6 to 8 servings.

Marti Moehlau, Xi Delta
Silver Spring, Maryland

CHICKEN JUBILEE

4 chicken breasts,	1/2 cup raisins
skinned	1/2 cup packed light
Garlic powder, salt and	brown sugar
pepper to taste	1 tablespoon
Vegetable oil	Worcestershire sauce
2 medium onions,	1 cup sherry
thinly sliced	1 16-ounce can pitted
1 12-ounce bottle of	dark cherries, drained
chili sauce	Hot cooked rice

Preheat oven to 325 degrees. Rinse chicken and pat dry; sprinkle with garlic powder, salt and pepper. Brown lightly on both sides in oil in skillet; remove to 9-by-13-inch baking dish. Combine onions, chili sauce, raisins, brown sugar and Worcestershire sauce in bowl; mix well. Pour over chicken; cover with foil. Bake for 1 hour or until tender. Add wine and cherries. Bake, covered, for 15 minutes longer. Serve with rice. Yield: 4 servings.

Julie Bruey, Xi Kappa Mu
Keystone Heights, Florida

HONEY-MUSTARD BAKED CHICKEN

2 chickens, cut up	1/4 cup Dijon mustard
1/2 cup butter or	1 teaspoon curry powder
margarine	1/2 teaspoon salt
1/2 cup honey	

Preheat oven to 350 degrees. Rinse chicken and pat dry; arrange in large shallow baking pan. Melt butter in saucepan. Stir in honey, mustard, curry powder and salt. Cook until heated through. Brush over chicken. Bake for 1 hour and 15 minutes or until golden brown. Yield: 6 to 8 servings.

Bernadine Kohler, Laureate Delta Alpha
Aurora, Colorado

GRANDMA'S DELICIOUS CHICKEN

6 to 8 chicken breast filets	1/4 cup chopped onion
All-purpose flour	1 clove of garlic, chopped
1/2 cup vegetable oil	1 teaspoon dry mustard
1 10-ounce can beef consommé	1 teaspoon parsley flakes
1/2 cup catsup	1 tablespoon vinegar
1/4 cup water	Salt and pepper to taste
1/4 cup sherry	Steamed rice

Preheat oven to 350 degrees. Rinse chicken and pat dry. Coat with flour. Brown on both sides in oil in skillet; drain. Combine consommé, catsup, water, wine, onion, garlic, dry mustard, parsley flakes, vinegar, salt and pepper in saucepan. Bring to a boil; reduce heat. Simmer for 15 minutes. Pour over chicken in 3-quart baking dish. Bake, covered, for 30 minutes. Bake, uncovered, for 30 minutes longer. Serve over steamed rice. Yield: 6 to 8 servings.

Susanne Watson, Xi Gamma Xi
Oroville, California

LOUISIANA CHICKEN

6 to 8 chicken breasts	3/4 cup currant jelly
1/2 cup all-purpose flour	1/4 cup orange juice
1/2 teaspoon salt	1 teaspoon dry mustard
Pepper to taste	1/8 teaspoon ginger
1/4 cup melted margarine	

Preheat oven to 375 degrees. Rinse chicken and pat dry. Coat with mixture of flour, salt and pepper. Arrange in baking pan sprayed with nonstick cooking spray. Drizzle with melted margarine. Bake, covered, for 20 minutes. Combine jelly, orange juice, dry mustard and ginger in saucepan. Bring to a boil, stirring to mix well. Pour over chicken. Bake, uncovered, for 30 minutes, turning after 20 minutes and basting with pan juices. Yield: 6 to 8 servings.

Gail Cox, Delta Xi
Knoxville, Tennessee

CHICKEN LOUIE SUPREME

2 cups thinly sliced celery	1 10-ounce can cream of chicken soup
8 chicken breast filets	2 tablespoons chopped pimento
All-purpose flour	
1/4 cup vegetable oil	2 tablespoons sliced stuffed green olives
1 cup fresh bread crumbs	1 cup shredded medium Cheddar cheese
1/2 cup slivered almonds	
1/2 cup half and half	

Preheat oven to 350 degrees. Sprinkle celery in greased 9-by-13-inch baking dish. Rinse chicken and pat dry. Coat with flour. Brown on both sides in oil in skillet; drain. Arrange in prepared baking dish. Add bread crumbs and almonds to drippings in skillet; mix well. Cook until brown; set aside. Pour mixture of remaining ingredients over chicken. Top with bread crumb mixture. Bake for 1 hour or until tender. Yield: 6 to 8 servings.

Karen B. Little, Preceptor Alpha Delta
Kennewick, Washington

CHICKEN MARBELLA

1 head garlic, finely puréed	6 bay leaves
1 cup pitted prunes	Salt and pepper to taste
1/2 cup pitted large green olives	4 2 1/2-pound chickens, cut into quarters
1/2 cup undrained capers	1 cup packed light brown sugar
1/2 cup red wine vinegar	1 cup white wine
1/2 cup olive oil	1/4 cup finely chopped Italian parsley
1/4 cup oregano	

Combine first 10 ingredients in large bowl. Rinse chicken and pat dry. Add to marinade, coating well. Marinate, covered, overnight. Preheat oven to 350 degrees. Drain chicken, reserving marinade. Arrange chicken in 1 or 2 large shallow baking dishes. Spoon marinade evenly over chicken. Sprinkle with brown sugar; pour wine over top. Bake for 50 minutes or until tender, basting frequently with pan juices. Remove chicken, prunes, olives and capers to serving platter, discarding bay leaves; sprinkle with parsley. Spoon a small amount of pan juices over chicken. Pour remaining juices into bowl; serve with chicken. Yield: 10 to 12 servings.

Shirley Shea, Laureate Beta
Victoria, British Columbia, Canada

CHICKEN PARMIGIANA

2 eggs	1/8 teaspoon garlic powder
1 teaspoon salt	1 tablespoon butter or margarine
1/8 teaspoon pepper	
6 chicken breast filets	1/2 cup grated Parmesan cheese
3/4 cup crushed club crackers	8 ounces mozzarella cheese, thinly sliced, cut into triangles
1/2 cup vegetable oil	
1 15-ounce can tomato sauce	
1/4 teaspoon basil	

Preheat oven to 350 degrees. Beat eggs with salt and pepper in bowl. Rinse chicken and pat dry. Dip into egg mixture; roll in cracker crumbs, coating well. Brown in hot oil in skillet; drain chicken and skillet well. Arrange chicken in lightly greased 9-by-13-inch baking dish. Bring tomato sauce, basil and garlic powder to a boil in skillet. Simmer for 10 minutes or until thickened. Stir in butter. Pour over chicken; sprinkle with Parmesan cheese. Bake, covered, for 30 minutes. Arrange mozzarella cheese slices over top. Bake, uncovered, for 10 minutes. Yield: 6 servings.

Becky Bradley, Xi Alpha Kappa
Clarksville, Arkansas

HEART-HEALTHY BAKED CHICKEN PARMESAN

1/3 cup water	1/4 teaspoon garlic
1/3 cup Italian bread	powder
crumbs	2 1/2 to 3 pounds chicken
1/4 cup grated Parmesan	breast filets
cheese	1 tablespoon vegetable
1 tablespoon minced	oil
parsley	1/4 cup melted margarine
1/8 teaspoon thyme	1/3 cup Marsala
1/4 teaspoon paprika	

Preheat oven to 350 degrees. Pour water into oiled shallow baking pan. Mix bread crumbs, cheese, parsley, thyme, paprika and garlic powder in bowl. Rinse chicken and pat dry. Coat with crumb mixture; arrange in prepared pan. Drizzle with oil and margarine. Bake for 30 minutes. Reduce oven temperature to 325 degrees. Pour wine over chicken. Bake, covered with foil, for 15 minutes. Increase oven temperature to 350 degrees. Bake, uncovered, for 10 minutes longer. Yield: 4 servings.

Janice Fiedler, Alpha Zeta
Apex, North Carolina

POPPY SEED CHICKEN

6 to 8 chicken breasts or	1 roll butter crackers,
2 chickens, cut up	crushed
1 cup sour cream	2 teaspoons poppy seed
2 10-ounce cans cream	3/4 cup melted margarine
of chicken soup	

Preheat oven to 350 degrees. Rinse chicken and pat dry. Arrange in greased 3-quart baking dish. Spread with mixture of sour cream and soup. Sprinkle with mixture of cracker crumbs and poppy seed. Drizzle with margarine. Bake for 30 to 40 minutes or until tender. Yield: 10 to 12 servings.

Roberta Snivley, Zeta Phi
Bryan, Ohio

ORANGE BRANDY CHICKEN

4 8-ounce chicken	2 tablespoons orange
breasts	juice
1 tablespoon olive oil	2 tablespoons butter or
2 tablespoons rosemary	margarine
Salt and pepper to taste	3 tablespoons chicken
2 tablespoons olive oil	stock
2 tablespoons brandy	Cooked wild rice or
1/4 cup Grand Marnier	pasta

Preheat oven to 450 degrees. Rinse chicken and pat dry. Sprinkle with 1 tablespoon olive oil, rosemary, salt and pepper. Brown skin side down in 2 tablespoons olive oil in skillet for 5 minutes. Arrange in baking dish. Bake for 20 minutes. Combine brandy, Grand Marnier, orange juice, butter and chicken stock in saucepan. Cook until heated through. Spoon over chicken. Bake for 2 minutes longer. Serve with wild rice or pasta. Yield: 4 servings.

Mary Ogren, Xi Alpha Sigma
Eagan, Minnesota

CHICKEN SCAMPI

2 pounds chicken breast	2 tablespoons lemon
filets	juice
1 1/2 cups bread crumbs	2 tablespoons minced
Salt and pepper to taste	garlic
2 eggs, beaten	12 ounces angel hair
3 tablespoons (or more)	pasta, cooked
vegetable oil	
1/2 cup butter or	
margarine	

Preheat oven to 325 degrees. Rinse chicken and pat dry; cut into bite-sized pieces. Mix bread crumbs with salt and pepper in bowl. Dip chicken in eggs; coat with crumbs. Brown 10 pieces at a time in oil in skillet; remove chicken to 2-liter baking dish. Add butter, lemon juice and garlic to drippings in skillet. Cook until butter melts, mixing well. Pour over chicken. Bake, covered, for 40 to 60 minutes or until tender. Serve over pasta. Yield: 3 to 4 servings.

Laura E. Kane, Alpha Rho
Sorrento, Maine

TAHITI CHICKEN

This recipe can easily be doubled or tripled.

6 chicken thighs,	3/4 cup orange juice
skinned	1/2 cup orange
1/4 cup all-purpose flour	marmalade
1 teaspoon paprika	3 tablespoons
1 teaspoon salt	cornstarch
1/8 teaspoon pepper	1/2 cup cold water
1/4 cup butter or	1/4 cup slivered almonds
margarine	

Preheat oven to 350 degrees. Rinse chicken and pat dry. Coat with mixture of flour, paprika, salt and pepper. Brown in butter in skillet; remove to 8-by-8-inch baking dish. Heat orange juice and marmalade in saucepan until marmalade melts. Stir in mixture of cornstarch and water. Cook until thickened, stirring constantly. Pour sauce over chicken; sprinkle with almonds. Bake for 50 minutes. Yield: 6 servings.

Joy Western, Laureate Beta Tau
Port Dover, Ontario, Canada

Mary Vitale, Zeta Phi, Bryan, Ohio, makes Easy Baked Chicken Breasts by layering 8 chicken breast filets and 8 slices Swiss cheese in baking dish. Top with mixture of 1 can chicken soup and 1/4 cup white wine. Sprinkle with 4 cups crushed stuffing mix and 1/4 cup melted butter or margarine. Bake in preheated 350-degree oven for 45 minutes.

CHICKEN AND BROCCOLI CASSEROLE

1 large bunch broccoli,
  cut into bite-sized
  pieces
2 10-ounce cans cream
  of chicken soup
3/4 cup mayonnaise
1/2 teaspoon garlic
  powder
Ginger and oregano to
  taste
1 teaspoon coriander
1 teaspoon freshly
  ground pepper
3 cups chopped cooked
  chicken
1/2 cup fine dry bread
  crumbs
1/2 cup shredded
  mozzarella cheese

Preheat oven to 350 degrees. Cook broccoli in boiling water to cover in saucepan for 2 minutes; drain. Combine next 7 ingredients in large saucepan. Heat for 5 minutes, whisking until smooth. Add broccoli and chicken; mix gently. Spoon into buttered 9-by-13-inch baking dish. Sprinkle with bread crumbs and cheese. Bake for 30 minutes or until bubbly and golden brown. Yield: 4 to 6 servings.

Ann Herron, Laureate Alpha Theta
Peterborough, Ontario, Canada

MONTEREY CHICKEN AND RICE BAKE

1/2 cup cottage cheese
3 ounces cream cheese,
  softened
1/2 cup sour cream
1 10-ounce can cream
  of chicken soup
1 4-ounce can chopped
  green chilies
3 cups chopped cooked
  chicken
3 cups cooked rice
1 cup shredded
  Monterey Jack cheese
2 tomatoes, chopped
1/8 teaspoon garlic
  powder
1 teaspoon salt
3/4 cup crushed corn
  chips

Preheat oven to 350 degrees. Combine cottage cheese, cream cheese and sour cream in bowl; mix well. Add next 8 ingredients; mix well. Spoon into shallow 2-quart baking dish. Sprinkle with corn chips. Bake for 25 to 30 minutes. Yield: 6 to 8 servings.

Karen J. Breigenzer, Alpha Alpha
Glasgow, Montana

CHICKEN AND WILD RICE CASSEROLE

1/2 cup uncooked wild
  rice
1/2 teaspoon salt
1 1/2 cups water
1 1/2 teaspoons butter or
  margarine
1 4-ounce can
  mushrooms, sliced
1/4 cup chicken broth
1 1/3 cups chopped
  cooked chicken
1/4 teaspoon pepper
1 10-ounce can cream
  of chicken soup
1/2 soup can milk
2/3 cup shredded cheese

Cook wild rice in salted water in saucepan for 45 minutes or until water is absorbed. Preheat oven to 325 degrees. Add butter, mushrooms, chicken broth, chicken and pepper to rice; mix well. Heat soup, milk and cheese in saucepan, stirring until smooth. Add

to rice mixture. Spoon into greased 1 1/2-quart baking dish. Bake for 1 hour. Yield: 4 servings.

Nancy Anderson, Xi Alpha
Moorhead, Minnesota

STAR OF TEXAS CHICKEN AND SPINACH CASSEROLE

1 chicken
1/4 cup margarine
1/4 cup all-purpose flour
1 teaspoon paprika
2 teaspoons seasoned
  salt
1/4 teaspoon cayenne
  pepper
2 teaspoons pepper
2 cups sour cream
1/3 cup lemon juice
1 8-ounce package egg
  noodles
1 10-ounce package
  frozen chopped spinach,
  thawed, drained
1 6-ounce can
  mushrooms, drained
1 8-ounce can water
  chestnuts, drained
1 4-ounce jar chopped
  pimento, drained
1/2 cup chopped onion
1/2 cup chopped celery
1 1/2 cups shredded
  Monterey Jack cheese

Preheat oven to 300 degrees. Rinse chicken inside and out. Cook in water to cover in saucepan until tender. Drain, reserving 1 cup stock. Chop chicken, discarding skin and bones. Melt margarine in saucepan. Blend in flour, paprika, seasoned salt, cayenne pepper and pepper. Add reserved stock, sour cream and lemon juice. Cook until thickened, stirring constantly. Add chicken. Cook noodles using package directions; drain. Add spinach, mushrooms, water chestnuts, pimento, onion and celery to noodles; mix well. Add chicken mixture; mix well. Spoon into 1 large or 2 medium baking dishes. Top with cheese. Bake for 25 to 30 minutes or until bubbly. Yield: 8 to 10 servings.

Shirley Ward, Eta Mu
Levelland, Texas

SCHLEMMERTOPF-STYLE FRIED CHICKEN

1 chicken, cut up
All-purpose flour
Salt and pepper to taste
1/2 cup butter or
  margarine
1/4 cup vegetable oil
1/4 cup wine vinegar
1 4-ounce can
  mushrooms
1 teaspoon rosemary
3 bouillon cubes
3 cups water
1 cup uncooked rice

Preheat oven to 350 degrees. Rinse chicken and pat dry. Coat with mixture of flour, salt and pepper. Brown in butter and oil in skillet; remove to 10-inch baking dish. Add vinegar, mushrooms and rosemary to chicken. Dissolve bouillon cubes in water in saucepan. Pour 1 cup bouillon into drippings in skillet; stirring to deglaze skillet. Pour over chicken. Bake for 1 hour. Stir rice into remaining bouillon in saucepan. Cook until tender. Serve with chicken. Yield: 4 to 5 servings.

Helen Walls, Xi Alpha Omega
Ladson, South Carolina

OVEN-FRIED GINGER CHICKEN

This was a hit at one of our Potluck Dinners.

1 cup all-purpose flour	1/2 cup butter or
2 teaspoons ginger	margarine
1/2 teaspoon cinnamon	1 chicken, cut up
2 teaspoons salt	1/2 cup soy sauce
1/2 teaspoon pepper	

Preheat oven to 400 degrees. Mix flour, ginger, cinnamon, salt and pepper in bowl. Melt butter in 9-by-13-inch baking dish. Rinse chicken and pat dry. Coat with flour mixture; arrange meaty side down in prepared dish. Bake for 45 minutes. Turn chicken over. Reduce oven temperature to 350 degrees. Pour soy sauce over chicken. Bake for 20 to 25 minutes or until done to taste. Yield: 6 servings.

Laura Fisher, Laureate Alpha Iota
Nanoose Bay, British Columbia, Canada

CHICKEN KABOBS

1 cup vegetable oil	2 cloves of garlic,
1/2 cup soy sauce	minced
1/3 cup lemon juice	Pepper to taste
2 tablespoons	6 chicken breast filets
Worcestershire sauce	1 large red bell pepper
2 tablespoons prepared	1 large green bell pepper
mustard	Cooked rice

Combine first 7 ingredients in shallow dish; mix well. Rinse chicken and pat dry; cut into 1 1/2-inch pieces. Add to marinade. Marinate in refrigerator for 3 hours or longer, turning chicken occasionally. Preheat grill. Cut bell peppers into squares. Drain chicken, reserving marinade. Thread chicken and peppers onto skewers. Grill for 20 minutes, turning skewers and basting occasionally with reserved marinade. Serve over rice. May use vegetables of choice, parboiling vegetables for easier skewering if desired. Yield: 4 to 6 servings.

Bev Sammut, Eta Upsilon
Bolton, Ontario, Canada

OVEN-BARBECUED CHICKEN

1 chicken, cut up	1 cup water
1/2 cup all-purpose flour	1/4 cup barbecue sauce
2 teaspoons salt	2 tablespoons light
Vegetable oil	brown sugar
1 onion, chopped	1 teaspoon instant beef
1/4 cup chopped celery	bouillon or
1/4 cup chopped green	beef-in-a-mug
bell pepper	1 teaspoon
1 cup catsup or 1	Worcestershire sauce
10-ounce can tomato	Hot cooked rice
soup	

Preheat oven to 350 degrees. Rinse chicken and pat dry. Coat with mixture of flour and salt. Brown in oil in skillet; remove to 3-liter baking dish with cover.

Sauté onion, celery and green pepper in drippings in skillet. Stir in next 6 ingredients. Pour over chicken. Bake, covered, for 1 to 1 1/2 hours or until tender. Serve with rice. Yield: 4 servings.

Betty Scharfenberg, Beta Kappa
Bonnyville, Alberta, Canada

MICROWAVE BARBECUED CHICKEN

1 cup catsup	1 cup packed light
3 tablespoons vinegar	brown sugar
3 tablespoons	1 tablespoon dry
Worcestershire sauce	mustard
3 tablespoons lemon	1 teaspoon salt
juice	1 chicken, cut up
2 tablespoons margarine	Hot cooked rice
1 tablespoon paprika	

Combine first 9 ingredients in 2-quart glass dish; mix well. Microwave on High for 2 1/2 minutes. Rinse chicken and pat dry. Add to sauce, coating well. Microwave, covered, on High for 25 to 30 minutes or until tender. Serve with rice. Yield: 5 servings.

Joni Eggen, Psi
Regina, Saskatchewan, Canada

MICROWAVE FIESTA CHICKEN KIEV

8 chicken breast filets	1 teaspoon MSG
3 tablespoons butter or	(optional)
margarine, softened	1/4 cup melted butter or
3 tablespoons Old	margarine
English sharp cheese	1 cup crushed Cheddar
spread	cheese-flavored butter
2 teaspoons onion flakes	crackers
2 tablespoons chopped	1 1/2 tablespoons taco
green chilies (optional)	seasoning mix

Rinse chicken and pat dry. Pound with meat mallet to flatten. Blend butter and cheese spread in small bowl. Add onion flakes, green chilies and MSG; mix well. Spoon onto ends of chicken filets. Roll chicken to enclose filling, tucking in ends; secure with wooden picks. Dip in melted butter; coat with mixture of cracker crumbs and taco seasoning mix. Arrange in 8-by-12-inch glass dish. Microwave, covered with waxed paper, on High for 10 to 12 minutes or until tender, rotating dish after 5 minutes. Let stand for 5 minutes. Remove wooden picks. Yield: 8 servings.

Kathryn Biss, Preceptor Delta Gamma
Nobleton, Ontario, Canada

B. J. McKenzie, Xi Gamma Xi, Beverly, West Virginia, combines 16 ounces Catalina salad dressing and 1/2 cup packed light brown sugar in 9-by-13-inch baking dish and adds 4 large boned chicken breasts, turning to coat. Bake, covered with foil, in preheated 350-degree oven for 45 minutes.

CHICKEN STUFFED WITH POTATOES AND OLIVES

3 or 4 medium red or new potatoes, peeled, chopped, cooked	2 cloves of garlic, crushed
8 to 10 stuffed green olives, chopped	1 tablespoon chopped capers
Rosemary to taste	3 tablespoons olive oil
3 to 4 tablespoons chopped parsley	1 3-pound chicken
	Salt and pepper to taste

Preheat oven to 375 degrees. Combine potatoes, olives, rosemary, parsley, garlic, capers and olive oil in bowl; mix well. Rinse chicken and pat dry. Season inside and out with salt and pepper. Stuff potato mixture into chicken. Place in baking dish. Bake for 1 hour and 10 minutes to 1 hour and 20 minutes or until tender. Cut chicken into quarters. Serve with potato dressing. Yield: 4 servings.

Janice Inlow, Xi Delta Gamma
Raytown, Missouri

ROASTED CHICKEN BREASTS WITH PROSCIUTTO AND LEMON

1 cup whipping cream	2 large shallots, minced
1 tablespoon buttermilk	2 tablespoons olive oil
3/4 cup unsalted butter or margarine, softened	2 cloves of garlic, crushed
4 ounces thinly sliced prosciutto or boiled ham, finely chopped	2 carrots, minced
	1 small green bell pepper, minced
1 tablespoon grated lemon rind	6 cups chicken stock or low-sodium canned broth
1/4 cup finely chopped parsley	Juice of 1 lemon
1/2 teaspoon salt	1 1/2 teaspoons arrowroot
1/2 teaspoon pepper	1 tablespoon water
4 large whole 1- to 1 1/4-pound chicken breasts	Salt and pepper to taste
	1/4 cup chopped parsley

Combine whipping cream and buttermilk in medium bowl; mix well. Let stand, covered with plastic wrap, at room temperature overnight. Chill, tightly covered, for 4 hours or longer to thicken. Store crème fraîche in refrigerator for several days. Preheat oven to 450 degrees. Combine butter and next 5 ingredients in bowl; mix well. Rinse chicken and pat dry. Loosen skin carefully from chicken. Spread butter mixture evenly between skin and chicken. Arrange on rack on baking sheet. Roast on center rack of oven for 30 minutes or until golden brown and tender but juicy, basting frequently with drippings. Cover with foil and keep warm. Sauté shallots in olive oil in large skillet for 3 minutes. Add garlic. Cook for 1 minute. Stir in carrots and green pepper. Cook for 2 minutes or until slightly tender. Add chicken stock, lemon juice and 1/2 cup crème

fraîche. Bring to a boil over high heat. Boil for 15 to 20 minutes or until reduced to 2 cups. Blend arrowroot in water in small bowl. Add to sauce gradually. Cook for 1 minute or until thickened, stirring constantly. Season with salt and pepper to taste. Cut chicken from bone in 1 piece, using sharp thin knife. Place on warmed plates; spoon sauce over top. Garnish with 1/4 cup parsley. Yield: 6 to 8 servings.

Maureen T. Gitschier, Zeta Theta
Lee's Summit, Missouri

YUMMY CHICKEN LIVERS

2 containers chicken livers	1/2 cup white wine
4 to 6 medium onions, sliced	1 teaspoon Italian seasoning
1/2 cup unsalted butter or margarine	Melba toast rounds or crackers

Rinse chicken livers and pat dry; cut into quarters. Sauté onions in butter in large skillet until transparent. Add wine and Italian seasoning. Simmer, covered, just until tender. Add livers. Sauté until cooked through, stirring gently. Serve immediately with Melba toast rounds. May prepare in advance and reheat in oven or microwave. May add to scrambled eggs. Yield: 8 to 10 servings.

Bobbie M. Singer, Laureate Delta
North Charleston, South Carolina

CORNISH HENS

1 envelope Italian salad dressing mix	2/3 cup vegetable oil
1/4 cup red or white wine vinegar	2 tablespoons Dijon mustard
2 tablespoons water	4 Cornish game hens

Prepare salad dressing mix with vinegar, water and oil in covered container, using package directions. Add mustard; shake to mix well. Rinse Cornish hens and pat dry. Combine with marinade in airtight container; mix well. Chill, covered, overnight, shaking container several times. Preheat oven to 350 degrees. Drain hens, reserving marinade. Place hens in shallow roasting pan. Drizzle with reserved marinade. Roast for 1 hour. Yield: 4 servings.

Christine Stutzman, Theta Theta
Goshen, Indiana

Paula B. Mathias, Alpha Kappa, Moorhead, Minnesota, makes Parmesan Chicken by arranging floured chicken breast strips in 1/4 cup melted butter or margarine in baking dish. Season with salt, pepper and 2 tablespoons lemon juice. Top with 1 cup whipping cream and 1/2 cup Parmesan cheese. Sprinkle with paprika. Bake in preheated 400-degree oven for 20 minutes.

BREAKFAST PIE

8 ounces ground turkey	4 cups shredded
2 4-ounce cans	Cheddar cheese
chopped green chilies,	2 cups milk
drained	4 eggs
1/2 cup sliced olives	1 cup baking mix

Preheat oven to 425 degrees. Brown turkey in skillet sprayed with nonstick cooking spray, stirring until tender; drain. Layer green chilies, olives, turkey and cheese in greased 10-inch pie plate. Beat milk, eggs and baking mix in bowl until smooth or process in blender for 15 seconds. Pour over layers. Bake for 30 minutes or until knife inserted in center comes out clean. Let stand for 10 minutes before serving. Yield: 8 servings.

Esther Hallock, Laureate Lambda
Salmon, Idaho

CURRIED TURKEY BREAST

1 2-pound boneless	1 10-ounce can cream
turkey breast, skinned	of chicken or cream of
Seasoned bread crumbs	celery soup
2 tablespoons vegetable	2 teaspoons curry
oil	powder (or to taste)
1/2 soup can milk	Salt and pepper to taste
16 ounces sour cream	

Preheat oven to 350 degrees. Rinse turkey and pat dry. Cut into 4 or 5 thick slices. Coat with bread crumbs. Brown in oil in skillet for 8 to 10 minutes on each side. Remove to 9-by-13-inch baking dish. Combine remaining ingredients in bowl; mix well. Pour over turkey. Bake for 15 to 20 minutes or until done to taste. Yield: 5 servings.

Robin Dowty, Delta Kappa Gamma
Malin, Oregon

IOWA GRILLED TURKEY TENDERLOIN

My brother, who is on the Iowa Turkey Federation Board, serves this at the Iowa State Fair.

1 pound turkey	1/4 cup dry sherry
tenderloins, 3/4 to	2 tablespoons onion
1 inch thick	flakes
1/4 cup soy sauce	Dash of garlic sauce
1/4 cup vegetable oil	1/4 teaspoon ginger
2 tablespoons lemon	Pepper to taste
juice	

Rinse turkey and pat dry; place in shallow dish. Combine remaining ingredients in blender container. Process until blended. Pour over turkey, turning to coat well. Marinate, covered, in refrigerator for several hours. Preheat grill. Drain turkey. Grill over hot coals for 6 to 8 minutes on each side or until done to taste. Do not overcook. Yield: 3 to 4 servings.

Karen Thada, Xi Kappa
Crawfordsville, Indiana

GOURMET LEMON TURKEY

4 turkey breast filets	Butter or margarine
All-purpose flour	1/2 cup wine
1 large onion, chopped	1 tablespoon lemon juice
10 large mushrooms,	Garlic powder and
sliced or chopped	pepper to taste

Rinse turkey and pat dry. Coat lightly with flour. Sauté onion and mushrooms in butter in large skillet. Add turkey. Cook for 2 to 3 minutes on each side. Add wine, lemon juice, garlic powder and pepper. Cook just until heated through. Serve with steamed broccoli and rice. Yield: 4 servings.

Jill Warren, Xi Alpha Lambda
Asheboro, North Carolina

PERFECT TURKEY LOAF

2 pounds ground turkey	1/4 cup minced green bell
3 slices day-old bread,	pepper
crumbled	1/4 cup catsup
2 eggs, lightly beaten,	2 tablespoons prepared
or egg substitute	horseradish
1/4 cup evaporated milk	1 teaspoon dry mustard
1 medium onion,	2 teaspoons salt
chopped	1/2 cup catsup

Preheat oven to 375 degrees. Combine first 10 ingredients in bowl; mix well. Shape into loaf; place in loaf pan. Spread with remaining 1/2 cup catsup. Bake for 1 hour and 15 minutes. Unmold onto serving plate. Yield: 6 to 8 servings.

Joan B. Stout, Laureate Alpha Phi
Tacoma, Washington

SMOTHERED TURKEY CUTLETS

4 turkey cutlets	1 cup sliced mushrooms
All-purpose flour	1/4 cup Madeira
1 tablespoon minced	1/4 cup chicken broth
garlic	4 slices prosciutto
1 tablespoon butter	4 slices Gruyère cheese

Rinse turkey and pat dry. Coat with flour. Sauté garlic in butter in skillet. Add turkey. Cook until brown on both sides. Add mushrooms, wine and broth. Cook for 3 to 5 minutes or until turkey is done to taste. Layer prosciutto and cheese over cutlets. Steam, covered, for 2 minutes. Yield: 2 servings.

Judy Silver, Delta Eta Beta
Sacramento, California

J'Ann Gray, Laureate Delta Eta, Abilene, Texas, layers 10 slices cooked turkey and 10 ounces cooked broccoli in baking dish. Top with mixture of 1/2 can cream of chicken soup, 1/3 cup each chopped celery and onion, 1/2 teaspoon seasoned salt, 1 egg and 10 canned biscuits cut into tenths. Bake in preheated 350-degree oven for 35 minutes. Serve with sauce of 1/2 can chicken soup and 1/4 cup water.

TURKEY PATTIES PAPRIKA

1½ pounds ground turkey	2 teaspoons instant chicken bouillon
⅔ cup bread crumbs	1 tablespoon paprika
1 egg	½ cup water
½ cup milk	1 tablespoon all-purpose flour
1 teaspoon garlic powder	1 cup milk
Butter or margarine	½ cup sour cream
1 cup chopped onion	Salt and pepper to taste

Combine turkey, bread crumbs, egg, ½ cup milk and garlic powder in bowl; mix well. Shape into 6 patties. Brown on both sides in butter in skillet; remove to plate. Sauté onion in drippings in skillet. Stir in instant bouillon, paprika and water. Return patties to skillet. Bring to a boil; reduce heat. Simmer, covered, for 10 minutes; remove from heat. Stir in mixture of flour and 1 cup milk. Cook over medium heat until thickened to desired consistency. Stir in sour cream, salt and pepper. Yield: 6 servings.

Patricia Anderson, Xi Iota Upsilon
Fort Lauderdale, Florida

TURKEY PATTIES PARMIGIANA

1 to 1½ pounds ground turkey	1 teaspoon instant chicken bouillon
1 egg	¼ cup water
¼ cup chopped parsley	1 8-ounce can tomato sauce
¼ teaspoon poultry seasoning	1 4-ounce can mushrooms, drained
Garlic powder, salt and pepper to taste	½ teaspoon oregano
1 slice reduced-calorie bread	¼ teaspoon Italian seasoning
6 crackers	Dash of garlic powder
½ teaspoon Italian seasoning	1 cup shredded mozzarella cheese

Preheat oven to 450 degrees. Combine turkey, egg, parsley, poultry seasoning, garlic powder, salt and pepper in bowl; mix well. Shape into 4 to 6 oval patties. Process bread, crackers and ½ teaspoon Italian seasoning in blender until crumbly. Coat patties in crumb mixture, pressing lightly. Arrange in 6-by-10-inch baking pan sprayed with nonstick cooking spray. Bake for 15 minutes. Dissolve instant bouillon in water in saucepan. Add tomato sauce, mushrooms, oregano, ¼ teaspoon Italian seasoning and garlic powder. Cook until heated through. Pour over patties. Bake for 15 minutes longer. Sprinkle with cheese. Bake just until cheese melts. Yield: 4 to 6 servings.

Patricia McConnell, Preceptor Lambda
Excelsior Springs, Missouri

BAKED FISH WITH MUSHROOM SAUCE

2 teaspoons margarine	2 tablespoons lemon juice
1 cup chopped mushrooms	10 ounces cod or haddock filets
1 small clove of garlic, minced	¼ cup chopped scallions
Salt and pepper to taste	¼ cup dry vermouth

Preheat oven to 400 degrees. Heat margarine in small skillet. Add next 5 ingredients. Cook until most of the liquid has evaporated, stirring occasionally. Spoon over fish in 1-quart baking dish. Add scallions and wine. Bake for 10 to 15 minutes or until fish flakes easily. Yield: 2 servings.

Anita L. Karl, Preceptor Laureate Zeta
Cheyenne, Wyoming

STUFFED CATFISH

8 fresh mushrooms, sliced	1 egg
½ onion, chopped	½ cup mayonnaise
2 shallots, chopped	1 tablespoon English mustard
¼ cup butter or margarine	½ teaspoon salt
8 farm-raised catfish filets	¼ teaspoon white pepper
1 green bell pepper, finely chopped	2 pounds lump crab meat
1 pimento, finely chopped	5 ounces white wine
	Salt and black pepper to taste

Preheat oven to 400 degrees. Sauté mushrooms, onion and shallots in butter in skillet. Spoon into shallow baking dish. Arrange filets in prepared dish. Mix next 7 ingredients in bowl. Stir in crab meat gently. Spoon into mound on filets. Add wine. Sprinkle with seasonings. Bake for 15 to 20 minutes or until fish flakes easily. Yield: 8 servings.

Martha Hallman, Mu
Jackson, Tennessee

OCEAN PERCH SUPREME

2 tablespoons butter or margarine, softened	1 10-ounce can cream of mushroom soup
1½ pounds frozen ocean perch	½ cup dry wine or water
2 tablespoons fresh lemon juice	1 teaspoon tarragon
½ cup milk	2 tablespoons toasted sliced almonds

Preheat oven to 400 degrees. Spread half the butter in 9-by-13-inch baking dish. Arrange fish in dish. Spread with remaining butter; sprinkle with lemon juice. Combine milk, soup, wine and tarragon in bowl; mix well. Spoon over fish. Bake for 30 minutes. Sprinkle with almonds. Yield: 4 servings.

September Leuthard, Xi Alpha Tau
Kemmerer, Wyoming

HALIBUT STEAK IN WINE SAUCE

1/4 cup melted butter or margarine	2 tablespoons melted butter or margarine
2 tablespoons lemon juice	1/2 cup dry white wine
1/2 teaspoon salt	1 teaspoon lemon juice
1/4 teaspoon pepper	1 cup milk or cream
1 to 2 pounds halibut steaks	1/2 teaspoon salt
3 tablespoons all-purpose flour	1/4 teaspoon pepper

Preheat broiler. Blend first 4 ingredients in small bowl. Place fish on rack in broiler pan; brush with half the butter mixture. Broil for 5 minutes on each side, brushing with remaining butter mixture when turned. Place fish in baking dish. Set oven temperature to 350 degrees. Blend flour into 2 tablespoons butter in saucepan. Stir in wine and remaining ingredients. Cook until thickened, stirring constantly. Pour over fish. Bake for 45 to 60 minutes or until done to taste. Yield: 2 to 4 servings.

Joanna Paul, Preceptor Beta Alpha
Portland, Oregon

BAKED RED SNAPPER IN CREOLE SAUCE

1 tablespoon shortening	2 tablespoons butter or margarine
1 teaspoon salt	
1/2 teaspoon pepper	1 29-ounce can tomatoes
4 to 6 pounds red snapper	1/2 teaspoon sugar
1/2 cup chopped onion	1 bay leaf
2 stalks celery, chopped	Salt and pepper to taste
1 clove of garlic, chopped	Steamed rice

Preheat oven to 450 degrees. Blend shortening, 1 teaspoon salt and 1/2 teaspoon pepper in small bowl. Rub fish inside and out with mixture. Place in 12-by-18-inch baking dish. Bake for 30 minutes. Reduce oven temperature to 350 degrees. Sauté onion, celery and garlic in butter in saucepan. Add tomatoes, sugar, bay leaf, salt and pepper. Simmer for 40 minutes, stirring occasionally. Pour over fish. Bake for 30 minutes or until fish flakes easily. Remove bay leaf. Serve over steamed rice. Yield: 4 to 8 servings.

Joy S. Thibodeaux, Preceptor Alpha Alpha
Westwego, Louisiana

BARBECUED SALMON

1 cup soy sauce	1 to 2 cloves of garlic, crushed
1/2 cup packed light brown sugar	1 lemon, sliced
3/4 cup white wine	1 1-inch piece gingerroot, crushed
1 medium onion, chopped	1 1/2 bay leaves
2 stalks celery, chopped	1 cup water
	6 to 8 salmon filets

Combine soy sauce, brown sugar, wine, onion, celery, garlic, lemon, gingerroot, bay leaves and water in shallow dish. Add salmon. Marinate in refrigerator for 4 hours or longer. Discard bay leaves. Preheat grill; line with foil sprayed with nonstick cooking spray. Grill salmon on both sides until done to taste. Serve with green salad, baked potato, corn on the cob and fresh buns. May serve cold. Yield: 6 to 8 servings.

Joyce Wenner, Preceptor Lambda
Nanaimo, British Columbia, Canada

ROAST SALMON DELIGHT IN SAUCE

The secret to cooking salmon is simple: cook it hot and fast.

1 fresh salmon, head removed	1 13-ounce can evaporated milk
Salt to taste	

Preheat oven to 400 degrees. Sprinkle cut ends and inside of salmon with salt. Place on rack in baking dish just larger than fish. Bake for 20 minutes. Pour evaporated milk over fish. Bake for 20 to 25 minutes longer or until fish flakes easily, basting occasionally. Yield: 4 to 8 servings.

Virginia Hedderly Cox, Beta Master
Oregon City, Oregon

SWEET AND SOUR FISH

1 medium onion, thinly sliced	1/4 cup sugar
1/2 medium green bell pepper, thinly sliced	1/4 cup vinegar
Vegetable oil	2 tablespoons catsup
1 pound frozen codfish, partially thawed	1 tablespoon soy sauce
Cornstarch	1/4 teaspoon ginger
1 8-ounce can pineapple chunks	1 1/2 teaspoons cornstarch
	1 1/2 teaspoons water
	Cooked rice

Sauté onion and green pepper in a small amount of oil in skillet. Remove to bowl. Cut fish into cubes. Toss with cornstarch in bowl, coating well. Brown in oil in skillet; keep warm. Drain pineapple, reserving 1/3 cup juice. Combine reserved juice with sugar, vinegar, catsup, soy sauce and ginger in saucepan. Stir in 1 1/2 teaspoons cornstarch dissolved in water. Cook until thickened, stirring constantly. Stir in pineapple and sautéed vegetables. Place fish on serving platter; spoon sauce over top. Serve with rice. Yield: 4 servings.

Barbara Owen, Epsilon
Winchester, Virginia

Sandra Ainsworth, Marietta, Georgia, marinates 10 pounds shrimp in mixture of 5 ounces soy sauce and 16 ounces Italian salad dressing. Bake on baking sheet in preheated 350-degree oven for 15 minutes.

EASY CHEESY TUNA MUFFINETTES

1 6-ounce can tuna	1 teaspoon seasoned salt
1 cup cooked rice	1 teaspoon lemon pepper
1 cup shredded Cheddar	1/4 cup melted butter or
cheese	margarine
1 egg	1/2 cup lemon juice
2 tablespoons milk	Lemon pepper to taste
1/2 small onion, chopped	

Preheat oven to 350 degrees. Combine tuna, rice, cheese, egg, milk, onion, seasoned salt and 1 teaspoon lemon pepper in bowl; mix well. Mound into muffin shapes in 6 muffin cups sprayed with nonstick cooking spray. Bake for 15 to 20 minutes or until cooked through. Combine butter, lemon juice and lemon pepper to taste in small bowl. Spoon over muffinettes at serving time. Yield: 6 servings.

Debbie Oglesby, Xi Gamma Omicron
Martinez, Georgia

TUNA RING WITH CHEESE SAUCE

1 egg, slightly beaten	2/3 cup milk
2 6-ounce cans tuna	1/4 cup margarine
1/2 cup chopped onion	1/4 cup baking mix
1/2 cup shredded	2 cups milk
Cheddar cheese	1/2 cup shredded
1/2 cup chopped celery	Cheddar cheese
1/2 teaspoon salt	1/4 teaspoon salt
1/4 teaspoon pepper	1/4 teaspoon pepper
2 cups baking mix	

Preheat oven to 375 degrees. Reserve 1 tablespoon egg. Mix remaining egg with tuna, onion, 1/2 cup cheese, celery, 1/2 teaspoon salt and 1/4 teaspoon pepper in bowl; set aside. Combine 2 cups baking mix with 2/3 cup milk in bowl; mix well. Roll into 10-by-15-inch rectangle on floured surface. Spread with tuna mixture. Roll from long side to enclose filling. Place seam side down on greased baking sheet, shaping into ring; pinch ends to seal. Make 12 cuts at 1-inch intervals in ring, cutting 2/3 of the way through. Turn slices onto sides. Brush with reserved egg. Bake for 25 to 30 minutes or until brown. Combine remaining ingredients in saucepan; mix well. Cook until smooth and bubbly, stirring constantly. Serve over tuna ring. Yield: 4 to 6 servings.

Teresa Koehn, Xi Gamma Tau
Canton, Kansas

TURBOT WITH GRAPEFRUIT BUTTER

1 fresh turbot filet	2 tablespoons white wine
Lemon juice to taste	2 ounces fresh
Salt and pepper to taste	grapefruit juice
Unsalted butter	Salt and pepper to taste
Juice of 1/2 lemon	10 1/2-inch sprigs of dill
1 teaspoon chopped	6 tablespoons unsalted
shallot	butter

Sprinkle filet with lemon juice, salt and pepper. Sauté in a small amount of butter in saucepan until nearly done to taste. Remove to warm plate; fish will continue to cook in hot juices. Combine juice of 1/2 lemon, shallot, wine, grapefruit juice, salt and pepper in small saucepan. Cook over medium heat until reduced to 2 tablespoons; remove from heat. Add dill and 6 tablespoons butter. Swirl pan until well mixed. Pour onto plate, pushing dill sprigs to outer edge. Place fish filet in center. Yield: 1 serving.

Joanne Watts, Xi Gamma Theta
Waterloo, Ontario, Canada

LINGUINE WITH CLAM SAUCE

1 10-ounce can clams	2 tablespoons
2 tablespoons minced	all-purpose flour
onion	1 cup milk
2 tablespoons minced	1 tablespoon chopped
celery	parsley
3 tablespoons margarine	Salt and pepper to taste
3/4 cup sliced	1 16-ounce package
mushrooms	linguine, cooked

Drain clams, reserving liquid; chop clams. Sauté onion and celery in margarine in small saucepan. Add mushrooms. Cook for 2 to 3 minutes or until tender. Stir in flour. Add reserved clam liquid and milk. Cook until thickened, stirring constantly. Add clams, parsley, salt and pepper. Cook until heated through. Serve over linguine. Serve with tossed salad and dinner rolls. Yield: 8 servings.

Elaine A. Ainsworth, Preceptor Beta
Piedmont, South Dakota

DEVILED CRAB CASSEROLE

1/2 cup finely chopped	2 cups crushed seasoned
green bell pepper	croutons
1/2 cup finely chopped	2 teaspoons
onion	Worcestershire sauce
1 cup finely chopped	1 pound crab meat or
celery	imitation crab meat
Butter or margarine	1 to 2 tablespoons
1 10-ounce can cream	butter or margarine
of shrimp soup	Cracker crumbs
1/2 cup mayonnaise	

Preheat oven to 350 degrees. Sauté green pepper, onion and celery in a small amount of butter in saucepan. Combine with soup, mayonnaise, crouton crumbs, Worcestershire sauce and crab meat in bowl; mix well. Spoon into greased 1 1/2-quart baking dish. Top with 1 to 2 tablespoons butter. Sprinkle with cracker crumbs. Bake for 20 to 30 minutes or until bubbly. Yield: 6 to 8 servings.

Betty Rollins, Preceptor Beta Tau
Grafton, Virginia

SCALLOPS SAUTÉ

2/3 cup chili sauce	1 1/2 pounds sea
1/3 cup catsup	scallops, drained
1 tablespoon prepared	2 tablespoons butter or
horseradish	margarine
1 tablespoon	Finely chopped parsley
Worcestershire sauce	Cooked noodles
1 tablespoon lemon juice	Melted butter or
2 teaspoons prepared	margarine
mustard	Grated Parmesan cheese
1/8 teaspoon garlic salt	

Combine chili sauce, catsup, horseradish, Worcestershire sauce, lemon juice, mustard and garlic salt in bowl; mix well. Sauté scallops in 2 tablespoons butter in medium skillet over high heat for 5 to 8 minutes or until browned and tender. Pour sauce over scallops. Cook just until bubbly. Sprinkle with parsley. Toss noodles with melted butter and Parmesan cheese in serving bowl. Serve with scallops. Yield: 4 to 6 servings.

Charlotte Zeiller, Xi Mu Nu
Dunnellon, Florida

CRAB AND SHRIMP AU GRATIN

1/4 cup all-purpose flour	1/8 teaspoon hot sauce
1 cup milk	8 ounces cooked shrimp
1/2 teaspoon salt	4 ounces crab meat or
1/2 teaspoon pepper	imitation crab meat
1/3 cup processed cheese	1 cup shredded Cheddar
spread	cheese
1 cup milk	4 cups cooked rice

Preheat oven to 350 degrees. Blend flour, 1 cup milk, salt and pepper in saucepan. Cook until thickened, stirring constantly. Combine cheese spread and 1 cup milk in double boiler. Cook over hot water until cheese melts, stirring to mix well. Stir in white sauce and hot sauce; mix well. Add shrimp and crab meat. Spoon into greased 1 1/2-quart baking dish. Top with Cheddar cheese. Bake for 20 minutes. Serve over rice. Yield: 4 servings.

Margareth Anderson, Xi Mu
Rochester, Minnesota

NEW ORLEANS BARBECUED SHRIMP

This was served at our cooking school fund-raiser, which was a sell-out. After everyone was served, members stood around the skillet, sopping up the sauce and peeling leftover shrimp.

3 to 4 pounds uncooked	5 ounces white wine
shrimp in shells	1/4 cup Worcestershire
1 teaspoon chopped	sauce
garlic	1 teaspoon lemon juice
2 tablespoons cajun	1/2 cup butter or
spice	margarine
1 1/2 cups butter or	French bread or cooked
margarine	rice

Sauté shrimp and garlic with cajun spice in 1 1/2 cups butter in large skillet for 2 to 3 minutes. Add wine, Worcestershire sauce and lemon juice. Cook for 3 to 6 minutes or until done to taste. Add 1/2 cup butter. Shake skillet until butter melts and mixes well. Serve with French bread or rice to soak up sauce. Yield: 10 servings.

Mary F. Kirigin, Xi Alpha Sigma
Stansbury Park, Utah

SHRIMP CREOLE

1/2 cup chopped onion	1 8-ounce can tomato
2/3 cup chopped green	sauce
bell pepper	1/4 teaspoon hot sauce
1/2 cup chopped celery	2 bay leaves
1/4 cup margarine	1/2 teaspoon salt
1 tablespoon chopped	1 1/2 pounds uncooked
parsley	shrimp, peeled
1 16-ounce can	Cooked rice
tomatoes	

Sauté onion, green pepper and celery in margarine in skillet over medium heat. Add parsley, tomatoes, tomato sauce, hot sauce, bay leaves and salt; mix well. Simmer for 20 minutes. Add shrimp. Simmer for 10 minutes or until shrimp turn pink. Remove bay leaves. Serve over cooked rice. Serve with salad and hot rolls. Yield: 4 to 5 servings.

Mable Bolchoz, Preceptor Upsilon
Charleston, South Carolina

SHRIMP ÉTOUFÉE

1 large onion, finely	1 16-ounce can tomato
chopped	purée
2 green onions, finely	2 bay leaves
chopped	1 teaspoon
3 cloves of garlic,	Worcestershire sauce
minced	4 drops of Tabasco sauce
1/2 cup finely chopped	1/2 teaspoon each
celery	thyme, sugar, salt and
1/2 cup unsalted butter	pepper
or margarine	1 pound cooked peeled
2 tablespoons	shrimp
all-purpose flour	Cooked rice
2 1/2 cups water	

Sauté onion, green onions, garlic and celery in butter in skillet. Add flour, water, tomato purée, bay leaves, Worcestershire sauce, Tabasco sauce, thyme, sugar, salt and pepper; mix well. Simmer for 25 minutes, stirring occasionally. Add shrimp. Cook just until heated through. Remove bay leaves. Serve over rice. Yield: 2 to 4 servings.

Denny Porter, Xi Mu Theta
Coral Springs, Florida

SHRIMP MARILYN

20 uncooked shrimp
1 cup bread crumbs
1 tablespoon grated
   Parmesan cheese
1 tablespoon parsley
   flakes
1 teaspoon oregano
1 teaspoon minced garlic
1 tablespoon extra-
   virgin olive oil

6 medium mushrooms,
   sliced
3 tablespoons extra-
   virgin olive oil
1 teaspoon minced garlic
10 1½-inch scallops
½ cup Chablis

Preheat broiler. Peel and devein shrimp, leaving tails intact. Mix bread crumbs, cheese, parsley flakes, oregano and 1 teaspoon garlic in bowl. Sauté bread crumb mixture in 1 tablespoon olive oil in small sauté pan for 5 minutes. Sauté mushrooms in remaining 3 tablespoons olive oil in medium sauté pan over medium heat for 5 minutes. Add 1 teaspoon garlic, shrimp and scallops. Cook until shrimp turn pink, stirring constantly. Stir in wine; remove from heat. Spoon into 2 shallow baking dishes. Sprinkle with crumb mixture. Broil just until bread crumbs begin to brown. Serve immediately with crisp salad and crusty French bread. Yield: 4 servings.

Floyd J. Bydalek, Xi Alpha Epsilon
Two Rivers, Wisconsin

QUICK NEPTUNE TEMPURA

7 ounces fresh
   mushrooms, sliced
2 tablespoons margarine
2 cloves of garlic,
   chopped
1 white onion, cut into
   2-inch pieces
2 green bell peppers, cut
   into 2-inch pieces
2 tablespoons margarine
2 pounds fish filets
2 pounds large shrimp
½ teaspoon seasoned
   salt
½ teaspoon salt
½ teaspoon pepper
½ teaspoon cajun
   seasoned salt
2 tablespoons
   all-purpose flour

¼ cup cornstarch
1 cup all-purpose flour
½ teaspoon baking
   powder
¼ teaspoon soda
½ teaspoon seasoned
   salt
1 teaspoon salt
½ teaspoon cajun
   seasoned salt
¼ teaspoon pepper
1 egg
1 cup water
4 cups corn oil
Mushroom Rice
   (page 149)
Sweet and sour sauce or
   tartar sauce

Sauté mushrooms in 2 tablespoons margarine in cast-iron skillet until brown. Add garlic. Sauté for 2 minutes; set aside. Sauté onion and green peppers in 2 tablespoons margarine until onion becomes transparent; set aside. Cut fish into 2-inch pieces. Alternate fish, shrimp and sautéed vegetables on skewers. Sprinkle with ½ teaspoon seasoned salt, ½ teaspoon salt, ½ teaspoon pepper, ½ teaspoon cajun

seasoned salt and 2 tablespoons flour. Combine cornstarch, remaining 1 cup flour, baking powder, soda, remaining ½ teaspoon seasoned salt, 1 teaspoon salt, ½ teaspoon cajun seasoned salt, ¼ teaspoon pepper, egg and water in bowl; mix well. Dip skewers into batter. Deep-fry in 375-degree corn oil in tempura pan or electric skillet for 1 to 3 minutes or until golden brown. Drain on paper towel. Preheat oven to 325 degrees. Place skewers over Mushroom Rice in large casserole. Bake for 20 minutes. Serve with sweet and sour sauce or tartar sauce.
Yield: 6 to 8 servings.

Aline B. Lewis, Preceptor Beta Mu
Port Arthur, Texas

TIME-SAVER SEAFOOD CASSEROLE

1 6-ounce can shrimp
1 6-ounce can crab
   meat
1 6-ounce can lobster
1 10-ounce can cream
   of mushroom soup
⅓ cup vermouth

1 tablespoon
   mayonnaise
1 cup bread crumbs
1 cup shredded Cheddar
   cheese
¼ cup melted butter or
   margarine

Preheat oven to 350 degrees. Rinse and flake seafoods. Combine with soup, vermouth and mayonnaise in bowl; mix well. Mix bread crumbs and 1 cup cheese in bowl. Pour butter into of 9-by-9-inch casserole. Line with half the cheese mixture. Add mixture of seafood; top with remaining cheese mixture. Sprinkle with additional cheese. Bake for 30 minutes. Yield: 8 servings.

Betty J. Green, Laureate Nu
Macon, Georgia

WEST COAST SEAFOOD LINGUINE

24 medium tiger prawns
24 small bay scallops
2 cups boiling water
¼ cup white wine
2 cloves of garlic,
   crushed
12 fresh mushrooms,
   sliced
2 cups whipping cream

1 tablespoon grated
   Parmesan cheese
1 tablespoon grated
   Romano cheese
1 tablespoon chopped
   fresh basil
2 teaspoons salt
27 ounces linguine,
   cooked

Cook prawns and scallops in boiling water in saucepan for 1 to 1½ minutes or just until cooked through. Drain, reserving cooking liquid. Cook reserved cooking liquid in saucepan until reduced to 1 cup. Add wine and garlic. Cook until reduced by ⅓. Add mushrooms, whipping cream, cheeses, basil and salt. Stir in seafood. Cook until heated through. Serve over pasta. Yield: 5 to 6 servings.

Lenore M. Hamers, Xi Phi
Melville, Saskatchewan, Canada

The Vegetable Patch

ASPARAGUS QUICHE

This quiche reminds me of a breakfast my dad made for us when I was little.

1/2 cup milk
1/2 cup mayonnaise
2 eggs
1 tablespoon cornstarch
1/2 cup chopped yellow onion
2 cups chopped asparagus
1/2 cup chopped green bell pepper
Bacon drippings for sautéing
1/2 pound bacon, crisp-fried, crumbled
2 cups shredded hot pepper cheese
Salt and pepper to taste
1 unbaked 9-inch pie shell

Preheat oven to 350 degrees. Combine milk, mayonnaise, eggs and cornstarch in bowl; mix well. Sauté onion, asparagus and green pepper in a small amount of bacon drippings in skillet. Add to milk mixture. Stir in bacon and cheese. Add salt and pepper. Pour into pie shell. Bake for 30 minutes. May reduce calories by baking in greased pie plate without pie shell. Yield: 6 to 8 servings.

Lorinda Lawson, Xi Gamma Xi
Oroville, California

ASPARAGUS STIR-FRY

1 pound fresh asparagus
1 or 2 cloves of garlic, chopped
1 tablespoon olive oil
Lemon pepper to taste

Trim asparagus; cut into 1 1/2-inch diagonal pieces. Stir-fry garlic in hot olive oil in wok until golden brown. Add asparagus. Stir-fry for 3 to 5 minutes or until tender-crisp. Sprinkle generously with lemon pepper. Yield: 6 servings.

June Avis, Epsilon Xi
Unionville, Ontario, Canada

CALICO BEANS

My aunt brought this to every family dinner because it was everyone's favorite. Tastes great!

1 28-ounce can pork and beans
1 16-ounce can lima beans, drained
1 16-ounce can kidney beans, drained
1/4 pound bacon
1/4 cup chopped onion
1/2 pound ground beef
2/3 cup packed light brown sugar
1/2 cup sugar
1/2 cup catsup
2 teaspoons vinegar
1 teaspoon prepared mustard
Pinch of salt

Combine pork and beans, lima beans and kidney beans in large bowl; mix well. Sauté bacon, onion and ground beef in skillet, stirring until ground beef is crumbly; drain. Add sautéed mixture to beans. Add brown sugar, sugar, catsup, vinegar, mustard and salt; mix well. Spoon into 2 1/2-quart casserole. Chill overnight. Preheat oven to 325 degrees. Bake for 1 1/2 hours. Yield: 8 to 10 servings.

Susan Peters, Zeta Beta
Maryville, Missouri

SPEEDY BAKED BEANS

1 16-ounce can pork and beans
1/2 cup chopped onion
2 tablespoons light brown sugar
1/3 cup catsup
1 tablespoon molasses
1 1/2 teaspoons dry mustard
Pinch of cloves

Preheat oven to 350 degrees. Combine all ingredients in 1 1/2-quart casserole. Bake, covered, for 30 minutes. Yield: 4 to 6 servings.

Lizabeth Peters
Kerrville, Texas

"BEST-IN-THE-WEST" BEANS

A favorite meal of our family, especially our son Scott! Great with fresh buns!

1/2 pound ground beef	2 tablespoons molasses
10 slices lean bacon, chopped	1/2 teaspoon salt
1/2 cup chopped onion	1/2 teaspoon chili powder
1/3 cup packed light brown sugar	1/2 teaspoon pepper
1/3 cup sugar	1 16-ounce can pork and beans
1/4 cup catsup	1 16-ounce can kidney beans, drained
1/4 cup barbecue sauce	
2 tablespoons prepared mustard	1 16-ounce can butter beans, drained

Preheat oven to 350 degrees. Brown ground beef and bacon in skillet, stirring until ground beef is crumbly; drain. Add onion. Cook until onion is tender. Stir in brown sugar, sugar, catsup, barbecue sauce, mustard, molasses, salt, chili powder and pepper. Add pork and beans, kidney beans, and butter beans; mix well. Pour into 3-quart casserole. Bake for 1 hour. May be cooked in slow cooker using manufacturer's directions. Yield: 10 to 12 servings.

Darlene J. Koetke, Preceptor Zeta
Minnedosa, Manitoba, Canada

MOCK TOURTIÈRE

Great served with coleslaw, relish tray, baked beans or crusty bread.

1/2 cup small brown lentils	1/2 cup sunflower seed
2 cups water	2 eggs
1/4 cup millet	1 cup grated Parmesan cheese
1/4 cup bulgur	1/4 teaspoon ground cloves
3/4 teaspoon salt	
1 teaspoon basil	1/4 teaspoon cinnamon
1 clove of garlic, minced	1/4 teaspoon cayenne pepper
1 onion, chopped	
1 stalk celery, chopped	1/4 teaspoon savory
1/4 green or red bell pepper, chopped	1 recipe 2-crust pie pastry

Preheat oven to 350 degrees. Cook lentils with 2 cups water in saucepan for 20 minutes. Add millet and bulgur. Cook for 15 minutes longer. Stir in salt and basil. Sauté garlic, onion, celery and green pepper in skillet coated with nonstick cooking spray. Add to lentil mixture. Purée sunflower seed, eggs and Parmesan cheese in blender. Add to lentil mixture with cloves, cinnamon, cayenne pepper and savory; mix well. Pour into pastry-lined 10-inch pie plate. Top with remaining pastry, sealing edge and cutting vents. Bake for 35 to 40 minutes or until golden brown. Yield: 6 to 8 servings.

Anna Rozestraten, Xi Alpha
Quebec, Canada

DEVILED GREEN BEANS

1 large onion, chopped	1 cup shredded Cheddar cheese
1/2 green bell pepper, chopped	3 tablespoons butter or margarine, softened
1 2-ounce jar pimento	1/4 pound bacon, crisp-fried, crumbled
1 cup chopped celery	
1 10-ounce can tomato soup	1 16-ounce can green beans
2 teaspoons prepared mustard	

Preheat oven to 350 degrees. Mix onion, green pepper, pimento and celery in 3-quart casserole. Add soup, mustard, cheese, butter, bacon and green beans; mix well. Bake for 30 minutes. Yield: 6 to 8 servings.

Jane Elizabeth O'Hare, Nu Mu
Salina, Kansas

GREEN BEANS WITH WATER CHESTNUTS

1/2 pound green beans	1 teaspoon sesame oil
1/2 cup water chestnuts, sliced	2 1/2 teaspoons soy sauce
1/2 cup fresh mushrooms	1/2 teaspoon salt
1/2 clove of garlic, crushed	1/4 teaspoon pepper
	1 teaspoon sugar
1 teaspoon vegetable oil	2 teaspoons sesame seed

Stir-fry green beans, water chestnuts, mushrooms and garlic in vegetable and sesame oils in skillet. Add soy sauce, salt, pepper, sugar and sesame seed; mix well. Cook, covered, for 4 to 5 minutes or until green beans are tender. Yield: 4 servings.

Jan Thorne, Alpha Chi
Glendive, Montana

SPICY ITALIAN GREEN BEANS

1/2 onion, chopped	1 16-ounce can chopped tomatoes
4 cloves of garlic, chopped	1 tablespoon oregano
1/4 cup olive oil	1 teaspoon basil
2 16-ounce cans green beans, drained	1 tablespoon parsley
	Salt and pepper to taste

Sauté onion and garlic in olive oil in large saucepan until onion is tender. Add green beans, undrained tomatoes, oregano, basil, parsley, salt and pepper; mix well. Simmer for 1 hour. Yield: 6 to 8 servings.

Judy Aucoin
Independence, Missouri

Peggy MacDougall, Xi Alpha Epsilon, Whitecourt, Alberta, Canada, adds 1 can each drained green beans and mushrooms to cream sauce made with 1 chopped onion sautéed in 1/2 cup butter or margarine, 1/4 cup all-purpose flour, 1 1/2 cups milk and 2 tablespoons Cheez Whiz. Season with pepper, 1/8 teaspoon Tabasco sauce, 1 teaspoon MSG and 1 tablespoon soy sauce.

GREEN BEANS WITH GARLIC OIL

2 pounds fresh or frozen green beans	2 tablespoons olive oil
1 small onion, thinly sliced into rings	1/2 teaspoon cumin
	1/4 teaspoon coriander
2 cloves of garlic, minced	1/4 teaspoon salt
	1/4 cup toasted slivered almonds

Cook green beans in a small amount of water in large saucepan for 10 to 12 minutes or until tender-crisp; drain. Cook onion and garlic in olive oil in skillet until tender. Stir in cumin, coriander and salt. Cook for 1 minute. Combine with green beans in bowl; mix well. Sprinkle with almonds. Yield: 12 servings.

Annemarie M. Johnson, Preceptor Alpha Phi
Arkansas City, Kansas

GREEN BEANS WITH SWISS CHEESE

1 tablespoon butter or margarine	1/2 cup sour cream
	2 16-ounce cans green beans, drained
1 tablespoon all-purpose flour	
1/2 teaspoon salt	1 1/2 cups shredded Swiss cheese
1/2 teaspoon sugar	
1/8 teaspoon pepper	1/3 cup cornflake crumbs
1/2 cup milk	1 tablespoon melted butter or margarine
1/2 teaspoon grated onion	

Preheat oven to 400 degrees. Melt 1 tablespoon butter in skillet. Blend in flour, salt, sugar and pepper. Cook until bubbly, stirring constantly. Add milk gradually, stirring constantly. Remove from heat. Stir in onion and sour cream. Add green beans and cheese to sauce; mix well. Spoon into buttered 1 1/2-quart baking dish. Sprinkle with cornflake crumbs; drizzle with remaining 1 tablespoon butter. Bake for 20 minutes. Yield: 6 to 8 servings.

Rebecca Culp, Xi Upsilon
Salem, Oregon

RO-TEL AND GREEN BEANS

1 small onion, chopped	1 tablespoon sugar
Bacon drippings for sautéing	1 10-ounce can Ro-Tel tomatoes with green chilies
2 16-ounce cans French-style green beans, drained	
	6 slices crisp-fried bacon, crumbled
1 teaspoon salt	

Sauté onion in bacon drippings in large skillet just until tender. Add green beans, stirring to coat with bacon drippings. Cook, covered, for several minutes. Add salt, sugar, undrained tomatoes and crumbled bacon; mix well. Reduce heat to low. Cook for 15 minutes longer. Yield: 6 to 8 servings.

Debbie Seab, Alpha Kappa
Moss Point, Mississippi

CREAMY BROCCOLI BAKE

1 cup sliced mushrooms	1/4 cup sour cream
3 tablespoons butter or margarine	1 cup 2% milk
	1/8 teaspoon marjoram
2 tablespoons all-purpose flour	1/4 cup chopped pimento
	Flowerets of 1 bunch broccoli, cooked
3 ounces cream cheese, softened	1/4 cup bread crumbs
1/4 cup crumbled bleu cheese	

Preheat oven to 350 degrees. Sauté mushrooms in butter in large skillet for 2 minutes. Stir in flour, cream cheese and bleu cheese. Add mixture of sour cream, milk and marjoram. Bring to a boil, stirring constantly. Remove from heat. Stir in pimento and broccoli. Spoon into 1 1/2-quart baking dish; sprinkle with bread crumbs. Bake for 30 minutes. May substitute two 10-ounce packages frozen chopped broccoli for fresh broccoli. Yield: 6 servings.

Dorene Botkins, Preceptor Chi
Covington, Virginia

BROCCOLI BAKE

This has been a good recipe to take to covered dish dinners. I have been asked for the recipe many times.

2 10-ounce packages frozen chopped broccoli	Salt and pepper to taste
	1 cup grated sharp cheese
1 10-ounce can cream of mushroom soup	
1 cup mayonnaise	1/4 cup margarine, softened
2 eggs, well beaten	1/2 6-ounce package herb-seasoned stuffing mix
1 medium onion, chopped	

Preheat oven to 350 degrees. Cook broccoli using package directions; drain. Combine soup, mayonnaise, eggs, onion, salt and pepper in large bowl; mix well. Stir in broccoli. Spoon into greased 9-by-13-inch baking dish. Sprinkle with cheese. Combine margarine and stuffing mix in bowl; mix well. Sprinkle over broccoli mixture. Bake for 45 minutes. Yield: 15 servings.

Valerie Rankin, Preceptor Epsilon Theta
Pinellas Park, Florida

Addie Heck, Laureate Gamma Psi, Westcliffe, Colorado, combines 8 ounces melted Velveeta cheese with 1 can mushroom soup, 1 small can mushrooms, 1 chopped onion and 4 cups cooked broccoli in casserole. Bake in preheated 350-degree oven for 25 minutes.

BROCCOLI-ONION CASSEROLE

2 10-ounce packages frozen chopped broccoli	Dash of pepper
3 medium onions, cut into quarters	1 cup milk
2 tablespoons butter or margarine	3 ounces cream cheese, softened
2 tablespoons all-purpose flour	1/2 cup shredded sharp American cheese
1/2 teaspoon salt	2 tablespoons melted butter or margarine
	1 cup soft bread crumbs

Preheat oven to 350 degrees. Cook broccoli using package directions; drain. Cook onions in salted water in saucepan until tender; drain. Melt 2 tablespoons butter in skillet. Stir in flour, salt and pepper. Add milk gradually. Cook until thickened, stirring constantly. Reduce heat to low. Add cream cheese, blending well. Place broccoli and onions in 1 1/2-quart baking dish; pour sauce over vegetables. Sprinkle with cheese. Combine remaining 2 tablespoons butter with bread crumbs in bowl; sprinkle over cheese layer. Bake for 40 to 45 minutes or until center is bubbly. Yield: 6 servings.

Jean Reed, Xi Gamma Upsilon
Alma, Nebraska

BROCCOLI-CHEESE CASSEROLE

3 tablespoons butter or margarine	1 10-ounce package frozen chopped broccoli, thawed
3 tablespoons all-purpose flour	8 ounces American cheese slices, cut into pieces
6 eggs, beaten	
4 cups cottage cheese	

Preheat oven to 350 degrees. Melt butter in 9-by-13-inch baking dish. Combine remaining ingredients in bowl; mix well. Spoon into baking dish. Bake for 45 minutes or until golden brown. Yield: 10 servings.

Carolyn Ray, Xi Alpha Sigma
Ashland, Ohio

DANISH RED CABBAGE

1/4 cup butter or margarine	Salt and pepper to taste
1 medium head red cabbage, shredded	1/2 cup currant jelly
2 tablespoons sugar	Additional sugar (optional)
1/2 cup cider vinegar	Additional vinegar (optional)
2 tart apples, chopped	

Melt butter in heavy saucepan. Add next 6 ingredients. Cook over low heat until apples are tender-crisp, stirring often. Stir in jelly. Adjust flavor with additional sugar or vinegar for desired sweet and sour taste. Yield: 8 to 10 servings.

Alice Treadway, Laureate Kappa
New Orleans, Louisiana

MAPLE-APPLE-CARROT MÉLANGE

3 medium unpeeled tart apples	1 large onion, sliced
6 medium carrots, diagonally sliced	2 tablespoons maple syrup
3 tablespoons butter or margarine	1/2 teaspoon salt

Cut apples into 1/4- to 1/2-inch wedges. Sauté carrots in butter in skillet until partially done. Stir in onion, syrup and salt. Reduce heat to low. Cook, covered, for 5 to 7 minutes. Add apples. Simmer just until carrots are tender. Stir well before serving.
Yield: 5 or 6 servings.

Mary Cashour, Alpha Rho
Bel Air, Maryland

WINTER CARROT CASSEROLE

4 1/2 cups sliced carrots, cooked tender-crisp	2 tablespoons prepared horseradish
2/3 cup mayonnaise	1/4 cup crushed saltine crackers
1/4 cup cottage cheese	2 tablespoons melted butter or margarine
2 tablespoons chopped onion	
1/4 teaspoon salt	

Preheat oven to 350 degrees. Place carrots in 1 1/2-quart baking dish. Combine mayonnaise, cottage cheese, onion, salt and horseradish in bowl; mix well. Stir into carrots. Sprinkle with cracker crumbs; drizzle with butter. Bake for 30 minutes.
Yield: 4 to 6 servings.

Lois Smith, Zeta Lambda
LaBelle, Florida

COMPANY CARROTS

Everyone who has eaten these is amazed at how delicious a carrot can be.

1/2 cup butter or margarine	1/4 teaspoon celery salt
2 tablespoons dried onion	1/4 teaspoon pepper
1/4 cup all-purpose flour	2 cups milk
1 teaspoon salt	12 carrots, sliced, cooked
1/2 teaspoon dry mustard	1/2 pound sharp Cheddar cheese slices
	Bread crumbs

Preheat oven to 350 degrees. Melt butter in saucepan over medium heat. Add onion, flour, salt, mustard, celery salt and pepper; mix well. Add milk gradually. Cook until thickened, stirring constantly. Layer carrots and cheese slices alternately in 1-quart baking dish until all ingredients are used, ending with carrots. Pour sauce over top; sprinkle with bread crumbs. Bake for 25 minutes. Yield: 8 to 10 servings.

Joy Sellers, Xi Epsilon
Newport News, Virginia

SWEET AND SOUR CARROTS

I took this dish to our Christmas dinner once and now I get "assigned" to bring it to the dinner every year.

1 8-ounce can chunk pineapple	1 tablespoon cornstarch
1 pound carrots, cut into 1-inch diagonal slices	2 tablespoons vinegar
	2 tablespoons soy sauce
1 medium green bell pepper, cut into 1/2-inch squares	1/2 cup sugar

Drain pineapple, reserving juice. Cook carrots in water to cover in medium saucepan over medium-high heat until tender-crisp. Add green pepper and pineapple; mix well. Cook for 3 minutes longer. Combine cornstarch, vinegar, reserved pineapple juice and soy sauce in small saucepan; blend well. Add sugar. Cook over medium heat until thickened, stirring constantly. Add carrot mixture, stirring well. Cook until heated through. Yield: 6 servings.

Paula J. Wilson, Gamma Theta
Cedar Rapids, Iowa

CAULIFLOWER WITH TART CREAM SAUCE

This is a family favorite, especially on holidays.

Cauliflowerets of 1 head cauliflower	2 tablespoons sugar
1 egg, beaten	1/2 teaspoon salt
1/2 cup sour cream	1/4 teaspoon paprika
2 tablespoons lemon juice	1/2 cup sliced pitted olives

Cook cauliflower in a small amount of water in saucepan until tender; drain. Combine egg, sour cream, lemon juice, sugar, salt and paprika in medium saucepan. Cook over low heat, stirring often until heated through. Do not boil. Pour over cauliflower and black olives in serving bowl. Yield: 6 servings.

Carrie L. Fletcher, Beta Gamma
Siloam Springs, Arkansas

COMPANY CAULIFLOWER

Always a hit at dinner parties and requested by my family at family get-togethers.

Cauliflowerets of 1 head cauliflower	1/4 cup all-purpose flour
1/2 pound sliced mushrooms	1 teaspoon salt
	2 cups milk
1/4 cup chopped green bell pepper	6 slices pimento cheese
1/3 cup butter or margarine	Dash of paprika

Preheat oven to 350 degrees. Cook cauliflower in salted water in saucepan for 10 to 15 minutes or just until tender; do not overcook. Drain. Sauté mushrooms and green pepper in butter in skillet. Stir in flour and salt gradually. Add milk gradually, stirring constantly. Cook until thickened, stirring constantly. Layer cauliflower, cheese and sauce 1/2 at a time into 1 1/2-quart baking dish. Sprinkle with paprika. Bake for 25 minutes. Yield: 6 servings.

Dee E. Borger, Preceptor Upsilon
Centerville, Ohio

GARLIC CORN

My niece makes this for family gatherings. The kids like it and don't realize they are eating their vegetables.

1 10-ounce package frozen corn	8 ounces cream cheese
	Garlic salt to taste

Combine corn and cream cheese in glass dish. Microwave using package directions for corn. Add garlic salt; stir well. Yield: 8 servings.

Sherry Savely, Theta Zeta
Greensburg, Kansas

CALICO CORN CUSTARD

This recipe was a second place winner in the 1990 Jacksonville Daily Progress Cooking Contest.

2 12-ounce cans whole kernel corn	3 eggs
	2 tablespoons sugar
1 small red bell pepper, chopped	1/4 teaspoon nutmeg
	1/2 teaspoon salt
1 small green bell pepper, chopped	1/8 teaspoon pepper
	1 cup half and half
Milk	1 green bell pepper ring

Preheat oven to 350 degrees. Drain corn, reserving liquid. Place corn in large bowl. Add red and green peppers; toss to mix. Add enough milk to reserved corn liquid to measure 1 cup. Beat eggs in mixer bowl. Add sugar, nutmeg, salt, pepper, half and half, and milk mixture, beating constantly. Stir in corn mixture. Spoon into greased 1 1/2-quart baking dish gently. Place baking dish in center of 9-by-13-inch baking pan. Fill pan with enough boiling water to measure 1 inch in depth. Bake for 40 minutes. Do not overbake. Garnish with pepper ring. Yield: 8 servings.

Pat Baggett, Preceptor Zeta Gamma
Gallatin, Texas

Doreen Brenner, Preceptor Gamma Epsilon, De Bary, Florida, combines 11 ounces whole kernel corn, 15 ounces cream-style corn, 1 cup sour cream, 1/2 cup melted margarine and 8 1/2 ounces corn muffin mix in casserole for a Triple-Corn Casserole. Bake in preheated 325-degree oven for 1 hour.

VEGETARIAN "HIPPIE-STYLE" EGGPLANT

3 medium eggplant
8 ounces mushrooms,
 chopped
2 cloves of garlic, minced
1 cup chopped onion
Salt and pepper to taste
3 tablespoons butter or
 margarine
1½ cups cottage cheese
1 cup cooked brown rice

1 cup grated Cheddar
 cheese
½ teaspoon thyme
Several drops of Tabasco
 sauce
¼ cup toasted
 sunflower seed
Paprika to taste
¼ cup chopped fresh
 parsley

Preheat oven to 350 degrees. Slice eggplant lengthwise. Scoop out centers, leaving ¼-inch shells. Reserve and chop centers. Sauté reserved eggplant with mushrooms, garlic, onion, salt and pepper in butter until onion is tender. Stir in next 6 ingredients. Stuff eggplant shells with mixture; sprinkle with paprika and parsley. Arrange in buttered baking dish. Bake for 40 minutes. Yield: 6 servings.

Dee Dee Daley, Xi Delta
Truckee, California

BAKED MUSHROOMS

12 large or 24 small
 mushrooms
Salt and pepper to taste

1 tablespoon butter
⅔ cup whipping cream
Hot buttered toast

Preheat oven to 400 degrees. Cut large mushrooms into quarters; leave small mushrooms whole. Arrange mushrooms close together stem side down in greased shallow baking dish. Sprinkle with salt and pepper; dot with butter. Pour cream over mushrooms. Bake for 20 minutes, stirring gently twice. Spoon over hot buttered toast to serve. Yield: 3 or 4 servings.

Connie Kovats, Alpha Zeta
Harrisburg, Pennsylvania

SCALLOPED MUSHROOMS

1½ pounds mushrooms
2½ cups soft bread
 crumbs
⅔ cup melted butter or
 margarine

1 teaspoon salt
½ teaspoon pepper
⅓ cup chopped leeks
6 tablespoons vermouth
 or dry white wine

Preheat oven to 325 degrees. Layer ⅓ of the mushrooms, ⅓ of the bread crumbs, ⅓ of the butter, ⅓ of the salt and ⅓ of the pepper and all leeks into buttered 2-quart baking dish. Repeat layers, ending with pepper. Sprinkle with remaining mushrooms, salt and pepper. Pour vermouth evenly over layers. Bake, covered, for 40 minutes. Combine remaining bread crumbs and remaining butter in bowl; sprinkle over top. Bake, uncovered, for 10 minutes longer. Yield: 8 servings.

Lonnie Lang, Iota
Nelson, British Columbia, Canada

THE BEST-EVER ONION RINGS

1½ cups all-purpose
 flour
1½ cups beer

3 large yellow onions
3 to 4 cups vegetable
 shortening

Combine flour and beer in large bowl; blend well. Let stand, covered, for 3 hours at room temperature. Cut onions into ¼-inch rings. Preheat shortening to 375 degrees in electric skillet. Dip onion rings into beer batter; place in hot oil. Fry until golden brown; drain. Place on paper towel-lined plate. Keep warm in preheated 200-degree oven until all onion rings are done. Yield: 6 servings.

Barbara Brown, Xi Psi
Jonesboro, Arkansas

BAKED ONION DELIGHT

12 medium or 6 large
 sweet onions, thinly
 sliced into rings
1 7½-ounce package
 potato chips, crushed
½ pound Cheddar
 cheese, grated

2 10-ounce cans cream
 of mushroom soup
½ cup milk
⅛ teaspoon cayenne
 pepper

Preheat oven to 350 degrees. Alternate layers of onion rings, crushed potato chips and cheese into buttered 9-by-13-inch baking dish. Pour mixture of soup and milk over layers. Sprinkle with cayenne pepper. Bake for 45 minutes or until bubbly at center. Yield: 10 to 12 servings.

Lois Mortensen, Alpha Eta
Green River, Wyoming

SCALLOPED ONIONS

6 large yellow onions,
 thinly sliced into rings
½ cup margarine
2 teaspoons all-purpose
 flour
1 teaspoon dry mustard
1 teaspoon salt

½ teaspoon pepper
1 cup milk
8 ounces Cheddar
 cheese, shredded
1 7-ounce package corn
 bread stuffing mix
2 tablespoons margarine

Preheat oven to 400 degrees. Sauté onions in ¼ cup margarine in skillet. Melt ¼ cup margarine in saucepan over medium heat. Stir in flour, dry mustard, salt and pepper. Add milk and cheese. Cook until cheese is melted, stirring constantly. Alternate onions and sauce in greased 9-by-13-inch baking dish. Sprinkle with stuffing mix; dot with remaining 2 tablespoons margarine. Bake for 20 minutes. Yield: 8 to 10 servings.

Peggy Adams, Preceptor Tau
Bowling Green, Kentucky

SNIFFLES AND PEAS

This recipe came from my husband's family and we enjoy the new twist on peas. It is a German recipe.

3 eggs, beaten
2 cups all-purpose flour
Salt and pepper to taste

2 cups fresh or frozen
peas
Milk

Mix eggs, flour, salt and pepper in small bowl until a stiff dough is formed. Simmer peas in milk to cover in saucepan until peas are tender. Drop small pieces of dough into peas. Cook until dumplings are done. Yield: 4 servings.

Julie Boettcher, Beta Iota
Custer, South Dakota

ORANGE-GLAZED PEA PODS

8 ounces fresh pea pods
2 teaspoons sugar
3/4 teaspoon cornstarch
Dash of salt
1/4 cup orange juice
1/2 teaspoon grated
orange rind

2 teaspoons unsalted
butter or margarine
1/2 cup sliced almonds,
toasted

Cook peas in a small amount of water in saucepan until tender-crisp; drain. Combine sugar, cornstarch and salt in double boiler. Add orange juice, blending until smooth. Add orange rind. Cook until mixture begins to thicken, stirring constantly. Stir in butter until melted. Spoon over peas in serving dish; sprinkle with almonds. Yield: 4 servings.

Peg Baldwin, Laureate Beta Mu
Kenton, Ohio

CHILI SALSA POTATO SKINS

5 large russet potatoes,
scrubbed
1/3 cup melted margarine
3/4 cup shredded mild
Cheddar cheese
3/4 cup shredded
Monterey Jack cheese

1   8-ounce can tomato
sauce
1   4-ounce can green
chilies
1/4 cup chopped green
onions

Preheat oven to 400 degrees. Pierce potatoes several times with fork. Bake until soft. Let stand until cooled. Scoop out center of potatoes, leaving 1/8-inch thick shell. Brush skins inside and out with margarine. Place potatoes skin side down on 12-by-15-inch baking sheet. Increase oven temperature to 500 degrees. Bake for 12 minutes. Sprinkle with Cheddar and Monterey Jack cheeses. Preheat broiler. Broil 4 inches from heat source for 2 minutes or until cheeses are melted. Combine tomato sauce, green chilies and green onions in bowl; mix well. Spoon over potato skins just before serving. Yield: 6 servings.

Brenda Shive, Gamma Pi
Burrton, Kansas

EXTRAORDINARY WHIPPED POTATOES

5 pounds potatoes,
peeled, cubed
8 ounces cream cheese,
cubed
1/4 cup butter or
margarine, softened

1 cup sour cream
1 tablespoon onion salt
1 teaspoon salt
1/4 teaspoon pepper
Butter or margarine
Paprika

Preheat oven to 350 degrees. Boil potatoes in salted water until tender. Drain; mash well. Combine potatoes and cream cheese in mixer bowl; mix well. Stir in 1/4 cup butter, sour cream, onion salt, salt and pepper. Beat until smooth and fluffy. Spoon into 2-quart baking dish. Dot with butter; sprinkle with paprika. Bake until heated through. Yield: 12 servings.

Terri Jones, Delta Delta
Christina Lake, British Columbia, Canada

GRILLED CHEESY POTATOES

1 1/2 pounds small red
potatoes
1/2 cup chopped onion
1 large green bell
pepper, cut julienne-
style (optional)
1/2 teaspoon salt

1/4 teaspoon pepper
2 tablespoons butter or
margarine
8 ounces Cheddar
cheese, sliced or
shredded

Preheat grill. Peel potatoes; slice 1/4-inch thick. Oil two 15-inch long strips of aluminum foil lightly. Combine potatoes, onion, green pepper, salt and pepper in bowl; mix well. Place half the mixture on one end of each strip of aluminum foil. Dot with butter. Fold other end of foil over potatoes; seal. Grill 6 inches above hot coals for 15 minutes on each side. Fold back foil; sprinkle cheese over potatoes. Grill for 3 minutes longer or until cheese melts. Yield: 6 servings.

Bonnie Koel, Xi Zeta Kappa
Rock Rapids, Iowa

OVEN-BAKED STUFFED POTATOES

5 pounds potatoes,
peeled, cubed
1 pound bacon, cut into
pieces
1 medium onion,
chopped

1/2 cup butter
2 cups shredded
Cheddar cheese
1 egg, beaten
1/2 cup (about) shredded
Cheddar cheese

Preheat oven to 350 degrees. Boil potatoes in salted water until tender; drain. Fry bacon until crispy; drain. Sauté onion in bacon drippings until tender; drain. Mix potatoes and butter in bowl; mash until smooth. Add 2 cups shredded cheese, bacon bits and onion; mix well. Stir in egg. Spoon into 3-quart glass baking dish. Top with remaining 1/2 cup shredded cheese. Bake, uncovered, for 30 minutes.
Yield: 6 to 8 servings.

Kathy Brown, Preceptor Iota Phi
Fort Worth, Texas

PARTY POTATOES

1/2 cup chopped green bell pepper	2 teaspoons salt
1/4 cup chopped green onions	1/4 teaspoon pepper
1/4 cup chopped pimento	1 teaspoon paprika
1/2 cup margarine	3 to 4 cups milk
6 tablespoons all-purpose flour	1 cup shredded Cheddar cheese
1 tablespoon parsley flakes	6 cups chopped cooked potatoes
	1 cup shredded Cheddar cheese

Preheat oven to 350 degrees. Sauté green pepper, green onions and pimento in margarine in skillet for 1 minute. Stir in flour, parsley flakes, salt, pepper and paprika. Add milk gradually, stirring constantly. Cook over medium heat until thickened, stirring constantly. Add 1 cup cheese; mix well. Spoon potatoes into 9-by-13-inch baking pan. Pour sauce over potatoes, stirring to coat. Sprinkle with remaining 1 cup cheese. Bake for 30 to 40 minutes or until potatoes are tender. Yield: 12 servings.

Nancy D. Hunt, Zeta Alpha
Fredonia, Kentucky

POTATOES ROMANOFF

6 large potatoes	1 1/2 teaspoons salt
5 cups sour cream	1/4 teaspoon pepper
1 bunch green onions, chopped	1/2 cup shredded sharp Cheddar cheese
1 cup shredded sharp Cheddar cheese	Paprika

Cook potatoes in jackets until tender. Peel potatoes; shred into large bowl. Add sour cream, green onions, 1 cup cheese, salt and pepper; mix well. Spoon into buttered 2-quart baking dish. Top with remaining 1/2 cup cheese; sprinkle with paprika. Chill, covered, for several hours to overnight. Preheat oven to 350 degrees. Bake, uncovered, for 30 to 40 minutes or until heated through. Yield: 8 servings.

LaVerna Harris, Laureate Lambda
Salmon, Idaho

BAKED POTATO SALAD

8 medium potatoes, peeled, cooked, diced	Salt and pepper to taste
8 ounces Velveeta cheese, cubed	1/2 pound bacon, chopped, partially fried, drained
1 cup mayonnaise	1/4 cup sliced olives
1/2 cup chopped onion	

Preheat oven to 325 degrees. Combine first 6 ingredients in bowl; mix well. Spoon into 9-by-13-inch baking dish. Top with bacon and olives. Bake, uncovered, for 1 hour. Yield: 10 servings.

Sharon Buntrock, Preceptor Beta Kappa
Benbrook, Texas

CREAMY RADISHES

3/4 pound red radishes, sliced	1/2 teaspoon salt
3 tablespoons butter or margarine	Dash of pepper
	1/4 cup milk
1 tablespoon all-purpose flour	Snipped chives or parsley

Place radishes in water to cover in 2-quart saucepan. Bring to a boil. Simmer for 5 to 7 minutes or until tender-crisp. Drain, reserving 1/2 cup liquid. Melt butter in skillet over low heat. Blend in flour, salt and pepper. Cook over low heat until mixture is thick and bubbly, stirring constantly. Remove from heat; stir in milk and reserved 1/2 cup liquid. Simmer for 1 minute, stirring constantly. Add radishes. Cook for 5 minutes longer or until heated through. Pour into serving dish; sprinkle with chives or parsley. Yield: 4 to 6 servings.

Mary Beauregard, Xi Iota Sigma
Sarasota, Florida

SPINACH CASSEROLE

1 10-ounce package frozen spinach	1 3-ounce can French-fried onion rings
1 10-ounce can cream of mushroom soup	8 butter crackers, crushed
8 ounces light cream cheese, cubed	

Preheat oven to 375 degrees. Cook spinach using package directions; drain. Heat soup and cream cheese in saucepan until blended, stirring frequently. Add onion rings and spinach; mix well. Pour into 8-by-8-inch baking dish. Sprinkle with cracker crumbs. Bake for 20 minutes. Yield: 8 servings.

Virginia M. Hamilton, Laureate Alpha Epsilon
Hays, Kansas

SPINACH ENCHILADAS

1 cup sour cream	1/2 clove of garlic
1 10-ounce can cream of chicken soup	12 flour tortillas
1 4-ounce can green chilies, chopped	2 cups shredded Colby cheese
1 10-ounce package frozen spinach, thawed, drained	1 medium onion, chopped
	Snipped chives

Preheat oven to 350 degrees. Combine sour cream, soup, green chilies, spinach and garlic in blender container. Purée at high speed until smooth. Pour 1/3 of the sauce into 9-by-13-inch baking pan. Sprinkle each tortilla with cheese and onion. Roll up to enclose filling; arrange in pan. Pour remaining sauce over tortillas. Bake for 25 minutes. Garnish with chives. Yield: 6 servings.

Sally Sutherlin, Preceptor Delta
La Mesa, New Mexico

SPINACH PÂTÉ

I cherish this recipe which came from my husband's grandmother, who was a wonderful cook. As it is very rich, we serve it on holidays.

2 10-ounce packages chopped spinach	1/2 to 1 cup bread crumbs
4 eggs, lightly beaten	1/3 cup vegetable oil
12 ounces Cheddar cheese, shredded	1/3 cup grated Romano cheese
12 ounces Velveeta cheese, shredded	1/3 cup grated Parmesan cheese
16 ounces cottage cheese, drained	1/3 cup cracker crumbs

Preheat oven to 350 degrees. Cook spinach using package directions; drain. Combine eggs, Cheddar cheese, Velveeta cheese and cottage cheese in large bowl; mix well. Add spinach gradually, stirring well. Add enough bread crumbs to thicken mixture. Spoon into well greased 9-by-13-inch baking dish. Sprinkle with oil. Top with mixture of Romano cheese, Parmesan cheese and cracker crumbs. Bake for 1 hour. Yield: 12 servings.

Marguerite Benet, Xi Beta Omicron
Yorba Linda, California

SPINACH-FILLED CRÊPES

1 cup milk	1 1/2 cups shredded sharp Cheddar cheese
3/4 cup all-purpose flour	
1 teaspoon sugar	2 10-ounce packages frozen chopped spinach, thawed
1/2 teaspoon salt	
2 tablespoons salad oil	
4 eggs	1/2 pound fresh mushrooms, chopped
1/3 cup butter or margarine	
1/3 cup all-purpose flour	6 tablespoons butter or margarine, coarsely chopped
1 teaspoon salt	
1/8 teaspoon pepper	1 whole mushroom, sliced
1/2 teaspoon dry mustard	
2 1/2 cups milk	1 tablespoon chopped parsley

Combine 1 cup milk, 3/4 cup flour, sugar, 1/2 teaspoon salt and oil in mixer bowl; beat well. Add eggs; beat until blended. Chill in refrigerator overnight. Pour 1/4 cup batter at a time onto hot, lightly greased nonstick 8-inch skillet, tilting skillet to cover bottom with batter. Bake until top side is dry; turn to brown other side. Cool on wire rack. Stack crêpes with waxed paper between them. Preheat oven to 350 degrees. Melt 1/3 cup butter in saucepan. Remove from heat. Add 1/3 cup flour, 1 teaspoon salt, pepper and mustard, stirring until mixture is smooth. Add milk gradually, stirring well. Bring to a boil, stirring constantly. Simmer for 1 minute. Add cheese; stir over low heat until melted. Remove from heat; set aside. Cook spinach using package directions; drain. Sauté spinach and chopped mushrooms in 6 tablespoons butter in 10-inch skillet for 2 minutes, stirring frequently. Pour cheese sauce over spinach, reserving 1/2 cup sauce for topping. Place 1/2 cup spinach mixture in center of each crêpe; roll up to enclose filling. Arrange crêpes on buttered baking sheet or heatproof serving platter. Bake, covered with aluminum foil, for 20 minutes. Spoon reserved cheese sauce over each crêpe. Garnish with sliced mushroom and parsley. Yield: 10 servings.

Marilyn A. Reitmeyer, Xi Zeta Tau
Pittsburgh, Pennsylvania

SPINACH ROC

2 or 3 fresh tomatoes, thickly sliced	1 tablespoon minced onion
2 10-ounce packages frozen spinach, cooked, drained	1/2 cup grated Parmesan cheese
	Pepper to taste
1 1/2 cups herb-seasoned stuffing mix	Garlic powder to taste
	1/2 cup margarine
6 eggs, beaten	Bread crumbs
1 teaspoon salt	

Preheat oven to 350 degrees. Line bottom of greased 9-by-9-inch baking pan with tomato slices. Combine spinach, stuffing mix, eggs, salt, onion, Parmesan cheese, pepper and garlic powder in large bowl; mix well. Spoon over tomato slices. Bake, uncovered, for 30 minutes. Dot with margarine and sprinkle with bread crumbs; serve hot. Yield: 6 to 8 servings.

Terry McLaughlin, Preceptor Nu
Orlando, Florida

HOLIDAY SQUASH CASSEROLES

6 cups cooked squash	1 1/2 cups shredded sharp Cheddar cheese
1 cup melted margarine	
4 eggs, beaten	1 teaspoon lemon pepper
1 cup cream of chicken soup	1 1/2 teaspoons black pepper
1 cup cream of mushroom soup	1/2 teaspoon salt
	1 tablespoon MSG
1/2 cup chopped green bell pepper	1/2 cup shredded Cheddar cheese
1/2 cup chopped pimento	1 cup butter-flavored cracker crumbs
1 cup chopped onion	

Preheat oven to 350 degrees. Combine squash, margarine, eggs and soups in large bowl; mix well. Stir in green pepper, pimento, onion, 1 1/2 cups cheese, lemon pepper, black pepper, salt and MSG. Spoon mixture into two 2-quart casseroles sprayed with nonstick cooking spray. Sprinkle with remaining 1/2 cup cheese and cracker crumbs. Bake, covered with aluminum foil, for 25 minutes. Remove foil. Bake for 10 minutes longer. Yield: 18 to 20 servings.

Mary Earle Watson, Laureate Mu
Albany, Georgia

SWEET POTATO YAM YUM

2½ cups mashed cooked
   sweet potatoes
1 cup sugar
1 egg, beaten
1 tablespoon vanilla
   extract
1 cup flaked coconut

1 8-ounce can crushed
   pineapple, drained
1 4-ounce jar
   maraschino cherries
1 cup sugar
3 tablespoons
   all-purpose flour

Preheat oven to 350 degrees. Combine sweet potatoes, 1 cup sugar, egg, vanilla and coconut in bowl;
mix well. Spoon into greased 2-quart casserole. Bake
for 45 minutes. Mix pineapple, undrained cherries,
remaining 1 cup sugar and flour in saucepan. Simmer until thickened, stirring constantly. Spread over
cooked potatoes; serve hot. Yield: 6 to 8 servings.

Doris Bame, Xi Gamma Pi
Carolina Beach, North Carolina

SWEET POTATO SOUFFLÉ

*This recipe has become a Thanksgiving tradition. A
lighter, healthier way to enjoy sweet potatoes.*

1 cup milk
¼ cup sugar
½ teaspoon salt
3 tablespoons butter or
   margarine, softened
1 teaspoon nutmeg

2 cups cooked sweet
   potatoes
2 egg yolks, beaten
2 egg whites
¼ teaspoon cream of
   tartar

Preheat oven to 350 degrees. Scald milk in saucepan.
Add sugar, salt, butter and nutmeg; mix well. Whip
sweet potatoes in large bowl until smooth. Add milk
mixture; beat until fluffy. Stir in egg yolks until
blended. Beat egg whites with cream of tarter in
mixer bowl until stiff peaks form. Fold into sweet
potato mixture gently. Pour into greased 1½-quart
soufflé dish. Bake for 50 to 60 minutes or until puffed
and golden brown. Yield: 8 servings.

Aurie Jo Salfen, Preceptor Beta Kappa
Rifle, Colorado

SWEET POTATOES KOOLAU

6 medium sweet
   potatoes, cooked,
   mashed
½ cup melted butter or
   margarine

¼ cup chopped pecans
½ cup orange juice
1 teaspoon salt
Crushed cornflakes

Preheat oven to 350 degrees. Combine cooked sweet
potatoes with butter, pecans, orange juice and salt in
bowl; mix well. Add more juice and butter if necessary. Shape into medium-sized balls; roll in crushed
cornflakes. Arrange in 9-by-13-inch baking dish.
Bake just until light brown. Yield: 6 servings.

Florence P. Stevens, Xi Phi
Butte, Montana

BUTTERSTUFFING TOMATOES

⅓ cup butter or
   margarine
½ teaspoon salt
1 teaspoon basil
¼ teaspoon pepper
½ cup green bell pepper
   strips

½ cup sliced celery
¼ cup chopped onion
4 tomatoes
1 cup herb-seasoned
   croutons
2 teaspoons sugar

Melt butter in large saucepan. Stir in salt, basil and
pepper. Sauté green pepper, celery and onion in
seasoned butter until tender. Cut tomatoes into 8
wedges each. Add to sautéed mixture with croutons
and sugar. Cook, covered, over medium-low heat
until heated through. Yield: 4 to 6 servings.

Linda Fricka, Xi Zeta Gamma
Chino Hills, California

TURNIP PUFF

6 cups cubed, cooked
   turnips
2 tablespoons butter or
   margarine, softened
2 eggs, beaten
2 tablespoons
   all-purpose flour
1 tablespoon light
   brown sugar

1 teaspoon baking
   powder
¾ teaspoon salt
⅛ teaspoon pepper
Pinch of nutmeg
½ cup fine bread crumbs
2 tablespoons melted
   butter or margarine

Preheat oven to 375 degrees. Mash cooked turnips in
large bowl. Add butter and eggs; beat well. Combine
flour, brown sugar, baking powder, salt, pepper and
nutmeg in small bowl; mix well. Stir into mashed
turnips. Spoon mixture into buttered 6-by-10-inch
baking dish. Sprinkle with bread crumbs. Drizzle with
melted butter. Bake for 25 minutes or until topping is
golden brown. Yield: 8 servings.

Eileen L. Davis, Laureate Phi
Ottawa, Ontario, Canada

CHEESE-STUFFED ZUCCHINI

4 medium zucchini
2 tablespoons sour
   cream
2 tablespoons melted
   butter or margarine

2 tablespoons cottage
   cheese
Salt and pepper to taste
Grated Parmesan cheese

Preheat oven to 350 degrees. Cook whole zucchini in
boiling water until almost done. Slice off top
lengthwise. Scoop out center of zucchini; strain pulp
to remove water. Combine pulp with sour cream,
butter, cottage cheese, salt and pepper; mix well.
Spoon into zucchini shells. Arrange in glass baking
dish. Sprinkle with Parmesan cheese. Bake until
heated through. Yield: 4 servings.

Cecil Rose, Beta Epsilon
Austin, Nevada

VEGETARIAN CHILI

1 large clove of garlic, minced	2 cups fresh or canned tomatoes
1 large onion, finely chopped	1/4 cup Italian-style tomato sauce
1 large carrot, chopped	1 1/2 cups corn
2 teaspoons safflower oil	1 tablespoon paprika
2 cups crumbled tofu	3/4 teaspoon chili powder
3 cups kidney beans, drained	Low-fat shredded Cheddar cheese

Sauté garlic, onion and carrot in hot oil in large deep skillet until tender. Add tofu. Sauté for 3 minutes longer. Add beans, tomatoes, tomato sauce, corn, paprika and chili powder; mix well. Simmer, covered, for 45 to 60 minutes, stirring occasionally. Garnish with low-fat shredded Cheddar cheese. Serve with corn bread. Yield: 8 to 9 servings.

Kathy Ryan, Epsilon Omega
Fairmont, West Virginia

VEGETABLE CASSEROLE DELUXE

1 16-ounce package frozen mixed vegetables, thawed	1 4-ounce can sliced mushrooms, drained
1 4-ounce can sliced bamboo shoots, drained	1 10-ounce can cream of mushroom soup
1 4-ounce can water chestnuts, drained, sliced	1 10-ounce can cream of celery soup
1 2-ounce jar pimento, drained, chopped	1/3 cup sour cream
	Salt and pepper to taste
	1 cup shredded Swiss cheese
	2 8-ounce cans French-fried onion rings

Preheat oven to 350 degrees. Combine mixed vegetables, bamboo shoots, water chestnuts, pimento, mushrooms, soups, sour cream, salt, pepper, cheese and 1 can onion rings in large bowl; mix well. Spoon into greased 2-quart baking dish. Bake, covered, for 30 minutes. Top with remaining 1 can onion rings. Bake, uncovered, for 10 minutes longer. Yield: 10 to 12 servings.

Esther Hess, Tau Theta
Harrisonville, Missouri

GARDEN GOODIES

4 cups shredded zucchini	1/2 cup grated Parmesan cheese
2 cups shredded carrots	
1/2 cup all-purpose flour	1/4 cup chopped onion
3/4 cup mayonnaise-type salad dressing	1 teaspoon crushed dried basil
1 cup shredded Monterey Jack cheese	Dash of pepper
	4 eggs, beaten

Preheat oven to 375 degrees. Combine zucchini, carrots and flour in large bowl; toss to coat. Add salad dressing, cheeses, onion, basil and pepper; mix well.

Stir in eggs. Press mixture into lightly greased 9-by-13-inch baking pan. Bake for 30 to 35 minutes or until set. Cool slightly; cut into squares. Yield: 48 servings.

Willa Swanson, Gamma Xi
Savannah, Missouri

VEGETABLE TRIO

1 10-ounce package frozen baby lima beans	2 hard-cooked eggs, chopped
1 10-ounce package frozen peas	3 tablespoons lemon juice
1 10-ounce package frozen French-style green beans or	2 tablespoons minced onion
1 20-ounce can French-style green beans	1 teaspoon Worcestershire sauce
1 cup mayonnaise-type salad dressing	1 teaspoon prepared mustard
	Dash of hot pepper sauce

Cook lima beans using package directions in large saucepan. Add peas. Cook for 5 minutes longer. Add green beans. Cook until vegetables are tender. Combine salad dressing, eggs, lemon juice, onion, Worcestershire sauce, mustard and pepper sauce in small saucepan. Simmer until thoroughly heated. Drain vegetables; place in serving dish. Pour sauce over vegetables; mix well. Serve immediately. Yield: 8 to 10 servings.

Myrna Schroder, Gamma Xi
Savannah, Missouri

CAJUN VEGETABLES

1/2 pound bacon	1 large onion, sliced into rings
2 1/2 pounds potatoes, peeled, sliced	2 large tomatoes, sliced
1 pound yellow squash, sliced	Cajun seasoning to taste
	Lemon pepper to taste
1 pound zucchini squash, sliced	1/2 cup butter or margarine
8 ounces whole okra	

Preheat oven to 275 degrees. Layer bacon, potatoes, squash, zucchini, okra, onion and tomatoes in 9-by-13-inch greased baking dish, sprinkling each layer with Cajun seasoning and lemon pepper. Dot with butter. Bake, covered with aluminum foil, for 3 to 4 hours or until vegetables are tender. Yield: 8 servings.

Cindy Hansard, Alpha Phi Rho
Electra, Texas

Lori Hollick, Psi, Regina, Saskatchewan, Canada, makes simple Onion Potatoes by layering 6 sliced potatoes, 3 tablespoons melted butter or margarine and 1 package onion soup mix in baking dish. Bake in preheated 350-degree oven for 1 hour.

GREEN-WHITE VEGETABLE CASSEROLE

1 6-ounce jar marinated artichoke hearts	³/₄ teaspoon oregano
2 tablespoons butter or margarine	1 10-ounce can cream of celery or mushroom soup
1 medium onion, chopped	4 eggs, beaten
1 clove of garlic, minced	¹/₈ teaspoon pepper
2 10-ounce packages frozen chopped spinach, thawed, drained	8 ounces cream cheese, softened
¹/₄ teaspoon ground nutmeg	¹/₃ cup milk
	¹/₃ cup grated Parmesan cheese

Preheat oven to 325 degrees. Drain and chop artichokes, reserving 2 tablespoons marinade. Heat reserved marinade with butter in skillet over medium heat. Add onion and garlic. Cook until tender. Stir in spinach, chopped artichokes, nutmeg, oregano, soup, eggs and pepper; mix well. Spoon into greased 2-quart baking dish. Beat cream cheese, milk and Parmesan cheese in bowl until smooth. Spread over spinach mixture. Bake for 35 minutes or until set. Yield: 8 to 10 servings.

Joan M. Gordon, Preceptor Mu Beta
Santa Rosa, California

SUMMER VEGETABLE BOWL

Last year I had a beautiful garden and used fresh vegetables for my meals. It was great.

4 slices bacon	1 tablespoon salt
12 small white onions	2 teaspoons sugar
2 green bell peppers, chopped	¹/₄ teaspoon pepper
2 cups hot water	6 zucchini, diced
1¹/₂ pounds green beans	2 large celery stalks, chopped
8 ears of corn, cut into thirds	2 tomatoes, cut into wedges

Fry bacon in 6-quart saucepan until crisp. Remove bacon to paper towel to drain. Add onions and green peppers to bacon drippings. Sauté until golden brown. Add hot water, green beans, corn, salt, sugar and pepper. Bring to a boil. Simmer, covered, for 10 minutes. Add zucchini and celery. Simmer, covered, for 10 minutes longer or until all vegetables are tender. Drain vegetables; arrange on large serving platter. Crumble bacon on top; garnish with tomato wedges. Yield: 8 to 10 servings.

Dena R. Meyer, Beta Epsilon Omega
Tuscola, Illinois

Elaine Trimmell, Republic, Missouri, wraps cooked Tater Tots with cheese slices and partially cooked bacon strips. Microwave until cheese melts.

VEGETARIAN SUPPER PIE

1 cup cracker crumbs	¹/₄ teaspoon tarragon, crushed
¹/₄ cup wheat germ	¹/₂ cup wheat germ
6 tablespoons melted butter or margarine	1 cup shredded Monterey Jack cheese
2 medium zucchini, sliced	¹/₂ cup grated Parmesan cheese
1 medium onion, sliced	2 eggs
2 tablespoons butter or margarine	¹/₂ cup milk
1 teaspoon marjoram	1 medium tomato, thinly sliced
¹/₂ teaspoon salt	
¹/₄ teaspoon pepper	

Preheat oven to 400 degrees. Combine cracker crumbs, ¹/₄ cup wheat germ and 6 tablespoons melted butter in small bowl; mix well. Press mixture onto sides and bottom of 9-inch springform pan. Bake for 7 to 9 minutes or until very lightly browned. Sauté zucchini and onion in 2 tablespoons butter in skillet until tender-crisp. Add marjoram, salt, pepper and tarragon; mix well. Arrange half the vegetables on crust. Sprinkle with 3 tablespoons wheat grem. Layer half the cheeses, remaining vegetables and 3 tablespoons wheat germ over top. Beat eggs and milk in small bowl. Pour into center of vegetables. Arrange tomato slices over layers; sprinkle with remaining cheeses and wheat germ. Reduce oven temperature to 325 degrees. Bake for 40 to 45 minutes or until hot and bubbly. Let stand for 5 minutes; cut into servings. Yield: 6 servings.

Barbara Bardin, Xi Kappa
Tulsa, Oklahoma

VEGETABLE SUPREME

2 cups fresh broccoli flowerets, cooked	1 cup cream of mushroom soup
2 cups fresh cauliflowerets, cooked	¹/₂ cup shredded sharp Cheddar cheese
1 cup sliced carrots, cooked	¹/₄ cup margarine, softened
1 medium onion, coarsely chopped, cooked	¹/₂ package herb-flavored croutons, crushed
2 eggs, beaten	¹/₂ cup shredded sharp Cheddar cheese
¹/₂ cup mayonnaise	¹/₄ cup pine nuts

Preheat oven to 350 degrees. Arrange cooked broccoli flowerets, cauliflowerets, carrots and onion in greased 9-by-9-inch baking dish. Combine eggs, mayonnaise, soup and ¹/₂ cup cheese in bowl; mix well. Pour over vegetables. Mix margarine and croutons in bowl. Sprinkle casserole with remaining ¹/₂ cup cheese, crouton mixture and pine nuts. Bake for 30 minutes. Yield: 8 servings.

Linda Bertram, Preceptor Zeta
Minnedosa, Manitoba, Canada

AUTUMN MEDLEY

2 cups cubed peeled peaches	1 14-ounce can pineapple chunks
1 cup cubed peeled plums	1 orange, unpeeled, thinly sliced
2 cups seedless green grape halves	Sugar
	1 cup small pecan halves
	Paraffin

Combine peaches, plums, grapes, undrained pineapple and orange slices in bowl; measure. Measure an equal amount of sugar. Combine fruit and sugar in saucepan. Simmer, uncovered, for 40 minutes, stirring occasionally. Add pecans. Bring mixture to a boil. Cook for 1 to 2 minutes, stirring constantly. Pour into sterilized 5-ounce jelly jars, leaving 1/4-inch headspace. Seal with 2 thin coats paraffin; cover with 2-piece lids. Yield: 10 jars.

Linda Alkema, Theta Epsilon
Elmvale, Ontario, Canada

FRUIT SALSA

1 large green bell pepper, chopped	1 large papaya or mango, cubed
1 large yellow bell pepper, chopped	1 pineapple, cored, cubed
1 large red bell pepper, chopped	1/2 cup finely chopped cilantro
1 medium jalapeño pepper, chopped	1 medium purple onion, chopped

Mix bell peppers, jalapeño pepper, papaya, pineapple, cilantro and onion thoroughly in large bowl. Serve with corn chips or over grilled fish or chicken breasts. May add more jalapeño pepper to make salsa hotter. Yield: 2 quarts.

Ann M. Lang, Lambda
Boise, Idaho

HOT CURRIED FRUIT

1 16-ounce can peaches, drained	1 21-ounce can cherry pie filling
1 20-ounce can pineapple chunks, drained	1/2 cup packed light brown sugar
1 16-ounce can pear halves	1/4 cup rum
	1 teaspoon curry powder
1 17-ounce can apricot halves, drained	

Preheat oven to 325 degrees. Mix peaches, pineapple, pears, apricots and pie filling together in large bowl. Add brown sugar, rum and curry powder; mix well. Pour into 1 1/2-quart baking dish. Bake for 1 hour. Serve hot. Yield: 8 to 10 servings.

Debbie Jones, Xi Beta Xi
Paris, Missouri

ZUCCHINI RELISH

10 cups coarsely ground zucchini	1 tablespoon dry mustard
4 cups chopped onions	2 tablespoons cornstarch
5 tablespoons canning salt	2 teaspoons celery seed
6 cups sugar	1/4 teaspoon pepper
2 1/4 cups cider vinegar	2 red bell peppers, chopped
1 tablespoon nutmeg	2 green bell peppers, chopped
1 tablespoon (scant) turmeric	

Combine zucchini, onions and canning salt in bowl. Let stand, covered, overnight. Drain; rinse well. Mix sugar, vinegar, nutmeg, turmeric, mustard, cornstarch, celery seed, pepper and bell peppers together in large saucepan. Stir in zucchini mixture. Bring to a boil. Simmer for 35 minutes or until thickened, stirring constantly. Pack into hot sterilized relish jars, leaving 1/2-inch headspace; seal with 2-piece lids. Yield: 10 to 12 jars.

Carol G. Davis, Preceptor Upsilon
Story, Wyoming

BING CHERRY JAM

4 cups pitted chopped Bing cherries	1/2 teaspoon cloves
1 envelope pectin	1/4 cup almond liqueur or 1 teaspoon almond extract
1/4 cup lemon juice	4 1/2 cups sugar
1/4 teaspoon salt	
1/2 teaspoon cinnamon	

Combine cherries, pectin, lemon juice, salt, cinnamon, cloves and almond liqueur in 6-quart saucepan. Bring to a full, rolling boil. Stir in sugar. Boil for 2 minutes. Remove from heat; skim. Pour into hot sterilized half-pint jars, leaving 1/4-inch headspace; seal with 2-piece lids. Process in boiling water bath for 10 minutes. Yield: 5 to 6 jars.

Karla Wilkinson, Xi Alpha Omega
Story, Wyoming

RHUBARB-BLUEBERRY JAM

5 cups finely cut rhubarb	2 3-ounce packages raspberry gelatin
1 cup water	
5 cups sugar	
1 21-ounce can blueberry pie filling	

Cook rhubarb in water in saucepan until tender. Add sugar. Simmer for 2 to 5 minutes, stirring constantly. Add pie filling. Simmer gently for 8 minutes longer. Remove from heat. Add gelatin, stirring until dissolved. Pour into hot sterilized jelly jars, leaving 1/4-inch headspace; seal with 2-piece lids. Store in refrigerator or freezer. Yield: 6 to 7 jars.

Janet Hansen, Xi Gamma Zeta
Harvard, Nebraska

CRANBERRY CHUTNEY

This is excellent served with turkey at Thanksgiving.

1 12-ounce package cranberries	1 cup chopped celery
1 cup water	1 apple, chopped
1½ cups sugar	1½ teaspoons grated orange zest
1 cup orange juice	¼ to ½ teaspoon ginger
1 cup chopped walnuts	1 cup raisins

Combine cranberries, water and sugar in large saucepan. Bring to a boil. Simmer for 15 minutes, stirring occasionally. Add orange juice, walnuts, celery, apple, orange zest, ginger and raisins; mix well. Remove from heat. Store, covered, in refrigerator. May plump raisins in a small amount of warm brandy while mixture is cooking; add raisins with brandy to mixture. Yield: 2½ quarts.

Sharon Timpe, Xi Alpha Theta
Mequon, Wisconsin

LEMON PASTA

This is great served with baked, broiled or steamed seafood.

1 12-ounce package any type pasta	½ cup grated Parmesan cheese
2 cups whipping cream	Salt and pepper to taste
Grated zest of 1 large lemon	

Cook pasta using package directions; drain. Heat whipping cream in large skillet over medium heat. Add lemon zest and Parmesan cheese, stirring well. Add cooked pasta, salt and pepper; toss to coat. Cream will thicken slightly. Yield: 4 servings.

Laura Sutherland, Epsilon Psi
Helena, Alabama

FOUR-CHEESE VEGETABLE LASAGNA

This is a family favorite. I have used it several times for special occasions. Low-fat dairy products may be used.

½ cup chopped onion	Flowerets of 1 bunch broccoli, steamed
½ cup margarine or butter	Flowerets of 1 head cauliflower, steamed
¼ cup all-purpose flour	
2½ cups milk	8 carrots, sliced, parboiled
3 cnps cottage cheese	12 uncooked lasagna noodles
1 teaspoon salt	
½ teaspoon pepper	12 ounces mozzarella cheese, sliced
1 tablespoon dried parsley	
8 ounces cream cheese, softened	¾ cup grated Parmesan cheese

Preheat oven to 350 degrees. Sauté onion in margarine in large saucepan. Stir in flour. Add milk and cottage cheese; mix well. Stir in salt, pepper and parsley. Add cream cheese slowly; mix until blended. Mix in broccoli flowerets, cauliflowerets and carrots.

Cook lasagna noodles using package directions; drain. Spoon a small amount of vegetable-cheese sauce in bottom of lasagna pan. Arrange 4 noodles over sauce. Spoon ⅓ of the remaining sauce over noodles. Top with ⅓ of the mozzarella cheese and ¼ cup Parmesan cheese. Repeat layers using remaining ingredients ½ at a time ending with Parmesan cheese. Bake, covered, for 30 minutes. Bake, uncovered, for 15 minutes longer or until bubbly and browned. Let stand for 15 minutes before serving. Yield: 15 servings.

Marty Jo Warner, Xi Epsilon Sigma
Mill Hall, Pennsylvania

PASTA WITH ASPARAGUS

2 pounds fresh asparagus, cut into 1-inch pieces	½ teaspoon pepper
	¼ cup margarine, softened
1 pound thin spaghetti	½ cup half and half
8 slices bacon, cut into 1-inch pieces	½ to ¾ cup grated Parmesan cheese
½ cup chopped green onions	

Cook asparagus in boiling salted water for 3 minutes; drain. Cook spaghetti using package directions; drain. Fry bacon in large skillet until crisp; drain. Sauté green onions in bacon drippings until soft. Add pepper and asparagus. Heat until warmed through. Toss spaghetti, asparagus, green onions, bacon, margarine, half and half, and Parmesan cheese together in large serving bowl. Serve immediately. May substitute broccoli for asparagus. Yield: 6 to 8 servings.

Rosemary Derksen, Xi Alpha Psi
South Bend, Indiana

PASTA PRIMAVERA

4 to 8 ounces uncooked spaghetti	½ green bell pepper, sliced
2 tablespoons chopped onion	8 to 12 fresh snow peas
	6 to 8 broccoli flowerets
½ to ¾ cup diagonally sliced celery	4 mushrooms, sliced
	⅓ to ½ cup yogurt
1 cup diagonally sliced carrots	Basil
	Garlic powder
¼ cup olive oil	Salt and pepper to taste

Cook spaghetti using package directions; drain. Sauté onion, celery and carrots in olive oil in large skillet or wok for 5 minutes. Add green pepper, snow peas, broccoli and mushrooms. Stir-fry until tender-crisp. Add spaghetti to stir-fried vegetables; toss well. Add yogurt, basil, garlic powder, salt and pepper. Cook until heated through, stirring constantly. Yield: 2 to 4 servings.

Betty Thorpe, Preceptor Kappa Xi
Universal City, Texas

MEATLESS ITALIAN MANICOTTI

16 uncooked manicotti shells
2 cups low-fat cottage cheese
1 cup grated Parmesan cheese
1 cup shredded low-fat mozzarella cheese
2 eggs, slightly beaten
1 teaspoon oregano
1/4 cup fresh chopped parsley
1/4 teaspoon cayenne pepper
2 16-ounce cans stewed tomatoes
1 1/2 tablespoons Italian seasoning
2 tablespoons cornstarch

Preheat oven to 350 degrees. Cook manicotti using package directions. Drain; place in cold water. Combine cottage cheese, Parmesan and mozzarella cheeses, eggs, oregano, parsley and cayenne pepper in bowl; mix well. Drain manicotti. Stuff shells with cheese mixture. Arrange in lightly oiled 9-by-13-inch baking pan. Combine stewed tomatoes, Italian seasoning and cornstarch in saucepan; mix well. Bring to a boil. Cook until thickened, stirring constantly. Pour over stuffed manicotti. Bake, covered, for 40 to 50 minutes. Yield: 8 servings.

Sharon Cullen, Xi Alpha Iota
Rochester, Minnesota

ANGEL'S HAIR PASTA WITH FRESH TOMATO SAUCE

This was a big hit with everyone at our family gathering last summer.

1 cup fresh basil
2 pounds Roma tomatoes, chopped
5 cloves of garlic, minced
1/2 cup olive oil
1 teaspoon salt
1/2 teaspoon freshly ground pepper
1/4 cup olive oil
16 ounces angel's hair pasta

Chop basil, reserving a few leaves for garnish. Combine with tomatoes, garlic, 1/2 cup olive oil, salt and pepper in bowl; mix well. Marinate for 4 hours to overnight. Heat remaining 1/4 cup olive oil in large saucepan. Add marinated tomato mixture. Simmer on medium-high for 5 minutes, stirring occasionally. Cook pasta in boiling salted water for 2 minutes or until slightly firm; drain. Toss with tomato mixture to coat. Garnish with reserved basil leaves cut into strips. Yield: 6 servings.

Helen M. Williams, Preceptor Kappa Psi
Sebastopol, California

Bernice Chrzan Cornmesser, Epsilon Psi, Pelham, Alabama, makes Infallible Rice by sautéing 1 minced onion in 2 tablespoons butter or margarine and combining with 1 cup rice and 2 cups hot chicken broth in casserole. Bake, covered, in preheated 325-degree oven for 20 minutes.

TORTELINI WITH SUN-DRIED TOMATO PESTO

1/2 stick pepperoni, cut into small pieces
3 tablespoons Dijon mustard
4 cloves of garlic, minced
1 tablespoon fennel seed
1 7-ounce jar sun-dried tomatoes, drained
1 1/2 cups olive oil
2 tablespoons lemon juice
Salt and pepper to taste
2 pounds meat or cheese tortelini, cooked, drained
2 ripe tomatoes, seeded, chopped
1 yellow bell pepper, chopped
1 stick pepperoni, thinly sliced
Lettuce leaves
1/2 cup chopped fresh parsley
3 tablespoons chopped fresh basil
Black olives

Combine 1/2 stick cut-up pepperoni, mustard, garlic, fennel seed and sun-dried tomatoes in blender container. Add oil in fine stream, processing constantly at high speed until mixture is smooth. Mix in lemon juice, salt and pepper. Combine cooked tortelini, tomatoes, yellow pepper and remaining 1 stick sliced pepperoni in large bowl. Add sauce; toss well. Serve in large lettuce-lined salad bowl. Sprinkle with parsley, basil and black olives. Yield: 8 servings.

Jane M. Goulet, Alpha Iota
Westport Island, Maine

GREEN AND GOLD CASSEROLE

This recipe won Best of Show and Grand Prize in the 1983 Rice Festival Colusa County Fair.

1 cup uncooked medium grain rice
1 green bell pepper, chopped
1/2 cup chopped yellow onion
1 tablespoon butter or margarine
1 cup whipping cream, whipped
4 egg yolks, well beaten
1 cup chopped broccoli, cooked
2/3 cup grated Parmesan cheese
4 egg whites
1 cup sour cream
3 tablespoons chopped green onions

Preheat oven to 350 degrees. Cook rice using package directions; drain. Sauté green pepper and onion in butter in saucepan until tender. Combine rice, green pepper, onion, whipped cream, beaten egg yolks, broccoli and Parmesan cheese in large bowl; mix well. Beat egg whites in mixer bowl until stiff peaks form. Fold into mixture gently. Spoon into 2-quart casserole; place casserole in pan of hot water in oven. Bake for 45 minutes. Top with sour cream and sprinkle with green onions. Yield: 6 to 8 servings.

Karen Mayberry, Kappa Epsilon
Colusa, California

ARKANSAS CUMIN RICE

This recipe was a specialty of the Riceland Hotel in Stuttgart, Arkansas.

1/3 cup chopped onion	2 10-ounce cans
1/4 cup chopped green bell pepper	consommé, any flavor
1 cup uncooked enriched rice	1 tablespoon Worcestershire sauce
1 tablespoon bacon drippings	3/4 teaspoon salt
	3/4 teaspoon cumin seed

Sauté onion, green pepper and rice in bacon drippings in large skillet until golden brown. Add consommé, Worcestershire sauce, salt and cumin seed; mix well. Cover tightly. Bring to a boil; reduce heat. Simmer gently for 20 minutes. Yield: 6 servings.

*Karen Hollanger, Phi Sigma
Humphrey, Arkansas*

AUNTIE INEZ'S RICE

1 cup uncooked rice	1 7-ounce can green
2 10-ounce cans chicken broth	chilies, drained, diced Dash of Worcestershire
3 cups sour cream	sauce
1 2-ounce jar pimento, drained	1 pound Monterey Jack cheese, shredded

Preheat oven to 325 degrees. Cook rice using package directions, substituting chicken broth for water. Combine sour cream, pimento, chilies and Worcestershire sauce in large bowl; mix well. Stir in cooked rice. Spoon into 9-by-12-inch glass baking dish. Sprinkle with cheese. Bake for 25 to 30 minutes or until bubbly and lightly browned.
Yield: 6 servings.

*Helen Fisk, Delta Kappa Psi
Escondido, California*

FESTIVE RICE

1 cup long grain rice	1 1/4 cups sour cream
1 4-ounce can green chilies, drained, chopped	Salt and pepper to taste 2 tablespoons butter or margarine
1 pound Monterey Jack or Cheddar cheese, shredded	

Preheat oven to 350 degrees. Cook rice using package directions; drain. Combine rice, chilies, 3/4 of the cheese, sour cream, salt and pepper in large bowl; mix thoroughly. Spoon into 2-quart baking dish. Sprinkle with remaining cheese; dot with butter. Bake for 35 minutes. Yield: 6 to 8 servings.

*Donna McCloud, Xi Lambda Chi
Robinson, Illinois*

FRIED RICE

I have used water chestnuts, bamboo shoots and bean sprouts. Let your imagination be your guide.

1 cup thinly sliced celery and/or mushrooms	1 cup shredded cooked pork, ham or chicken
3 tablespoons vegetable oil	1/2 cup peas 2 tablespoons soy sauce
3 cups cooked rice	1/2 teaspoon sugar
4 to 6 medium green onions, cut into 2-inch lengths	2 eggs, beaten

Stir-fry celery in hot oil in wok or large skillet for 1 to 2 minutes. Add rice, stirring to coat with oil. Add green onions. Stir-fry for 1 minute. Add cooked pork, peas, soy sauce and sugar. Stir-fry until heated through. Add eggs. Stir-fry just until set. Serve immediately. Yield: 4 servings.

*Bonnie Gray, Laureate Lambda
Salmon, Idaho*

MUSHROOM RICE

8 fresh mushrooms, sliced	1/4 teaspoon red pepper 1/4 teaspoon black
1 tablespoon margarine	pepper
1 tablespoon chopped celery	1/4 teaspoon onion salt 1 tablespoon fresh
1 teaspoon chopped green onion tops	chopped parsley 3 cups cooked rice
Few slices of garlic	1/2 cup canned peas

Sauté mushrooms in margarine in cast-iron skillet until brown. Add celery. Sauté for 2 minutes. Stir in green onions, garlic, red pepper, black pepper, onion salt and parsley. Add rice and peas; toss lightly. Yield: 6 to 8 servings.

*Aline B. Lewis, Preceptor Beta Mu
Port Arthur, Texas*

RICE AND CELERY CASSEROLE

2 cups cooked rice	2 10-ounce cans cream
1 1/2 cups chopped celery	of mushroom soup
1 small onion, minced	2 tablespoons lemon
4 hard-cooked eggs, chopped	juice 1 teaspoon salt
3/4 cup slivered almonds	1 cup mayonnaise
1 8-ounce can mushrooms, drained	1/3 cup bread crumbs

Preheat oven to 350 degrees. Combine rice, celery, onion, eggs, almonds and mushrooms in large bowl; mix well. Mix soup, lemon juice, salt and mayonnaise together in small bowl. Stir into rice mixture. Spoon into 3-quart baking dish. Top with bread crumbs. Bake for 45 minutes. Yield: 4 to 6 servings.

*Elaine K. Benton, Laureate Beta Eta
Lorain, Ohio*

SOUR CREAM RICE PILAF

3 10-ounce cans chicken broth	1½ cups uncooked rice
¼ cup butter or margarine	¼ cup butter or margarine
1 tablespoon lemon juice	1 8-ounce can mushrooms, drained
½ teaspoon pepper	1 cup sour cream
1½ teaspoons salt	2 tablespoons chopped parsley
½ bay leaf	

Preheat oven to 325 degrees. Combine chicken broth, ¼ cup butter, lemon juice, pepper, salt and bay leaf in casserole. Bake until heated through. Add rice. Bake, covered, for 1 hour. Remove bay leaf. Add remaining ¼ cup butter, mushrooms, sour cream and parsley. Bake until heated through. Yield: 6 to 8 servings.

Betty Mershon, Xi Omicron Beta
San Andreas, California

LAZY VEGETABLE PILAF

I make this pilaf recipe to accompany any meat for dinner, especially when I'm late from work and my family is hungry.

½ cup chopped green bell pepper	½ teaspoon salt
1 cup sliced carrots	½ teaspoon pepper
½ cup chopped celery	1 teaspoon garlic powder
1 cup chopped tomatoes	2 cups cooked rice
1 cup chopped onions	½ cup soy sauce
⅓ cup bacon drippings	
1 pound sliced bacon, crisp-fried, crumbled	

Sauté green pepper, carrots, celery, tomatoes and onions in bacon drippings in skillet until tender. Add bacon, salt, pepper, garlic powder and rice; mix well. Stir in soy sauce. Cook until heated through, stirring constantly. Yield: 6 to 8 servings.

Norma T. Mejia, Xi Alpha
Mayaguez, Puerto Rico

CHEESE RISOTTO

1 cup uncooked rice	1 12-ounce can evaporated milk
2½ cups water	1 2-ounce jar chopped pimento
1 envelope chicken and rice soup mix	1 cup shredded sharp Cheddar cheese
1 10-ounce can cream of chicken soup	

Preheat oven to 350 degrees. Cook rice, 2½ cups water and 1 package chicken and rice soup mix in saucepan using package directions. Add soup, evaporated milk, pimento and cheese; mix well. Pour into 9-by-12-inch baking dish. Bake for 20 minutes. Yield: 12 servings.

Joyce Sanford, Sigma Rho
Twinsburg, Ohio

SPANISH RICE

2 tablespoons olive oil	1½ cups water
½ cup chopped onion	1 tomato, chopped
½ cup chopped green bell pepper	½ teaspoon salt
1½ cups rice	¼ teaspoon chopped garlic
1½ cups chicken broth	

Heat oil in 2-quart saucepan. Sauté onion and green pepper until tender. Add rice; stir to coat with oil. Add chicken broth, water, tomato, salt and garlic. Bring to a boil; reduce heat. Simmer, covered, for 20 minutes or until all liquid has been absorbed. Yield: 4 servings.

Dixie Jordan, Eta Upsilon
Midland, Texas

PECAN BROWN RICE

3¼ cups cold water	⅛ teaspoon pepper
1½ cups brown rice	¾ cup coarsely chopped pecans, toasted
2 tablespoons butter or margarine	¼ cup chopped parsley
2 teaspoons instant chicken bouillon	

Combine water, brown rice, butter, instant bouillon and pepper in large saucepan; cover tightly. Bring to a boil; reduce heat. Cook for 40 minutes; do not remove cover. Remove from heat. Let stand, covered, for 10 minutes. Stir in toasted pecans and parsley. Yield: 4 servings.

Leona Lanthier, Laureate Nu
Comox, British Columbia, Canada

BARLEY BAKE

This is a favorite recipe of mine. It was shared with me by a close friend and Beta sister, Inez Asta. This dish goes especially well with baked poultry.

1 cup chopped onion	2 10-ounce cans chicken broth
1 cup chopped celery	5 ounces water
1 cup chopped fresh parsley	2 cups uncooked barley
8 ounces fresh mushrooms, sliced	Seasoned salt to taste
1 cup butter or margarine	Pepper to taste

Preheat oven to 325 degrees. Sauté onion, celery, parsley and mushrooms in butter in large saucepan. Add chicken broth and water. Cook over medium heat until heated through, stirring frequently. Pour over barley in 9-by-13-inch baking dish. Bake for 1¼ hours. Stir in seasoned salt and pepper just before serving. Yield: 6 to 8 servings.

Sharon M. Fox, Preceptor Alpha
Missoula, Montana

CHILI HOMINY CASSEROLE

2 20-ounce cans hominy, drained	1½ cups sour cream
3 tablespoons grated onion	1 4-ounce can green chilies, drained, chopped
1½ cups shredded Monterey Jack cheese	¾ teaspoon salt
	½ cup bread crumbs

Preheat oven to 350 degrees. Combine hominy, onion, cheese, sour cream, chilies and salt in large bowl; mix well. Spoon into 2½-quart casserole. Sprinkle with bread crumbs. Bake for 30 to 40 minutes or until bubbly. Yield: 6 to 8 servings.

Tami Bond, Xi Pi
Oakwood, Georgia

ISABELLE'S CREOLE SEASONING

This makes a great present. Once someone tries it they'll keep asking you for more. Use as you would salt and pepper. It's terrific in stews, gumbos and casseroles.

26 ounces salt	2 tablespoons MSG
1 1½-ounce container ground black pepper	2 tablespoons chili powder
¼ cup red pepper	2 tablespoons onion powder
2 tablespoons garlic powder	

Combine salt, black pepper, red pepper, garlic powder, MSG, chili powder and onion powder in bowl; mix well. Pour into salt shakers or covered jars. Yield: 4 cups.

Isabelle Bahan, Eta Rho
Mandeville, Louisiana

MEATY SPINACH STUFFING

1 10-ounce package frozen chopped spinach	1 clove of garlic, minced
1 pound bulk pork sausage	4 eggs, slightly beaten
8 ounces ground veal	¾ cup grated Parmesan cheese
8 ounces ground pork	1 8-ounce package herb-seasoned stuffing mix
1 cup chopped onion	
1 cup chopped celery with leaves	1 cup chicken broth
¼ cup snipped parsley	½ teaspoon rubbed sage

Preheat oven to 350 degrees. Cook spinach using package directions; drain. Brown sausage, veal and pork in large skillet until crumbly; drain. Add onion, celery, parsley and garlic; stir well. Cook, covered, for 20 minutes. Combine eggs, spinach and Parmesan cheese in large bowl; mix well. Add meat mixture and stuffing mix, stirring well. Stir in broth and sage. Spoon into 2-quart baking dish. Bake for 1 hour. Yield: 10 cups.

Nancy Bachellerie, Xi Phi Phi
Oroville, California

HOLIDAY STUFFING

I take this to our family's potluck turkey dinners.

⅔ cup chopped onion	10 cups bread cubes
1 cup chopped celery	½ cup golden raisins
⅔ cup butter or margarine	1 large apple, chopped
Salt and pepper to taste	½ cup chopped almonds, toasted
2½ teaspoons poultry seasoning	1½ cups chicken broth

Preheat oven to 325 degrees. Sauté onion and celery in butter until tender. Add salt, pepper and poultry seasoning. Combine bread cubes, raisins, chopped apple and almonds in large bowl; mix well. Stir in seasoned butter mixture. Pour in broth, stirring well. Spoon into large 5-quart baking pan. Bake for 1 hour. Yield: 36 servings.

Kelly Jensen-Webster
Meeteetse, Wyoming

BARBECUE SAUCE

6 or 7 green onions, chopped	3 tablespoons sugar
1 small onion, chopped	3 tablespoons liquid smoke
½ cup margarine	3 tablespoons vinegar
1 14-ounce bottle of hot catsup	3 tablespoons Worcestershire sauce
14 ounces water	1 tablespoon parsley flakes
3 tablespoons chili powder	Salt and pepper to taste

Sauté green onions and onion in margarine in large saucepan until limp and tender. Add catsup, water, chili powder, sugar, liquid smoke, vinegar, Worcestershire sauce, parsley flakes, salt and pepper; mix well. Simmer for 30 minutes or until mixture thickens. Yield: 7½ cups.

Eva Mae Keller, Laureate Gamma Xi
Sweeney, Texas

FRENCH ONION SAUCE

2 large onions, thinly sliced	1 10-ounce can condensed beef broth
2 tablespoons butter or margarine	¼ teaspoon Worcestershire sauce
2 tablespoons cornstarch	2 tablespoons grated Parmesan cheese

Sauté onions in butter in 2-quart saucepan for 20 minutes or until lightly browned. Stir in cornstarch. Add beef broth and Worcestershire sauce; mix well. Cook over medium heat until thickened and bubbly, stirring constantly. Add Parmesan cheese. Cook until heated through, stirring constantly. Yield: 2 cups.

Karen Loyd, Eta Rho
Covington, Louisiana

Bread Winners

PARKER HOUSE-STYLE BISCUITS

2 envelopes dry yeast
2 tablespoons warm
    (105- to 115- degree)
    water
5 cups self-rising flour
¼ cup sugar
1 cup shortening
2 cups buttermilk
½ to ¾ cup melted
    butter or margarine

Dissolve yeast in warm water. Mixture will be thick. Sift together flour and sugar into large bowl. Cut in shortening until crumbly. Add buttermilk and yeast mixture, stirring well. Chill, covered, in refrigerator overnight. Preheat oven to 400 degrees. Roll out dough on floured surface. Cut with biscuit cutter; place on baking sheet. Brush with butter. Bake for 15 minutes or until golden brown. Yield: 3 dozen.

Virginia Tyler, Delta Tau
Thomaston, Georgia

PRALINE BISCUITS

½ cup butter or
    margarine
½ cup packed light
    brown sugar
36 pecan halves
Cinnamon
2 cups baking mix
⅓ cup applesauce
⅓ cup milk

Preheat oven to 400 degrees. Divide butter into 12 pieces. Place 1 piece butter, 2 teaspoons brown sugar and 3 pecan halves in each cup of greased muffin pan. Sprinkle cinnamon in each cup. Heat in oven until butter and sugar are melted. Combine baking mix, applesauce and milk in bowl; beat 20 strokes. Drop by spoonfuls onto mixture in muffin cups. Bake for 10 minutes or until golden brown. Invert onto serving plate immediately. Yield: 1 dozen.

Janice Vogt, Lambda Sigma
Centralia, Missouri

SWEET POTATO BISCUITS

4 cups unsifted
    all-purpose flour
¼ cup packed light
    brown sugar
2 tablespoons baking
    powder
1 teaspoon soda
1 teaspoon salt
1 teaspoon cinnamon
1¼ cups buttermilk
1 cup melted butter or
    margarine
2 cups mashed cooked
    sweet potatoes

Preheat oven to 450 degrees. Combine flour, brown sugar, baking powder, soda, salt and cinnamon in bowl; mix well. Add buttermilk and melted butter; mix well. Add mashed sweet potatoes; mix well. Drop by tablespoonfuls onto greased baking sheet. Bake for 15 to 20 minutes or until golden brown. Yield: 3 dozen.

Nancy H. McCoy, Gamma Theta
Gulfport, Mississippi

BREADSTICKS FANTASTIC

1 tablespoon yeast
1½ cups warm water
2 tablespoons sugar
½ teaspoon salt
3 cups all-purpose flour
1 cup margarine
½ cup grated Parmesan
    cheese
2 tablespoons garlic salt

Dissolve yeast in warm water in bowl. Add sugar, salt and enough flour to make a soft dough. Let dough rest for 10 minutes. Preheat oven to 350 degrees. Place half the margarine in each of two 9-by-13-inch baking pans. Heat in oven until melted. Roll out dough to shape of pans on floured surface. Cut into strips. Roll strips in melted margarine; twist and place in pan. Sprinkle with Parmesan cheese and garlic salt. Let rise for 15 minutes. Bake for 20 to 25 minutes or until brown. Yield: 2 dozen.

Susan Townsend, Beta Zeta
Pierce, Idaho

FABULOUS ITALIAN STICKS

1 loaf frozen bread dough, thawed	*1/2 teaspoon thyme*
3 tablespoons olive oil	*3 cups shredded mozzarella cheese*
1 tablespoon basil	*Spaghetti sauce*

Preheat oven to 350 degrees. Press out bread dough to fill greased 10-by-15-inch jelly roll pan. Brush with olive oil. Sprinkle with basil and thyme. Top with cheese. Bake for 35 to 40 minutes or until light brown. Cut into 1-by-4-inch strips. Serve with spaghetti sauce. Yield: 4 to 6 servings.

Joy Strasser, Delta Chi
Mukwonago, Wisconsin

CINNAMON BUNS

For as long as I can remember Mom made these rolls for holiday and family dinners. Now my own family requests them, but they are never as good as Mom's.

2 teaspoons sugar	*1/4 cup light corn syrup*
1/2 cup lukewarm water	*1/2 cup water*
2 envelopes dry yeast	*2 eggs, beaten*
1 cup milk	*1 teaspoon cinnamon*
2/3 cup shortening	*7 to 8 cups sifted all-purpose flour*
1 teaspoon salt	
1/2 cup sugar	

Dissolve 2 teaspoons sugar in lukewarm water. Add yeast; stir well. Let stand for 10 minutes. Scald milk in saucepan. Combine milk, shortening, salt, 1/2 cup sugar and corn syrup in mixer bowl; mix well. Stir in 1/2 cup water. Cool to lukewarm. Stir yeast mixture well; add to milk mixture. Add eggs 1 at a time, beating well after each addition. Add cinnamon and half the flour; mix well. Add enough remaining flour to form stiff dough. Knead on floured surface until dough is soft but not sticky. Place dough in greased bowl. Let rise, covered, in warm place until doubled in bulk. Pinch off dough in walnut-sized pieces; place on greased baking sheet. Let rise. Preheat oven to 350 degrees. Bake for 15 minutes or until light brown. Yield: 24 rolls.

Claudia M. Long, Kappa Kappa
Meriden, Kansas

HOT CROSS BUNS

2 envelopes dry yeast	*1/4 teaspoon nutmeg*
Pinch of sugar	*4 to 4 1/2 cups all-purpose flour*
1/2 cup lukewarm water	
1/2 cup lukewarm milk	*1 cup raisins*
3/4 cup mashed potatoes	*1/2 cup chopped candied fruit*
1/2 cup sugar	
1 1/4 teaspoons salt	*1/4 cup all-purpose flour*
1/2 cup butter or margarine, softened	*1/4 cup butter or margarine, softened*
2 eggs	*1 to 1 1/2 teaspoons water*
1 tablespoon cinnamon	

Add yeast and pinch of sugar to lukewarm water in bowl; mix well. Let stand for 10 minutes. Combine yeast mixture, milk, potatoes, 1/2 cup sugar, salt, 1/2 cup butter, eggs, cinnamon and nutmeg in mixer bowl; mix well. Add 2 cups flour. Beat for 4 to 6 minutes or until dough is clinging to beaters. Stir in enough remaining 2 1/2 cups flour to form stiff dough. Work in raisins and chopped fruit. Cover bowl with greased plastic wrap. Let dough rise in warm place for 1 1/2 hours or until doubled in bulk. Punch dough down. Break off egg-sized pieces of dough. Flatten slightly; place on greased baking sheet. Place 2 inches apart for firm sides; place closer together for soft sides. Grease tops of rolls lightly; cover with greased plastic wrap. Let rise until doubled in bulk. Mark top with X. Mix 1/4 cup flour with 1/4 cup butter in bowl until smooth. Add enough remaining water until of spreading consistency. Pipe through pastry bag with 1/4-inch round tip onto X. Preheat oven to 375 degrees. Bake buns for 15 to 20 minutes or until light brown. May mark X with confectioners' sugar icing after baking. Yield: 15 to 20 buns.

Tammie McRae, Alberta Betta Kappa
Bonnyville, Alberta, Canada

GRANDMA'S CRUMB CAKE

4 cups all-purpose flour	*Pinch of salt*
2 cups sugar	*1/4 cup margarine, softened*
3 tablespoons cinnamon	
1/2 teaspoon salt	*2/3 cup sugar*
1 1/2 cups melted margarine, cooled	*1 egg, beaten*
	1 teaspoon vanilla extract
2 cups all-purpose flour	
1 tablespoon baking powder	*3/4 cup milk*
	Confectioners' sugar

Combine 4 cups flour, 2 cups sugar, cinnamon and 1/2 teaspoon salt in bowl; mix well. Cut in melted margarine with fork until crumbly. Mix 2 cups flour, baking powder and salt together. Cream 1/4 cup margarine and 2/3 cup sugar in mixer bowl until light and fluffy. Add egg and vanilla; mix well. Add dry mixture alternately with milk, mixing well after each addition. Spread in greased 10-by-15-inch baking dish. Sprinkle crumb mixture over top. Place in cold oven. Bake at 350 degrees for 30 minutes. Cool. Sprinkle with confectioners' sugar. Yield: 24 servings.

Nancy Feikes, Xi Alpha Beta
LaPorte, Indiana

Carol A. Johannigmeiek, Fort Collins, Colorado, makes a Lemon-Cheese Spread by combining 8 ounces softened cream cheese, 1 teaspoon grated lemon rind, 1 tablespoon lemon juice and 1 tablespoon confectioners' sugar.

LEMON-CHEESE COFFEE CAKE

1 2-layer package
   lemon supreme cake
   mix
2 eggs
1 cup all-purpose flour
1 envelope dry yeast
2/3 cup warm water
16 ounces cream cheese,
   softened
2 eggs
1/4 cup sugar

1 tablespoon
   all-purpose flour
1 tablespoon milk
1/4 cup plus 2
   tablespoons butter or
   margarine, softened
1 cup confectioners'
   sugar
1 tablespoon light corn
   syrup
1 tablespoon water

Preheat oven to 350 degrees. Combine 1 1/2 cups cake mix, 2 eggs, 1 cup flour, yeast and warm water in mixer bowl. Beat at medium speed for 2 minutes. Spread in greased 9-by-13-inch baking pan. Combine cream cheese, 2 eggs, sugar, 1 tablespoon flour and milk in mixer bowl; beat until well blended. Spoon over yeast batter. Cut butter into remaining cake mix in bowl until crumbly. Sprinkle over batter. Bake for 40 to 45 minutes or until golden brown. Combine remaining ingredients in bowl; beat until well blended. Drizzle over hot cake. Yield: 16 to 20 servings.

Mary C. Oglesbee, Laureate Alpha Delta
Cincinnati, Ohio

JALAPEÑO CORN BREAD

1 8-ounce can cream-
   style corn
1 cup yellow cornmeal
1 cup shredded sharp
   Cheddar cheese
3 cups milk
1/2 cup chopped
   jalapeño peppers

3 eggs, beaten
1 3-ounce can hot
   green chili peppers
1 teaspoon salt
1/2 teaspoon soda
2 tablespoons butter or
   margarine

Preheat oven to 400 degrees. Combine corn, cornmeal, half the cheese, milk, jalapeño peppers, eggs, chili peppers, salt and soda in mixer bowl; mix well. Place butter in 1 1/2-quart casserole or cast-iron skillet. Heat in oven until melted; do not brown. Pour batter into hot butter. Sprinkle with remaining cheese. Bake for 40 to 50 minutes. Cover with foil if top browns after baking for 35 minutes.
Yield: 9 to 10 servings.

Nadene Rankin, Xi Eta Gamma
Brazil, Indiana

MEXICAN CORN BREAD

1 cup self-rising
   cornmeal
1/2 cup self-rising flour
1 medium onion,
   chopped

1/2 cup vegetable oil
1 cup cream-style corn
1/2 cup shredded cheese
2 eggs
1 cup buttermilk

Preheat oven to 350 degrees. Combine cornmeal and flour in mixer bowl; mix well. Add onion, oil, corn and cheese; mix well. Mix eggs and buttermilk together. Stir into batter until just mixed. Pour into greased 8-inch square pan. Bake for 45 minutes or until bread tests done. Yield: 12 servings.

Edith Clendennen
San Angelo, Texas

CHEESE BREAD

1/2 cup margarine,
   softened
8 ounces cream cheese,
   softened

1 5-ounce jar Old
   English cheese spread
1 loaf French bread

Preheat oven to 350 degrees. Combine margarine, cream cheese and Old English cheese spread in mixer bowl; mix well. Split French bread into halves lengthwise. Spread cheese mixture over bottom half; replace top. Place on baking pan. Bake for 30 minutes. Cool for several minutes before slicing. Yield: 8 to 10 servings.

Lorri Saracini, Xi Beta Kappa
Hot Springs, Arkansas

GARLIC HERB FRENCH BREAD

1/2 cup margarine,
   softened
1 green onion, finely
   chopped
2 tablespoons grated
   Parmesan cheese

2 cloves of garlic,
   minced
2 teaspoons oregano
1 loaf French bread

Preheat oven to 350 degrees. Combine margarine, green onion, Parmesan cheese, garlic and oregano in bowl; mix well. Cut French bread almost to bottom in diagonal slices. Spread mixture between slices. Wrap in foil. Bake for 30 minutes.
Yield: 2/3 cup spread.

Helen M. Williams, Preceptor Kappa Psi
Sebastopo, California

SIMPLY DELICIOUS HOT BREAD

1 loaf French bread
8 ounces sliced Swiss
   cheese
1/2 cup margarine,
   softened
1 tablespoon poppy seed

1/4 cup finely chopped
   onion
1 tablespoon prepared
   mustard
4 slices uncooked
   bacon, chopped

Preheat oven to 400 degrees. Cut French bread almost to bottom in 16 slices. Cut cheese slices diagonally. Place 1 triangle of cheese in each opening in bread. Place bread on foil-covered baking sheet. Combine margarine, poppy seed, onion and mustard in bowl; mix well. Spread over top and sides of bread. Sprinkle chopped bacon on top. Bake for 20 to 25 minutes or until brown. Yield: 8 servings.

Pam Matlock, Laureate Alpha Rho
Wichita, Kansas

APPLE BREAD

1/2 cup shortening	1 teaspoon salt
1 cup sugar	1 cup apple cider
1 1/2 tablespoons	2 cups all-purpose flour
buttermilk	1 1/2 cups shredded
2 eggs	peeled apples
1 teaspoon vanilla	1/2 cup chopped walnuts
extract	2 teaspoons sugar
1 teaspoon soda	1/2 teaspoon cinnamon

Preheat oven to 350 degrees. Cream shortening and 1 cup sugar in mixer bowl until light and fluffy. Add buttermilk, eggs, vanilla, soda and salt, mixing well after each addition. Add cider and flour alternately, mixing well after each addition. Stir in apples and walnuts. Pour into greased 5-by-9-inch loaf pan. Sprinkle with mixture of remaining 2 teaspoons sugar and cinnamon. Bake for 1 hour or until loaf tests done. Remove to wire rack to cool.
Yield: 10 to 12 servings.

Linda J. Perry, Xi Epsilon Mu
Toledo, Ohio

CANDY BREAD

Mother made this at holidays for kids who didn't care for fruitcake.

2/3 cup shortening	1 teaspoon soda
2 cups packed light	1 teaspoon cinnamon
brown sugar	1 cup sour milk
2 eggs	1 cup raisins
4 cups all-purpose flour	1 cup chopped pecans
1 1/2 teaspoons salt	1 pound small gumdrops

Preheat oven to 350 degrees. Cream shortening, brown sugar and eggs in mixer bowl until light and fluffy. Add mixture of flour, salt, soda and cinnamon alternately with sour milk, mixing well after each addition. Add raisins, pecans and gumdrops; mix well. Pour into 2 greased 5-by-9-inch loaf pans. Bake for 1 hour or until loaves test done. Yield: 2 loaves.

Judi Stasko, Theta Psi
Ames, Iowa

CHEDDAR CHEESE AND ONION MINI-LOAVES

1 cup milk	1 cup shredded Cheddar
1 cup water	cheese
1 envelope onion soup	5 1/4 cups (about)
mix	all-purpose flour
3 tablespoons butter or	2 tablespoons melted
margarine	butter or margarine
2 tablespoons sugar	1/8 teaspoon garlic salt
1 envelope dry yeast	2 tablespoons grated
1 teaspoon salt	Parmesan cheese

Combine milk, water, onion soup mix and 3 tablespoons butter in 1-quart saucepan. Cook over low heat until butter melts. Let stand for 10 minutes or until cooled to 120 degrees. Combine sugar, yeast, salt, Cheddar cheese and 2 cups flour in mixer bowl. Add cooled milk mixture. Beat at medium speed for 2 minutes. Add 1 cup flour. Beat at high speed for 2 minutes. Stir in 2 cups flour. Knead in remaining 1/4 cup flour on floured surface for 10 to 12 minutes or until smooth and elastic. Place in greased bowl, turning to coat surface. Let rise, covered, in warm place for 1 1/2 hours or until doubled in bulk. Divide into 6 portions on floured surface. Shape into loaves. Place in greased 3-by-5-inch loaf pans. Let rise, covered, for 40 minutes or until almost doubled in bulk. Preheat oven to 350 degrees. Brush loaves with mixture of melted butter and garlic salt. Sprinkle with Parmesan cheese. Place loaf pans on baking sheet. Bake for 35 minutes or until loaves test done. Remove to wire rack to cool. Yield: 6 small loaves.

Ruth S. Pitman, Xi Beta Omicron
Littleton, Colorado

CHEDDAR-ONION BUNDT BREAD

2 8-ounce loaves	1/2 cup melted
frozen bread dough,	margarine
thawed	1/2 envelope onion soup
2 cups shredded	mix
Cheddar cheese	

Cut bread into 24 pieces. Make indentation in each. Fill with cheese; seal. Dip in mixture of margarine and soup mix. Place in bundt pan. Let rise, covered, until doubled in bulk. Preheat oven to 350 degrees. Bake for 30 to 35 minutes or until brown.
Yield: 16 servings.

DeVee Dietz, Gamma
Huron, South Dakota

CRANBERRY AND APPLE BREAD

1/4 cup butter or	3 cups all-purpose flour
margarine, softened	1/2 teaspoon soda
1 cup sugar	1/2 teaspoon salt
2 eggs	1 1/2 cups chopped
1 cup sour cream	cranberries
2 teaspoons grated	1 1/2 cups chopped
lemon rind	golden Delicious
4 teaspoons baking	apples
powder	1/2 cup chopped walnuts

Preheat oven to 350 degrees. Cream butter and sugar in mixer bowl until light and fluffy. Add eggs, sour cream and lemon rind; mix well. Sift in dry ingredients; mix well. Fold in cranberries, apples and walnuts. Pour into greased 5-by-9-inch loaf pan. Bake for 60 to 70 minutes or until loaf tests done. Cool on wire rack for 15 minutes. Remove to wire rack to cool completely. Wrap in foil. Let stand for 24 hours to mellow before slicing. Yield: 1 loaf.

Margaret Doherty, Xi Alpha Alpha Omicron
Ennis, Texas

BUTTERSCOTCH BANANA BREAD

2 cups mashed ripe bananas	4 teaspoons baking powder
1½ cups sugar	1 teaspoon cinnamon
2 eggs	1 teaspoon nutmeg
½ cup melted butter or margarine	1 teaspoon salt
	½ cup milk
3½ cups all-purpose flour	2 cups butterscotch chips
1 teaspoon soda	2⅔ cups chopped pecans

Preheat oven to 350 degrees. Combine bananas, sugar, eggs and butter in mixer bowl. Beat until creamy. Add mixture of flour, soda, baking powder, spices and salt alternately with milk, mixing well after each addition. Stir in butterscotch chips and 2 cups pecans. Pour into 2 greased and floured 5-by-9-inch loaf pans. Sprinkle with remaining ⅔ cup pecans. Bake for 60 to 70 minutes or until loaves test done. Cool in pans for 15 minutes. Remove to wire rack to cool completely. Yield: 2 loaves.

Shelly Ann Fry, Zeta Phi
Bryan, Ohio

BISHOP BREAD

A favorite restaurant of ours serves this at every meal.

½ cup butter or margarine, softened	1 tablespoon baking powder
1 cup packed light brown sugar	1 teaspoon salt
	½ cup sugar
2 eggs	½ cup all-purpose flour
1 cup milk	¼ cup butter or margarine
2¾ cups all-purpose flour	1 tablespoon cinnamon

Preheat oven to 375 degrees. Cream butter, brown sugar and eggs in mixer bowl until very light and fluffy. Blend in milk at low speed. Add mixture of next 3 dry ingredients; mix just until moistened. Pour into greased 9-by-13-inch baking pan. Combine sugar, remaining ½ cup flour and ¼ cup butter and cinnamon in small bowl; mix until crumbly. Sprinkle over batter. Bake for 25 minutes or until bread tests done. Let stand on wire rack for several minutes to cool slightly. Cut into squares. Serve warm. Yield: 16 servings.

Judy Kutcher, Xi Zeta Mu
Eldridge, Iowa

Kathy Witchey, Preceptor Alpha Eta, Sulphur, Oklahoma, makes easy Vegetable Bread by sautéing 1 cup chopped green bell pepper and 1 cup chopped onion in 1 cup margarine. Add 1 tablespoon chopped chives, 3 ounces bacon bits, ½ cup Parmesan cheese and 3 cans biscuits cut into quarters. Place in buttered bundt pan. Bake in preheated 375-degree oven for 30 minutes.

BLUEBERRY AND PINEAPPLE BREAD

⅔ cup shortening	½ cup milk
1⅓ cups sugar	1½ teaspoons lemon juice
4 eggs	
3 cups all-purpose flour	1 cup crushed pineapple, drained
2 teaspoons baking powder	2 cups blueberries
1 teaspoon soda	1 cup chopped pecans
½ teaspoon salt	½ cup shredded coconut

Preheat oven to 350 degrees. Cream shortening and sugar in mixer bowl until light and fluffy. Add eggs; mix well. Sift flour, baking powder, soda and salt together. Add to creamed mixture alternately with milk and lemon juice, mixing well after each addition. Add pineapple; mix well. Fold in blueberries, pecans and coconut. Pour into 3 greased and floured 4-by-8-inch loaf pans. Bake for 40 to 45 minutes or until loaves test done. Cool in pans for 10 minutes. Remove to wire rack to cool completely. Yield: 3 loaves.

Marilyn Borras, Epsilon Tau
Stafford, Virginia

CHEESE BRAIDS

I give this pastry as Christmas gifts.

2 envelopes dry yeast	32 ounces cream cheese, softened
½ cup warm water	
6 tablespoons sugar	10 tablespoons sugar
1 cup margarine, softened	4 teaspoons vanilla extract
3 eggs	2⅔ cups confectioners' sugar
1 cup sour cream	
5 cups all-purpose flour	½ cup orange juice
4 egg yolks	¼ cup lemon juice

Dissolve yeast in warm water in bowl. Add 6 tablespoons sugar; set aside. Cream margarine, eggs and sour cream in mixer bowl until fluffy. Add flour and yeast mixture; mix well. Chill in refrigerator overnight. Let stand at room temperature for 1 hour. Divide into 4 portions. Roll each portion into 9-by-12-inch rectangle on floured surface. Place each rectangle on greased baking sheet. Combine egg yolks, cream cheese, 10 tablespoons sugar and vanilla in bowl; mix well. Spread filling down centers of rectangles. Cut each side into 1-inch strips; fold alternately over center to enclose filling and make braided loaves. Let rise, covered, for 1 hour. Preheat oven to 350 degrees. Bake for 25 minutes. Drizzle mixture of confectioners' sugar, orange juice and lemon juice over hot braids. Yield: 4 braids.

Kathy Wilkinson, Xi Delta Beta
York, Nebraska

CHEESE-PEPPER BREAD

1 envelope dry yeast	1 egg
1/4 cup warm water	2 1/3 cups all-purpose
2 tablespoons sugar	flour
1 teaspoon salt	1 cup shredded Cheddar
1/4 teaspoon soda	cheese
1 cup sour cream	1/2 teaspoon pepper

Dissolve yeast in warm water in mixer bowl. Add sugar, salt, soda, sour cream, egg and 1 1/2 cups flour. Beat at low speed for 30 seconds, scraping bowl constantly. Beat at high speed for 2 minutes, scraping bowl occasionally. Stir in remaining ingredients. Spoon into 2 greased 1-pound coffee cans. Let rise in warm place for 50 minutes. Dough will rise only slightly. Preheat oven to 350 degrees. Bake for 40 minutes or until golden brown. Remove from cans. Cool slightly before slicing. Yield: 2 loaves.

Rondalyn Draper
Price, Utah

CINNAMON RAISIN BREAD

2 cups all-purpose flour	1 cup raisins
2 envelopes dry yeast	3 1/2 to 4 cups
1 cup milk	all-purpose flour
3/4 cup water	2 tablespoons melted
1/4 cup sugar	butter or margarine
1/4 cup vegetable oil	1 cup sugar
2 teaspoons salt	1 tablespoon cinnamon
1 egg	

Combine 2 cups flour and yeast in mixer bowl. Heat milk, water, 1/4 cup sugar, oil and salt in saucepan over low heat to 120 to 130 degrees. Add to flour mixture. Beat at medium speed for 3 minutes. Add egg; mix well. Add raisins and enough remaining flour to make soft dough. Knead on floured surface for 8 minutes or until smooth and elastic. Let rest, covered, for 20 minutes. Divide into 2 portions. Roll each portion into 7-by-14-inch rectangle. Brush with melted butter. Sprinkle with mixture of 1 cup sugar and cinnamon. Roll as for jelly roll from narrow end, sealing edges. Place seam side down in greased 4-by-8-inch loaf pans. Let rise in warm place until doubled in bulk. Preheat oven to 375 degrees. Bake for 35 minutes or until loaves test done. Remove to wire rack to cool. Yield: 2 loaves.

Diane Kindt, Beta Omega
Glenham, South Dakota

CHOCOLATE CHIP BREAD

1/2 cup shortening	1/4 teaspoon cloves
1 cup sugar	1/2 teaspoon allspice
2 eggs	1 teaspoon cinnamon
1 3/4 cups all-purpose	1 cup applesauce
flour	1/2 cup raisins
1 teaspoon soda	1/2 cup chopped pecans
1/4 teaspoon salt	1 cup chocolate chips

Preheat oven to 325 degrees. Cream shortening and sugar in mixer bowl until light and fluffy. Add eggs; mix well. Add mixture of flour, soda, salt and spices alternately with applesauce, mixing well after each addition. Stir in raisins, pecans and 1/2 cup chocolate chips. Pour into greased and floured 5-by-8-inch loaf pan. Sprinkle remaining 1/2 cup chocolate chips on top. Bake for 1 1/4 hours or until loaf tests done. Remove to wire rack to cool. Let stand, tightly covered with foil, overnight before serving. Yield: 1 loaf.

Marcia Nestler, Xi Zeta Mu
Eldridge, Iowa

COCONUT-PECAN LOAVES

2 cups butter or	1 22-ounce pound cake,
margarine, softened	crumbled
4 cups sugar	3/4 cup packed light
1 4-ounce bottle of	brown sugar
vanilla extract	3/4 cup butter or
2 eggs	margarine
1 16-ounce package	1 1/2 cups all-purpose
flaked coconut	flour
4 cups chopped pecans	

Preheat oven to 325 degrees. Cream 2 cups butter and sugar in mixer bowl until light and fluffy. Add vanilla and eggs; mix well. Stir in coconut, pecans and pound cake crumbs. Pour into 9 ungreased 3-by-5-inch loaf pans. Sprinkle mixture of brown sugar, remaining 3/4 cup butter and flour over batter. Bake for 45 to 50 minutes or until loaves test done. Chill in refrigerator overnight. Loaves will sink in middle. Yield: 9 miniature loaves.

Beverly Walker, Xi Delta Gamma
Ada, Oklahoma

DATE-NUT WHISKEY BREAD

1 cup chopped dates	1 egg, beaten
1 teaspoon instant	1 3/4 cups all-purpose
coffee	flour
1 teaspoon soda	1 teaspoon baking
1 cup boiling water	powder
1/4 cup shortening	1 2-ounce jigger of
1 cup sugar	whiskey
1/2 teaspoon salt	1 cup chopped pecans

Preheat oven to 325 degrees. Sprinkle dates with coffee powder and soda in bowl. Add water; mix well. Let stand until cool. Cream shortening and sugar in mixer bowl until light and fluffy. Add salt and egg; mix well. Add sifted flour and baking powder alternately with dates, mixing well after each addition. Stir in whiskey and pecans. Pour into greased 5-by-9-inch loaf pan. Bake for 1 1/2 hours or until loaf tests done. Yield: 1 loaf.

Fran Bogar, Xi Kappa Epsilon
St. Charles, Missouri

HEART BREADS

1 envelope dry yeast	3/4 cup chopped pecans
2/3 cup warm water	1 tablespoon grated
1/2 cup honey	lemon rind
1/3 cup melted butter or	1 teaspoon vanilla
margarine	extract
1 teaspoon salt	1 teaspoon almond
2 eggs	extract
4 to 41/2 cups	3/4 cup confectioners'
all-purpose flour	sugar
1/3 cup packed light	1 tablespoon milk
brown sugar	Red cinnamon candies
3 tablespoons butter or	or toasted sliced
margarine, softened	almonds
1 medium apple, chopped	

Dissolve yeast in water in bowl. Add honey, melted butter, salt and eggs; mix well. Add flour; mix well. Let rise in warm place until doubled in bulk. Combine brown sugar and next 6 ingredients in bowl; mix well. Roll dough 3/8 inch thick on floured surface. Cut with 3-inch round cutter. Place rounded teaspoon apple mixture in center of each circle. Bring edge up, sealing to enclose filling. Place seam side down along sides of greased heart-shaped baking pans; rolls should touch slightly. Let rise, covered, for 45 minutes. Preheat oven to 350 degrees. Bake for 30 minutes. Brush tops with additional melted butter or margarine. Frost with mixture of confectioners' sugar and milk. Decorate with candies or toasted almonds. Yield: 28 servings.

Gail I. Persson, Epsilon Iota
Blair, Nebraska

HONEY NUT BREAD

2 cups all-purpose flour	1 teaspoon ginger
1 teaspoon baking	1/2 cup honey
powder	1 egg, slightly beaten
1 teaspoon soda	1 cup milk
1 teaspoon salt	1/2 cup chopped pecans
1/2 teaspoon cinnamon	

Preheat oven to 350 degrees. Combine flour, baking powder, soda, salt and spices in bowl; mix well. Add honey, egg and milk. Beat for 3 minutes or until smooth. Fold in pecans. Spoon into buttered 5-by-9-inch loaf pan. Bake for 50 minutes or until loaf tests done. Cool in pan for 10 minutes. Remove to wire rack to cool completely. Yield: 12 servings.

Joanne Tauber, Preceptor Delta Sigma
Tampa, Florida

GOUDA CHEESE MONKEY BREAD

3 pounds frozen bread	2 tablespoons onion
dough, thawed	flakes
10 ounces Gouda cheese,	6 tablespoons melted
shredded	butter or margarine
3/4 cup chopped parsley	

Knead dough with cheese, parsley and onion flakes on floured board until ingredients are well incorporated. Shape into 1-inch balls. Dip into melted butter. Arrange in well greased tube pan with removable bottom. Let rise, covered with plastic wrap, in warm place for 1 hour or until dough reaches top of pan. Preheat oven to 350 degrees. Bake for 45 minutes or until golden brown. Let stand on wire rack for 5 minutes. Loosen edges with knife. Remove to wire rack to cool completely. Yield: 1 loaf.

Sandra H. Brasier, Xi Phi Gamma
Katy, Texas

OATMEAL SESAME BREAD

3/4 cup boiling water	21/2 to 3 cups
1/2 cup quick-cooking	all-purpose flour
oats	2 tablespoons butter or
1 envelope dry yeast	margarine
1/4 cup warm water	1 teaspoon salt
1/4 cup packed light	1/4 cup sesame seed
brown sugar	

Combine boiling water and oats in bowl. Let stand until cool. Dissolve yeast in warm water. Add 1 tablespoon brown sugar. Let stand for 5 minutes. Combine remaining brown sugar, flour, butter and salt in large bowl; mix well. Add yeast mixture; mix well. Add oatmeal and sesame seed; mix well. Shape into ball. Place in greased bowl, turning to coat surface. Let rise until doubled in bulk. Punch dough down; place in greased 5-by-9-inch loaf pan. Let rise for 1 hour. Preheat oven to 375 degrees. Bake for 30 to 35 minutes or until loaf tests done. Remove to wire rack to cool. Yield: 1 loaf.

Susan Fredenberg, Rho
Kalispell, Montana

JESSICA'S PEAR BREAD

2 16-ounce cans pears,	3 cups all-purpose flour
drained, chopped	1 teaspoon salt
3 eggs, beaten	1 teaspoon soda
1 cup vegetable oil	1/4 teaspoon baking
11/2 cups sugar	powder
1/2 teaspoon grated	11/2 teaspoons cinnamon
lemon rind	1 cup chopped walnuts
1 teaspoon vanilla	
extract	

Preheat oven to 325 degrees. Combine pears, eggs, oil, sugar, lemon rind and vanilla in bowl; mix well. Sift in flour, salt, soda, baking powder and cinnamon; mix well. Fold in walnuts. Pour into 2 greased 5-by-9-inch loaf pans. Bake for 11/4 hours or until loaves test done. Yield: 24 servings.

Patricia Leffew, Xi Lambda Xi
Clarenden, Texas

FAMOUS ONION-DILL BREAD

1 envelope dry yeast
1/4 cup warm water
3/4 cup cottage cheese
3/4 cup sour cream
3 tablespoons sugar
3 tablespoons minced
  dried onion
2 tablespoons whole
  dillseed

1 1/2 tablespoons butter
  or margarine
1 egg
3 1/3 cups all-purpose
  flour
1/4 teaspoon soda
1 1/2 teaspoons salt

Dissolve yeast in warm water in large bowl. Combine cottage cheese, sour cream, sugar, onion, dillseed and butter in saucepan. Heat until warm. Add to yeast mixture. Beat in egg. Add mixture of flour, soda and salt 1 cup at a time, beating well after each addition. Beat for 5 to 10 minutes or until dough is smooth and elastic. Knead on floured surface for 10 to 15 minutes or until elastic. Place in greased bowl, turning to coat surface. Let rise, covered, in warm dark place for 1 1/2 hours or until doubled in bulk. Divide into 2 portions; shape into loaves. Place in 2 greased 4-by-8-inch loaf pans. Let rise, covered, for 45 minutes or until doubled in bulk. Preheat oven to 350 degrees. Bake for 40 to 45 minutes or until brown. Remove to wire rack to cool. Yield: 2 loaves.

Peggy Carey, Xi Delta Kappa
Grand Blanc, Michigan

POPPY SEED BREAD

1 2-layer package
   yellow cake mix
1 6-ounce package
   lemon instant
   pudding mix
4 eggs
1 cup hot water

1/2 cup vegetable oil
1/4 cup poppy seed
1 tablespoon milk
1 tablespoon lemon juice
1 cup (or more)
   confectioners' sugar

Preheat oven to 350 degrees. Combine cake mix, lemon pudding mix and eggs in mixer bowl; beat well. Add hot water, oil and poppy seed; mix well. Pour into 2 greased and floured 5-by-9-inch loaf pans. Bake for 45 minutes or until bread tests done. Invert onto wire rack to cool. Mix milk, lemon juice and enough confectioners' sugar in bowl to form a glaze. Drizzle over hot bread. Yield: 12 to 15 servings.

Kathy Barrow, Epsilon Psi
Bassett, Virginia

CRANBERRY AND PUMPKIN BREAD

2 eggs, beaten
2 cups sugar
1/2 cup vegetable oil
1 cup solid pack
   pumpkin
2 1/4 cups all-purpose
   flour

1 tablespoon pumpkin
   pie spice
1 teaspoon soda
1/2 teaspoon salt
1 cup chopped
   cranberries

Preheat oven to 350 degrees. Combine eggs, sugar, oil and pumpkin in mixer bowl; beat well. Mix flour, pumpkin pie spice, soda and salt together in large bowl. Make well in center. Add pumpkin mixture, stirring just until dry ingredients are moistened. Stir in cranberries. Spoon batter into 2 greased and floured in 3-by-8-inch loaf pans. Bake for 1 hour or until bread tests done. Invert onto wire rack to cool. Yield: 2 loaves.

Rosemary Battaglia, Xi Chi
Waterbury, Connecticut

PRUNE NUT BREAD

3 cups all-purpose flour
1 1/2 cups whole wheat
   flour
2 teaspoons baking
   powder
1 teaspoon salt
1 1/2 teaspoons soda
1 cup chopped walnuts
2 eggs, beaten

1 cup packed light
   brown sugar
3 tablespoons vegetable
   oil
1 1/2 cups buttermilk
3/4 cup prune juice or
   apple juice
2 cups chopped prunes

Preheat oven to 350 degrees. Combine first 5 ingredients in large bowl; mix well. Add walnuts; toss to coat. Mix eggs, brown sugar, oil, buttermilk and juice in bowl. Stir in prunes. Pour into flour mixture, stirring just until moistened. Spoon into 2 greased 5-by-9-inch loaf pans. Bake for 50 minutes or until loaves test done. Invert onto wire rack to cool. Yield: 2 loaves.

Jacqueline Reitz, Laureate Gamma
Pittsfield, Massachusetts

PUMPKIN SWIRL BREAD

8 ounces cream cheese,
   softened
1/4 cup sugar
1 egg, beaten
1 3/4 cups all-purpose
   flour
1 1/2 cups sugar
1 teaspoon soda

1 teaspoon cinnamon
1/2 teaspoon salt
1/4 teaspoon nutmeg
1 cup canned pumpkin
1/2 cup melted margarine
1 egg, beaten
1/3 cup water

Preheat oven to 350 degrees. Combine cream cheese, sugar and 1 egg in bowl; mix well. Mix flour, sugar, soda, cinnamon, salt and nutmeg in large bowl. Add pumpkin, melted margarine, 1 egg and water, mixing just until moistened. Reserve 2 cups pumpkin batter. Pour remaining pumpkin batter into 1 greased and floured 9-by-15-inch loaf pan. Spoon in cream cheese batter; top with reserved pumpkin batter. Cut through batter with knife to marbleize. Bake for 1 hour and 10 minutes or until bread tests done. Cool in pan for 10 minutes. Invert onto wire rack to cool. Yield: 1 loaf.

Jerry Louise Clark, Xi Sigma
Dodge City, Kansas

REUBEN BRAID

3 tablespoons yellow cornmeal	1½ teaspoons caraway seed
1 12-ounce can beer	¼ cup bread flour
1 tablespoon butter or margarine	½ cup Thousand Island dressing
1 tablespoon salt	1 16-ounce can sauerkraut, drained
1 envelope dry yeast	8 ounces corned beef, thinly sliced
1 tablespoon sugar	
1 tablespoon honey	
2 cups bread flour	8 ounces Swiss cheese, thinly sliced
1½ cups rye flour	

Combine cornmeal and beer in medium saucepan. Simmer for 2 minutes. Stir in butter and salt. Cool to 105 to 115 degrees. Stir in yeast, sugar and honey. Let stand for 5 minutes. Pour into large mixer bowl. Add 2 cups bread flour; mix well. Add rye flour and caraway seed; mix well. Place on lightly floured surface. Work in enough remaining ¼ cup bread flour to reduce stickiness. Place dough in oiled bowl, turning to grease surface. Let rise in warm place until doubled in bulk. Punch dough down. Let rest for 10 minutes. Divide dough into 2 portions. Roll each portion into rectangle on lightly floured surface. Place on greased baking sheet. Score lightly each rectangle into thirds lengthwise. Spread Thousand Island dressing down center third, leaving 1 inch at top and bottom. Top with sauerkraut, corned beef and Swiss cheese. Cut 1-inch strips from outer edge to filling. Fold strips alternately across filling sealing each strip. Let rest, covered, for 30 minutes. Preheat oven to 350 degrees. Place on greased baking sheet. Bake for 30 minutes or until bread tests done. Cut into slices. Yield: 16 to 20 servings.

Joan Froelich, Laureate Epsilon
Abilene, Kansas

STRAWBERRY BREAD

1½ cups all-purpose flour	1 10-ounce package frozen strawberries, thawed
1 cup sugar	
½ teaspoon soda	
½ teaspoon salt	3 ounces cream cheese, softened
½ teaspoon cinnamon	
½ cup vegetable oil	4 ounces whipped topping
2 eggs, beaten	

Combine flour, sugar, soda, salt and cinnamon in bowl; mix well. Make a well in center. Add oil and eggs; mix well. Reserve ¼ cup strawberry juice. Add remaining strawberries and juice to batter; whip until well mixed. Grease and flour 5-by-9-inch loaf pan; line bottom with waxed paper. Preheat oven to 350 degrees. Spoon batter into prepared pan. Bake for 1 hour or until bread tests done. Cool in pan for several minutes. Invert onto wire rack to cool. Mix cream cheese and reserved strawberry juice in bowl. Fold in whipped topping. Slice bread. Serve with cream cheese spread. Yield: 10 servings.

Michelle Lynn, Alpha Zeta
Moberly, Missouri

SWEET POTATO BREAD

1 cup boiling water	½ cup warm water
1 cup milk, scalded	2 eggs, beaten
½ cup honey	1 16-ounce can sweet potatoes, mashed
2 tablespoons sugar	
3 tablespoons vegetable oil	3 cups all-purpose flour
2 teaspoons salt	3 cups whole wheat flour
2 envelopes dry yeast	

Combine boiling water, scalded milk, honey, sugar, oil and salt in bowl; mix well. Let cool to room temperature. Dissolve yeast in ½ cup warm water. Add to cooled mixture; mix well. Combine eggs and mashed sweet potatoes in mixer bowl; mix well. Add yeast mixture; beat well. Add all-purpose flour and whole wheat flour gradually, mixing well. Turn out onto floured surface. Knead well, adding additional flour as needed to smooth dough. Place in greased bowl, turning to grease surface. Let rise, covered, until doubled in bulk. Punch down, kneading well. Divide into 2 portions. Place in 2 greased 5-by-9-inch loaf pans. Let rise until doubled in bulk. Preheat oven to 350 degrees. Bake for 50 to 60 minutes or until bread tests done. Cool in pan for several minutes. Invert onto wire rack to cool. Yield: 2 loaves.

Ava Swan, Laureate Pi
Roswell, New Mexico

SHREDDED WHEAT BREAD

3 large shredded wheat cereal biscuits, crushed	2¾ cups boiling water
	1 envelope yeast
¼ cup melted shortening	1 teaspoon sugar
	½ cup warm water
⅔ cup molasses	Whole wheat flour

Combine crushed shredded wheat, shortening, molasses and boiling water in large bowl. Dissolve yeast and sugar in ½ cup warm water. Let stand for 10 minutes. Stir into mixture. Stir in enough whole wheat flour to make a soft dough. Knead until smooth on lightly floured surface. Place in greased bowl, turning to grease surface. Let rise in warm place until doubled in bulk. Shape into 3 loaves. Place in greased 5-by-9-inch loaf pans. Let rise, covered, until doubled in bulk. Preheat oven to 350 degrees. Bake for 20 to 30 minutes or until bread tests done. Cool in pan for several minutes. Invert onto wire rack to cool. Yield: 3 loaves.

Kim MacNeil, Zeta
Dartmouth, Nova Scotia, Canada

ZUCCHINI AND CHEDDAR BREAD

1 cup chopped onion	1/4 cup milk
1/4 cup butter or margarine	3 eggs
2 1/2 cups baking mix	1 1/2 cups shredded zucchini
1 tablespoon chopped parsley	1 cup shredded Cheddar cheese
1/2 teaspoon basil	3/4 cup chopped almonds, toasted
1/2 teaspoon thyme	

Preheat oven to 400 degrees. Grease and flour 9-inch round baking pan. Sauté onion in butter in skillet until tender. Cool to room temperature. Combine baking mix, parsley, basil and thyme in mixer bowl. Add milk and eggs. Beat for 1 minute. Stir in onion, zucchini, cheese and almonds. Spread in prepared pan. Bake for 40 minutes or until bread tests done. Cool in pan for several minutes. Invert onto wire rack. Yield: 12 to 16 servings.

Sandra L. Utz, Psi Beta
Plattsburg, Missouri

PUFFY MAPLE BARS

2 envelopes dry yeast	2 eggs, beaten
1/2 cup warm water	5 cups all-purpose flour
6 tablespoons sugar	Vegetable oil for deep frying
1 1/4 cups warm milk	Maple-flavored confectioners' sugar frosting
1/3 cup margarine, softened	
2 teaspoons salt	

Dissolve yeast in warm water in large bowl. Add 1 tablespoon sugar. Let stand until bubbly. Add remaining 5 tablespoons sugar, warm milk, margarine, salt and eggs; beat until smooth. Add 3 cups flour gradually; beat until smooth. Add enough remaining 2 cups flour to make soft dough. Place in greased bowl. Let rise, covered, for 1 to 1 1/2 hours or until doubled in bulk. Roll to 3/4-inch thickness on floured surface. Cut into rectangles. Placed on greased baking sheet. Let rise for 30 to 40 minutes or until doubled in bulk. Preheat oil in deep-fryer. Deep-fry several at a time until evenly browned; drain on paper towels. Frost with maple-flavored confectioners' sugar frosting. Yield: 3 dozen.

Lois A. Bennett, Preceptor Iota
Helena, Montana

MAKE-YOUR-OWN ENGLISH MUFFINS

2 cups all-purpose flour	1 tablespoon butter or margarine
2 tablespoons sugar	1 egg
2 teaspoons salt	4 cups all-purpose flour
1 envelope dry yeast	1/2 cup (about) cornmeal
1 3/4 cups milk	
1/4 cup water	

Combine 2 cups flour, sugar, salt and dry yeast in large mixer bowl. Heat milk, water and butter in

saucepan to 120 to 130 degrees. Add to yeast mixture gradually. Beat at medium speed for 2 minutes. Add egg and 1 cup flour. Beat at high speed for 2 minutes. Stir in just enough remaining 3 cups flour to make soft dough. Knead on lightly floured surface until smooth and elastic. Place in greased bowl, turning to coat surface. Let rise, covered, for 1 hour or until doubled in bulk. Punch dough down. Let rise, covered, for 45 minutes or until doubled in bulk. Roll 1/2 inch thick on lightly floured surface; cut with 3 1/4-inch tuna can with both ends removed. Arrange muffins 1 inch apart on greased baking sheet sprinkled with cornmeal. Sprinkle with cornmeal. Let rise, covered, for 45 minutes or until doubled in bulk. Preheat griddle over very low heat. Place muffins on lightly greased griddle with wide spatula. Bake for 8 minutes on each side or until light brown. Cool on wire rack. Split with fork tines before toasting. Yield: 2 dozen.

Mary Smrcka, Preceptor Lambda
Glasgow, Montana

NO-EGG CINNAMON APPLE MUFFINS

1 cup whole wheat flour	1/8 teaspoon salt
1 tablespoon baking powder	1/3 cup skim milk
1 1/2 cups raisin bran cereal	3 tablespoons honey
1 teaspoon cinnamon	3 tablespoons vegetable oil
	1 apple, peeled, grated

Preheat oven to 400 degrees. Mix first 5 ingredients in large bowl. Mix milk, honey and oil in small bowl. Add to flour mixture; stir just until moistened. Stir in apple. Fill paper-lined muffin cups 3/4 full. Bake for 25 minutes or until golden brown. Yield: 1 dozen.

Patricia Baker, Tau
Benton, Illinois

BEST-OF-ALL BLUEBERRY MUFFINS

1/2 cup margarine, softened	1/2 teaspoon salt
1 1/4 cups sugar	1/2 cup milk
2 eggs	1/2 cup crushed blueberries
2 cups all-purpose flour	2 cups whole blueberries
2 teaspoons baking powder	1/4 cup (about) sugar

Preheat oven to 375 degrees. Cream margarine and 1 1/4 cups sugar in bowl until light and fluffy. Beat in eggs 1 at a time. Mix flour, baking powder and salt together. Add to creamed mixture alternately with milk, mixing well after each addition. Stir in crushed blueberries. Fold in whole blueberries gently. Spoon into paper-lined muffin cups. Sprinkle with remaining 1/4 cup sugar. Bake for 25 to 30 minutes or until golden brown. Yield: 22 to 24 muffins.

Dolores Durnwald, Xi Beta Nu
Whitesburg, Georgia

SUPER BRAN MUFFINS

2 cups warm milk
2 cups bran flakes cereal
2 cups baking mix
3/4 cup honey
2 eggs, beaten
1/3 cup vegetable oil
1 teaspoon cinnamon
1 teaspoon nutmeg
1 cup chopped pecans
1 cup chopped fruit,
  such as apples,
  bananas, blueberries,
  raisins or dates

Preheat oven to 350 degrees. Pour warm milk over cereal in bowl. Let stand for 10 minutes. Combine baking mix, honey, eggs, oil and spices in bowl; mix well. Add to cereal mixture; mix well. Add pecans and fruit in any combination; stir just until mixed. Spoon into greased muffin cups. Bake for 20 to 25 minutes; do not overbake. Yield: 2 dozen.

Betty S. Jones, Xi Eta Rho
Camdenton, Missouri

SPICED CARROT MUFFINS

1 cup all-purpose flour
1 cup whole wheat flour
2 1/2 teaspoons baking
  powder
1 teaspoon cinnamon
1/2 teaspoon soda
1/2 teaspoon nutmeg
1/4 teaspoon salt
1/4 teaspoon cloves
1 cup coarsely shredded
  carrots
1/2 cup raisins
3/4 cup low-fat milk
1/4 cup honey
3 tablespoons vegetable
  oil
2 egg whites

Preheat oven to 400 degrees. Combine dry ingredients in bowl. Stir in carrots and raisins. Combine milk, honey, oil and egg whites in bowl; mix well. Add to carrot mixture; stir just until moistened. Spoon into greased muffin cups. Bake for 20 to 25 minutes or until brown. Yield: 1 dozen.

Carolyn Zaza, Xi Chi
Waterbury, Connecticut

CHOCOLATE ZUCCHINI MUFFINS

1 cup sugar
3 eggs
1 cup vegetable oil
3 cups shredded zucchini
2 teaspoons vanilla
  extract
3 cups all-purpose flour
2 teaspoons soda
1 1/2 teaspoons baking
  powder
2 teaspoons cinnamon
1/4 cup baking cocoa
1/2 teaspoon salt
1 cup chocolate chips
1 cup carob chips

Preheat oven to 350 degrees. Combine sugar, eggs, oil, zucchini and vanilla in large bowl; mix well. Combine flour, soda, baking powder, cinnamon, cocoa, salt, chocolate chips and carob chips in medium bowl; mix well. Add to zucchini mixture; stir just until moistened. Spoon into greased muffin cups. Bake for 20 minutes. Yield: 2 dozen.

Marilyn Chalmers, Gamma Mu
Belleville, Ontario, Canada

FRENCH BREAKFAST PUFFS

1/3 cup shortening
1/2 cup sugar
1 egg
1 1/2 cups all-purpose
  flour
1 1/2 teaspoons baking
  powder
1/2 teaspoon salt
1/4 teaspoon nutmeg
1/2 cup milk
1/2 cup melted margarine
1/2 cup sugar
1 teaspoon cinnamon

Preheat oven to 350 degrees. Cream shortening, 1/2 cup sugar and egg in bowl until light and fluffy. Add mixture of flour, baking powder, salt and nutmeg alternately with milk. Fill greased muffin cups 2/3 full. Bake for 20 to 25 minutes or until golden brown. Roll hot muffins in melted margarine; coat with mixture of 1/2 cup sugar and cinnamon. Yield: 15 muffins.

Toni Foley, Phi Epsilon Eta
Salem, Illinois

MARVELOUS MUFFINS

2 cups baking mix
3/4 teaspoon soda
1/2 cup packed light
  brown sugar
1/2 cup chopped
  macadamia nuts
1 egg, beaten
1 cup crushed pineapple

Preheat oven to 400 degrees. Combine baking mix, soda, brown sugar and macadamia nuts in bowl. Beat egg with undrained pineapple in small bowl. Stir into dry ingredients. Fill greased muffin cups 3/4 full. Bake for 12 to 15 minutes or until golden brown. Yield: 12 to 15 muffins.

Nancy F. Otte, Preceptor Laureate
Freeport, Illinois

PIÑA COLADA MUFFINS

1 2-layer package
   yellow cake mix
1/3 cup vegetable oil
3 eggs
1 teaspoon coconut
  extract
1 teaspoon rum extract
1 cup flaked coconut
1/2 cup chopped walnuts
1 cup crushed pineapple

Preheat oven to 350 degrees. Prepare cake mix using package directions using oil and eggs. Add flavorings, coconut, walnuts and pineapple. Mix for 1 minute; do not over mix. Fill greased muffin cups 3/4 full. Bake for 15 to 20 minutes or until golden brown. Yield: 2 1/2 dozen.

Katy Rosolowski, Xi Nu Alpha
Orlando, Florida

Kim Hedine, Lambda, Walla Walla, Washington, makes Zucchini Pancakes by mixing 2 cups grated zucchini, 2 eggs, 1/2 cup baking mix, 1 tablespoon vegetable oil and 1 tablespoon sugar. Bake on hot greased griddle.

SUNSHINE PINEAPPLE CARROT MUFFINS

1½ cups all-purpose flour	1 cup sugar
1 teaspoon baking powder	⅔ cup vegetable oil
1 teaspoon soda	2 eggs
2 teaspoons cinnamon	1 teaspoon vanilla extract
½ teaspoon nutmeg	1 cup crushed pineapple
½ teaspoon salt	1½ cups grated carrots

Preheat oven to 350 degrees. Mix dry ingredients in bowl. Beat sugar, oil, eggs and vanilla in bowl. Stir in undrained pineapple and carrots. Stir into dry ingredients. Fill greased muffin cups ⅔ full. Bake for 25 minutes. Yield: 1 dozen.

Mary Hall, Laureate Delta
Lethbridge, Alberta, Canada

POPPY SEED POUND CAKE MUFFINS

2 cups all-purpose flour	2 eggs
1 tablespoon poppy seed	1 cup plain yogurt
½ teaspoon salt	1 teaspoon vanilla extract
¼ teaspoon soda	1 to 1½ teaspoons almond extract
1 cup sugar	
½ cup butter or margarine, softened	

Preheat oven to 400 degrees. Mix first 4 ingredients together. Cream sugar and butter in bowl until light and fluffy. Beat in eggs, yogurt and flavorings. Stir in flour mixture until moistened. Spoon into paper-lined muffin cups. Bake for 15 to 20 minutes. Cool on wire rack. Yield: 12 to 16 muffins.

Shari Goode, Xi Beta Lambda
Soda Springs, Idaho

PUMPKIN APPLE STREUSEL MUFFINS

2½ cups all-purpose flour	2 cups chopped peeled apples
2 cups sugar	1 cup chopped pecans
1 tablespoon pumpkin pie spice	2 tablespoons all-purpose flour
1 teaspoon soda	¼ cup sugar
½ teaspoon salt	½ teaspoon cinnamon
2 eggs, beaten	4 teaspoons butter or margarine
1 cup pumpkin	
½ cup vegetable oil	

Preheat oven to 350 degrees. Combine first 5 ingredients in large bowl. Beat eggs with pumpkin and oil in bowl. Add to dry ingredients; stir just until moistened. Stir in apples and pecans. Fill greased muffin cups ¾ full. Combine 2 tablespoons flour, ¼ cup sugar and cinnamon in small bowl. Cut in butter until crumbly. Sprinkle over batter. Bake for 35 to 40 minutes or until golden brown. Yield: 1½ dozen.

Terri Bruch, Epsilon Delta
Mt. Pleasant, Iowa

SAUSAGE AND CHEESE MUFFINS

8 ounces sausage	½ cup shredded Cheddar cheese
¼ cup finely chopped onion	1 egg, beaten
¾ cup all-purpose flour	1 cup buttermilk
½ cup cornmeal	Salt and pepper to taste
1 teaspoon soda	

Preheat oven to 400 degrees. Cook sausage with onion in skillet until brown and crumbly, stirring frequently; drain. Combine with flour, cornmeal, soda and cheese in bowl; mix well. Beat egg with buttermilk. Add to sausage mixture; mix well. Add salt and pepper. Spoon into greased muffin cups. Bake for 25 to 30 minutes or until golden brown. Yield: 6 muffins.

Mary Perroni, Chi Phi
Vandenberg AFB, California

APPLE PANCAKES

2 cups baking mix	2 tablespoons cornstarch
1 teaspoon cinnamon	¼ teaspoon nutmeg
1 egg	2 tablespoons lemon juice
1⅓ cups milk	¼ cup butter or margarine
¾ cup grated apple	Hot syrup
2 cups apple cider	
1 cup sugar	
¼ teaspoon cinnamon	

Preheat griddle. Combine baking mix, 1 teaspoon cinnamon, egg, milk and apple in bowl; mix well. Combine cider, sugar, ¼ teaspoon cinnamon, cornstarch, nutmeg and lemon juice in saucepan; mix well. Bring to a boil, stirring constantly. Boil for 1 minute; remove from heat. Add butter; stir until melted. Stir into apple mixture. Ladle batter onto hot lightly greased griddle. Bake until golden brown on both sides, turning once. Serve with hot syrup. Yield: 4 servings.

Joyce Picht, Chi
Waterloo, Iowa

OATMEAL PANCAKES

1½ cups oats	1 tablespoon baking powder
2 cups milk	1 teaspoon salt
½ cup whole wheat flour	½ teaspoon cinnamon
½ cup all-purpose flour	2 eggs, beaten
1 tablespoon light brown sugar	¼ cup melted butter or margarine

Preheat griddle. Combine oats and milk in bowl. Let stand for 5 minutes. Add flours, brown sugar, baking powder, salt and cinnamon; mix well. Add eggs and butter; mix well. Ladle onto hot lightly greased griddle. Bake until golden brown on both sides, turning once. Yield: 10 pancakes.

Tracy L. Kew, Xi Delta Upsilon
Golden, British Columbia, Canada

BANANA BREAD FRENCH TOAST

2 cups sifted
    all-purpose flour
1 teaspoon soda
1/2 teaspoon salt
1/2 cup unsalted butter
    or margarine, softened
1 cup sugar
2 eggs
1 cup mashed bananas
1 teaspoon lemon juice
1/3 cup milk
1/2 cup chopped pecans

4 eggs
1/4 cup whipping cream
2 tablespoons light
    brown sugar
1 teaspoon vanilla
    extract
1/4 teaspoon nutmeg
1/4 teaspoon cinnamon
3 tablespoons butter or
    margarine
Maple syrup

Preheat oven to 350 degrees. Sift flour, soda and salt together. Cream unsalted butter and sugar in bowl until light and fluffy. Beat in 2 eggs 1 at time. Add bananas and lemon juice. Beat in sifted dry ingredients alternately with milk. Stir in pecans. Pour into buttered 5-by-9-inch loaf pan. Bake for 1 hour and 20 minutes or until loaf tests done. Cool on wire rack. May refrigerate for up to 2 days. Cut into 3/4-inch slices. Preheat skillet over medium heat. Combine next 6 ingredients in bowl; whisk until blended. Melt 1 tablespoon butter in skillet. Dip banana bread slice into egg mixture; place in buttered skillet. Bake for 3 minutes on each side or until golden brown. Place on baking sheet in 250-degree oven to keep warm. Repeat with remaining butter and banana bread. Serve with maple syrup. Yield: 6 servings.

Diane Heyman, Mu Theta
Paxton, Illinois

PAIN PERDU

2 eggs
1/2 cup sugar
1 cup milk
1 teaspoon vanilla
    extract
1/2 teaspoon grated
    lemon rind
8 slices day-old French
    bread
2 tablespoons butter or
    margarine

6 tablespoons
    confectioners' sugar
1/2 cup butter or
    margarine, softened
1 teaspoon cinnamon or
    2 teaspoons grated
    orange rind
Nutmeg
Preserves or syrup

Beat eggs with sugar in bowl. Stir in milk, vanilla and lemon rind. Arrange bread slices in single layer in shallow dish. Pour egg mixture over bread. Let stand for 30 minutes. Preheat large skillet. Cook bread in 2 tablespoons butter in hot skillet for 6 minutes on each side or until golden brown. Blend confectioners' sugar, softened butter and cinnamon in bowl. Place toast on serving plate. Spread with butter mixture. Sprinkle with additional confectioners' sugar and nutmeg. Serve with preserves or syrup. Yield: 8 servings.

Diane Frame, Xi Delta Gamma
Manassas, Virginia

BLUEBERRY BREAKFAST PIZZA

1 loaf frozen bread
    dough, thawed
8 ounces cream cheese,
    softened
1/2 cup sugar
1 egg, beaten
1 teaspoon vanilla
    extract
2 cups blueberries
3/4 cup all-purpose flour

1/2 cup sugar
6 tablespoons margarine
1/4 teaspoon butter
    extract
1 cup confectioners'
    sugar
2 tablespoons milk
1/2 teaspoon vanilla
    extract

Press dough into 14-inch pizza pan. Beat cream cheese with 1/2 cup sugar in mixer bowl until light and fluffy. Beat in egg and 1 teaspoon vanilla. Spread over bread dough. Sprinkle with blueberries. Combine flour and 1/2 cup sugar in small bowl. Cut in margarine and butter extract until crumbly. Sprinkle over blueberries. Let rise for 30 minutes. Preheat oven to 375 degrees. Bake pizza for 30 to 40 minutes or until golden brown. Blend confectioners' sugar with milk and 1/2 teaspoon vanilla in bowl. Drizzle over warm pizza. Yield: 10 to 12 servings.

Jean Fick, Xi Zeta Kappa
Rock Rapids, Iowa

BED AND BREAKFAST ROLLS

12 ounces cream cheese,
    softened
1 tablespoon
    mayonnaise
1/4 cup (about) milk
1 loaf sliced white
    bread, crusts trimmed

1/2 cup melted margarine
1 cup sugar
1 to 2 tablespoons
    cinnamon

Combine cream cheese, mayonnaise and enough milk to make of spreading consistency in bowl; beat until creamy. Spread on bread slices; roll each as for jelly roll. Place seam side down on baking sheet. Chill overnight. Preheat oven to 325 degrees. Brush rolls with melted margarine; coat with mixture of sugar and cinnamon. Cut into quarters; place on baking sheet. Bake for 15 minutes. Broil for several seconds or until bubbly. Yield: 40 servings.

Linda King, Beta Beta Chi
Cedar Hill, Texas

Ginger Brown, Xi Xi Tau, Lubbock, Texas, prepares Easy Breakfast Rolls by dipping 20 canned flaky biscuits into 1/2 cup melted butter or margarine. Place buttered side up on baking sheet. Make indentation in each; fill with favorite canned pie filling. Sprinkle with mixture of 2 tablespoons butter or margarine, 1/4 cup sugar and 3 tablespoons all-purpose flour. Bake in preheated 375-degree oven for 15 minutes or until golden brown. Serve warm.

HEAVENLY ROLLS

If heaven had a taste, this would be it.

1 envelope dry yeast	1/2 cup sugar
1/4 cup warm water	1 teaspoon salt
2 eggs	1/2 cup vegetable oil
1 cup milk, scalded	4 cups all-purpose flour

Dissolve yeast in warm water. Beat eggs in large bowl. Add milk, sugar and salt. Stir in yeast and oil. Add flour; mix well. Let stand overnight. Turn dough onto floured board. Turn dough several times; do not knead in flour. Divide into 2 portions. Roll each into circle; cut into wedges. Roll up from wide end; place 1 1/2 inches apart on greased baking sheet. Let rise for 2 to 3 hours. Preheat oven to 375 degrees. Bake for 12 minutes. Yield: 32 rolls.

Cricket Cobb, Xi Alpha Gamma
Las Vegas, Nevada

HAY HAND ROLLS

1 envelope dry yeast	3 eggs, beaten
4 cups warm water	1 cup melted margarine
1 tablespoon sugar	1 cup sugar
1 tablespoon salt	6 cups all-purpose flour
4 cups all-purpose flour	

Dissolve yeast in warm water in large bowl. Add 1 tablespoon sugar, salt and 4 cups flour; mix well. Let stand, covered, at room temperature for several hours to overnight. Add eggs, margarine, 1 cup sugar and enough remaining 6 cups flour to make soft dough. Knead on lightly floured surface until smooth. Place in greased bowl, turning to coat surface. Let rise, covered, until doubled in bulk. Shape into rolls; place in greased baking pans. Let rise until doubled in bulk. Preheat oven to 400 degrees. Bake for 15 to 20 minutes or until golden brown. Dough may be refrigerated for up to 1 week before baking. Yield: 3 dozen.

Suzanne Mansell, Kappa Sigma
Richmond, Missouri

HONEY PECAN CRESCENTS

3 cups all-purpose flour	1/2 cup honey
1/2 cup sugar	1/2 teaspoon vanilla
1 teaspoon cinnamon	extract
1/2 teaspoon salt	1 1/2 cups finely chopped
1 envelope fast-rising	pecans
yeast	1 egg
1 cup milk	1 tablespoon milk
1/2 cup butter or	1 cup sifted
margarine	confectioners' sugar
2 eggs	1/8 teaspoon salt
1 1/2 to 2 cups	1/2 teaspoon vanilla
all-purpose flour	extract
2 tablespoons butter or	4 to 5 tablespoons milk
margarine	

Combine 3 cups flour, sugar, cinnamon, salt and dry yeast in large mixer bowl. Heat 1 cup milk and 1/2 cup butter in saucepan to 130 degrees. Add to flour mixture; beat at low speed until blended. Add 2 eggs. Beat at medium speed for 3 minutes. Stir in enough remaining 1 1/2 to 2 cups flour to make soft dough. Knead on floured surface for 5 minutes or until smooth and elastic. Place in greased bowl, turning to coat surface. Let rise for 1 1/2 hours or until doubled in bulk. Punch dough down. Let rest for 10 minutes. Divide into 2 portions. Roll each into 13-inch circle. Cut each into 12 wedges. Heat 2 tablespoons butter and honey in saucepan, stirring constantly until well blended. Mix in 1/2 teaspoon vanilla and pecans. Let stand until cool. Spoon 2 teaspoons mixture onto wide end of each wedge. Roll as for jelly roll. Shape into crescents on greased baking sheet. Let rise until doubled in bulk. Preheat oven to 375 degrees. Brush crescents with mixture of egg and 1 tablespoon milk. Bake for 15 minutes. Cool on baking sheet for 5 minutes. Remove to wire rack to cool completely. Blend confectioners' sugar with salt, vanilla and enough milk to make of drizzling consistency. Drizzle over crescents. Yield: 2 dozen.

Shirley Wheatley, Laureate Alpha Kappa
King City, Missouri

PEPPERONI PLUS ROLLS

5 loaves frozen bread	1 pound provolone
dough, thawed	cheese, sliced
1 pound pepperoni,	1 pound mozzarella
sliced	cheese, sliced
1 pound chipped ham,	Melted margarine
chopped	
1 pound Velveeta	
cheese, sliced	

Let bread dough rise. Knead 1 loaf at a time. Divide each loaf into 3 portions; roll each into 5-by-9-inch rectangle. Alternate meats and cheeses down center of rectangle; fold one side over center. Brush with a small amount of water; fold ends toward center. Brush with water; fold remaining side over center; press to seal. Place folded side down on greased baking sheet. Preheat oven to 350 degrees. Bake for 10 minutes or until golden brown. Brush with margarine. May freeze and reheat. Yield: 15 rolls.

Billie Eileen Rakushin, Laureate Alpha Chi
Struthers, Ohio

Diane Harris-Wakeling, Xi Gamma Mu, Aurora, Ontario, Canada, makes Giant Golden Popovers by beating 2 extra large eggs with 1 cup milk and adding 1 cup all-purpose flour and 1/4 teaspoon salt. Fill buttered custard cups 3/4 full. Bake in preheated 475-degree oven for 30 minutes. Reduce temperature to 350 degrees. Bake for 20 minutes.

CHEDDAR AND CORN SCONES

2¼ cups all-purpose flour	1 cup shredded Cheddar cheese
4 teaspoons baking powder	1 10-ounce can cream-style corn
½ teaspoon salt	1 egg, beaten
½ teaspoon dry mustard	1 tablespoon milk
½ cup butter or margarine, softened	

Preheat oven to 425 degrees. Combine flour, baking powder, salt and dry mustard in bowl. Cut in butter until crumbly. Add cheese, corn, egg and milk; mix with fork until soft dough forms. Knead 10 to 12 times on floured surface. Roll into circle; cut into wedges. Brush with additional milk. Place on greased baking sheet. Bake for 15 minutes or until golden brown. Yield: 12 scones.

Barb Cowell, Upsilon
Rosetown, Saskatchewan, Canada

GRIDDLE SCONES

2 cups all-purpose flour	¼ cup butter
¼ teaspoon salt	¾ cup buttermilk
1 teaspoon soda	1 teaspoon cream of tartar
2 teaspoons sugar	

Preheat electric skillet to 350 degrees. Sift flour, salt, soda and sugar into bowl. Rub in butter with fingertips until mixture resembles crumbs. Add mixture of buttermilk and cream of tartar to flour; mix quickly to form soft dough. Turn onto floured surface. Divide into 2 portions. Shape into two ½-inch thick rounds. Cut each round into quarters. Cook in hot skillet for 5 minutes; turn. Cook for 5 minutes longer. Serve hot. Yield: 8 servings.

Sandy Leveille, Alpha Zeta
Thunder Bay, Ontario, Canada

SCONES

⅓ cup margarine	¼ cup sugar
2 cups all-purpose flour	1 cup raisins
2 teaspoon baking powder	1 teaspoon vanilla extract
⅓ teaspoon soda	1 cup sour cream
1 teaspoon salt	1 egg yolk

Preheat oven to 375 degrees. Cut margarine into mixture of flour, baking powder, salt and sugar in bowl until crumbly. Add raisins, vanilla and sour cream; mix well. Shape mixture into two 1-inch thick rounds on ungreased baking sheet. Score each into 4 or 6 wedges. Brush with beaten egg yolk. Bake for 15 minutes. Yield: 8 to 12 servings.

Marjorie M. Buckner, Preceptor Gamma Delta
Welland, Ontario, Canada

SOUR CREAM TWISTS

1 cup sour cream	⅓ cup packed light brown sugar
1 envelope dry yeast	1 teaspoon cinnamon
¼ cup warm water	1½ cups confectioners' sugar
2 tablespoons margarine, softened	2 tablespoons butter or margarine
3 tablespoons sugar	1½ teaspoons vanilla extract
1 teaspoon salt	
1 egg	1 to 2 tablespoons hot water
3 cups bread flour	
2 tablespoons butter or margarine, softened	

Heat sour cream in saucepan to lukewarm. Dissolve yeast in warm water in large bowl. Add sour cream, 2 tablespoons margarine, sugar, salt, egg and 1 cup flour; beat until smooth. Add remaining flour; mix well. Knead on floured surface for 10 minutes or until smooth and elastic. Place in greased bowl, turning to coat surface. Let rise, covered, until doubled in bulk. Punch dough down. Let rest for 10 minutes. Roll into 6-by-24-inch rectangle. Brush with 2 tablespoons butter; sprinkle half the dough lengthwise with mixture of brown sugar and cinnamon. Fold dough over lengthwise; cut into 1-inch strips. Twist 1 strip at a time; place 2 inches apart on greased baking sheet. Let rise, covered, until doubled in bulk. Preheat oven to 375 degrees. Bake for 12 to 15 minutes or until golden brown. Blend confectioners' sugar with 2 tablespoons butter, vanilla and enough hot water to make of spreading consistency. Spread over warm twists.
Yield: 2 dozen.

Loretta Freepons, Laureate Beta Iota
Prosser, Washington

SPOON BREAD

I can remember when I could eat this spoon bread drenched in butter! Mmm. Now I have to count calories and watch cholesterol.

2 eggs	1½ teaspoons baking powder
1 teaspoon salt	2 cups hot water
1 tablespoon sugar	¼ cup butter or margarine
1 cup milk	
1 cup cornmeal	

Preheat oven to 400 degrees. Combine eggs, salt, sugar and milk in small bowl. Mix cornmeal and baking powder in bowl. Pour in hot water slowly, stirring constantly. Add egg mixture; mix well. Melt butter in 2-quart casserole. Pour most of melted butter into batter; mix well. Pour batter into prepared casserole. Bake for 30 to 40 minutes or until knife inserted into center comes out clean.
Yield: 8 to 10 servings.

Mary Gemski, Preceptor Alpha Pi
Hampton, Virginia

SOUTHERN-STYLE SPOON BREAD

2 cups water
2 cups cornmeal
3 tablespoons butter or
shortening, melted
3/4 teaspoon salt
1 1/2 cups milk
3 eggs, separated
Butter or margarine

Preheat oven to 350 degrees. Bring water to a rolling boil in saucepan. Sift cornmeal twice. Add to water, stirring until smooth. Add butter and salt. Stir in milk. Beat egg yolks until light; add to cornmeal mixture. Beat egg whites until stiff peaks form. Fold gently into batter. Pour into greased baking dish. Bake for 30 to 40 minutes or until golden brown. Serve hot with butter. Yield: 6 to 8 servings.

Juanita B. Chancey, Beta Master
Wilmington, Ohio

SPUDNUTS

4 cups milk
1 cup shortening
1 cup sugar
1 cup mashed potatoes
2 envelopes dry yeast
1 cup warm potato
water
1 teaspoon soda
1 teaspoon baking
powder
1 tablespoon vanilla
extract
4 eggs, well beaten
1 tablespoon salt
12 cups all-purpose
flour
Vegetable oil for deep
frying
1 1-pound package
confectioners' sugar
1/2 cup water
1 tablespoon butter or
margarine, softened
Vanilla extract to taste

Combine milk and shortening in saucepan. Bring to a boil. Let stand until cooled to lukewarm. Combine with sugar and mashed potatoes in large bowl. Dissolve yeast in warm potato water. Add to potato mixture. Add soda, baking powder and 1 tablespoon vanilla; mix well. Let stand for 30 minutes or until frothy. Add eggs, salt and flour; mix well. Let rise until doubled in bulk. Roll on floured surface; cut with doughnut cutter. Let rise until doubled in bulk. Preheat oil to 365 degrees. Deep-fry spudnuts until golden brown; drain on paper towels. Blend confectioners' sugar, water, butter and vanilla to taste in bowl. Spread over spudnuts. Yield: 12 dozen.

V. Dale Green, Xi Gamma Tau
Shirley, Arkansas

SWEET PUFFS

2 cups all-purpose flour
1 cup butter or
margarine
1/2 cup sour cream
1 egg yolk
1/2 cup sugar
1 teaspoon vanilla
extract
1 teaspoon grated
lemon rind
8 ounces cream cheese,
softened
1 egg
Confectioners' sugar

Process flour and butter in food processor until mixture resembles coarse cornmeal. Add sour cream and egg yolk. Process until dough leaves side of bowl. Divide dough into 2 portions. Chill, covered, for 8 hours. Preheat oven to 375 degrees. Beat sugar, vanilla, lemon rind, cream cheese and egg in bowl until smooth and fluffy. Roll chilled pastry to 1/8-inch thickness; cut into 3-inch squares. Press into muffin cups. Spoon 1 teaspoon cream cheese mixture into each shell. Fold and seal corners in center. Bake for 20 to 25 minutes or until golden. Remove from pan. Let stand until cool. Sprinkle with confectioners' sugar. Yield: 3 1/2 dozen.

Rosetta Guess, Zeta Alpha
Marion, Kentucky

RAISED WAFFLES

1 envelope dry yeast
1/4 cup warm water
1 3/4 cups lukewarm milk
2 tablespoons sugar
2 cups all-purpose flour
1 teaspoon salt
3 eggs
1/4 cup butter or
margarine, softened

Dissolve yeast in warm water in bowl. Beat in remaining ingredients until smooth. Let rise, covered, for 1 1/2 hours. Stir batter down. Chill, covered, for 8 to 12 hours. Preheat waffle iron. Stir batter down. Pour batter onto center of hot waffle iron. Bake for 5 minutes or until steaming stops. Yield: 8 waffles.

Agnes Ann Hanson, Xi Eta
Newcastle, Wyoming

WALK-AWAY WALNUT WAFFLES

2 cups buttermilk
pancake mix
1 tablespoon sugar
1 teaspoon cinnamon
1/2 cup finely chopped
walnuts
1 1/2 cups milk
1 egg
2 tablespoons vegetable
oil
1 tablespoon butter
flavoring

Preheat waffle iron sprayed with corn oil cooking spray. Combine pancake mix, sugar, cinnamon, walnuts, milk, egg, oil and flavoring in bowl; beat until well mixed. Pour onto hot waffle iron. Bake until steaming stops. Yield: 6 servings.

Roxanne Bell, Alpha Phi
Chanute, Kansas

Priscilla Brower, Los Alamos, New Mexico, makes Sour Milk Waffles by sifting 2 cups all-purpose flour, 1 teaspoon salt, 3/4 teaspoon soda and 1 teaspoon baking powder together in bowl. Combine 2 egg yolks, 1/4 cup melted butter or margarine and 1 1/2 cups sour milk in bowl. Stir mixture into dry ingredients until smooth. Fold in 2 stiffly beaten egg whites. Bake on hot greased waffle iron.

World Champions

AFRICAN BOBOTI

I lived in South Africa for one year and this is a dish they served a lot.

2 medium onions, sliced
2 teaspoons margarine
2 pounds lean ground beef
1 egg
¼ cup milk
2 slices white bread, cubed
¼ cup chopped dried apricots
¼ cup dark raisins
2 tablespoons sugar
1 tablespoon curry powder
2 tablespoons lemon juice
2 teaspoons salt
¼ teaspoon pepper
5 bay leaves
2 eggs
¾ cup milk
¼ teaspoon turmeric

Preheat oven to 350 degrees. Sauté onions in margarine in skillet until golden brown. Add ground beef. Cook until brown, stirring frequently; drain. Combine 1 egg, ¼ cup milk and bread cubes in large bowl; mix well. Add next 7 ingredients; mix well. Add meat mixture; mix gently. Spoon mixture into 2-quart baking dish; place bay leaves on top. Bake for 30 minutes. Remove bay leaves. Beat remaining 2 eggs with remaining ¾ cup milk in small bowl. Add turmeric, stirring until just blended. Pour over casserole. Bake for 10 to 12 minutes longer or until topping is set. Serve with rice and chutney.
Yield: 8 to 10 servings.

Joyce Parker, Preceptor Beta Pi
Delta, British Columbia, Canada

CHIMICHANGAS

6 large flour tortillas
3 cups Beef for Chimichangas
Vegetable oil for frying
Shredded lettuce
1 7-ounce can green chili salsa
2 tomatoes, chopped
1 cup sour cream

Preheat oven to 350 degrees. Warm tortillas in oven for 5 minutes. Warm Beef For Chimichangas in small saucepan. Preheat ½-inch oil to 400 degrees in electric skillet. Spread ½ cup beef mixture on lower ⅓ of each tortilla. Fold bottom edge over filling. Fold both sides toward center; roll as for jelly roll. Secure with a pick. Fry in hot oil for 2 minutes or until golden and crisp. Drain on paper towels. Serve on shredded lettuce; top with green chili salsa, tomatoes and sour cream. Yield: 6 servings.

BEEF FOR CHIMICHANGAS

1 5-pound beef roast
1 tablespoon vegetable shortening
1 onion, chopped
1 4-ounce can chopped green chilies
2 7-ounce cans green chili salsa
¼ teaspoon garlic powder
¼ cup all-purpose flour
4 teaspoons salt
1 teaspoon ground cumin

Preheat oven to 200 degrees. Place roast in deep baking pan. Do not add salt or water. Bake, tightly covered, for 12 hours or until well done. Drain, reserving liquid. Let roast stand until cool. Remove bones; shred meat. Melt shortening in large skillet. Add onion and green chilies. Sauté for 1 minute. Add chili salsa, garlic powder, flour, salt and cumin. Cook for 1 minute over medium-low heat. Stir in reserved pan liquid and shredded meat. Cook for 5 minutes or until slightly thickened. Let stand until cool. May freeze. Yield: 30 servings.

Debbie Newcomb, Xi Epsilon
Washington, Iowa

REAL MEXICAN ENCHILADAS

1²/₃ cups masa flour	1 tablespoon Tequila
¹/₃ cup all-purpose flour	1 tablespoon chili powder
³/₄ teaspoon salt	1 16-ounce can kidney
1 cup water	beans
1 pound ground chuck	Sauce for Enchiladas
1 clove of garlic, minced	1 cup shredded sharp
2 teaspoons salt	Cheddar cheese

Combine masa flour, flour and ³/₄ teaspoon salt in bowl; mix well. Stir in water. Knead on floured surface for 5 minutes or until dough is no longer sticky. Divide into 12 portions. Let stand, covered, for 20 minutes. Preheat griddle. Roll each portion into 6¹/₂-inch circle; trim evenly, using a saucer as a guide. Bake on ungreased griddle for 1 minute on each side. Brown ground chuck with garlic, remaining 2 teaspoons salt, Tequila and chili powder in medium skillet over low heat, stirring frequently. Stir in kidney beans. Preheat oven to 350 degrees. Place ¹/₃ cup beef filling in center of each tortilla; roll up. Arrange seam side down in 9-by-13-inch baking dish. Pour Sauce for Enchiladas over top; sprinkle with cheese. Bake for 25 minutes. Yield: 12 servings.

SAUCE FOR ENCHILADAS

1 clove of garlic, minced	1 beef bouillon cube
¹/₂ cup chopped onion	³/₄ cup boiling water
¹/₄ cup chopped green	2 to 3 tablespoons
bell pepper	finely chopped green
3 tablespoons olive oil	chilies
1 35-ounce can Italian	Dash of ground cumin
tomatoes	¹/₂ teaspoon salt
1 6-ounce can tomato	¹/₈ teaspoon pepper
paste	

Sauté garlic, onion and green pepper in olive oil in large skillet for 5 minutes or until tender. Stir in undrained tomatoes and tomato paste. Bring to a boil over medium heat, stirring constantly. Add bouillon cube dissolved in boiling water, chilies and seasonings; mix well. Simmer for 5 minutes or until thickened, stirring occasionally. Yield: 12 servings.

Diane Polansky Ward, Xi Gamma Psi
Ankeny, Iowa

Sharon Schwartzkopf, Alpha Alpha, Boulder, Colorado, makes Boulder Beta Salsa by combining 6 pounds chopped canned tomatoes, 6 ounces tomato paste, 3 tablespoons each oregano and chopped garlic, 2 to 3 cups chopped fresh cilantro, 1¹/₂ cups white vinegar, 3 cups chopped onions, 2 tablespoons chopped canned jalapeño peppers and 2 cups chopped Anaheim peppers in kettle. Simmer to blend flavors; pour into hot sterilized jars and seal with 2-piece lids. Process in hot water bath for 20 minutes.

CAUDILLO (Mexican Stew)

3 pounds beef cubes	¹/₂ cup chicken stock
1¹/₂ cups chopped onions	2 teaspoons salt
Bacon drippings for	2 teaspoons pepper
frying	2 teaspoons garlic salt
3 cups chopped tomatoes	2 teaspoons cumin
1¹/₂ cups green chili	2 pounds potatoes,
strips	cubed
¹/₂ cup beef stock	

Sauté beef and onions in bacon drippings in large saucepan; drain. Add tomatoes, chili strips, beef stock, chicken stock, salt, pepper, garlic salt and cumin. Cook over low heat until meat is tender. Add potatoes. Cook for 30 minutes longer or until potatoes are tender. Yield: 8 servings.

Mary A. Shook, Xi Zeta Iota
Wagoner, Oklahoma

ITALIAN PARTY FLANK STEAK

¹/₄ cup olive oil	6 to 8 slices of
¹/₄ cup red wine vinegar	prosciutto or other
2 cloves of garlic, finely	cured ham
chopped	24 medium fresh
2 tablespoons chopped	basil leaves
parsley	2 tablespoons chopped
¹/₄ teaspoon coarsely	parsley
ground pepper	2 tablespoons grated
1 1¹/₄-pound flank	Parmesan cheese
steak, ³/₄-inch thick,	Ground pepper to taste
butterflied	1 bunch watercress
2 red bell peppers	
1 tablespoon chopped	
parsley	

Combine olive oil, vinegar, garlic, 2 tablespoons parsley and ¹/₄ teaspoon pepper in shallow dish; mix well. Add flank steak. Marinate at room temperature for 2 hours. Split peppers; remove seeds. Preheat broiler. Place skin side up on rack in broiler pan. Broil 4 inches from heat source until skins are charred black. Seal peppers in plastic bag for 15 minutes. Remove skins. Preheat oven to 350 degrees. Remove steak, reserving marinade; remove excess marinade from steak. Place steak on flat surface. Layer pepper halves, 1 tablespoon parsley and prosciutto over surface of steak. Cover with basil leaves. Sprinkle with remaining 2 tablespoons parsley, Parmesan cheese and pepper to taste. Roll as for jelly roll from long side. Secure with six 8-inch long strings, tying at 2- to 3-inch intervals. Place steak in shallow baking dish; pour marinade over top. Bake for 30 minutes, basting twice. Let stand for 15 minutes before slicing. Cut into ¹/₂-inch slices to serve, discarding string. Arrange on serving platter; garnish with watercress. Yield: 8 servings.

Mary Tetreault, Xi Chi
Waterbury, Connecticut

KRAUT KUGAS

I first tasted these pies at a bluegrass festival in Iowa, while camping next to some friends of ours. I think the dish is Greek.

2 envelopes dry yeast	2 pounds ground beef
1/2 cup warm water	1 pound ground pork
1/2 cup sugar	1/2 cup margarine
3 tablespoons vegetable	1 large onion, finely
shortening	chopped
1 cup boiling water	1 clove of garlic, minced
1 cup cold water	1 medium head cabbage,
1/2 teaspoon salt	shredded
2 eggs, well beaten	1/2 teaspoon salt
7 cups all-purpose flour	1/2 teaspoon pepper
Swiss cheese (optional)	

Dissolve yeast in warm water. Cream sugar and shortening in large bowl until light and fluffy. Add boiling water, cold water and 1/2 teaspoon salt, mixing well after each addition. Add eggs, mix well. Add yeast, stirring well. Add all the flour and cheese at once; mix well. Dough will be sticky. Place in greased bowl. Chill, tightly covered, overnight. Remove dough from refrigerator 1 hour before using. Brown ground beef and pork in margarine in large saucepan, stirring until crumbly. Add onion, garlic, cabbage, salt and pepper; mix well. Cook over low heat until heated through. Preheat oven to 350 degrees. Pinch off tennis ball-sized portion of dough. Roll 1/4 inch thick on floured surface. Place 3 tablespoons meat mixture in center of circle. Fold up edge; pinch to seal. Place pinched side down in greased baking pan. Let stand for 30 minutes. Bake for 30 minutes. Yield: 25 to 35 servings.

Mary Long, Lambda Rho
Queen City, Missouri

AUSTRIAN PAPRIKA GOULASH

This was one of my favorite meals while I lived in Austria.

2 pounds stewing beef	2 beef bouillon cubes
All-purpose flour for	1 bay leaf
coating	2 tablespoons paprika
Vegetable oil for frying	1 clove of garlic, minced
6 large onions, finely	3 cups water
chopped	Salt and pepper to taste

Preheat oven to 325 degrees. Cut beef into bite-sized pieces; coat with flour. Brown in a small amount of oil in Dutch oven. Sauté onions in a small amount of oil in large skillet until tender. Add onions, bouillon cubes, bay leaf, paprika, garlic, water, salt and pepper to beef; stir well. Bake, covered, for 2 hours. Remove bay leaf. Serve over parslied potatoes or noodles. Yield: 4 to 6 servings.

Sherry Freel, Xi Gamma Nu
Gallatin, Texas

RIGATONI AL FORNO

After many attempts, this is my version of a dish that was served at one of our favorite restaurants in New Jersey.

1 large onion, finely	1 bay leaf
chopped	1/2 teaspoon oregano
1/4 pound mushrooms,	1/4 cup chopped parsley
sliced	1 teaspoon salt
2 tablespoons margarine	1/4 teaspoon pepper
2 tablespoons olive oil	11/2 pounds ground
2 large cloves of garlic,	turkey or very lean
crushed	ground beef
1 16-ounce can tomato	1 pound rigatoni
purée	11/2 cups shredded
2 16-ounce cans stewed	mozzarella cheese
tomatoes	1/2 cup grated Parmesan
1/2 cup dry red wine	

Cook onion and mushrooms in mixture of margarine and oil in large saucepan until onion is tender. Add garlic, tomato purée, undrained tomatoes, wine, bay leaf, oregano, parsley, salt and pepper; mix well. Bring to a boil. Brown ground beef in large skillet, stirring until crumbly; drain. Add to tomato sauce. Simmer for 11/2 hours or until sauce is reduced to about 5 cups. Remove bay leaf. Preheat oven to 350 degrees. Cook rigatoni using package directions; drain. Add to sauce mixture. Spoon into lasagna pan. Cover with mozzarella cheese; sprinkle with Parmesan cheese. Bake for 30 to 35 minutes or until top is golden. Yield: 8 servings.

Betty Carmichael, Laureate Phi
Sun City West, Arizona

STUFFED POTATOES

My husband was a career Air Force pilot. Many recipes bring memories of our 21/2 years in Puerto Rico. Puerto Rican potato balls are a treat!

2 cups cooked ground	1 tablespoon salt
beef	1/4 cup all-purpose flour
Sofrito to taste	1 egg, beaten
11/2 pounds potatoes,	Oil for frying
cooked	

Combine ground beef with Sofrito in bowl; mix well. Mash potatoes in large bowl. Add salt, flour and egg; mix well. Divide potato mixture into 8 to 10 portions. Roll into circles on floured surface. Place 1 tablespoon ground beef on each circle. Shape dough around ground beef, forming a ball. Fry in 1/2 inch hot oil in cast-iron skillet until brown; drain. Yield: 8 to 10 servings.

Louise Long, Laureate Beta Lambda
Bethany, Missouri

ROULADEN (Beef Birds)

This is an old German family recipe. I serve it with a clear gravy made from the pan drippings. The horse-radish mustard gives it a spicy flavor.

2 pounds round steak, 1/4 inch thick	2 teaspoons minced onion
Salt and pepper to taste	1/4 teaspoon paprika
2 slices bacon, finely chopped	1/4 cup fresh bread crumbs
2 ounces ground beef	1 tablespoon salad oil
1/2 teaspoon prepared horseradish mustard	1 bay leaf
	1 cup water

Preheat oven to 350 degrees. Cut steak into 8 portions. Tenderize with meat mallet; season with salt and pepper. Combine chopped bacon, ground beef, mustard, minced onion, paprika and bread crumbs in bowl; mix well. Spread 1 tablespoon of mixture on each portion of steak. Roll up; secure with kitchen string. Brown in oil in skillet over medium heat; drain. Place in roasting pan. Add bay leaf and water. Bake, covered, for 2 to 2 1/2 hours or until tender. Remove bay leaf and string before serving. Yield: 8 servings.

JoAnn Hannig, Beta
Blaine, Minnesota

RUSSIAN STEW

This is an old family recipe handed down to me by my mother and to her by her grandmother.

2 pounds stew beef, cut into 1/2-inch pieces	1 pound apricots
1 onion, thinly sliced	1 pound prunes
2 tablespoons vegetable oil	32 ounces borsch
	4 cups water
4 carrots, cut into 1/4-inch slices	2 lemons, sliced
	Salt and pepper to taste
4 red or white potatoes, cubed	

Brown beef and onion in oil in large saucepan for 10 minutes. Add carrots, potatoes, apricots, prunes, borsch, water, lemon slices, salt and pepper; mix well. Simmer, covered, for 1 1/2 hours. Stir every 30 minutes, adding water if needed. Adjust seasonings before serving. Yield: 6 to 8 servings.

Alison Maartensen, Kappa Phi
Dunsmuir, California

Darlene Kokinakis, Xi Omega, Albion, Idaho, makes Greek Chicken by basting chicken with mixture of 1/4 cup lemon juice, 1/2 teaspoon oregano and 1/4 teaspoon garlic powder during grilling. Add salt and pepper to taste.

SAUERBRATEN AND CADOFFLE KLASE

2 cups red wine vinegar	All-purpose flour for coating
2 onions, sliced	
1 lemon, sliced	2 tablespoons vegetable shortening
10 whole cloves	
4 bay leaves	6 tablespoons butter or margarine
6 peppercorns	
2 tablespoons salt	6 tablespoons all-purpose flour
2 tablespoons sugar	
1 4-pound rump or sirloin roast	1 tablespoon sugar
	8 gingersnaps, crushed

Combine vinegar, onions, lemon slices, cloves, bay leaves, peppercorns, salt and 2 tablespoons sugar in large bowl; mix well. Place beef roast in mixture. Marinate, tightly covered, in refrigerator for 36 to 48 hours, turning roast twice a day. Remove roast. Pat dry; coat with flour. Brown roast in shortening and 1 tablespoon butter in large saucepan. Strain and reserve marinade. Add 2 cups reserved marinade to roast in saucepan. Simmer roast, covered, for 3 hours. Melt remaining 5 tablespoons butter in skillet. Blend in flour and remaining 1 tablespoon sugar. Cook until browned, stirring constantly. Add remaining reserved marinade gradually, stirring constantly. Cook until slightly thickened, stirring constantly. Add to pan juices with roast. Simmer for 1 hour longer. Remove beef to warm platter. Add gingersnaps to pan juices. Cook until thickened, stirring constantly. Serve with roast. Yield: 8 servings.

Ella M. Taylor, Xi Iota Theta
St. Petersburg, Florida

CHINESE PEPPER STEAK

1 1/2 pounds sirloin steak, 1 inch thick	1/4 cup soy sauce
	1/2 teaspoon sugar
Garlic powder to taste	1/2 cup beef bouillon
1 teaspoon ginger	1 4-ounce can mushrooms
1 teaspoon salt	
1/2 teaspoon pepper	4 green onions, sliced
1/4 cup vegetable oil	1 tablespoon cornstarch
3 large green bell peppers, sliced	1/4 cup cold water
	Hot cooked rice
2 large onions, thinly sliced	

Freeze steak for 1 hour; cut into 1/8-inch slices. Sauté garlic powder, ginger, salt and pepper in oil in skillet until garlic powder is golden. Add steak slices. Stir-fry for 2 minutes or until steak is lightly browned. Remove steak. Add green peppers and sliced onions. Stir-fry for 3 minutes. Return steak to skillet. Add soy sauce, sugar, bouillon, mushrooms, green onions and cornstarch dissolved in water; mix well. Simmer for 5 minutes or until sauce thickens. Serve over hot rice. Yield: 6 to 8 servings.

Joan M. Thompson, Preceptor Alpha Omega
Oklahoma City, Oklahoma

KOREAN STEAK AND RICE

A good friend who spoke very little English introduced this dish to me. The title is a literal translation and the recipe is my original interpretation.

1 4- to 5-pound chuck roast	2 tablespoons vegetable oil
2 teaspoons salt	3 cups cooked rice
1 teaspoon pepper	1 tablespoon garlic salt
1 green bell pepper, sliced into strips	1/3 cup soy sauce
1 medium onion, sliced	1 teaspoon ginger
1/2 medium head cabbage, sliced	2 tablespoons vegetable oil
	2/3 cup soy sauce

Freeze beef until partially frozen; cut into very thin strips. Sprinkle with salt and pepper. Stir-fry green pepper, onion and cabbage in 2 tablespoons oil in large skillet just until tender. Add rice, garlic salt, 1/3 cup soy sauce and ginger; mix well. Stir-fry beef in remaining 2 tablespoons oil in medium skillet until done to taste. Sprinkle with remaining 2/3 cup soy sauce. Stir-fry for 1 minute longer. Spoon rice mixture onto serving platter; surround with beef strips. Yield: 6 servings.

Connie Rhoades, Xi Beta Omega
Valentine, Nebraska

BASQUE-STYLE CHICKEN

Being of Basque descent, and raised in a community of Basques in northern Nevada, I learned to appreciate this distinct type of food early on.

1 2-pound chicken, cut up, skinned	1/2 cup chopped fresh parsley
All-purpose flour for coating	1 cup pimentos, sliced
Salt and pepper to taste	1 cup ham strips (not smoked)
Vegetable oil for frying	11/2 cups dry white wine
Olive oil for frying	2 teaspoons paprika
3 to 4 cloves of garlic, sliced	1 8-ounce can tomato sauce
2 medium onions, chopped	1 cup dry white wine

Soak chicken pieces in water in a bowl for 30 minutes. Preheat oven to 325 degrees. Drain chicken; pat dry. Coat chicken lightly in mixture of flour, salt and pepper. Brown in mixture of equal amounts of vegetable oil and olive oil in large skillet; drain. Place browned chicken in large baking dish. Sauté garlic, onions, parsley, pimentos and ham strips in pan drippings in heavy skillet. Add 11/2 cups wine and paprika; mix well. Pour mixture over chicken. Bake for 30 minutes. Turn chicken. Combine tomato sauce and remaining 1 cup wine; pour over chicken. Bake for 1 hour longer. Chicken will be very tender. Yield: 6 to 8 servings.

Judy M. Burke, Preceptor Alpha Sigma
Beaverton, Oregon

THAI CHICKEN AND VEGETABLES

3/4 cup vegetable oil	Garlic salt to taste
1/4 cup white vinegar	1 10-ounce package frozen mixed vegetables of choice
2 tablespoons soy sauce	
2 tablespoons peanut butter	1 tablespoon vegetable or peanut oil
3/8 teaspoon cayenne pepper	4 cups shredded lettuce
1/2 teaspoon garlic powder	1/4 to 1/2 cup sliced green onions
2 boneless chicken breasts	1 tomato, cut into wedges
1 tablespoon vegetable or peanut oil	

Combine 3/4 cup oil, vinegar, soy sauce, peanut butter, cayenne pepper and garlic powder in blender container. Process until blended. Wash chicken; pat dry. Cut into 1-by-1/4-inch pieces. Stir-fry chicken in 1 tablespoon oil in wok over high heat for 4 to 5 minutes or until done. Drain on paper towels; sprinkle with garlic salt. Stir-fry frozen vegetables in remaining 1 tablespoon oil until vegetables are tender-crisp. Place 1 cup shredded lettuce on each serving plate. Top with green onions, cooked vegetables and cooked chicken. Garnish with tomato. Serve with blended salad dressing. Yield: 3 to 4 servings.

Kathryn J. Roberts, Theta Omega
Beloit, Kansas

HAM LINGUINE FLORENTINE

1/2 cup slivered almonds	1 13-ounce can beef broth
11/2 cups sliced mushrooms	3/4 cup light cream or milk
3/4 cup chopped onion	
3 tablespoons butter or margarine	11/2 cups julienne ham
	1/2 cup snipped parsley
3 tablespoons vegetable oil	3 tablespoons Dijon mustard
3 tablespoons all-purpose flour	6 ounces linguine, cooked
3/4 teaspoon thyme	8 ounces fresh spinach, coarsely chopped

Brown almonds in heavy skillet over medium heat for 5 minutes or until golden, stirring constantly. Remove from skillet; set aside. Sauté mushrooms and onion in butter and oil in skillet until onion is tender but not brown. Stir in flour and thyme. Add beef broth and cream. Cook over medium heat until thickened and bubbly, stirring constantly. Cook for 1 minute, stirring constantly. Stir in 1/4 cup almonds, ham, parsley and mustard. Stir in hot cooked linguine. Place spinach on platter or on individual dinner plates. Top with hot linguine mixture. Sprinkle with remaining almonds. Yield: 6 servings.

Felicia Pancoast, Theta Theta
Everett, Washington

PIZZA RUSTICA

2 cups all-purpose flour
2 egg yolks
Pinch of salt
Pinch of cinnamon
1/2 cup butter or
  margarine, cut into
  pieces
3 tablespoons ice water
2 egg yolks
3/4 pound ricotta cheese
3 tablespoons grated
  Parmesan cheese
1/4 pound mozzarella
  cheese, cut into small
  pieces
1/4 pound each salami,
  prosciutto and Parma
  ham, cut into small
  pieces
Salt and pepper to taste
1 egg white, beaten
1 1/2 to 2 tablespoons
  sugar

Combine flour, 2 egg yolks, salt, cinnamon, butter and ice water in food processor container. Process using manufacturer's instructions for dough making. Wrap dough in waxed paper. Chill for 1 hour. Preheat oven to 375 degrees. Beat remaining 2 egg yolks in large bowl. Add ricotta cheese; beat until smooth. Add next 5 ingredients; mix well. Roll out 2/3 of the dough; cut into strips. Fit around side of well greased 1-quart soufflé dish. Pour in cheese and meat filling. Roll out remaining dough for top. Press edges down to seal. Brush with mixture of egg white and sugar. Bake for 45 minutes or until golden brown. Cool slightly; unmold onto serving dish. Yield: 6 to 8 servings.

Cindy Lewandowski
Bowling Green, Kentucky

KIBBI

1/2 cup bulgur wheat
1 medium onion, ground
1 pound ground lamb
1 teaspoon salt
1/8 teaspoon pepper
1/4 teaspoon allspice
Butter or margarine
Pocket Bread

Wash bulgur wheat; soak in water for 2 hours or until soft; drain. Preheat oven to 375 degrees. Combine wheat, ground onion, ground lamb, salt, pepper and allspice in large bowl; mix well. Press mixture firmly into 8-by-8-inch baking pan. Score into triangles. Dot each triangle with butter. Bake for 45 minutes. Serve with Pocket Bread. Yield: 4 to 5 servings.

POCKET BREAD

1 envelope dry yeast
1 1/3 cups warm water
1 teaspoon salt
1 tablespoon vegetable
  or olive oil
1/4 teaspoon sugar
3 1/2 cups all-purpose
  flour
Cornmeal

Dissolve yeast in warm water in large mixer bowl. Stir in salt, oil, sugar and 1 1/2 cups flour. Beat until smooth. Stir in enough remaining flour to make dough easy to handle. Turn onto lightly floured surface. Knead for 10 minutes or until dough is smooth and elastic. Place in greased bowl, turning to grease surface. Let rise, covered, in warm place for 1 hour.

Dough is ready if an indentation remains when touched. Punch dough down. Divide into 12 equal portions; shape into balls. Let rise for 30 minutes. Sprinkle 3 ungreased baking sheets with cornmeal. Roll each ball into a 1/8-inch thick circle, leaving center area of dough untouched (this will form the pocket). Place on prepared baking sheets. Let rise for 30 minutes. Preheat oven to 500 degrees. Bake for 10 minutes or until loaves are puffed and light brown. Remove from baking sheet; cool on wire rack. Yield: 12 servings.

Linda L. Swenson, Alpha Kappa
Moorhead, Minnesota

ARABIAN LAMB

2 1/2 pounds lamb
  shoulder chops
1/4 cup olive oil
2 cloves of garlic,
  minced
2 onions, chopped
1/2 cup raisins
1 teaspoon ground ginger
  or 1-inch piece of fresh
  ginger, peeled, chopped
Salt and pepper to taste
1 bay leaf
2 whole cloves
1 14-ounce can
  tomatoes
3 hard-cooked eggs,
  halved
1/2 cup toasted slivered
  almonds
Chopped parsley

Preheat oven to 325 degrees. Brown lamb chops on both sides in hot oil in Dutch oven. Add next 9 ingredients; stir well. Add enough water to cover lamb chops. Bake, covered, for 1 hour or until chops are tender; skim off grease. Remove bay leaf. Garnish with eggs, almonds and parsley. Yield: 4 to 6 servings.

Dora Martin, Preceptor Beta
Vancouver, British Columbia, Canada

COSTOLETTE DI MAIALE UBRIACHE
(Drunken Pork Chops)

6 thick pork chops
1 1/2 to 2 cups uncooked
  rice
1 large onion, chopped
2 tablespoons butter or
  margarine
1/4 cup chopped celery
1 20-ounce can tomatoes
Salt and pepper to taste
1 cup red vermouth
1 green bell pepper,
  sliced into 6 rings

Preheat oven to 350 degrees. Trim pork chops. Render fat in large heavy skillet, discarding unrendered trimmings. Sear chops on both sides in pan drippings in skillet. Pour uncooked rice into 9-by-13-inch casserole. Arrange pork chops on top of rice. Sauté onion in skillet with remaining pan drippings plus 2 tablespoons butter. Add celery. Sauté until tender. Press tomatoes through sieve. Add to onion and celery. Add salt, pepper and vermouth, mixing well. Pour sauce over pork chops and rice. Place green pepper ring on each chop. Bake, covered with aluminum foil, for 1 hour. Serve immediately. Yield: 6 servings.

Mary Novotne, Preceptor Xi
Aurdea, Nebraska

NASI GORENG

On cold winter nights, my husband and I curl up in front of the TV and eat this.

2 cups long grain rice	4 large onions, sliced
1 16-ounce package	into rings
frozen mixed	1/4 cup butter or
vegetables, thawed	margarine
1/4 cup butter or	3 tablespoons soy sauce
margarine	1 1/2 teaspoons mild
1 1/4 pounds pork	curry powder
shoulder, cut into cubes	Salt and pepper to taste

Cook rice in boiling salted water for 12 minutes; drain. Place mixed vegetables in microwave-safe dish. Microwave on High for 5 to 6 minutes. Melt 1/4 cup butter in large skillet. Add cubed pork and onions. Cook over medium heat for 20 minutes or until pork is cooked through, stirring occasionally. Add remaining 1/4 cup butter, cooked rice, mixed vegetables, soy sauce, curry powder, salt and pepper. Cook until mixture is heated through, stirring frequently. Yield: 4 servings.

Leslie White, Kappa Pi
Carleton Place, Ontario, Canada

OKTOBERFEST GERMAN SAUERKRAUT

I went to Germany in July, 1990, with my daughter and her family and was a guest of Max and Emma Burkard in Gross Krotzenburg. Emma served this dish for my birthday party there. I served this at an Oktoberfest party at my home, along with some German wine I brought back.

4 32-ounce jars	1 3-pound pork loin
sauerkraut, rinsed,	tip roast, trimmed,
drained	cubed
3 apples, peeled, cut	1 large onion, chopped
into wedges	2 to 4 cups water
2 large baking potatoes,	Caraway seed to taste
cubed	
1 pound bacon, cut into	
1-inch pieces	

Preheat electric roaster to 250 degrees. Place sauerkraut in electric roaster. Add apple wedges and potato cubes. Sauté bacon in skillet sprayed with nonstick cooking spray; drain, reserving pan drippings. Add bacon to sauerkraut. Sauté cubed pork and onion in reserved pan drippings. Add to sauerkraut; mix well. Stir in 2 cups water. Cook, covered, for 1 hour. Add caraway seed. Cook for 7 hours longer, adding water as needed to prevent scorching. Yield: 20 servings.

Louise DeMaet, Mu Master
Texas City, Texas

POLISH STUFFED CABBAGE

1 large head cabbage	1 small onion, chopped
1 cup water	Salt and pepper to taste
1 cup cooked rice	2 14-ounce cans
1 pound ground pork	stewed tomatoes
1 pound ground beef	1 cup water
2 eggs, beaten	

Preheat oven to 350 degrees. Place cabbage in large saucepan; add 1 cup water. Cook, covered, over medium-high heat for 20 minutes or until cabbage leaves are tender; drain. Let stand for 15 minutes or until cool enough to handle. Combine rice, pork, ground beef, eggs, onion, salt and pepper in bowl; mix well. Remove cabbage leaves carefully. Place 1 tablespoon meat mixture in center of each cabbage leaf, folding sides up to enclose filling. Arrange cabbage rolls in large baking pan lined with extra cabbage leaves. Pour in tomatoes and 1 cup water. Bake, covered, for 3 1/2 to 4 hours, basting frequently. Add more water if needed. Yield: 6 to 8 servings.

Mary Dudek, Xi Iota Psi
Bryan, Texas

HOMEMADE TAMALES

1 4- to 5-pound pork	1 teaspoon garlic
or beef roast	powder
Salt and pepper to taste	5 pounds masa cornmeal
Garlic powder to taste	1 pound lard
1 1/2 to 2 large onions,	2 tablespoons salt
chopped	2 to 3 packages corn
Chili powder to taste	husks
2 teaspons cumin	

Sprinkle roast with salt and pepper to taste and garlic powder to taste. Place in large saucepan; cover with water. Boil until meat falls from bone. Remove bone and fat; chop meat. Skim and strain broth; set aside. Combine chopped pork, onions, salt and pepper to taste, chili powder, cumin and 1 teaspoon garlic powder in large saucepan. Cover with water. Simmer for several hours, stirring occasionally. Mix masa cornmeal, lard and 2 tablespoons salt in large bowl. Add reserved broth gradually, stirring until mixture becomes spreadable. Soak corn husks in warm water for 30 minutes; drain. Layer 1 heaping tablespoon masa mixture and 1 tablespoon meat mixture in center of each corn husk. Roll to enclose filling. Fold ends to seal. Place on wire rack in baking pan filled with 1/4-inch water. Pour remaining liquid from meat mixture over tamales; cover tightly. Steam for several hours or until tamales separate from husks. May store in freezer. May substitute 4 pounds chopped cooked chicken for roast. Yield: 96 servings.

Jeanne Sweet, Alpha Sigma
Russellville, Arkansas

VIETNAMESE SKEWERED PORK BROCHETTE

Everyone who tries this recipe raves about it. It is one of my husband's favorites and is very easy to do.

1 green onion, chopped	3 tablespoons sugar
1 tablespoon pepper	3 pounds pork tenderloin
1 tablespoon salt	1 onion
6 to 8 tablespoons fish	1 green bell pepper
sauce	13 wooden skewers
2 teaspoons garlic	Cooked rice or Chinese
powder	noodles

Combine green onion, pepper, salt, fish sauce, garlic powder and sugar in bowl; mix well. Cut pork into 1-inch cubes. Cut onion and green pepper into wedges. Marinate pork, onion and green pepper in prepared sauce for at least 2 hours. Soak wooden skewers in water for 30 minutes. Preheat broiler. Thread pieces of pork, onion and green pepper alternately on skewers. Broil for 5 minutes on 1 side; turn. Broil for 2 minutes longer. Serve with rice or Chinese noodles. Yield: 13 servings.

Janice Porter, Xi Psi
North Vancouver, British Columbia, Canada

RUSSIAN KIELBASA AND SAUERKRAUT

This recipe was given to me by a Russian lady at the Russian Church's potluck dinner. Add a green salad and Russian rye bread for a really good meal.

1 32-ounce jar	2 teaspoons caraway
sauerkraut	seed
1 large kielbasa sausage	1/2 teaspoon marjoram
1 large onion, chopped	2 to 3 tablespoons light
2 medium apples,	brown sugar
chopped	3/4 to 1 cup white wine
1 tablespoon olive oil	

Rinse and drain sauerkraut. Cut kielbasa into chunks. Brown in skillet; drain. Sauté onion and apples in olive oil in large skillet. Add sauerkraut, caraway seed, marjoram and brown sugar; stir well. Cook over medium heat for 2 minutes. Place kielbasa in slow cooker. Spoon sauerkraut mixture over top. Pour in wine. Cook on High for 4 to 6 hours or on Low for 8 to 10 hours. Yield: 4 to 6 servings.

Ellie Halter, Kappa Zeta
Redding, California

PORTUGUESE BEAN SOUP

2 cups dried Great	1/4 pound ham, cubed
Northern beans	1 teaspoon salt
4 cups water	1/2 onion, chopped
1/2 pound Polish	1 cup water
sausage, thinly sliced	1 large potato, cubed
3 slices bacon, cut into	1 cup shredded cabbage
pieces	

Combine beans and 4 cups water in large saucepan. Bring to a boil. Cook for 2 minutes; remove from heat. Cover and let stand for 1 hour. Add sausage, bacon, ham, salt, onion and 1 cup water; mix well. Cover; bring to a boil. Simmer for 1 1/2 hours. Add potato and cabbage. Cook for 30 minutes longer, adding water if necessary. Yield: 10 servings.

Nancy Hale, Omicron Xi
Dexter, Missouri

TUFOLIS

16 manicotti shells	1/2 pound mozzarella
1 medium onion,	cheese, shredded
chopped	1 egg, beaten
1 1/2 cloves of garlic,	1 cup bread crumbs
minced	1/4 teaspoon oregano
1 4-ounce can	Salt and pepper to taste
mushrooms, chopped	2 15-ounce cans
2 tablespoons butter or	tomato sauce
margarine	Grated Parmesan cheese
1 pound Italian	
sausage, chopped	

Preheat oven to 350 degrees. Cook manicotti shells using package directions; drain. Brown onion, garlic and mushrooms in butter in skillet. Add sausage, cheese, beaten egg, bread crumbs, oregano and salt and pepper; mix well. Pour a small amount of tomato sauce in 9-by-12-inch baking pan. Stuff each shell with mixture. Arrange in pan. Pour remaining tomato sauce over shells; sprinkle with Parmesan cheese. Bake for 45 to 50 minutes or until lightly browned. Yield: 8 servings.

Patricia M. Janulewicz, Preceptor Kappa
Grand Island, Nebraska

BOUILLABAISSE

1/2 cup chopped onion	Red pepper to taste
1/2 cup chopped celery	1 20-ounce can
1 clove of garlic, minced	tomatoes
1/4 cup butter or	1 cup fish stock or
margarine	water
1 pound fresh fish filets,	1/2 pint fresh oysters,
skinned, cubed	shelled
1 bay leaf, crushed	1/2 pound shrimp, peeled
1/4 teaspoon thyme	French bread
Salt and black pepper	
to taste	

Sauté onion, celery and garlic in butter in 6-quart saucepan until tender. Add cubed fish, bay leaf, thyme, salt, black pepper, red pepper, tomatoes and fish stock; mix well. Simmer for 10 minutes. Add oysters and shrimp. Simmer for 10 minutes longer. Serve with French bread. Yield: 6 to 8 servings.

Marcia A. Hunter, Alpha Xi Lambda
Cleveland, Texas

SEVICHE

2 pounds delicate, white, firm fish filets	1 or 2 hot peppers, finely chopped
Salt	1 clove of garlic, minced
Ice cubes	1/2 to 1 cup lime juice
1 cup finely chopped onion	1/4 cup vinegar
	1 teaspoon sugar

Cut fish into 3/8-inch pieces. Place fish in crock; sprinkle heavily with salt. Cover with ice cubes. Chill in refrigerator overnight. Rinse thoroughly; drain. Place layer of fish 2-inches deep in bowl. Cover with 1/2 of the onion and all the peppers; sprinkle with garlic. Layer remaining fish and onions over top. Combine lime juice, vinegar and sugar in small bowl; mix well. Pour over layers. Let stand for 2 1/2 hours, stirring every 30 minutes. Chill in refrigerator until serving time. Yield: 4 servings.

Adelaide M. (Cindy) Seldon, Preceptor Eta Theta
Panama City, Florida

CLAMS MEDITERRANEAN

1 cup olive oil	Dash of red pepper
5 to 7 cloves of garlic, minced	2 6-ounce cans chopped clams, drained
1 bay leaf	1/2 pound fresh mushrooms, sliced
1 tablespoon crushed, dried oregano	4 to 6 ounces spaghetti, cooked
1 tablespoon crushed, dried parsley	1/4 cup grated Romano cheese
1 teaspoon crushed, dried basil	

Heat oil in skillet. Add garlic. Stir-fry over medium heat for 30 seconds. Reduce temperature. Add bay leaf, oregano, parsley, basil and red pepper. Cook for 2 to 3 minutes, stirring constantly. Add clams and mushrooms. Simmer gently over low heat for 5 minutes. Do not overcook. Toss with cooked spaghetti; sprinkle with Romano cheese. Serve immediately. Yield: 2 to 3 servings.

Pamela Andrew, Alpha Omega
Eagar, Arizona

SAUDI ARABIAN GREEN BEANS AND SHRIMP

8 ounces fresh shrimp, peeled	3/4 teaspoon salt
1 pound green beans, cut French-style	1/4 teaspoon ground coriander
1 large onion, sliced	1/4 teaspoon cinnamon
2 tablespoons vegetable oil	1/8 teaspoon cumin
1/4 cup tomato sauce	Dash of pepper
	2 medium tomatoes, cut into wedges

Cut shrimp into halves lengthwise. Cook beans, covered, in a small amount of boiling water in saucepan for 10 minutes or until tender-crisp; drain.

Sauté onion in hot oil in large skillet until tender but not brown. Stir in green beans, shrimp, tomato sauce, salt, coriander, cinnamon, cumin and dash of pepper. Cook, covered, over medium heat for 3 to 5 minutes or until shrimp turn pink, stirring occasionally. Add tomato wedges. Cook for 2 minutes longer or until heated through, stirring constantly. Yield: 6 servings.

Cassandra A. Lathe, Preceptor Iota Alpha
Canyon Lake, Texas

TROUT MEUNIÈRE AMANDINE

2 tablespoons (heaping) all-purpose flour	1 teaspoon salt
1/4 cup margarine	4 ounces slivered almonds
2 tablespoons (heaping) instant beef bouillon	2 tablespoons margarine
1 1/2 cups hot water	4 large trout filets
2 lemons	1 egg
2 tablespoons Worcestershire sauce	1/4 cup evaporated milk
	1 cup all-purpose flour
	3/4 to 1 cup margarine

Brown 2 tablespoons flour in heavy 1-quart saucepan. Add 1/4 cup margarine, stirring well to make roux. Dissolve beef bouillon in hot water. Add to roux. Stir in juice and pulp of lemons, Worcestershire sauce and salt. Cut 1/4 of lemon peel into slivers. Add to roux. Cook for 10 minutes, stirring frequently. Remove from heat. Cover to keep warm. Toast almonds in 2 tablespoons margarine in small skillet; set aside. Dip fish filets into mixture of egg and evaporated milk. Coat with 1 cup flour. Fry in 3/4 cup margarine in heavy skillet, browning on both sides. Arrange on individual serving plates. Pour 1/4 cup sauce over each portion; sprinkle with toasted almonds. Yield: 4 servings.

Sylvia Barham, Xi Pi
Decatur, Alabama

AVOCADO SALAD

3 large ripe avocados	1/3 to 1/2 cup mayonnaise
4 hard-cooked eggs	Salt and pepper to taste
1/2 medium white onion	1 teaspoon seasoned salt
1/2 cup sliced dill pickles	Lettuce leaves
2 teaspoons lemon juice	Picante sauce
1 large ripe tomato, cut into halves	Corn chips

Process 2 avocados, eggs, onion, dill pickles, lemon juice, tomato half, mayonnaise, salt, pepper and seasoned salt in food processor until chopped to medium-sized pieces. Mashed remaining avocado in bowl. Chop remaining tomato half finely. Stir avocado and tomato into mixture. Serve on lettuce-lined salad plates with picante sauce and corn chips. Yield: 6 servings.

Brenda Rex, Preceptor Alpha Omega
Oklahoma City, Oklahoma

BRAZILIAN VEGETABLE SALAD

3 potatoes	1/2 onion, chopped
3 carrots	3/4 cup corn, cooked
2 whole beets	Mayonnaise to taste
1 chayote squash	

Combine potatoes, carrots, beets and squash in water half the depth of vegetables in saucepan. Cook until tender, stirring occasionally. Peel vegetables; chop into small pieces. Add onion and corn. Add mayonnaise to taste; toss to mix. Yield: 8 to 10 servings.

Pat Nelson, Xi Nu
Springfield, Missouri

BLACK BEAN CHILI

1 pound dried black beans, rinsed	1/4 cup canola oil
2 cloves of garlic, minced	1 4-ounce can chopped green chilies
1 large green bell pepper, chopped	1/4 cup chili powder
2 medium onions, chopped	1 tablespoon cumin
2 large tomatoes, chopped	1/2 teaspoon red pepper
	8 ounces Monterey Jack cheese, shredded
	Cold Dos Equis beer

Combine beans and water to cover in saucepan. Simmer on low heat for 6 to 8 hours or until tender, stirring occasionally. Drain beans, reserving liquid. Sauté garlic, green pepper, onions and tomatoes in hot canola oil in skillet until green pepper is tender-crisp. Add green chilies, chili powder, cumin and red pepper. Simmer for 2 hours, stirring occasionally. Add to cooked beans. Simmer for 2 hours longer, stirring occasionally and adding bean liquid as needed for desired degree of thickness. Spoon into bowls; sprinkle with cheese. Serve with Dos Equis beer to put out the fire. Yield: 6 servings.

Al Connarn, Xi Gamma Zeta
Pisgah Forest, North Carolina

EGGPLANT PARMIGIANA

1 pound Italian sausage	1/4 cup red wine
1 28-ounce can crushed tomatoes	2 tablespoons sugar
1 16-ounce can tomato sauce	1 medium eggplant
	1 1/2 cups all-purpose flour
1 10-ounce can tomato paste	Pepper to taste
1 tablespoon oregano	2 eggs, beaten
2 teaspoons basil	Vegetable oil
1 tablespoon minced garlic	Grated Parmesan cheese
	3 cups shredded mozzarella cheese

Remove casing from sausage. Brown sausage in skillet, stirring until crumbly; drain. Add tomatoes, tomato sauce, tomato paste, oregano, basil, garlic, wine and sugar. Simmer for 1 hour, stirring occasionally. Slice eggplant into 1/4-inch slices. Mix flour and pepper in bowl. Dip eggplant slices into flour to coat; dip into beaten eggs. Dip in flour again to coat. Brown eggplant several slices at a time, on both sides in hot vegetable oil in skillet. Preheat oven to 350 degrees. Alternate layers of tomato sauce, eggplant, Parmesan cheese and mozzarella cheese in 9-by-13-inch baking dish, ending with tomato sauce. Bake, uncovered, for 1 hour. Yield: 8 to 10 servings.

Cathy Astrella, Gamma Nu
Sturbridge, Maine

SWISS FONDUE

While we were living in Hong Kong, a friend from Georgia treated us to an elegant fondue feast. This was one of my favorites.

1 cup dry white wine	1 teaspoon cornstarch
1 1/2 pounds Swiss cheese, shredded	1/4 teaspoon soda
	Dash of pepper, nutmeg and paprika
1 clove of garlic, minced	1 loaf French bread
1/4 teaspoon kirsch, cherry or grape brandy	

Bring white wine to a simmer in saucepan. Remove from heat. Stir in cheese and garlic. Mix kirsch and cornstarch together. Add to cheese mixture. Heat for 3 minutes, stirring constantly. Stir in soda, pepper, nutmeg and paprika. Serve in fondue pot. Cut French bread into cubes for dipping. May add Gouda cheese to improve consistency of fondue. Yield: 4 to 6 servings.

Ann Rupprecht, Xi Alpha Rho
Grand Island, Nebraska

KUGELIS (Lithuanian Potato Pudding)

This is always served with our Christmas meal. No one in our family wants to miss a meal when Kugelis is being served. I make extra and freeze it.

10 large peeled, potatoes, finely grated	2 teaspoons salt
	1/4 teaspoon pepper
1 pound bacon, finely chopped	3 eggs, beaten
	Sour cream or applesauce
1 medium onion, finely chopped	

Preheat oven to 400 degrees. Place potatoes in bowl. Sauté bacon in skillet. Add onion. Cook until tender. Pour bacon, onion and bacon drippings over potatoes; mix well. Add salt, pepper and eggs; mix well. Pour into greased 9-by-13-inch baking dish. Bake for 15 minutes. Reduce oven temperature to 375 degrees. Bake until golden brown. Cut into squares. Serve with sour cream or applesauce. Yield: 12 servings.

Joanne Kazakevicius, Xi Rho
Brantford, Ontario, Canada

FETTUCINI WITH CLAM SAUCE

This recipe is one of my husband's favorites.

1 envelope original
  ranch dressing mix
3/4 cup milk
1/2 cup mayonnaise
1/4 cup melted butter or
  margarine

1 10-ounce can whole
  clams, drained
1/2 cup sliced black
  olives
8 ounces fettucini,
  cooked

Combine dressing mix, milk and mayonnaise in bowl; mix well. Let stand for 30 minutes or until thickened. Combine butter, clams and olives in saucepan. Heat to serving temperature. Toss fettucini with sauce and clam mixture in serving bowl. Serve warm. Yield: 6 servings.

Linda McConnell
Dallas, Texas

FETTUCINI FLORENTINE

16 ounces uncooked
  fettucini
1 teaspoon salt
1/2 cup butter or
  margarine
1 10-ounce package
  frozen chopped
  spinach, thawed,
  drained

1 pound bacon, crisp-
  fried, crumbled
1 1/2 cups whipping cream
1 egg, beaten
2 cups grated Parmesan
  cheese
2 teaspoons salt
1/4 teaspoon pepper

Cook noodles with 1 teaspoon salt using package directions; drain. Melt butter in large chafing dish. Add spinach and crumbled bacon; mix well. Cook until heated through. Add noodles; toss lightly. Combine cream, egg, Parmesan cheese, remaining 2 teaspoons salt and pepper in saucepan; toss to mix. Cook, covered, for 5 minutes or until heated through. Yield: 6 to 8 servings.

Karen Gall, Sigma Kappa
Milpitas, California

PAKORAS

Deep frying veggies Indian style, is a good way to get husbands and kids to eat their veggies.

2 cups Chana flour
  (chick-pea flour)
1 to 1 1/4 cups water
1 tablespoon cumin
1 tablespoon coriander
1 teaspoon ground red
  chilies
1 teaspoon garlic
  powder
1/2 teaspoon turmeric

1/2 teaspoon ginger
Salt and pepper to taste
4 cups thin, bite-sized
  pieces of assorted firm
  vegetables such as
  cauliflower, potato,
  onion, zucchini, green
  bell pepper and
  eggplant
Oil for frying

Combine Chana flour, water, cumin, coriander, red chilies, garlic powder, turmeric, ginger, salt and pepper in bowl; mix well. The mixture should look like thick pancake batter. Let stand for several minutes. Add vegetables to batter, stirring to coat. May add water if more moisture is needed. Heat 3 inches of oil in skillet. Drop vegetables by teaspoonfuls into hot oil. Cook for 5 minutes or until vegetables are tender. Drain on paper towels. Yield: 6 to 8 servings.

Mary Anne Skill, Zeta Iota
Chetwynd, British Columbia, Canada

REAL SPANISH RICE

1 cup uncooked rice
2 tablespoons salad oil
  or olive oil
1 chicken and tomato
  bouillon cube

2 cups hot water
1/2 cup chopped fresh
  tomato
1/4 large onion, chopped
1 clove of garlic, minced

Brown rice in oil in skillet over medium heat, stirring constantly. Stir bouillon cube into hot water in bowl until dissolved. Add tomato, onion and garlic to rice; mix well. Stir in bouillon. Simmer, covered, over low heat for 20 to 30 minutes or until water is absorbed. For spicy rice, decrease water to 1/2 cup and add 1/2 cup picante sauce. Yield: 6 to 8 servings.

Cheryl Spencer, Beta Upsilon
Medford, Oregon

SWEET POTATOES KHMER CAMBODIA

This has been a Thanksgiving or Christmas Day tradition in our family for 30 years.

2 8-ounce cans sweet
  potatoes, drained,
  mashed
1 9-ounce can crushed
  pineapple, drained
2 cooking apples,
  chopped
1 8-ounce can water
  chestnuts, drained,
  finely chopped

1 8-ounce can sliced
  pineapple
3 tablespoons butter or
  margarine
1/3 cup packed light
  brown sugar
1/2 teaspoon cinnamon
1 jigger rum
1/2 teaspoon ground
  ginger

Preheat oven to 350 degrees. Combine mashed sweet potatoes, crushed pineapple, apples and water chestnuts in bowl; mix well. Drain sliced pineapple, reserving juice. Melt butter in skillet. Add brown sugar, cinnamon, rum, ginger and reserved pineapple juice; mix well. Pour half the brown sugar syrup into sweet potatoes; mix well. Layer pineapple slices and sweet potatoes in buttered casserole. Top with remaining brown sugar syrup. Bake for 45 minutes. Yield: 9 to 12 servings.

Dolores Lindell, Xi Phi Phi
Oroville, California

TORTILLA SOUP

My husband always cooks this when we need a cheap vacation. Serve with margaritas and you can escape to Mexico for dinner.

1 small onion, chopped	1½ cups tomato juice
3 cloves of garlic, crushed	1 tablespoon chopped cilantro
2 tablespoons vegetable oil	1 teaspoon cumin
1 15-ounce can peeled tomatoes	1 teaspoon salt
	⅛ teaspoon pepper
1 10-ounce can beef bouillon	2 teaspoons Worcestershire sauce
1 10-ounce can chicken broth	1 tablespoon steak sauce
1½ cups water	4 tortillas, cut into ½-inch strips
1 10-ounce can Ro-Tel tomatoes and green chilies	¼ cup shredded Cheddar cheese

Sauté onion and garlic in vegetable oil in soup pot until soft. Add tomatoes, beef bouillon, chicken broth, water, Ro-Tel tomatoes, tomato juice, cilantro, cumin, salt, pepper, Worcestershire sauce and steak sauce. Simmer, covered, for 1 hour. Add tortilla strips and cheese. Simmer for 10 minutes longer. Yield: 6 servings.

Rebecca Vandervoort, Iota Tau
Pryor, Oklahoma

DANISH AEBELSKIVARS

Aebelskivar-and-Sausage supper was an annual church fund-raiser in our community when I was growing up. Our family always went and filled up on these delectable little pancake balls. I learned to make them and eventually made them for my fiancé.

3 egg yolks, beaten	2 cups all-purpose flour
2 teaspoons sugar	1 teaspoon soda
½ teaspoon salt	3 egg whites, stiffly beaten
2 cups buttermilk	
1 teaspoon baking powder	Vegetable oil
	Applesauce

Combine egg yolks, sugar, salt and buttermilk in mixer bowl; beat well. Mix baking powder, flour and soda together. Add to batter, mixing well. Fold in egg whites. Heat aebelskivar pan over medium high heat. Add ½ teaspoon vegetable oil to each section of hot pan. Fill each section ⅔ full with batter. Add 1 teaspoon applesauce, covering with several drops of batter. Cook until bubbly and bottom of each ball is baked. Turn with 2 forks. Bake until brown. Serve hot with butter and syrup, applesauce or honey. Yield: 20 aebelskivars.

Dorothy E. Eyberg, Laureate Tau
Arispe, Iowa

FOOGEN

1 envelope yeast	½ cup sugar
½ cup lukewarm water	½ cup vegetable oil
1 cup water	Pinch of salt and nutmeg
1 cup milk	
3 to 4 cups all-purpose flour	Raisins
	Vegetable oil
2 eggs	Sugar

Dissolve yeast in ½ cup lukewarm water. Add 1 cup water, milk and enough flour to make soft dough. Let rise for 1 hour. Add eggs, ½ cup sugar, ½ cup oil, salt, nutmeg and raisins; mix well. Let rise for 1½ hours. Grease each section of iron foogen pan. Heat pan. Fill each section ½ full with dough. Cook until bottom is baked; turn foogen. Bake until brown. This makes round sponge bread or cakes. Roll in sugar. Yield: 36 to 48 servings.

Beverly Miller, Laureate Tau
Creston, Iowa

PIEROGI (Polish)

2½ cups all-purpose flour	6 potatoes, cooked, mashed
1 egg, beaten	8 ounces Cheddar cheese, shredded
1 cup hot water	
1 teaspoon vegetable oil or melted butter or margarine	Melted butter or margarine
	Bacon drippings
¼ teaspoon salt	Sour cream or yogurt
1 onion, finely chopped	Chopped parsley or chives
2 tablespoons butter or margarine	

Combine flour and egg in bowl; mix well. Add water, oil and salt; mix well. Knead until firm. Let stand, covered, for 10 minutes. Sauté onion in 2 tablespoons butter in skillet until tender. Combine with mashed potatoes and cheese in bowl; mix well. Roll out dough until thin on floured surface; cut with biscuit cutter. Spoon potato filling onto 1 side of pierogi; fold to enclose. Pinch edges together to seal. Drop pierogi into large saucepan of salted boiling water. Simmer gently for 5 minutes or until pierogi rise to top. Remove with slotted spoon. Spread a small amount of melted butter on pierogi to prevent sticking. Fry pierogi in hot bacon drippings until golden brown on both sides. Serve with sour cream; top with parsley. Yield: 4 to 6 servings.

Laurie Van Straalen, Xi Delta Upsilon
Simcoe, Ontario, Canada

Sue Badstibner, Upsilon Kappa, Knob Noster, Missouri, makes Teriyaki Sauce by mixing 1 cup each soy sauce and sherry, 2 cloves of garlic, ½ chopped onion, ½ teaspoon ginger and 2 tablespoons sugar in blender container. Marinate meat for 1 hour before grilling.

LEFSE (Norwegian)

4 cups milk	1 teaspoon salt
1/2 cup whipping cream	4 cups all-purpose flour
6 tablespoons	Butter or margarine
butter or margarine	Sugar and cinnamon

Combine milk, whipping cream, butter and salt in 4-quart heavy saucepan. Bring to a full rolling boil almost to top of pan. Remove from heat. Stir in flour quickly. Cool to room temperature. May hasten cooling by dropping large spoonfuls onto tray. Knead on floured surface, adding a small amount of flour if needed to form stiff dough. Shape into long roll. Roll out paper-thin with corrugated rolling pin. Cut into shape of round salad plate. Layer on tray. Preheat griddle or lefse baker to 450 degrees. Bake each lefse until light brown on both sides. Serve with butter, sugar and cinnamon. Yield: 9 to 12 servings.

Kathleen Lee, Delta Upsilon
Albion, Nebraska

TURKISH POCA

When I was in elementary school I loved my aunt's visits and her famous Turkish Pocas. One day I couldn't wait for school to be out so I just left to go home and hug my aunt. She returned me to school the next day and explained to my teacher why I disappeared. That evening I was happily eating pocas while I wrote my homework—10 pages of "I love my aunt's pocas."

1 envelope active dry	1/2 cup yogurt or milk
yeast	1/2 cup olive oil
1 teaspoon sugar	1 egg
1/2 cup lukewarm water	1 cup (about) warm
4 cups all-purpose flour	water
1 1/2 teaspoons salt	

Dissolve yeast and sugar in 1/2 cup water. Mix flour and salt in large bowl. Make a well in center. Add yogurt, olive oil, egg and yeast mixture; mix well. Add remaining water gradually, mixing until dough is sticky. Chill, covered, in refrigerator overnight. Preheat oven to 415 degrees. Shape dough into 12 balls, dipping hands in water as necessary to prevent sticking. Place on baking sheet. Bake for 20 to 25 minutes or until brown. Yield: 12 servings.

Ann Aydemir, Beta Nu
Kitimat, British Columbia, Canada

Elaine Smith, Delta Omicron, Lexington, South Carolina, makes Italian Zabaglione by beating 4 egg yolks with 2 tablespoons confectioners' sugar until thick. Cook over hot water until very thick, adding 2 tablespoons sherry a small amount at a time and beating constantly.

WANGBERG DARK RAISIN BREAD

This is my native Norwegian grandfather's recipe which my mother learned to bake when she was 10 years old. My 5-year-old son bakes it with me.

1/2 cup melted	1/2 cup honey
margarine	4 cups scalded potato
1 cup oats	water, milk or water
1 cup raisins	1 1/2 tablespoons yeast
1 tablespoon salt	6 cups (about)
1/2 cup molasses	all-purpose flour
2 cups whole wheat	1/2 cup margarine,
flour	softened

Combine melted margarine, oats, raisins, salt, molasses, whole wheat flour and honey in large mixer bowl; mix well. Add scalded potato water; mix well. Let stand for 10 minutes or until mixture feels very warm, not hot. Sprinkle yeast over top; mix gently. Let mixture stand for 10 minutes or until mixture bubbles. Add all-purpose flour 1 cup at a time, mixing well after each addition until very thick. Grease hands with portions of remaining margarine. Mix in remaining flour 1/4 to 1/2 cup at a time until dough is no longer sticky and most of remaining margarine has been added. Let rise, covered, in warm place until doubled in bulk. Punch dough down; let rise again. Punch dough down; cut into 5 portions. Shape into squares; roll into loaves. Place loaves in five 5-by-9-inch loaf pans. Let rise until about 1/2 inch over pan. Preheat oven to 350 degrees. Bake loaves for 30 minutes or until loaves test done. Cool in pan for several minutes. Invert onto towel. Brush surface with margarine. Cover with towel. Let stand until cool. Grandfather often made Norwegian open-faced sandwiches on this bread. Yield: 5 loaves.

Naomi Bentzinger, Mu Iota
Williams, Iowa

BIRCHERMÜESLI

This recipe was given to me by friends from Switzerland who visited me.

2 cups plain yogurt	1/2 cup sliced grapes
4 ounces cream cheese,	1 banana, sliced
softened	1 apple, chopped
3/4 cup quick oats	2 teaspoons lemon juice
3/4 cup sliced hazelnuts	1/2 cup coconut
1/3 cup raisins	3/4 cup whipping cream,
1/2 cup sliced	whipped
strawberries	Sugar to taste

Combine yogurt and cream cheese in bowl; mix well. Add oats, hazelnuts, raisins, strawberries, grapes, banana, apple, lemon juice and coconut; mix well. Fold in whipped cream and sugar. Yield: 6 to 8 servings.

Carol Arnet, Xi Zeta
Waldron, Kansas

CAPIROTADA (Bread Pudding)

This recipe comes from Mexico where Catholics did no baking or cooking from Ash Wednesday to Easter Sunday and all foods were prepared ahead and had to last without refrigeration. Each family had its own variation.

1 15-ounce package raisins	4 cups water
2 cups packed dark brown sugar	15 slices white bread, toasted
1 tablespoon allspice	1 pound Monterey Jack cheese, shredded

Rinse raisins; drain. Combine brown sugar, allspice and water in saucepan. Simmer over medium heat for 5 to 10 minutes or until sugar is dissolved and mixture thickens, stirring constantly. Alternate layers of toasted bread, cheese and raisins in 3-quart casserole. Pour sugar mixture gradually over layers, soaking all bread. Use only amount of mixture needed. Preheat oven to 350 degrees. Bake bread pudding for 30 minutes or until all liquid is absorbed. Serve warm or cold. Store at room temperature. May add 1 cup peanuts and/or 1 cup coconut. Yield: 10 to 12 servings.

Cecilia C. Hurlbut, Alpha Omega
Eagar, Arizona

CUBAN FLAN

My father brought this recipe from Cuba and translated it for me. I think of him each time I make it.

Sugar	1 14-ounce can
3 large eggs	sweetened condensed
1/2 teaspoon almond extract	milk
1/2 cup evaporated milk	1 tablespoon water

Sprinkle sugar over bottom of metal mold. Cook on high until sugar is caramelized, stirring constantly. Cool to room temperature. Process eggs, almond extract, evaporated milk, condensed milk and water in blender on High for 2 minutes. Pour over sugar in mold. Preheat oven to 325 degrees. Place mold in pan of water. Bake for 20 to 25 minutes. Turn off oven. Let flan stand in oven for 2 or more hours. Chill in refrigerator overnight. Unmold onto serving plate. Yield: 4 to 6 servings.

Mary Vaujin LeDoux, Upsilon Kappa
Inverness, Florida

DENMARK KRINGLES

1 cup butter or margarine, softened	3 3/4 cups all-purpose flour
6 tablespoons sugar	1 1/2 teaspoons baking
1/4 teaspoon salt	powder
1 cup whipping cream	Sugar

Preheat oven to 400 degrees. Cream butter, sugar and salt in mixer bowl until light and fluffy. Add cream; mix well. Mix flour and baking powder together. Add to mixture 1/2 at a time, mixing well after each addition. Dough will be stiff. Roll out dough 1/2 at a time on floured surface to 1/8-inch thickness. Sprinkle with sugar. Cut into desired shapes. Place on cookie sheet. Bake for 10 to 12 minutes or until light brown. These cookies freeze well. Yield: 4 1/2 dozen.

Mary Jo Kellogg, Alpha Zeta
Nevada, Iowa

DUTCH ALMOND BARS

My 93-year-old grandmother who came from Holland taught me how to make these. She always made almond patties at Christmas time until she found this version.

1 cup butter or margarine	3/4 cup sugar
2 cups all-purpose flour	2 eggs, beaten
1/2 cup ice water	1/4 teaspoon almond extract
8 ounces almond paste	Sugar

Cut butter into flour in bowl until crumbly. Add ice water, stirring until mixture forms a ball. Cut dough into 2 portions. Wrap each in foil. Chill in refrigerator overnight. Crumble almond paste into mixer bowl. Add sugar, eggs and almond extract; beat well. Chill, covered, overnight. Let dough stand at room temperature for 30 minutes. Preheat oven to 400 degrees. Roll 1 portion of dough into 10-by-14-inch rectangle on floured surface. Place in 9-by-13-inch baking dish, spreading up sides of dish. Spread with filling. Roll remaining dough. Place over filling, trimming edges. Pierce surface with fork. Sprinkle lightly with sugar. Bake for 30 minutes or until brown. Cut into bars. Yield: 12 to 15 servings.

Becky Hasselmann, Xi Zeta Kappa
Rock Rapids, Iowa

FRIED MEXICAN ICE CREAM

1 pint ice cream	1 egg
1/2 cup crushed corn flakes or cookie crumbs	Oil for deep frying
1 teaspoon cinnamon	Honey
2 teaspoons sugar	Whipped cream

Scoop 4 or 5 balls of ice cream into bowl. Place in freezer. Mix crumbs, cinnamon and sugar in bowl. Roll ice cream balls in half the crumb mixture; return to freezer. Beat egg in bowl. Dip ice cream balls in egg; roll in remaining crumbs. Return to freezer. Preheat oil to 350 degrees in deep-fryer. Cook ice cream balls 1 at a time in fryer basket or slotted spoon for 1 minute. Remove to dessert compote. Drizzle with honey; top with whipped cream. Yield: 4 to 5 servings.

Wilma Neville, Preceptor Beta Alpha
Portland, Oregon

FRUIT DUMPLINGS (Czechoslovakian)

1 cup small curd creamy cottage cheese	Dried prunes, plums or apricots
2 eggs	Water
1 teaspoon margarine, softened	1/2 to 1 teaspoon salt
1 teaspoon baking powder	Melted butter or margarine
1 teaspoon salt	Cinnamon-sugar
1 teaspoon sugar	Bread crumbs
2 cups (about) all-purpose flour	Cinnamon
	Butter or margarine

Combine cottage cheese, eggs and margarine in bowl; mix well. Mix baking powder, 1 teaspoon salt, 1 teaspoon sugar and flour together. Add to cottage cheese mixture; stir until slightly sticky soft ball is formed. Flour ball of dough lightly. Rinse and dry fruit. Roll dough out on floured surface to 1/4-inch thickness. Cut into squares large enough to wrap fruit. Wrap around fruit, sealing edges; place on tray. Cover with towel to prevent drying. Bring water with remaining salt to a boil in large deep saucepan. Drop dumplings into water. Cook for several minutes. Release dumplings from bottom of pan gently. Cook for 10 minutes; turn dumplings. Cook for 10 minutes longer. Remove to wire rack to cool; pierce steam hole with fork. Drizzle with butter; sprinkle with cinnamon-sugar. Brown bread crumbs with cinnamon in butter in skillet. Sprinkle over dumplings. Yield: 9 to 12 servings.

Patricia A. Harstad
Toddville, Iowa

GALATOBOURIKA

This is one of my favorite Greek desserts.

3 cups milk	1 pound phyllo dough
1 cup sugar	1 pound melted butter or margarine
1/2 cup cream of wheat	3 cups water
4 eggs, at room temperature	2 1/2 cups sugar
1 tablespoon butter or margarine	1 cinnamon stick
1 teaspoon vanilla extract	1 cup honey

Combine milk, 1 cup sugar, cream of wheat and eggs in saucepan; mix well. Cook over medium heat until thickened, stirring constantly. Remove from heat. Stir in 1 tablespoon butter and vanilla. Cool to room temperature. Preheat oven to 350 degrees. Separate phyllo dough sheets; brush with melted butter. Layer phyllo dough into 8-by-8-inch baking dish to 1/4-inch thickness. Spread cream of wheat filling over dough. Cover with layers of buttered phyllo dough to 1/4-inch thickness. Bake for 20 minutes or until brown. Combine water, remaining 2 1/2 cups sugar and cinnamon stick in saucepan. Cook for 30 minutes or until thickened, stirring frequently. Remove cinnamon stick. Stir in honey. Pour over hot Galatobouriko. Yield: 12 to 16 servings.

Nancy Burkhardt, Xi Gamma Gamma
Richmond, Indiana

GERMAN PEPPERNUTS

1 cup sugar	1 teaspoon cinnamon
1 cup margarine	7 teaspoons (heaping) ground aniseed
1 cup dark molasses	1 teaspoon salt
1 teaspoon soda	5 to 6 cups all-purpose flour
1/2 cup hot water	
1/2 teaspoon ground cloves	

Combine sugar, margarine and molasses in saucepan. Bring to a boil, stirring constantly. Cool to room temperature. Dissolve soda in water. Add with cloves, cinnamon, aniseed and salt to sugar mixture; mix well. Add enough flour to form stiff dough. Shape into long 3/4-inch rolls on lightly floured surface. Place in freezer container. Freeze until firm. Preheat oven to 350 degrees. Slice dough into 1/4-inch slices; place on lightly greased cookie sheet. Bake for 8 to 10 minutes or until brown. Cool for several minutes on cookie sheet. Remove to wire rack to cool completely. Store, tightly sealed. Yield: 11 to 12 dozen.

Alice Hummel, Xi Alpha Rho
Grand Island, Nebraska

HUNGARIAN CHOCOLATE WALNUT CAKE

2 cups ground walnuts	7 egg whites, stiffly beaten
1 cup milk	1 cup margarine, softened
7 egg yolks	2 cups confectioners' sugar
7 tablespoons berry sugar or sugar	1 teaspoon vanilla extract
3 tablespoons baking cocoa	
5 tablespoons sifted all-purpose flour	

Combine ground walnuts and milk in saucepan. Cook over low heat until thickened, stirring constantly. This will burn easily. Chill in refrigerator for 2 hours. Preheat oven to 350 degrees. Combine egg yolks and sugar in mixer bowl; beat well. Add cocoa and flour; mix well. Fold in egg whites. Spoon into 3 greased and floured cake pans. Bake for 15 minutes or until layers test done. Cool in pan for several minutes. Invert onto wire rack to cool completely. Cream margarine and confectioners' sugar in mixer bowl until light and fluffy. Add vanilla and cold walnut mixture; beat well. Spread icing between layers and over side and top of cake. Chill cake to set frosting. Yield: 12 servings.

Kim Borbely, Lambda
Yorkton, Saskatchewan, Canada

ITALIAN CASSATA

6 tablespoons
  shortening
4 cups all-purpose flour
¾ cup sugar
4 eggs
½ cup water
3 dozen eggs

3 cups sugar
3 pounds ricotta cheese
2 1-ounce chocolate
  candy bars, grated
2 teaspoons cinnamon
2 packages chopped
  candied green citron

Cut shortening into flour and ¾ cup sugar in bowl until crumbly. Add 4 eggs and water; mix well. Roll out on lightly floured surface. Line 6-by-12-inch baking dish. Preheat oven to 325 degrees. Combine 3 dozen eggs, 3 cups sugar, ricotta cheese, grated chocolate bars and cinnamon in mixer bowl; beat well. Stir in citron. Pour into pastry-lined baking dish. Bake, uncovered, for 1 hour. Reduce oven temperature to 300 degrees. Bake for 2 hours. Yield: 20 servings.

Elaine Marie Vatalaro, Xi Nu Omicron
Gilroy, California

KOURAMBIETHES
(Greek Butter Finger Cookies)

2 cups unsalted butter
  or margarine
½ cup confectioners'
  sugar
1 ounce whiskey
1 egg yolk

4 cups cake flour, sifted
1 cup toasted finely
  chopped almonds
All-purpose flour
Confectioners' sugar

Melt butter in saucepan; pour off butter into mixer bowl, discarding sediment in saucepan. Chill in refrigerator until firm. Beat until light and creamy. Add ½ cup confectioners' sugar, whiskey and egg yolk; beat well. Beat in 3 cups cake flour. Stir in remaining 1 cup cake flour. Stir in almonds. Stir in enough all-purpose flour to form soft dough that is not sticky. Preheat oven to 325 degrees. Shape into small crescents; place on ungreased cookie sheet. Bake for 15 to 20 minutes or until light brown. Remove to wire rack; sprinkle with additional confectioners' sugar while warm. Yield: 4 dozen.

Rita Bertler, Chi Nu
Englewood, Florida

NORWEGIAN ALMOND TARTS

14 tablespoons butter
  or margarine
1½ cups all-purpose
  flour
3 to 4 tablespoons
  whipping cream

3 egg whites
1 cup confectioners'
  sugar
1 cup ground almonds

Cut butter into flour in bowl until crumbly. Add cream, stirring until mixture forms a ball. Chill for several hours. Divide dough into 18 portions, reserving a small amount for top of tarts. Press each portion into bottom and up sides of individual tart pans. Beat egg whites until soft peaks form. Add confectioners' sugar gradually, beating until stiff. Add almonds. Beat for 10 minutes or until thick. Spoon into tart shells. Preheat oven to 400 degrees. Roll out reserved pastry on floured surface. Cut into strips. Arrange lattice-fashion on top of tarts. Bake for 20 minutes or until brown. Yield: 18 servings.

Katherine Sergeant, Kappa Eta
Lindsay, Ontario, Canada

SCHWARZWÄLDER KIRSCHTORTE
(Black Forest Cherry Torte)

2 cups cake flour
2 teaspoons baking
  powder
½ cup baking cocoa
6 eggs
2 cups sugar
4 teaspoons lemon juice
¾ cup hot milk
1 16-ounce can tart red
  cherries in heavy syrup
2 tablespoons
  cornstarch
8 to 10 drops red food
  coloring

1 8-ounce bar
  German's sweet
  chocolate
1 cup whipping cream,
  whipped
3 cups whipping cream
Pinch of salt
3 tablespoons
  confectioners' sugar
3 tablespoons
  Kirschwasser
Maraschino cherries
German's sweet
  chocolate curls

Preheat oven to 350 degrees. Sift flour, baking powder and cocoa together. Beat eggs in mixer bowl for 10 minutes or until thick and lemony. Add sugar gradually, beating well after each addition. Add lemon juice; mix well. Add flour mixture gradually. Add hot milk, mixing quickly until batter is smooth. Pour batter into 3 greased and floured cake pans. Bake for 25 minutes or until cake tests done. Cool in pan for several minutes. Invert onto wire rack to cool completely. Cut each layer crosswise into 2 layers. Combine cherries and cornstarch in saucepan; mix well. Tint with red food coloring. Cook over medium heat until thickened and sauce is clear, stirring constantly. Cool to room temperature. Melt chocolate bar in double boiler over hot water. Cool to room temperature. Fold into whipped cream. Chill for 15 to 20 minutes in refrigerator. Beat remaining 3 cups whipping cream in mixer bowl until soft peaks form. Add salt and sugar gradually, beating until stiff. Fold in Kirschwasser. Layer cake layer, half the chocolate filling, cake layer, ⅓ of the Kirschcreme, cake layer, remaining chocolate filling, cake layer, half the remaining Kirschcreme, cake layer, cherry filling and cake layer on cake plate. Spread remaining Kirschcreme over top and side of cake. Garnish with maraschino cherries and shaved chocolate. Chill in refrigerator for 1 hour. Yield: 12 to 14 servings.

Shirley Welch, Psi Iota
Ocie, Missouri

Cookies and Candies

ALMOND SQUARES

2 cups graham cracker
  crumbs
2 tablespoons light
  brown sugar
1/2 cup melted butter
  or margarine
1 14-ounce can
  sweetened condensed
  milk
1 7-ounce package
  flaked coconut

1 teaspoon vanilla
  extract
1 cup semisweet
  chocolate chips
1 cup butterscotch chips
1/4 cup butter or
  margarine
6 tablespoons chunky
  peanut butter
1/3 cup chopped
  almonds

Preheat oven to 325 degrees. Combine graham cracker
crumbs, brown sugar and melted butter in small
bowl; mix well. Press into greased 9-by-13-inch
baking pan. Bake for 10 minutes; cool. Combine condensed milk, coconut and vanilla in bowl; mix well.
Pour over prepared crust. Bake for 25 minutes; cool.
Combine chocolate chips, butterscotch chips, butter,
peanut butter and almonds in top of double boiler.
Cook until melted, stirring constantly. Spread over
cooled layer. Cool; cut into squares.
Yield: 36 servings.

Lori Espinosa, Xi Alpha Rho
Hermiston, Oregon

DUTCH ALMOND SQUARES

1/2 cup butter or
  margarine, softened
1/2 cup shortening
2/3 cup sugar
3/4 cup packed light
  brown sugar
1 tablespoon almond
  extract

1 egg, beaten
2 cups all-purpose flour
1 teaspoon baking
  powder
Pinch of salt
3/4 cup slivered almonds
Maraschino cherries

Preheat oven to 350 degrees. Cream butter, shorten-
ing and sugars in mixer bowl until light and fluffy.
Add almond extract and egg; beat well. Stir flour,
baking powder and salt into creamed mixture.
Spread evenly into 9-by-13-inch greased baking pan.
Bake for 20 to 25 minutes or until golden brown.
Decorate with slivered almonds or maraschino cher-
ries. Cut into squares while warm. Yield: 36 servings.

Joan Wilby, Xi Epsilon Delta
Pickering, Ontario, Canada

APRICOT COOKIES

1 cup margarine,
  softened
1/2 cup sugar
2 cups all-purpose flour
Pinch of salt
1 21-ounce can apricot
  pie filling
1 4-ounce jar apricot
  preserves

1/3 cup margarine,
  softened
1/4 cup sugar
1/4 cup packed light
  brown sugar
1/4 teaspoon salt
3/4 cup all-purpose flour

Preheat oven to 350 degrees. Cream 1 cup margarine
and 1/2 cup sugar in mixer bowl until light and fluffy.
Cut in 2 cups flour and salt until crumbly. Press into
greased 11-by-16-inch baking pan. Bake for 10
minutes; cool slightly. Spread with mixture of apricot
pie filling and apricot preserves while warm. Combine remaining 1/3 cup margarine, 1/4 cup sugar,
brown sugar, 1/4 teaspoon salt and 3/4 cup flour in
small bowl; mix well. Sprinkle over top layer. Bake
for 30 to 35 minutes longer. Cut into bars. May drizzle with vanilla glaze while warm. Yield: 24 servings.

Marian J. Bonnom, Preceptor Alpha Lambda
Winston-Salem, North Carolina

APRICOT SPICE BARS

1/2 cup water	1 teaspoon baking
1 1/3 cups packed light	powder
brown sugar	1 teaspoon cinnamon
1/2 cup butter or	1/4 teaspoon ginger
margarine, softened	1/4 teaspoon nutmeg
1 teaspoon vanilla	1 cup chopped dried
extract	apricots
1 egg, beaten	1 cup chopped pecans
1 cup all-purpose flour	Confectioners' sugar

Preheat oven to 350 degrees. Combine water, brown sugar, butter, vanilla, and egg in bowl; mix well. Mix flour, baking powder, cinnamon, ginger and nutmeg together. Add to egg mixture; mix well. Stir in apricots and pecans. Spoon into greased 9-by-13-inch baking pan. Bake for 30 minutes. Sprinkle with confectioners' sugar while warm; cut into squares. Yield: 15 servings.

Lisa Thomsen, Preceptor Sigma
Grand Island, Nebraska

BUTTERSCOTCH BROWNIES WITH CHOCOLATE ICING

1/4 cup melted butter	1 teaspoon baking
or margarine	powder
1 cup packed light	1/4 teaspoon salt
brown sugar	1/2 cup chopped pecans
1 egg, beaten	1/2 cup semisweet
1/2 teaspoon vanilla	chocolate chips
extract	1/4 cup peanut butter
3/4 cup all-purpose flour	1/4 cup flaked coconut

Preheat oven to 350 degrees. Cream butter and brown sugar in mixer bowl until light and fluffy. Add egg and vanilla; mix well. Add flour, baking powder, salt and pecans, stirring well after each addition. Spread into greased 8-by-8-inch baking pan. Bake for 30 minutes or until edges come away from sides of pan. Cool on wire rack. Combine chocolate chips, peanut butter and coconut in top of double boiler. Cook until chocolate is melted, stirring constantly. Spread over cooled brownies; cut into squares. Yield: 20 servings.

Joanne Dodge, Xi Beta Nu
Prince George, British Columbia, Canada

BROWNIES WITH A TWIST

1 cup margarine	2 eggs, beaten
1/4 cup baking cocoa	1 teaspoon vanilla
1 cup water	extract
2 cups all-purpose flour	1 14-ounce can
1 1/2 cups packed light	sweetened condensed
brown sugar	milk
1 teaspoon soda	1/4 cup margarine
1/2 teaspoon cinnamon	1/4 cup baking cocoa
1/2 teaspoon salt	

Preheat oven to 350 degrees. Melt 1 cup margarine in saucepan. Stir in 1/4 cup cocoa and water. Bring to a boil; remove from heat. Combine flour, brown sugar, soda, cinnamon and salt in mixer bowl. Add cocoa mixture. Beat at high speed until smooth. Stir in eggs, vanilla and 1/3 of the condensed milk. Pour mixture into greased 10-by-15-inch baking pan. Bake for 15 minutes. Melt 1/4 cup margarine in saucepan. Add remaining 1/4 cup cocoa and remaining condensed milk, stirring constantly until smooth. Spread over warm cake. Cut into bars when cool. Yield: 48 servings.

Deborah Wood, Theta
Fredericton, New Brunswick, Canada

PEANUT SWIRL BROWNIES

1 cup semisweet	1/2 cup peanut butter
chocolate chips	chips
1/2 cup butter or	1 cup semisweet
margarine	chocolate chips
2/3 cup sugar	1 teaspoon vegetable
2 eggs, beaten	oil
1 teaspoon vanilla	1/4 cup peanut butter
extract	chips
1/2 teaspoon baking	1 tablespoon vegetable
powder	oil
3/4 cup all-purpose flour	
1/4 teaspoon salt	

Place 1 cup chocolate chips and butter in microwave-safe dish. Microwave on Medium for 3 to 4 minutes or until melted. Stir well; cool slightly. Beat sugar and eggs together in large bowl. Stir in chocolate mixture and vanilla. Add mixture of baking powder, flour and salt; mix well. Stir in 1/2 cup peanut butter chips. Spread mixture into 8-by-8-inch glass dish. Microwave on High for 4 1/2 to 6 minutes or until top is no longer sticky, turning once. Let stand for 10 minutes. Place on wire rack to cool completely. Combine remaining 1 cup chocolate chips and 1 teaspoon oil in small glass bowl. Microwave on Medium for 2 to 2 1/2 minutes or until chocolate is melted; stir to blend. Combine remaining 1/4 cup peanut butter chips with remaining 1 tablespoon oil in glass bowl. Microwave on High for 1 to 2 minutes or until melted; stir well. Spread chocolate mixture over brownies. Drizzle peanut butter mixture over top at 1-inch intervals. Swirl together with tip of knife. Chill in refrigerator for 1 hour; cut into squares. Yield: 24 servings.

Glenda St. John, Preceptor Pi
Kindersley, Saskatchewan, Canada

CHEERY CHERRY BARS

1 cup all-purpose flour	1 4-ounce jar
1/2 cup shortening or	maraschino cherries,
margarine	drained, cut into
3 tablespoons	halves
confectioners' sugar	2 egg whites
Salt to taste	1/2 cup sugar

Preheat oven to 350 degrees. Combine first 4 ingredients in bowl; mix well. Press into 8-by-8-inch greased baking pan. Bake for 10 minutes. Cover crust with cherry halves. Beat egg whites in bowl until stiff. Beat in sugar. Spread over cherries. Bake for 20 minutes or until golden brown. Cool; cut into squares. Yield: 15 servings.

Ruth Young, Laureate Beta Mu
Dunsford, Ontario, Canada

CHOCOLATE CRINKLES

4 ounces unsweetened	2 cups sugar
chocolate	4 large eggs, beaten
2 cups all-purpose flour	2 teaspoons vanilla
2 teaspoons baking	extract
powder	2 cups semisweet
1/2 teaspoon salt	chocolate chips
1 cup vegetable oil	Confectioners' sugar

Melt chocolate in top of double boiler; cool. Sift flour, baking powder and salt together. Mix oil, cooled chocolate and sugar in bowl. Beat in eggs 1 at a time. Add vanilla and sifted dry ingredients; mix well. Fold in chocolate chips. Chill, covered, for 4 hours to overnight. Preheat oven to 350 degrees. Roll mixture by teaspoonfuls in confectioners' sugar. Arrange on greased cookie sheet. Bake for 9 to 11 minutes or until cookies test done. Cool on cookie sheet for 5 minutes. Remove to wire rack to cool completely. Yield: 72 servings.

Karen Barwick, Epsilon Nu
Birmingham, Alabama

CHOCOLATE NINJA TURTLE COOKIES

1/2 cup all-purpose flour	4 ounces unsweetened
1/2 teaspoon baking	chocolate, chopped
powder	1/4 cup butter or
1/2 teaspoon salt	margarine
1 tablespoon plus 1	1/2 cup sugar
teaspoon instant	4 eggs, slightly beaten
coffee	1 cup sugar
2 teaspoons vanilla	2 cups chopped walnuts
extract	2 cups semisweet
2 cups semisweet	chocolate chips
chocolate chips	2 cups pecan halves

Preheat oven to 350 degrees. Sift flour, baking powder and salt together. Dissolve coffee in vanilla in small bowl. Combine 2 cups chocolate chips, unsweetened chocolate and butter in top of double boiler. Cook until chocolate is melted, stirring constantly. Pour into bowl. Stir in 1/2 cup sugar. Beat in eggs 1 at a time. Add remaining 1 cup sugar and coffee mixture; mix well. Stir in sifted dry ingredients. Fold in walnuts and remaining 2 cups chocolate chips. Drop dough by 1/4 cupfuls onto foil-lined cookie sheet, leaving 2 inches between each cookie. Arrange 5 pecans around edge of each cookie to form head and legs. Bake for 12 to 13 minutes or until cookies begin to crack. Remove to wire rack to cool. Yield: 20 to 24 servings.

Kathy Verchick, Delta Chi
Tampa, Florida

DAD'S COOKIE CAKE

24 oatmeal cookies,	1/2 cup butter or
crushed	margarine
1/2 cup melted butter or	1 egg, beaten
margarine	2 cups confectioners'
3 ounces semisweet	sugar
baking chocolate	

Preheat oven to 350 degrees. Mix crushed cookies with 1/2 cup melted butter in bowl. Press 3/4 of the crumb mixture into 8-by-8-inch greased baking pan. Bake for 5 minutes. Melt chocolate with 1/2 cup butter in saucepan. Add egg; mix well. Add confectioners' sugar; mix well. Spread over prepared crust. Sprinkle remaining crumb mixture over top. Chill in refrigerator; cut into bars. Yield: 15 servings.

Heather Bellamy, Xi Alpha Theta
Medicine Hat, Alberta, Canada

COCONUT MACADAMIA COOKIES

1 cup butter or	3 1/2 cups all-purpose
margarine, softened	flour
1/2 cup shortening	2 teaspoons soda
2/3 cup sugar	1 1/2 teaspoons salt
1 2/3 cups packed light	2 1/2 cups shredded
brown sugar	coconut
4 eggs	1 1/2 cups coarsely
1 tablespoon vanilla	chopped macadamia
extract	nuts
1 teaspoon lemon juice	

Preheat oven to 325 degrees. Beat butter, shortening and sugars in mixer bowl for 5 minutes. Beat in eggs 1 at a time. Beat in vanilla and lemon juice. Mix flour, soda and salt together. Beat into creamed mixture gradually. Add coconut and macadamia nuts; mix well. Drop by tablespoonfuls onto greased cookie sheet. Bake for 22 to 25 minutes or until golden brown. Yield: 48 servings.

Jan Schmidt, Xi Zeta Kappa
Rock Rapids, Iowa

GINGER GIANTS

1 cup all-purpose flour	1/2 cup butter, softened
1/2 teaspoon soda	1/2 cup packed light
1/2 teaspoon baking	brown sugar
powder	1/3 cup sugar
1/2 teaspoon cinnamon	1 egg, beaten
1/2 teaspoon nutmeg	1 teaspoon vanilla
1/2 teaspoon ground	extract
ginger	1 cup oats
1/2 teaspoon salt	1 cup raisins

Preheat oven to 350 degrees. Combine first 7 ingredients in bowl; mix well. Cream butter, sugars, egg and vanilla at high speed in mixer bowl until light and fluffy. Add dry ingredients gradually to creamed mixture, beating at low speed until blended. Stir in oats and raisins. Drop dough by 1/4 cupfuls onto ungreased cookie sheet. Bake for 15 to 17 minutes or until golden brown. Cool on wire rack.
Yield: 8 to 10 cookies.

Denise LaPalme, Xi Delta Lambda
Windsor, Ontario, Canada

"GOOD AS GOLD" BARS

1 1/2 cups all-purpose	1 teaspoon vanilla
flour	extract
1 teaspoon salt	1 8-ounce can crushed
1 teaspoon nutmeg	pineapple
3/4 teaspoon soda	1 cup finely chopped
1/2 teaspoon cinnamon	apple
1/4 cup margarine,	1/2 cup raisins
softened	Cream cheese frosting
3/4 cup sugar	(optional)
2 eggs	

Preheat oven to 350 degrees. Combine flour, salt, nutmeg, soda and cinnamon in medium bowl. Cream margarine and sugar in large bowl until light and fluffy. Add eggs and vanilla; mix well. Drain pineapple, reserving 1 teaspoon juice for frosting. Mix pineapple and dry ingredients with creamed mixture. Stir in apple and raisins. Spread onto greased and floured 10-by-15-inch baking pan. Bake for 20 minutes or until toothpick inserted near center comes out clean. Cool on wire rack; cut into small bars. Frost with cream cheese frosting flavored with reserved pineapple juice.
Yield: 64 servings.

Doris Grigsby Byers, Xi Pi
Terre Haute, Indiana

COCONUT-LEMON SQUARES

2 cups all-purpose flour	1 teaspoon baking
1/2 cup packed light	powder
brown sugar	1/4 cup all-purpose flour
1 cup butter, softened	3 eggs, beaten
1/2 teaspoon vanilla	1 cup flaked coconut
extract	2/3 cup lemon juice
2 cups sugar	Grated zest of 2 lemons

Preheat oven to 350 degrees. Combine 2 cups flour and brown sugar in bowl. Cut in butter until crumbly. Stir in vanilla. Press into greased 9-by-13-inch baking pan. Bake for 15 minutes. Combine sugar, baking powder and 1/4 cup flour in bowl. Stir in remaining ingredients. Pour over prepared crust. Bake for 20 minutes. Cool on wire rack; cut into squares.
Yield: 36 squares.

Margaret Cater, Zeta Delta
Prescott, Ontario, Canada

THE ULTIMATE SOUR LEMON BARS

1 1/2 cups all-purpose	5 large eggs
flour	2 cups sugar
1/4 cup confectioners'	1 cup fresh lemon juice,
sugar	strained
Pinch of salt	3 tablespoons
1/2 cup chilled unsalted	all-purpose flour
butter, cut into squares	2 1/2 tablespoons grated
1/2 teaspoon vanilla	lemon zest
extract	

Preheat oven to 350 degrees. Line 9-by-9-inch baking pan with aluminum foil, extending foil 1 inch above 2 sides. Butter the 2 uncovered sides of pan. Combine 1 1/2 cups flour, confectioners' sugar, salt and butter in blender container. Process at high speed, pulsing until mixture is finely crumbled. Add vanilla. Process until dough begins to form. Press into bottom of prepared pan. Bake for 28 minutes. Whisk eggs and 2 cups sugar in bowl. Add lemon juice and 3 tablespoons flour, stirring constantly. Strain into another bowl. Stir in lemon zest. Pour over baked crust. Reduce oven temperature to 325 degrees. Bake for 22 minutes or until filling is set. Cool on wire rack. Chill, covered, for 4 hours to overnight. Lift from pan using foil sides onto serving plate; cut into bars. Yield: 16 servings.

Eddie G. Nichols, Xi Beta Alpha
Great Bend, Kansas

MINT MELT-AWAY COOKIES

1 cup sugar	2 eggs, beaten
1 cup vegetable oil	2 teaspoons vanilla
1/2 cup confectioners'	extract
sugar	4 cups all-purpose flour
3/4 cup butter or	1/2 teaspoon salt
margarine, softened	1 teaspoon soda
1 cup crushed candy	1 cup crushed pecans
canes	

Preheat oven to 375 degrees. Cream sugar, oil, confectioners' sugar and butter in large bowl. Stir in crushed candy. Add eggs and vanilla; mix well. Stir flour, salt and soda into creamed mixture. Fold in pecans. Drop mixture by teaspoonfuls onto ungreased cookie sheet. Bake for 10 minutes. Cool on wire rack.
Yield: 36 servings.

Marilynn L. Buxton, Xi Gamma Nu
Waverly, Iowa

ORANGE-CARROT COOKIES

1 cup margarine, softened	2 cups all-purpose flour
3/4 cup sugar	1/2 teaspoon salt
1 cup mashed cooked carrots	3/4 cup flaked coconut
2 eggs, beaten	Juice of 1/2 orange
1 teaspoon vanilla extract	Grated rind of 1 orange
2 teaspoons baking powder	1 cup confectioners' sugar
	1/2 teaspoon butter or margarine, softened

Preheat oven to 350 degrees. Cream 1 cup margarine and sugar in mixer bowl until light. Add carrots, eggs and vanilla; mix well. Stir in baking powder, flour, salt and coconut. Drop by teaspoonfuls onto greased cookie sheet. Bake for 20 minutes. Cool on wire rack. Beat orange juice, orange rind, confectioners' sugar and 1/2 teaspoon butter in small bowl until creamy. Spread frosting over cooled cookies. Yield: 36 servings.

Barb Westgate, Xi Gamma Nu
Grand Forks, British Columbia, Canada

PECAN PIE BARS

2 cups all-purpose flour	1 egg, beaten
1/2 cup confectioners' sugar	1 teaspoon vanilla extract
1 cup margarine	1 cup almond brickle chips
1 14-ounce can sweetened condensed milk	1 cup chopped pecans

Preheat oven to 350 degrees or 325 degrees for glass dish. Combine flour and confectioners' sugar in bowl. Cut in margarine until crumbly. Press into bottom of 9-by-13-inch greased baking pan. Bake for 15 minutes. Beat condensed milk, egg and vanilla in small bowl. Stir in almond brickle chips and pecans. Spread over baked crust. Bake for 25 minutes longer or until golden brown. Cool on wire rack; cut into bars. Store, covered, in refrigerator or freezer. Yield: 36 servings.

Marguerite Wells, Alpha Lambda
Carroll, Iowa

MAGIC PEANUT BUTTER MIDDLES

1 1/2 cups all-purpose flour	1/4 cup creamy peanut butter
1/2 cup unsweetened baking cocoa	1 teaspoon vanilla extract
1/2 teaspoon soda	1 egg, beaten
1/2 cup sugar	3/4 cup confectioners' sugar
1/2 cup packed light brown sugar	3/4 cup creamy peanut butter
1/2 cup margarine, softened	Sugar

Preheat oven to 375 degrees. Mix flour, cocoa and soda together. Cream sugar, 1/2 cup brown sugar, margarine and 1/4 cup peanut butter in mixer bowl until light and fluffy. Beat in vanilla and egg. Stir in dry ingredients. Set dough aside. Mix confectioners' sugar and 3/4 cup peanut butter in small bowl, stirring until creamy. Roll into thirty 1-inch balls. Envelop with about 1 tablespoon dough to cover completely. Arrange 2 inches apart on ungreased cookie sheet. Flatten with bottom of glass dipped in sugar. Bake for 7 to 9 minutes or until set and slightly cracked. Cool on wire rack. Decorate as desired. Yield: 30 servings.

Sandra Guthrie, Preceptor Kappa Tau
Diamond Bar, California

PERSIMMON COOKIES

1 cup shortening	1/4 teaspoon ground cloves
1 cup sugar	1/4 teaspoon nutmeg
1 egg, beaten	1 teaspoon baking powder
1 teaspoon vanilla extract	
1 cup persimmon pulp	1 teaspoon soda
2 cups all-purpose flour	1 cup raisins
1/4 teaspoon salt	1 cup chopped pecans
1/4 teaspoon cinnamon	

Preheat oven to 350 degrees. Cream shortening and sugar in mixer bowl until light and fluffy. Add egg; mix well. Stir in vanilla and persimmon pulp. Sift dry ingredients together. Add to creamed mixture, stirring well. Add raisins and pecans; mix well. Drop dough by teaspoonfuls onto greased cookie sheet. Bake for 12 minutes. Cool on wire rack. Yield: 42 servings.

Lila A. Neher, Xi Delta Zeta
Akron, Colorado

GORP BARS

1 cup light corn syrup	2 cups granola cereal
1/2 cup packed light brown sugar	1 cup dark seedless raisins
1/4 teaspoon salt	1 cup semisweet chocolate chips
1 1/2 cups peanut butter	1/3 cup orange-flavored instant drink mix (optional)
1 teaspoon vanilla extract	
1 cup nonfat dry milk	

Combine corn syrup, brown sugar and salt in saucepan. Bring to a boil. Stir in peanut butter; remove from heat. Add vanilla, stirring well. Add dry milk, cereal, raisins and chocolate chips; mix well. Add orange-flavored drink mix if desired. Press mixture into greased 9-by-13-inch pan. Chill for 30 minutes; cut into 40 bars. Chill, covered, for 30 minutes longer. Store in refrigerator. Yield: 40 servings.

Diann Kellestine, Xi Gamma Theta
Kitchener, Ontario, Canada

POTATO CHIP COOKIES

2 cups butter or margarine, softened	1 cup crushed potato chips
1 cup sugar	3 1/4 cups all-purpose flour
2 teaspoons vanilla extract	Confectioners' sugar

Preheat oven to 350 degrees. Cream butter and sugar in mixer bowl until light. Stir in vanilla, potato chips and flour. Drop mixture by teaspoonfuls 2 inches apart onto greased cookie sheet. Bake for 10 minutes or until golden brown. Cool on wire rack. Dust cookies with confectioners' sugar. Yield: 24 servings.

Kim Swinford, Beta Omicron
Cambria, Illinois

SOUR CREAM RAISIN BARS

1 3/4 cups oats	4 egg yolks, beaten
1 3/4 cups all-purpose flour	3 tablespoons cornstarch
1 cup packed light brown sugar	2 cups raisins
1 teaspoon soda	1 1/2 cups sugar
1 cup margarine, softened	2 cups sour cream

Preheat oven to 350 degrees. Combine oats, flour, brown sugar and soda in bowl. Cut in margarine until crumbly. Reserve 1 1/2 cups crumb mixture. Pat remaining crumb mixture into 9-by-13-inch greased baking pan. Bake for 15 minutes. Combine remaining ingredients in saucepan. Simmer over low heat for 5 to 10 minutes or until thickened, stirring constantly. Pour over baked crust. Sprinkle reserved crumb mixture over top. Bake for 20 minutes. Cool on wire rack; cut into bars. Yield: 24 servings.

Darlene Gudgeon, Xi Alpha Sigma
Thermopolis, Wyoming

ROLO COOKIES

1 cup margarine, softened	3/4 cup baking cocoa
1 cup sugar	1 teaspoon soda
1 cup packed light brown sugar	1/2 cup chopped pecans
2 eggs, beaten	1 9-ounce package Rolo caramels
2 teaspoons vanilla extract	1 tablespoon sugar
2 1/2 cups all-purpose flour	1/2 cup chopped pecans
	1 cup vanilla candy coating wafers or chopped almond bark

Cream margarine, 1 cup sugar and brown sugar in mixer bowl until light and fluffy. Add eggs and vanilla; mix well. Mix flour, cocoa and soda together. Stir into creamed mixture. Add 1/2 cup pecans; mix well. Chill dough for 1 hour. Preheat oven to 375 degrees. Divide dough into 4 portions; shape each portion into 12 balls. Press 1 unwrapped Rolo cara-mel into each ball, shaping to enclose completely. Combine remaining 1 tablespoon sugar and remaining 1/2 cup pecans in small bowl. Dip top of each ball into mixture. Arrange on greased cookie sheet. Bake for 8 to 10 minutes or until golden brown. Cool on wire rack. Melt vanilla candy wafers in saucepan. Drizzle over cookies. Yield: 48 cookies.

Julie J. Bargman, Iota Phi
Redman, Iowa

RUM BALLS

2 cups semisweet chocolate chips	1/2 cup dark rum
1/2 cup almond paste, softened	3/4 cup water
1 cup sour cream	2 cups finely chopped pecans
8 cups crushed vanilla wafers	3 cups sifted confectioners' sugar
1 1/2 cups melted butter or margarine	16 ounces chocolate sprinkles

Melt chocolate chips in top of double boiler; cool. Mix with almond paste and sour cream in bowl. Combine crushed wafers, butter, rum, water, pecans and confectioners' sugar in large bowl; mix until dough holds its shape. Add chocolate mixture to dough; mix well. Chill in refrigerator for 6 hours to overnight. Shape into 1 1/2-inch balls, using only enough mixture to form 12 balls at a time. Keep remaining mixture chilled until ready to use. Roll in chocolate sprinkles to cover. Arrange on cookie sheet. Freeze until firm. Store, covered, in freezer. Serve frozen or very cold. Yield: 108 to 120 servings.

Sherry Bennett, Eta Delta
MacKenzie, British Columbia, Canada

FESTIVE RUM BALLS

1 2-layer package yellow cake mix	3 ounces rum or to taste
1 pound ground almonds	2 ounces rum extract
1 cup melted shortening	6 cups confectioners' sugar
2 cups semisweet chocolate chips, melted	Graham cracker crumbs or colored sprinkles

Prepare and bake cake mix using package directions. Crumble cooled cake. Let stand for 2 days or until dry, stirring occasionally. Combine dried cake with almonds, shortening and melted chocolate in large bowl; mix well. Stir in rum and rum extract. Add confectioners' sugar gradually, mixing well after each addition. Form dough into 1-inch balls. Roll in graham cracker crumbs or sprinkles. Chill in refrigerator. Store in refrigerator for 1 week before serving. Yield: 100 servings.

Joan Petainen, Preceptor Delta Iota
Sault Ste. Marie, Ontario, Canada

TRIPLE GOOD BARS

2 cups raisins	1¹/₃ cups packed light
1 14-ounce can	brown sugar
sweetened condensed	1¹/₂ teaspoons vanilla
milk	extract
1 tablespoon grated	2¹/₂ cups oats
lemon zest	1 cup all-purpose flour
1 tablespoon lemon	1¹/₂ cups chopped
juice	walnuts
1 cup margarine,	¹/₂ teaspoon soda
softened	¹/₄ teaspoon salt

Preheat oven to 375 degrees. Combine raisins, condensed milk, lemon zest and lemon juice in saucepan. Cook over medium heat until mixture begins to boil, stirring constantly. Remove from heat; set aside to cool. Cream margarine, brown sugar and vanilla in large mixer bowl until light and fluffy. Add oats, flour, walnuts, soda and salt; mix well. Reserve 2 cups mixture for topping. Press remaining mixture into bottom of greased 9-by-13-inch baking pan. Spread raisin-lemon sauce over crust to within ¹/₂ inch of edge. Sprinkle reserved mixture over top. Bake for 25 to 30 minutes or until golden brown. Cool on wire rack. Cut into bars. Yield: 30 servings.

Lillie Mae Merriman, Gamma Delta
Martinsville, Virginia

GRANDMA'S WHIPPED SHORTBREAD

2 cups margarine,	3 cups all-purpose flour
softened	1 cup cornstarch
1 cup confectioners'	
sugar	

Preheat oven to 300 degrees. Beat margarine and confectioners' sugar in mixer bowl for 3 minutes or until light and fluffy. Add flour 1 cup at a time, beating well after each addition. Add cornstarch. Beat for 4 to 5 minutes longer. Drop dough by teaspoonfuls onto ungreased cookie sheet. Bake for 15 to 17 minutes or until light brown. Cool on wire rack. Yield: 72 servings.

Brenda Legge, Lambda Alpha
Welland, Ontario, Canada

WORLD'S BEST COOKIES

1 cup butter or	1 cup oats
margarine, softened	1 cup crushed cornflakes
1 cup sugar	¹/₂ cup shredded coconut
1 cup packed light	¹/₂ cup chopped walnuts
brown sugar	3¹/₂ cups sifted
1 egg, beaten	all-purpose flour
1 cup vegetable oil	1 teaspoon soda
1 teaspoon vanilla	1 teaspoon salt
extract	

Preheat oven to 325 degrees. Cream butter and sugars together in mixer bowl until light and fluffy. Add egg; mix well. Stir in oil and vanilla. Add oats, cornflakes, coconut and walnuts; mix well. Add mixture of flour, soda and salt gradually, mixing well after each addition. Shape dough into 1-inch balls. Place on ungreased cookie sheet. Flatten with fork dipped in water. Bake for 12 minutes or until golden brown. Cool on cookie sheet; remove to wire rack to cool completely. Yield: 72 to 96 servings.

Sheila Ollar, Sigma
Mission Viejo, California

HICKORY NUT BRITTLE

2 cups sugar	2 cups chopped hickory
1 cup light corn syrup	nuts
1 cup water	2 teaspoons soda
1 tablespoon butter or	2 teaspoons vanilla
margarine	extract

Combine sugar, corn syrup and water in 3-quart saucepan. Cook over medium heat until sugar dissolves completely, stirring constantly. Bring to a boil; stir in butter. Cook to 230 degrees on candy thermometer, spun thread stage; do not stir. Cook to 280 degrees on candy thermometer, soft-crack stage, stirring constantly. Add hickory nuts. Cook to 300 degrees on candy thermometer, hard-crack stage, stirring constantly. Remove from heat. Stir in soda and vanilla quickly. Pour mixture into two buttered 10-by-15-inch pans, spreading to even thickness. Stretch thinner by lifting and pulling with two forks as candy cools. Break into pieces when cool.
Yield: 2 pounds.

Iva Polley
Bethany, Missouri

MICROWAVE CARAMELS

1 cup butter or	1 teaspoon vanilla
margarine, melted	extract
1 1-pound package	1 12-ounce package
light brown sugar	semisweet chocolate
1 14-ounce can	chips or chocolate
sweetened condensed	almond bark candy
milk	coating
1 cup light corn syrup	

Pour butter into large microwave-safe bowl. Add brown sugar, condensed milk and corn syrup; stir well. Microwave on High for 17 to 18 minutes, stirring every 3 minutes. Add vanilla; mix well. Pour into buttered 9-by-13-inch pan. Chill in refrigerator overnight. Melt chocolate chips in glass bowl in microwave. Pour over caramel mixture. Cut into 1-inch squares. May cut caramels and dip into chocolate if desired. Yield: 108 to 120 servings.

Julie A. Myhre, Beta Omega
Menomonie, Wisconsin

COCONUT DAINTIES

4 cups confectioners' sugar	1 cup finely shredded coconut
8 ounces cream cheese, softened	1 12-ounce package colored mints

Cream confectioners' sugar and cream cheese in mixer bowl until light and fluffy. Stir in coconut. Shape into small balls; arrange on waxed paper. Press mint into center of each ball. Chill in refrigerator until firm. Freezes well. Yield: 100 servings.

Roselyn Farmer, Alpha Mu
Comox, British Columbia, Canada

FRENCH CARAMEL CANDY

2 cups sugar	3/4 cup light corn syrup
1/2 cup butter or margarine	2 cups sour cream

Combine sugar, butter, corn syrup and 1 cup sour cream in 3-quart saucepan; mix well. Cook over medium heat just to the boiling point, stirring constantly. Stir in remaining 1 cup sour cream gradually. Cook to 250 to 268 degrees on candy thermometer, hard-ball stage, stirring constantly. Pour into buttered 9-by-9-inch pan. Cool until firm. Cut into small squares. Wrap in waxed paper. Yield: 2 1/2 pounds.

Mary Schiefert, Beta Lambda
Rochester, Minnesota

STRAWBERRY DIVINITY

A really different candy that always attracts attention.

3 cups sugar	2 egg whites
3/4 cup light corn syrup	1 3-ounce package strawberry gelatin
3/4 cup water	

Combine sugar, corn syrup and water in saucepan; mix well. Cook over high heat to 250 to 268 degrees on candy thermometer, hard-ball stage. Beat egg whites in bowl until stiff peaks form. Add gelatin; beat well. Add hot syrup gradually, beating at high speed constantly until very stiff. Drop by spoonfuls onto waxed paper or pour into buttered dish. Cool. Yield: 2 1/2 pounds.

Sherry Ripperger, Kappa Tau
Savannah, Missouri

FRUIT COTLETS

2 envelopes unflavored gelatin	1 cup finely chopped pecans
1/2 cup grated apple or chopped dried apricots	1 teaspoon vanilla extract
3/4 cup grated apple or chopped dried apricots	1/2 cup confectioners' sugar
2 cups sugar	1 tablespoon cornstarch
1 teaspoon lemon juice	

Soften gelatin using package directions. Combine 1/2 cup apple with gelatin in bowl. Let stand for 10 minutes. Combine remaining 3/4 cup apple, sugar and lemon juice in large saucepan; mix well. Stir in gelatin-apple mixture. Bring to a boil. Simmer for 15 minutes. Cool for 30 minutes. Add pecans and vanilla; mix well. Pour into greased 8-by-8-inch pan. Let stand for 24 hours. Cut into squares. Roll in mixture of confectioners' sugar and cornstarch.
Yield: 20 servings.

 Susan K. McDonald, Xi Alpha Omega
Story, Wyoming

FUDGE

1/2 cup butter or margarine, softened	2 cups semisweet chocolate chips
1 12-ounce can evaporated milk	3 ounces German's chocolate
4 1/2 cups sugar	1 tablespoon vanilla extract
32 marshmallows	2 cups chopped pecans
2 ounces unsweetened chocolate	

Combine butter, evaporated milk and sugar in saucepan. Bring to a boil. Cook for 5 minutes or until sugar is dissolved. Remove from heat. Add marshmallows, stirring until dissolved. Add chocolates, vanilla and pecans, stirring until chocolates are melted. Pour into greased 9-by-13-inch pan. Chill in refrigerator until firm. Cut into squares.
Yield: 6 pounds.

Martha Hallman, Mu
Jackson, Tennessee

PERFECT FUDGE

This recipe was given to me the first year I was married. I have prepared it for my husband at Christmas for 19 years now.

4 cups semisweet chocolate chips	2 cups miniature marshmallows
2 ounces unsweetened chocolate	1 12-ounce can evaporated milk
1 cup butter or margarine, softened	4 cups sugar

Combine chocolate chips, unsweetened chocolate, butter and marshmallows in large bowl. Mix evaporated milk and sugar in saucepan. Bring to a boil; reduce heat. Simmer for 10 minutes, stirring constantly. Pour into chocolate mixture; mix well to blend. Pour into buttered 9-by-13-inch pan. Chill in refrigerator until firm. Yield: 5 pounds.

Guyla M. Krum, Xi Mu Eta
Sugar Land, Texas

FUDGE-MALLOW RAISIN CANDY

2 cups semisweet chocolate chips	3 cups miniature marshmallows
1 cup chunky peanut butter	3/4 cup raisins

Melt chocolate and peanut butter in saucepan over low heat, stirring constantly until smooth. Fold in marshmallows and raisins. Pour mixture into aluminum foil-lined 8-by-8-inch pan. Chill in refrigerator until firm; cut into small squares. Yield: 24 servings.

Carol LaTulippe, Omicron
Milton, Vermont

THREE-LAYER FUDGE

3 recipes Basic Fudge	1 teaspoon vanilla extract
2 ounces unsweetened chocolate	1 cup mixed chopped dates, figs and pecans
12 marshmallows	
1 7-ounce can flaked coconut	

Prepare 1 recipe Basic Fudge, except add chocolate with sugar and milk in saucepan. Add marshmallows when mixture is removed from heat. Beat until thick and creamy. Spread into buttered 9-by-13-inch pan. Prepare second recipe Basic Fudge. Add coconut and vanilla when mixture is removed from heat. Beat until thick and creamy. Spread over chocolate layer. Prepare third recipe Basic Fudge, adding dates, figs and pecans when mixture is removed from heat. Beat until thick and creamy. Spread over coconut layer. Cool until firm. Cut into squares. Yield: 5 pounds.

BASIC FUDGE

2 cups sugar	1 tablespoon butter or margarine, softened
3/4 cup milk	

Combine sugar and milk in saucepan. Cook over medium heat to 234 to 240 degrees on candy thermometer, soft-ball stage, stirring constantly. Add butter; remove from heat. Beat constantly until mixture thickens. Yield: 1 1/2 pounds.

Rowena M. Key, Laureate Eta
Clarksville, Tennessee

HOMEMADE HARD CANDY

3 3/4 cups sugar	1 teaspoon red or green food coloring
1 1/2 cups light corn syrup	
1 cup water	1 1-pound package confectioners' sugar
1 teaspoon cinnamon oil extract	

Combine sugar, corn syrup and water in saucepan; stir until sugar is dissolved. Cook to 310 degrees on candy thermometer, hard-crack stage. Remove from heat. Add cinnamon extract and food coloring; mix well. Tear foil into 36-inch length; roll up sides and ends to form pan. Sprinkle with confectioners' sugar. Pour hot mixture into foil. Let stand until cool. Break into pieces; store in covered jar. Yield: 4 pounds.

Kim Michael, Theta Theta
Goshen, Indiana

KIT KAT BARS

1 cup butter or margarine	1/2 cup semisweet chocolate chips
1/3 cup sugar	1/2 cup butterscotch chips
1 cup packed light brown sugar	2/3 cup creamy peanut butter
2 cups finely crushed graham cracker crumbs	1 28-ounce package butter-flavored crackers
1/2 cup milk	

Mix butter, sugars, graham cracker crumbs and milk in saucepan. Bring to a boil, stirring constantly. Cook for 5 minutes; cool. Melt chocolate chips, butterscotch chips and peanut butter in top of double boiler, stirring constantly until blended. Line bottom of 9-by-13-inch pan with 1/3 of the butter-flavored crackers. Layer sauce and butter-flavored crackers 1/2 at a time over butter-flavored crackers. Top with chocolate mixture. Chill in refrigerator until topping is firm. Yield: 24 servings.

Sue E. Sohrweide, Alpha Beta
White Bear Lake, Minnesota

LEMON PUDDING CANDY CLUSTERS

1 3-ounce package lemon pudding and pie filling mix	1/2 cup evaporated milk
	1 tablespoon butter or margarine, softened
1 cup sugar	1 cup flaked coconut

Combine pudding mix and sugar in saucepan. Stir in evaporated milk and butter. Cook over medium heat until mixture comes to a boil, stirring constantly. Simmer for 3 minutes. Remove from heat. Add coconut; beat well. Drop mixture by spoonfuls onto waxed paper. Stir in a few drops of hot water if mixture begins to harden. Yield: 1 pound.

Lois Main, Laureate Zeta
Duluth, Minnesota

Ann Doucet, Xi Rho Zeta, Deer Park, Texas, makes Spiced Pecans by combining 1 egg white, 2 tablespoons water, 1/2 cup sugar, 1/2 teaspoon salt, 1/4 teaspoon each cinnamon, cloves and allspice and 2 1/2 cups pecan halves. Place on greased baking sheet and bake in preheated 250-degree oven for 1 hour.

EASY-DO PRALINES

1 4-ounce package butterscotch pudding and pie filling mix	1 cup sugar
1/2 cup packed light brown sugar	1/2 cup evaporated milk
	1 tablespoon margarine, softened
	1 1/2 cups pecans

Combine pudding mix, sugars, evaporated milk and margarine in saucepan; mix well. Cook over low heat until sugar is dissolved. Add pecans. Simmer until mixture reaches 234 degrees to 240 degrees on candy thermometer, soft-ball stage, stirring constantly. Remove from heat. Beat until mixture thickens. Drop by spoonfuls onto waxed paper to form 4-inch patties; cool. Yield: 15 servings.

Dorothy Howell, Preceptor Kappa
Kenai, Alaska

MIRACULOUS PRALINES

1 cup whipping cream	1 teaspoon vanilla extract
1 1-pound package light brown sugar	2 tablespoons butter or margarine
2 cups pecan halves or pieces	

Combine whipping cream and brown sugar in microwave-safe bowl; mix well. Microwave on High for 13 to 15 minutes or until mixture boils. Stir in pecans, vanilla and butter. Drop by spoonfuls onto aluminum foil-lined pan. Yield: 36 servings.

Gary Lou Geddes, Xi Omicron Omega
Fort Worth, Texas

SNOWBALLS

1/2 cup chopped pecans	3 tablespoons butter or margarine, softened
1/2 cup chopped cherries	1/4 teaspoon vanilla extract
1/2 cup peanut butter	1/4 cup (about) hot milk
1/2 cup confectioners' sugar	Flaked coconut
1 tablespoon butter or margarine, softened	
2 cups confectioners' sugar	

Combine pecans, cherries, peanut butter, 1/2 cup confetioners' sugar and 1 tablespoon butter in bowl; mix well. Form mixture into 1-inch balls. Chill in refrigerator until firm. Cream remaining 2 cups confectioners' sugar and 3 tablespoons butter in small mixer bowl until light and fluffy. Stir in vanilla and enough hot milk to make mixture smooth. Dip candy in confectioners' sugar frosting; roll in coconut flakes. Chill in refrigerator.
Yield: 20 servings.

Sheryle Blackwood, Zeta Sigma
Elkford, British Columbia, Canada

TIGER BUTTER

1 cup white chocolate candy coating wafers	1 cup chocolate candy coating wafers
1/2 cup peanut butter	

Melt white chocolate wafers in top of double boiler, stirring constantly. Stir in peanut butter. Melt chocolate wafers in top of another double boiler, stirring constantly. Alternate strips of white chocolate-peanut butter mixture with melted chocolate on waxed paper-lined tray. Swirl with a knife. Cool. Break into pieces. Yield: 1 1/4 pounds.

Carol Steele, Delta
Brandon, Manitoba, Canada

TINY TASTY TURTLES

4 cups semisweet chocolate chips	1 tablespoon vanilla extract
1 14-ounce can sweetened condensed milk	4 cups (about) pecan pieces
1 13-ounce jar marshmallow creme	1 24-ounce package caramels, cut into halves or quarters

Melt chocolate chips in top of double boiler. Add condensed milk, marshmallow creme, vanilla and pecan pieces; stir well. Roll caramel pieces in chocolate mixture. Place on waxed paper; cool in refrigerator. Yield: 5 pounds.

Candace Steigelman, Xi Kappa Epsilon
Columbus, Ohio

TRUFFLE MICE

I made these with the children at Christmas. It was fun creating this together.

4 ounces semisweet chocolate, chopped	1/3 cup confectioners' sugar
1/3 cup sour cream	Gold or silver beads
1 cup finely crumbled chocolate wafers	Slivered almonds
	Small round licorice

Melt chocolate in top of double boiler, stirring constantly. Remove from heat. Blend in sour cream, stirring well. Add chocolate wafer crumbs; mix well. Refrigerate, covered, for 1 hour or until firm. Roll scant 1 tablespoon of chocolate mixture in confectioners' sugar. Form into oval for body of mouse. Place 2 beads for eyes, almonds for ears, and licorice strip for tail. Yield: 12 servings.

Carol Zurevinski, Kappa
North Battleford, Saskatchewan, Canada

Happy Endings

ANGEL LIGHT PUDDING

1 4-ounce package
   vanilla pudding and
   pie filling mix
1 envelope unflavored
   gelatin
1/3 cup cold
   water

1 8-ounce can crushed
   pineapple, drained
4 egg whites
1/2 cup sugar
1 large angel food cake
Strawberries or
   raspberries

Cook pudding mix using package directions. Soften gelatin in cold water. Stir into hot pudding until dissolved. Add pineapple; mix well. Cool to room temperature. Beat egg whites until soft peaks form. Add sugar gradually, beating until stiff peaks form. Fold into pudding mixture. Break angel food cake into bite-sized pieces. Layer cake and pudding 1/2 at a time in 9-by-13-inch glass dish. Chill, covered, overnight. Cut into squares. Top with strawberries or raspberries. Yield: 10 to 12 servings.

Marge Pope, Preceptor Beta Alpha
Kenmore, New York

APRICOT AND BERRY MARBLE

1 3-ounce package
   raspberry gelatin
1 cup boiling water
1/2 cup cold water
2 cups fresh or frozen
   raspberries
1 3-ounce package
   apricot gelatin

1 cup boiling water
1 cup lemon sherbet
1 tablespoon lemon juice
10 fresh apricots,
   pitted, chopped
Apricot halves
Raspberries

Dissolve raspberry gelatin in 1 cup boiling water. Add cold water; mix well. Chill until partially set. Fold in 2 cups raspberries. Dissolve apricot gelatin in remaining 1 cup boiling water. Add lemon sherbet 1 spoonful at a time, stirring until melted. Stir in lemon juice. Chill until partially set. Stir in chopped apricots. Alternate layers of raspberry gelatin and apricot gelatin in 6 1/2-cup ring mold. Swirl with spoon to marbleize. Chill for several hours or until set. Unmold onto serving plate. Fill center with apricot halves. Garnish with raspberries. Yield: 12 servings.

Ann Poe, Epsilon Nu
Birmingham, Alabama

BANANA WELLINGTON

1 10-ounce package
   frozen raspberries in
   light syrup, thawed
1 tablespoon sugar
1 teaspoon cornstarch
2 firm ripe bananas
8 12-by-17-inch sheets
   phyllo dough

1/2 cup coarsely chopped
   white chocolate
1/2 cup toasted sliced
   almonds
Vegetable oil for frying
Confectioners' sugar

Purée raspberries, sugar and cornstarch in blender. Strain through fine sieve into saucepan. Cook over medium heat for 5 minutes or until thickened, stirring constantly. Chill. Cut bananas into halves; cut each half lengthwise. Open phyllo dough, keeping damp towel over unused portion. Fold each piece of dough crosswise so short ends meet. Place 1 banana quarter in center of dough. Sprinkle with 1 tablespoon white chocolate and 1 tablespoon almonds. Brush edges of dough with water. Fold sides to center; roll from short end, pressing edge to seal. Heat 1 inch oil in large heavy saucepan to 325 degrees. Fry 4 phyllo rolls at a time for 3 to 4 minutes or until golden brown, turning to brown evenly. Drain on paper towels. Keep warm in oven. Place phyllo rolls on dessert plates. Spoon raspberry sauce over rolls. Sprinkle with confectioners' sugar. Serve hot. Yield: 8 servings.

Helen Plummer, Gamma Delta
Bridgeport, Nebraska

BANANA AND BERRY BROWNIE PIZZA

1 family-size package brownie mix	1 pint strawberries, sliced
8 ounces cream cheese, softened	2 ounces semisweet chocolate
1 egg	1 14-ounce can sweetened condensed milk
1 teaspoon vanilla extract	
1 or 2 bananas, cut into 1/4-inch slices	

Preheat oven to 350 degrees. Prepare brownie mix using package directions. Spread batter on greased pizza pan. Bake for 15 minutes. Combine cream cheese, egg and vanilla in mixer bowl. Beat at medium speed until well blended. Spread over baked brownie crust, leaving 1/2-inch to 1-inch space around edge. Bake for 15 minutes longer. Cool to room temperature. Spread bananas and strawberries over baked crust. Microwave chocolate and condensed milk until chocolate is melted, stirring occasionally. Microwave for several minutes longer or until thickened, stirring occasionally. Drizzle over fruit. Yield: 8 to 12 servings.

Julie Straub, Phi Alpha Epsilon
Great Bend, Kansas

BAKLAVA

I grew up in a very ethnic area and spent much of my time in my friends' mothers' kitchens. I adopted this recipe years ago and it simply would not be Christmas without it.

4 cups finely chopped walnuts	3 cups sugar
1 cup sugar	1 16-ounce jar honey
1 1/2 teaspoons ground cinnamon	3 tablespoons lemon juice
1 16-ounce package phyllo dough	1 cinnamon stick
2 cups melted sweet cream butter	1 long strip lemon rind
	1 long strip orange rind
	4 whole cloves
	2 cups water

Combine walnuts, 1 cup sugar and ground cinnamon in bowl; mix well. Open phyllo dough. Layer phyllo dough in buttered 9-by-13-inch baking dish 8 leaves at a time, brushing with butter every 2 leaves. Spread half the walnut mixture on top of 8 leaves. Repeat layers, ending with phyllo dough. Brush top with remaining butter. Preheat oven to 300 degrees. Trim excess dough from side of baking dish. Score top in diamond pattern. Bake for 1 hour and 20 minutes or until golden brown. Cool in baking dish. Combine remaining 3 cups sugar, honey, lemon juice, cinnamon stick, lemon rind, orange rind, cloves and water in saucepan. Simmer for 10 minutes. Remove cinnamon stick, cloves and lemon and orange rinds. Pour half the mixture over cooled baklava. Store remaining syrup in covered jar in refrigerator. May keep baklava for 1 month in cool place. May freshen it by heating remaining syrup and pouring over baklava as needed. May freeze baklava before baking; thaw completely. Serve from baking dish or cut into servings and place in paper muffin cup liners. Yield: 28 servings.

Karen Shelly-Genther, Eta Iota
West Chester, Pennsylvania

BLUEBERRY CREAM CAKE

My husband took this dessert to Moosehead Lake on an ice fishing trip with a group of men and everyone loved it. So when the women were invited to go they asked me to make this dessert again. It was all eaten before lunch.

1 14-ounce can sweetened condensed milk	2 cups whipping cream
	Sugar to taste
	Vanilla extract to taste
1 cup cold water	1 loaf pound cake, cut into 1/4-inch slices
1 teaspoon almond extract	4 cups blueberries
1 4-ounce package vanilla instant pudding mix	

Combine condensed milk, water and almond extract in large mixer bowl; beat well. Add pudding mix; beat until well mixed. Chill for 5 minutes. Beat whipping cream until soft peaks form. Add sugar and vanilla, beating until stiff. Fold into pudding mixture. Layer cake slices, pudding mixture and blueberries 1/2 at a time in 9-by-13-inch dish. Chill for 4 hours or until set. Cut into squares.
Yield: 12 servings.

Dawn M. Dugas
Ellsworth, Maine

MIDSUMMER BERRIES

1 10-ounce package Lorna Doone cookies	2 eggs
3/4 cup butter or margarine, softened	1/3 cup chopped walnuts
	1 quart blueberries
1 cup confectioners' sugar	1 cup unsweetened whipped cream

Roll cookies into crumbs. Sprinkle half the crumbs in 9-inch square dish. Cream butter and confectioners' sugar in mixer bowl until light and fluffy. Add eggs 1 at a time, beating well after each addition. Spread in prepared dish. Sprinkle with walnuts; top with blueberries. Spread whipped cream over blueberries. Sprinkle with remaining crumbs. Chill for 2 hours. Cut into squares. Yield: 9 to 12 servings.

Rita Maitland, Laureate Gamma
Lenox, Maine

LEMON AND BLUEBERRY FLUFF

1 3-ounce package lemon gelatin	1 9-ounce package frozen unsweetened blueberries, thawed
1 cup boiling water	
1/4 teaspoon grated lemon rind	1 tablespoon cornstarch
	1/2 cup cold water
2 tablespoons lemon juice	2 tablespoons sugar
	Several drops of vanilla extract
3/4 cup cold water	
2 egg whites	

Dissolve gelatin in boiling water in large bowl. Add lemon rind, lemon juice and 3/4 cup cold water. Chill until partially set. Add egg whites. Beat with mixer for 1 to 2 minutes or until light and fluffy. Pour into eight 5-ounce custard cups. Chill until firm; mixture may separate slightly. Crush 1/2 cup blueberries in saucepan. Stir in mixture of cornstarch and remaining 1/2 cup cold water. Add sugar. Cook over medium heat until thick and bubbly, stirring constantly. Cook for 1 minute longer, stirring constantly. Remove from heat. Stir in remaining blueberries and vanilla. Chill in refrigerator. Unmold gelatin onto dessert plates. Spoon blueberry sauce over each. Yield: 8 servings.

Muriel Patricia Thompson, Laureate Alpha Pi
Stroud, Ontario, Canada

OLD-FASHIONED BREAD PUDDING WITH LEMON SAUCE

3/4 cup raisins	Cinnamon
3 eggs	1 cup water
1 cup sugar	1/2 cup sugar
Pinch of salt	1 tablespoon cornstarch
1 teaspoon vanilla extract	1/4 cup butter or margarine
1/2 teaspoon nutmeg	2 teaspoons grated lemon rind
1 cup cold milk	
2 cups scalded milk	Dash of salt
2 tablespoons melted margarine	1/4 cup lemon juice
5 slices cinnamon-raisin bread, crusts trimmed	

Place raisins and water to cover in small bowl. Combine eggs, 1 cup sugar, salt, vanilla, nutmeg and cold milk in mixer bowl; beat well. Add a small amount of scalded milk. Stir egg mixture into hot milk. Add melted margarine; mix well. Cut bread into cubes. Toast until light brown. Preheat oven to 350 degrees. Place toasted bread in 11/2-quart shallow casserole. Drain raisins; sprinkle over bread. Pour egg mixture into casserole, pushing bread down to coat. Sprinkle with cinnamon. Place casserole in baking pan with 1/2 inch of warm water. Bake for 1 hour or until set. Combine water, remaining 1/2 cup sugar and cornstarch in saucepan; mix well. Simmer for 5 minutes or until thickened, stirring constantly. Remove from heat. Stir in butter until melted. Add lemon rind, salt and lemon juice; mix well. Serve warm over bread pudding. Yield: 8 to 12 servings.

Doris Fontaine, Preceptor Delta
Long Beach, Mississippi

BUTTERFINGER DESSERT

2 eggs	2 large Butterfinger candy bars, crushed
2 cups confectioners' sugar	
	1 medium angel food cake
1/2 cup melted margarine	
9 ounces whipped topping	

Beat eggs in mixer bowl. Add confectioners' sugar and margarine; beat well. Fold in whipped topping. Reserve 1/4 of the candy bar crumbs. Add remaining crumbs to whipped topping mixture. Tear cake into bite-sized pieces. Alternate layers of cake pieces and whipped topping mixture in 9-by-13-inch glass dish. Sprinkle with reserved crumbs. Freeze until firm. Yield: 12 servings.

Barb Duncan, Preceptor Chi
Rapid City, South Dakota

BOSTON CREAM CHEESECAKE

1 9-ounce package yellow cake mix	2 ounces unsweetened chocolate
16 ounces cream cheese, softened	3 tablespoons margarine
	1 cup confectioners' sugar
1/2 cup sugar	
1 teaspoon vanilla extract	1 teaspoon vanilla extract
2 eggs	Strawberries
1/3 cup sour cream	
2 tablespoons cold water	

Preheat oven to 350 degrees. Grease bottom of 9-inch springform pan. Prepare cake mix using package directions. Pour batter into prepared pan. Bake for 20 minutes. Combine cream cheese, sugar and 1 teaspoon vanilla in mixer bowl; beat until well blended. Add eggs 1 at a time, beating well after each addition. Add sour cream; mix well. Spread over baked layer. Bake for 35 minutes longer. Cool in pan for several minutes. Loosen cake from rim. Cool completely; remove rim of pan. Bring water to a boil in saucepan. Add chocolate and margarine. Cook until melted, stirring frequently. Combine chocolate mixture and confectioners' sugar in mixer bowl; beat well. Add remaining 1 teaspoon vanilla; mix well. Spread over cheesecake. Chill for several hours. Garnish with strawberries. Yield: 10 to 12 servings.

Becky Zielinski, Tau Omega
Freeman, Missouri

FUDGE TRUFFLE CHEESECAKE

1½ cups vanilla wafer crumbs	1 14-ounce can sweetened condensed milk
½ cup confectioners' sugar	4 eggs
⅓ cup baking cocoa	2 teaspoons vanilla extract
⅓ cup melted butter or margarine	Whipped cream
2 cups semisweet chocolate chips	Shaved chocolate
24 ounces cream cheese, softened	

Preheat oven to 300 degrees. Combine crumbs, confectioners' sugar and cocoa in bowl; mix well. Stir in melted butter. Press into greased 9-inch springform pan. Melt chocolate chips in heavy saucepan over low heat, stirring constantly. Combine cream cheese and condensed milk in mixer bowl; beat well. Add melted chocolate, eggs and vanilla; beat well. Pour over crumb mixture. Bake for 1 hour and 5 minutes or until center is set. Cool to room temperature. Garnish with dollops of whipped cream and shaved chocolate. Yield: 10 to 12 servings.

Dorothy M. Peabody, Beta Master
Portland, Oregon

STRAWBERRY AMARETTO CHEESECAKE

¼ cup Amaretto cookie crumbs	4 egg whites, at room temperature
24 ounces low-fat cottage cheese	⅛ teaspoon cream of tartar
16 ounces cream cheese, softened	¼ cup sugar
¾ cup sugar	¾ cup strawberry halves
2 tablespoons Amaretto	1 tablespoon sugar
2 eggs	2 cups strawberry halves

Preheat oven to 325 degrees. Coat bottom of 10-inch springform pan with nonstick cooking spray. Sprinkle with cookie crumbs. Process cottage cheese and cream cheese in food processor until smooth. Add ¾ cup sugar, Amaretto and eggs. Process until smooth. Pour into large bowl. Beat egg whites with cream of tartar in mixer bowl until soft peaks form. Add ¼ cup sugar 1 tablespoonful at a time, beating well after each addition. Fold into cottage cheese mixture ¼ at a time. Pour into prepared pan. Bake for 50 minutes. Cool in pan for 15 minutes. Chill, covered, for 8 hours. Process ¾ cup strawberry halves and 1 tablespoon sugar in blender until smooth. Arrange remaining 2 cups strawberries over cheesecake. Drizzle with strawberry glaze. Yield: 14 servings.

Virginia Wade, Preceptor Beta Omicron
Smithfield, Virginia

IRISH CREAM MOCHA CHEESECAKE

1½ cups chocolate wafer crumbs	¼ cup chocolate syrup
2 tablespoons sugar	½ cup Irish Cream
⅓ cup melted butter or margarine	1 tablespoon instant coffee
16 ounces cream cheese, softened	1 teaspoon hot water
1 14-ounce can sweetened condensed milk	1 cup whipping cream, whipped
	12 dark chocolate-covered Irish Cream sticks

Combine crumbs and sugar in bowl; mix well. Add melted butter, stirring until well mixed. Press onto bottom and halfway up side of greased 9-inch springform pan. Chill in refrigerator. Combine cream cheese and condensed milk in bowl. Beat until smooth. Add chocolate syrup and liqueur; mix well. Mix instant coffee and hot water. Add to chocolate mixture; mix well. Fold in whipped cream. Pour over crumb mixture. Freeze, covered, for 6 hours. Decorate with Irish Cream sticks in spoke fashion. Yield: 12 servings.

Stephanie Wilson, Preceptor Alpha Alpha
St. Albert, Alberta, Canada

MANDARIN ORANGE CHEESECAKE

1¾ cups graham cracker crumbs	½ cup sugar
1 tablespoon sugar	1 teaspoon vanilla extract
½ teaspoon cinnamon	2 cups sour cream
½ cup melted butter or margarine	¼ cup sugar
16 ounces cream cheese, softened	1 10-ounce can mandarin oranges
2 eggs	¼ cup sugar
	1 tablespoon cornstarch

Preheat oven to 350 degrees. Combine crumbs, 1 tablespoon sugar and cinnamon in bowl; mix well. Stir in melted butter until well mixed. Press onto bottom and side of greased 8-inch springform pan. Bake for 5 minutes. Combine cream cheese and eggs in mixer bowl; beat well. Add ½ cup sugar and vanilla; mix well. Spoon over crumb crust. Bake for 30 minutes longer. Combine sour cream and ¼ cup sugar in bowl; mix well. Spread over cheesecake. Bake for 15 to 20 minutes longer. Cake should be firm to touch and side should pull away from pan. Cool in pan for several minutes. Remove pan side. Drain mandarin oranges, reserving ⅓ cup orange juice. Combine reserved orange juice, ¼ cup sugar and cornstarch in saucepan. Cook over medium heat until thick and clear, stirring constantly. Cool to room temperature. Decorate cooled cheesecake with mandarin oranges. Spread glaze over top. Chill for 6 hours. Yield: 8 to 10 servings.

Iris Sutherland, Xi Rho
Coldbrook, Nova Scotia, Canada

WHITE RUSSIAN BLACKBERRY CHEESECAKE

1/2 cup butter or margarine	1 cup sugar
2 tablespoons Kahlua	3 eggs
2 cups shortbread cookie crumbs	1 cup sour cream
	1/2 cup whipping cream
1 cup blackberries	1/4 cup Kahlua
1 to 2 tablespoons sugar	3 tablespoons vodka
2 to 3 tablespoons Minute tapioca	1/2 cup blackberry jelly
	1 tablespoon vodka
16 ounces cream cheese, softened	1 cup whipped topping
	3 tablespoons Kahlua

Preheat oven to 350 degrees. Heat butter in saucepan over medium heat until light brown, stirring constantly. Remove from heat. Stir in 2 tablespoons Kahlua. Add cookie crumbs; mix well. Press onto bottom and halfway up side of greased 10-inch springform pan. Spread blackberries over crumbs. Sprinkle with 1 to 2 tablespoons sugar and tapioca. Combine cream cheese and 1 cup sugar in mixer bowl; mix well. Add eggs 1 at a time, beating well after each addition. Add sour cream, whipping cream, 1/4 cup Kahlua and 3 tablespoons vodka; mix well. Pour over blackberries. Place shallow pan half full of hot water on lower rack of oven. Bake cheesecake for 1 hour to 1 hour and 15 minutes or until center is set. Chill for several hours to overnight. Remove side of pan. Bring blackberry jelly to a boil in saucepan, stirring frequently. Stir in 1 tablespoon vodka. Drizzle by teaspoonfuls over side of cheesecake. Pour remaining jelly mixture over top of cheesecake, spreading to edge. Chill until set. Garnish with mixture of whipped topping and 3 tablespoons Kahlua. Yield: 16 servings.

Karen Cross, Delta Iota
Mt. Shasta, California

CHERRY BERRY ON A CLOUD

6 egg whites	2 cups whipping cream, whipped
1/2 teaspoon cream of tartar	
	2 cups miniature marshmallows
1/4 teaspoon salt	
1 3/4 cups sugar	1 21-ounce can cherry pie filling
6 ounces cream cheese, softened	
	2 cups drained sliced strawberries
1 cup sugar	
1 teaspoon vanilla extract	1 teaspoon lemon juice

Preheat oven to 275 degrees. Beat egg whites with cream of tartar and salt in mixer bowl until foamy. Add 1 3/4 cups sugar 1 tablespoon at a time, beating well after each addition until stiff and glossy. Spread in greased 9-by-13-inch baking dish. Bake for 1 hour. Turn off oven. Let stand in closed oven for 12 hours. Combine cream cheese, 1 cup sugar and vanilla in mixer bowl; mix well. Fold whipped cream and marshmallows into cream cheese mixture. Spread over meringue. Chill for 12 hours or longer. Cut into servings. Combine pie filling, strawberries and lemon juice in bowl; mix well. Spoon over dessert. Yield: 15 to 24 servings.

Phyllis A. Case, Preceptor Beta Omicron
Paola, Kansas

CHERRY CREAM PUFF RING

This is great looking for the holidays. You can put decoration in center of ring.

1 cup water	2 4-ounce packages French vanilla instant pudding mix
1/2 cup butter or margarine	
	1/2 teaspoon vanilla extract
1 cup all-purpose flour	
4 eggs	
2 cups milk	1 21-ounce can cherry pie filling
2 cups sour cream	

Preheat oven to 400 degrees. Bring water and butter to a boil in 1-quart saucepan. Stir in flour. Cook for 1 minute or until mixture forms a ball, stirring vigorously. Remove from heat. Add eggs. Beat at low speed with electric mixer for 2 minutes or until smooth. Drop by tablespoonfuls onto greased baking sheet to form 8-inch ring. Smooth with spatula. Bake for 50 to 60 minutes or until puffed and golden brown. Cool in pan for several minutes. Invert onto wire rack to cool completely. Cut top off cream puff ring; remove any soft dough inside. Combine milk and sour cream in mixer bowl; mix well. Add pudding mix and vanilla; beat well. Place cream puff ring on serving plate. Fill with pudding mixture. Spoon half the pie filling over pudding. Replace top. Spoon remaining pie filling over all. Chill until serving time. Yield: 15 servings.

Gloria Walker, Xi Beta Zeta
Barnhart, Missouri

DOUGHNUT HOLE CUSTARD PUDDING

6 doughnut holes	1/4 teaspoon nutmeg
3 eggs	1 3/4 cups milk
1/3 cup sugar	1 teaspoon vanilla extract
1/4 teaspoon salt	

Preheat oven to 450 degrees. Cut doughnut holes into halves. Arrange in 1 1/2-quart baking dish. Combine eggs and sugar in mixer bowl; mix well. Add salt, nutmeg, milk and vanilla; beat well. Pour over doughnut holes. Bake for 20 minutes or until knife inserted near center comes out clean. Doughnut holes will rise to top while baking. Yield: 6 servings.

Deborah Wilson, Preceptor Delta Phi
Jefferson City, Missouri

CHERRY MASH ICE CREAM

4 eggs	2 tablespoons vanilla
1½ cups sugar	extract
2 cups whipping	1 12-ounce can
cream	evaporated milk
1 14-ounce can	8 Cherry Mash candy
sweetened condensed	bars
milk	Whole milk

Beat eggs in large mixer bowl until foamy. Add sugar gradually, beating until thickened. Add whipping cream, condensed milk, vanilla and evaporated milk; mix well. Heat candy bars in saucepan until soft. Add to milk mixture; mix well. Pour into ice cream freezer. Add whole milk to fill line. Freeze using manufacturer's instructions. Yield: 4 to 6 servings.

Missy McClure, Alpha Rho Delta
Olton, Texas

CHOCOLATE MALT ICE CREAM TORTE

1 cup finely crushed	½ gallon vanilla or
graham cracker crumbs	marble fudge ice
3 tablespoons sugar	cream
1 teaspoon cinnamon	½ cup malted milk
3 tablespoons melted	powder
butter or margarine,	4 ounces chocolate-
cooled	covered malted milk
2 tablespoons finely	balls, coarsely
grated semisweet	chopped
chocolate	

Combine crumbs, sugar and cinnamon in bowl; mix well. Stir in butter and chocolate until well mixed. Press onto bottom and halfway up side of greased springform pan. Let ice cream stand in bowl until soft but not melted. Add malted milk powder; beat until well blended. Spread over crumb mixture. Sprinkle with chopped malted milk balls, patting lightly into ice cream. Freeze, covered, for 4 hours or until firm. Loosen from side of pan with knife dipped in hot water. Remove pan ring. Cut into wedges. Yield: 10 to 12 servings.

Carlye Seitz, Beta Theta
Redmond, Oregon

OREO-CHERRY DELIGHT

36 Oreo cookies, crushed	1 to 2 21-ounce cans
½ cup butter or	cherry pie filling
margarine, softened	4 cups whipped topping
½ gallon vanilla ice	Chocolate syrup
cream	Chopped pecans

Combine cookie crumbs and butter in bowl; mix well. Press into 9-by-13-inch glass dish. Slice ice cream; arrange over crust. Layer pie filling and whipped topping over ice cream. Drizzle with chocolate syrup; sprinkle with pecans. Freeze, covered, until firm. Remove from freezer several minutes before serving. Yield: 8 to 10 servings.

Mary Ann Minton, Chi Preceptor
Hopkinsville, Kentucky

COFFEE BRANDY FREEZE

1 quart coffee-flavored	½ cup brandy
ice cream, softened	Shaved milk chocolate

Process ice cream and brandy in blender until blended. Spoon into goblets. Garnish with shaved chocolate. Serve at once. Yield: 4 servings.

Bev Sammut, Eta Upsilon
Bolton, Ontario, Canada

CRÈME BRÛLÉE AMANDINE

2 cups whipping cream	⅛ teaspoon salt
7 egg yolks	½ cup finely chopped
1 teaspoon vanilla	toasted blanched
extract	almonds
⅓ cup packed light	¾ cup packed light
brown sugar	brown sugar

Scald whipping cream in double boiler. Remove from heat. Beat egg yolks in mixer bowl until thick and lemony. Stir in vanilla, ⅓ cup brown sugar and salt. Add a small amount of hot cream to egg yolks. Stir egg yolks into hot cream. Cook over hot water to the consistency of mayonnaise, stirring constantly. Stir in almonds. Spoon into greased 8-inch round baking dish. Chill thoroughly. Sift remaining ¼ cup brown sugar over top to about ¼-inch thickness 2 hours before serving time. Place under preheated broiler for a few seconds or until brown sugar melts into an even glaze. Chill until serving time. Break through hard top crust with spoon to serve.
Yield: 4 to 6 servings.

Colette Iberg, Rho Chi
Pocahontas, Illinois

CHOCOLATE MOUSSE TORTE

2 cups chocolate wafer	12 ounces semisweet
crumbs	chocolate
½ cup melted unsalted	3 egg yolks
butter	3 tablespoons orange
1 cup whipping cream	liqueur

Combine crumbs and butter in bowl; mix well. Press onto bottom and side of greased 10-inch springform pan. Chill for 1 hour. Scald whipping cream in saucepan. Combine chocolate, egg yolks and liqueur in blender container. Process at medium speed while gradually adding hot whipping cream. Blend until smooth. Pour into prepared crust. Chill overnight. Yield: 12 servings.

Carol Ann Sweeney, Xi Delta Omega
Santa Rosa, California

DESSERT ROYALE

4 egg yolks	1/2 cup water
3/4 cup sugar	1/4 cup rum or Tia Maria
16 ounces cream cheese, softened	1 16-ounce package ladyfingers or vanilla wafers
4 egg whites	
1 teaspoon instant coffee	2 ounces semisweet chocolate, finely grated

Beat egg yolks in mixer bowl. Add sugar gradually, beating well after each addition. Add cream cheese; beat well. Beat egg whites in bowl until soft peaks form. Fold into cream cheese mixture. Mix coffee in water in bowl until dissolved. Add rum; mix well. Spread 1/4 of the cream cheese mixture in 12-cup glass bowl. Dip 1/3 of the ladyfingers into rum mixture to coat; arrange over cream cheese mixture. Sprinkle with 1/3 of the chocolate. Repeat until all ingredients are used ending with cream cheese mixture and chocolate. Chill for 6 hours to overnight. Yield: 8 to 10 servings.

Liz Cyr, Lambda
Kingston, Ontario, Canada

FRUIT PIZZA

1 2-layer package white cake mix	Assorted fruit for topping such as pineapple chunks and green or red grapes
8 ounces cream cheese, softened	
1 21-ounce can cherry pie filling	1 4-ounce package slivered almonds

Preheat oven to 350 degrees. Grease and flour pizza pan. Prepare cake mix using package directions. Pour batter onto pizza pan to depth of 1/4 inch. Bake for 10 minutes or until light brown. Cool. Spread cream cheese over crust. Separate cherries from pie filling. Spread pie filling over cream cheese layer. Arrange cherries and remaining fruit in circles over pie filling. Sprinkle with almonds. Chill until serving time. May also use banana slices, fresh strawberries, cherries, kiwi slices or blueberries as toppings. Yield: 12 servings.

Betty Jo Ellis, Xi Gamma Beta
Lumberton, Texas

ENGLISH TRIFLE PUNCH BOWL CAKE

1 angel food cake	1 10-ounce package frozen strawberries, thawed, drained
1 6-ounce package vanilla pudding and pie filling mix	
1 teaspoon almond extract	1 package strawberry glaze
1 8-ounce can crushed pineapple	1 16-ounce can juice-pack peach slices
1 8-ounce can pineapple chunks	12 ounces whipped topping
2 bananas, sliced	Pineapple chunks
	Strawberries

Tear angel food cake into bite-sized pieces. Cook pudding using package directions. Add almond extract; mix well. Drain pineapple juice into bowl. Add banana slices, stirring to coat. Layer half the angel food cake pieces, pineapple, strawberries, half the strawberry glaze, half the pudding, remaining cake, drained peaches, banana slices and remaining strawberry glaze into glass punch bowl. Cover with remaining pudding. Spread with whipped topping. Garnish with additional pineapple and strawberries. Chill until serving time. Yield: 15 to 20 servings.

Ann Herbert Floyd, Preceptor Phi
Franklin, Tennessee

GRAND MARNIER MOUSSE

6 egg whites	1 1/2 cups whipping cream
1/4 teaspoon cream of tartar	
1 1/2 cups sugar	1 teaspoon vanilla extract
4 drops of red and 12 drops of yellow food coloring	1/4 cup Grand Marnier
	Grated rind of 3 oranges
	Shaved chocolate

Beat egg whites with cream of tartar in mixer bowl until frothy. Add sugar gradually, beating until stiff but not dry. Combine food colorings, whipping cream and vanilla in large bowl; beat until thickened. Fold in liqueur, orange rind and beaten egg whites. Spoon into glass bowl. Freeze, covered with plastic wrap, overnight. Remove from freezer 20 minutes before serving. Garnish with shaved chocolate. Yield: 8 servings.

Patti Ann Zaharis, Xi Alpha
Beaconsfield, Quebec, Canada

LEMON MOUSSE

3/4 to 1 cup sugar	2 tablespoons orange liqueur
1 envelope unflavored gelatin	
1 1/2 teaspoons cornstarch	1 1/2 cups whipping cream, whipped
2 teaspoons finely shredded lemon rind	6 egg whites, stiffly beaten
1 cup lemon juice	Lemon slices
4 egg yolks, beaten	Almond slivers

Combine first 6 ingredients in saucepan; mix well. Cook until thickened and bubbly, stirring constantly. Remove from heat. Cover surface with plastic wrap. Cool to room temperature. Chill in refrigerator. Process chilled lemon mixture and liqueur in blender until smooth. Pour into large bowl. Fold in whipped cream and egg whites. Spoon into serving bowl. Chill, covered, for 4 hours to overnight. Garnish with lemon slices and almonds. Yield: 12 to 16 servings.

Anne Bluemel, Beta Alpha
Kemmerer, Wyoming

MARSHMALLOW ICEBOX CAKE

2 cups milk
1/4 cup sugar
3 egg yolks
1 tablespoon
   all-purpose flour
1 3-ounce package
   lemon gelatin
3 egg whites, stiffly
   beaten
1 cup whipping cream,
   whipped

1 1-pound package
   miniature
   marshmallows
1 cup finely chopped
   pecans
1 13-ounce jar
   maraschino cherries,
   drained
1 1-pound package
   vanilla wafers,
   crushed

Combine milk, sugar, egg yolks and flour in saucepan; mix well. Bring to a boil, stirring constantly. Stir in gelatin. Cool. Fold in next 5 ingredients. Alternate layers of cookie crumbs and marshmallow mixture in tube pan. Chill for 6 to 12 hours. Unmold onto serving plate. Yield: 20 to 25 servings.

Jacqueline S. Tramel, Xi Alpha Delta
Knoxville, Tennessee

MINCEMEAT AND VANILLA ICE CREAM TORTE

1 cup sliced almonds
3 tablespoons melted
   butter or margarine
1 1/4 cups vanilla wafer
   crumbs

5 pints vanilla ice cream
1 28-ounce jar
   mincemeat

Preheat oven to 375 degrees. Spread almonds in 10-by-15-inch baking pan. Bake for 5 minutes or until light brown, stirring several times. Cool to room temperature. Mix butter and vanilla wafer crumbs in bowl. Press onto bottom and side of greased 9-inch springform pan. Chill in freezer for 30 minutes or until firm. Soften ice cream in refrigerator for 30 minutes. Combine ice cream and mincemeat in bowl; mix well. Spoon over prepared crust. Sprinkle with toasted almonds. Freeze, covered, until firm. Loosen from side of pan with knife dipped in hot water. Remove side of springform pan. Let stand at room temperature for 10 minutes. Yield: 16 servings.

Colette Carrothers, Laureate Alpha Rho
Oakville, Ontario, Canada

MOCHA RIPPLE BARS

1 1/2 cups chocolate
   cookie crumbs
1 1/2 teaspoons instant
   coffee
1/2 cup melted butter or
   margarine
1 1/4 teaspoons
   unflavored gelatin
1/2 cup water
1/2 cup sugar

1/2 cup whipping cream
8 ounces cream cheese,
   softened
1/2 cup sugar
1 1/2 teaspoons vanilla
   extract
1 cup whipping cream
1/4 cup baking cocoa
1 tablespoon instant
   coffee

Combine cookie crumbs and 1 1/2 teaspoons instant coffee in bowl; mix well. Stir in melted butter until well mixed. Press into 7-by-10-inch dish. Chill in refrigerator. Soften gelatin in water in saucepan. Heat until gelatin dissolves, stirring constantly. Add 1/2 cup sugar and 1/2 cup cream; mix well. Combine cream cheese, remaining 1/2 cup sugar and vanilla in bowl; mix well. Add gelatin mixture; mix well. Whip remaining 1 cup cream until thickened. Fold into cream cheese mixture. Place 1/3 of the mixture in small bowl. Add cocoa and remaining 1 tablespoon instant coffee; mix well. Alternate layers of cream cheese mixture and mocha cream cheese mixture onto prepared cookie crumb crust. Stir layers with knife to marbleize. Chill for 8 hours to overnight. Yield: 8 to 10 servings.

Shirley Melnychuk, Alpha Upsilon
Esterhazy, Saskatchewan, Canada

BROILED PEACHES FLAMBÉ

8 peach halves
1/2 cup packed light
   brown sugar
8 dots of butter or
   margarine

1/2 cup brandy
Ice cream

Arrange peach halves cut side up in oven-proof dish. Place 1 tablespoon brown sugar and 1 dot of butter in center of each. Preheat boiler. Broil 3 inches from heat source until sugar melts and peaches are heated through. Heat brandy in saucepan. Spoon ice cream into serving dishes. Pour hot brandy over peaches; ignite. Spoon over ice cream. Serve immediately. Yield: 8 servings.

Wendy Pelech, Xi Delta Upsilon
Golden, British Columbia, Canada

SMASHING MYSTERY DESSERT

2 cups packed light
   brown sugar
2 eggs
2/3 cup all-purpose flour
1 teaspoon soda

1 cup chopped pecans
1 cup miniature
   chocolate chips
2 cups whipping cream
2 tablespoons brandy

Preheat oven to 350 degrees. Combine brown sugar and eggs in mixer bowl; beat well. Add mixture of flour and soda; mix well. Stir in pecans and chocolate chips. Spoon into lightly greased 9-by-13-inch baking dish. Bake for 25 minutes. Cool for 2 hours. Whip cream in bowl until soft peaks form. Fold in brandy. Break cake into bite-sized pieces. Stir into whipped cream mixture. Spoon into 9-by-13-inch dish. Freeze for 4 hours to overnight or until firm. Yield: 8 to 10 servings.

Cindy Warrick, Zeta Kappa
Topeka, Kansas

PASADENA PEACH DELIGHT

1 10-count package ladyfingers	1 cup whipping cream
Peach brandy	1 tablespoon sugar
2 10-ounce packages frozen sliced peaches, partially thawed	4 to 5 drops of vanilla or almond extract
	1 cup toasted almonds

Split ladyfingers into halves lengthwise. Layer in freezer dish. Sprinkle with brandy. Add peach slices. Whip cream in mixer bowl until soft peaks form. Add sugar and flavoring; beat until thick. Spread over peaches. Sprinkle with almonds. Freeze, covered with waxed paper, for 6 hours. Cut into pieces. Yield: 6 servings.

Marie Crosby, Preceptor Chi
Fanwood, New Jersey

PEANUT BUSTER PARFAIT

1½ cups sweetened condensed milk	1 16-ounce package Oreo cookies, crushed
2 cups confectioners' sugar	½ cup butter or margarine, softened
⅔ cup chocolate chips	2 cups Spanish peanuts
½ cup butter or margarine	½ gallon vanilla ice cream, softened

Combine condensed milk and confectioners' sugar in saucepan; mix well. Add chocolate chips and ½ cup butter. Simmer for 8 minutes, stirring constantly. Cool to room temperature. Combine cookie crumbs and remaining ½ cup butter in bowl; mix well. Press into 9-by-13-inch dish. Sprinkle with peanuts. Spread softened ice cream over cookie crust. Drizzle with chocolate mixture. Freeze until firm. Yield: 12 servings.

Doris White, Epsilon Iota
Memphis, Missouri

FRESH PEARS IN WINE

6 small fresh pears	2 tablespoons lemon juice
1 cup Sauterne	
1 cup sugar	Sour cream
½ cup water	Cheese
1 teaspoon ginger (optional)	

Peel pears, leaving pears whole with stems. Place upright in slow cooker. Combine wine, sugar, water, ginger and lemon juice in bowl; mix well. Pour over pears. Cook, covered, in slow cooker for 4 to 6 hours or until tender. Serve warm. Garnish with sour cream and cheese. Yield: 6 servings.

Nancy Carlson, Eta Eta
Sandspit, British Columbia, Canada

FROZEN RASPBERRY DESSERT

½ cup margarine	1 10-ounce package frozen raspberries, partially thawed
1 cup all-purpose flour	
½ cup packed light brown sugar	16 ounces whipped topping
3 egg whites	
½ cup sugar	
2 tablespoons lemon juice	

Preheat oven to 350 degrees. Cut margarine into flour in bowl until crumbly. Add brown sugar; mix well. Spread in 9-by-13-inch baking dish. Bake for 5 minutes. Stir well. Bake for 5 minutes longer. Remove and reserve half the crumbs. Press down remaining crumbs in baking dish. Beat egg whites until soft peaks form. Add sugar gradually, beating until stiff peaks form. Fold in lemon juice and raspberries. Fold in whipped topping. Spread over crust. Sprinkle with reserved crumbs. Freeze, covered, until firm. May substitute strawberries or blueberries for raspberries. Yield: 12 to 15 servings.

Alberta Crary, Beta Master
Deadwood, South Dakota

RASPBERRY SWIRL

⅓ cup melted butter or margarine	1 cup sour cream
1 7-ounce package coconut, toasted	1 cup whipping cream, whipped
1 envelope unflavored gelatin	1 10-ounce package frozen raspberries in syrup, thawed
¼ cup water	4 teaspoons cornstarch
1 14-ounce can sweetened condensed milk	

Combine butter and coconut in bowl; mix well. Press onto bottom and side of greased 8-inch springform pan. Chill in refrigerator. Sprinkle gelatin into water in saucepan. Let stand for 1 minute. Cook over low heat until gelatin is dissolved, stirring constantly. Combine condensed milk, sour cream and gelatin in mixer bowl; mix well. Fold in whipped cream. Chill, covered, for 30 minutes or until partially set. Purée raspberries in blender. Combine raspberries and cornstarch in saucepan; mix well. Cook until thick and glossy, stirring constantly. Cool to room temperature. Layer gelatin mixture and raspberries ½ at a time over coconut crust. Swirl gently with knife. Chill for 4 hours or until set. Remove side of springform pan. Yield: 8 to 10 servings.

Dawn D. Walker, Xi Lambda
Clarksburg, West Virginia

SNOWBALL CAKE

2 envelopes unflavored gelatin	1½ cups sugar
¼ cup cold water	16 ounces whipped topping
1 cup boiling water	1 angel food cake, torn into pieces
3 cups sliced fresh strawberries	1 7-ounce can coconut

Soften gelatin in cold water in bowl. Add boiling water, stirring until dissolved. Stir in strawberries and sugar. Chill for 1 hour. Fold in 1 cup whipped topping. Spoon cake in 9-by-13-inch dish. Spoon gelatin mixture over cake; top with remaining whipped topping. Sprinkle with coconut.
Yield: 12 servings.

Jane C. Newman, Epsilon Psi
Martinsville, Virginia

STRAWBERRY-LEMON BAVARIAN CAKE

½ cup unsalted butter or margarine, softened	2 tablespoons water
¼ cup sugar	¾ cup strained lemon juice
½ teaspoon vanilla extract	1 cup sugar
1 cup all-purpose flour	2 tablespoons orange liqueur
½ teaspoon baking powder	2 cups whipping cream, chilled
¼ teaspoon salt	1½ pints strawberries, chopped
2 envelopes unflavored gelatin	

Preheat oven to 350 degrees. Cream butter and ¼ cup sugar in mixer bowl until light and fluffy. Add vanilla. Add mixture of flour, baking powder and salt; mix well. Pour into greased 10-inch springform pan. Bake for 20 minutes or until golden brown. Cool in pan. Chill for 15 minutes. Soften gelatin in water. Combine lemon juice, remaining 1 cup sugar, liqueur and gelatin in saucepan; mix well. Cook over medium heat until gelatin and sugar are dissolved, stirring constantly. Set pan in large bowl of cold water. Stir just until cool. Pour whipping cream into chilled mixer bowl. Beat until soft peaks form. Add lemon gelatin mixture, beating just until mixed. Fold in strawberries. Spoon over crust. Chill, covered, for 4 hours or until set. Yield: 10 to 12 servings.

Jan Perigard, Xi Chi
Waterbury, Connecticut

Willie Treichler, Laureate Mu, Mesa, Arizona, makes Sherbet Dessert by rolling 1 package Mother's Macaroon Cookies into fine crumbs. Reserving a small amount of crumbs for topping, place in 9-by-12-inch glass dish. Fold 16 ounces whipped topping gently into ½ gallon softened rainbow sherbet. Spoon into prepared dish; top with reserved crumbs. Freeze until fiirm. Cut into squares.

TACO COOKIES WITH FRESH FRUIT

⅔ cup sugar	3 cups assorted chopped fresh fruit
½ cup melted butter or margarine	2 tablespoons sugar
2 tablespoons water	1 cup whipping cream, whipped
2 eggs	18 ounces semisweet chocolate
½ teaspoon vanilla extract	¼ cup butter or margarine
⅓ cup all-purpose flour	¼ cup milk
⅓ cup baking cocoa	

Preheat oven to 325 degrees. Grease and flour 3 large cookie sheets. Cover spines of two ⅝-inch thick books with foil. Stand books, foil side up, between 2 books. Combine ⅔ cup sugar, melted butter, water, eggs and vanilla in mixer bowl; beat until smooth. Add flour and cocoa gradually; beat well. Drop 2 tablespoonfuls batter for each taco onto prepared cookie sheets. Spread into 4-inch circle. Bake for 15 minutes. Remove from cookie sheet immediately. Drape 2 tacos over each book, pressing gently to fold. Let stand until cool. Combine fruit and 2 tablespoons sugar in bowl; mix well. Fill each cooled taco with whipped cream and ¼ cup fruit. Break chocolate into pieces. Combine chocolate, ¼ cup butter and milk in saucepan. Cook over low heat until chocolate is melted, stirring constantly until smooth. Spoon over filled tacos. Yield: 10 servings.

Patricia Dewey, Xi Gamma Tau
Nacogdoches, Texas

ANGEL FOOD SWISS CAKE ROLLS

1 package angel food cake mix	½ cup grated chocolate chips
3 tablespoons baking cocoa	1 tablespoon butter or margarine, softened
Confectioners' sugar	⅓ cup chocolate chips
8 ounces whipped topping	

Preheat oven to 350 degrees. Line two 10-by-15-inch baking pans with foil. Prepare cake mix using package directions, adding cocoa. Spread evenly in prepared pans; cut through batter to release air bubbles. Bake for 15 minutes or until cakes test done. Invert onto towels sprinkled with confectioners' sugar. Roll up in towels. Cool in refrigerator. Unroll cakes. Spread with mixture of whipped topping and grated chocolate. Reroll cakes to enclose filling. Place seam side down on serving plates. Combine butter and chocolate chips in airtight plastic bag. Place in warm water until melted, squeezing gently to mix well. Cut off corner of bag. Drizzle chocolate over rolls. Cut into slices. Yield: 20 servings.

Dodie Grachek, Gamma
Omaha, Nebraska

LEMON ANGEL CAKE

1 package 2-step angel food cake mix	3 eggs
1 cup water	2/3 teaspoon grated lemon rind
3/4 cup canola oil	2 tablespoons fresh lemon juice
1/4 cup all-purpose flour	Confectioners' sugar
1/2 teaspoon vanilla extract	

Place oven rack in lowest position. Preheat oven to 375 degrees. Beat egg whites package from cake mix according to package directions, using 1 cup water. Combine dry ingredients package from cake mix with oil, flour, vanilla, eggs and lemon rind in mixer bowl. Beat at low speed for 30 seconds or until blended. Beat for 2 minutes. Fold gently into egg whites. Spoon into ungreased 10-inch tube pan. Bake for 40 to 50 minutes or until cake tests done. Invert onto cake plate. Blend lemon juice with enough confectioners' sugar in bowl to make of glaze consistency. Drizzle over cake. Yield: 16 servings.

Shirley B. Griffin, Laureate Mu
Crawley, Louisiana

APPLE SPICE CUSTARD CAKE

1 2-layer package spice cake mix	1 14-ounce can sweetened condensed milk
2 medium apples, peeled, finely chopped	1/4 cup lemon juice
8 ounces sour cream, at room temperature	Cinnamon to taste

Preheat oven to 350 degrees. Prepare cake mix using package directions, adding apples. Spoon into greased and floured 9-by-13-inch cake pan. Bake for 30 minutes or until wooden pick inserted in center comes out clean. Combine sour cream, condensed milk and lemon juice in bowl; mix well. Spread over cake. Bake for 10 minutes or until topping is set. Sprinkle with cinnamon. Cool on wire rack. Store in refrigerator. Yield: 15 servings.

Mary Braly, Preceptor Beta Kappa
Fort Worth, Texas

APPLE HARVEST TORTE

4 cups chopped unpeeled apples	1 tablespoon melted butter or margarine
1 cup sugar	1 teaspoon vanilla extract
1/2 cup all-purpose flour	1/2 cup chopped walnuts
2 teaspoons baking powder	1/2 cup chopped dates
1 egg, beaten	

Preheat oven to 400 degrees. Combine apples, sugar, flour, baking powder, egg, butter, vanilla, walnuts and dates in bowl; mix well. Spoon into greased and floured 8-by-8-inch cake pan. Bake for 40 minutes. Serve warm with vanilla ice cream. Yield: 9 servings.

Sharon Fick, Mu Pi
Fort Wayne, Indiana

APRICOT CAKE

1 2-layer package orange cake mix	1/4 cup apricot brandy
1 4-ounce package vanilla instant pudding mix	1 cup confectioners' sugar
1/2 cup vegetable oil	2 tablespoons apricot nectar
4 eggs	2 tablespoons vodka
1/4 cup apricot nectar	2 tablespoons apricot brandy
1/4 cup vodka	

Preheat oven to 350 degrees. Combine cake mix, pudding mix, oil, eggs, 1/4 cup apricot nectar, 1/4 cup vodka and 1/4 cup apricot brandy in mixer bowl. Beat for 4 minutes. Spoon into greased and lightly floured 12-cup bundt pan. Bake for 45 to 50 minutes or until cake tests done. Cool in pan for 15 minutes. Invert onto serving plate. Combine confectioners' sugar, 2 tablespoons apricot nectar, 2 tablespoons vodka and 2 tablespoons apricot brandy in saucepan. Heat until confectioners' sugar dissolves, stirring to mix well. Pour over warm or cooled cake. Yield: 16 servings.

Debbie Baley, Delta Kappa Gamma
Malin, Oregon

BLACK WALNUT CAKE WITH LEMON CREAM CHEESE FROSTING

2 cups unsalted butter or margarine, softened	5 eggs
2 cups sugar	1 1/2 cups chopped black walnuts
1 1/2 cups sifted all-purpose flour	16 ounces cream cheese, softened
1/2 cup whole wheat flour	2 tablespoons lemon juice
1 tablespoon vanilla extract	Grated rind of 1 lemon
	4 cups confectioners' sugar

Preheat oven to 330 degrees. Cream butter in large mixer bowl until light and fluffy. Add sugar, beating until smooth. Add all-purpose and whole wheat flours; beat until smooth. Add vanilla. Beat in eggs 1 at a time. Fold in walnuts. Spoon into 3 greased and floured 9-inch cake pans. Bake for 20 minutes. Cool in pans for 10 minutes. Remove to wire rack to cool completely. Combine cream cheese, lemon juice and lemon rind in large mixer bowl; beat until smooth. Add confectioners' sugar; mix well. Spread between layers and over top and side of cake. Yield: 16 to 20 servings.

Denise L. Shibley, Omega Kappa
Holt, Missouri

LEMON BLUEBERRY BRUNCH CAKE

1   2-layer package
    lemon cake mix
1/4 cup butter or
    margarine, softened
3 ounces cream cheese,
    softened
1/3 cup water
2 eggs
1   21-ounce can
    blueberry pie filling

1/2 cup finely chopped
    almonds or pecans
1/2 cup confectioners'
    sugar
1 tablespoon butter
    or margarine, softened
2 to 3 teaspoons milk
1/4 teaspoon lemon
    extract

Preheat oven to 350 degrees. Combine cake mix, 1/4 cup butter and cream cheese in mixer bowl. Beat at low speed until mixture resembles fine crumbs. Reserve 1 cup for topping. Add water and eggs to remaining crumb mixture. Beat at high speed for 2 minutes. Pour into greased and floured 9-by-13-inch cake pan. Spoon pie filling over top, spreading gently to cover batter. Mix reserved crumbs with almonds in bowl. Sprinkle over pie filling. Bake for 35 to 45 minutes or until cake tests done. Blend confectioners' sugar, 1 tablespoon butter, milk and lemon extract in bowl. Drizzle over warm cake. Serve warm or cool. Store in refrigerator. Yield: 12 servings.

Vera MacGillivray, Beta Delta
Clinton, Illinois

PALMER HOUSE CARROT CAKE

2 cups all-purpose flour
2 cups sugar
2 teaspoons soda
1 tablespoon cinnamon
Allspice to taste
Salt to taste
4 eggs
1 cup vegetable oil
4 cups finely shredded
    carrots

1/2 cup apricot preserves
8 ounces cream cheese,
    softened
1/3 cup unsalted butter
    or margarine,
    softened
1/2 teaspoon vanilla
    extract
3 cups (about) sifted
    confectioners' sugar

Preheat oven to 350 degrees. Sift flour, sugar, soda, cinnamon, allspice and salt together. Beat eggs in mixer bowl until light and foamy. Add oil very gradually, beating constantly at medium speed. Add dry ingredients; mix until smooth. Stir in carrots. Spoon into 3 greased and floured 8-inch cake pans. Bake for 20 to 25 minutes or until layers test done. Cool in pans for 10 minutes. Remove to wire rack to cool completely. Spread apricot preserves between layers. Beat cream cheese, butter and vanilla in mixer bowl until light and fluffy. Add enough confectioners' sugar to make of spreading consistency. Spread over top and side of cake. Store, covered, in refrigerator. Yield: 16 servings.

 Nancy L. Harris, Preceptor Beta Gamma
Fort Wayne, Indiana

CARROT AND PINEAPPLE CHEER CAKE

3 eggs
2 cups sugar
1 1/2 cups vegetable oil
1 cup grated carrots
2 cups drained crushed
    pineapple
1 cup coconut
1 cup chopped pecans
2 1/2 cups all-purpose
    flour
2 teaspoons soda
2 teaspoons cinnamon

1 teaspoon salt
2 teaspoons vanilla
    extract
1/2 cup margarine,
    softened
8 ounces cream cheese,
    softened
1   1-pound package
    confectioners' sugar
1 teaspoon vanilla
    extract
1 cup chopped pecans

Preheat oven to 350 degrees. Combine eggs, sugar and oil in saucepan. Cook until sugar dissolves, stirring constantly; do not boil. Combine with carrots, pineapple, coconut and pecans in bowl; mix well. Add flour, soda, cinnamon, salt and 2 teaspoons vanilla; mix well. Spoon into greased and floured bundt pan. Bake for 30 to 40 minutes or until cake tests done. Cool on wire rack. Invert onto serving plate. Cream margarine and cream cheese in large mixer bowl until light and fluffy. Add confectioners' sugar and remaining 1 teaspoon vanilla; mix well. Mix in pecans. Spread over cooled cake. Yield: 16 servings.

Rhonda E. Boales, Alpha Xi
Casa Grande, Arizona

BIENENSTICH (Bee Sting Cake)

4 eggs
2 cups sugar
2 cups all-purpose flour
2 teaspoons baking
    powder
1/2 teaspoon salt
1 cup milk
2 tablespoons margarine
1/2 cup packed light
    brown sugar

1/4 cup margarine
6 tablespoons whipping
    cream
3/4 cup coconut
3/4 cup sliced almonds
1 1/2 cups whipping
    cream
1/4 cup sugar
3 tablespoons vanilla
    instant pudding mix

Preheat oven to 400 degrees. Beat eggs and 2 cups sugar in mixer bowl until foamy. Add flour, baking powder and salt; mix well. Heat milk and 2 tablespoons margarine in saucepan until margarine melts. Add to batter; mix well. Spoon into greased 9-by-13-inch cake pan. Bake for 20 minutes. Combine brown sugar, 1/4 cup margarine and 6 tablespoons whipping cream in saucepan. Cook until bubbly, stirring constantly. Stir in coconut and almonds. Spread over hot cake. Broil until golden brown. Chill in refrigerator. Whip remaining 1 1/2 cups whipping cream in mixer bowl until soft peaks form. Add 1/4 cup sugar and pudding mix; mix well. Cut cake into halves lengthwise. Spread whipped cream mixture between halves of cake. Yield: 12 servings.

Pauline McLean, Beta Mu
Abbotsford, British Columbia, Canada

BLACKBERRY WINE CAKE

1 2-layer package yellow cake mix	1 cup blackberry wine
1 3-ounce package blackberry gelatin	1 cup confectioners' sugar
1/2 cup vegetable oil	1 teaspoon vegetable oil
4 eggs	1/4 cup (or more) blackberry wine

Preheat oven to 350 degrees. Combine cake mix, gelatin, 1/2 cup oil, eggs and 1 cup wine in mixer bowl. Beat at medium speed for 2 minutes, scraping bowl after 1 minute. Spoon into greased and floured tube or bundt pan. Bake for 45 minutes. Combine confectioners' sugar, remaining 1 teaspoon oil and 1/4 cup wine in bowl; mix well. Pour over hot cake. Cool cake in pan on wire rack. Remove to serving plate. Yield: 16 servings.

Debbie Beahm, Preceptor Rho
Haughton, Louisiana

BLACK FOREST CAKE

This recipe won First Place for desserts in a local baking contest.

2 egg whites	1 cup milk
1/2 cup sugar	2 egg yolks
1 3/4 cups all-purpose flour	2 ounces unsweetened chocolate, melted
1 cup sugar	Cream Center Filling
3/4 teaspoon soda	1 21-ounce can cherry pie filling
1 teaspoon salt	Chocolate curls
1/3 cup vegetable oil	

Preheat oven to 350 degrees. Beat egg whites in mixer bowl until soft peaks form. Add 1/2 cup sugar gradually, beating until stiff peaks form. Sift flour, 1 cup sugar, soda and salt into bowl. Add oil and half the milk; beat for 1 minute. Add remaining milk, egg yolks and melted chocolate. Beat for 1 minute longer. Fold in egg whites. Spoon into 2 greased and floured 9-inch cake pans. Bake for 30 to 35 minutes or until layers test done. Cool in pans for 10 minutes. Remove to wire rack to cool completely. Split each layer into halves horizontally. Alternate Cream Center Filling and cherry pie filling between layers of cake. Top with remaining Cream Center Filling and/or pie filling. Garnish with chocolate curls. Yield: 16 servings.

CREAM CENTER FILLING

1/4 cup margarine, softened	1/2 cup sugar
1/2 cup shortening	1/2 cup milk
1 teaspoon vanilla extract	2 tablespoons all-purpose flour

Combine margarine, shortening, vanilla and sugar in mixer bowl; beat for 4 minutes. Blend milk and flour in saucepan. Cook until thickened, stirring constantly. Add to margarine mixture; beat for 4 minutes longer. Yield: 1 1/2 cups.

Shelly Lindahl, Xi Zeta Upsilon
Platte City, Missouri

CHERRY RICOTTA LOVE CAKE

1 2-layer package yellow cake mix	1 teaspoon vanilla extract
Skim milk	1 4-ounce package vanilla instant pudding mix
1 21-ounce can cherry pie filling	
1 teaspoon vanilla extract	1 cup milk
2 pounds ricotta cheese	8 ounces whipped topping
4 eggs	Cherries
1 cup sugar	

Preheat oven to 350 degrees. Prepare cake mix using package directions, substituting skim milk for water and adding half the pie filling and 1 teaspoon vanilla. Spoon into greased 9-by-13-inch cake pan. Combine cheese, eggs, sugar and 1 teaspoon vanilla in bowl; mix until smooth. Spoon evenly over cake batter. Bake for 1 hour and 10 minutes or until golden brown. Cool in pan for 10 minutes. Invert onto platter. Let stand for 1 hour. Combine pudding mix and milk in mixer bowl. Beat at low speed for 1 minute or until thickened. Fold in remaining pie filling and whipped topping. Spread over top and sides of cake. Garnish with additional cherries. Store in refrigerator. Yield: 20 servings.

Pauline B. Romano, Laureate Pi
Rome, New York

ALMOND JOY CAKE

1 2-layer package chocolate cake mix	1/2 cup margarine
26 large marshmallows	1 1/2 cups sugar
1 cup evaporated milk	1/2 cup evaporated milk
1 cup sugar	6 ounces semisweet chocolate chips
14 ounces coconut	1 cup sliced almonds

Preheat oven to 350 degrees. Prepare and bake cake mix using package directions for 10-by-15-inch cake pan. Combine marshmallows, 1 cup evaporated milk and 1 cup sugar in saucepan. Heat until marshmallows melt, stirring to mix well. Stir in coconut. Pour over hot cake. Bring margarine, remaining 1 1/2 cups sugar and 1/2 cup evaporated milk to a boil in saucepan, stirring to mix well. Remove from heat. Stir in chocolate chips until melted. Stir in almonds. Pour over top. Let stand until cool. Yield: 12 to 16 servings.

Denise Kammlah, Xi Omega Psi
Waco, Texas

CHOCOLATE-CREAM CHEESE CAKE

3 cups all-purpose flour	2/3 cup vegetable oil
2 cups sugar	2 teaspoons vanilla
3/4 cup baking cocoa	extract
2 teaspoons soda	8 ounces cream cheese,
1 teaspoon salt	softened
2 cups water	1/4 cup sugar
2 tablespoons white	1 egg
vinegar	6 ounces chocolate chips

Preheat oven to 350 degrees. Mix flour, 2 cups sugar, cocoa, soda and salt in bowl. Add water, vinegar, oil and vanilla; mix well. Spoon into well greased 9-by-13-inch cake pan. Combine cream cheese and remaining 1/4 cup sugar in mixer bowl; beat until smooth. Add egg; mix well. Drop by spoonfuls over batter. Sprinkle with chocolate chips. Bake for 25 to 30 minutes or until cake tests done. Cool on wire rack. May omit cream cheese mixture and just sprinkle with chocolate chips.
Yield: 15 to 20 servings.

Debbie Ford, Xi Gamma Pi
Paso Robles, California

EARTHQUAKE CAKE

1 cup chopped pecans	1/2 cup margarine,
1 cup coconut	softened
1 2-layer package	1 1-pound package
German chocolate	confectioners' sugar
cake mix	1 teaspoon vanilla
8 ounces cream cheese,	extract
softened	

Preheat oven to 350 degrees. Spread mixture of pecans and coconut in greased 10-by-14-inch glass cake pan. Prepare cake mix using package directions. Pour into prepared pan. Combine cream cheese, margarine, confectioners' sugar and vanilla in bowl; mix well. Spoon over cake batter. Bake for 45 to 50 minutes or just until cake tests done; do not overbake. Cool on wire rack. Yield: 15 servings.

Marty Tharp, Preceptor Beta Sigma
Yukon, Oklahoma

MACADAMIA FUDGE CAKE

1 cup all-purpose flour	1/2 teaspoon baking
3/4 cup sugar	powder
1 cup sour cream	1 egg
1/2 cup butter or	1/2 teaspoon vanilla
margarine, softened	extract
1/4 cup baking cocoa	1/4 teaspoon salt
1 1/2 teaspoons instant	Macadamia Fudge
coffee	Frosting
1/2 teaspoon soda	

Preheat oven to 350 degrees. Line greased 9-inch round cake pan with greased waxed paper. Combine flour, sugar, sour cream, butter, cocoa, coffee powder, soda, baking powder, egg, vanilla and salt in mixer bowl; mix until smooth. Spoon into prepared pan. Bake for 30 to 35 minutes or until cake tests done. Cool in pan for 10 minutes. Remove to wire rack to cool completely. Place on serving plate. Pour Macadamia Fudge Frosting over cake. Chill until frosting is firm. Yield: 12 servings.

MACADAMIA FUDGE FROSTING

1 cup whipping cream	4 ounces sweet
1/2 cup sugar	chocolate
2 tablespoons butter or	1 teaspoon vanilla
margarine	extract
1 tablespoon light corn	7 ounces chopped
syrup	macadamia nuts

Combine whipping cream, sugar, butter, corn syrup and chocolate in saucepan. Bring to a boil, stirring constantly. Cook for 5 minutes, stirring constantly. Remove from heat. Stir in vanilla. Cool for 10 minutes. Stir in macadamia nuts. Yield: 2 cups.

Leslie Comis, Rho
Lacombe, Alberta, Canada

CRANBERRY UPSIDE-DOWN CAKE

2/3 cup sugar	1 tablespoon baking
4 cups fresh cranberries	powder
2/3 cup sugar	1 teaspoon salt
5 egg yolks	7 egg whites, at room
1 1/2 cups sugar	temperature
3/4 cup water	1/2 teaspoon cream of
1/2 cup vegetable oil	tartar
2 teaspoons grated	2 cups whipping cream
lemon rind	2 tablespoons
2 teaspoons vanilla	confectioners' sugar
extract	2 teaspoons cream
2 cups all-purpose flour	sherry

Preheat oven to 350 degrees. Sprinkle 1/3 cup sugar in each of 2 greased 8-inch square cake pans. Spread cranberries in prepared pans. Sprinkle 1/3 cup sugar over cranberries in each pan. Bake, covered with foil, for 30 minutes. Cool, uncovered, on wire rack. Combine egg yolks, 1 1/2 cups sugar, water, oil, lemon rind and vanilla in mixer bowl; mix well. Stir in mixture of flour, baking powder and salt. Beat egg whites with cream of tartar in mixer bowl until soft peaks form. Fold into batter. Spoon over cranberries. Bake for 35 to 40 minutes or until layers test done. Cool in pans for 5 minutes. Invert onto wire rack to cool completely. Combine whipping cream, confectioners' sugar and sherry in mixer bowl. Beat until soft peaks form. Spread between layers of cake; spread or pipe around sides of cake.
Yield: 20 servings.

Ruth Corley, Preceptor Beta Phi
College Station, Texas

GARDEN EGGPLANT PUDDING CAKE

1 2-layer package pudding-recipe yellow cake mix	1/4 cup vegetable oil
	2 cups grated peeled eggplant
1 4-ounce package vanilla instant pudding mix	1/2 teaspoon nutmeg
	1/4 teaspoon cinnamon
	1/8 teaspoon cloves
4 eggs	1/8 teaspoon salt
1/2 cup sour cream	Confectioners' sugar

Preheat oven to 350 degrees. Combine cake mix, pudding mix, eggs, sour cream, oil, eggplant, nutmeg, cinnamon, cloves and salt in large mixer bowl; mix until moistened. Beat at medium speed for 4 minutes. Spoon into greased and floured 10-inch bundt pan. Bake for 50 to 55 minutes or until cake tests done; do not underbake. Cool in pan for 15 minutes. Invert onto serving plate. Sprinkle with confectioners' sugar. Yield: 12 servings.

Glynda Endsley, Xi Delta Delta
Kearney, Missouri

MAMA'S HONEY CAKE

3 eggs	1 teaspoon each baking powder, soda and cinnamon
1 cup sugar	
1 cup vegetable oil	
1 cup honey	1 cup raisins
1 cup cold black coffee	1/2 cup chopped walnuts
3 cups all-purpose flour	Confectioners' sugar

Preheat oven to 375 degrees. Beat eggs and sugar in mixer bowl until thick and lemon-colored. Add oil, honey and coffee; mix well. Add flour, baking powder, soda and cinnamon; mix well. Stir in raisins and walnuts. Spoon into greased and floured bundt pan. Bake for 55 to 60 minutes or until cake tests done. Cool in pan for 10 minutes. Invert onto serving plate. Sprinkle with confectioners' sugar. Yield: 12 servings.

Dolores LaChance-Faglier, Preceptor Alpha Mu
Martinez, Georgia

ITALIAN CREAM CAKE

1/2 cup butter or margarine, softened	1 cup buttermilk
	1 teaspoon vanilla extract
1/2 cup shortening	
2 cups sugar	1 cup coconut
5 egg yolks	1 cup chopped pecans
2 cups all-purpose flour	5 egg whites, stiffly beaten
1 teaspoon soda	
Salt to taste	Italian Cream Frosting

Preheat oven to 350 degrees. Cream butter, shortening and sugar in mixer bowl until light and fluffy. Beat in egg yolks. Add flour, soda, salt and buttermilk; beat for 2 minutes. Add vanilla; mix well. Fold in coconut, pecans and stiffly beaten egg whites. Spoon into 3 greased and floured 8- or 9-inch cake pans. Bake for 20 to 25 minutes or until layers test done. Cool in pans for several minutes. Remove to wire rack to cool completely. Spread Italian Cream Frosting between layers and over top and side of cake. Yield: 16 servings.

ITALIAN CREAM FROSTING

8 ounces cream cheese, softened	1 1/2 teaspoons vanilla extract
1/2 cup butter or margarine, softened	1 cup chopped pecans
	1/2 cup coconut
1 1-pound package confectioners' sugar	

Beat cream cheese and butter in mixer bowl until light and fluffy. Add confectioners' sugar; beat well. Add vanilla, pecans and coconut; mix well. Yield: 5 cups.

Rita H. Millen, Psi
Taylors, South Carolina

LEMON PECAN CAKES

2 cups butter, softened	1 2-ounce bottle of lemon extract
2 cups sugar	
6 eggs	1 pound pecans
4 cups all-purpose flour	8 ounces red and green candied cherries
1 teaspoon baking powder	
	8 ounces candied pineapple
1 cup golden raisins	

Preheat oven to 275 degrees. Cream butter in mixer bowl until light and fluffy. Add sugar, beating well. Beat in eggs. Sift in flour and baking powder; mix well. Add remaining ingredients; mix well. Spoon into 2 greased and floured 5-by-9-inch cake pans. Place in preheated oven with pan of water on lower rack. Bake for 1 hour. Remove pan of water. Bake for 30 to 45 minutes longer or until cakes test done. Cool in pans. Yield: 2 cakes.

Linda Gladfelder, Xi Tau Tau
Valencia, California

PIÑA COLADA CAKE

1 2-layer package white cake mix	1/2 cup vegetable oil
	1/3 cup water
1 4-ounce package coconut cream instant pudding mix	1/3 cup rum
	Piña Colada Frosting (page 209)
4 eggs	2/3 cup coconut (optional)

Preheat oven to 350 degrees. Combine cake mix, pudding mix, eggs, oil, water and rum in mixer bowl. Beat for 4 minutes; batter will be stiff. Spoon into greased and floured 9-by-13-inch cake pan. Bake for 25 to 30 minutes or until cake tests done. Cool in pan for 10 minutes. Remove to wire rack to cool completely. Slice horizontally into 2 layers. Spread Piña Colada Frosting between layers and over top and sides of cake. Sprinkle with coconut. Store in refrigerator. Yield: 12 to 15 servings.

PIÑA COLADA FROSTING

1 8-ounce can crushed
   pineapple
1 4-ounce package
   coconut cream instant
   pudding mix
1/3 cup rum
12 ounces whipped
   topping

Combine undrained pineapple with pudding mix and rum in bowl; mix well with spoon. Fold in whipped topping. Yield: 4 cups.

Vicki Brashears, Xi Omicron
Frostburg, Maryland

POUND CHRISTMAS CAKE

2 cups butter or
   margarine, softened
2 cups sugar
6 egg yolks, beaten
4 cups pecan pieces
1 pound candied
   cherries, chopped
1 pound candied
   pineapple, chopped
4 cups sifted all-purpose
   flour
1 1-ounce bottle of
   vanilla extract
1 teaspoon baking
   powder
6 egg whites, stiffly
   beaten

Preheat oven to 250 degrees. Cream butter and sugar in mixer bowl until light and fluffy. Beat in egg yolks. Add pecans; mix well. Dredge cherries and pineapple with part of flour. Add to batter with vanilla; mix well. Add remaining flour and baking powder, mixing with hands if batter becomes too stiff to stir. Fold in egg whites. Spoon into greased and floured tube pan. Place in oven with pan of water on racks above and below cake. Bake for 5 hours. Cool in pan for 10 minutes. Invert onto serving plate. May let stand for 24 to 36 hours and freeze until serving time. Yield: 20 servings.

Frances Hood, Laureate Delta
Northport, Alabama

COCONUT-PECAN POUND CAKE

1 cup butter or
   margarine, softened
1/3 cup shortening
3 cups sugar
5 eggs
3 cups cake flour
1 cup milk
1 teaspoon baking
   powder
1 teaspoon coconut
   extract
1 7-ounce can coconut
1 1/2 cups chopped pecans
1 cup confectioners'
   sugar
1/2 teaspoon coconut
   extract
1 tablespoon (about)
   milk

Preheat oven to 325 degrees. Cream butter, shortening and sugar in mixer bowl until light and fluffy. Beat in eggs 1 at a time. Add flour, milk, baking powder and 1 teaspoon coconut extract; mix well. Stir in coconut and pecans. Spoon into greased and floured tube pan. Bake for 1 1/2 hours. Cool in pan for 25 minutes. Invert onto cake plate. Combine confec-

tioners' sugar with 1/2 teaspoon coconut extract and enough milk to make of glaze consistency in bowl; mix well. Drizzle over cake. Yield: 16 servings.

Linda B. Freeney, Laureate Mu
Albany, Georgia

RASPBERRY CHOCOLATE MOUSSE TIARA CAKE

1 2-layer package
   Swiss chocolate cake
   mix
3 eggs
1 1/3 cups water
1/2 cup vegetable oil
1 cup red raspberry
   preserves
1/2 cup milk chocolate
   chips
2 tablespoons water
8 ounces whipped
   topping

Preheat oven to 350 degrees. Combine cake mix, eggs, 1 1/3 cups water and oil in mixer bowl; blend at low speed. Beat at medium speed for 2 minutes. Spoon 3 1/2 cups batter into greased tiara pan. Bake for 21 to 24 minutes or until toothpick inserted in center comes out clean. Cool in pan for 5 to 10 minutes. Remove to wire rack to cool completely. Place on serving plate. Spread preserves in well of cake. Combine chocolate chips and 2 tablespoons water in glass dish. Microwave on Medium-Low for 1 1/2 minutes or until melted; stir to mix well. Reserve 2 tablespoons chocolate mixture. Chill remaining chocolate mixture for 10 minutes or until thickened but still creamy. Fold into whipped topping in bowl. Spread evenly over preserves. Drizzle with reserved chocolate. Chill for 4 hours to overnight. May spoon remaining cake batter into paper-lined muffin cups and bake using package directions. Yield: 12 servings.

Ginger Mottu, Xi Delta
Montgomery, Alabama

QUEEN ELIZABETH LAMB CAKE

2 cups all-purpose flour
1/4 cup baking cocoa
1 cup sugar
2 teaspoons soda
1 cup mayonnaise or
   salad dressing
1 cup water
1 teaspoon vanilla
   extract
1 recipe seven-minute
   frosting
Coconut
Raisins

Preheat oven to 350 degrees. Sift flour, cocoa, sugar and soda into bowl. Add mayonnaise, water and vanilla; mix well. Spoon into greased and floured lamb mold cake pan. Bake for 45 minutes. Cool in pan for 30 minutes. Remove to serving plate. Spread with seven-minute frosting. Sprinkle with coconut, add raisins for eyes and mouth and tie ribbon around neck. Yield: 12 servings.

Eleanor Parker, Xi Alpha Xi
North Bridgton, Maine

ARABY SPICE CAKE

3/4 cup shortening	1 teaspoon cinnamon
1 1/2 cups sugar	3/4 teaspoon salt
3 eggs	3/4 cup buttermilk
2 cups sifted cake flour	1 teaspoon vanilla
1/4 teaspoon baking	extract
powder	1 teaspoon lemon
1/2 teaspoon soda	extract
2 tablespoons baking	1/2 cup coarsely chopped
cocoa	almonds
3/4 teaspoon nutmeg	Araby Spice Icing

Preheat oven to 350 degrees. Cream shortening and sugar in mixer bowl until light and fluffy. Beat in eggs. Sift flour, baking powder, soda, cocoa, nutmeg, cinnamon and salt together. Add to creamed mixture alternately with mixture of buttermilk and flavorings, mixing well after each addition. Stir in almonds. Spoon into 2 greased and floured 9-inch cake pans. Bake for 30 to 35 minutes or until layers test done. Cool in pans for 10 minutes. Remove to wire rack to cool completely. Spread Araby Spice Icing between layers and over top and side of cake. May bake in 9-by-13-inch cake pan for 35 to 45 minutes if preferred. Yield: 16 servings.

ARABY SPICE ICING

3 cups sifted	6 tablespoons butter or
confectioners' sugar	margarine, softened
4 1/2 teaspoons baking	1 egg yolk
cocoa	4 1/2 teaspoons hot coffee
1 teaspoon cinnamon	

Mix confectioners' sugar, cocoa and cinnamon in bowl. Add butter, egg yolk and hot coffee; mix until smooth. Yield: 3 1/2 cups.

Patricia R. Davis, Laureate Alpha Iota
Bowser, British Columbia, Canada

STRAWBERRY SURPRISE CAKE

1 angel food cake	1/3 cup milk
1 4-ounce package	1 quart strawberries
French vanilla	16 ounces whipped
instant pudding mix	topping
8 ounces cream cheese,	
softened	

Cut off top of cake and reserve. Hollow out bottom, leaving shell. Prepare pudding mix using package directions. Beat cream cheese with milk in mixer bowl until smooth. Fold into pudding. Layer pudding and strawberries 1/2 at a time in cake shell. Replace top. Spread whipped topping over top and side of cake. Garnish with additional strawberries. Yield: 8 to 10 servings.

Karen Hagerman, Xi Delta Psi
Erie, Pennsylvania

DUTCH APPLE PIE

4 cups sliced peeled	1/2 cup oats
apples	2/3 cup melted butter or
1 cup sugar	margarine
1 teaspoon cinnamon	1 1/2 cup packed light
2 tablespoons	brown sugar
all-purpose flour	1 1/2 cups all-purpose
1/2 teaspoon salt	flour
1 unbaked 9-inch pie	1/2 teaspoon soda
shell	

Preheat oven to 350 degrees. Combine apples, sugar, cinnamon, 2 tablespoons flour and salt in bowl; mix well. Place in pie shell. Mix oats, butter, brown sugar, remaining 1 1/2 cups flour and soda. Sprinkle over pie. Bake for 45 minutes to 1 hour or until apples are tender. May wrap aluminum foil around edge of pie shell before baking to prevent burning. Yield: 8 servings.

Diana Kooima
Rock Valley, Iowa

BLUE RIBBON CREAMY APPLE PIE

1/2 cup butter or	1/2 teaspoon vanilla
margarine, softened	extract
1/4 cup sugar	4 cups thinly sliced
1/2 teaspoon vanilla	apples
extract	1/2 teaspoon cinnamon
1 cup all-purpose flour	2/3 cup sugar
8 ounces cream cheese,	1 tablespoon butter or
softened	margarine
1/4 cup sugar	1/2 cup chopped pecans
1 egg	or hickory nuts

Preheat oven to 400 degrees. Combine 1/2 cup butter, 1/4 cup sugar and 1/2 teaspoon vanilla in mixer bowl; beat well. Add flour gradually, beating constantly. Beat until soft dough is formed. Press onto bottom and side of 9-inch pie plate. Beat cream cheese, 1/4 cup sugar, egg and remaining 1/2 teaspoon vanilla in bowl until smooth. Spread over prepared pie plate. Layer mixture of apples, cinnamon and remaining 2/3 cup sugar over cream cheese mixture. Dot with remaining 1 tablespoon butter. Sprinkle with pecans. Bake for 15 minutes. Reduce temperature to 350 degrees. Bake for 30 minutes longer. Yield: 6 to 8 servings.

 Jeanne R. Patterson, Laureate Alpha Epsilon
Bloomsburg, Pennsylvania

Ida May Humke, Iota Masters, Quincy, Illinois, makes No-Cook Caramel Pecan Pie by melting 8 ounces vanilla caramels in 3/4 cup milk and adding 1 envelope unflavored gelatin softened in 1/4 cup cold water and pinch of salt. Chill until thick. Fold in chopped pecans and 1/2 cup whipping cream, whipped. Pour into graham cracker pie shell and chill.

AVOCADO PIE

2 large ripe avocados, chopped	1½ cups chopped walnuts
1 cup sweetened condensed milk	1 teaspoon nutmeg
Juice of 2 limes	1 9-inch graham cracker pie shell

Combine all ingredients in blender container. Process until smooth. Pour into pie shell. Chill for 2 hours. Yield: 8 servings.

Jennifer Dory, Beta Epsilon
Austin, Nevada

BLACK RUSSIAN PIE

14 Oreo cookies, crushed	½ cup milk
2 tablespoons melted butter or margarine	⅓ cup Kahlua
24 marshmallows	1 cup whipping cream, whipped
⅛ teaspoon salt	Chocolate curls

Combine cookie crumbs and butter in 8-inch pie plate; mix well. Press over bottom and side of pie plate. Freeze until firm. Cook marshmallows, salt and milk in double boiler until marshmallows are melted. Cool until partially set. Stir in Kahlua and whipped cream. Chill for 30 minutes. Pour into prepared pie plate. Freeze until firm. Garnish with chocolate curls. Yield: 6 to 7 servings.

Paulette Klaja, Preceptor Alpha Chi
Pittsburgh, Pennsylvania

CARAMEL PIES

1 24-ounce package caramels	16 ounces whipped topping
½ cup water	2 9-inch butter cookie crumb pie shells
1 cup sour cream	

Place caramels and water in saucepan. Cook over low heat until caramels are melted, stirring constantly. Let stand until cool. Fold in sour cream and whipped topping. Spoon into pie shells. Chill until serving time. Yield: 12 to 14 servings.

Lori Higginbotham, Epsilon Nu
Birmingham, Alabama

CHOCOLATE MOUSSE PIE

3 cups chocolate cookie crumbs	2 cups whipping cream
½ cup melted margarine	6 tablespoons confectioners' sugar
2 cups semisweet chocolate chips	4 egg whites, at room temperature
2 eggs	2 cups whipping cream
4 egg yolks, at room temperature	

Combine cookie crumbs and margarine in bowl; mix well. Press over bottom and halfway up side of 10-inch springform pan. Chill for 30 minutes. Soften chocolate chips in double boiler. Cool slightly. Add eggs; mix well. Add egg yolks; mix well. Whip 2 cups whipping cream until soft peaks form. Add confectioners' sugar; mix well. Beat egg whites until stiff but not dry. Fold a small amount of whipped cream and beaten egg whites into melted chocolate. Fold in remaining whipped cream and beaten egg whites until completely incorporated. Spoon into prepared springform pan. Chill for 6 hours to overnight. Remove side of springform pan. Whip remaining 2 cups whipping cream. Spread over mousse. Yield: 10 servings.

Paula Horsley, Preceptor Tau
Elko, Nevada

CRANBERRY-PECAN PIE

1½ cups sugar	⅛ teaspoon salt
3 tablespoons cornstarch	½ cup chopped pecans
½ cup water	1 baked 10-inch pie shell
3 cups cranberries	3 egg whites
2 tablespoons butter or margarine	¼ teaspoon cream of tartar
	⅓ cup sugar

Combine 1½ cups sugar and cornstarch in saucepan. Stir in water until smooth. Add cranberries. Cook until cranberries open, stirring frequently. Add butter, salt and pecans; mix well. Spoon into pie shell. Beat egg whites, cream of tartar and remaining ⅓ cup sugar until stiff. Spoon over pie. Broil until lightly browned. Yield: 8 servings.

Kathy Proctor
Everett, Washington

GRAPE-CRUMB PIE

This recipe was my grandmother's. She ran her own catering home for 37 years here in Chillicothe, Ohio, called "The Lynne House."

3½ cups Concord grapes	1 unbaked 9-inch pie shell
1 cup sugar	
¼ cup all-purpose flour	¾ cup all-purpose flour
¼ teaspoon salt	½ cup sugar
1 tablespoon lemon juice	⅓ cup butter or margarine
4½ teaspoons butter or margarine	

Preheat oven to 400 degrees. Remove skins from grapes, reserving skins. Bring pulp to a boil; press through sieve to remove seeds. Combine 1 cup sugar, ¼ cup flour and salt in a small bowl; add to strained pulp. Stir in grape skins, lemon juice and 4½ teaspoons butter. Spoon into pie shell. Sift remaining ¾ cup flour and ½ cup sugar together. Cut in remaining ⅓ cup butter until crumbly. Sprinkle over pie. Bake for 40 to 50 minutes or until pie tests done. Yield: 8 servings.

Vicki Hempstead, Preceptor Epsilon Omega
Chillicothe, Ohio

HUCKLEBERRY STRATA PIE

1 8-ounce can crushed pineapple	1 baked 10-inch pie shell
4 cups huckleberries	1½ cups sugar
8 ounces cream cheese, softened	2 tablespoons cornstarch
3 tablespoons sugar	¼ teaspoon salt
1 tablespoon milk	1 teaspoon lemon juice
1 teaspoon vanilla extract	1¼ cup whipping cream, whipped

Drain pineapple, reserving syrup and 2 tablespoons pineapple. Drain huckleberries, reserving juice. Blend cream cheese, 3 tablespoons sugar, milk and vanilla in bowl. Stir in pineapple. Spread in pie shell. Chill in refrigerator. Combine remaining 1½ cups sugar, cornstarch and salt in bowl. Add reserved pineapple syrup; mix well. Combine 1½ cups syrup mixture with reserved huckleberry juice in saucepan. Cook until thickened, stirring constantly. Stir in huckleberries and lemon juice. Pour over creamy layer in pie shell. Chill in refrigerator. Top with whipped cream and reserved 2 tablespoons pineapple. Yield: 8 servings.

Ella Leinwebber, Laureate Alpha Iota
Spokane, Washington

BEST-EVER LEMON PIE

1¼ cups sugar	1½ teaspoons lemon extract
6 tablespoons cornstarch	2 teaspoons vinegar
2 cups water	1 baked 9-inch pie shell
3 egg yolks	3 egg whites
⅓ cup lemon juice	6 tablespoons sugar
3 tablespoons butter or margarine	1 teaspoon vanilla extract

Preheat oven to 350 degrees. Combine 1¼ cups sugar and cornstarch in double boiler. Add water, mixing well. Combine egg yolks and lemon juice in bowl; beat well. Add to cornstarch mixture. Cook until thickened, stirring frequently. Stir in butter, lemon extract and vinegar. Pour into pie shell. Let stand until cool. Beat egg whites in mixer bowl until stiff. Add remaining 6 tablespoons sugar 1 tablespoon at a time, beating constantly. Add vanilla, beating until stiff peaks form. Top pie with meringue. Bake for 10 minutes. Yield: 8 servings.

Pamela Scism, Beta Gamma
Siloam Springs, Arkansas

MAPLE SYRUP PIE

1 recipe 2-crust pie pastry	2 tablespoons cold water
1 cup maple syrup	¼ cup chopped walnuts
½ cup water	1 tablespoon butter or margarine
3 tablespoons cornstarch	

Preheat oven to 450 degrees. Line 8-inch pie plate with half the pastry. Boil maple syrup and ½ cup water in saucepan for 5 minutes. Add cornstarch mixed with 2 tablespoons cold water. Cook until thickened, stirring constantly. Add walnuts and butter. Pour into prepared pie plate. Top with remaining pastry. Seal edges; cut vents. Bake for 30 minutes or until golden brown. Yield: 8 servings.

Leanna Linski, Xi Beta Upsilon
Sedalia, Missouri

MARGARITA PIE

½ cup melted butter or margarine	⅓ cup lime juice
1½ cups finely crushed pretzels	2 tablespoons Tequila
¼ cup sugar	2 tablespoons Triple Sec
1 14-ounce can sweetened condensed milk	1 cup whipping cream, whipped
	Whipped cream
	Orange twists

Combine butter, pretzel crumbs and sugar in bowl; mix well. Press onto bottom and side of pie plate. Chill in refrigerator. Combine condensed milk, lime juice, Tequila and Triple Sec in bowl; mix well. Fold in whipped cream. Pour into chilled pie crust. Freeze for 2 hours or chill for 4 hours or until firm. Remove from freezer 15 minutes before serving. Garnish with dollops of whipped cream and orange twists. Yield: 8 servings.

Marg Barton, Laureate Mu
North Bay, Ontario, Canada

MINCEMEAT PIES WITH RUM SAUCE

1 cup ground beef	⅔ cup chopped dried apricots (optional)
2 cups water	2 baked 9-inch pie shells
1 teaspoon salt	
1½ cups raisins	½ cup butter or margarine
3 cups chopped peeled apples	¼ cup water
1 teaspoon nutmeg	1 cup sugar
1 teaspoon cinnamon	¼ cup light rum
½ cup margarine	

Preheat oven to 350 degrees. Boil ground beef, 2 cups water and salt in saucepan until ground beef is cooked through. Add raisins and apples. Cook until heated through. Stir in nutmeg, cinnamon and margarine. Cook for 5 to 10 minutes longer. Pour into pie shells. Bake for 45 minutes. Boil butter, remaining ¼ cup water, sugar and rum in saucepan for 3 minutes. Serve warm over mincemeat pie slices. Yield: 16 servings.

Ruth Anne Gray, Laureate Chi
Macon, Missouri

PEACHES AND CREAM CHEESE PIE

2 16-ounce cans sliced peaches	3 tablespoons margarine, softened
3/4 cup all-purpose flour	1/2 cup milk
1 teaspoon baking powder	8 ounces cream cheese, softened
1/2 teaspoon salt	1/2 cup sugar
1 4-ounce package vanilla pudding and pie filling mix	1/2 teaspoon cinnamon
1 egg	1 tablespoon sugar

Preheat oven to 350 degrees. Drain peaches, reserving 3 tablespoons juice. Combine flour, baking powder, salt, pudding mix, egg, margarine and milk in mixer bowl. Beat at medium speed for 2 minutes. Pour into lightly greased 10-inch pie plate. Top with peaches. Combine cream cheese, 1/2 cup sugar and reserved peach juice in bowl. Mix until smooth. Mixture will be thick. Spoon over peaches, leaving a margin around edge. Sprinkle with mixture of cinnamon and remaining 1 tablespoon sugar. Bake for 30 to 35 minutes. Do not use instant pudding mix in this recipe. Yield: 6 to 8 servings.

Theresa Fields
Villa Grove, Illinois

PAMPERED PUMPKIN PIES

We have lived in a lot of different states and this has been very well liked everywhere we've lived. It's quick and easy.

1 pint vanilla ice cream, softened	1/2 teaspoon ground cloves
1 16-ounce can pumpkin	1 teaspoon vanilla extract
11/4 cups sugar	1 cup whipping cream, whipped
1/2 teaspoon salt	2 baked 10-inch pie shells
1 teaspoon cinnamon	
1/2 teaspoon ginger	

Beat ice cream, pumpkin, sugar, salt, cinnamon, ginger, cloves, vanilla and whipped cream in large mixer bowl until smooth. Pour into pie shells. Freeze for 4 hours. Remove from freezer 10 to 15 minutes before serving. Yield: 14 to 16 servings.

Norma Komrofske, Beta Xi
Colorado Springs, Colorado

PUMPKIN CHIFFON PIE

1 cup pumpkin	2 cups whipping cream, whipped
1 11-ounce package marshmallows	1 baked 9- or 10-inch deep-dish pie shell
11/2 teaspoons cinnamon	Whipped cream
11/2 teaspoons nutmeg	
1 teaspoon ground cloves	

Combine pumpkin and marshmallows in large saucepan. Cook over medium heat until marshmallows melt, stirring frequently. Stir in cinnamon, nutmeg and cloves. Let stand for 1 hour. Fold whipped cream into pumpkin mixture gently. Pour into pie shell. Chill for 1 hour. Top with additional whipped cream. Yield: 6 to 8 servings.

Carolyn Salminen, Xi Beta Alpha
Port Coquitlam, British Columbia, Canada

STRAWBERRY CHEESE PIE

8 ounces cream cheese, softened	1/3 cup lemon juice
1 14-ounce can sweetened condensed milk	1 baked 9-inch pie shell
	4 cups fresh strawberries
1 teaspoon vanilla extract	1 16-ounce package strawberry glaze, chilled

Beat cream cheese in large mixer bowl until light and fluffy. Add condensed milk gradually, beating until smooth. Stir in vanilla and lemon juice. Pour into baked 9-inch pie shell. Chill for 3 hours or until set. Top with strawberries and desired amount of glaze. Yield: 6 to 8 servings.

Sandy Dustman, Chi Eta
Jamesport, Missouri

DOUBLE SWEET POTATO PIE

1 cup all-purpose flour	1/2 cup sugar
1 teaspoon baking powder	3 tablespoons lemon juice
1/2 teaspoon salt	1 tablespoon grated lemon rind
1 cup cold mashed cooked sweet potatoes	3 egg yolks
1/3 cup melted margarine	1/4 teaspoon nutmeg
1 egg, well beaten	3 large sweet potatoes, cooked, mashed
1/4 cup margarine, softened	1 cup evaporated milk
1/4 teaspoon salt	3 egg whites

Preheat oven to 425 degrees. Sift flour, baking powder and 1/2 teaspoon salt into bowl. Mix in 1 cup sweet potatoes, melted margarine and egg. Roll 1/4 inch thick on floured cloth. Fit into 9-inch pie plate. Trim and flute edge. Cream remaining 1/4 cup margarine, 1/4 teaspoon salt and sugar in large bowl until light and fluffy. Add lemon juice and lemon rind, mixing well. Beat egg yolks, nutmeg, remaining 3 sweet potatoes and evaporated milk in mixer bowl. Stir into creamed mixture. Beat egg whites until stiff peaks form. Fold into creamed mixture gently. Spoon into prepared pie plate. Bake for 10 minutes. Reduce temperature to 350 degrees. Bake for 40 minutes longer or until knife inserted near center comes out clean. Yield: 8 to 10 servings.

Mary Gemski, Preceptor Alpha Pi
Hampton, Virginia

Metric Equivalents

Although the United States has opted to postpone converting to metric measurements, most other countries, including England and Canada, use the metric system. The following chart provides convenient approximate equivalents for allowing use of regular kitchen measures when cooking from foreign recipes.

Volume

These metric measures are approximate benchmarks for purposes of home food preparation.
1 milliliter = 1 cubic centimeter = 1 gram

Liquid	Dry
1 teaspoon = 5 milliliters	1 quart = 1 liter
1 tablespoon = 15 milliliters	1 ounce = 30 grams
1 fluid ounce = 30 milliliters	1 pound = 450 grams
1 cup = 250 milliliters	2.2 pounds = 1 kilogram
1 pint = 500 milliliters	

Weight

1 ounce = 28 grams
1 pound = 450 grams

Length

1 inch = 2½ centimeters
¹⁄₁₆ inch = 1 millimeter

Formulas Using Conversion Factors

When approximate conversions are not accurate enough, use these formulas to convert measures from one system to another.

Measurements	Formulas
ounces to grams:	# ounces x 28.3 = # grams
grams to ounces:	# grams x 0.035 = # ounces
pounds to grams:	# pounds x 453.6 = # grams
pounds to kilograms:	# pounds x 0.45 = # kilograms
ounces to milliliters:	# ounces x 30 = # milliliters
cups to liters:	# cups x 0.24 = # liters
inches to centimeters:	# inches x 2.54 = # centimeters
centimeters to inches:	# centimeters x 0.39 = # inches

Approximate Weight to Volume

Some ingredients which we commonly measure by volume are measured by weight in foreign recipes. Here are a few examples for easy reference.

flour, all-purpose, unsifted	1 pound = 450 grams = 3½ cups
flour, all-purpose, sifted	1 pound = 450 grams = 4 cups
sugar, granulated	1 pound = 450 grams = 2 cups
sugar, brown, packed	1 pound = 450 grams = 2¼ cups
sugar, confectioners'	1 pound = 450 grams = 4 cups
sugar, confectioners', sifted	1 pound = 450 grams = 4½ cups
butter	1 pound = 450 grams = 2 cups

Temperature

Remember that foreign recipes frequently express temperatures in Centigrade rather than Fahrenheit.

Temperatures	Fahrenheit	Centigrade
room temperature	68°	20°
water boils	212°	100°
baking temperature	350°	177°
baking temperature	375°	190.5°
baking temperature	400°	204.4°
baking temperature	425°	218.3°
baking temperature	450°	232°

Use the following formulas when temperature conversions are necessary.

Centigrade degrees x ⁹/₅ + 32 = Fahrenheit degrees
Fahrenheit degrees - 32 x ⁵/₉ = Centigrade degrees

American Measurement Equivalents

1 tablespoon = 3 teaspoons	12 tablespoons = ¾ cup
2 tablespoons = 1 ounce	16 tablespoons = 1 cup
4 tablespoons = ¼ cup	1 cup = 8 ounces
5 tablespoons + 1 teaspoon = ⅓ cup	2 cups = 1 pint
8 tablespoons = ½ cup	4 cups = 1 quart
	4 quarts = 1 gallon

Merit Winners

MEMORABLE MOMENTS
First Prize
Chase, Sue, page 26
Second Prize
Gervais, Brenda, page 24
Third Prize
Harrison, Lavada, page 20

FRESH BEGINNINGS
First Prize
Poveromo, Hope Rose,
 page 63
Second Prize
Echols, Maureen, page 56
Third Prize
Monarchi, Ardis, page 59

THIRST QUENCHERS
First Prize
Zieler, Donna C., page 79
Second Prize
Davis, Peggy, page 77
Third Prize
Fife, Renee, page 75

SALADS AND SUCH
First Prize
Behnke, Judy, page 89
Second Prize
Ross, Betty, page 92
Third Prize
Bressler, Mrs. Loy,
 page 86

THE MEAT MARKET
First Prize
Luna, Jill, page 118
Second Prize
Breigenzer, Karen J.,
 page 125
Third Prize
Adamson, Marsha, page 109

THE VEGETABLE PATCH
First Prize
Lang, Ann M., page 146
Second Prize
Bertram, Linda, page 145
Third Prize
Benet, Marguerite, page 142

BREAD WINNERS
First Prize
Heyman, Diane, page 164
Second Prize
Oglesbee, Mary C., page 154
Third Prize
Fick, Jean, page 164

WORLD CHAMPIONS
First Prize
Roberts, Kathryn J., page 172
Second Prize
Arnet, Carol, page 180
Third Prize
Pancoast, Felicia, page 172

COOKIES AND CANDIES
First Prize
Espinosa, Lori, page 184
Second Prize
LaPalme, Denise, page 187
Third Prize
McDonald, Susan K., page 191

DESSERTS
First Prize
Patterson, Jeanne R., page 210
Second Prize
Seitz, Carlye, page 199
Third Prize
Harris, Nancy L., page 205

HONORABLE MENTION
Ackley, Alice, page 113
Adams, Kim, page 58
Alkema, Linda, page 146
Annett, Harlene, page 96
Audras, Gail E., page 54
Awtry, Sue, page 100
Bachellerie, Nancy, page 151
Baker, Jean, page 82
Bamsey, Madeline, page 108
Bardin, Barbara, page 145
Bargman, Julie J., page 189
Barham, Sylvia, page 176
Bell, Roxanne, page 167
Benton, Elaine K., page 149
Berthe, Dianne V., page 47
Biedermann, Jane, page 101
Boor, Joyce, page 105

Borbely, Kim, page 182
Borras, Marilyn, page 156
Botkins, Dorene, page 136
Bounds, Lisa, page 101
Bowe, Karen, page 57
Bower, Cindy, page 77
Bowles, Deana, page 23
Bradley, Melany, page 48
Brashears, Vicki, page 208
Brasier, Sandra H., page 158
Brown, Debra Jo, page 103
Brown, Ginger, page 164
Bruch, Terri, page 163
Bruey, Julie, page 122
Bryant, Donna, page 121
Buchele, Marilyn R., page 67
Bulis-Stanion, Carol, page 78
Burke, Elizabeth, page 78
Burns, Mildred, page 114
Burns, Patricia M., page 72
Burrell, Ginger, page 114
Busse, Jenelle, page 85
Byrne, Starr, page 97
Capodagli, Jan, page 117
Carmichael, Betty, page 170
Cashour, Mary, page 137
Christiansen, Dorothy J.,
 page 112
Coartney, Brenda, page 75
Comis, Leslie, page 207
Cone, Alice, page 86
Connarn, Al, page 177
Cook, Janice, page 89
Cooper, Kay, page 77
Corley, Ruth, page 207
Cowell, Barb, page 166
Crosby, Marie, pages 76, 202
Cross, Karen, page 198
Cyr, Liz, page 77
Daehler, Jeannette, page 60
Davis, Judi, page 119
Dennis, Pauline, page 91
Derksen, Rosemary, page 147
Doherty, Margaret, page 155
Douglass, Beverly S., page 93
Farnsworth, Betty, page 70
Fisher, Betsy, page 31
Fisk, Helen, page 149
Fletcher, Carrie L., page 138
Freepons, Loretta, page 166

Index

Beta Sigma Phi Cookbooks

available from *Favorite Recipes® Press* are chock-full of home-tested recipes from Beta Sigma Phi members that earn you the best compliment of all... "More Please!"

Every cookbook includes:

☆ color photos or black-and-white photos

☆ delicious, family-pleasing recipes

☆ lay-flat binding

☆ wipe-clean color covers

☆ easy-to-read format

☆ comprehensive index

To place your order, call our **toll free** number **1-800-251-1520** or clip and mail the convenient form below.

BETA SIGMA PHI COOKBOOKS	Item #	Qty.	U.S. Retail Price	Canadian Retail Price	Total
Beta Sigma Phi Celebrations Cookbook	84573		$9.95	$12.95	
All-Occasion Casseroles Cookbook with Menus	28037		$4.50	$4.50	
The Dining Room	10006		$5.95	$5.95	
Save & Win	70017		$5.95	$5.95	
Shipping and Handling		1	$1.95	$2.95	
TOTAL AMOUNT					

☐ Payment Enclosed
☐ Please Charge My ☐ MasterCard ☐ Visa
                    ☐ Discover

Signature _____

Account Number _____

Name _____

Address _____

City _____ State ____ Zip _____

No COD orders please.
Call our toll free number for faster ordering.
Prices subject to change.
Books offered subject to availability.
Please allow 30 days for delivery.

Mail completed order form to:

Favorite Recipes® Press
P.O. Box 305141
Nashville, TN 37230